R. Gupta's®

POPULAR MASTER GUIDE

National Testing Agency **(NTA)**

UGC-NET/JRF

Junior Research Fellowship & Assistant Professor Eligibility Exam

PSYCHOLOGY

PAPER II

by

Dr. SWATI MAHARSHI

RAMESH PUBLISHING HOUSE, NEW DELHI

Published by
O.P. Gupta *for* Ramesh Publishing House

Admin. Office
12-H, New Daryaganj Road, Opp. Officers' Mess,
New Delhi-110002 ✆ 23275224, 23245124
E-mail: info@rameshpublishinghouse.com
For Online Shopping: www.rameshpublishinghouse.com

Showroom
• Balaji Market, Nai Sarak, Delhi-110006 ✆ 23282525 📱 9354373464
• 4457, Nai Sarak, Delhi-110006

Book Code: R-1754

ISBN: 978-93-87604-96-4

Price: ₹ 470

Printed at: Nidhi Enterprises, Delhi

CONTENTS

PREVIOUS PAPERS (SOLVED)

PART-A

PART-B

Previous Years' Paper

National Testing Agency (NTA)

UGC-NET Junior Research Fellowship & Assistant Professor Eligibility Exam

PSYCHOLOGY, JANUARY-2026

(Exam held on 02-01-2026)

PAPER-II

1. The relation between 't' ratio and 'F' ratio is:

1. t = Square of F
2. t = F
3. t = Square root of F
4. t = 1/2 F

2. Match the List-I with List-II.

List-I	List-II
A. Two factor theory of intelligence	I. Howard Gardner
B. Primary mental abilities	II. Thurstone
C. Triarchic theory of intelligence	III. Charles Spearman
D. Theory of multiple intelligence	IV. Sternberg

Choose the ***correct*** answer from the options given below:

1. A-III, B-IV, C-I, D-II
2. A-III, B-II, C-IV, D-I
3. A-III, B-I, C-II, D-IV
4. A-III, B-II, C-I, D-IV

3. Given below are two statements : one is labelled as Assertion (A) and the other is labelled as Reason (R).

Assertion (A): Creative thinking always requires divergent thinking.

Reason (R): Divergent thinking helps in generating multiple solutions to a single problem.

In the light of the above statements, choose the ***most appropriate*** answer from the options given below:

1. Both (A) and (R) are correct and (R) is the correct explanation of (A).
2. Both (A) and (R) are correct, but (R) is not the correct explanation of (A).
3. (A) is correct, but (R) is not correct.
4. (A) is not correct, but (R) is correct.

4. Arrange the development of the following personality tests in chronological order:

A. Rorschach Inkblot Test
B. Draw-A-Man task
C. Thematic Apperception Test
D. 16 Personality factor

Choose the ***correct*** answer from the options given below:

1. A, B, C, D
2. A, C, B, D
3. A, C, D, B
4. A, D, B, C

5. Research by Steven Maier suggest that learned helplessness may be due to a higher-level region of the brain known as the ______ which helps subject determine what is controllable.

1. Amygdala
2. Ventromedial prefrontal cortex
3. Hippocampus
4. Dorsal raphe nucleus

6. The gaps between section of myelin is called ______.

1. Myelin Sheath
2. Axon Hillock
3. Dendrites
4. Nodes of Ranvier

7. During which of the following Psycho-sexual stages, the male child develops the Oedipus Complex?

1. Anal stage
2. Latency stage
3. Phallic stage
4. Genital stage

8. Arrange the following theories of motivation in chronological order with respect to the year of development:

A. Deci's self-determination theory
B. McClelland's need achievement theory
C. Maslow's hierarchy of needs
D. Dweck's self-theory

Choose the ***correct*** answer from the options given below:

1. B, C, A, D 2. D, A, C, B
3. C, B, D, A 4. A, B, D, C

9. Arrange the sequence of the steps in the synthesis of catecholamines from tyrosine:

A. Tyrosine B. Epinephrine
C. Dopamine D. L-dopa
E. Norepinephrine

Choose the ***correct*** answer from the options given below:

1. A, B, C, D, E 2. A, D, C, E, B
3. A, D, C, B, E 4. A, C, B, D, E

10. The following two are the major contributions of Thorndike's doctrine in the field of Psychology.

A. Associative shifting
B. Law of similarity
C. Law of effect
D. Extinction

Choose the ***correct*** answer from the options given below:

1. A and B only 2. A and C only
3. B and C only 4. A and D only

11. ______ is the assumption that everything that happen in the universe can be accounted for by definite laws of causation.

1. Mechanism 2. Operationism
3. Naturalmonism 4. Determinism

12. Which of the following statements are true in the context of sampling?

A. Purposive sampling is probability sampling
B. Snowball sampling is based upon sociometry
C. 'G' power is used to estimate sample size
D. Sampling error increases with sample size
E. Standard deviation of sampling distribution is sampling error

Choose the ***correct*** answer from the options given below:

1. A, C and D only
2. B, C and D only
3. B, C and E only
4. A, D and E only

13. In which of the following statistical analysis there will be more than one dependent/ criterion variables:

1. Multiple Regression
2. Simple Regression
3. Canonical Correlation
4. Three way Analysis of variance

14. The human belly button is a ______; it serves no adaptive function and is merely the by product of the umbilical cord.

1. Homologus 2. Analogus
3. Spandrels 4. Exaptations

15. Match the List-I with List-II.

List-I	List-II
A. Confluence	I. Absence of difference between self and others
B. Retroflection	II. Lack of discrimination or assimilation of new information gained
C. Deflection	III. Avoidance of contact with others
D. Introjection	IV. Suppression of behaviour and the redirection back onto the self

Choose the ***correct*** answer from the options given below:

1. A-I, B-IV, C-III, D-II
2. A-I, B-III, C-IV, D-II
3. A-II, B-III, C-I, D-IV
4. A-III, B-II, C-I, D-IV

16. Which motivational theory relies heavily on the concept of homeostasis?

1. Instinctual theory
2. Need for affiliation theory
3. Drive reduction theory
4. Need for achievement theory

17. What would be the correct sequence while developing a robust questionnaire?

A. Curricular Validity
B. Confirmatory Factor Analysis
C. Item Discrimination Index
D. Exploratory Factor Analysis
E. Norm Development

Choose the ***correct*** answer from the options given below:

1. C, A, B, D, E
2. C, D, B, A, E
3. C, D, A, B, E
4. C, A, D, B, E

18. Match the List-I with List-II.

List-I	List-II
A. Allport	I. 16 PF (Surface and source traits)
B. Cattell	II. Cardinal, central, secondary trait
C. H.J. Eysenck	III. Psychosexual stages of development
D. Sigmund Freud	IV. Extraversion-Neuroticism-psychoticism dimensions

Choose the ***correct*** answer from the options given below:

1. A-I, B-III, C-IV, D-II
2. A-III, B-I, C-II, D-IV
3. A-II, B-I, C-IV, D-III
4. A-IV, B-II, C-I, D-III

19. Correct sequence in Lazarus's Cognitive Mediational Theory of emotion.

A. Appraisal
B. Bodily response
C. Stimulus
D. Emotional response

Choose the ***correct*** answer from the options given below:

1. A, D, B, C
2. C, D, B, A
3. C, A, D, B
4. B, C, D, A

20. ______ Test is a Non reading and motor reduced Test.

1. 16 Personality Factor Test
2. Big Five Personality Test
3. Thematic Apperception Test
4. Peabody Picture Vocabulary Test-IV

21. According to Wundt, the ability to arrange willfully the elements of thought into any number of configurations is called:

1. Cognitive map
2. Confirmable proposition
3. Creative synthesis
4. Wishful thinking

22. Arrange Prochaska's stage model:

A. Contemplation
B. Precontemplation
C. Action
D. Preparation
E. Maintenance

Choose the ***correct*** answer from the options given below:

1. B, A, C, D, E 2. B, C, A, E, D
3. B, D, A, E, C 4. B, A, D, C, E

23. Given below are two statements : one is labelled as Assertion (A) and the other is labelled as Reason (R).

Assertion (A): One psychologist changed the level of significance from 0.05 to 0.01. This can increase the probability of Type II error.

Reason (R): Type II error is caused by wrongful acceptance of Null hypothesis.

In the light of the above statements, choose the ***most appropriate*** answer from the options given below :

1. Both (A) and (R) are correct and (R) is the correct explanation of (A).
2. Both (A) and (R) are correct, but (R) is not the correct explanation of (A).
3. (A) is correct, but (R) is not correct.
4. (A) is not correct, but (R) is correct.

24. Match the List-I with List-II.

List-I	List-II
A. Biographical Research	I. Lived Experiences
B. Ethnography	II. Theoretical Saturation
C. Grounded Theory	III. Retrospective Studies
D. Phenomenological Approach	IV. Cultural Anthropology

Choose the ***correct*** answer from the options given below:

1. A-II, B-IV, C-III, D-I
2. A-III, B-IV, C-II, D-I
3. A-IV, B-III, C-I, D-II
4. A-I, B-III, C-IV, D-II

25. Given below are two statements : one is labelled as Assertion (A) and the other is labelled as Reason (R).

Assertion (A): In a memory experiment, participants were found to use both verbal and visual encoding while performing the given task.

Reason (R): Episodic buffer, a component of working memory, is used to integrate and to store briefly the information from phonological loop and visuospatial sketch-pad.

In the light of the above statements, choose the ***most appropriate*** answer from the options given below:

1. Both (A) and (R) are correct and (R) is the correct explanation of (A).
2. Both (A) and (R) are correct, but (R) is not the correct explanation of (A).
3. (A) is correct, but (R) is not correct.
4. (A) is not correct, but (R) is correct.

26. According to Richard Lazarus, when someone asks himself, "How can I deal with this potentially harmful stressor ?" The individual is focused on a ______ appraisal.

1. Primary 2. Secondary
3. Tertiary 4. Minimal

27. Which of the following is non-parametric counter part of two-way ANOVA?

1. Wilcoxon Sign Test
2. Kruskal-Wallis Test
3. Spearman's Rank order Test
4. Friedman's Test

28. ______ Psychophysiological Technique measures the Skin Conductance Response (SCR).

1. Electroencephalagraphy
2. CT-Scan
3. Electromyography
4. Electro Dermal Activity

29. Given below are two statements : one is labelled as Assertion (A) and the other is labelled as Reason (R).

Assertion (A) : Classical conditioning is faster when UCS is presented immediately after CS rather than before.

Reason (R): According to cognitive perspective, classical conditioning occurs because CS provides expectancy about the coming of UCS.

In the light of the above statements, choose the ***most appropriate*** answer from the options given below:

1. Both (A) and (R) are correct and (R) is the correct explanation of (A).
2. Both (A) and (R) are correct, but (R) is not the correct explanation of (A).
3. (A) is correct, but (R) is not correct.
4. (A) is not correct, but (R) is correct.

30. Which one of the following is not included in four skills of Dialectical Behaviour Therapy?

1. Core mindfulness skills
2. Emotional Regulation skills
3. Intrapersonal Effectiveness skills
4. Distress Tolerance skills

31. Context dependent forgetting explains:

A. Forgetting occurs when context at retrieval differs from encoding.
B. It is supported by the encoding specificity principle.
C. It only applies to procedural memory.
D. It is unrelated to environmental cues.

Choose the ***correct*** answer from the options given below:

1. A and D only 2. A, B and C only
3. A and B only 4. B and C only

32. How many emotions are identified as basic emotions that are universal across cultures by Paul Ekman?

1. Five 2. Six
3. Four 4. Seven

33. Rorschach Inkblot Test consists of ______ inkblots devised by Herman Rorschach (1884-1922).

1. 05 2. 10
3. 13 4. 30

34. Which is not the core conditions of Effective Counselling?

1. Reflection
2. Empathy
3. Unconditional Positive regard
4. Congruence

35. World Health Organization (WHO) has defined five key principles to outline the areas of health promotion. Which is not **correct** according to WHO?

1. Health professionals should be consulted and involved in health promotion.
2. Health promotion should be focused on specific target groups.
3. Promotion should include public participation and encourage the formation of self-help groups.
4. The promotion should be focused on the cause of health problem, including the individuals environment.

36. Given below are two statements : one is labelled as Assertion (A) and the other is labelled as Reason (R).

Assertion (A): Adaptation is the developing skills required by one's particular environment.

Reason (R): Successful adaptation will differ from one culture to the next.

In the light of the above statements, choose the ***most appropriate*** answer from the options given below:

1. Both (A) and (R) are correct and (R) is the correct explanation of (A).
2. Both (A) and (R) are correct, but (R) is not the correct explanation of (A).
3. (A) is correct, but (R) is not correct.
4. (A) is not correct, but (R) is correct.

37. Method of limit, a specialized technique chiefly useful in the determination of sensory threshold, is contributed by ______.

1. Ernst Weber
2. Gustav Fechner
3. Hermann Von Helmholtz
4. Wilhelm Wundt

38. Given below are two statements : one is labelled as Assertion (A) and the other is labelled as Reason (R).

Assertion (A): Resilience refers to the ability to adapt positively despite adversity.

Reason (R): It is simply the absence of stress in one's life.

In the light of the above statements, choose the ***most appropriate*** answer from the options given below:

1. Both (A) and (R) are correct and (R) is the correct explanation of (A).
2. Both (A) and (R) are correct, but (R) is not the correct explanation of (A).
3. (A) is correct, but (R) is not correct.
4. (A) is not correct, but (R) is correct.

39. Bhabesh plays violent videogames not because of their violent content, rather he enjoys feeling of mastery and competence it provides. This explanation of aggression is put forth by:

1. Frustration-aggression hypothesis
2. General aggression model
3. Catharsis hypothesis
4. Cognitive Evaluation theory

40. Which one of the following combination is **not correct**?

1. Physical World - Umwelt
2. Psychological World - Eigen welt
3. Social World - Life welt
4. Spiritual World - Uber welt

41. Carrol Ryff's Psychological well-being model includes six dimensions. Which one of the following is correct according to this model.

1. Self Acceptance, Environment Mastery, Personal growth, Purpose in life, Autonomy
2. Environmental Mastery, Autonomy, Positive relationship, Self Acceptance, Optimism
3. Autonomy, Purpose in life, Positive relationship, Personal growth, Grit
4. Life purpose, Environmental Mastery, Resilience, Autonomy, Relationship

42. Which is the correct option for Flynn effect?

1. Intelligence scores are relatively stable in developed countries
2. Intelligence scores are decreasing due to over reliance on technology
3. Intelligence scores are steadily increasing in modernized countries
4. Intelligence scores are cumulative based on different culture

43. One day I lost my ear ring. To keep from losing earrings, further I used to thermocool to keep the earring in place. Using the thermocool as a temporary earring back showed that I overcome from the following:

1. Confirmation bias
2. A mental set
3. Functional Fixedness
4. Transformation bias

44. Sense organs in the muscles, tendons and joints tell us about the position of our limbs and the state of tension in the muscles. They serve the sense called:

1. Reflector
2. Kinesthesis
3. Simulation
4. Transduction

45. Match the List-I with List-II.

List-I	List-II
A. Kaivalya	I. Intellect
B. Asuya	II. Reasoning
C. Buddhi	III. Self realization
D. Tarka	IV. Jealousy

Choose the ***correct*** answer from the options given below:

1. A-I, B-IV, C-II, D-III
2. A-I, B-II, C-III, D-IV
3. A-III, B-IV, C-I, D-II
4. A-III, B-I, C-IV, D-II

46. Which factors influence encoding into long term memory?

A. Attention at the time of learning
B. Emotional salience of the material
C. Repetition alone, regardless of meaning
D. Use of retrieval cues during learning

Choose the ***correct*** answer from the options given below:

1. A, B and C only
2. A and C only
3. A and B only
4. A and D only

47. Match the List-I with List-II.

List-I (*Theories*)	List-II (*Psychologists*)
A. Correspondent Interference	I. Kelley
B. Covariation Theory	II. Ajzen & Fishbein
C. Planned Behaviour	III. Festinger
D. Social Comparison	IV. Jones & Davis

Choose the ***correct*** answer from the options given below:

1. A-I, B-IV, C-III, D-II
2. A-I, B-II, C-III, D-IV
3. A-IV, B-III, C-II, D-I
4. A-IV, B-I, C-II, D-III

48. Guilford's theory of intelligence known as cubical model of intelligence consists of 120 small cubes representing primary abilities those are some combination of operations, products and contents. Which one of the following is included in product dimension?

1. Evaluation
2. Convergent Production
3. Memory
4. Transformations

49. The correct sequence for engagement in pro-social behaviour as suggested by Latane and Darley (1970).

A. Notice that something unusual is happening
B. Decide that you have the knowledge or skills needed to help
C. Decide to actually help
D. Interpret the event as an emergency
E. Accept responsibility for helping

Choose the ***correct*** answer from the options given below:

1. D, A, B, C E
2. D, A, C, B, E
3. A, D, E, B, C
4. A, D, B, C, E

50. Tanmaya has low self-esteem and high interpersonal trust. She will show ______ attachment style.

1. Pre-occupied
2. Fearful-avoidant
3. Dismissing
4. Secure

51. Match the List-I with List-II.

List-I	List-II
A. Abrahm Maslaw	I. Achievement, affiliation, power motives
B. McClelland	II. Expectancy-Valence model
C. Herzberg	III. Hierarchy of needs
D. Vroom	IV. Two-factor theory (Hygiene & Motivators)

Choose the ***correct*** answer from the options given below:

1. A-IV, B-II, C-III, D-I
2. A-III, B-I, C-IV, D-II
3. A-II, B-IV, C-I, D-III
4. A-I, B-III, C-II, D-IV

52. Which of the following levels of functioning in the '*citta*' is considered the central processor?

1. Buddhi
2. Manas
3. Ahankara
4. Vasana

53. Match the List-I with List-II.

List-I	List-II
A. Dialectical Behaviour Therapy	I. Glasser
B. Reality Therapy	II. Kierkegaard
C. Existential Psycho Therapy	III. Marsha Linehan
D. Solution focused Therapy	IV. Shazer

Choose the ***correct*** answer from the options given below:

1. A-III, B-II, C-IV, D-I
2. A-IV, B-III, C-II, D-I
3. A-III, B-I, C-II, D-IV
4. A-II, B-III, C-I, D-IV

54. The limb (anga), which signifies concentration according to Yog-sutra is:

1. Dhyana
2. Dharana
3. Samadhi
4. Pranayam

55. The two genes that control the same trait are called ______.

1. Homozygous
2. Alleles
3. Heterozygous
4. Genetic recombination

56. Match the List-I with List-II.

List-I	List-II
A. Law of proximity	I. We group close to each other together
B. Law of similarity	II. Perceiving familiar shapes even when incomplete
C. Law of closure	III. Distinguishing object from background
D. Law of figure-ground	IV. Grouping similar items together in perception

Choose the ***correct*** answer from the options given below:

1. A-IV, B-II, C-III, D-I
2. A-I, B-III, C-II, D-IV
3. A-I, B-IV, C-II, D-III
4. A-II, B-I, C-IV, D-III

57. Which of the following best describes eudaimonic well-being?

1. Achievement of financial stability
2. Living in accordance with one's values and realizing potential
3. Pursuit of pleasure and avoidance of pain
4. Reduction of stress through lifestyle changes

58. Given below are two statements : one is labelled as Assertion (A) and the other is labelled as Reason (R).

Assertion (A): Health Psychology interventions are limited only to clinical treatment of patients.

Reason (R): They focus on prevention, promotion of healthy behaviour and improving quality of life.

In the light of the above statements, choose the ***most appropriate*** answer from the options given below:

1. Both (A) and (R) are correct and (R) is the correct explanation of (A).
2. Both (A) and (R) are correct, but (R) is not the correct explanation of (A).
3. (A) is correct, but (R) is not correct.
4. (A) is not correct, but (R) is correct.

59. Two dorsal arms of the spinal gray matter are called:

A. Dorsal root ganglia
B. Dorsal horn
C. Basal ganglia
D. Ventral horns

Choose the ***correct*** answer from the options given below:

1. A and B only
2. A and C only
3. A and D only
4. B and D only

60. Which of the following tactics of compliance is based upon Commitment or Consistency?

1. Ingratiation
2. Door-in-the-face technique
3. Low ball pressure
4. Dead-line technique

61. What are the three distinct types of intelligence by Sternberg?

A. Progressive Intelligence
B. Componential Intelligence
C. Experiential Intelligence

D. Contextual Intelligence
E. Exponential Intelligence

Choose the ***correct*** answer from the options given below:

1. A, C, D only
2. B, C, E only
3. B, C, D only
4. C, D, E only

62. According to Panchkosha Theory, what is the correct sequence:

A. Vijnanamaya Kosha
B. Annamaya Kosha
C. Manomaya Kosha
D. Pranamaya Kosha
E. Anandamaya Kosha

Choose the ***correct*** answer from the options given below:

1. B, C, A, D, E
2. B, D, C, A, E
3. C, B, E, A, D
4. C, E, A, B, D

63. Match the List-I with List-II.

List-I	**List-II**
A. Availability heuristic	I. Presentation of information concerning potential outcomes
B. Representativeness heuristic	II. Reference points that may lead us for problem solving
C. Anchoring-and-Adjustment heuristic	III. What comes to mind first
D. Framing	IV. Assuming that what is typical is also likely the solution

Choose the ***correct*** answer from the options given below:

1. A-I, B-III, C-II, D-IV
2. A-II, B-III, C-I, D-IV
3. A-III, B-IV, C-II, D-I
4. A-IV, B-II, C-III, D-I

64. Given below are two statements : one is labelled as Assertion (A) and the other is labelled as Reason (R).

Assertion (A): Saumya, a learned singer, sang with more excitement in the presence of a groups of audience owing to social facilitation.

Reason (R): When a group of people perform additive tasks, that leads to social facilitation.

In the light of the above statements, choose the ***most appropriate*** answer from the options given below :

1. Both (A) and (R) are correct and (R) is the correct explanation of (A).
2. Both (A) and (R) are correct, but (R) is not the correct explanation of (A).
3. (A) is correct, but (R) is not correct.
4. (A) is not correct, but (R) is correct.

65. Arrange the brain divisions in correct sequence:

A. Myelencephalon
B. Metencephalon
C. Mesencephalon
D. Telencephalon
E. Diencephalon

Choose the ***correct*** answer from the options given below:

1. A, B, C, D, E
2. A, B, C, E, D
3. A, C, B, D, E
4. A, D, E, C, B

66. Given below are two statements : one is labelled as Assertion (A) and the other is labelled as Reason (R).

Assertion (A): The working memory index (WMI) in Wechsler's Adult Intelligence Scale is comprised of subtests sensitive to attention and immediate memory.

Reason (R): A relatively low score on working memory index may signify that, the examinee has attentional or memory problem, especially with orally presented materials.

In the light of the above statements, choose the ***most appropriate*** answer from the options given below :

1. Both (A) and (R) are correct and (R) is the correct explanation of (A).
2. Both (A) and (R) are correct, but (R) is not the correct explanation of (A).
3. (A) is correct, but (R) is not correct.
4. (A) is not correct, but (R) is correct.

67. Which of the following are true with reference to Ashtanga Yagasutra?

A. Dharana is the last limb/stage

B. The first five limbs/stages are preparatory stage

C. The practice of last three stages reduces cognitive distraction

D. Yama refers to sensory withdrawal

Choose the ***correct*** answer from the options given below:

1. A, B only
2. B, C only
3. A, C only
4. B, D only

68. Arrange the following according to Piaget's theory:

A. Knowledge that an object exists even when it is not in sight.

B. The object remains same when there is a superficial change of the object.

C. Thinking about possibilities and even impossibilities.

D. Ask questions and explore their surroundings without relying on senses and motor skills relying.

Choose the ***correct*** answer from the options given below:

1. A, C, B, D
2. A, D, B, C
3. B, A, C, D
4. B, C, A, D

69. Match the List-I with List-II.

List-I	List-II
A. Right View	I. Samma - Samadhi
B. Right Effort	II. Samma - Sankalpa
C. Right Concentration	III. Samma - Ditthi
D. Right Intention	IV. Samma - Vayama

Choose the ***correct*** answer from the options given below:

1. A-II, B-III, C-I, D-IV
2. A-I, B-IV, C-II, D-III
3. A-II, B-I, C-IV, D-III
4. A-III, B-IV, C-I, D-II

70. Match the List-I with List-II.

List-I	List-II
A. Primary motor cortex	I. Disorder of attention
B. Motor nuclei of the cranial nerves	II. Habit learning
C. Basal ganglia	III. Astereognosia
D. Simultanagnosia	IV. Controlling the muscles of the face

Choose the ***correct*** answer from the options given below:

1. A-III, B-II, C-I, D-IV
2. A-I, B-II, C-III, D-IV
3. A-III, B-IV, C-II, D-I
4. A-II, B-III, C-IV, D-I

71. According to Bandura's observational learning theory, what is the correct sequence of key elements for learner?

A. Have the motivation repeat the action

B. Able to remember what was done

C. Capable of reproducing of imitating the actions of the model

D. Pay attention to the model

Choose the ***correct*** answer from the options given below:

1. C, D, B, A
2. D, B, C, A
3. A, D, B, C
4. B, C, A, D

72. Arrange the following developmental task according to the Psychosexual stages of developmental:

A. Toilet Training

B. Recognising adult role models

C. Weaning

D. Beginning intimate relationships

E. Developing interpersonal relationship

Choose the ***correct*** answer from the options given below:

1. C, A, B, E, D
2. A, C, D, B, E
3. A, B, D, E, C
4. C, A, D, B, E

73. Match the List-I with List-II.

List-I	List-II
A. Visual system	I. Tympanic membrane
B. Auditory system	II. Fovea
C. Somatosensory system	III. Chemotopic map
D. Olfactory system	IV. Rubber hand illusion

Choose the ***correct*** answer from the options given below:

1. A-II, B-I, C-IV, D-III
2. A-II, B-III, C-IV, D-I
3. A-II, B-I, C-III, D-IV
4. A-II, B-IV, C-III, D-I

74. Which of the following is not included in verbal tests of Wechslers Adult intelligence scale?

1. Information
2. Digit symbol
3. Comprehension
4. Arithmetic

75. The moon is often perceived as 'racing' through a thin layer of clouds which is an example of:

1. Induced Movement
2. Real Movement
3. Apparent Movement
4. Autokinetic Movement

76. Which model explains how patients adapt to chronic illness based on their perceptions and beliefs about illness?

1. Promotion and Motivation model
2. Theory of reasoned action and planned behaviour
3. Self regulation model or common sense model
4. Health belief model

77. The academic aptitude and achievement test assess:

A. The student's potential for academic work
B. The candidate's knowledge in various subjects
C. The moral behaviour of the candidate
D. The pupile's ability to understand and apply that knowledge

Choose the ***correct*** answer from the options given below:

1. A, B and C only
2. A, C and D only
3. A, B and D only
4. B, C and D only

78. Persons having IQ level in between 20-25 to 35-40 require ______ during test administration.

1. Intermittent support
2. Limited support
3. Extensive support
4. Pervasive support

79. What are the ethics in counselling?

A. Trustworthiness
B. Directing
C. Autonomy
D. Justice
E. Moralising

Choose the ***correct*** answer from the options given below:

1. A, B, C only
2. A, B, D only
3. A, B, E only
4. A, C, D only

80. What are true from the following about Factorial Design?

A. There are more than one dependent variable.
B. There are more than one independent variable.
C. Dependent variable is continuous in nature.
D. Independent variable is continuous in nature.
E. Factors are extracted through factor loadings.

Choose the ***correct*** answer from the options given below:

1. A, B, C only
2. B, C only
3. B, D only
4. B, D, E only

81. Which theory of emotion relies heavily on cognition and labelling?

1. The original or common-sense, theory
2. Schachter-Singer's theory
3. Cannon-Bard's theory
4. James-Lange's theory

82. The most suitable method to verify construct validity of a psychological test is ______.

1. Calculating Cronbach alpha
2. Exploratory Factor Analysis
3. Multitrait - Multimethod Matrix
4. Computing Discrimination Index

83. Arrange the Kohlberg's stages of moral development in chronological order:

A. Instrumental relationism orientation
B. Interpersonal concordance orientation
C. Punishment and obedience orientation
D. Law-and-order orientation
E. Social contract-legalistic orientation

Choose the ***correct*** answer from the options given below:

1. C, A, B, D, E
2. C B, A, D, E
3. C, D, E, B, A
4. C, E, A, B, D

84. Arrange in sequence the stages of Kubler Ross theory of Death and Dying.

A. Anger
B. Denial
C. Bargain
D. Acceptance
E. Depression

Choose the ***correct*** answer from the options given below:

1. B, A, C, D, E
2. A, B, D, C, E
3. E, A, B, C, D
4. B, A, C, E, D

85. Arrange Erikson's stages of development in sequential manner:

A. Initiative vrs. Guilt
B. Industry vrs. Inferiority
C. Identify vrs. Role confusion
D. Intimacy vrs. Isolation

Choose the ***correct*** answer from the options given below:

1. A, B, C, D
2. A, C, B, D
3. C, A, B, D
4. C, B, D, A

86. The assumption that personal interpretation of ambiguous stimuli must necessarily reflect the unconscious needs, motives and conflicts of the examinee is known as:

1. Projective hypothesis
2. Semi-projective hypothesis
3. Non-projective hypothesis
4. Research hypothesis

87. Given below are two statements : one is labelled as Assertion (A) and the other is labelled as Reason (R).

Assertion (A): Prosopagnosia is a visual agnosia with specific to recognizing the face.

Reason (R): The diagnosis of prosopagnosia is associated with damage to the ventral surface to the brain, known as Fusiform face area at the boundary between the occipital and temporal lobes.

In the light of the above statements, choose the ***most appropriate*** answer from the options given below:

1. Both (A) and (R) are correct and (R) is the correct explanation of (A).
2. Both (A) and (R) are correct, but (R) is not the correct explanation of (A).
3. (A) is correct, but (R) is not correct.
4. (A) is not correct, but (R) is correct.

88. Tarun working as a server in a retail outlet, flirts with the customer. Which of the following represents 'consistency' domain of the Covariation Theory?

1. Many other servers in the retail outlet also flirt with the customers.
2. Tarun flirts with this customers at other times.
3. Tarun does not flirt with other customers.
4. No other servers flirt with the customer.

89. Match the List-I with List-II.

List-I (*Correlation Method*)	List-II (*Nature of the Variables*)
A. Biserial	I. Both the variables are continuous
B. Point Biserial	II. Both the variables are apparent dichotomous
C. Tetrachoric	III. One continuous and one genuinely dichotomous
D. Product moment	IV. One continuous and one apparently dichotomous

Choose the ***correct*** answer from the options given below:

1. A-IV, B-III, C-II, D-I
2. A-IV, B-II, C-III, D-I
3. A-III, B-II, C-IV, D-I
4. A-III, B-IV, C-I, D-II

90. Match the List-I with List-II.

List-I	List-II
A. Broadbent's Filter Theory	I. Attention is limited by cognitive resources, influenced by arousal
B. Treisman's Attentuation Theory	II. Unattended information is weakened but not completely blocked
C. Deutsch & Deutsch Late Selection Theory	III. Selection occurs after semantic analysis of all inputs
D. Kahneman's Capacity Model	IV. Attention works as an early filter, blocking unattended information completely

Choose the ***correct*** answer from the options given below:

1. A-IV, B-II, C-III, D-I
2. A-III, B-IV, C-I, D-II
3. A-I, B-III, C-II, D-IV
4. A-II, B-I, C-IV, D-III

Directions (Qs. No. 91 to 95): *Read the following passage and answer the questions:*

Ishita, a Psychometrician generated 120 items in July 2021 to develop a tool on pro-environmental behaviour with five response patterns starting from 'Strongly Disagree' to 'Strongly Agree'. She retained 85 items based upon item-total correlation Then she verified internal consistency of the items using data collected from 800 respondents in Dec, 2021. Ms. Ishita named five dimensions extracted by her through exploratory factor analysis in March 2022. Thereafter she collected data from 400 respondents and accomplished measurement model analysis through confirmatory factor analysis in November, 2022.

91. Which of the following method has been used to verify reliability?

1. Test-Retest method
2. Spearman-Brown prophecy method
3. Kuder-Richardson method
4. Cronbach-Alfa method

92. Which type of scale has been developed by Ishita?

1. Q-Short Scale
2. Semantic Differential Scale
3. Likert type Scale
4. Bogardus Scale

93. Square root of AVE (Average Variance Extracted) can be used to assess ______.

1. Composite Reliability
2. Inter-rater Reliability
3. Convergent Validity
4. Discriminant Validity

94. Confirmatory factor Analysis can help in examining:

1. Composite Validity
2. Face Validity
3. Convergent Validity
4. Criton-related Validity

95. Which type of validity has been established bv Ishita in March, 2022?

1. Content Validity
2. Construct Validity
3. Concurrent Validity
4. Predictive Validity

Directions (Qs. No. 96 to 100): *Read the following passage and answer the questions:*

Motivational Interviewing (MI) is a counselling technique where the counsellor provides information and leaves the decision to the client. It helps individuals explore and resolve ambivalence about change by drawing out their own motivation and goals. The process of MI follows four steps-planning, focusing, engaging and evolving. The skills of MI are not drastically different from the general skills of counselling. However, as in the case of counselling in general contextualising the skills is very important.

96. The first step of Motivational Interviewing (MI) is:

1. Evolving
2. Engaging
3. Focusing
4. Planning

97. In Evolving stage, the role of the counsellor is to:

1. Empower and instruct the client to initiate change
2. Instruct the client how to over come short comings
3. Assume the clients perspective
4. Encourage the client to express reasons for change

98. Who developed the principles of Motivational Interviewing (MI)?

1. Cormier, Nurius and Osborn
2. Rollnick, Miller and Butler
3. Roger, Butcher and Harlow
4. Gold, Sticker and Helms

99. Which principle is central to Motivational Interviewing (MI)?

1. Educative and Autonomy
2. Confrontative and Evocative
3. Collaborative and Educative
4. Autonomy and Collaborative

100. Which one of the following is not the correct principles for the practitioner of MI?

1. Challenges the client for resistance to change
2. Listening with empathy
3. Empowering the client
4. Resisting the righting reflex

ANSWERS

1	2	3	4	5	6	7	8	9	10
3	2	1	1	2	4	3	3	2	2
11	**12**	**13**	**14**	**15**	**16**	**17**	**18**	**19**	**20**
4	3	3	3	1	3	4	3	3	4
21	**22**	**23**	**24**	**25**	**26**	**27**	**28**	**29**	**30**
3	4	1	2	1	2	4	4	1	3
31	**32**	**33**	**34**	**35**	**36**	**37**	**38**	**39**	**40**
3	2	2	1	2	2	2	3	4	3
41	**42**	**43**	**44**	**45**	**46**	**47**	**48**	**49**	**50**
1	3	3	2	3	3	4	4	3	1
51	**52**	**53**	**54**	**55**	**56**	**57**	**58**	**59**	**60**
2	2	3	2	2	3	2	4	4	3

61	62	63	64	65	66	67	68	69	70
3	2	3	3	2	2	2	2	4	3
71	**72**	**73**	**74**	**75**	**76**	**77**	**78**	**79**	**80**
2	1	1	2	1	3	3	3	4	2
81	**82**	**83**	**84**	**85**	**86**	**87**	**88**	**89**	**90**
2	2	1	4	1	1	1	2	1	1
91	**92**	**93**	**94**	**95**	**96**	**97**	**98**	**99**	**100**
4	3	4	3	2	2	4	2	4	1

EXPLANATORY ANSWERS

1. In hypothesis testing, the direct relationship between the two statistics is $F = t^2$ when the comparison involves only two groups. Therefore, if we express the same relation in terms of t, it becomes $t = \sqrt{F}$. This is why the square-root relation is the correct one, not equality, half, or square of F. The question asks the relation between the two ratios, and among the given options, option 3 matches that exact mathematical relation.

2.
- **A-III:** Two-factor theory is associated with Charles Spearman because he proposed that intelligence has a general factor g along with specific factors s. This is the classical two-factor view of intelligence, so A must match III.
- **B-II:** Primary mental abilities are linked with Thurstone, who argued that intelligence is made up of several relatively independent mental abilities rather than only one general factor. Hence B correctly matches II.
- **C-IV:** Triarchic theory of intelligence was given by Sternberg, who described intelligence in analytical, creative, and practical forms. So C must match IV.
- **D-I:** Theory of multiple intelligence is associated with Howard Gardner, who proposed multiple distinct intelligences instead of a single general intelligence. Therefore D matches I.

3. Creative thinking refers to the ability to generate novel, original and useful ideas. One of the fundamental cognitive processes involved in creativity is divergent thinking, a concept strongly associated with J.P. Guilford's work on creativity research. Divergent thinking enables a person to produce numerous possible ideas, alternatives or solutions to a single problem, rather than converging quickly on one fixed answer. This mental flexibility expands the range of possibilities and increases the probability of arriving at an innovative idea. Because creativity essentially involves originality, fluency and flexibility of ideas, divergent thinking becomes a central mechanism through which creative thinking operates. The assertion states that creative thinking requires divergent thinking, which is valid because generating multiple potential ideas is a core step in creative ideation. The reason correctly explains this by stating that divergent thinking produces multiple solutions to a problem. Since the reason clearly describes the mechanism through which creative thinking operates, it directly explains the assertion. Therefore both statements are correct and the reason appropriately explains the assertion.

4. **A. Rorschach Inkblot Test:** This came first in 1921, when Hermann Rorschach published Psychodiagnostik. So A is the earliest among the four.

B. Draw-A-Man task: Florence Goodenough introduced this test in 1926. Therefore it comes after the Rorschach test and before the TAT.

C. Thematic Apperception Test: The TAT was introduced in 1935 by Henry Murray and Christiana Morgan. Hence it follows the Draw-A-Man task.

D. 16 Personality factor: The 16PF questionnaire was first published in 1949, making it the latest among the listed tests.

Thus the correct chronological order is A, B, C, D.

5. Steven Maier's later neuroscience work on learned helplessness showed that the ventromedial prefrontal cortex (vmPFC) has an important role in detecting controllability. When a subject can detect that a stressor is controllable, this brain region helps regulate the helplessness-related response system. That is why the blank is filled by ventromedial prefrontal cortex. The amygdala and hippocampus are important brain regions, and the dorsal raphe nucleus is involved in helplessness circuitry, but the specific higher-level region helping determine controllability is the vmPFC.

6. In a myelinated neuron, the axon is wrapped by insulating layers of myelin sheath produced by Schwann cells (in the peripheral nervous system) or oligodendrocytes (in the central nervous system). However, this myelin covering is not continuous along the entire length of the axon. Small periodic gaps occur between adjacent myelin segments, and these gaps are known as Nodes of Ranvier. These nodes play a crucial physiological role in nerve impulse conduction. Electrical impulses jump from one node to the next through a process called saltatory conduction, which greatly increases the speed of neural transmission compared to unmyelinated fibers. At these nodes, voltage-gated sodium and potassium channels are highly concentrated, allowing rapid regeneration of the action potential. The other options do not represent such gaps: the myelin sheath itself is the insulating covering, the axon hillock is the region where action potentials usually originate, and dendrites are branching structures receiving incoming signals.

7. Sigmund Freud's psycho-sexual theory of personality development proposed five sequential stages: oral, anal, phallic, latency and genital. The phallic stage, typically occurring between about 3 and 6 years of age, is the stage in which the child's attention is focused on the genital region and where significant psychodynamic conflicts emerge. During this period, Freud proposed that a male child develops an unconscious emotional attachment to the mother and perceives the father as a rival for maternal affection. This psychological conflict is termed the Oedipus complex. The child eventually resolves this conflict through identification with the father, which contributes to the formation of the superego and gender role development. The anal stage relates mainly to toilet training, the latency stage involves relative calm in sexual drives, and the genital stage occurs in adolescence; therefore none of those stages are associated with the Oedipus complex.

8. C. **Maslow's hierarchy of needs:** Abraham Maslow introduced this motivational theory in 1943, proposing that human motivation follows a hierarchy beginning with physiological needs and progressing to safety, love/belonging, esteem and self-actualization. It is the earliest among the listed theories.

   B. **McClelland's need achievement theory:** David McClelland developed the Need for Achievement theory in the 1950s (around 1953–1961). It emphasized three learned needs—achievement, power and affiliation—as major drivers of human motivation.

   D. **Dweck's self-theory:** Carol Dweck's work on implicit theories of intelligence and motivation (mindset theory) emerged mainly during the 1970s–1980s, focusing on fixed vs. growth mindsets and their impact on motivation and learning.

   A. **Deci's self-determination theory:** Edward Deci and Richard Ryan developed Self-Determination Theory in the mid-1980s (1985), emphasizing intrinsic motivation and the psychological needs of autonomy, competence and relatedness.

   The chronological order based on development years is therefore Maslow → McClelland → Dweck → Deci, which corresponds to option 3.

9. A. **Tyrosine:** Catecholamine synthesis begins with the amino acid tyrosine, which serves as the biochemical precursor for the pathway.

   D. **L-dopa:** Tyrosine is first converted into L-DOPA (L-dihydroxyphenylalanine) through the action of the enzyme tyrosine hydroxylase, which is the rate-limiting step in catecholamine synthesis.

   C. **Dopamine:** L-DOPA is then converted into dopamine by the enzyme DOPA decarboxylase. Dopamine itself functions as an important neurotransmitter.

   E. **Norepinephrine:** Dopamine is further converted into norepinephrine (noradrenaline) through the enzyme dopamine β-hydroxylase, mainly in sympathetic neurons and adrenal medulla.

B. **Epinephrine:** Finally, norepinephrine is converted into epinephrine (adrenaline) by the enzyme phenylethanolamine N-methyltransferase, especially in the adrenal medulla.

Thus the biochemical pathway proceeds as Tyrosine → L-DOPA → Dopamine → Norepinephrine → Epinephrine, matching option 2.

10. Edward L. Thorndike was a pioneering psychologist in the study of learning and animal behavior. Two of the most important principles emerging from his connectionist learning theory were Associative Shifting and the Law of Effect. The Law of Effect states that responses followed by satisfying consequences are more likely to be repeated, whereas responses followed by discomfort are less likely to recur. This principle became foundational in later behaviorist learning theories and operant conditioning research. Associative shifting refers to the process by which a response initially connected with one stimulus gradually becomes associated with another stimulus through repeated pairings during learning. These contributions significantly influenced the understanding of stimulus–response learning. The law of similarity belongs more to Gestalt learning principles, and extinction was primarily elaborated later within classical and operant conditioning frameworks rather than being one of Thorndike's main doctrinal contributions.

11. Determinism is the philosophical and scientific assumption that every event occurring in the universe happens according to definite laws of causation. According to this principle, no event occurs randomly; instead, each phenomenon is the inevitable result of preceding conditions governed by causal laws. In psychology and natural sciences, determinism implies that behaviour and mental processes can be explained through identifiable causes such as biological, environmental, or psychological factors. This viewpoint underlies much of scientific research because it assumes that events follow lawful patterns that can be studied and predicted. Mechanism refers more broadly to explaining processes through mechanical or physical systems, operationism relates to defining concepts through observable operations, and natural monism concerns metaphysical unity of nature. Only determinism precisely describes the belief that all events are governed by causal laws.

12. B. **Snowball sampling is based upon sociometry:** Snowball sampling is a non-probability sampling technique in which existing participants help recruit further participants from their social networks. Because recruitment occurs through interpersonal links, the method relies on sociometric connections among individuals, making this statement valid.

C. **'G' power is used to estimate sample size:** G'Power is a statistical software widely used for power analysis, which helps researchers determine the appropriate sample size required to detect an effect with a specified level of statistical power. Therefore this statement is correct.

E. **Standard deviation of sampling distribution is sampling error:** In statistical theory, the standard deviation of the sampling distribution of a statistic is called the standard error, which represents sampling error. It quantifies how much a sample statistic is expected to vary from the true population parameter.

Statements A and D are incorrect because purposive sampling is a non-probability method and sampling error generally decreases rather than increases with larger sample sizes.

13. Canonical correlation analysis is a multivariate statistical technique designed to examine the relationship between two sets of variables simultaneously. Each set can contain multiple variables, meaning the analysis involves more than one dependent (criterion) variable and more than one independent (predictor) variable. The procedure constructs canonical variates—linear combinations of variables from each set—and then measures the correlation between these variates. In contrast, simple regression involves one dependent variable and one predictor; multiple regression still retains only one dependent variable despite multiple predictors; and three-way ANOVA studies the effect of three independent variables on a single dependent variable. Therefore canonical correlation is the correct option.

14. In evolutionary biology, spandrels refer to traits that arise as incidental by-products of the evolution of other structures rather than through direct adaptive selection. The concept was introduced by Stephen Jay Gould and Richard Lewontin to explain biological features that exist not because they provide survival advantages but because they are unavoidable structural consequences of other evolutionary changes. The human navel (belly button) is an example because it is simply the scar left after the umbilical cord detaches following birth. It does not contribute to survival or reproduction and therefore has no adaptive function. Homologous structures share a common evolutionary origin, analogous structures perform similar functions despite different origins, and exaptations are traits that evolved for one function but were later co-opted for another. The navel fits the concept of a spandrel.

15. • **A–I (Confluence – Absence of difference between self and others):** In Gestalt therapy, confluence occurs when an individual experiences a blurred boundary between oneself and others, losing awareness of personal identity and merging psychologically with others.
   • **B–IV (Retroflection – Suppression of behaviour and redirection onto the self):** Retroflection involves turning impulses meant for others back toward oneself, often resulting in self-directed behaviour such as self-criticism or internalized aggression.
   • **C–III (Deflection – Avoidance of contact with others):** Deflection refers to strategies used to avoid direct emotional contact, such as changing the subject, joking, or intellectualizing instead of engaging authentically.
   • **D–II (Introjection – Lack of discrimination or assimilation of new information gained):** Introjection occurs when individuals uncritically accept beliefs or attitudes from others without properly assimilating or evaluating them, leading to unexamined internalized rules or values.

16. Drive reduction theory, proposed by Clark Hull, explains motivation primarily in terms of homeostasis, the body's tendency to maintain internal physiological balance. When a biological imbalance occurs (for example hunger, thirst, or fatigue), it produces a psychological state called a drive. This drive motivates behaviour aimed at reducing the imbalance and restoring equilibrium. For instance, lack of food creates hunger drive, which motivates eating; lack of water produces thirst drive, motivating drinking. Once the need is satisfied, the physiological balance is restored and the drive is reduced. Because the central mechanism of this theory is restoring internal balance, the concept of homeostasis is fundamental to drive reduction theory. Instinct theory focuses on innate patterns of behaviour, while need for affiliation and need for achievement theories emphasize social and learned motivations rather than biological equilibrium.

17. **C. Item Discrimination Index:** In questionnaire construction, after drafting items, the first empirical step is item analysis. The item discrimination index evaluates how well each item differentiates between respondents with high and low overall scores. Items that fail to discriminate effectively are revised or eliminated so that only useful items remain in the instrument.

A. Curricular (Content) Validity: After identifying workable items, content or curricular validity is examined through expert judgement. Specialists check whether the selected items adequately represent the theoretical construct or subject domain that the questionnaire is intended to measure. This step ensures conceptual relevance and coverage.

D. Exploratory Factor Analysis (EFA): With items verified for relevance, EFA is conducted to explore the underlying structure of the questionnaire. It statistically groups items into latent factors or dimensions without imposing a prior model, helping researchers understand how items naturally cluster.

B. Confirmatory Factor Analysis (CFA): Once EFA suggests a factor structure, CFA is used to test and confirm whether the hypothesized factor model fits the data. This step validates the measurement structure, usually using a different dataset or sample.

E. Norm Development: After the questionnaire's structure and validity are established, norms are developed by administering the instrument to a large representative population. These norms provide reference values (means, percentiles, standard scores) for interpreting individual results.

The correct sequence is C → A → D → B → E.

18. • **A–II (Allport – Cardinal, central, secondary traits):** Gordon Allport proposed a trait theory distinguishing cardinal traits, central traits,

and secondary traits to describe the structure of personality characteristics.

- **B–I (Cattell – 16 PF (Surface and source traits)):** Raymond Cattell developed factor-analytic personality research and created the 16 Personality Factor (16PF) questionnaire, differentiating between surface traits and underlying source traits.
- **C–IV (H.J. Eysenck – Extraversion–Neuroticism–Psychoticism dimensions):** Hans J. Eysenck proposed a biologically oriented model of personality consisting of three major dimensions: Extraversion, Neuroticism, and Psychoticism (PEN model).
- **D–III (Sigmund Freud – Psychosexual stages of development):** Freud's psychoanalytic theory described personality development through psychosexual stages such as oral, anal, phallic, latency, and genital stages.

19. **C. Stimulus:** According to Lazarus's cognitive mediational theory, an emotional process begins with an environmental stimulus, which may be internal or external.

A. Appraisal: The individual then performs cognitive appraisal, evaluating whether the stimulus is threatening, beneficial, or irrelevant to personal well-being.

D. Emotional response: Based on this appraisal, a specific emotion such as fear, anger, or happiness is experienced. The emotional experience is therefore mediated by cognitive evaluation.

B. Bodily response: After the emotion is generated, physiological responses such as increased heart rate, sweating, or hormonal changes occur as part of the emotional reaction.

20. The Peabody Picture Vocabulary Test–IV (PPVT-IV) is designed to measure receptive vocabulary and verbal ability in individuals from early childhood to adulthood. It is specifically structured as a non-reading and motor-reduced test, meaning that the participant does not need to read words or produce complex motor responses. Instead, the examiner speaks a word and the participant selects the picture that best represents that word from a set of images. Because responses involve simply pointing or indicating a picture, the test minimizes the influence of reading ability, writing skills, or motor coordination. This feature makes it especially useful for assessing language ability in young children, individuals with reading difficulties, or persons with motor impairments.

21. Wilhelm Wundt proposed the concept of creative synthesis as part of his voluntaristic theory of mind. According to Wundt, mental elements such as sensations and feelings combine in consciousness through an active mental process rather than through mere mechanical association. The mind has the capacity to willfully organize and rearrange these elements into new patterns, producing experiences that are qualitatively different from the individual components. Thus the resulting conscious experience becomes more complex than the simple sum of its parts. This active organization of mental contents by the mind is called creative synthesis, and it laid the groundwork for later ideas emphasizing holistic perception in psychology.

22. **B. Precontemplation:** This is the initial stage in Prochaska and DiClemente's Transtheoretical Model where individuals have no intention to change behaviour in the foreseeable future and may not yet recognize that a problem exists.

A. Contemplation: Individuals become aware of the problem and begin thinking about behavioural change. They evaluate the advantages and disadvantages of changing but have not yet committed themselves to action.

D. Preparation: At this stage individuals intend to take action soon and start making preliminary steps such as gathering information or planning strategies for behavioural modification.

C. Action: This stage involves actively implementing behavioural change. Individuals modify behaviour, environment, or experiences to overcome the problem and adopt healthier practices.

E. Maintenance: The final stage focuses on sustaining the behavioural change for a long period and preventing relapse by reinforcing new habits and coping strategies.

23. When the level of significance (α) is reduced from 0.05 to 0.01, the rejection criterion for the null hypothesis becomes more stringent. This means stronger statistical evidence is required to reject the null hypothesis. Because the rejection region becomes smaller, the probability of failing to reject a false null hypothesis increases, thereby increasing the chance of a Type II error (β). Hence the assertion is correct. The reason is also correct because Type II error occurs when a false null hypothesis is wrongly accepted or not rejected. The stricter significance level makes it more likely that the null hypothesis will be retained even when it is false, which directly corresponds to the definition of Type II error. Therefore the reason correctly explains the assertion.

24.
- **A–III (Biographical Research – Retrospective Studies):** Biographical research investigates an individual's life history by examining past events, personal narratives, and life experiences, usually through retrospective accounts and historical records.
- **B–IV (Ethnography – Cultural Anthropology):** Ethnography originates from cultural anthropology and involves detailed observation and description of the culture, traditions, and behaviour of particular groups within their natural settings.
- **C–II (Grounded Theory – Theoretical Saturation):** Grounded theory aims to develop theoretical explanations directly from empirical data. Data collection continues until theoretical saturation is reached, meaning no new categories or insights emerge.
- **D–I (Phenomenological Approach – Lived Experiences):** Phenomenological research focuses on understanding individuals' lived experiences and how people perceive and interpret particular phenomena in their everyday lives.

25. In Baddeley and Hitch's working memory model, verbal information is processed through the phonological loop, while visual and spatial information is processed through the visuospatial sketchpad. During many cognitive tasks, individuals may therefore encode information using both verbal and visual strategies simultaneously, which makes the assertion correct. The episodic buffer, introduced later by Baddeley, acts as an integrative system that temporarily stores and binds information from the phonological loop, visuospatial sketchpad, and long-term memory into a unified representation. Because it integrates and holds information from both verbal and visual subsystems, it allows these different types of encoded information to function together during memory tasks. Thus the reason correctly explains how both forms of encoding can operate simultaneously.

26. Richard Lazarus' Cognitive Appraisal Theory explains that individuals evaluate stressful situations through two major stages of appraisal. In primary appraisal, a person evaluates whether an event is irrelevant, benign, or threatening to well-being. In secondary appraisal, the individual evaluates available coping resources and possible strategies to manage the stressor. When a person asks the question "How can I deal with this potentially harmful stressor?", the focus is clearly on assessing coping options, resources, and strategies. This reflects the evaluation of what can be done to manage or control the threat, which is the defining feature of secondary appraisal. Thus the statement describes the secondary appraisal stage.

27. The Friedman Test is a non-parametric statistical test used when the assumptions of parametric repeated-measures ANOVA are violated. It serves as the non-parametric alternative to two-way ANOVA with repeated measures, particularly when the same subjects are measured under different conditions and the data are ordinal or not normally distributed. The Friedman test works by ranking the scores within each participant across conditions and then analyzing whether the ranks differ significantly across treatments. The other tests listed do not correspond to a two-way ANOVA counterpart: Wilcoxon sign test compares two related samples, Kruskal–Wallis is the non-parametric alternative to one-way ANOVA, and Spearman's rank test measures correlation rather than group differences.

28. Electrodermal Activity (EDA) is a psychophysiological technique used to measure changes in the electrical conductance of the skin, which occur due to activity of the sweat glands controlled by the sympathetic nervous system. The Skin Conductance Response (SCR) reflects momentary changes in skin conductivity associated with emotional arousal, stress, or attention. Electrodes are placed on the skin, usually on the fingers or palm, and small variations in electrical conductance are recorded. Because sweat gland activity increases with sympathetic activation, SCR is widely used in studies of emotion, stress, lie detection, and autonomic nervous system functioning. The other options measure different physiological processes: EEG records brain electrical activity, CT scan provides structural brain imaging, and EMG measures muscle activity.

29. In classical conditioning, the most effective learning occurs when the conditioned stimulus (CS) precedes the unconditioned stimulus (UCS) by a short interval. This arrangement, known as forward conditioning, allows the organism to use the CS as a reliable signal predicting the UCS. If the UCS appears before the CS, learning is weaker because the CS does not provide useful predictive information. Therefore the assertion is correct because conditioning occurs faster when the UCS follows the CS. The reason is also correct because, according to the cognitive perspective of conditioning, learning occurs when the CS creates an expectancy that the UCS will occur. When the CS precedes the UCS, the CS functions as a predictor of the UCS, strengthening the association. Hence the reason correctly explains the assertion.

30. Dialectical Behaviour Therapy (DBT), developed by Marsha Linehan, teaches four major categories of behavioural skills that help individuals regulate emotions and cope with distress. These four skill modules are Core Mindfulness, Emotion Regulation, Distress Tolerance, and Interpersonal Effectiveness. Core mindfulness focuses on awareness and acceptance of the present moment. Emotion regulation skills help individuals understand and manage intense emotions. Distress tolerance skills teach methods for surviving crises without making situations worse. Interpersonal effectiveness skills focus on maintaining healthy relationships while asserting personal needs. The option "Intrapersonal Effectiveness skills" is not one of the four DBT skill modules, making it the correct answer.

31. Context-dependent forgetting refers to the phenomenon in which recall of information becomes more difficult when the environmental context during retrieval differs from the context present during encoding. Memory retrieval is facilitated when the same contextual cues that were present at the time of learning are available again at the time of recall. This idea is strongly supported by the encoding specificity principle, which states that memory is best retrieved when the cues available at recall match those present during encoding. Therefore statement A is correct because forgetting increases when contexts differ. Statement B is also correct because encoding specificity provides the theoretical basis for context-dependent memory. Statement C is incorrect since context effects apply to episodic memory rather than only procedural memory, and D is incorrect because context-dependent forgetting is directly related to environmental cues.

32. Psychologist Paul Ekman proposed that certain emotional expressions are biologically innate and universal across cultures. Through cross-cultural research involving participants from different societies, including isolated communities, Ekman identified six basic universal emotions that are expressed through similar facial expressions worldwide. These emotions are happiness, sadness, fear, anger, surprise, and disgust. Because people from very different cultural backgrounds recognize these expressions in the same way, they are considered universal emotional expressions.

33. The Rorschach Inkblot Test, developed by Swiss psychiatrist Hermann Rorschach, is a projective personality assessment technique consisting of 10 standardized inkblot cards. Participants are shown each inkblot and asked to describe what they see in the ambiguous image. Their responses are interpreted to understand underlying personality characteristics, emotional functioning, and thought processes. The ambiguity of the inkblots encourages individuals to project their internal thoughts, motives, and feelings onto the stimulus, which forms the basis of the interpretation.

34. In Carl Rogers' person-centered counselling approach, three core conditions are considered essential for effective therapeutic change. These are empathy, unconditional positive regard, and congruence (genuineness). Empathy refers to the therapist's ability to understand the client's internal frame of reference. Unconditional positive regard involves accepting the client without judgment, and congruence refers to authenticity and transparency of the counsellor. Reflection is a counselling technique used by therapists to paraphrase or clarify clients' statements, but it is not one of the three fundamental core conditions required for effective counselling according to Rogers.

35. According to the World Health Organization's Ottawa Charter for Health Promotion (1986), health promotion is aimed at the entire population within the context of their everyday lives, rather than concentrating only on particular high-risk groups or narrowly defined target groups. The goal of health promotion is to enable people to increase control over and improve their health by addressing broad determinants such as social conditions, environmental factors, and lifestyle influences. Thus limiting health promotion only to specific target groups contradicts this broader population-based perspective. WHO principles emphasize public participation and empowerment, encouraging communities to take active roles in improving health conditions and forming self-help initiatives. They also stress addressing the causes of health problems, including environmental and social determinants, rather than focusing solely on disease treatment. Additionally, health professionals and primary health-care workers play an important supportive role in enabling and guiding health promotion activities. Therefore the statement suggesting that health promotion should be restricted to specific target groups is inconsistent with WHO's principles.

36. Adaptation refers to the process through which individuals develop behaviours, skills, and strategies that allow them to function effectively within their environment. It involves learning or acquiring abilities that help a person cope with environmental demands, solve problems, and maintain effective functioning in a particular setting. Thus the assertion correctly defines adaptation as the development of skills required by one's environment. The reason is also correct because successful adaptation varies across cultures and environments; different societies value different competencies depending on ecological, social, and cultural conditions. For example, adaptation in technologically advanced urban societies may require digital and analytical skills, whereas adaptation in rural agricultural settings may involve agricultural knowledge and ecological awareness. However, the reason only describes variation in adaptation across cultures and does not explain why adaptation itself is defined as the development of environment-specific skills. Therefore both statements are correct, but the reason does not explain the assertion.

37. The method of limits is one of the classical psychophysical methods used to determine sensory thresholds such as the absolute threshold (RL) and the difference threshold (DL). In this technique, stimuli are presented either in ascending order (increasing intensity) or descending order (decreasing intensity). The observer indicates the point at which the stimulus becomes detectable or undetectable, and the threshold is calculated from these transition points. This method was developed by Gustav Fechner, the founder of psychophysics, who attempted to establish a quantitative relationship between physical stimuli and psychological sensation. Fechner also introduced other important psychophysical methods such as the method of constant stimuli and the method of adjustment, making significant contributions to the scientific measurement of sensory experience.

38. Resilience refers to the capacity to adapt positively and recover effectively in the face of adversity, stress, trauma, or challenging life circumstances. Psychological research defines resilience as the ability to maintain or regain mental health despite experiencing significant stressors. Therefore the Assertion is correct because resilience specifically involves positive adaptation during difficult conditions. The Reason is incorrect because resilience does not mean the absence of stress in a person's life. In fact, resilience can only be observed when stress, adversity, or risk is present, since it reflects how effectively individuals cope with and recover from those challenges. Thus resilience represents the capacity to "bounce back" from stress rather than the avoidance of stress.

39. Cognitive Evaluation Theory (CET), proposed by Edward Deci and Richard Ryan as part of Self-Determination Theory, explains motivation in terms of intrinsic psychological needs such as competence, autonomy, and relatedness. According to this perspective, individuals engage in activities not merely because of external rewards or the nature of the activity, but because the activity provides a sense of mastery, competence, and personal satisfaction. In the example given, Bhabesh plays violent video games not because he is attracted to the violent content but because the activity gives him a feeling of mastery and competence. This intrinsic motivation aligns with cognitive evaluation theory rather than aggression-based theories such as the frustration–aggression hypothesis or catharsis hypothesis.

40. In existential psychology, particularly in the work of Ludwig Binswanger and Rollo May, human existence is understood through several dimensions of "being-in-the-world." These include Umwelt, the physical or biological world representing interaction with the natural environment; Mitwelt, the social world involving relationships with other people; Eigenwelt, the psychological or inner world reflecting self-awareness and personal identity; and Überwelt, the spiritual or ideal world related to values, beliefs, and meaning. The option stating "Social World – Life welt" is incorrect because the correct existential term for the social world is Mitwelt, not "Life welt." Therefore the given combination is not correct.

41. Carol Ryff's model of Psychological Well-Being (1989) proposes six dimensions describing optimal psychological functioning: Self-acceptance, Environmental mastery, Personal growth, Purpose in life, Autonomy, and Positive relations with others. These dimensions represent different aspects of positive psychological functioning. Self-acceptance refers to having a positive attitude toward oneself; environmental mastery refers to the ability to effectively manage life situations and surrounding environments; personal growth indicates continuous development and realization of potential; purpose in life involves having goals and meaning in life; and autonomy reflects independence and self-determination in thinking and behaviour. Although Positive relations with others is the sixth dimension not listed in option 1, the five components given in option 1 are all genuine dimensions of Ryff's model. The other options include constructs such as optimism, grit, and resilience, which belong to other psychological theories and are not part of Ryff's framework.

42. The Flynn Effect, identified by psychologist James R. Flynn, refers to the observed long-term rise in average intelligence test scores across many countries over the twentieth century. Studies of IQ test results showed that each generation tends to perform better than the previous one on standardized intelligence tests. The increase has been attributed to factors such as improved nutrition, better education, more cognitively stimulating environments, technological advancement, and increased familiarity with abstract reasoning tasks. This phenomenon was observed primarily in modernized and industrialized societies, making option 3 the correct description of the Flynn Effect.

43. Functional fixedness is a cognitive bias in which individuals have difficulty seeing alternative uses for familiar objects because they are accustomed to thinking of them only in their conventional roles. Overcoming functional fixedness occurs when a person successfully identifies a novel or unconventional use for an object. In the given example, thermocol is used as a temporary substitute for an earring back, which represents a creative alternative use for the material. By using thermocol in a way different from its usual purpose, the individual demonstrates the ability to overcome functional fixedness.

44. Kinesthesis (or kinesthetic sense) refers to the sensory system that provides information about the position and movement of body parts. Specialized receptors located in muscles, tendons, and joints send signals to the brain regarding muscle tension, limb position, and body movement. This information allows individuals to coordinate movement and maintain posture without necessarily relying on visual input. The kinesthetic sense is therefore essential for performing coordinated motor activities such as walking, writing, or maintaining balance.

45.
- **A–III (Kaivalya – Self realization):** In Indian philosophical traditions, especially Yoga philosophy, Kaivalya refers to the ultimate state of liberation or spiritual isolation of the self, often interpreted as self-realization or complete spiritual freedom.
- **B–IV (Asuya – Jealousy):** Asuya in classical Indian thought denotes jealousy or envy, referring to resentment toward the success or qualities of others.
- **C–I (Buddhi – Intellect):** Buddhi represents the faculty of intellect or discriminative intelligence that enables understanding, decision-making, and discernment between right and wrong.

- **D–II (Tarka – Reasoning):** Tarka refers to logical reasoning or analytical argument used to arrive at valid conclusions in philosophical discourse.

46. Encoding into long-term memory is influenced by several cognitive and emotional factors that determine how effectively information is processed and stored. Attention at the time of learning (A) is essential because information must first be actively attended to before it can be encoded into memory. Divided attention weakens encoding and reduces later recall. Emotional salience of the material (B) also enhances encoding because emotionally meaningful information activates stronger cognitive processing and is often supported by amygdala involvement, leading to stronger memory traces. Repetition alone regardless of meaning (C) is not sufficient for effective long-term encoding because simple rote rehearsal without semantic processing usually leads to shallow encoding. Use of retrieval cues during learning (D) primarily facilitates recall rather than the encoding process itself. Therefore only A and B are correct.

47.
- **A–IV (Correspondent Inference – Jones & Davis):** The Correspondent Inference Theory was proposed by Edward Jones and Keith Davis, explaining how people infer internal dispositions from observed behaviour.
- **B–I (Covariation Theory – Kelley):** Harold Kelley proposed the Covariation Model of attribution, which explains how individuals attribute behaviour to internal or external causes based on consensus, consistency and distinctiveness information.
- **C–II (Planned Behaviour – Ajzen & Fishbein):** The Theory of Planned Behaviour, developed by Icek Ajzen and earlier work with Martin Fishbein, explains how attitudes, subjective norms and perceived behavioural control influence behavioural intentions.
- **D–III (Social Comparison – Festinger):** Leon Festinger proposed Social Comparison Theory, which suggests individuals evaluate their own opinions and abilities by comparing themselves with others.

48. Guilford's Structure of Intellect (SI) model, often called the cubical model of intelligence, proposed that intellectual abilities arise from combinations of three dimensions: Operations, Contents, and Products. Operations include processes such as cognition, memory, convergent production, divergent production, and evaluation. Contents refer to types of information such as figural, symbolic, semantic, and behavioural. The product dimension represents the form in which information is organized or processed and includes categories such as units, classes, relations, systems, transformations, and implications. Among the options provided, transformations belongs to the product dimension.

49. **A. Notice that something unusual is happening:** According to Latane and Darley's model of helping behaviour, the first step is noticing that an unusual event or potential problem is occurring in the environment.

D. Interpret the event as an emergency: After noticing the event, the individual must interpret the situation as one requiring assistance or intervention.

E. Accept responsibility for helping: If the event is perceived as an emergency, the individual must decide that they personally are responsible for providing help.

B. Decide that you have the knowledge or skills needed to help: The individual evaluates whether they possess the necessary competence or resources to assist effectively.

C. Decide to actually help: Finally, the individual chooses to implement helping behaviour.

50. Attachment theory applied to adult relationships suggests that different attachment styles arise from combinations of self-esteem (view of self) and interpersonal trust (view of others). Individuals with low self-esteem but high trust in others tend to develop a preoccupied attachment style. Such individuals often seek high levels of approval, closeness, and reassurance from others because they doubt their own self-worth but believe others are valuable and trustworthy. This results in dependence on relationships for validation and emotional security.

51.
- **A–III (Abraham Maslow – Hierarchy of needs):** Abraham Maslow proposed the Hierarchy of Needs theory, which explains human motivation as progressing through five levels of needs: physiological, safety, love/belonging, esteem, and self-actualization.

These needs are arranged hierarchically, with lower-level needs generally requiring satisfaction before higher-level needs become motivationally important.

- **B–I (McClelland – Achievement, affiliation, power motives):** David McClelland developed the Need Theory of Motivation, identifying three primary learned needs: need for achievement (nAch), need for affiliation (nAff), and need for power (nPow). These motives influence behaviour, work performance, and leadership styles.
- **C–IV (Herzberg – Two-factor theory):** Frederick Herzberg proposed the Two-Factor Theory of Motivation, distinguishing between hygiene factors (such as salary, working conditions, and job security) and motivator factors (such as achievement, recognition, and responsibility). Hygiene factors prevent dissatisfaction, whereas motivators promote job satisfaction.
- **D–II (Vroom – Expectancy–Valence model):** Victor Vroom developed the Expectancy Theory of Motivation, which explains motivation as a function of three components: expectancy (belief that effort leads to performance), instrumentality (belief that performance leads to outcomes), and valence (value placed on the outcome).

52. In Indian psychological and philosophical traditions related to cittá (mind-stuff), mental functioning is often described through components such as manas, buddhi, and ahankara. Manas functions as the coordinating center of sensory processing and mental activity, integrating information received from the sense organs and directing attention. Because it organizes and processes incoming sensory information before further evaluation, it is often described as the central processor within this system of mental functioning. Buddhi represents higher intellect or discriminative reasoning, ahankara refers to the ego sense or sense of individuality, and vasana refers to latent impressions or tendencies.

53. • **A–III (Dialectical Behaviour Therapy – Marsha Linehan):** Dialectical Behaviour Therapy (DBT) was developed by Marsha Linehan to treat individuals with severe emotional dysregulation, especially borderline personality disorder.

- **B–I (Reality Therapy – Glasser):** William Glasser developed Reality Therapy, which focuses on personal responsibility and fulfilling basic psychological needs through effective behaviour.
- **C–II (Existential Psycho Therapy – Kierkegaard):** Existential psychotherapy draws heavily from the philosophical ideas of Søren Kierkegaard, who emphasized individuality, freedom, and personal responsibility in human existence.
- **D–IV (Solution-focused Therapy – Shazer):** Steve de Shazer developed Solution-Focused Brief Therapy, which concentrates on identifying solutions and strengths rather than analysing problems extensively.

54. In Patanjali's Yoga Sutras, the eight limbs of yoga (Ashtanga Yoga) describe progressive stages of spiritual discipline. Dharana refers to concentration, the stage in which the practitioner focuses the mind on a single object or point of attention. It follows pratyahara (withdrawal of senses) and precedes dhyana (meditation). Dharana represents the development of sustained attention and mental control, which eventually leads to deeper meditative states.

55. In genetics, alleles are alternative forms of a gene that occupy the same position (locus) on homologous chromosomes and control the same trait. For example, different alleles may determine variations of a particular characteristic such as eye colour or blood type. An individual inherits one allele from each parent, and the interaction between these alleles determines the expressed trait. Homozygous refers to having identical alleles for a trait, heterozygous refers to having different alleles, and genetic recombination refers to the process of genetic material exchange during meiosis.

56. • **A–I (Law of proximity – We group close to each other together):** According to Gestalt psychology, the law of proximity states that objects located near each other are perceived as belonging to the same group. Spatial closeness leads individuals to organize elements into unified perceptual groups.

- **B–IV (Law of similarity–Grouping similar items together in perception):** The law of similarity explains that elements sharing similar features such as shape, color, or size tend to be perceived as belonging together. Similarity therefore becomes a basis for perceptual organization.

- **C – II (Law of closure–Perceiving familiar shapes even when incomplete):** The law of closure states that the perceptual system tends to fill in missing parts of a figure so that incomplete patterns are perceived as complete and meaningful wholes.
- **D–III (Law of figure–ground – Distinguishing object from background):** The figure–ground principle describes how the perceptual system separates the focal object (figure) from the surrounding environment (background), allowing clear perception of the object.

57. Eudaimonic well-being refers to a form of well-being that emphasizes self-realization, personal growth, and living in accordance with one's true values and purpose. The concept originates from Aristotelian philosophy, where happiness arises from fulfilling one's potential and functioning optimally as a human being. In psychology, this perspective focuses on meaning, self-development, autonomy, and the pursuit of life goals consistent with personal values rather than simply maximizing pleasure or avoiding discomfort.

58. Health psychology is a field that studies how psychological, behavioural, and social factors influence health, illness, and healthcare. Its interventions are not limited to clinical treatment of patients; instead, they include health promotion, disease prevention, stress management, and improvement of quality of life. Therefore the Assertion is incorrect. The Reason is correct because health psychology indeed focuses on prevention, promotion of healthy behaviour, and enhancement of quality of life, often through behavioural interventions, education, and lifestyle modification.

59. The gray matter of the spinal cord has a characteristic H-shaped structure consisting of different horns. The dorsal horns (posterior horns) form the two dorsal arms of this structure and are primarily responsible for processing sensory information entering the spinal cord. The ventral horns are the anterior projections of gray matter that contain motor neurons responsible for sending signals to skeletal muscles. Dorsal root ganglia are clusters of sensory neuron cell bodies located outside the spinal cord, and basal ganglia are brain structures involved in motor control. Therefore the dorsal arms correspond to the dorsal horns, while ventral horns form the anterior arms.

60. The low-ball technique is a compliance strategy based on the principle of commitment and consistency, described by Robert Cialdini. In this technique, a person first agrees to a request or commitment under attractive initial conditions. After the commitment is made, the conditions are changed (for example, a higher cost or additional requirement is introduced). Because people prefer to remain consistent with their previous commitments and decisions, they often continue with the agreement even after the change. This psychological desire for consistency explains why the low-ball technique is effective in gaining compliance.

61. Sternberg's Triarchic Theory of Intelligence proposes three major types of intelligence describing how individuals process information and adapt to their environment. Componential intelligence (B) refers to analytical abilities involved in problem solving, evaluating ideas, and performing academic tasks. Experiential intelligence (C) refers to creative abilities that enable individuals to deal with novel situations and generate innovative solutions. Contextual intelligence (D) refers to practical intelligence, which involves adapting to, shaping, or selecting environments to meet personal goals. The other options listed, Progressive intelligence and Exponential intelligence, are not components of Sternberg's triarchic model. Therefore the correct set is B, C, and D.

62. The Panchakosha theory described in the Taittiriya Upanishad explains human existence through five successive sheaths or layers of consciousness that cover the inner self. The outermost layer is the Annamaya Kosha (B), the physical sheath associated with the material body sustained by food. The next is Pranamaya Kosha (D), the vital energy sheath that regulates physiological processes and life force (prana). The third layer is Manomaya Kosha (C), the mental sheath responsible for thoughts, emotions, and sensory processing. The fourth layer is Vijnanamaya Kosha (A), the intellectual sheath associated with discrimination, wisdom, and higher knowledge.

The innermost sheath is Anandamaya Kosha (E), the bliss sheath representing deep spiritual awareness and inner joy. Thus the correct order from outermost to innermost is Annamaya → Pranamaya → Manomaya → Vijnanamaya → Anandamaya.

63. • **A–III (Availability heuristic – What comes to mind first):** The availability heuristic involves judging the likelihood of events based on how easily examples come to mind, often influenced by recent or vivid experiences.

• **B–IV (Representativeness heuristic – Assuming that what is typical is also likely the solution):** This heuristic occurs when individuals judge probabilities based on how much something resembles a typical case or prototype.

• **C–II (Anchoring-and-adjustment heuristic – Reference points that may guide problem solving):** People rely on an initial reference value (anchor) and make adjustments from that point when estimating unknown quantities.

• **D–I (Framing – Presentation of information concerning potential outcomes):** Framing refers to how the presentation or wording of information influences decisions and judgments.

64. Social facilitation refers to the tendency for individuals to perform better on well-learned or simple tasks when in the presence of others. In the given situation, Saumya is a trained singer performing before an audience, and the presence of others increases her excitement and improves performance, illustrating social facilitation. Therefore the Assertion is correct. The Reason is incorrect because additive tasks relate to social loafing and group productivity, not social facilitation. Additive tasks involve combining individual efforts in group work, which is conceptually different from the audience effect responsible for social facilitation.

65. The major divisions of the brain can be arranged developmentally from lower to higher structures. The Myelencephalon (A) forms the medulla oblongata and represents the lowest part of the hindbrain. Above it lies the Metencephalon (B), which includes the pons and cerebellum and plays an important role in coordination and regulation of movement. The Mesencephalon (C) corresponds to the midbrain and functions in visual and auditory reflexes and motor control. The Diencephalon (E) includes structures such as the thalamus and hypothalamus involved in sensory relay and homeostasis. The highest division is the Telencephalon (D), which forms the cerebral hemispheres responsible for higher cognitive processes such as thinking, reasoning, and voluntary behaviour.

66. In the Wechsler Adult Intelligence Scale (WAIS), the Working Memory Index (WMI) measures the ability to hold, maintain, and mentally manipulate information for short periods. It includes subtests such as Digit Span, Arithmetic, and Letter–Number Sequencing, which are sensitive to attention, concentration, and immediate auditory memory. These tasks require individuals to temporarily store and manipulate verbally presented information, making the Assertion correct. The Reason is also correct because a relatively low WMI score often indicates difficulties with attention control or short-term/working memory, particularly with orally presented material, since these subtests rely heavily on auditory processing and mental manipulation. However, the reason does not explain why WMI is composed of subtests sensitive to attention and immediate memory; instead, it describes the interpretation of low scores on the index. Therefore both statements are correct, but the reason is not the correct explanation of the assertion.

67. **B. The first five limbs/stages are preparatory stage:** In Patanjali's Ashtanga Yoga, the eight limbs consist of Yama, Niyama, Asana, Pranayama, Pratyahara, Dharana, Dhyana, and Samadhi. The first five limbs are considered preparatory practices that discipline the body and mind before deeper meditative states.

C. The practice of last three stages reduces cognitive distraction: The final three limbs—Dharana (concentration), Dhyana (meditation), and Samadhi (absorption)—are collectively called Samyama. These stages involve deep mental focus and progressively reduce cognitive distractions.

Statements A and D are incorrect because Samadhi, not Dharana, is the final limb, and Pratyahara (not Yama) refers to sensory withdrawal.

68. Piaget's theory of cognitive development describes four sequential stages of cognitive growth. A (Knowledge that an object exists even when it is not in sight) refers to object permanence, which develops in the sensorimotor stage. D (Asking questions and exploring surroundings without relying only on sensory–motor actions) reflects the preoperational stage, where children begin symbolic thinking and curiosity. B (Understanding that objects remain the same despite superficial changes) refers to conservation, which develops in the concrete operational stage. C (Thinking about possibilities and hypothetical situations) represents the formal operational stage, where abstract and hypothetical reasoning emerges. Therefore the correct developmental order is sensorimotor → preoperational → concrete operational → formal operational.

69. • **A–III (Right View – Samma Ditthi):** In the Buddhist Eightfold Path, Right View refers to understanding reality correctly and recognizing the Four Noble Truths.

- **B–IV (Right Effort – Samma Vayama):** Right Effort involves cultivating wholesome mental states and preventing unwholesome states from arising.
- **C–I (Right Concentration – Samma Samadhi):** Right Concentration refers to deep meditative absorption and focused mental states developed through meditation practices.
- **D–II (Right Intention – Samma Sankalpa):** Right Intention refers to commitment to ethical and mental self-improvement, including intentions of renunciation, goodwill, and harmlessness.

70. • **A–III (Primary motor cortex – Astereognosia):** Damage affecting cortical sensory–motor integration can lead to astereognosia, the inability to recognize objects by touch despite intact basic sensory perception.

- **B–IV (Motor nuclei of cranial nerves – Controlling the muscles of the face):** The motor nuclei of cranial nerves control voluntary movements of facial muscles, jaw, tongue, and other structures of the head and neck.
- **C–II (Basal ganglia – Habit learning):** The basal ganglia are heavily involved in motor control, procedural learning, and habit formation, supporting automatic behavioural patterns.
- **D–I (Simultanagnosia – Disorder of attention):** Simultanagnosia is a neuropsychological condition in which a person cannot perceive multiple elements of a visual scene simultaneously, reflecting a disturbance of visual attention and perceptual integration.

71. According to Albert Bandura's observational learning (social learning) theory, learning occurs through observing and imitating the behaviour of others. Bandura proposed four sequential processes required for observational learning. The first step is attention (D), where the learner must pay attention to the model's behaviour. The second step is retention (B), where the observer must remember the observed behaviour through mental representation or symbolic coding. The third step is reproduction (C), where the individual must have the physical and cognitive ability to reproduce or imitate the observed behaviour. The final step is motivation (A), where the learner must have sufficient incentive or motivation to perform the behaviour. Without motivation, even learned behaviour may not be performed. Therefore the correct sequence is Attention → Retention → Reproduction → Motivation.

72. Freud's psychosexual stages of development describe how personality develops through a sequence of stages associated with different erogenous zones and developmental tasks. C (Weaning) corresponds to the oral stage, where infants transition from breastfeeding to other forms of nourishment. A (Toilet training) corresponds to the anal stage, where children learn control over bodily functions. B (Recognising adult role models) corresponds to the phallic stage, where identification with the same-sex parent or adult role models occurs. E (Developing interpersonal relationships) corresponds to the latency stage, where social relationships with peers become important and sexual impulses are relatively dormant. D (Beginning intimate relationships) corresponds to the genital stage, which emerges in adolescence and involves mature sexual relationships and intimacy.

73. • **A–II (Visual system – Fovea):** The fovea is the small central region of the retina responsible for high-acuity vision and detailed visual perception.

- **B–I (Auditory system – Tympanic membrane):** The tympanic membrane (eardrum) is a key structure of the auditory system that vibrates in response to sound waves and transmits them to the middle ear bones.
- **C–IV (Somatosensory system – Rubber hand illusion):** The rubber hand illusion demonstrates how the somatosensory system integrates tactile and visual information to create a sense of body ownership.
- **D–III (Olfactory system – Chemotopic map):** The olfactory system organizes odor information through patterns known as chemotopic maps in the olfactory bulb.

74. In the Wechsler Adult Intelligence Scale (WAIS), tests are divided into verbal and performance (or processing speed/perceptual) subtests. Information, Comprehension, and Arithmetic are verbal subtests because they involve language comprehension, general knowledge, and verbal reasoning. Digit Symbol (Digit Symbol Coding), however, is part of the performance or processing speed index, requiring quick visual–motor coordination rather than verbal reasoning. Therefore it is not included among the verbal tests.

75. Induced movement occurs when the movement of one object causes another stationary object to appear as if it is moving. In the example given, when clouds move across the sky, the stationary moon appears to move or race through the clouds. The motion of the surrounding clouds creates the illusion that the moon itself is moving. This perceptual phenomenon demonstrates how relative motion cues influence visual perception, leading to the experience of induced movement rather than actual movement.

76. The Self-Regulation Model (SRM), also called the Common Sense Model of illness representation, was proposed by Leventhal and colleagues. It explains how individuals understand and respond to illness based on their personal beliefs and perceptions about the disease. According to this model, patients form cognitive representations of illness including beliefs about its identity, cause, timeline, consequences, and controllability. These beliefs influence emotional reactions and coping strategies, which in turn affect health behaviours and adaptation to chronic illness. Therefore the model specifically explains how patients adjust to chronic diseases according to their own perceptions and interpretations of the illness.

77. Academic aptitude tests measure a student's potential ability to learn or perform academic tasks (A). These tests assess capacities such as reasoning ability, problem-solving skills, and readiness for academic learning. Achievement tests, on the other hand, evaluate the knowledge and skills already acquired in specific subjects (B). Together, aptitude and achievement assessments also measure the ability to understand, apply, and use acquired knowledge effectively (D). However, such tests do not evaluate moral behaviour (C) of the candidate. Therefore statements A, B, and D are correct.

78. Individuals with IQ levels approximately between 20–25 and 35–40 fall within the category of moderate intellectual disability. According to classifications used in adaptive functioning frameworks, such individuals generally require extensive support for daily functioning and structured assistance in educational or testing situations. Extensive support involves regular, consistent assistance across several life activities but not necessarily continuous support in every setting. Therefore during test administration and everyday functioning, individuals within this IQ range typically require extensive support.

79. Ethical principles in counselling guide professional conduct and ensure client welfare. Trustworthiness (A) refers to maintaining honesty, reliability, and confidentiality in the therapeutic relationship. Autonomy (C) emphasizes respecting the client's right to make independent decisions and exercise personal choice. Justice (D) involves fairness, equality, and impartiality in providing counselling services. In contrast, directing (B) and moralising (E) are not ethical principles; counselling emphasizes facilitating client self-understanding rather than imposing the counsellor's values or judgments.

80. A factorial design in experimental research involves studying the effects of two or more independent variables (factors) simultaneously on a dependent variable. Therefore statement B is correct because factorial designs require more than one independent variable. Statement C is also correct since the dependent variable in such experiments is typically continuous or measurable to allow statistical comparison of groups. Statement A is incorrect because factorial designs usually have a single dependent variable (though multiple can exist in complex designs). Statement D is incorrect because independent variables are generally categorical factors rather than continuous variables. Statement E refers to factor analysis, not factorial experimental design.

81. The Schachter–Singer two-factor theory of emotion emphasizes the combined role of physiological arousal and cognitive interpretation (labelling) in emotional experience. According to this theory, an emotion occurs when a person first experiences physiological arousal and then cognitively interprets or labels that arousal based on environmental cues. For example, an increased heart rate might be interpreted as fear or excitement depending on the context. Because this model explicitly relies on cognitive appraisal and labelling of physiological states, it is the theory most strongly associated with cognition in emotional experience.

82. Construct validity refers to the degree to which a psychological test actually measures the theoretical construct it claims to measure. Exploratory Factor Analysis (EFA) is one of the most commonly used statistical methods for examining construct validity because it identifies the underlying latent factors that explain the correlations among test items. When items designed to measure the same theoretical construct cluster together into a common factor, it provides empirical support that the test is capturing the intended construct. Thus EFA helps reveal the internal structure of the test and verifies whether the item groupings correspond to the hypothesized dimensions of the construct.

Other options serve different purposes. Cronbach's alpha measures internal consistency reliability rather than validity. Multitrait–Multimethod Matrix is a broader framework used to examine convergent and discriminant validity across different methods but is not typically the primary statistical technique used to initially verify the internal construct structure of a test. Discrimination index is part of item analysis and assesses how well individual items differentiate high and low scorers, not whether the test measures the intended construct.

83. **C. Punishment and obedience orientation:** This is Kohlberg's Stage 1, where moral reasoning is based on avoiding punishment and obeying authority.

A. Instrumental relativist orientation: This corresponds to Stage 2, where behaviour is guided by self-interest and reciprocal benefits.

B. Interpersonal concordance orientation: This represents Stage 3, where individuals seek approval and try to be seen as "good" by others.

D. Law-and-order orientation: This is Stage 4, emphasizing maintaining social order, obeying laws, and fulfilling duties.

E. Social contract–legalistic orientation: This corresponds to Stage 5, where moral reasoning is based on social contracts, rights, and democratic principles.

84. **B. Denial:** The first stage in Kübler-Ross's model, where individuals initially refuse to accept the reality of impending loss or death.

A. Anger: The second stage involves feelings of frustration, resentment, and anger about the situation.

C. Bargaining: In this stage individuals attempt to negotiate or make deals in hopes of postponing the loss.

E. Depression: This stage involves sadness, grief, and emotional withdrawal as the reality of the loss becomes more apparent.

D. Acceptance: The final stage occurs when individuals come to terms with the reality of death and experience a sense of peace or resolution.

85. **A. Initiative vs. Guilt:** This stage occurs during early childhood when children begin to assert themselves and initiate activities.

B. Industry vs. Inferiority: During the school-age years, children develop competence through learning and productive activities.

C. Identity vs. Role Confusion: In adolescence individuals explore personal identity and develop a coherent sense of self.

D. Intimacy vs. Isolation: In early adulthood individuals seek close relationships and emotional intimacy with others.

86. The projective hypothesis is the basic assumption underlying projective techniques in personality assessment. It states that when a person is presented with ambiguous, unstructured, or vague stimuli, the person's interpretation of that material tends to reflect his or her unconscious needs, motives, wishes, conflicts, and personality dynamics. This idea is the foundation of tests such as the Rorschach Inkblot Test and the Thematic Apperception Test (TAT). Since the question specifically refers to the assumption that personal interpretations of ambiguous stimuli reveal unconscious material of the examinee, the correct term is projective hypothesis.

87. Prosopagnosia is a form of visual agnosia specifically related to difficulty or inability in recognizing faces, even though basic vision may remain intact. Therefore the Assertion is correct. The Reason is also correct because prosopagnosia is commonly associated with damage to the fusiform face area (FFA) on the ventral surface of the brain, particularly near the boundary of the occipital and temporal lobes. This brain region is especially important for face perception and recognition. Since damage to this area explains why an individual loses the ability to recognize faces, the reason directly explains the assertion.

88. In Kelley's Covariation Theory, consistency refers to whether the same person behaves in the same way toward the same stimulus or person across time and situations. In this question, the issue is whether Tarun shows the same flirting behaviour with this customer on other occasions as well. If he does, then consistency is high. Option 2 exactly reflects this meaning because it asks whether Tarun flirts with this customer at other times. The other options represent different attributional dimensions such as consensus or distinctiveness, not consistency.

89.
- **A–IV (Biserial – One continuous and one apparently dichotomous):** Biserial correlation is used when one variable is continuous and the other appears dichotomous artificially, though it is assumed to come from an underlying continuous distribution.
- **B–III (Point Biserial – One continuous and one genuinely dichotomous):** Point biserial correlation is used when one variable is continuous and the other is truly dichotomous, such as male/female or pass/fail.
- **C–II (Tetrachoric – Both the variables are apparent dichotomous):** Tetrachoric correlation is used when both variables are artificially dichotomized, though both are assumed to originate from continuous distributions.
- **D–I (Product moment – Both the variables are continuous):** Pearson's product moment correlation is used when both variables are continuous and measured on interval or ratio scales.

90.
- **A–IV (Broadbent's Filter Theory – Attention works as an early filter, blocking unattended information completely):** Broadbent proposed an early selection model in which unattended information is filtered out before semantic processing.
- **B–II (Treisman's Attenuation Theory – Unattended information is weakened but not completely blocked):** Treisman modified Broadbent's view by suggesting that unattended messages are attenuated, not fully eliminated, so some important stimuli may still be noticed.
- **C–III (Deutsch & Deutsch Late Selection Theory – Selection occurs after semantic analysis of all inputs):** According to this model, all incoming information is processed up to the semantic level, and selection occurs only at a later stage.
- **D–I (Kahneman's Capacity Model – Attention is limited by cognitive resources, influenced by arousal):** Kahneman explained attention in terms of limited mental capacity, where available attentional resources vary with arousal and task demands.

91. In the passage, Ishita verified the internal consistency of the items using responses from 800 participants. Internal consistency reliability examines how closely related the items of a scale are in measuring the same construct. The most widely used statistic for measuring internal consistency is Cronbach's alpha, which estimates reliability by examining the average inter-item correlations among scale items. Since the description clearly states that internal consistency was tested, the method used corresponds to Cronbach's alpha reliability.

92. Ishita developed items with five response patterns ranging from "Strongly Disagree" to "Strongly Agree." This format represents the typical structure of a Likert-type scale, where respondents indicate their level of agreement with statements using ordered response categories. Likert scales are widely used in psychological and behavioural research for measuring attitudes, beliefs, and behavioural tendencies such as pro-environmental behaviour.

93. In structural equation modelling and factor analysis, Average Variance Extracted (AVE) measures the amount of variance captured by a construct relative to measurement error. The square root of AVE is commonly compared with correlations between constructs to determine discriminant validity. If the square root of AVE for a construct is greater than its correlations with other constructs, it indicates that the construct is more strongly related to its own indicators than to other constructs, thus confirming discriminant validity.

94. Confirmatory Factor Analysis (CFA) is used to test whether observed variables adequately represent the hypothesized latent constructs in a measurement model. Through factor loadings, AVE values, and composite reliability, CFA helps determine whether items that are intended to measure the same construct actually converge on that construct. Therefore CFA is commonly used to examine convergent validity, which assesses whether multiple indicators of the same construct are strongly related.

95. In March 2022, Ishita extracted five dimensions through Exploratory Factor Analysis (EFA). EFA identifies the underlying factor structure of a scale and shows whether items cluster into theoretical constructs as expected. Demonstrating that items group together into meaningful factors provides evidence that the scale measures the intended psychological constructs. Therefore the validity established through this process is construct validity.

96. Motivational Interviewing (MI) follows four sequential processes: Engaging, Focusing, Evoking (Evolving), and Planning. The engaging stage is the first step and involves building a trusting and collaborative relationship between the counsellor and the client. In this stage the counsellor uses empathy, active listening, and rapport-building techniques to create a supportive environment where the client feels comfortable discussing concerns and ambivalence about change.

97. During the evoking (evolving) stage of Motivational Interviewing, the counsellor's role is to draw out the client's own motivations, reasons, and readiness for change. Rather than instructing or directing the client, the counsellor encourages the client to verbalize personal reasons for change, often referred to as "change talk." This helps strengthen intrinsic motivation and commitment to behaviour change.

98. Motivational Interviewing was originally developed by William R. Miller and Stephen Rollnick, and later elaborated in healthcare contexts with the contribution of Christopher Butler. Their work established MI as a client-centered counselling approach designed to enhance motivation for behavioural change by resolving ambivalence.

99. Motivational Interviewing is grounded in several guiding principles, among which collaboration and support for client autonomy are central. Collaboration means that the counsellor works with the client rather than directing or confronting them, creating a partnership in the counselling process. Autonomy refers to respecting the client's right and responsibility to make decisions about change, emphasizing that the ultimate choice lies with the client.

100. Motivational Interviewing discourages confrontation or challenging the client directly. Instead, MI principles emphasize empathy, supporting self-efficacy, rolling with resistance, and resisting the "righting reflex." Challenging the client for resistance contradicts the MI philosophy, which focuses on understanding and gently guiding the client toward change rather than confronting or pressuring them.

Previous Years' Paper

National Testing Agency (NTA)

UGC-NET Junior Research Fellowship and Assistant Professor Eligibility Exam

PSYCHOLOGY, JUNE-2025

(Exam held on 28-06-2025)

PAPER-II

1. Tanmaya, a school-going girl, helped a blind person crossing the road and felt happy to see smile on the blind person's face. This can be explained through:

1. Defensive helping phenomenon
2. Negative-state relief model
3. Empathic-Joy hypothesis
4. Reciprocal-altruism theory

2. In which of the following statistical analysis we have more than one dependent/outcome variables?

1. Simple regression
2. Multiple regression
3. Multi-variate analysis of variance
4. Three way analysis of variance

3. In Yoga, three levels of functioning in '*Citta*' (functional mind) are distinguished. Which of the following level represents the principles of individuation?

1. *Buddhi* 2. *Ahamkar*
3. *Manas* 4. *Prakriti*

4. Write the appropriate sequence for causes of forgetting:

A. Encoding failure
B. Interference
C. Retrieval failure
D. Decay

Choose the **correct** answer from the options given below:

1. B, D, C, A 2. A, D, B, C
3. D, B, C, A 4. A, B, D, C

5. Which of the following is the commonly identified sequence for characteristics of cyber bullying?

A. Anonymity embolden perpetrators
B. Increased risk of depression and anxiety in victims
C. 24/7 accessibility and difficulty in escaping harassment
D. Potential for long term psychological trauma

Choose the **correct** answer from the options given below:

1. A, B, C, D 2. C, B, D, A
3. D, A, B, C 4. B, A, C, D

6. In a cloth store Tarun was deciding about whether to purchase or not a dress whose cost was coming to be ₹ 4000. That point the sales person suggested that if he (Tarun) purchases clothes amounting ₹ 5000, he would get a T-shirt free of cost. In this situation, which of the following techniques has been used by the sales person to influence Tarun?

1. Foot-in-the-Door Technique
2. Lowball procedure
3. That's-not-all technique
4. Door-in-the-Face technique

7. The 'orthogonal rotation' is carried out in factor analysis, when factors are:

1. Uncorrelated
2. Correlated
3. Dependent upon each other
4. Placed at 180 degree to each other

8. Which model of attention suggest that information is filtered based on physical characteristics?

1. Treisman's Attention Model
2. Broadbent's Filter Model
3. Deutsch and Deutsch's Late Selection Model
4. Koohneman's Capacity Model

9. Which of the following influences perception?

A. Attention
B. Past experience
C. Sensory adaptation
D. Language

Choose the **most appropriate** answer from the options given below:

1. D and C only
2. A and B only
3. D, B and C only
4. A, B and D only

10. Arrange these personality assessment tools in chronological order of their development.

A. MBTI
B. MMPI
C. Rorschach Inkblot Test
D. 16 PF
E. NEO-PI

Choose the **correct** answer from the options given below:

1. A, C, E, B, D
2. B, A, D, E, C
3. D, E, A, B, C
4. C, A, D, B, E

11. A common logical error that people make is to seek information that support their ideas rather than evidence that would invalidate those ideas. This error is called:

1. Deductive reasoning
2. Affirming the consequent
3. The confirmation bias
4. Affirming the antecedent

12. According to Tittiraiya Upanishad, '*Jiva*' (Human Being) is a multi-layered entity. Arrange those layers in order:

A. *Vigyanamaya Kosa*
B. *Annamaya Kosa*
C. *Manomaya Kosa*
D. *Anandamaya Kosa*
E. *Pranamaya Kosa*

Choose the **correct** answer from the options given below:

1. C, B, A, D, E
2. C, D, A, B, E
3. B, E, C, A, D
4. B, C, A, D, E

13. Match the following:

List-I	List-II
A. Processing speed	I. Perceptual speed
B. Fluid intelligence	II. Spelling ability
C. Broad cognitive speediness	III. Semantic processing speed
D. Crystalized intelligence	IV. Quantitative reasoning

Choose the **correct** answer from the options given below:

1. A-II, B-III, C-IV, D-I
2. A-III, B-IV, C-I, D-II
3. A-I, B-III, C-IV, D-II
4. A-IV, B-II, C-I, D-III

14. Cooking something by following the directions in a recipe exactly is an example of the use of:

1. A heuristic
2. An analogy
3. An algorithm
4. A functional strategy

15. Match the following:

List-I	List-II
A. Test of Intelligence	I. Robert Woodworth
B. Personal Data Sheet	II. Henry Murray
C. Thematic Apperception Test	III. Krumboltz
D. Career Beliefs Inventory	IV. Alfred Binet

Choose the **correct** answer from the options given below:

1. A-IV, B-II, C-III, D-I
2. A-II, B-III, C-IV, D-I
3. A-III, B-IV, C-II, D-I
4. A-IV, B-I, C-II, D-III

16. Once complex behaviours are learned, they can be maintained using different schedules of reinforcement. Which type of schedule produces the highest response rate?

1. Fixed schedule
2. Variable schedule
3. Interval schedule
4. Ratio schedule

17. Which of the following is the non-parametric counterpart of two-way ANOVA?

1. Mann-Whitney Test
2. Wilcoxon-Sign Test
3. Kruskal-Wallis Test
4. Friedman Test

18. Who among the following are the key researchers in motivation theory?

A. Abraham Maslow B. B.F. Skinner
C. Albert Bandura D. Edward Deci

Choose the **most appropriate** answer from the options given below:

1. C and D only 2. A and D only
3. B and C only 4. A and B only

19. When systematic desensitization is used to overcome a phobia, the desensitizing activities:

1. Become increasingly more intense as the treatment progresses
2. Become less intense as the treatment progresses
3. Are presented in a random but counterbalanced order
4. Are not directly related to the phobia

20. Arrange the following needs according Maslow's hierarchy from lowest to highest:

A. Esteem B. Self-actualization
C. Physiological D. Safety
E. Love and belongingness

Choose the **correct** answer from the options given below:

1. A, D, B, C, E
2. B, A, C, E, D
3. C, D, E, A, B
4. D, C, A, E, B

21. Which domains of Biopsychology studies the psychological effects of brain damage in human patients?

1. Physiological Psychology
2. Cognitive Neuroscience
3. Neuropsychology
4. Psychophysiology

22. How do mind-body interventions affect stress?

1. Mind-body interventions have no effect on stress
2. Only mind-body interventions that involve vigorous exercise reduce stress
3. Mind-body interventions help reduce the physical effects of stress
4. Mind-body interventions increase autonomic reactivity and thus stress

23. Which of the Eastern-Western combination about psychotherapeutic processes are correct?

A. *Asana* - Breathing Exercise
B. *Vipasana* - Mindfulness Meditation
C. *Manana* - Reflection
D. *Upayoga* - Argumentation
E. *Sabasana* - Progressive Muscle Relaxation

Choose the **most appropriate** answer from the options given below:

1. A, B and D only
2. A, C and D only
3. B, C and E only
4. B, D and E only

24. The assumption that everything happens in the Universe can be accounted for by definite laws of causation in called:

1. Determinism 2. Operationism
3. Mechanism 4. Natural Monism

25. There are several schools of Yoga. Which of the following represent some of those schools?

A. *Dwanda Yoga* (Path of conflict)
B. *Bhakti Yoga* (Path of devotion)
C. *Karma Yoga* (Path of selfless service)
D. *Gyana Yoga* (Intellectual path)

Choose the **most appropriate** answer from the options given below:

1. A, B and C only
2. B, C and D only
3. C, D and A only
4. D, A and B only

26. Square root of AVE (Average Variance Extracted) can be used to verify .... validity of a psychological questionnaire.

1. Criterion-related
2. Convergent
3. Discriminant
4. Predictive

27. Arrange the sequence of the Central Nervous System:

A. Dura matter
B. Sub-arachnoid space
C. Cerebrospinal Fluid
D. Arachnoid membrane

Choose the **correct** answer from the options given below:

1. A, B, D, C 2. A, D, B, C
3. A, D, C, B 4. A, C, B, D

28. What are some applications of personality assessment?

A. Employment section
B. Clinical diagnosis
C. Neurological diagnosis
D. Developmental disabilities

Choose the **most appropriate** answer from the options given below:

1. B and C only
2. A and D only
3. A and B only
4. C and D only

29. Arrange the following core principles of peace psychology in sequential manner.

A. Conflict resolution and reconciliation
B. Promotion of human rights
C. Understanding the psychological roots of violence
D. Building culture of peace

Choose the **correct** answer from the options given below:

1. A, B, C, D
2. B, A, C, D
3. B, D, A, C
4. C, A, D, B

30. What is not a health protective behaviour?

1. Avoid getting chilled
2. Get enough sleep
3. Eat as you like
4. Destroy old or unused medicines

31. The crises of psychosocial development during childhood to adolescence:

A. Industry vs Inferiority
B. Self-concept vs Self-actualization
C. Trust vs Mistrust
D. Initiative vs Guilt

Choose the **most appropriate** answer from the options given below:

1. B, C and D only
2. B, A and D only
3. A, C and D only
4. C, B and D only

32. Max-min-con principle in the context of research methodology denotes:

1. Maximizing systematic variance, minimizing extraneous variance, controlling error variance
2. Maximizing systematic variance, minimizing error variance, controlling extraneous variance
3. Maximizing extraneous variance, minimizing systematic variance, controlling error variance
4. Maximizing extraneous variance, minimizing error variance, controlling systematic variance

33. 'Origence' is related to .... aspect of Personality?

1. Creativity 2. Openness
3. Introversion 4. Neuroticism

34. Which of the following combination accurately portrays one phase of Selye's General Adaptation Syndrome?

1. Resistance: Internal efforts to restore homeostasis
2. Exhaustion: Fight or Flight response
3. Alarm: Bodily image
4. Alarm: Mobilization of resources to achieve homeostasis

35. An organism's observable traits are referred to as:

1. Genotype 2. Dominant traits
3. Recessive Trait 4. Phenotype

36. The most recent reported evolutionary development of the brain convulsions has two main regions:

A. Dorsal portion
B. Ventral portion
C. Gyri
D. Sulci

Choose the **most appropriate** answer from the options given below:

1. A and B only 2. A and C only
3. A and D only 4. C and D only

37. According to Maslow's theory which need in the hierarchy must be met first before needs higher up become the focus of concerns:

1. Safety needs 2. Physiological needs
3. Esteem needs 4. Belonging needs

38. Which of the following are forms of learning?

A. Classical conditioning
B. Operant conditioning
C. Observational learning
D. Genetic inheritance
E. Habituation

Choose the **most appropriate** answer from the options given below:

1. B, E, A and D only
2. D, C, B and E only
3. A, B, C and D only
4. A, C, B and E only

39. Proteins that bind to DNA and influence the extent to which genes are expressed are called:

1. Transcription factor
2. Replication
3. Translation
4. Genetic recombination

40. Which of the following are the laws of learning?

A. Law of effect
B. Law of recency
C. Law of primacy
D. Law of exercise
E. Law of readiness

Choose the **most appropriate** answer from the options given below:

1. A, B and C only
2. A, C and D only
3. A, B and E only
4. A, D and E only

41. Which among the following components belong to psychological wellbeing?

A. Sense of self
B. Safety and security

C. Sense of purpose
D. Independence
E. Cultural activities

Choose the **most appropriate** answer from the options given below:

1. A, D and E only
2. B, C and D only
3. A, B and C only
4. A, C and D only

42. How many categories of disabilities are mentioned in the Right to Persons with Disabilities (RPwD) Act 2016?

1. 07
2. 14
3. 21
4. 24

43. Match the following:

List-I	List-II
A. Maslow's Hierarchy of Need	I. Proposes that motivation arises from intrinsic factors
B. McClelland's Acquired Needs Theory	II. Suggests that basic needs must be fulfilled before higher level needs
C. Herzberg's Two-factor Theory	III. Identifies needs for achievement, affiliation and power as motivators
D. Self-determination Theory	IV. Distinguishes between hygiene and motivators

Choose the **correct** answer from the options given below:

1. A-III, B-II, C-IV, D-I
2. A-II, B-I, C-III, D-IV
3. A-IV, B-III, C-II, D-I
4. A-II, B-III, C-IV, D-I

44. Match the following:

List-I	List-II
A. Discriminative Conditioning	I. Rudlof Lotze
B. Apperceptive Mass	II. J.B. Watson
C. Unconscious Inference	III. Wilhelm Wundt
D. Local Signs	IV. Helmholtz

Choose the **correct** answer from the options given below:

1. A-II, B-III, C-IV, D-I
2. A-III, B-II, C-I, D-IV
3. A-I, B-II, C-III, D-IV
4. A-IV, B-III, C-II, D-I

45. .... index is the useful tool for identifying proportion of respondents giving correct response to an item.

1. Item reliability
2. Item validity
3. Item discrimination
4. Item difficulty

46. The James-Lange theory and the Cannon-Bird theory differ in the relationship they assume between bodily arousal and emotion. Which of the following matches a theory and its proposed relationship correctly.

1. James-Lange theory: Bodily arousal and emotion happen simultaneously
2. James-Lange theory: Bodily arousal results from emotion
3. Cannon-Bard theory: Bodily arousal and emotion happen simultaneously
4. Cannon-Bard theory: Bodily arousal precedes emotions

47. Higher-order knowledge about your own thinking as well as your ability to use this knowledge to manage your own cognitive processes such as comprehension and problem solving is called:

1. Metacognition
2. Higher Cognition
3. Planning
4. Self-Regulation

48. We want to be like that, because they are successful and have a positive status explains:

1. Social-cognitive domain theory
2. Social bond theory
3. Social media hypothesis
4. Social competition hypothesis

49. According to Wilhelm Wundt, the analysis of consciousness is known as:

1. Analytical psychology
2. Comparative psychology
3. Content psychology
4. Individualistic psychology

50. The moon illusion is best explained by:

1. Linear perspective
2. Atmospheric perspective
3. Size-Distance scaling
4. Retinal disparity

51. Which of the following is/are true about- *Patanjali Yoga-Sutra*?

A. The practice of '*Asana*' (posture) precedes '*Pranayama*' (control of breath)
B. Instructions of *Yoga-Sutra* are not relevant for psychological wellbeing
C. It consists of eight limbs (*Astangas*)
D. Diligent engagement in Yogic practices can lead to '*Kaivalya*'
E. *Yoga-Sutra* is based upon ancient '*Nyaya*' system

Choose the **most appropriate** answer from the options given below:

1. B, D and E only
2. A, B and D only
3. B, C and E only
4. A, C and D only

52. PASS theory of intelligence does not include:

1. Regulation of cortical arousal and attention
2. Autonomous system of the cerebral cortex
3. Codes information using simultaneous and successive processes
4. Planning, self-monitoring and structuring of cognitive activities

53. Dr. Upadhaya has carried out two way ANOVA with 'intensity of light' and 'font size' as independent variables and 'visual acuity' as the dependent variable. Which of the following are true?

A. Interaction effect can be checked
B. It is a factorial design
C. Independent variables have been taken up as continuous variables in this study
D. This is a suitable example to establish causal effect

Choose the **most appropriate** answer from the options given below:

1. A, B and C only
2. B, C and D only
3. C, D and A only
4. B, D and A only

54. Identify the correct sequence for an action research:

A. Observation B. Reflection
C. Plan D. Action

Choose the **correct** answer from the options given below:

1. A, D, B, C 2. A, C, D, B
3. C, A, D, B 4. C, D, A, B

55. Unlike Sigmund Freud, the humanistic psychology Rogers and Maslow focused on the innate human motivation to achieve to one's fullest potential, called as:

1. Self-actualization
2. Will to strive
3. Superiority complex
4. Unconditional self-concept

56. Match the following as enumerated in Mimansa to explain personality:

List-I	List-II
A. Inference	I. 'Anupalabdhi'
B. Analogy	II. 'Arthapatti'
C. Implication	III. 'Anumana'
D. Negation	IV. 'Upamana'

Choose the **correct** answer from the options given below:

1. A-I, B-III, C-II, D-IV
2. A-I, B-IV, C-III, D-II
3. A-III, B-IV, C-II, D-I
4. A-III, B-II, C-I, D-IV

57. Which of the neuron parts are in correct sequence:

A. Dendrite B. Cell body
C. Axon D. End Brush
E. Terminal Bottom

Choose the **correct** answer from the options given below:

1. A, E, C, D, B
2. A, B, C, D, E
3. A, C, B, E, D
4. A, D, C, E, B

58. Match the following:

List-I	List-II
A. Social persuasion	I. Past success and failure in similar situation as perceived by the individual
B. Physiological arousal	II. Seeing other people like you succeed on a task that is similar to the one you face
C. Mastery experience	III. Sense of anxiety and forbidding
D. Vicarious experience	IV. Encouragement, informational feedback, useful guidance from a trusted source

Choose the **most appropriate** answer from the options given below:

1. A-I, B-II, C-III, D-IV
2. A-IV, B-III, C-I, D-II
3. A-III, B-I, C-II, D-IV
4. A-II, B-III, C-IV, D-I

59. Arrange the following steps of Sigmund Freud's psychosexual development.

A. Oral Sensory B. Latency Stage
C. Phallic Stage D. Anal Stage
E. Genital Stage

Choose the **correct** answer from the options given below:

1. A, C, D, E, B
2. A, D, B, E, C
3. A, D, C, B, E
4. A, B, E, D, C

60. Arrange the steps of scientific research.

A. General research questions
B. Collection of data
C. Analysis of data
D. Review of related literature

Choose the **correct** answer from the options given below:

1. A, B, C, D 2. B, A, D, C
3. D, A, B, C 4. C, B, D, A

61. The inner most meninx which adheres to the surface of the central nervous system is:

1. Dura mater
2. Arachnoid Membrane
3. Subarachnoid Space
4. Pia Mater

62. The basal ganglia structures dominate the entire motor functions of:

A. Elephant B. Human
C. Birds D. Reptiles

Choose the **most appropriate** answer from the options given below:

1. A and B only 2. C and D only
3. A and C only 4. B and D only

63. Match the following:

List-I	List-II
A. Distance from the mean in standard deviation units	I. Skewness
B. Asymmetry of frequency distribution	II. Reliability coefficient
C. The ratio of true score variance to the total variance of test score	III. Criterion
D. Any outcome measure against which a test is validated	IV. Standard Score

Choose the **correct** answer from the options given below:

1. A-IV, B-I, C-II, D-III
2. A-I, B-II, C-III, D-IV
3. A-II, B-III, C-IV, D-I
4. A-III, B-IV, C-I, D-II

64. What are correct according to Jean Piaget?

A. The emergence of logical thought

B. Dealing with abstractions as well as reality

C. Learning to represent the world internally

D. Morality judged in terms of consequences

Choose the **most appropriate** answer from the options given below:

1. C, D and A only
2. A, B and C only
3. B, D and A only
4. A, D and B only

65. Match the following:

List-I	List-II
A. E.L. Thorndike	I. Observation
B. B.F. Skinner	II. Extinction
C. I.P. Pavlov	III. Law of effect
D. Bandura	IV. Shaping

Choose the **correct** answer from the options given below:

1. A-II, B-I, C-III, D-IV
2. A-III, B-IV, C-II, D-I
3. A-I, B-II, C-IV, D-III
4. A-IV, B-III, C-I, D-II

66. Which of the following is the correct sequence of group development?

A. Storming B. Adjourning

C. Performing D. Forming

E. Norming

Choose the **correct** answer from the options given below:

1. D, A, B, C, E
2. D, C, A, B, E
3. D, C, A, E, B
4. D, A, E, C, B

67. A standardized test in psychology consists of:

A. Reliability

B. Validity

C. Maximum items

D. Difficult languages

Choose the **most appropriate** answer from the options given below:

1. A and B only
2. A and C only
3. B and C only
4. C and D only

68. Match the following:

List-I	List-II
A. Synaptic Plasticity	I. Strengthening of neural connection through repeated stimulation
B. Long Term Potentiation (LTP)	II. Ability of neural connections to change and adapt
C. Neuro-transmitters	III. Chemical massagers that transmit signals between neurons
D. Neurogenesis	IV. Growth of new neurons in certain parts of the brain

Choose the **correct** answer from the options given below:

1. A-II, B-I, C-III, D-IV
2. A-III, B-II, C-IV, D-I
3. A-IV, B-III, C-II, D-I
4. A-II, B-IV, C-I, D-III

69. Cattell and Horn's theory postulates two kinds of intelligence. A person who is good at using and combining familiar facts has high:

1. Emotional intelligence
2. Crystalized intelligence
3. Fluid intelligence
4. Primary intelligence

70. Match the type of correlation with the nature of the variables.

List-I	List-II
A. Product Moment Correlation	I. One continuous variable and one apparently dichotomous variable
B. Biserial Correlation	II. Two dichotomous variables

C. Phi-Coefficient	III. Two continuous variables
D. Point Biserial Correlation	IV. One continuous variable and one genuinely dichotomous variable

Choose the **correct** answer from the options given below:

1. A-III, B-IV, C-I, D-II
2. A-III, B-I, C-II, D-IV
3. A-III, B-II, C-I, D-IV
4. A-III, B-I, C-IV, D-II

71. According to Buddhist perspective, which of the following represents, the cognitive aspects of the personality?

1. *Rupa*
2. *Sanna*
3. *Vedana*
4. *Sukha*

72. Match the following:

List-I	List-II
A. Weber's Law	I. Sensation grows as a logarithmic concern of stimulus intensity
B. Fetchner's Law	II. JND is proportional to the original stimulus
C. Absolute Threshold	III. Minimum Intensity needed to detect a stimulus
D. Just Noticeable Difference (JND)	IV. Smallest detectable difference between two stimuli

Choose the **most appropriate** match from the options given below:

1. A-I, B-III, C-II, D-IV
2. A-II, B-IV, C-III, D-I
3. A-II, B-I, C-III, D-IV
4. A-IV, B-II, C-III, D-I

73. In .... Validity the criterion measure are obtained at approximately the same time is the test scores.

1. Concurrent validity
2. Predictive validity
3. Content validity
4. Criterion related validity

74. Which of the following is/are true about 'Factor Analysis'?

A. Factor extraction is stopped when Eigen value becomes less than one

B. It is an interdependent statistics

C. It is a Non-parametric analysis

D. Scree plot can be used to determine the number of factors to be extracted

Choose the **most appropriate** answer from the options given below:

1. A and D only
2. B and C only
3. A, B and D only
4. B, C and D only

75. According to Goddard (1910)'s study on residents of the Vineland facility and their categorization by diagnosis and mental age, the residents having the mental age of 3 to 7 years are termed as:

1. Idiots
2. Imbeciles
3. Feebleminded
4. Mild mental retardation

76. Arrange the following intelligence tests according to their first introduction:

A. Binet and Simon Simple 30 Item Test

B. Wechsler Intelligence Test

C. Army Alpha Test

D. Army Beta Test

Choose the **correct** answer from the options given below:

1. C, B, A, D
2. C, A, D, B
3. C, D, A, B
4. C, B, D, A

77. Arrange the Sequence of the Memory Process:

A. Encoding

B. Perception

C. Storing

D. Retrieval

Choose the **correct** answer from the options given below:

1. A, C, D, B   2. B, D, C, A
3. C, B, A, D   4. B, A, C, D

78. Match the following:

List-I	List-II
A. Theory of Correspondent Inference	I. Kelley
B. Balance Theory of Liking	II. Festinger
C. Covariation Theory	III. Jones and Davis
D. Social Comparison Theory	IV. Newcomb

Choose the **correct** answer from the options given below:

1. A-I, B-IV, C-III, D-II
2. A-II, B-III, C-IV, D-I
3. A-IV, B-III, C-I, D-II
4. A-III, B-IV, C-I, D-II

79. Match the form of intelligence with profession.

List-I	List-II
A. Naturalist	I. Law
B. Spatial	II. Programming Language
C. Logical-Mathematical	III. Forest Conservation
D. Linguistic	IV. Architecture

Choose the **correct** answer from the options given below:

1. A-I, B-II, C-IV, D-III
2. A-II, B-III, C-I, D-IV
3. A-III, B-IV, C-II, D-I
4. A-IV, B-I, C-III, D-II

80. Mnemonics work to improve memory because:

1. Rote processing improves memory automatically
2. Memory is linear and thus reinforced by repetitive practice
3. Mnemonics have not been found to improve memory
4. Active organization and integration improves memory

81. Which of the following are goals of humanistic therapy?

A. Increase self-awareness
B. Promote personal growth
C. Develop coping skills
D. Promote interpersonal growth

Choose the **most appropriate** answer from the options given below:

1. A and B only   2. A and D only
3. C and D only   4. B and C only

82. Epileptic seizures can be a consequence of:

A. Head trauma   B. Nose running
C. Eye flue   D. Brain tumor

Choose the **most appropriate** answer from the options given below:

1. A and D only
2. A and B only
3. A and C only
4. B and C only

83. Standard deviation of sampling distribution is known as:

1. Level of significance
2. Sampling error
3. Standardized coefficient
4. Parameter

84. The ethical guidelines during the test administration does not include:

A. Helping the examinee by answering the questions
B. Maintaining confidentiality
C. Favouring the examinee
D. Taking consent from the participant

Choose the **most appropriate** answer from the options given below:

1. A and B only   2. B and C only
3. A and D only   4. A and C only

85. Match the following:

List-I	List-II
A. Bias	I. Taunting, teasing, and using threatening language
B. Verbal	II. Excluding victim systematically and directly from peer involvements
C. Indirect	III. Racial, faith based sexual and homophobic harassment
D. Social exclusion	IV. Informing other peers not to engage with someone, spreading nasty untruths.

Choose the **correct** answer from the options given below:

1. A-IV, B-III, C-II, D-I
2. A-I, B-II, C-III, D-IV
3. A-II, B-III, C-IV, D-I
4. A-III, B-I, C-IV, D-II

86. Match the following:

List-I	List-II
A. Classical Conditioning	I. G.A. Miller
B. Nonsense Syllables	II. Ivan P. Pavlov
C. Magical number	III. Ebbinghaus
D. Law of Acquisition	IV. Edwin Guthrie

Choose the **correct** answer from the options given below:

1. A-II, B-IV, C-III, D-I
2. A-II, B-III, C-I, D-IV
3. A-III, B-II, C-IV, D-I
4. A-IV, B-III, C-I, D-II

87. .... is the useful index of central tendency which is the middle most score when all the scores have been ranked.

1. Mean
2. Median
3. Mode
4. Range

88. According to Miller, which are the types of internal conflict?

A. Avoidance-Avoidance conflict
B. Approach-Approach conflict
C. Antecedent-Consequence conflict
D. Approach-Consequence conflict
E. Approach-Avoidant conflict

Choose the **most appropriate** answer from the options given below:

1. A, B and C only
2. B, E and A only
3. B, D and E only
4. A, D and E only

89. The four *Brahmavihars* are relevant in the context of workplace relationship. Which of the following *Brahmavihars* corresponds to compassion?

1. *Maitri*
2. *Karuna*
3. *Mudita*
4. *Upeksha*

90. Arrange the following theories of Leadership chronologically in terms of their evolution:

A. Behavioural theory by Michigan studies
B. Transformational leadership theory
C. Trait theory
D. Contingency theory
E. Servant-leadership theory

Choose the **correct** answer from the options given below :

1. A, B, C, E, D
2. A, C, B, E, D
3. C, A, D, B, E
4. C, D, B, A, E

Directions (Qs. No. 91-95): *Read the following passage and answer the questions.*

Rahul, a 22-year-old university student had always feared public speaking. As a child, he once froze on the stage during a school recital, and since then the thought of speaking in front of an audience made him anxious. In the college, his fear became a serious obstacle when he had to give presentations for his classes. His palms would sweat, his heart would race and his mind would go blank. After discussing his problem with a counsellor, Rahul learned that he was experiencing performance anxiety. He was advised by the therapist to start with simple steps like speaking in front of a mirror, and then to a small group of friends. Gradually, he progressed to deliver short talks in his classroom. Overtime, Rahul gained confidence and even began to enjoy public speaking. He learned to challenge negative thoughts and replace them with positive self-talk.

91. As Rahul began to enjoy speaking, his experience reflects:

1. Self-efficacy
2. Regression
3. Learned helplessness
4. Repression

92. Rahul's fear of public speaking can be classified as.

1. Agoraphobia 2. Anthrophobia
3. Glossophobia 4. Hematophobia

93. Speaking in front a mirror by Rahul is an example of which therapy?

1. Catharsis
2. Insight building
3. Spontaneous recovery
4. Exposure Hierarchy

94. The heart-racing and sweaty palms, Rahul experienced before speaking, are examples of:

1. Hallucinations
2. Physiological symptoms of anxiety
3. Delusions
4. Positive reinforcement

95. Which psychological theory is most associated with gradual exposure and behavioural change?

1. Psychoanalysis 2. Humanistic
3. Behaviourism 4. Biological

Directions (Qs. No. 96-100): *Read the following passage and answer the questions.*

Aisha, a 30-year-old project manager, works in a high stress environment where she makes dozens of decisions daily. By late afternoon, she often feels mentally exhausted and starts making impulsive choices or delaying decisions altogether. She began skipping her meals, neglecting exercise, and found it harder to concentrate in tasks. Aisha's supervisor suggested her to meet an organizational psychologist. Through consultation, Aisha learned that she was experiencing decision fatigue, a condition where cognitive resources are depleted after too many choices. The psychologist helped her apply time management strategies, prioritize self-care and use chunking to reduce mental load. She also began practicing mindfulness meditation to restore her focus. After some months, Aisha reported improved mental clarity, better decision making, and less stress.

96. Aisha's changes in work behaviour following new strategies represent which of the following learning type?

1. Classical conditioning
2. Vicarious conditioning
3. Trial and error learning
4. Cognitive learning

97. As advised by the Psychologist, chunking strategy helps in:

1. Encouraging multi-tasking
2. Improving attention
3. Breaking tasks into manageable parts
4. Breaking time into parts to achieve success

98. Aisha's difficulty in concentrating is most directly related to issues with:

1. Cognitive load 2. Implicit memory
3. Stereotype threat 4. Operant behaviour

99. Skipping meals and lack of exercise by Aisha contributed to:

1. Displacement
2. Reduced cognitive performance
3. Trait-anxiety
4. Self-actualization

100. Practicing mindfulness meditation by Aisha helped her improve:

1. Motor coordination
2. Focus and emotional regulation
3. Long-term memory
4. Creativity

ANSWERS

1	**2**	**3**	**4**	**5**	**6**	**7**	**8**	**9**	**10**
3	3	2	2	1	3	1	2	4	4
11	**12**	**13**	**14**	**15**	**16**	**17**	**18**	**19**	**20**
3	3	2	3	4	4	4	2	1	3
21	**22**	**23**	**24**	**25**	**26**	**27**	**28**	**29**	**30**
3	3	3	1	2	3	2	3	4	3
31	**32**	**33**	**34**	**35**	**36**	**37**	**38**	**39**	**40**
3	2	1	1	4	4	2	4	1	4
41	**42**	**43**	**44**	**45**	**46**	**47**	**48**	**49**	**50**
4	3	4	1	4	3	1	4	3	3
51	**52**	**53**	**54**	**55**	**56**	**57**	**58**	**59**	**60**
4	2	4	4	1	3	2	2	3	3
61	**62**	**63**	**64**	**65**	**66**	**67**	**68**	**69**	**70**
4	2	1	2	2	4	1	1	2	2
71	**72**	**73**	**74**	**75**	**76**	**77**	**78**	**79**	**80**
2	3	1	3	2	3	4	4	3	4
81	**82**	**83**	**84**	**85**	**86**	**87**	**88**	**89**	**90**
1	1	2	4	4	2	2	2	2	3
91	**92**	**93**	**94**	**95**	**96**	**97**	**98**	**99**	**100**
1	3	4	2	3	4	3	1	2	2

EXPLANATORY ANSWERS

1. Tanmaya helped a blind person and felt happy after seeing the smile on his face, which reflects the Empathic-Joy hypothesis.

- This hypothesis states that individuals help others because they experience personal joy and emotional satisfaction when they see the positive outcome of their help.
- The motivation here is not obligation, reward, or relieving personal discomfort but the pleasure gained from witnessing someone else's well-being.
- Tanmaya's happiness came from empathy—she emotionally connected with the blind person—and joy—she felt happy seeing his smile.

Therefore, the event fits Empathic-Joy hypothesis most accurately.

2. This analysis involves more than one dependent/outcome variable simultaneously.

- MANOVA examines the effect of one or more independent variables on multiple dependent variables at the same time, making it multivariate.
- Example: studying the impact of teaching method on achievement, motivation, and creativity together.
- Simple regression and multiple regression both use only one dependent variable.
- Three-way ANOVA also includes only one dependent variable, not multiple.

Hence MANOVA is the only option that satisfies the condition.

3. In Yoga, Ahamkar is the level of 'Citta' that represents the principle of individuation — the sense of "I" or "self-identity."

- According to Yoga-philosophy, Citta functions through Manas, Buddhi, and Ahamkar.

- Ahamkar generates the feeling of "I-ness," the sense of being a distinct individual, separate from others.
- This role of distinguishing one's own identity is called "principle of individuation."

Hence Ahamkar is the correct level representing individuation.

4. The appropriate sequence of causes of forgetting is Encoding failure → Decay → Interference → Retrieval failure.
   - **Encoding failure:** The information is never stored properly; forgetting begins right at the input stage.
   - **Decay:** Memory traces weaken over time when they are not rehearsed or used.
   - **Interference:** New or old information disrupts recall, causing confusion.
   - **Retrieval failure:** The information exists in memory but cannot be accessed due to missing retrieval cues.

   This is the widely accepted cognitive sequence of forgetting processes.

5. This is the commonly identified sequence describing characteristics and consequences of cyber-bullying.

   A. **Anonymity emboldens perpetrators:** Online space often hides identity, making bullies more aggressive.

   B. **Increased risk of depression and anxiety in victims:** Research consistently shows psychological harm among affected individuals.

   C. **24/7 accessibility with no escape:** Victims can be harassed anytime, making cyber-bullying continuous and pervasive.

   D. **Potential for long-term psychological trauma:** Prolonged distress, low self-esteem, social withdrawal, and PTSD-like symptoms may occur.

   The sequence A → B → C → D captures how cyber-bullying originates and how its harmful impact unfolds.

6. The salesperson first presented the dress costing ₹ 4000, and then added an extra benefit — a free T-shirt — only if Tarun increases his purchase to ₹ 5000. This is a classic example of the that's-not-all technique.
   - In this technique, after giving the initial offer, the seller immediately adds an additional incentive (free gift/bonus/discount) before the customer responds.
   - The purpose is to make the customer feel the revised offer is more attractive and difficult to refuse.
   - Here the free T-shirt is presented as an added benefit to encourage Tarun to increase his spending.
   - The offer is structured to create urgency and perceived value, which increases compliance.

7. Orthogonal rotation in factor analysis is used when the extracted factors are assumed to be uncorrelated with each other.
   - Orthogonal rotation (e.g., Varimax) keeps the angle between factors at 90°, meaning zero correlation.
   - It simplifies interpretation by maximizing variance of loadings and ensuring each factor remains statistically independent.
   - If factors were correlated, an oblique rotation (e.g., Promax, Oblimin) would be used instead.

   Therefore, orthogonal rotation is appropriate only when factors are uncorrelated.

8. This model proposes that attention filters information early based on physical characteristics such as pitch, loudness, or sensory modality.
   - According to Broadbent (1958), all incoming information initially enters a sensory buffer.
   - A selective filter then blocks unattended stimuli and allows only the attended channel to pass forward for processing.
   - Filtering occurs before meaning is processed, and the key basis for selection is physical features like voice tone or ear of presentation.

   Thus it is the earliest and most classical "physical characteristic–based" attention model.

9. Attention, past experience, and language significantly influence perception; sensory adaptation does not directly influence perception in this context.
   - **Attention:** Determines which stimuli are processed, shaping how information is perceived.
   - **Past experience:** Prior learning influences interpretation of new sensory input.

- **Language:** Labels, vocabulary, and categorical distinctions modify how we perceive objects and events (linguistic relativity).

Sensory adaptation changes sensitivity (e.g., getting used to smell), but it does not systematically shape perception across contexts like the other three do.

10. The chronological order is Rorschach Inkblot Test → MBTI → 16 PF → MMPI → NEO-PI.

C. Rorschach Inkblot Test (1921): Developed by Hermann Rorschach; one of the earliest projective personality tests.

A. MBTI (1940s): Developed by Katharine Briggs and Isabel Briggs Myers based on Jung's typology.

D. 16 PF (1949–1950): Developed by Raymond Cattell using factor-analytic approach.

B. MMPI (1943; revised 1989): Standardized objective personality inventory used clinically.

E. NEO-PI (1980s–1990s): Developed by Costa & McCrae to assess the Big Five traits.

Hence the correct developmental sequence is: C → A → D → B → E.

11. This bias refers to the tendency of people to seek, notice, and remember information that supports their already existing beliefs while ignoring or discounting information that contradicts those beliefs.

- In cognitive psychology, confirmation bias is one of the most common errors in reasoning.
- People selectively look for supportive evidence and avoid data that may disprove their views.
- This leads to flawed decision-making, rigid thinking, and resistance to change even when strong contradictory evidence exists.

Therefore, the described error matches confirmation bias accurately.

12. According to Taittiriya Upanishad, the five koshas are arranged as Annamaya → Pranamaya → Manomaya → Vigyanamaya → Anandamaya.

B. Annamaya Kosa: The physical sheath—body made of food; outermost layer.

E. Pranamaya Kosa: Vital energy sheath—life force (prana) that sustains physiological functions.

C. Manomaya Kosa: Mental sheath—thoughts, emotions, and basic mental processes.

A. Vigyanamaya Kosa: Intellectual sheath—wisdom, discrimination (buddhi).

D. Anandamaya Kosa: Bliss sheath—innermost layer, source of deep happiness and peace.

The established Upanishadic order is from gross to subtle: Annamaya → Pranamaya → Manomaya → Vigyanamaya → Anandamaya.

13. Each cognitive ability appropriately matches with the definition provided in List-II.

A. Processing speed → I. Perceptual speed: Processing speed often reflects how quickly a person can perceive and mentally process simple stimuli.

B. Fluid intelligence → III. Semantic processing speed: Fluid intelligence involves reasoning and problem-solving, which depend partly on rapid processing of meaning-based information.

C. Broad cognitive speediness → IV. Quantitative reasoning: This factor includes fast performance in cognitive tasks including numerical operations and reasoning.

D. Crystallized intelligence → II. Spelling ability: Crystallized intelligence reflects accumulated knowledge and vocabulary, which includes proper spelling and language skills.

Hence the matches form set A-I, B-III, C-IV, D-II.

14. Following a recipe step-by-step represents the use of an algorithm because it is a fixed, rule-based sequence that guarantees a correct outcome if followed properly.

- Algorithms are systematic procedures with clear rules that produce accurate solutions every time.
- Recipes give exact measurements, steps, timing, and methods—mirroring algorithmic procedures in problem solving.
- Heuristics, in contrast, are shortcuts and do not guarantee correct results.

Therefore, cooking strictly by recipe is algorithmic behavior.

15. These psychological tools correctly match with their respective creators.

A. Test of Intelligence → IV. Alfred Binet: Binet developed the first widely used intelligence test (Binet-Simon), foundation of all modern IQ testing.

B. **Personal Data Sheet → I. Robert Woodworth:** Woodworth created the first personality inventory called the Woodworth Personal Data Sheet for assessing emotional instability.

C. **Thematic Apperception Test → II. Henry Murray:** Murray and Morgan developed TAT, a projective test to study motives, needs, and personality themes.

D. **Career Beliefs Inventory → III. Krumboltz:** Krumboltz developed CBI to measure beliefs influencing career decision making.

Therefore the correct matching set is A-IV, B-I, C-II, D-III.

16. Ratio schedules produce the highest response rate because reinforcement depends on the number of responses, not on time, and especially the variable-ratio schedule generates extremely high, steady, and persistent responding.

- In ratio schedules, reinforcement is delivered after a certain number of responses, motivating fast responding.
- Among all schedules, variable-ratio reinforcement produces the highest and most consistent response rate because reinforcement is unpredictable yet directly tied to performance.
- Examples include gambling, slot machines, and lottery systems, where people respond rapidly due to uncertain reward timing.
- Interval schedules (fixed or variable) are slower because reinforcement depends on time, not number of responses.

Therefore, ratio schedules—particularly variable-ratio—maintain the maximum response rate.

17. The Friedman Test is the non-parametric equivalent of the two-way ANOVA when repeated measures or ranked data are used.

- Two-way ANOVA evaluates effects of two independent variables on a continuous dependent variable; Friedman tests the same structure but for ordinal or non-normally distributed data.
- Mann-Whitney and Wilcoxon-Sign are for two groups only, not two-way designs.
- Kruskal-Wallis is the non-parametric counterpart of one-way ANOVA, not two-way.

Hence Friedman Test best corresponds to non-parametric two-way analysis.

18. Abraham Maslow and Edward Deci are major figures in motivation theory, contributing humanistic and self-determination perspectives.

- **Abraham Maslow:** Proposed the Hierarchy of Needs, a foundational model explaining human motivation from basic needs to self-actualization.
- **Edward Deci:** Developed Self-Determination Theory (SDT) focusing on intrinsic motivation and the needs for autonomy, competence, and relatedness.
- Skinner focused on behaviorism and reinforcement, not specifically motivation theory in psychological sense.
- Bandura contributed to learning and self-efficacy, not primarily motivation theory.

Therefore, A and D are the correct motivational theorists.

19. Systematic desensitization uses a graded hierarchy of anxiety-producing stimuli from least to most intense.

- It begins with relaxation training and exposure to mild fear-evoking situations.
- As the client masters lower levels without anxiety, progressively stronger or more fear-related scenarios are introduced.
- This gradual exposure paired with relaxation reduces learned fear responses and prevents overwhelming the individual.

Thus, intensity increases step-by-step as therapy moves forward.

20. Maslow's hierarchy arranges needs from lowest (basic survival) to highest (growth-based self-actualization).

C. **Physiological needs:** Food, water, sleep—foundation of survival; lowest level.

D. **Safety needs:** Physical security, stability, protection from harm.

E. **Love and belongingness:** Relationships, acceptance, affection.

A. **Esteem:** Respect, confidence, achievement.

B. **Self-actualization:** Realizing one's full potential; highest growth need.

The correct order from lowest to highest is: Physiological → Safety → Love/Belonging → Esteem → Self-actualization.

21. This domain of Biopsychology specifically studies the psychological effects of brain damage in human patients.

- Neuropsychology investigates how injuries, lesions, or diseases of the brain affect cognition, behavior, language, memory, and emotional functioning.
- It uses standardized tests to assess deficits after strokes, trauma, tumors, or degenerative disorders.
- Physiological psychology generally uses animals; cognitive neuroscience studies neural underpinnings of mental processes; psychophysiology studies physiological responses (e.g., heart rate).

Hence, neuropsychology is the correct field.

22. These techniques reduce autonomic arousal and promote relaxation.

- Mind-body interventions include meditation, yoga, breathing exercises, progressive relaxation, and guided imagery.
- These practices decrease heart rate, muscle tension, cortisol levels, and sympathetic activation.
- Regular practice improves stress management, emotional regulation, and physiological calmness.

Therefore, they have strong positive effects on reducing stress responses.

23. Vipasana–Mindfulness Meditation, Manana–Reflection, and Savasana–Progressive Muscle Relaxation correctly represent Eastern–Western therapeutic combinations.

B. Vipasana – Mindfulness Meditation: Vipassana is the ancient Buddhist practice of mindful awareness; directly linked to Western mindfulness-based therapies.

C. Manana – Reflection: Manana involves introspective contemplation; matches reflective therapeutic approaches.

E. Savasana – Progressive Muscle Relaxation: Savasana encourages deep relaxation; aligns with Western PMR techniques.

Asana is not equal to breathing exercises; Upayoga is not argumentation.

Thus, correct combination is B, C and E.

24. This assumption states that all events in the universe occur according to definite laws of cause and effect.

- Determinism proposes that nothing happens randomly; every phenomenon has prior conditions that determine its occurrence.
- In psychology and science, it supports the idea that behavior can be studied, predicted, and explained through lawful principles.
- Operationism defines concepts by measurement; mechanism refers to body as machine; natural monism concerns unity of nature.

Thus, determinism matches the statement perfectly.

25. These represent Bhakti Yoga, Karma Yoga, and Gyana Yoga — the classical schools of Yoga.

B. Bhakti Yoga: Path of devotion; emphasizes love and surrender to the divine.

C. Karma Yoga: Path of selfless service; performing actions without attachment to outcome.

D. Gyana Yoga: Path of knowledge; uses inquiry and wisdom to attain liberation.

Dwanda Yoga is not a recognized classical school; the traditional four paths are Bhakti, Karma, Gyana, and Raja.

Therefore, the valid schools among the options are B, C, and D.

26. Square root of AVE is compared with inter-construct correlations to establish discriminant validity in psychological questionnaires.

- Discriminant validity ensures that constructs meant to be different are indeed statistically distinct.
- According to the Fornell–Larcker criterion, the square root of AVE for each construct must be greater than its correlations with other constructs.
- If this condition is met, it indicates that the construct shares more variance with its own items than with other variables.
- Convergent validity uses AVE itself (not its square root); criterion and predictive validity use external outcomes.

Hence, square root of AVE verifies discriminant validity.

27. The correct anatomical sequence is Dura mater → Arachnoid membrane → Sub-arachnoid space → Cerebrospinal Fluid.

A. **Dura mater:** The tough, outermost protective meningeal layer.

D. **Arachnoid membrane:** Located beneath dura; web-like middle layer.

B. **Sub-arachnoid space:** Lies under the arachnoid membrane.

C. **Cerebrospinal Fluid (CSF):** Flows within the sub-arachnoid space, protecting brain and spinal cord.

This outer-to-inner sequence matches CNS protective layers accurately.

28. Personality assessment is mainly applied in employment selection and clinical diagnosis.

A. **Employment selection:** Personality tests help assess traits such as responsibility, emotional stability, and teamwork, improving hiring decisions.

B. **Clinical diagnosis:** Clinicians use personality inventories (MMPI, TAT) to understand psychopathology, coping patterns, and personality disorders.

Neurological diagnosis uses neuropsychological tests, not personality tools.

Developmental disabilities are assessed through developmental and cognitive scales, not personality.

Therefore, applications correctly include A and B only.

29. Peace psychology proceeds in the sequence—understanding roots of violence → conflict resolution → building culture of peace → promoting human rights.

C. **Understanding the psychological roots of violence:** First step is identifying causes—aggression, prejudice, trauma, social conditions.

A. **Conflict resolution and reconciliation:** Once causes are understood, strategies are developed to reduce conflict and repair relationships.

D. **Building culture of peace:** Long-term work to create peaceful norms, empathy, cooperation, and nonviolence.

B. **Promotion of human rights:** Final step emphasizes justice, dignity, equality—essential for sustainable peace.

Thus, the correct progression is: C → A → D → B.

30. This is not a health-protective behaviour, because unregulated eating increases risks of obesity, diabetes, and cardiovascular issues.

- Health-protective behaviours include taking precautions that prevent illness or promote well-being.
- Avoiding getting chilled, getting adequate sleep, and safely discarding expired medicines all reduce health risks.
- However, "eat as you like" implies ignoring nutritional balance and health guidelines, which harms rather than protects health.

Hence, option 3 is not a health-protective behaviour.

31. The crises during childhood to adolescence in Erikson's psychosocial theory include Industry vs. Inferiority, Trust vs. Mistrust, and Initiative vs. Guilt.

Erikson proposed eight stages of psychosocial development; several of these occur from infancy to adolescence.

C. **Trust vs. Mistrust - infancy stage (0–1 year)**, where basic trust develops through caregiving.

D. **Initiative vs. Guilt - early childhood (3–6 years)**, involving planning, decision-making, and self-direction.

A. **Industry vs. Inferiority - middle childhood (6–12 years)**, focusing on mastery of skills and competence.

B. **Self-concept vs. Self-actualization** is not an Eriksonian crisis; it does not belong to the theory.

Therefore, the correct set of crises is A, C, and D.

32. The Max-Min-Con principle is a fundamental guideline in experimental research design, formulated by Fred N. Kerlinger, and it enhances internal validity by managing three types of variance.

- **Maximize systematic variance:** This is the variance produced by the independent variable. It is increased by using strong, clearly defined, and distinct treatment levels so that the effect of the independent variable becomes highly visible.

- **Minimize error variance:** This is random, unpredictable variation caused by measurement error, temporary subject states, or chance factors. It is reduced by using reliable instruments, consistent procedures, and stable testing conditions.
- **Control extraneous variance:** This is systematic variance produced by variables other than the independent variable. It is controlled through random assignment, matching, or including the extraneous variable in the design (blocking) to prevent confounding.

Thus, the Max–Min–Con strategy maximizes the meaningful signal, reduces noise, and eliminates alternative explanations, ensuring that observed effects are genuinely due to the independent variable.

33. 'Origence' refers to a personality aspect associated with creativity and originality.

- Origence was proposed in personality research to describe a person's preference for spontaneity, innovation, and creative expression.
- People high in origence enjoy novelty, artistic exploration, imagination, and unconventional ideas.
- It does not correspond to openness, introversion, or neuroticism directly, although it may relate conceptually to creative tendencies.

Therefore, origence is linked to creativity.

34. Internal efforts to restore homeostasis: This accurately describes the resistance phase of Selye's General Adaptation Syndrome (GAS).

- The alarm stage triggers immediate fight-or-flight activation through the sympathetic nervous system.
- The resistance stage maintains physiological arousal but shifts toward stabilizing and coping to restore balance (homeostasis).
- The exhaustion stage appears when prolonged stress depletes energy resources, leading to breakdown.

Thus, "Resistance: Internal efforts to restore homeostasis" correctly portrays one phase.

35. Observable traits of an organism, such as height, eye color, or behavior, are referred to as the phenotype.

- Phenotype represents the expression of genes interacting with the environment.
- Genotype refers to the genetic makeup that underlies these traits but is not directly observable.
- Dominant and recessive traits describe patterns of inheritance, not the visible characteristics themselves.

Therefore, observable traits correspond to phenotype.

36. The recent evolutionary development of the brain's convolutions refers to the folded structure of the cerebral cortex, and this structure is defined by two main features—gyri and sulci.

C. **Gyri** are the raised ridges or folds on the cortical surface. These allow more neural tissue to be packed into the limited space of the skull, greatly increasing processing capacity.

D. **Sulci** are the grooves or furrows between the gyri. These divisions help organize cortical areas and contribute to the complex architecture of the neocortex.

Together, the pattern of gyri and sulci (gyrification) is considered one of the most recent and advanced evolutionary features of the human brain, strongly associated with higher cognitive functions.

Dorsal and ventral regions (A and B) are general directional terms and do not specifically represent the structural components of cortical convolutions.

37. According to Maslow, basic physiological needs must be satisfied first before any higher-level need becomes motivationally significant.

- Physiological needs include food, water, sleep, and the biological requirements for survival.
- Only after these are met does the individual seek safety, belongingness, esteem, and finally self-actualization.

These needs form the foundational level of Maslow's hierarchy.

38. Classical conditioning, observational learning, operant conditioning, and habituation are all recognized forms of learning.

A. Classical conditioning: Learning through associations of stimuli (Pavlov).

C. Observational learning: Learning by watching others' behavior and consequences (Bandura).

B. Operant conditioning: Learning through reinforcement and punishment (Skinner).

E. Habituation: Decrease in response after repeated exposure to a stimulus.

Genetic inheritance is biological transmission, not learning.

Therefore, A, C, B, and E are valid learning forms.

39. These proteins bind to DNA and regulate gene expression by promoting or inhibiting transcription.

- Transcription factors attach to specific DNA sequences, controlling how much mRNA is produced.
- Replication, translation, and recombination are cellular processes, not DNA-binding regulatory proteins.

Thus, transcription factors are responsible for influencing gene expression levels.

40. The laws of learning include the law of effect, the law of exercise, and the law of readiness.

A. Law of effect: Behavior followed by satisfying consequences is likely to be repeated (Thorndike).

D. Law of exercise: Practice strengthens learning and lack of practice weakens it.

E. Law of readiness: Learning is most effective when the learner is physically and mentally prepared.

Laws of primacy and recency relate to memory, not foundational laws of learning.

Therefore, A, D, and E constitute the laws of learning.

41. Psychological wellbeing includes the internal psychological components that contribute to mental health and optimal functioning, such as sense of self, sense of purpose, and independence.

A. Sense of self involves self-awareness, self-acceptance, and a stable identity, which are core elements of psychological wellbeing.

C. Sense of purpose provides direction, meaning, and motivation in life, strongly linked to positive psychological functioning.

D. Independence reflects autonomy and the ability to make one's own choices, an essential dimension of wellbeing.

B. Safety and security are basic needs, not psychological wellbeing components.

E. Cultural activities are environmental or social experiences rather than core psychological components.

42. The Right to Persons with Disabilities (RPwD) Act, 2016 recognizes 21 disability categories. The act expanded the earlier 7 categories to 21, including benchmark disabilities such as intellectual disability, autism spectrum disorder, specific learning disability, acid attack victims, thalassemia, hemophilia, and others.

This expansion ensured broader legal protection and service coverage for diverse disability groups.

43. Each motivational theory corresponds to the description in List-II as follows.

- **A-II: Maslow's Hierarchy of Needs** suggests that basic needs must be fulfilled before higher-level needs such as esteem and self-actualization.
- **B-III: McClelland's Acquired Needs Theory** identifies the learned needs for achievement, affiliation, and power.
- **C-IV: Herzberg's Two-factor Theory** distinguishes between hygiene factors (which prevent dissatisfaction) and motivators (which create satisfaction).
- **D-I: Self-determination Theory** proposes that motivation arises from intrinsic factors such as autonomy, competence, and relatedness.

44. The correct matching between concepts and theorists is as follows.

- **A-II: Discriminative Conditioning – J.B. Watson**, who emphasized stimulus discrimination in classical conditioning.
- **B-III: Apperceptive Mass – Wilhelm Wundt**, who used the term for the total content of consciousness influencing perception.
- **C-IV: Unconscious Inference – Helmholtz**, who proposed that perception involves unconscious deductive processes.

- **D-I: Local Signs – Rudolf Lotze**, who proposed that each point on the skin gives a 'local sign' aiding spatial perception.

45. Item difficulty index is used to identify the proportion of respondents who answer an item correctly.

- It represents how "easy" or "hard" an item is, calculated as the percentage or proportion of individuals giving the correct answer.
- A high difficulty index means the item is easy (many answered correctly); a low index means it is difficult.

Item reliability, validity, and discrimination index measure different item characteristics, not proportion of correct responses.

46. Bodily arousal and emotion happen simultaneously: Cannon and Bard proposed that when a stimulus is perceived, the thalamus sends signals at the same time to the cortex (producing emotion) and to the autonomic system (producing bodily arousal).

- According to this theory, emotion and physiological reactions occur together, not one after the other.
- James-Lange theory instead states that bodily arousal precedes and produces emotion.

Therefore, Cannon-Bard theory correctly matches with simultaneous arousal and emotion.

47. Metacognition refers to knowledge about one's own thinking and the ability to use that knowledge to regulate cognitive processes such as learning, comprehension, and problem solving.

- It includes awareness of one's cognitive strengths and weaknesses, monitoring comprehension, and selecting strategies for effective thinking.
- Planning and self-regulation are components of metacognition, while higher cognition is a broader category.

Thus, the term for understanding and managing your own thinking is metacognition.

48. This hypothesis explains that individuals want to resemble or be like others who hold high status, prestige, or success, as a way of improving their own standing.

- It suggests that people model themselves on high-status individuals to gain social advantage.
- The explanation aligns with the idea that admiration of successful people motivates imitation due to competitive social motives.

Hence, it fits the description of wanting to be like someone because they are successful and possess positive status.

49. According to Wilhelm Wundt, the analysis of consciousness—breaking it into basic contents such as sensations and feelings—was referred to as content psychology.

- Wundt focused on identifying the contents and structure of conscious experience through introspection.
- Analytical psychology refers to Jung; comparative psychology studies cross-species behavior; individualistic psychology relates to single-person differences.

Therefore, analysis of consciousness in Wundt's system is content psychology.

50. The moon illusion is explained by the size-distance scaling hypothesis, which states that objects perceived as farther away appear larger when their retinal image is the same size.

- When the moon is near the horizon, depth cues make it appear farther; thus, the brain scales up its perceived size.
- When it is overhead, fewer cues are available, so it appears smaller despite the same retinal size.

This cognitive scaling mechanism best explains the illusion.

51. Patanjali's Yoga-Sutra includes eight limbs, places Asana before Pranayama, and teaches that committed practice leads to Kaivalya.

A. Asana precedes Pranayama: In the Eight-Limbed Path (Ashtanga Yoga), Asana comes before Pranayama.

C. Eight limbs: Yoga-Sutra consists of Yama, Niyama, Asana, Pranayama, Pratyahara, Dharana, Dhyana, and Samadhi.

D. Kaivalya: Patanjali describes Kaivalya as the ultimate liberation achieved through disciplined practice.

(B) is incorrect because Yoga-Sutra directly enhances psychological wellbeing.

(E) is incorrect because Yoga-Sutra aligns with Samkhya philosophy, not Nyaya.

52. PASS theory does not include an autonomous cortical system.

- PASS stands for Planning, Attention–Arousal, Simultaneous processing, and Successive processing.
- These four cognitive systems explain how humans plan, attend, and process information.

An autonomous system is not part of PASS theory.

53. A two-way ANOVA with light intensity and font size is a factorial design, allows checking interaction effects, and can establish causal relationships if manipulated.

A. Interaction effect: Two-way ANOVA always tests the interaction of the two independent variables.

B. Factorial design: Using two independent variables automatically forms a factorial design.

D. Causal effect: If intensity and font size are experimentally manipulated, causal inference is possible.

(C) is incorrect because intensity and font size here are treated as categorical manipulated variables, not continuous variables.

54. Action research proceeds through the sequence of planning, taking action, observing the results, and finally reflecting on the outcomes.

C. Plan: The cycle begins by identifying a problem, setting goals, and designing an intervention or strategy to address the issue.

D. Action: The planned intervention is implemented in the real setting.

A. Observation: During implementation, data is collected systematically to observe the effects of the action.

B. Reflection: The researcher evaluates the observations, reflects on the outcomes, and determines improvements or next steps, which then feed into the next cycle of planning.

55. Rogers and Maslow emphasized the inherent human drive to grow, develop, and reach one's fullest potential.

- Maslow placed self-actualization at the top of the hierarchy of needs.
- Rogers viewed self-actualization as the organismic drive toward growth and fulfillment.

Thus, the term describing innate human motivation for reaching potential is self-actualization.

56. The Mimansa correspondences match as follows.

A. Inference → III. 'Anumana': Anumana refers to logical inference based on reasoning.

B. Analogy → IV. 'Upamana': Upamana means knowledge gained through comparison or analogy.

C. Implication → II. 'Arthapatti': Arthapatti refers to presumption or necessary implication when direct evidence is lacking.

D. Negation → I. 'Anupalabdhi': Anupalabdhi means knowledge gained through non-perception, or recognition of absence.

57. The correct structural sequence of a neuron is dendrite → cell body → axon → end brush → terminal button.

A. Dendrite: Receives incoming signals.

B. Cell body (Soma): Integrates signals.

C. Axon: Conducts nerve impulse away from the cell body.

D. End Brush: Near the synaptic end of the axon, branches to form multiple contacts.

E. Terminal Button: Releases neurotransmitters into the synapse.

58. These correspond to Bandura's four sources of self-efficacy.

A. Social persuasion → IV: Encouragement, constructive feedback, and guidance strengthen belief in ability.

B. Physiological arousal → III: Feelings of anxiety or tension interpreted as signs of inability or threat.

C. Mastery experience → I: Past successes or failures directly influence confidence in performing similar tasks.

D. Vicarious experience → II: Observing similar others succeed builds belief in one's own capability.

59. Freud's psychosexual stages follow the sequence oral → anal → phallic → latency → genital.

A. Oral Sensory: First stage (0–1.5 years).

D. Anal Stage: Second stage (1.5–3 years).

C. **Phallic Stage:** Third stage (3–6 years).
B. **Latency Stage:** Fourth stage (6 years to puberty).
E. **Genital Stage:** Final stage (puberty onward).

60. The scientific research process begins with reviewing literature, followed by formulating research questions, collecting data, and analyzing data.

D. **Review of related literature:** Establishes background and identifies gaps.
A. **General research questions:** Formed based on understanding of the existing literature.
B. **Collection of data:** Empirical evidence is gathered.
C. **Analysis of data:** Data is interpreted to answer the research questions.

61. The pia mater is the innermost meninx and is tightly adhered to the brain and spinal cord surfaces.

It follows every fold (gyri and sulci) of the CNS closely.

Dura mater is the tough outer layer; arachnoid is the middle layer; subarachnoid space is a fluid-filled cavity, not a meninx.

62. In birds and reptiles, the basal ganglia dominate motor functions because these species rely heavily on subcortical structures for movement control.

C. **Birds:** Their motor system is largely governed by basal ganglia homologues, which regulate complex behaviors such as flight patterns and song production, with limited cortical involvement.
D. **Reptiles:** Reptilian motor control depends primarily on basal ganglia and related brainstem nuclei, which direct fundamental movements like posture, locomotion, and reflexive actions.

Elephants and humans (A and B) possess highly developed cerebral cortex and cerebellum, which share major roles in motor planning, coordination, and execution, meaning the basal ganglia do not dominate motor control in these mammals.

63. Each item correctly matches the statistical term to its description.

- **A → IV:** Standard score describes distance from the mean in standard deviation units (e.g., z-score).
- **B → I:** Skewness refers to asymmetry of a distribution.
- **C → II:** Reliability coefficient is the ratio of true score variance to total test score variance.
- **D → III:** Criterion is the external measure used to validate a test.

64. These statements correspond to Piaget's stages of cognitive development.

A. **Emergence of logical thought:** Occurs in the concrete operational stage.
B. **Dealing with abstractions and reality:** Occurs in the formal operational stage.
C. **Representing the world internally:** Occurs in the preoperational stage.

(D) describes Piaget's early moral realism but is not one of his primary cognitive stage characteristics.

Therefore, A, B, and C are correct according to Piaget.

65. The theorists and their contributions match as follows.

- **A → III: Thorndike – Law of effect**, basic principle of learning based on consequences.
- **B → IV: Skinner – Shaping**, gradual reinforcement of successive approximations.
- **C → II: Pavlov – Extinction**, disappearance of conditioned response when UCS is removed.
- **D → I: Bandura – Observation**, learning through observing models.

66. The correct sequence of group development follows forming → storming → norming → performing → adjourning.

D. **Forming:** Group members come together, roles clarify, and expectations are set.
A. **Storming:** Conflicts arise as individuals assert themselves and challenge roles.
E. **Norming:** The group establishes norms, cohesion increases, and cooperation strengthens.
C. **Performing:** The group becomes fully functional, working efficiently toward goals.
B. **Adjourning:** The group dissolves after completing its tasks.

67. A standardized psychological test must demonstrate reliability and validity.

A. **Reliability:** The test must produce consistent results across time and conditions.

B. **Validity:** The test must measure what it claims to measure.

Maximum items (C) and difficult language (D) do not define standardization.

68. Each neuroscientific concept matches its correct description.

- **A → II: Synaptic plasticity:** Ability of neural connections to change and adapt structurally or functionally.
- **B → I: Long-Term Potentiation (LTP):** Strengthening of neural connections after repeated stimulation.
- **C → III: Neurotransmitters:** Chemical messengers transmitting signals across synapses.
- **D → IV: Neurogenesis:** Formation of new neurons in specific brain areas (e.g., hippocampus).

69. This refers to using accumulated knowledge, learned facts, and past experiences.

People high in crystallized intelligence excel at solving problems using stored knowledge, vocabulary, and familiarity with past information. Fluid intelligence, in contrast, is the ability to think logically in new situations.

70. The correlations match the nature of the variables as follows.

- **A → III: Product Moment Correlation:** Used when both variables are continuous.
- **B → I: Biserial Correlation:** One continuous variable and one apparently dichotomous variable (artificial dichotomy).
- **C → II: Phi-Coefficient:** Used for two genuinely dichotomous variables.
- **D → IV: Point Biserial Correlation:** One continuous variable and one genuinely dichotomous variable.

71. In the Buddhist perspective, Sanna (Perception) represents the cognitive aspect of personality.

Rupa refers to physical form, Vedana refers to feeling or sensation, and Sukha refers to pleasantness, not cognition. Sanna involves recognition, categorization, and interpretation — the core mental processes related to cognition.

72. These psychophysical laws match as follows.

- **A → II: Weber's Law:** JND is proportional to the original stimulus magnitude.
- **B → I: Fechner's Law:** Sensation grows as a logarithmic function of stimulus intensity.
- **C → III: Absolute Threshold:** Minimum stimulus intensity required for detection.
- **D → IV: JND:** Smallest detectable difference between two stimuli.

73. In concurrent validity, the test scores and the criterion measures are obtained at approximately the same time.

It assesses how well test results match a current external criterion.

Predictive validity involves future performance, content validity checks test coverage, and criterion validity is the broader category.

74. Factor analysis includes factor extraction rules and is interdependent, and scree plot is used for deciding number of factors.

A. Extraction often uses the rule "Eigenvalue > 1."

B. It is an interdependent technique because all variables are analyzed together.

D. Scree plot helps determine factor count visually.

(C) is incorrect because factor analysis is a parametric multivariate technique, not non-parametric.

75. In Goddard's (1910) classification system, individuals with a mental age of 3 to 7 years were termed "Imbeciles."

Goddard adapted the Binet–Simon scale and categorized individuals into three groups:

- Idiots: Mental age 0–2 years
- Imbeciles: Mental age 3–7 years
- Morons: Mental age 8–12 years

The term Feebleminded was an umbrella label for all these categories combined.

"Mild mental retardation" is from later clinical classifications and was not used by Goddard.

76. The chronological order of introduction of these intelligence tests is Army Alpha → Army Beta → Binet & Simon Simple 30-Item Test (commonly adopted version) → Wechsler Intelligence Test.

C. Army Alpha Test (1917): Developed during World War I to screen large numbers of literate military recruits using verbal and numerical tasks.

D. Army Beta Test (1917): Introduced immediately afterward for illiterate or non-English-speaking recruits using nonverbal tasks.

A. Binet & Simon Simple 30-Item Test: Although Binet–Simon scales (1905, 1908, 1911) existed earlier, the simple 30-item version widely referenced in educational psychology was standardized and circulated after the influence of the Army testing programs.

B. Wechsler Intelligence Test (1939): David Wechsler introduced the Wechsler–Bellevue, the foundation of modern WAIS tests, much later than the others.

77. Memory processing follows the sequence perception → encoding → storage → retrieval.

B. Perception: Information first enters through the senses and is registered as raw data.

A. Encoding: The perceived information is transformed into mental codes—verbal, visual, or semantic—so the brain can store it.

C. Storing: The encoded information is kept in sensory memory, short-term memory, or long-term memory for later use.

D. Retrieval: Previously stored information is accessed when needed for thinking, recognition, or recall.

78. Each theory correctly matches its psychologist.

- **A → III: Correspondent Inference Theory – Jones & Davis:** Explains how people infer stable traits from observed behaviors.
- **B → IV: Balance Theory – Newcomb:** Suggests people seek cognitive balance in attraction and liking relationships.
- **C → I: Covariation Theory – Kelley:** States that people attribute causes based on consistency, distinctiveness, and consensus information.
- **D → II: Social Comparison Theory – Festinger:** Proposes that individuals compare themselves with others to evaluate their own abilities and opinions.

79. Each intelligence type fits the profession that depends most on that cognitive strength.

- **A → III: Naturalist → Forest conservation:** Involves classifying natural patterns, ecosystems, and living organisms.
- **B → IV: Spatial → Architecture:** Requires strong mental rotation, visualization, and spatial design abilities.
- **C → II: Logical–Mathematical → Programming:** Depends on reasoning, logic, abstraction, and complex problem-solving.
- **D → I: Linguistic → Law:** Legal work requires advanced verbal reasoning, persuasive speaking, reading, and writing skills.

80. Mnemonics enhance memory because they promote deeper, meaningful encoding rather than simple repetition.

- Mnemonics work by grouping information, forming associations, and creating vivid mental images, which strengthens long-term retention.
- They allow the brain to connect new material with existing knowledge networks, making retrieval easier.
- As a result, mnemonics consistently improve accuracy, recall speed, and memory durability far better than rote learning.

81. Humanistic therapy focuses on increasing self-awareness and promoting personal growth as its central goals.

A. Increase self-awareness: Humanistic therapy (Rogers, Maslow) emphasizes understanding one's inner experiences, feelings, and authentic self.

B. Promote personal growth: It aims to help individuals move toward self-actualization, fulfillment, and personal development.

C. Develop coping skills is more characteristic of cognitive–behavioral therapies.

D. Promote interpersonal growth is not the primary aim, although improved relationships may occur as a result.

82. Epileptic seizures can arise from head trauma and brain tumors because both disturb normal electrical brain activity.

Choose the **correct** answer from the options given below:

1. A, B and D only
2. A, D and E only
3. A, B and C only
4. A, B and E only

14. In terms of creativity, what does 'divergent thinking' refer to?

1. Coming with the most efficient solution to a problem.
2. Generating multiple possible solutions or ideas from a single straight point.
3. Following strict rules to solve problem.
4. Thinking within the limits of existing knowledge.

15. The correct sequence of the elements of observational learning is:

A. Motivation
B. Attention
C. Observation
D. Reproduction
E. Retention

Choose the **correct** answer from the options given below:

1. C, B, D, A, E
2. C, D, A, E, B
3. C, B, E, A, D
4. C, B, E, D, A

16. Arrange the following stages of group creativity in order of their occurrence.

A. Brainstorming
B. Confrontation of problem
C. Idea finding
D. Group interaction
E. Solution finding

Choose the **correct** answer from the options given below:

1. A, B, D, E, C
2. D, C, E, B, A
3. C, A, B, D, E
4. B, A, D, C, E

17. A major neural pathway that connects Broca's areas and Wernicke's area is called:

1. Anterior commissure
2. Arcuate fasciculus
3. Massa intermedia
4. Posterior commissure

18. Which one of the following are types of long term memory?

A. Echoic memory
B. Nondeclarative memory
C. Iconic memory
D. Semantic memory
E. Episodic memory

Choose the **correct** answer from the options given below:

1. B, D and E only
2. A, C and D only
3. C, D and E only
4. B, C and D only

19. Match the LIST-I with LIST-II.

LIST-I	LIST-II
A Locus coeruleus	I. Acetylcholine
B. Raphe nuclei	II. Dopamine
C. Substantia nigra	III. Serotonin
D. Basal forebrain	IV. Norepinephrine

Choose the **correct** answer from the options given below:

1. A-IV, B-III, C-II, D-I
2. A-III, B-I, C-II, D-IV
3. A-II, B-III, C-IV, D-I
4. A-I, B-III, C-II, D-IV

20. Which principle of research ethics emphasises the importance of disclosing the true nature of the study to participants after their participation?

1. Debriefing
2. Informed consent
3. Justification of deception
4. Right to withdraw

21. The concept of 'Glass Cliff' refers to:

1. When women and minorities are seen as better leaders because of their ability to manage crises.
2. When women and minorities are discriminated against because of their ability to manage crises.
3. When women and minorities are promoted in organizations that are thriving.
4. When women and minorities are given more time to solve organizational problems than others.

22. Match the LIST-I with LIST-II.

LIST-I	LIST-II
A. Luria Nebraska	I. Non-pictorial projective test
B. The Myers-Briggs type indicator	II. Non-verbal performance of intelligence
C. Porteus Maze Test	III. Neuropsychological battery
D. Word Association Test	IV. Testing in industrial and business setting

Choose the **correct** answer from the options given below:

1. A-I, B-III, C-II, D-IV
2. A-I, B-IV, C-III, D-II
3. A-III, B-IV, C-II, D-I
4. A-II, B-III, C-IV, D-I

23. Among the following choose the correct sequence of stages of group development.

A. Storming B. Norming
C. Forming D. Adjourning
E. Performing

Choose the **correct** answer from the options given below:

1. B, C, E, D, A
2. D, E, C, A, B
3. C, A, B, E, D
4. A, B, C, D, E

24. The common barriers to successful problem solving includes the following, EXCEPT:

1. Functional fixedness
2. Subgoals
3. Mental sets
4. Confirmation bias

25. Arrange the development of language through the examples given below:

A. Adding consonant sounds to the vowel.
B. Making vowel like sounds.
C. One word speech like some noun.
D. Use of grammatical terms and increase in length of sentence.
E. Simple sentence using nouns, verbs and adjectives.

Choose the **correct** answer from the options given below:

1. B, A, C, E, D
2. A, C, B, E, D
3. B, C, D, E, A
4. B, C, A, D, E

26. Who termed the body's response to stressors as the general adaptation syndrome?

1. Walter Cannon
2. Richard Lazarus
3. Hans Selye
4. Carl Lange

27. Match the LIST-I with LIST-II.

LIST-I	LIST-II
A. Semantics	I. Function of language in social intercourse
B. Morpheme	II. The rules that specify how words are arranged to yield grammatically acceptable sentences
C. Pragmatics	III. A minimal unit of speech used in a language to code a specific meaning
D. Syntax	IV. Study of meaning

Choose the **correct** answer from the options given below:

1. A-III, B-IV, C-II, D-I
2. A-II, B-IV, C-III, D-I
3. A-IV, B-III, C-I, D-II
4. A-IV, B-II, C-III, D-I

28. Which of the following is not a therapy based on classical conditioning?

1. Systematic desensitization
2. Exposure therapy
3. Behavioural activation
4. Aversion therapy

29. According to Festinger the three basic things that people can do to reduce cognitive dissonance:

A. Change their conflicting behaviour to make it match their attitude.
B. Change their conflicting attitude over trustworthy message.
C. Change their current conflicting cognition to justify their behaviour.
D. Form new cognitions to justify their behaviour.
E. Use the information processing peripheral route.

Choose the **correct** answer from the options given below:

1. A, B and C only
2. B, C and D only
3. C, D and E only
4. A, C and D only

30. Arrange the following steps in sequence to develop a standardized psychological test:

A. Preliminary administration
B. Planning and item writing
C. Reliability and validity testing
D. Test Manual preparation
E. Norm establishment

Choose the **correct** answer from the options given below:

1. A, B, E, C, D 2. B, C, A, E, D
3. B, A, C, E, D 4. A, B, D, E, C

31. Which of the following assumptions is **not** one of the underlying analysis of covariance?

1. Within groups variance must be appropriately equal
2. The treatment groups should be selected at random from the different population.
3. The contribution of variance in the total sample must be additive
4. There should be a linear relationship between X and Y

32. Which of the following characteristics of test determines whether the people who have done well on particular items, have also done well on the whole test?

1. Item difficulty
2. Item discriminability
3. Item reliability
4. Item validity

33. A conflict in which the most beneficial action for an individual will (if chosen by most people) have harmful effects on everyone is called:

1. Social conflict
2. Social dilemma
3. Tit for tat strategy
4. Integrative solution

34. The memory model derived from the work in the development of artificial intelligence (AI) is called:

1. Parallel distributed processing
2. Levels of processing model
3. Three stage model
4. Information processing model

35. Match the LIST-I with LIST-II.

LIST-I	LIST-II
A. Precentral gyrus	I. Subcortical motor area
B. Basal ganglia	II. Motor structure in hind brain
C. Postcentral gyrus	III. Cortical motor area
D. Cerebellum	IV. Somatosensory area

Choose the **correct** answer from the options given below:

1. A-IV, B-I, C-III, D-II
2. A-III, B-II, C-IV, D-I
3. A-IV, B-II, C-I, D-III
4. A-III, B-I, C-IV, D-II

36. Research on perceived fairness in group settings indicates that we make judgements by focusing on three distinct aspects or rules. These are:

A. Distributive justice
B. Collective justice
C. Procedural justice
D. Transactional justice
E. Transformational justice

Choose the **correct** answer from the options given below:

1. A, B and D only
2. A, C and D only
3. A, D and B only
4. A, B and E only

37. Arrange the following phases of basic motivation process in order of their occurrence.

A. Drive
B. Goal need fulfillment
C. Tension
D. Homeostasis
E. Action

Choose the **correct** answer from the options given below:

1. C, A, E, B, D
2. A, B, C, D, E
3. C, E, A, D, B
4. E, D, A, B, C

38. Match the LIST-I with LIST-II.

LIST-I	LIST-II
A. Fear as an acquired drive	I. Fritz Heider
B. Frustration	II. Kurt Lewin
C. The Life Space	III. Amsel
D. Balance Theory	IV. Miller

Choose the **correct** answer from the options given below:

1. A-I, B-II, C-III, D-IV
2. A-III, B-I, C-IV, D-II
3. A-II, B-IV C-I, D-III
4. A-IV, B-III, C-II, D-I

39. A child scolds her mother for littering because there is a sign saying not to do so. As per Kohlberg's theory of moral development, this example refers to which level of morality?

1. Pre conventional morality
2. Post conventional morality
3. Conventional morality
4. Unconventional morality

40. Ethnographic method is related to the strategies adopted ....

A. to explore the lived experience of the group.
B. to establish relations with people to be studied.
C. to study the socio-demographic process that shape an educated person.
D. to comprehend the 'other' vis-a-vis researcher's own self.
E. to be sensitive to the socio-cultural context.

Choose the **correct** answer from the options given below:

1. A, B and C only
2. B, C and E only
3. A, D and E only
4. B, D and E only

41. A person have fears of animals, the natural environment such as thunderstorms, specific situations such as flying. This person has:

1. Social anxiety disorder
2. Specific phobias
3. Panic disorder
4. Generalized anxiety disorder

42. Major phases involved in case study are given below. Arrange them in order of beginning to end.

A. Diagnosis and identification of causal factors.

B. Recognition and determination of status of the phenomenon.

C. Application of remedial measures.

D. Collection of data, examination and history of given phenomenon.

E. Follow up programme to determine effectiveness of the treatment applied.

Choose the **correct** answer from the options given below:

1. B, D, A, C, E 2. D, B, C, A, E
3. C, B, D, A, E 4. B, A, C, D, E

43. The large scale attempts to identify risk factors that predict the development of certain diseases are known as:

1. Epidemiological studies
2. Cohort studies
3. Cross-sectional studies
4. Case studies

44. Negative reinforcement is associated with which one of the following in Instrumental Conditioning?

1. Addition of noxious stimulus following a response.
2. Removal of a positive stimulus following a response.
3. Removal of a noxious stimulus following a response.
4. Addition of a positive stimulus following a response.

45. Ebbinghaus found that information is forgotten:

1. More rapidly as time goes by
2. Gradually at first, then increasing in speed of forgetting
3. Quickly at first, then tapering off gradually
4. Most quickly one day after learning

46. Choose the correct sequence of neuronal structures involved in synaptic transmission.

A. Post synaptic membrane

B. Synaptic vesicles

C. Terminal button

D. Axon

E. Synaptic cleft

Choose the **correct** answer from the options given below:

1. E, C, B, A and D
2. C, B, E, A and D
3. A, C, D, E and B
4. D, C, B, E and A

47. The key features of qualitative research methods include the following, EXCEPT:

1. It respects the subjectivity of the participants.
2. It considers the nature of reality as deterministic.
3. It provide rich or thick description of the phenomenon.
4. It views language central to communication.

48. Which of the following are true in relation to Piaget's Development Theory?

A. Children actively construct their understanding of the world through stages.

B. Culture and social interaction guide cognitive development.

C. Each of these stages is qualitatively different from other stages.

D. Knowledge is constituted through interaction.

E. Each developmental stage brings distinct way of thinking.

Choose the **correct** answer from the options given below:

1. A and E only
2. A and B only
3. C, D and E only
4. A, C and E only

49. Match the LIST-I with LIST-II.

LIST-I	LIST-II
A. Realistic Conflict theory	I. Feeling of discontent aroused by the belief that one fares poorly compared with others.
B. Social Identity theory	II. Stereotypes and prejudices arise from conflicts over limited resources.
C. Contact Hypothesis	III. The theory that people favour ingroup over outgroup in order to enhance self-esteem.
D. Relative Deprivation theory	IV. The theory that direct contact between hostile groups will reduce prejudice under certain conditions.

Choose the **correct** answer from the options given below:

1. A-I, B-III, C-IV, D-II
2. A-I, B-IV, C-III, D-II
3. A-III, B-II, C-IV, D-I
4. A-II, B-III, C-IV, D-I

50. Arrange the negotiation stages for resolving a conflict situation in their correct sequence.

A. Bargain
B. Prepare
C. Information exchange and validation
D. Execute
E. Conclude

Choose the **correct** answer from the options given below:

1. B, C, A, E, D
2. A, B, C, E, D
3. B, A, C, E, D
4. C, B, A, D, E

51. Which of the following statements are associated with the theory of emotion proposed by James-Lange?

A. Autonomic and somatic activities active due to emotional stimuli trigger the experience of emotion.
B. Experience of emotion triggers the autonomic reactions.
C. Visceral activities are too slow to be the sources of emotion.
D. Different patterns of autonomic arousal may be the source of the experience of different emotions.
E. Context is important to interpret the experienced emotion based on autonomic arousal.

Choose the **correct** answer from the options given below:

1. A and D only
2. A and C only
3. D and E only
4. B and C only

52. Which one of the following is INCORRECT regarding metacognitive knowledge?

1. It involves cognition about cognition.
2. It involves thinking about thinking.
3. It prevents monitoring progress while problem solving.
4. Poor thinkers lack metacognitive skills.

53. Deci and Ryan's (1985) self determination theory proposed that:

A. People have inclination towards spontaneous interest, mastery and exploration.
B. Intrinsic motivation occur when our need for importance and autonomy is satisfied.
C. The theory explains genesis of needs.
D. Intrinsic motivation is strengthened by goals, deadlines and directives.
E. There is an spectrum of intrinsic motivation starting from motivation.

Choose the **correct** answer from the options given below:

1. A, B and C only
2. B, C and D only
3. A, D and E only
4. A, B and E only

54. Which among the following is the correct sequential meaning of 'sat, cit and ananda' according to Upanisadic tradition?

1. bliss, existence and consciousness
2. existence, consciousness and bliss
3. consciousness, bliss and existence
4. truth, character and happiness

55. In terms of professional development in the field of psychology in India, arrange the following in chronological order based on the year of establishment.

A. Indian Psychological Association
B. National Institution of Mental Health and Neurosciences (NIMHANS)
C. Defense Science Organization
D. Indian Academy of Applied Psychology (IAAP)
E. National Academy of Psychology (NAOP)

Choose the **correct** answer from the options given below:

1. A, D, B, C, E
2. A, B, C, D, E
3. E, D, B, C, A
4. A, C, B, D, E

56. Match the LIST-I with LIST-II.

LIST-I	LIST-II
A. Structuralism	I. William James
B. Functionalism	II. Carl Rogers
C. Behaviourism	III. Edward Tichner
D. Humanism	IV. John B. Watson

Choose the **correct** answer from the options given below:

1. A-III, B-I, C-IV, D-II
2. A-III, B-IV, C-II, D-I
3. A-I, B-III, C-II, D-IV
4. A-II, B-I, C-IV, D-III

57. Syllogistic reasoning consists of:

A. Two premises and a conclusion
B. The terms within a syllogism are either stated positively or negatively
C. Syllogisms are either valid or invalid
D. Syllogisms are presented in 'if-then' reasoning form
E. People either affirm or deny the antecedent.

Choose the **correct** answer from the options given below:

1. D and E only
2. A and E only
3. C, D and E only
4. A, B and C only

58. Which of the following is NOT a property that make scales of measurement different from one another?

1. Magnitude
2. Triangulation
3. Equal intervals
4. An absolute zero

59. Which of the following approaches to motivation focuses on the idea that behaviour is driven by internal desires and biological needs?

1. Cognitive approach
2. Incentive approach
3. Instinct approach
4. Drive theories

60. As per Ayurveda, which of the following are considered to be 'dosha'?

A. Rasa
B. Vata
C. Pitta
D. Vairagya
E. Kapha

Choose the **correct** answer from the options given below:

1. B, C and E only
2. A, B and C only
3. B, C and D only
4. C, D and E only

61. Match the LIST-I with LIST-II.

LIST-I	LIST-II
A. Jiva	I. Agent capable of freely choosing a course of action
B. Karta	II. Knower
C. Jnata	III. Experience of pleasure and pain
D. Bhokta	IV. A living being

Choose the **correct** answer from the options given below:

1. A-IV, B-I, C-II, D-III
2. A-I, B-II, C-IV, D-III
3. A-III, B-IV, C-I, D-II
4. A-I, B-II, C-III, D-IV

62. According to the levels of processing theory which of the following levels of processing produced best recall?

A. Phonetic level
B. Semantic level
C. Structural level
D. Maintenance rehearsal
E. Elaborative rehearsal

Choose the **correct** answer from the options given below:

1. B and E only 2. D and E only
3. A and B only 4. C and D only

63. Which of the following methods of physiological psychology are considered as invasive methods?

A. Lesion
B. Electroencephalogram (EEG)
C. Electrocorticogram (ECoG)
D. Magnetoencephalogram (MEG)
E. Magnetic Resonance Imaging (MRI)

Choose the **correct** answer from the options given below:

1. B and C only
2. D and E only
3. A and C only
4. C and D only

64. Which of the following doctrine asserts that the individual person is neither part of, no different from, nor a modification of the supreme consciousness?

1. Ayurveda 2. Jainism
3. Adavita 4. Buddhism

65. The anterior pituitary gland secrets .... hormone and the posterior pituitary gland secrets .... hormone.

1. Gonadotropic, Somatotropic
2. Oxytocin, Gonadotropic
3. Somatotropic, Vasopressin
4. Vasopressin, Oxytocin

66. Traits that are influential but only within a narrow range of situations such as 'liking chocolate' are labelled as ....

1. Cardinal traits 2. Central traits
3. General traits 4. Secondary traits

67. Peterson and Seligman (2001) proposed that to be included in character strength in values in action classification a positive characteristics had to satisfy the following:

A. be trait like
B. lead to some form of fulfillment
C. need not to be supported by institutions
D. be morally valued
E. diminish other people

Choose the **correct** answer from the options given below:

1. A, B and C only
2. A, C and E only
3. A, B and D only
4. C, D and E only

68. Which of the following is defined by "the number of people who get a particular item correct" for a test that measures achievement or ability?

1. Item difficulty
2. Item validity
3. Criterion validity
4. Item reliability

69. The gender issues consists of many different perspectives, focusing a different aspect of female experiences, all feminist theories advocate the following, EXCEPT:

1. Gender is socially constructed
2. Gender is biological construct
3. Men exercise power and control over women
4. Women's problems are due to external factors

70. Every behaviour has a cause and that cause is to be found in the mind. This refers to:

1. Unconditional positive regard by Rogers
2. Collective unconscious by Jung
3. Psychic determinism by Freud
4. Idiographic psychology by Gordon Allport

71. Apgar Scale assess the health of newborns. The Apgar Scale evaluated the following:

A. Pupil Dialation
B. Body temperature
C. Heart rate
D. Muscle tone
E. Reflex irritability

Choose the **correct** answer from the options given below:

1. A and B only
2. C, D and E only
3. A, B and C only
4. D and E only

72. The professional issues alone not determine the appropriateness of testing. It is also shaped by moral issues listed below:

A. Human rights
B. Divided loyalties
C. Dehumanization
D. Labeling
E. Invasion of privacy

Choose the **correct** answer from the options given below:

1. A, D and E only
2. A, B and C only
3. C, D and E only
4. B, D and E only

73. Match the LIST-I with LIST-II.

LIST-I	LIST-II
A. Heteronomous morality	I. Justice and rules are conceived as unchangeable
B. Autonomous morality	II. If a rule is broken, punishment will be given out immediately.
C. Immanent justice	III. Child become aware that rules are created by people
D. Preconventional reasoning	IV. Moral reasoning is controlled primarily by external reward and punishment

Choose the **correct** answer from the options given below:

1. A-IV, B-III, C-II, D-I
2. A-II, B-IV, C-III, D-I
3. A-I, B-III, C-II, D-IV
4. A-III, B-I, C-IV, D-II

74. Match the LIST-I with LIST-II.

LIST-I	LIST-II
A. Stereotypes	I. Refer to hiring based on group membership
B. Prejudice	II. Negative emotional responses based on group membership
C. Discrimination	III. Beliefs about social groups in terms of traits that they are believed to share
D. Tokenism	IV. Differential (usually negative) behaviour towards members of different social groups

Choose the **correct** answer from the options given below:

1. A-IV, B-III, C-II, D-I
2. A-II, B-IV, C-I, D-III
3. A-IV, B-II, C-I, D-III
4. A-III, B-II, C-IV, D-I

75. Arrange the psychosexual stages of personality development in their correct order.

A. Latency stage B. Genital stage
C. Oral stage D. Phallic stage
E. Anal stage

Choose the **correct** answer from the options given below:

1. A, B, C, D, E
2. E, A, C, B, D
3. C, E, D, A, B
4. C, E, D, B, A

76. In Piaget's cognitive development stages, a fully developed sense of 'object permanence' appears at which stage?

1. The sensorimotor stage
2. The preoperational stage
3. The concrete operation stage
4. The formal operation stage

77. The positivist model of science is rooted in the following assumptions, except:

1. Empiricism
2. Determinism
3. Open mindedness
4. Parsimony

78. If a severe ear infection damages the bones of the middle ear, one may develop ……….. hearing impairment.

1. Stimulation 2. Nerve
3. Brain Pathway 4. Conduction

79. Match the LIST-I with LIST-II.

LIST-I	LIST-II
A. Multiple Regression	I. The formula to predict the Y variable values based on X variable
B. Regression	II. The straight line defining the relationship of X and Y variables by squaring deviations around it
C. Regression equation	III. Falling off the dependent values as a result of independent values
D. Regression line	IV. Prediction of dependent variable as a result of two or more variables

Choose the **correct** answer from the options given below:

1. A-IV, B-III, C-I, D-II
2. A-I, B-IV, C-II, D-III
3. A-II, B-III, C-I, D-IV
4. A-IV, B-II, C-III, D-I

80. Meditation as a state of mind can be achieved by the combined effect of:

A. Dharana B. Vasana
C. Dhyana D. Jugupsa
E. Samadhi

Choose the **correct** answer from the options given below:

1. C, B, D only
2. C, D, E only
3. A, B, C only
4. A, C, E only

81. The Thematic Apperception Test (TAT) is based on which of the following theory?

1. Atkinson's Theory of Achievement Motivation
2. Murray's Theory of Needs
3. Maslow's Theory of Needs
4. McClelland's Theory of Needs

82. An organisational behaviourist developed a tool to measure organisational loyality. Arrange the following steps he must have accomplished sequentially.

A. Computing croanback alpha
B. Establishing percentile norm

C. Item discrimination
D. Exploratory factor analysis
E. Item writing

Choose the **correct** answer from the options given below:

1. E, B, A, C, D
2. A, D, C, B, E
3. D, B, C, A, E
4. E, C A, D, B

83. Match the LIST-I with LIST-II.

LIST-I (Definition)	LIST-II (Theory)
A. Social context of an action has effect on the type of motivation existing for the action	I. Self theory of motivation
B. People are said to have an optimal level of tension leads to maintain by increasing or decreasing stimulation.	II. Drive reduction theory
C. Behaviour arises from internal drives to push the organism to satisfy physiological needs	III. Arousal theory
D. A person's view of himself can affect the individuals perception of success or failure	IV. Self determination theory

Choose the **correct** answer from the options given below:

1. A-IV, B-II, C-III, D-I
2. A-I, B-III, C-IV, D-II
3. A-IV, B-III, C-II, D-I
4. A-IV, B-I, C-III, D-II

84. The characteristics of groupthink includes the following, EXCEPT:

1. Invulnerability
2. Self deception
3. Lack of disagreement
4. Lack of self control

85. The PASS model of intelligence developed by J.P. Das and associates is based on the work of Luria (1973). The three functional units proposed by Luria are:

A. Object sensation
B. Cortical arousal and attention
C. Coding information using simultaneous processes
D. Motivation to pay attention
E. Structuring of cognitive abilities.

Choose the **correct** answer from the options given below:

1. A, B and C only
2. B, C and D only
3. B, C and E only
4. C, D and E only

86. Match the LIST-I with LIST-II.

LIST-I	LIST-II
A. Ethological theory	I. Development is the result of ongoing, bidirectional interchange between heredity and environment
B. Ecological theory	II. Adaption and survival of the fittest shape behaviour
C. Evolutionary psychology	III. Development is influenced by environmental systems
D. Epigenetic view	IV. Characterize by critical period and imprinting

Choose the **correct** answer from the options given below:

1. A-IV, B-III, C-II, D-I
2. A-I, B-III, C-IV, D-II
3. A-II, B-IV, C-I, D-III
4. A-I, B-II, C-III, D-IV

87. Match the LIST-I with LIST-II.

LIST-I	LIST-II
A. Systematic observation	I. Detailed information is gathered

B. Surveys	II. Can be used in field as well as in laboratory settings
C. Experimental research	III. Behaviour is observed in natural setting
D. Case study method	IV. Large amount of information can be acquired quickly

Choose the **correct** answer from the options given below:

1. A-I, B-III, C-II, D-IV
2. A-III, B-IV, C-II, D-I
3. A-IV, B-II, C-III, D-I
4. A-IV, B-III, C-II, D-I

88. Match the LIST-I with LIST-II.

LIST-I	LIST-II
A. Humoral immunity	I. Ingest microbes
B. Cell-mediated immunity	II. B-lymphocytes
C. Phagocytosis	III. Indicative of inflammatory activity
D. Cytokine level	IV. T-lymphocytes

Choose the **correct** answer from the options given below:

1. A-II, B-IV, C-I, D-III
2. A-IV, B-II, C-III, D-I
3. A-IV, B-I, C-II, D-III
4. A-I, B-II, C-III, D-IV

89. A tendency in which visual elements which are closer in time and space are grouped together is called:

1. Similarity
2. Closure
3. Common fate
4. Proximity

90. The mechanisms of Stigmatization includes the following, Except -

1. Negative treatment and direct discrimination
2. Negative reinforcement
3. Expectancy confirmation processes
4. Automatic stereotype activation

Directions (Qs. No. 91-95): *Read the following passage and answer the questions that follows:*

Panic disorder is defined and characterized by the occurrence of unexpected panic attacks. The person having panic disorder experiences recurrent unexpected attacks and must have been persistently concerned about having another attack. Most of the symptoms of panic attack are physical, although there are some cognitive symptoms also. Panic attacks are brief and intense with symptoms developing abruptly and usually reaching peak intensity within a short period. Panic attacks are often unexpected or uncued. They sometimes occur in situations in which they might be least expected such as during relaxation or during sleep. People suffer from panic disorder with or without Agoraphobia. In many studies gender difference has been found on prevalence of panic disorder. Once panic disorder develops it tends to have a chronic and disabling course. People with panic disorder have one or more additional diagnosis. It is estimated that 30 to 50 per cent of people with panic disorder develops some serious other disorders.

91. Which of the following brain structure plays a central role in panic attack?

1. Thalamus
2. Amygdala
3. Pons
4. Hypothalamus

92. When panic attack occurs in situations in which they might be least expected it is called:

1. Nocturnal panic
2. Situationally predisposed
3. Disorganized panic attack
4. Generalized panic

93. Which of the following is NOT a cognitive symptom for panic disorder?

1. Depersonalization or Derealization
2. Fear of dying

3. Fear of going crazy
4. Dissociative amnesia

94. Panic attacks are much more prevalent in the following:
1. Children
2. Aged
3. Women
4. Men

95. People with panic disorder will experience which of the following common disorder at some point in their lives?
1. Dissociative disorder
2. Somatization
3. Serious depression and avoidant personality disorder
4. Obsessive compulsive disorder

Directions (Qs. No. 96-100): *Read the following passage and answer the questions that follows:*

Health behaviours are practiced by people to maintain their health. A health habit is a health behaviour that is firmly established and often performed automatically. These habits usually develop in childhood and stabilize around the age of 11 or 12. Wearing a seat belt, brushing one's teeth daily, and eating a healthy diet are examples of such behaviours. Although a health habit many develop initially because it is reinforced by positive outcomes such a parental approval, it eventually becomes independent of reinforcement process. For example, brushing teeth automatically before going to bed. Belloc and Breslow (1972) conducted a study which focused on several important health habits: sleeping 7 to 8 hours a night, not smoking, eating breakfast each day, having no more than one or two peg of alcoholic drinks each day, getting regular exercise, not eating between meals, and being no more than 10% overweight. They found that more good health habits people practiced, fewer illnesses they had had, better they had felt, and less disabled.

96. Ramesh had a few drinks for the first time at a party, and he woke up the next day with a splitting headache, blurred vision, inability to remember plans, etc. He realised that he may be vulnerable to health risk because of alcohol and decided to quit drinking. His health habits are most likely to be controlled by:
1. His personal goals
2. Perceived symptoms
3. Social influence
4. Access to health care

97. A health habit is a health behaviour that:
1. is only performed under the supervision of health specialists
2. is specially important for at risk individuals to adopt
3. is not always beneficial to an individuals metabolism and immune system
4. is often performed without awareness

98. Health promotion efforts most commonly capitalize on:
1. Personal control
2. Personal goals
3. Values
4. Teachable moments

99. Most people do not perceive their risk correctly and view their poor health behaviours as shared by everyone. This perception is often:
1. Unrealistically optimistic
2. Unrealistically pessimistic
3. Socially influenced
4. Unambiguous

100. Focusing health promotions on at risk people is beneficial because:
1. It is obvious that people who are not at risk are more likely to stay healthy.
2. It is easier to prevent health problems among those who are not at risk.
3. It helps to identify other factors that may increase risk.
4. It helps to gradually reduce their risk.

EXPLANATORY ANSWERS

1. **(4):** The correct descending order of the human spinal column divisions is Cervical, Thoracic, Lumbar, Sacral, and Coccygeal.
   D. **Cervical:** This is the uppermost part of the spinal column, consisting of 7 vertebrae (C1–C7), located in the neck region.
   A. **Thoracic:** Located below the cervical spine, this section has 12 vertebrae (T1–T12), which connect to the ribs.
   E. **Lumbar:** Found in the lower back, this division contains 5 vertebrae (L1–L5), and supports much of the body's weight.
   C. **Sacral:** Below the lumbar spine, the sacral region is made up of 5 fused vertebrae forming the sacrum, which connects the spine to the hip bones.
   B. **Coccygeal:** This is the lowest part of the spinal column, usually made up of 3 to 5 fused vertebrae, forming the coccyx or tailbone.

   Hence, the descending sequence is Cervical → Thoracic → Lumbar → Sacral → Coccygeal, matching option 4.

2. **(3):** Point biserial correlation is used to measure the relationship between one continuous variable and one dichotomous variable (a variable that takes only two categories).
   - It is a special case of the Pearson correlation when the dichotomous variable is naturally or artificially divided into two groups (e.g., male/female, pass/fail).
   - It helps assess how strongly the continuous variable (like test scores) is associated with the two groups of the categorical variable.
   - Mathematically, it is computed similarly to the Pearson's r, but adapted for one variable being binary.
   - Example: Correlating gender (male/female) with performance scores (continuous) on a test.

3. **(3):** Aerobic exercises are characterized by rhythmic, continuous activity that increases heart and respiratory rate and improves cardiovascular endurance.
   A. **Bicycling:** A classic aerobic activity when done at a steady, moderate pace.
   C. **Rope jumping:** It is high-intensity and involves continuous rhythmic movement, hence an aerobic activity.
   D. **Swimming:** A total-body aerobic exercise involving endurance and controlled breathing.
   B. **Walking:** Although it can be aerobic, it is typically considered low to moderate intensity unless done b skly.
   E. **Weight exercises:** These are usually anaerobic as they involve short bursts of effort rather than sustained endurance.

   Therefore, the correct aerobic activities from the list are A, C, and D.

4. **(3):** The term "work of worrying" refers to a psychological coping mechanism where a patient mentally rehearses or anticipates an upcoming potentially unpleasant event (like surgery, chemotherapy, etc.) as a way to prepare themselves emotionally and cognitively.
   - This process often involves imagining scenarios, outcomes, or conversations related to the event.
   - It enables the patient to gain information, understand possible consequences, and better manage emotional responses.
   - This technique can reduce anxiety and give the patient a sense of control over the situation.
   - It is not the same as bottling up feelings (which involves suppression) or denial, but a cognitive preparation process.

5. **(1):** According to the Self-Determination Theory (SDT) proposed by Edward Deci and Richard Ryan, the fulfillment of three basic psychological needs—autonomy, competence, and relatedness—is essential for optimal human motivation and well-being.

   A supportive environment is key to satisfying these needs.
   - **Autonomy:** Supported when individuals feel volitional and self-directed.

- **Competence:** Enhanced when individuals receive positive feedback and optimal challenges.
- **Relatedness:** Fulfilled when individuals experience meaningful connections with others.

Environments such as responsive families, autonomy-supportive teachers, and empathetic healthcare professionals promote intrinsic motivation and healthy psychological functioning.

Research consistently shows that people thrive in environments that nurture these three needs, reinforcing the significance of external support systems.

6. **(3):** Learned helplessness is a psychological condition that occurs when a person has been subjected to repeated negative experiences (especially failures) and begins to believe they have no control over the situation, even when opportunities to change or escape the situation are available.

This phenomenon was first described by Martin Seligman in experiments with dogs, where the animals, after repeated exposure to unavoidable shocks, stopped trying to escape even when escape was possible.

In humans, it is often linked with depression, low motivation, and passivity.

The core idea is that past experiences of failure condition an individual to expect failure, thereby reducing the likelihood of future attempts to overcome challenges.

7. **(1):** Activation of the hypothalamic-pituitary-adrenal (HPA) axis is a central part of the body's stress response system.

When the body perceives stress, the hypothalamus releases corticotropin-releasing hormone (CRH), which stimulates the pituitary gland to secrete adrenocorticotropic hormone (ACTH).

ACTH then triggers the adrenal cortex to release cortisol, a glucocorticoid hormone.

Cortisol plays several roles:

- Increases blood sugar levels
- Suppresses the immune response
- Helps regulate metabolism
- Assists with memory formulation under stress

It is a primary stress hormone and a crucial marker of HPA axis activation.

8. **(2):** The correct order of steps in factor analysis (a statistical method used to identify underlying variables or factors that explain the pattern of correlations within a set of observed variables) is:

D. **Computation of Correlation Matrix:** Initial step where correlations among all variables are computed to assess interrelations.

B. **KMO Bartlett Test:** Kaiser-Meyer-Olkin Measure and Bartlett's Test of Sphericity are used to assess sampling adequacy and suitability of data for factor analysis.

E. **Factor Extraction:** Identifying the number of factors and extracting them using methods like Principal Component Analysis or Maximum Likelihood.

C. **Factor Rotation:** Helps in simplifying the structure and achieving a more interpretable solution, e.g., Varimax rotation.

A. **Factor Naming:** Final step where each factor is named based on the variables that load highly on it.

This sequence reflects the logical flow of conducting a robust factor analysis.

9. **(2):** According to Gordon Allport's theory of Proprium development (Proprium refers to the self or ego in his theory), the correct sequence of development through childhood is:

C. **Bodily self:** First awareness of one's body and its boundaries (around age 1).

D. **Self-identity:** Recognition of self as a distinct, consistent entity (around age 2).

E. **Self-esteem:** Developing feelings of worth and competence (around age 3).

B. **Extension of self:** Identifying with external objects or people as extensions of the self (around age 4–6).

A. **Self-image:** Formation of self-image based on how one is perceived by others (around age 6–12).

These stages are part of Allport's concept of the seven stages of proprium, illustrating the evolution of self-concept from infancy to adolescence.

10. **(4):** In neuropsychological and behavioural neuroscience studies, selective chemical lesions are used to understand brain-behaviour relationships.

B. **Kainic acid:** A neurotoxin that destroys neurons by overstimulating glutamate receptors; commonly used to model epilepsy and for hippocampal lesions.

D. **Ibotenic acid:** A neurotoxin that causes excitotoxic lesions by mimicking glutamate; often used to create targeted lesions in the brain.

E. **6-Hydroxydopamine (6-OHDA):** Specifically destroys dopaminergic and noradrenergic neurons; widely used to simulate Parkinson's disease in animals.

A. **Dopaminesterase** is not a recognized neurotoxin.

C. **Deoxyglucose** is used in brain metabolism imaging (e.g., PET scans) and is not used to produce lesions.

Hence, B, D, and E are the correct neurotoxins used for selective lesion studies.

11. (3): According to the General Aggression Model (GAM), aggression is the result of a combination of personal and situational variables that influence internal states (like arousal, cognition, and affect), which in turn affect appraisal and decision-making processes leading to aggressive behaviour.

Personal traits (e.g., personality, attitudes) and situational variables (e.g., provocation, presence of weapons) are both recognized as core inputs in the GAM.

Biological responses such as arousal or neurophysiological states are also considered as mediators within the model.

However, genetic predispositions, while relevant to aggression in broader biological or evolutionary theories, are not explicitly considered within the operational framework of the GAM as a primary factor contributing to aggression.

Therefore, genetic predispositions are not a core component in this model.

12. (3): Qualitative research methods focus on understanding phenomena from a holistic, contextual, and subjective standpoint. The following characteristics apply:

A. **They reduce the power differential between researcher and participants:** Qualitative approaches emphasize collaboration, giving participants a voice and reducing hierarchical barriers.

B. **The data is yielded in the form of words, pictures etc.:** Unlike quantitative research which uses numerical data, qualitative data is non-numeric, including interviews, narratives, and images.

E. **Reality is constructed through the process of communication:** Qualitative methods are based on constructivist epistemology, which assumes that reality is socially constructed through interaction and language.

C and D refer to experimental methods typically used in quantitative research, involving manipulation of independent variables and control groups.

Hence, only A, B, and E align with qualitative research methods.

13. (1): Farrell (1992) identified major applications of computers in cognitive-behavioral assessment, particularly in making the process more efficient and objective.

A. **Coding observational data:** Computers can help automate and standardize the coding process, reducing human error.

B. **Directly recording behaviour:** Computerized systems can capture responses in real time (e.g., reaction times, keypresses).

D. **Training:** Programs can be used to train individuals in specific behaviours or skills, especially in therapeutic or assessment contexts.

C. Indirectly recording behaviour and E. Report writing are not considered major applications in Farrell's classification—indirect recording is less precise, and report writing is often done by clinicians post-analysis.

Therefore, the valid applications per Farrell's framework are A, B, and D.

14. (2): Divergent thinking is a core component of creativity, where an individual generates multiple, unique, or varied solutions or ideas from a single starting point.

It involves flexibility, originality, fluency, and elaboration of ideas.

For example, when asked to name as many uses for a brick as possible, someone engaging in divergent thinking might say: paperweight, doorstop, weapon, tool for sculpting, etc.

This contrasts with convergent thinking, which focuses on finding the one best or correct answer. Hence, divergent thinking emphasizes expanding the range of possible ideas, not narrowing them down.

15. (4): The correct sequence of observational learning, as proposed by Albert Bandura, consists of the following stages:

C. **Observation:** First, the individual must be exposed to the behaviour demonstrated by a model.

B. **Attention:** The individual must pay attention to the important features of the model's behaviour.

E. **Retention:** The observer must retain the behaviour in memory for later reproduction.

D. **Reproduction:** The observer must be physically and mentally able to reproduce the observed behaviour.

A. **Motivation:** Finally, there must be motivation to perform the behaviour, which can be influenced by anticipated rewards or punishments.

This sequence outlines the cognitive and behavioral processes involved in learning through imitation.

16. (4): The correct order of stages in group creativity reflects how a team collaboratively arrives at innovative solutions through structured processes:

B. **Confrontation of problem:** This is the initial step where the group identifies and defines the problem clearly. It sets the direction for creative exploration.

A. **Brainstorming:** Once the problem is defined, members freely generate as many ideas as possible without judgment, encouraging divergent thinking.

D. **Group interaction:** Ideas are then discussed, refined, combined, and evaluated through group dialogue and collaboration.

C. **Idea finding:** In this phase, the group isolates the most promising ideas generated from brainstorming and discussion.

E. **Solution finding:** Final stage where the selected ideas are developed into feasible, actionable solutions.

This sequence ensures that creativity is structured and moves from ideation to implementation.

17. (2): The arcuate fasciculus is a major white matter tract in the brain that connects Broca's area (involved in speech production) in the frontal lobe to Wernicke's area (involved in language comprehension) in the temporal lobe.

It plays a crucial role in language processing and repetition.

Damage to this pathway results in conduction aphasia, where patients can understand and produce speech but struggle with repeating words or phrases.

This neural connection is vital for integrated language function, linking comprehension and production processes.

The other options (anterior/posterior commissure and massa intermedia) are midline structures with different roles, not involved in this specific language circuit.

18. (1): Long-term memory is typically divided into: **Declarative (explicit) memory,** which includes:

B. **Nondeclarative (implicit) memory:** Memory for skills and procedures, like riding a bike or typing, which does not require conscious recall.

D. **Semantic memory:** Memory for facts, concepts, and general knowledge (e.g., Paris is the capital of France).

E. **Episodic memory:** Memory of personal experiences and specific events in time (e.g., your last birthday).

A. **Echoic memory** and C. **Iconic memory** are not part of long-term memory; they are components of sensory memory, which stores auditory and visual information respectively for a few seconds or less.

Hence, B, D, and E are valid types of long-term memory.

19. (1): Matching the brain structures with their primary neurotransmitters:

A. Locus coeruleus – IV. Norepinephrine: The locus coeruleus is the main source of norepinephrine in the brain, involved in arousal, attention, and stress response.

B. Raphe nuclei – III. Serotonin: These nuclei, located in the brainstem, are the major producers of serotonin, which affects mood, sleep, and emotional regulation.

C. Substantia nigra – II. Dopamine: This midbrain structure produces dopamine, especially important for motor control; its degeneration is linked to Parkinson's disease.

D. Basal forebrain – I. Acetylcholine: This area is a key source of acetylcholine, crucial for learning, memory, and attention.

These pairings reflect the established neurochemical mapping of brain regions and their functions.

20. **(1):** Debriefing is an essential principle of research ethics, particularly when deception is involved in the study design.

- It involves disclosing the full purpose and nature of the study to participants after their participation is complete.
- The aim is to ensure that participants are fully informed, can ask questions, and have any misconceptions clarified.
- It also serves to minimize potential harm, especially if participants were misled or exposed to stress during the study.
- Ethical guidelines by organizations like APA and British Psychological Society (BPS) mandate debriefing to uphold participants' rights and dignity.

Debriefing supports the principle of respect for persons by maintaining transparency and trust in the research process.

21. **(1):** The term "Glass Cliff", introduced by researchers Michelle Ryan and Alex Haslam in 2005, refers to a phenomenon where women and minorities are more likely to be promoted or put into leadership roles during times of crisis or downturn, when the risk of failure is high.

- This creates a situation where they are set up to fail, as the context is unstable or risky.
- The idea is not necessarily because they are seen as better leaders in stable times, but because they are perceived as better suited for handling difficult situations — often because of stereotypical associations with empathy or nurturing.
- This differs from the Glass Ceiling, which refers to the invisible barrier preventing women from reaching top positions.

Thus, the Glass Cliff implies that women and minorities are offered leadership only under precarious conditions, aligning with option 1.

22. **(3):** Matching LIST-I with LIST-II:

A. Luria Nebraska – III. Neuropsychological battery: The Luria-Nebraska Neuropsychological Battery is a standardized test used to assess brain functioning across multiple domains, including motor skills, language, memory, and intellectual abilities.

B. The Myers-Briggs Type Indicator – IV. Testing in industrial and business setting: MBTI is a popular personality assessment tool used mainly in organizational and career counseling to improve team dynamics, leadership development, and career choice.

C. Porteus Maze Test – II. Non-verbal performance of intelligence: This test is used to assess planning and foresight and is especially helpful in assessing non-verbal intelligence. It involves tracing paths through mazes without lifting the pencil.

D. Word Association Test – I. Non-pictorial projective test: This is a type of projective technique where individuals respond with the first word that comes to mind when presented with a stimulus word, revealing unconscious thoughts or feelings.

Hence, the correct matching is A–III, B–IV, C–II, D–I.

23. **(3):** The correct sequence of group development is based on Tuckman's model (1965), which outlines five stages of group formation and functioning:

C. **Forming:** Initial stage where group members meet, orient themselves, and understand the task.

A. **Storming:** Conflict may arise as individuals assert opinions or compete for roles.

B. **Norming:** Group cohesion begins to develop, and norms are established.

E. **Performing:** Group functions smoothly toward achieving goals with effective cooperation.

D. **Adjourning:** Final stage where the group disbands after task completion.

This model helps in understanding team dynamics and optimizing group performance.

24. **(2):** In the context of problem solving, subgoals are not a barrier but rather a facilitating strategy.

Subgoals refer to breaking down a complex problem into smaller, more manageable steps, making the problem-solving process more efficient and structured.

In contrast, the following are barriers:

- **Functional fixedness:** Tendency to see objects only in their traditional use, which limits creative solutions.
- **Mental sets:** Tendency to approach problems in a familiar way even when a new approach is better.
- **Confirmation bias:** Tendency to seek out information that supports one's existing beliefs while ignoring contradictory data.

Thus, subgoals are helpful and do not hinder problem-solving.

25. (1): The development of language in children typically follows a universal sequence:

B. **Making vowel-like sounds:** Known as cooing, infants begin this around 6 to 8 weeks of age.

A. **Adding consonant sounds to the vowel:** This is called babbling (e.g., "ba", "da"), which begins around 4 to 6 months.

C. **One-word speech like some noun:** By about 12 months, children begin holophrastic speech, using single words to represent entire ideas.

E. **Simple sentence using nouns, verbs, and adjectives:** Around age 2, telegraphic speech appears with simple combinations (e.g., "want toy big").

D. **Use of grammatical terms and increase in length of sentence:** As grammar develops (ages 3+), children form complex sentences using proper syntax and grammar.

This sequence mirrors the typical milestones of early childhood language acquisition.

26. (3): Hans Selye, a pioneering endocrinologist, introduced the concept of the General Adaptation Syndrome (GAS) in 1936 to describe the body's physiological response to stressors.

GAS outlines a three-stage response to stress:

1. **Alarm stage**–immediate reaction to a stressor, activating the sympathetic nervous system.
2. **Resistance stage**–adaptation occurs, and the body tries to cope with the stressor.
3. **Exhaustion stage**–if the stress continues for too long, the body's resources become depleted, leading to fatigue and potential illness.

Selye's work was foundational in understanding the biological basis of stress and its impact on health.

27. (3): The correct matching of language components is:

A. Semantics – IV. Study of meaning: Semantics deals with the meaning of words and sentences in a language, including literal and figurative meanings.

B. Morpheme – III. A minimal unit of speech used in a language to code a specific meaning: A morpheme is the smallest grammatical unit, like "un-" or "-ing", which carries meaning.

C. Pragmatics – I. Function of language in social intercourse: Pragmatics involves the social rules and context governing how language is used in interaction (e.g., politeness, turn-taking).

D. Syntax – II. The rules that specify how words are arranged to yield grammatically acceptable sentences: Syntax refers to sentence structure and grammatical rules.

This pairing reflects the foundational aspects of linguistic structure and function.

28. (3): Behavioural activation is a therapeutic approach based on operant conditioning, not classical conditioning. It focuses on increasing engagement in positively reinforcing activities to combat depression, using principles like positive reinforcement and activity scheduling. In contrast, the following therapies are rooted in classical conditioning:

- **Systematic desensitization:** Gradual exposure paired with relaxation to reduce phobic responses.
- **Exposure therapy:** Involves confronting feared stimuli to extinguish the conditioned fear response.
- **Aversion therapy:** Pairs an unwanted behavior with an unpleasant stimulus to reduce its occurrence.

Thus, behavioural activation does not belong to the classical conditioning category.

29. (4): According to Leon Festinger's theory of cognitive dissonance, individuals experience discomfort when they hold conflicting cognitions (e.g., beliefs vs. actions) and are motivated to reduce this dissonance.

The three basic strategies to reduce dissonance include:

A. **Change their conflicting behaviour to match their attitude:** e.g., quitting smoking if one believes smoking is harmful.

C. **Change their current conflicting cognition to justify their behaviour:** e.g., rationalizing smoking by saying "it helps me reduce stress."

D. **Form new cognitions to justify their behaviour:** e.g., believing "my grandfather smoked and lived to 90."

B is about persuasion and message credibility, not directly part of dissonance reduction.

E refers to the elaboration likelihood model of persuasion, not dissonance theory.

Therefore, A, C, and D are the accurate strategies as per Festinger.

30. (3): The correct sequence in developing a standardized psychological test is:

B. **Planning and item writing:** Define test objectives, content domain, and write items based on psychological theories.

A. **Preliminary administration:** Conduct a pilot test to collect initial data and identify flaws in items.

C. **Reliability and validity testing:** Evaluate internal consistency, test-retest reliability, and establish construct, content, and criterion validity.

E. **Norm establishment:** Collect large-scale normative data to interpret individual scores meaningfully.

D. **Test Manual preparation:** Final step involves preparing a comprehensive manual covering administration, scoring, norms, and psychometric properties.

This structured process ensures that the test is both scientifically rigorous and practically useful.

31. (2): The statement (2) is not a necessary assumption for conducting Analysis of Covariance (ANCOVA).

ANCOVA has the following key assumptions:

1. **Homogeneity of within-group variances (option 1):** The variance within each group should be approximately equal.

3. **Additivity of variances:** The combined effect of independent variables and covariates on the dependent variable is assumed to be additive.

4. **Linearity between covariate (X) and dependent variable (Y):** A linear relationship must exist for the covariate to effectively adjust the dependent variable.

However, random selection of treatment groups from different populations (option 2) is not an assumption of ANCOVA. The focus is more on random assignment within the study sample, not across different populations.

Hence, option 2 is not a required assumption.

32. (2): Item discriminability measures how well a test item distinguishes between high and low scorers on the overall test.

- A highly discriminating item is one that people who scored well on the total test are more likely to get right, and those who scored poorly are more likely to get wrong.
- This is crucial for item analysis in test construction to ensure each item contributes meaningfully to assessing the intended construct.
- Item difficulty (option 1) tells how many test-takers got the item right, but doesn't assess its relationship with overall performance.
- Item reliability and item validity refer to other psychometric properties but not directly to this correlation between item and total score.

Thus, item discriminability is the correct characteristic.

33. (2): A social dilemma is a situation where an individual faces a conflict between personal benefit and collective welfare.

- It occurs when the most advantageous option for an individual, if adopted by many people, leads to negative consequences for the group.
- Classic examples include the Tragedy of the Commons (overuse of shared resources) and Prisoner's Dilemma.

- Social dilemmas are central to fields like social psychology and behavioral economics, as they reveal how cooperation and competition impact group outcomes.

Hence, the scenario described fits the definition of a social dilemma.

34. **(1):** The Parallel Distributed Processing (PDP) model, also known as the connectionist model, was inspired by the development of artificial intelligence (AI) and neural networks.

- It suggests that memory and cognitive processes arise from simultaneous activity across interconnected units (nodes), much like how neurons function in the brain.
- Knowledge is stored in the pattern of activation across a large number of units, rather than a single location.
- This model contrasts with older models like the Three-stage model (Atkinson-Shiffrin), and focuses on processing information in parallel, not sequentially.

Hence, the PDP model is directly derived from AI developments.

35. **(4):** Correct matching of brain structures and their functions:

A. Precentral gyrus – III. Cortical motor area: Located in the frontal lobe, the precentral gyrus contains the primary motor cortex, responsible for voluntary muscle movements.

B. Basal ganglia – I. Subcortical motor area: These deep brain nuclei are crucial for motor planning, control, and movement regulation, especially in initiating movements.

C. Postcentral gyrus – IV. Somatosensory area: Located in the parietal lobe, this region is responsible for processing touch, pressure, and proprioception.

D. Cerebellum – II. Motor structure in hind brain: The cerebellum coordinates balance, posture, and fine motor movements, functioning as part of the hindbrain.

This mapping aligns with both anatomical and functional neuropsychology.

36. **(2):** Research on perceived fairness in group settings identifies three major aspects of justice that influence how people judge fairness in social and organizational contexts:

A. **Distributive justice:** This refers to the perceived fairness of outcomes or resource distribution, such as salaries, rewards, or workload distribution.

C. **Procedural justice:** It involves the perceived fairness of the processes and rules used to make decisions, regardless of the outcome.

D. **Transactional justice:** Though less frequently cited than the other two, it refers to the fairness in the interpersonal treatment and communication during the decision-making process, often included under interactional justice in literature.

B. Collective justice and E. Transformational justice are not among the standard categories in organizational justice theories.

Thus, the valid components of perceived fairness are A, C, and D.

37. **(1):** The basic motivation process involves a sequence of internal and external events that lead to goal-directed behaviour:

C. **Tension:** It begins with a state of internal tension caused by an unmet need (e.g., hunger creates tension).

A. **Drive:** This tension creates a drive, which is an energized state pushing the individual to take action.

E. **Action:** The drive leads to behavioral activity aimed at fulfilling the need (e.g., looking for food).

B. **Goal need fulfillment:** The action results in satisfying the original need, thereby reducing the drive.

D. **Homeostasis:** Once the need is fulfilled, the organism returns to a state of physiological balance or equilibrium.

This sequence aligns with drive-reduction theory and homeostatic motivation models.

38. **(4):** Correct matching of theorists with their concepts:

A. Fear as an acquired drive – IV. Miller: Neal E. Miller proposed that fear can be learned as a secondary drive through classical conditioning.

B. Frustration – III. Amsel: Leonard Amsel expanded on frustration theory, introducing the idea of frustration as a motivating stimulus, particularly in learning paradigms.

C. The Life Space – II. Kurt Lewin: Lewin's field theory proposed that behaviour is a function of the person and their environment, represented as a "life space."

D. Balance Theory – I. Fritz Heider: Heider developed Balance Theory, which explains how individuals seek psychological consistency in their relationships and attitudes.

This matching reflects significant contributions to motivation and social cognition theories.

39. (3): According to Lawrence Kohlberg's theory of moral development, this example illustrates Conventional Morality, particularly Stage 4 – Law and Order orientation.

- In this stage, individuals conform to societal rules and laws because they value maintaining order.
- The child scolding her mother for violating a rule (sign that prohibits littering) reflects a respect for authority and adherence to societal rules, typical of conventional morality.
- Pre-conventional morality focuses on avoiding punishment or gaining reward.
- Post-conventional morality involves more abstract principles such as justice or human rights, which are not evident in this example.

Thus, the child is demonstrating conventional reasoning based on rule compliance.

40. (4): The ethnographic method is a qualitative research strategy from anthropology used to study people and cultures in their natural settings.

B. **To establish relations with people to be studied:** Ethnography requires building rapport and trust with participants, often through prolonged immersion.

D. **To comprehend the 'other' vis-a-vis researcher's own self:** Ethnography encourages reflexivity, where researchers examine their own influence and perspectives in the context of the study.

E. **To be sensitive to the socio-cultural context:** Ethnographers aim to understand the social meanings and cultural practices of the group from an insider's perspective.

A (exploring lived experience) is more aligned with phenomenology, and C is related to sociological studies of education.

Therefore, B, D, and E best reflect the core elements of ethnographic research.

41. (2): Specific phobia is characterized by an intense, irrational fear of a particular object or situation, which is actively avoided or endured with significant distress. The person in the question has fears of animals (zoophobia), natural environments (e.g., thunderstorms – astraphobia), and specific situations (e.g., flying – aviophobia). These are classic subtypes of specific phobias, as per the DSM-5, which categorizes them into five types: animal type, natural environment type, situational type, blood-injection-injury type, and other types. This disorder is different from:

- Social anxiety disorder, which involves fear of social or performance situations.
- Panic disorder, which involves sudden, unexpected panic attacks.
- Generalized anxiety disorder, which is characterized by chronic and excessive worry about various aspects of life.

Hence, the symptoms best fit specific phobias.

42. (1): The correct sequence of phases in a case study method generally follows these steps:

B. **Recognition and determination of status of the phenomenon:** Identifying the issue or subject under investigation.

D. **Collection of data, examination and history of given phenomenon:** Gathering relevant data including historical, psychological, or contextual information.

A. **Diagnosis and identification of causal factors:** Analyzing the data to understand causes and patterns.

C. **Application of remedial measures:** Intervening or treating based on the diagnosis.

E. **Follow up programme to determine effectiveness of the treatment applied:** Monitoring outcomes to evaluate the success of interventions.

This sequence ensures a comprehensive and systematic approach to understanding and addressing the case.

43. (1): Epidemiological studies aim to identify patterns, causes, and effects of health and disease conditions in defined populations. These studies often focus on large-scale investigations to determine risk factors associated with the development of diseases such as heart disease, cancer, or diabetes. Types of epidemiological studies include cohort studies, case-control studies, and cross-sectional studies.

These are distinct from:

- Cohort studies, which track specific groups over time.
- Cross-sectional studies, which assess data at one point in time.
- Case studies, which involve detailed examination of a single subject or case.

Therefore, the best broad term for large-scale disease prediction studies is epidemiological studies.

44. (3): In Instrumental (Operant) Conditioning, negative reinforcement occurs when a behaviour is strengthened because it removes or reduces an aversive (noxious) stimulus.

Example: Buckling a seatbelt to stop the annoying seatbelt alarm. The behaviour (buckling) increases because it removes the unpleasant sound.

This is different from:

- Positive reinforcement, which adds a pleasant stimulus to increase behaviour.
- Punishment, which can either add a negative stimulus (positive punishment) or remove a positive one (negative punishment) to decrease behaviour.

Hence, removal of a noxious stimulus is the correct definition of negative reinforcement.

45. (3): Hermann Ebbinghaus, through his studies on memory using nonsense syllables, discovered the "forgetting curve", which shows how information is lost over time when there is no attempt to retain it.

- The curve illustrates that forgetting happens rapidly at first, especially within the first hour or day after learning.
- After the initial steep drop, the rate of forgetting slows down, forming a gradual decline.
- This phenomenon highlights the importance of repetition and reinforcement for long-term memory retention.

Hence, the forgetting occurs quickly at first, then tapers off, aligning with option 3.

46. (4): The correct sequence of neuronal structures involved in synaptic transmission begins from the origin of the electrical signal and ends with the reception of the neurotransmitter by the next neuron.

D. **Axon:** The action potential travels down the axon of the presynaptic neuron.

C. **Terminal button:** At the end of the axon, the signal reaches the axon terminal or terminal button.

B. **Synaptic vesicles:** These vesicles in the terminal button contain neurotransmitters, which are released into the synapse upon stimulation.

E. **Synaptic cleft:** The neurotransmitters diffuse across this small gap between neurons.

A. **Post synaptic membrane:** Neurotransmitters bind to receptors on this membrane of the next neuron, initiating a new electrical signal.

This sequence explains the process of chemical synaptic transmission, crucial in neural communication.

47. (2): Option (2) is not a feature of qualitative research methods.

- Qualitative research is grounded in a constructivist or interpretivist paradigm, which views reality as subjective, multiple, and socially constructed, not deterministic.
- Determinism, which implies fixed causality and predictable outcomes, is a feature of quantitative research based on the positivist approach.

The other statements are key features of qualitative research:

- **Respects subjectivity (1):** Acknowledges participant perspectives.
- **Provides thick description (3):** Offers deep contextual details.
- **Views language as central (4):** Recognizes the role of discourse and meaning-making in human interaction.

Thus, the incorrect statement is option 2.

48. **(4):** The following statements are true in relation to Piaget's Cognitive Development Theory:

A. **Children actively construct their understanding of the world through stages:** Piaget emphasized that children are active learners who progress through four universal, sequential stages of development.

C. **Each of these stages is qualitatively different from other stages:** The stages—Sensorimotor, Preoperational, Concrete Operational, and Formal Operational—are defined by distinct cognitive abilities and thought processes.

E. **Each developmental stage brings distinct way of thinking:** For example, abstract thinking emerges only in the Formal Operational stage.

Incorrect statements:

B. Culture and social interaction guide cognitive development is aligned more with Vygotsky's sociocultural theory, not Piaget's.

D. Knowledge is constituted through interaction is vague but can be debated; Piaget emphasized interaction with the environment rather than social interaction per se.

Therefore, the valid Piagetian aspects are A, C, and E.

49. **(4):** The correct matchings of theories in social psychology with their descriptions are:

A. Realistic Conflict Theory – II. Stereotypes and prejudices arise from conflicts over limited resources: Proposed by Muzafer Sherif, this theory explains intergroup hostility as stemming from competition over scarce resources.

B. Social Identity Theory – III. The theory that people favour ingroup over outgroup in order to enhance self-esteem: Developed by Tajfel and Turner, it emphasizes the role of group membership in shaping self-concept and prejudice.

C. Contact Hypothesis – IV. The theory that direct contact between hostile groups will reduce prejudice under certain conditions: Formulated by Gordon Allport, it asserts that intergroup contact, under favourable conditions (equal status, cooperation), reduces prejudice.

D. Relative Deprivation Theory – I. Feeling of discontent aroused by the belief that one fares poorly compared with others: This theory explains how perceived inequality, rather than actual deprivation, leads to dissatisfaction and possible social unrest.

These pairings are well-established in intergroup relations and prejudice research.

50. **(1):** The correct sequence of negotiation stages for conflict resolution is:

B. **Prepare:** The initial stage involves planning, setting goals, and gathering relevant information.

C. **Information exchange and validation:** Both parties share their interests and validate each other's concerns, establishing transparency and building trust.

A. **Bargain:** This is the core negotiation phase where offers and counter-offers are made.

E. **Conclude:** Once a mutual agreement is reached, the negotiation is finalized.

D. **Execute:** The agreed terms are then implemented, and responsibilities are carried out.

This stepwise approach ensures that negotiations proceed from preparation to implementation, maximizing the chances of conflict resolution.

51. **(1):** The James-Lange theory of emotion proposes that physiological arousal precedes the emotional experience. According to this theory:

A. Autonomic and somatic activities active due to emotional stimuli trigger the experience of emotion: Correct. The body responds first (e.g., increased heart rate), and then the brain interprets these changes as an emotion.

D. Different patterns of autonomic arousal may be the source of the experience of different emotions: Correct. James-Lange suggests that each emotion arises from a distinct pattern of physiological response.

Incorrect statements:

B is more aligned with the Cannon-Bard theory, which posits that emotion and physiological responses occur simultaneously.

C is an argument against the James-Lange theory (used by Cannon-Bard).

E reflects ideas from Schachter-Singer's two-factor theory, which emphasizes cognitive context.

Hence, only A and D align with the James-Lange theory.

52. **(3):** The statement (3) is incorrect regarding metacognitive knowledge. Metacognition is defined as "thinking about thinking" or "cognition about cognition", and it plays a critical role in monitoring, evaluating, and regulating one's cognitive processes. It includes two main components:

- Metacognitive knowledge: awareness of one's cognitive processes.
- Metacognitive regulation: the ability to monitor progress, adjust strategies, and reflect during problem-solving.

Therefore, metacognition enables and improves monitoring, not prevents it.

The other statements correctly describe metacognitive concepts.

53. **(4):** Deci and Ryan's Self-Determination Theory (SDT) emphasizes autonomous motivation and the satisfaction of three basic psychological needs: autonomy, competence, and relatedness.

A. **People have inclination towards spontaneous interest, mastery and exploration:** Correct. SDT sees humans as inherently growth-oriented.

B. **Intrinsic motivation occurs when our need for importance and autonomy is satisfied:** Correct. Autonomy, in particular, is key to intrinsic motivation.

E. **There is a spectrum of intrinsic motivation starting from motivation:** Correct, though better stated as a continuum of self-determined motivation ranging from amotivation to intrinsic motivation.

Incorrect:

C is inaccurate: SDT does not focus on the genesis of needs, but assumes that autonomy, competence, and relatedness are innate.

D is also incorrect: Deadlines and directives, especially when controlling, undermine intrinsic motivation.

Thus, A, B, and E are correct under SDT.

54. **(2):** The phrase "Sat-Cit-Ananda" is a fundamental concept in Upanishadic philosophy that expresses the nature of Brahman or the absolute reality.

- **Sat:** Existence or absolute being — that which is eternal and unchanging.
- **Cit:** Consciousness or pure awareness — the ability to know and be aware.
- **Ananda:** Bliss or absolute joy — the state of supreme happiness or fulfillment.

The traditional sequence is: Sat (Existence) → Cit (Consciousness) → Ananda (Bliss), reflecting the ultimate non-dual realization in Vedanta.

55. **(4):** The chronological order based on year of establishment of key institutions in Indian psychology is:

A. **Indian Psychological Association (IPA)**–Established in 1924, it was the first professional psychological body in India.

C. **Defence Science Organization (DSO)**–Established in 1948, later evolved into DRDO, and supported applied psychological research in military settings.

B. **NIMHANS**–Originated from All India Institute of Mental Health in 1954, which merged in 1974 to become NIMHANS.

D. **Indian Academy of Applied Psychology (IAAP)**–Established in 1962, focusing on promoting applied psychology research and practice.

E. **National Academy of Psychology (NAOP)**–Formed in 1989, it serves as a national platform for psychological research and academic exchange.

This order reflects the historical trajectory of psychology's institutional growth in India.

56. **(1):** The correct matching of early psychological schools with their prominent founders or proponents is as follows:

A. Structuralism – III. Edward Titchener: Structuralism was introduced by Wilhelm Wundt but brought to the U.S. and further developed by Titchener, who focused on analyzing the structure of the mind through introspection.

B. Functionalism – I. William James: Functionalism, championed by William James, emphasized the purpose of mental processes and how they help individuals adapt to their environment.

C. Behaviourism - IV. John B. Watson: Watson is known as the father of behaviourism, advocating for psychology as the study of observable behaviour, rejecting introspection.

D. Humanism - II. Carl Rogers: One of the leading figures in humanistic psychology, Rogers emphasized self-actualization, unconditional positive regard, and a client-centered approach.

This matching accurately reflects the foundational figures of each psychological perspective.

57. (4): Syllogistic reasoning is a form of deductive reasoning involving logical structures.

A. **Two premises and a conclusion:** This is the basic form of a syllogism (e.g., All humans are mortal; Socrates is a human; therefore, Socrates is mortal).

B. **The terms within a syllogism are either stated positively or negatively:** Correct. Statements can be affirmative (e.g., All A are B) or negative (e.g., No A is B).

C. **Syllogisms are either valid or invalid:** Validity refers to whether the conclusion logically follows from the premises, regardless of the truth of the premises.

Incorrect options:

D: 'If-then' reasoning is more characteristic of conditional reasoning, not classical syllogisms.

E: Affirming or denying the antecedent is part of propositional logic, not syllogistic logic.

Thus, A, B, and C define syllogistic reasoning correctly.

58. (2): Triangulation is not a property of measurement scales—it is a research method used to enhance the validity and reliability of data by combining multiple methods, data sources, or researchers.

Properties that differentiate scales of measurement are:

1. **Magnitude:** Ordering of values from least to greatest (e.g., ranks in ordinal scales).

3. **Equal intervals:** The distance between values is consistent (e.g., in interval scales like temperature in Celsius).

4. **An absolute zero:** Presence of a true zero point (e.g., weight in kilograms), relevant in ratio scales.

Hence, triangulation is unrelated to measurement scales and is the correct answer here.

59. (4): Drive theories of motivation focus on biological needs and internal drives that push behaviour to maintain homeostasis.

- A drive is an internal state of tension (e.g., hunger, thirst) caused by unmet needs, which motivates behaviour to reduce that tension.
- This theory was first developed by Clark Hull, who proposed that behaviour is aimed at reducing internal physiological tension.

In contrast:

- Instinct theory emphasizes innate, fixed patterns of behaviour.
- Incentive theory highlights external stimuli pulling behaviour.
- Cognitive theory centers on expectations and goals, not biological urges.

Therefore, drive theories best explain internal, need-based motivation.

60. (1): In Ayurveda, the concept of "Doshas" refers to the three fundamental bodily humours or energies that govern physiological and psychological functions.

B. **Vata:** Composed of air and ether, responsible for movement and communication.

C. **Pitta:** Made of fire and water, governs digestion, metabolism, and transformation.

E. **Kapha:** Made of earth and water, provides structure, stability, and lubrication.

Incorrect options:

A. Rasa refers to taste or nutritive fluid, not a dosha.

D. Vairagya is a concept from Indian philosophy meaning detachment or dispassion, unrelated to doshas.

Thus, B, C, and E are the correct Ayurvedic doshas.

61. (1): In Indian philosophical terminology, these concepts reflect different roles of the self (Atman or soul) in its worldly experience:

A. Jiva - IV. A living being: Jiva refers to the individual embodied soul, subject to birth and rebirth, comprising the Atman and subtle body.

B. Karta – I. Agent capable of freely choosing a course of action: Karta means the doer or agent, the one who performs actions (karma) with intention.

C. Jnata – II. Knower: Jnata is the one who knows or perceives, representing the cognitive function of the self.

D. Bhokta – III. Experience of pleasure and pain: Bhokta is the experiencer, particularly of pleasure, pain, and other dualities, a key concept in Vedanta and Sankhya systems.

These four concepts help define the multidimensional nature of the self in Vedantic philosophy.

62. **(1):** According to the Levels of Processing Theory proposed by Craik and Lockhart (1972), the depth at which information is processed determines its memorability.

B. **Semantic level:** Involves processing the meaning of information, which leads to deep encoding and better recall.

E. **Elaborative rehearsal:** Involves linking new information with existing knowledge, which also leads to deeper semantic processing.

In contrast:

A. Phonetic level involves shallow processing based on sound.

C. Structural level refers to even more superficial processing like font or appearance.

D. Maintenance rehearsal keeps info in short-term memory through repetition but doesn't aid long-term retention.

Hence, semantic processing and elaborative rehearsal produce the best recall.

63. **(3):** In physiological psychology, invasive methods are those that involve direct intervention in the brain or body.

A. **Lesion:** Involves intentional damage or removal of brain tissue to study behavioral effects. This is clearly invasive.

C. **Electrocorticogram (ECoG):** A technique involving direct placement of electrodes on the exposed surface of the brain, typically during surgery. This is also invasive.

Non-invasive methods include:

B. **EEG:** Electrodes placed on the scalp to record electrical activity; non-invasive.

D. **MEG:** Measures magnetic fields produced by neural activity; non-invasive.

E. **MRI:** Uses magnetic fields and radio waves to produce brain images; non-invasive.

Hence, only lesion and ECoG are invasive techniques.

64. **(3):** The doctrine described—where the individual self (Atman) is neither part of, nor different from, nor a modification of the Supreme Consciousness (Brahman)—is central to Advaita Vedanta, a non-dualistic school of Indian philosophy. Founded by Adi Shankaracharya, Advaita teaches that Brahman is the only reality, and the Atman is identical to Brahman. It denies the ultimate reality of multiplicity and difference, affirming oneness (non-duality).

In contrast:

- Jainism asserts individual souls as eternal and separate.
- Buddhism denies a permanent self (Anatta).
- Ayurveda is a medical system, not a metaphysical doctrine.

Thus, the view matches Advaita perfectly.

65. **(3):** The pituitary gland, known as the "master gland", is divided into anterior and posterior lobes, each with distinct hormonal functions. Anterior Pituitary secretes somatotropic hormone (also called growth hormone), which regulates growth, metabolism, and cell regeneration. Posterior Pituitary stores and releases:

- Vasopressin (also known as antidiuretic hormone or ADH), which helps in water retention by kidneys and regulates blood pressure.
- Oxytocin, which influences uterine contractions and lactation.

Among the given options, somatotropic and vasopressin correctly correspond to anterior and posterior pituitary secretions, respectively.

66. **(4):** According to Gordon Allport's trait theory, secondary traits are those that are less consistent, more situational, and not central to personality.

These traits influence behavior in specific contexts or under certain conditions, such as preferences or attitudes (e.g., "liking chocolate" or "preferring jazz music").

In contrast:

- Cardinal traits dominate an individual's entire personality (e.g., Mother Teresa's compassion).
- Central traits are general characteristics present across many situations (e.g., honesty, sociability).
- General traits is not a recognized category in Allport's classification.

Hence, traits like "liking chocolate" fall under secondary traits.

67. **(3):** According to Peterson and Seligman (2001), in their Values in Action (VIA) classification of character strengths, a positive characteristic must meet several criteria to be considered a character strength.

Among the correct ones are:

A. **Be trait-like:** The strength should be stable and consistent over time.

B. **Lead to some form of fulfillment:** The strength should contribute to personal well-being or flourishing.

D. **Be morally valued:** The trait should be seen as intrinsically good, not just instrumental.

Incorrect:

C. **Need not be supported by institutions** – VIA actually emphasizes institutional support (like education, religion, or family) as a validation factor.

E. **Diminish other people** – This contradicts the VIA framework, which is based on uplifting and prosocial qualities.

Hence, only A, B, and D fulfill the criteria.

68. **(1):** Item difficulty in test construction refers to the proportion or number of individuals who answer a particular item correctly.

- It is commonly expressed as a p-value, where:
- p = number of people who answered the item correctly / total number of respondents
- For example, a p-value of 0.80 means 80% got the item correct, making it an easy item.
- It is a key index in achievement and aptitude testing, guiding item selection and test balance.

Other options refer to:

- **Item validity:** How well an item measures what it is intended to.
- **Criterion validity:** Whether the test correlates with a relevant external outcome.
- **Item reliability:** Consistency of responses to an item.

Thus, the definition fits item difficulty.

69. **(2):** Feminist theories broadly agree that gender is a social construct, not merely a product of biology.

- Feminism views gender as a set of socially learned roles, behaviours, and expectations, shaped by culture, institutions, and history.
- While biological sex refers to physical characteristics (male/female), gender is seen as a fluid, constructed identity (e.g., man, woman, nonbinary).

Other feminist core beliefs include:

- Patriarchal structures result in men's power over women.
- External systemic factors (not inherent flaws in women) cause women's problems (e.g., lack of representation, wage gaps).

Therefore, the idea that gender is a biological construct is rejected by most feminist theories, making it the correct answer here.

70. **(3):** Psychic determinism is a principle of Sigmund Freud's psychoanalytic theory stating that all mental processes are not spontaneous, but rather determined by the unconscious or pre-existing mental complexes.

- It asserts that every behaviour, thought, or emotion has a psychological cause, even slips of the tongue or dreams.
- This reflects Freud's belief in the unconscious mind as a powerful driver of behaviour.

The other options refer to different theories:

- Unconditional positive regard – Carl Rogers (Humanism)
- Collective unconscious – Carl Jung
- Idiographic psychology – Gordon Allport (focus on individual uniqueness)

Thus, the statement best matches Freud's concept of psychic determinism.

71. **(2):** The Apgar Scale, developed by Virginia Apgar in 1952, is used to assess the health and physical condition of newborns immediately after birth. It includes five criteria, each scored from 0 to 2, with a total score out of 10. The scale evaluates:

C. **Heart rate (Pulse)** – Indicates cardiovascular function.

D. **Muscle tone (Activity)** – Assesses flexion and movement.

E. **Reflex irritability (Grimace)** – Measured by response to stimulation (e.g., mild pinch or suctioning).

Other components include respiratory effort and skin colour.

A. Pupil dilation and B. Body temperature are not part of the Apgar assessment.

Thus, the correct components are C, D, and E.

72. **(1):** While professional standards guide the practice of psychological testing, ethical and moral concerns also significantly shape its appropriateness.

The key moral concerns include:

A. **Human rights** – Ensuring that participants are treated with dignity and are not exploited.

D. **Labeling** – Test results can lead to stereotyping and stigma, especially in educational or clinical settings.

E. **Invasion of privacy** – Tests may probe deeply into personal issues, raising concerns about confidentiality and informed consent.

Incorrect options:

B. Divided loyalties and C. Dehumanization are ethical challenges, but they are broader professional or contextual issues, not central moral concerns directly tied to test use.

Hence, A, D, and E are the correct answers regarding moral issues in testing.

73. **(3):** The correct match of moral development concepts is as follows:

A. Heteronomous morality – I. Justice and rules are conceived as unchangeable: As per Piaget's theory, younger children believe rules are fixed and handed down by authority.

B. Autonomous morality – III. Child becomes aware that rules are created by people: With age, children understand that rules are social agreements and can be changed by consensus.

C. Immanent justice – II. If a rule is broken, punishment will be given out immediately: Children believe in immediate retribution, even if no one witnessed the wrongdoing.

D. Preconventional reasoning – IV. Moral reasoning is controlled primarily by external reward and punishment: According to Kohlberg, at this level, behavior is guided by consequences, not internalized values.

This matching reflects key milestones in moral cognitive development.

74. **(4):** The correct matching of terms related to social bias and intergroup relations is:

A. Stereotypes – III. Beliefs about social groups in terms of traits that they are believed to share: These are cognitive generalizations, often oversimplified and resistant to change.

B. Prejudice – II. Negative emotional responses based on group membership: Refers to attitudinal bias, often irrational and emotionally charged.

C. Discrimination – IV. Differential (usually negative) behaviour towards members of different social groups: It involves actions, such as exclusion or unequal treatment.

D. Tokenism – I. Refer to hiring based on group membership: A symbolic effort to include minority group members, often to deflect criticism, without real inclusion.

This classification accurately reflects the cognitive, emotional, and behavioural components of prejudice.

75. **(3):** According to Sigmund Freud's theory of psychosexual development, personality is shaped through a series of sequential stages, each focusing on different erogenous zones and conflicts.

The correct order is:

C. **Oral stage (0–1 years):** Focus on mouth – sucking and feeding.

E. **Anal stage (1–3 years):** Focus on anus – toilet training, control.

D. **Phallic stage (3–6 years):** Focus on genitals, emergence of Oedipus/Electra complex.

A. **Latency stage (6–12 years):** Sexual impulses are dormant, energy directed to school and friendships.

B. **Genital stage (12+ years):** Focus on mature sexual intimacy and relationships.

This order outlines Freud's stages of personality development across childhood to adolescence.

76. **(1):** According to Jean Piaget's theory of cognitive development, the sensorimotor stage spans from birth to about 2 years of age.

- During this stage, infants learn through direct sensory and motor interactions with their environment.
- A major milestone achieved toward the end of this stage is the development of object permanence, which is the understanding that objects continue to exist even when they are not visible.
- Piaget demonstrated this concept using tasks such as hiding a toy under a cloth and observing whether the infant searches for it.

In contrast:

- The preoperational stage (2–7 years) involves symbolic thought and egocentrism.
- The concrete operational stage (7–11 years) involves logical reasoning with concrete objects.
- The formal operational stage (12+ years) introduces abstract reasoning.

Thus, object permanence develops in the sensorimotor stage.

77. **(3):** The positivist model of science emphasizes that knowledge should be based on observable, empirical, and measurable evidence. It relies on several core assumptions:

- **Empiricism:** Knowledge comes from sensory experience and observation.
- **Determinism:** All events are assumed to have causes that can be scientifically investigated.
- **Parsimony:** The preference for simplest explanations with fewer assumptions.

Open-mindedness, while valuable in scientific inquiry, is not a formal foundational assumption of positivism; it is more associated with general scientific attitude or philosophy, not the positivist framework itself.

Hence, open-mindedness is not a core assumption of positivism.

78. **(4):** Damage to the bones of the middle ear (malleus, incus, stapes) leads to conduction hearing loss. Conduction hearing impairment occurs when sound vibrations cannot efficiently travel from the outer ear through the middle ear to the inner ear.

Causes include:

- Ear infections
- Ossicle damage
- Fluid buildup
- Perforated eardrum

In contrast:

- Nerve hearing loss (sensorineural) involves damage to the cochlea or auditory nerve.
- Stimulation hearing loss and brain pathway impairment involve deeper neurological structures.

Therefore, middle ear damage leads to conduction hearing impairment.

79. **(1):** Correct matching of regression-related concepts is:

A. Multiple Regression – IV. Prediction of dependent variable as a result of two or more variables: This method uses multiple independent variables to predict a single dependent variable.

B. Regression – III. Falling off the dependent values as a result of independent values: This refers to the regression effect, where extreme scores tend to be closer to the mean upon retesting.

C. Regression equation – I. The formula to predict the Y variable values based on X variable: Typically written as $Y = a + bX$ in simple linear regression.

D. Regression line – II. The straight line defining the relationship of X and Y variables by squaring deviations around it: This is the line of best fit, minimizing the sum of squared errors.

This matching reflects the key constructs of regression analysis.

80. **(4):** In Indian yogic philosophy, meditation (Dhyana) is part of the eight limbs (Ashtanga Yoga) outlined by Patanjali, and is achieved through a sequence of mental disciplines:

A. **Dharana:** Concentration or holding attention on a single object or point.

C. **Dhyana:** Meditation itself — a state of uninterrupted flow of concentration.

E. **Samadhi:** The culmination, a state of deep absorption or union with the object of meditation.

Together, Dharana → Dhyana → Samadhi are referred to as the internal limbs of yoga (Antaranga Sadhana).

Incorrect:

B. Vasana refers to latent tendencies or impressions of past actions.

D. Jugupsa means disgust or aversion, and is not a meditative state.

Thus, meditation is achieved by the combination of A, C, and E.

81. **(2):** The Thematic Apperception Test (TAT) was developed by Henry A. Murray and Christiana Morgan in the 1930s, and it is directly based on Murray's Theory of Needs, particularly his concept of "psychogenic needs".

- The TAT is a projective test in which individuals are shown ambiguous pictures and asked to create a story.
- These stories are analyzed to uncover underlying motives, concerns, and the way the person sees the social world, especially in relation to Murray's need-press model.
- Unlike Maslow or McClelland, who emphasized a hierarchy or motivational typologies, Murray's theory focuses on personality through needs, including achievement, affiliation, aggression, etc.

Thus, the TAT is grounded in Murray's Theory of Needs.

82. **(4):** In constructing a psychological tool (like for organizational loyalty), the correct sequential steps include:

E. **Item writing:** Initially, items are generated based on theory and construct definition.

C. **Item discrimination:** After pilot testing, items are evaluated for how well they differentiate between high and low scorers.

A. **Computing Cronbach's alpha:** This assesses the internal consistency reliability of the scale.

D. **Exploratory factor analysis (EFA):** Conducted to identify underlying factor structure or dimensions within the items.

B. **Establishing percentile norm:** After finalizing the tool, norms are created using large samples for interpretation.

Hence, this logical sequence reflects standard psychometric test development.

83. **(3):** Correct matching of motivational theories with their descriptions is:

A. Social context of an action has effect on motivation - IV. Self-determination theory: Proposed by Deci and Ryan, this theory states that autonomy, competence, and relatedness in the social context influence motivation.

B. Optimal level of tension - III. Arousal theory: Suggests individuals are motivated to maintain an optimal arousal level, increasing or decreasing stimulation as needed.

C. Internal drives to satisfy needs - II. Drive reduction theory: A biological approach by Clark Hull, where behavior aims to reduce internal tension caused by unmet physiological needs.

D. View of self affecting success/failure - I. Self-theory of motivation: Suggests that self-perception, beliefs, and identity shape motivation, especially regarding goal-setting and achievement.

This mapping aligns with distinct theoretical perspectives on motivation.

84. **(4):** Groupthink is a concept introduced by Irving Janis that describes faulty decision-making in cohesive groups due to pressures for unanimity. Key characteristics include:

1. **Invulnerability:** Illusion that the group is immune to errors.
2. **Self-deception:** Group rationalizes decisions, ignoring warnings.
3. **Lack of disagreement:** Dissent is discouraged; members self-censor.

Pressure to conform, stereotyping outsiders, and illusion of unanimity are also common features.

However, lack of self-control is not a core characteristic of groupthink; it pertains more to impulsivity or behavioral dysregulation, not group dynamics.

Hence, this option is incorrect in this context.

85. **(3):** The PASS Model of Intelligence, proposed by J.P. Das, Jack Naglieri, and Kirby, is based on the work of Alexander Luria (1973). It outlines four core components of intelligence:

B. **Cortical arousal and attention:** This is the first functional unit, responsible for alertness and attentional control.

C. **Coding information using simultaneous processes:** Part of the second unit, simultaneous processing involves integrating information into meaningful wholes (e.g., understanding spatial relationships).

E. **Structuring of cognitive abilities:** Related to planning, which is the third functional unit, involving goal-setting, strategy formation, and evaluation.

Incorrect:

A. Object sensation and D. Motivation to pay attention are not core PASS model constructs.

Thus, B, C, and E accurately reflect Luria's foundational components in the PASS model.

86. **(1):** The correct matching of theories/views of development with their core principles is:

A. Ethological theory – IV. Characterized by critical period and imprinting: Associated with Konrad Lorenz, this theory emphasizes biologically sensitive periods where specific behaviours (e.g., imprinting in geese) are best learned.

B. Ecological theory – III. Development is influenced by environmental systems: Proposed by Urie Bronfenbrenner, this theory highlights the role of nested environmental contexts (microsystem, mesosystem, etc.) in shaping development.

C. Evolutionary psychology – II. Adaptation and survival of the fittest shape behaviour: Focuses on how evolutionary principles (natural selection) explain human behaviours and psychological traits.

D. Epigenetic view – I. Development is the result of ongoing, bidirectional interchange between heredity and environment: This modern view integrates genetic expression with environmental influence over time.

Thus, this option correctly aligns the four developmental frameworks.

87. **(2):** The correct matching of research methods with their descriptions is:

A. Systematic observation – III. Behaviour is observed in natural settings: This method involves structured, non-intrusive observation in real-life environments.

B. Surveys – IV. Large amount of information can be acquired quickly: Surveys are useful for gathering data from many people efficiently, often using questionnaires or interviews.

C. Experimental research – II. Can be used in field as well as in laboratory settings: Experiments involve manipulation of variables and controlled conditions, whether in lab or field.

D. Case study method – I. Detailed information is gathered: Case studies offer in-depth insights into a single individual or situation, often through interviews, tests, and archival records.

This sequence reflects the distinct characteristics of each method accurately.

88. **(1):** The correct matching of immune responses and their mediators is:

A. Humoral immunity – II. B-lymphocytes: B-cells are responsible for producing antibodies that circulate in body fluids (humour).

B. Cell-mediated immunity – IV. T-lymphocytes: T-cells attack infected cells directly and regulate immune responses.

C. Phagocytosis – I. Ingest microbes: Phagocytes like macrophages engulf and digest pathogens as part of innate immunity.

D. Cytokine level – III. Indicative of inflammatory activity: Cytokines are signaling proteins that regulate inflammation and immune responses; elevated levels indicate immune activity.

Hence, the immunological components are accurately paired.

89. **(4):** The Gestalt principle of proximity states that objects that are close together in space or time are perceived as belonging to the same group.

- It is one of several perceptual grouping principles that explain how we organize visual elements.

- For example, in a cluster of dots, those nearer each other are perceived as forming a shape or group.

Other principles include:

- **Similarity:** Grouping based on likeness.
- **Closure:** Filling in gaps to perceive complete figures.
- **Common fate:** Grouping items moving in the same direction.

Hence, grouping by spatial or temporal closeness is explained by proximity.

90. **(2):** Stigmatization involves various social-cognitive and behavioural processes that lead to the devaluation or discrimination of individuals based on certain characteristics (e.g., mental illness, race, disability).

Mechanisms include:

- **Negative treatment and direct discrimination:** Active exclusion or poor treatment.
- **Expectancy confirmation processes:** When people behave in ways that confirm stereotypes held about them.
- **Automatic stereotype activation:** Stereotypes can be triggered unconsciously and influence perceptions or behaviour.

Negative reinforcement, however, is a behavioural learning concept (removing an aversive stimulus to increase behaviour) and is not a recognized mechanism of stigmatization.

Thus, it is the correct exception in this context.

91. **(2):** The amygdala is a key brain structure involved in processing fear and emotional responses, and it plays a central role in the occurrence of panic attacks.

- Neuroimaging and clinical studies have shown that individuals with panic disorder often have hyperactivity in the amygdala, which may trigger the fight-or-flight response even in the absence of real threats.
- While the thalamus, pons, and hypothalamus also participate in emotional and autonomic regulation, the amygdala is most directly implicated in panic attacks and anxiety disorders.

Hence, the amygdala is the central structure associated with panic attacks.

92. **(1):** When panic attacks occur during unexpected or low-arousal states like sleep or relaxation, they are referred to as nocturnal panic attacks.

- These are uncued attacks that happen without a specific external trigger.
- The passage notes that panic attacks sometimes occur "in situations in which they might be least expected such as during relaxation or during sleep", which aligns with the definition of nocturnal panic.

Other options:

- Situationally predisposed refers to attacks that are more likely in certain contexts but not completely unexpected.
- Disorganized panic attack and generalized panic are not recognized clinical terms.

Hence, the correct term is nocturnal panic.

93. **(4):** Among the listed symptoms, dissociative amnesia is not a typical cognitive symptom of panic disorder.

Cognitive symptoms of panic disorder commonly include:

- Fear of dying
- Fear of going crazy or losing control
- Depersonalization or derealization (feeling detached from oneself or surroundings)

However, dissociative amnesia—the inability to recall important personal information, often following trauma—is a symptom of dissociative disorders, not panic disorder.

Thus, dissociative amnesia does not belong to the core cognitive symptom cluster of panic attacks.

94. **(3):** Research has consistently shown that panic disorder is more prevalent in women than men.

- According to epidemiological studies, women are twice as likely as men to be diagnosed with panic disorder.
- Hormonal differences, sociocultural expectations, and greater likelihood of seeking treatment may all contribute to this difference.
- The passage also refers to gender differences in prevalence rates.

Thus, panic attacks are more prevalent among women.

95. **(3):** Comorbidity is very common in individuals with panic disorder, and serious depressive episodes and avoidant personality disorder are two of the most frequently co-occurring conditions.

- The passage states that 30 to 50% of those with panic disorder develop other serious disorders.
- Major depressive disorder is one of the most common comorbid diagnoses.
- Avoidant personality disorder also often co-occurs due to the social withdrawal and fear of judgment that overlaps with anxiety symptoms.

Other listed options like OCD, somatization, or dissociative disorders may occur but are less commonly associated than depression and avoidant traits.

Hence, serious depression and avoidant personality disorder are most commonly experienced.

96. **(2):** In this scenario, Ramesh experienced negative physical symptoms such as splitting headache, blurred vision, and memory loss after drinking. These unpleasant consequences made him aware of his vulnerability and prompted him to decide to quit drinking.

- This aligns with the concept of "perceived symptoms" triggering behavioral change, as people often begin to modify habits when they notice or experience symptoms that signal health risk.
- Other options like personal goals or social influence may contribute later, but here the immediate physical discomfort was the motivator.

Therefore, his health habits are most likely controlled by perceived symptoms.

97. **(4):** A health habit is defined in the passage as a health behavior that is firmly established and performed automatically, which means without conscious thought or awareness.

- For example, brushing teeth before bed becomes a routine act, done even without remembering why or who taught it initially.
- It is not something that requires supervision (Option 1) or is limited to at-risk individuals (Option 2).
- Also, these habits are typically beneficial, not harmful, to metabolism or immunity.

Thus, the correct feature is that health habits are often performed without awareness.

98. **(4):** Health promotion efforts frequently use "teachable moments"—specific times or contexts when individuals are more receptive to adopting healthy behaviours.

- These moments can occur during major life events (e.g., pregnancy, diagnosis, recovery from illness), or when people experience health scares, or transitions like starting school or a new job.
- While personal control, goals, and values influence health behavior, teachable moments offer a strategic point for intervention.

Hence, health promotion efforts most commonly capitalize on teachable moments.

99. **(1):** Many individuals underestimate their personal health risk and assume that "it won't happen to me."

- This belief is referred to as unrealistic optimism, where a person views their own risk as lower than others, even when engaging in harmful behaviours.
- For example, smokers may believe they won't get cancer because they think "everyone smokes" or "I'm not as bad as others."
- This bias can hinder preventive health behaviours and accurate risk assessment.

Therefore, such perception is termed unrealistically optimistic.

100. **(3):** Focusing on at-risk individuals allows health professionals to:

- Deliver targeted interventions,
- Identify additional risk factors (like genetic vulnerability, environmental exposure, or behavioural patterns),
- Understand how multiple variables interact to produce disease, and
- Prevent progression to illness.
- The goal is not just prevention, but risk reduction and early detection.

Thus, this targeted approach helps to identify other contributing risk factors, making option 3 correct.

Previous Years' Paper

National Testing Agency (NTA)

UGC-NET Junior Research Fellowship & Assistant Professor Eligibility Exam

PSYCHOLOGY, AUGUST-2024

(Exam held on 30-08-2024)

PAPER-II

1. People living on railway platforms, crowded market area on the main roads with heavy traffic are likely to experience:

1. Energetic stress
2. Ergonomic stress
3. Anthropogenic stress
4. Tropical Stress

2. Which of the following is not included in Sullivan basic modes theory?

1. Prototaxic mode
2. Pretaxic mode
3. Parataxic mode
4. Syntaxic mode

3. The leading neuroscience theories of intelligence is called:

1. Parieto-Frontal interpolated theory
2. Frontal-Occipital integration theory
3. Parieto-Frontal integration theory
4. Frontal-Parietal symbolic theory

4. Which of the following is one of the non-parametric counterpart of ANOVA?

1. Kruskal-Wallis Test
2. Mann-Whitney Test
3. Kendell's Test
4. Wilcoxn's Test

5. In the equation for linear regression Y = $a + b$X, b stands for:

1. Y intercept on X
2. Regression coefficient
3. X intercept on Y
4. Constant

6. In case of normal probability curve, the graph curve is plotted for:

1. Scores and respective frequencies
2. Scores and respective deviations
3. 'z' scores and respective relative frequencies
4. 'z' scores and respective standard deviations

7. A psychologist was interested to conduct a study on gamblers. Identifying the gamblers, even with the help of police, is a challenging task. Which of the following sampling technique will be more appropriate to take up the study?

1. Quota sampling
2. Cluster sampling
3. Snowball sampling
4. Stratified sampling

8. Peterson and Seligman carried out their famous work on strengths, virtues and character. This work is referred as:

1. Characters in Action project
2. Strength in Action project
3. Virtues in Action project
4. Values in Action project

9. The situation of conflict arising upon allocation of funding to different groups is an example of conflict arising over issues of:

1. Interest
2. Values
3. Growth
4. Demand characteristics

10. Which of the following attribute, according to Mahatma Gandhi as well as Patanjali, is an essential condition for practicing non-violence?

1. Dukha 2. Vairagya
3. Krodha 4. Utsaha

11. Spreading rumours behind someone's back can most appropriately be referred as ....

1. Social aggression
2. Relation aggression
3. Indirect aggression
4. Physical aggression

12. Which one of the following is correct with regard to PASS model developed by J.P. Das and his associates?

1. Planning, Arousal, Successive and Simultaneous processing
2. Programing, Attentive, Sequencing and Simultaneous processing
3. Processing, Awakening, Simultaneous and Successive processing
4. Planning, Attention, Arousal, Simultaneous and Successive processing

13. Which one of the following is the preferred method for determining item bias?

1. Item difficutly level
2. Item discrimination index
3. Item characteristic curve
4. Inter item correlation matrix

14. The multitrait-multimethod design does not provide which one of the following?

1. Predictive evidence validity
2. Discriminant evidence validity
3. Convergent evidence validity
4. Reliability

15. The distribution, which is skewed to the left, has one high point and has many high scores is called:

1. Evenly distributed distribution
2. Platykurtic distribution
3. Negatively skewed distribution
4. Positively skewed distribution

16. In order to interpret individual test scores and to calculate confidence interval, which of the following is important and necessary?

1. Pearson product moment correlation
2. Test variance
3. Spearman-Brown formula
4. Standard error of measurement

17. In addition to tripartite system of working memory, Baddeley, Allen and Hitch (2011) added a fourth component which is called:

1. Iconic Sketchpad
2. Storage Rehearsal
3. Phonological loop
4. Episodic buffer

18. The theory which is used to compare judgements or the decisions we make under uncertain conditions is called:

1. Subliminal perception theory
2. Signal detection theory
3. Judgmental process theory
4. Decision processing theory

19. Hull's approach to theory construction is called:

1. Hypothetical deductive
2. Hypothetical inductive
3. Hypothetical intuitive
4. Hypothetical tautology

20. Who among the following is not considered as a reinforcement theorist?

1. Thorndike 2. Gutherie
3. Hull 4. Skinner

21. According to which theory of emotion the Physiological reaction and the emotion are assumed to occur simultaneously?
1. James-Lange Theory
2. Cannon-Bard Theory
3. Cognitive-Arousal Theory
4. Cognitive-Mediational Theory

22. Who is the Personality Theorist who believed that individuals are in the process of 'becoming' and nothing is predetermined?
1. Sigmund Freud 2. Alfred Adler
3. Carl Jung 4. B.F. Skinner

23. The disorder where an extra Sex chromosome in the 23rd pair resulting in XXY producing a male with reduced masculine characteristics resulting in enlarged breasts, obesity and excessive height is called:
1. Phenylketonuria (PKU)
2. Turner's syndrome
3. Tay-Sachs disorder
4. Klinefelter's syndrome

24. In the disease called Multiple Sclerosis (MS) ....
1. The myelin Sheath is destroyed
2. The myelin Sheath is thick
3. The myelin shows bumps in some places
4. The electrical signals jump

25. The functions of Gamma-aminobutyric acid (GABA) can be described in terms of:
1. Excitatory or inhibitory, involved in arousal, attention, memory
2. Mainly excitatory, involved in arousal and mood
3. Majorly inhibitory involved in sleep and inhibitory movement
4. Inhibitory neural regulation, involved in pain relief

26. The area responsible for interaction between frontal, temporal and motor areas in order to produce speech is called ....
1. Primary Auditory Cortex
2. Broca's Area
3. Spery's Area
4. Wernicke's Area

27. Which of the following are components of hardiness?
1. Control, Coherence, Challenge
2. Challenge, Constructivity, Confidence
3. Control, Commitment, Challenge
4. Commitment, Collaboration, Control

28. One behavioural scientist is developing a questionnaire to assess the attitude towards workplace support. Which of the following will be the best way to establish construct validity of the questionnaire?
1. Croanbach Alpha
2. Inter-item Correlation
3. Factor Analysis
4. Kuder-Richardson Formula

29. The four phases of forgiveness according to Enright, Freedman and Rique includes:
1. Undercovering, Contemplation, Work and Recovering
2. Uncovering, Decision, Work and Deepening
3. Uncovering, Covering, Contemplating, Recovering
4. Understanding, Balming, Generosity, Recovering

30. The first psychology department in India was formally started in 1916 by ....
1. Girindra Shekhar Bose
2. N.N. Sengupta
3. M.V. Gopalaswami
4. S.M. Mohsin

31. The different states of consciousness like wakefulness, dream, deep sleep as well as extraordinary state (turiya avastha) are described in ....
1. Mandukya Upanisad
2. Katha Upanisad
3. Svetasvatara Upanisad
4. Mimamsa

32. The five sheaths (pancha kosas) theory is explained in ....

1. Katha Upanisad
2. Mandukya Upanisad
3. Prasna Upanisad
4. Taittiriya Upanisad

33. A famous study called the 'Robber's Cave' conducted by Sherif *et al.* in 1961 demonstrated the social behaviour known as ....

1. Social comparison
2. Equal status contact
3. Self-fulfilling prophecy
4. Reciprocity of liking

34. According to social identity theory, formation of a person's identity within a particular social group is explained by the sequential process of ....

1. Social categorization, social identity and social comparison
2. Social identity, social categorization and social comparison
3. Social comparison, social identity and social categorization
4. Social comparison, social categorization and social identity

35. The process by which one person tries to change the belief, opinion, position or course of action of another person through argument, pleading or explanation is an example of:

1. Social influence
2. Deindividuation
3. Persuasion
4. Prosocial behaviour

36. Asking for a small commitment and after gaining compliance, asking for a bigger commitment is known as ....

1. Foot-in-the-door technique
2. Low-ball technique
3. Progressive ball technique
4. Door-in-the-face technique

37. Which one of the following is not a component of creativity according to Torrance?

1. Flexibility
2. Elaboration
3. Abstractness of titles
4. Verification

38. While Carkhuff's model describes conmnmication skills as pre-processing skills, Ivey and Ivey call it a ....

1. Basic communication skills
2. Life Skill model
3. Micro-Skill approach
4. DASIE model

39. A key element in all therapeutic process is the development of an effective:

1. Challenging
2. Personal integration
3. Advanced empathy
4. Working alliance

40. Some casual factors occurring relatively early in life may not show their effects for many years, that may contribute to a predisposition to develop a disorder. These would be considered as ....

1. Proximal risk factors
2. Distal risk factors
3. Fixed risk factors
4. Concomitant risk factors

41. Kohlberg's stages of moral development follows:

A. Being a moral person in the eyes of others
B. Makes moral choices based on beliefs
C. Behaves appropriately to avoid punishment
D. Conflicts with moral principles and individual rights
E. Makes choices based on what is right-behaviour

Choose the **correct** answer from the options given below:

1. C, E, A, B, D
2. D, E, B, A, C
3. A, D, C, E, B
4. B, E, C, D, A

42. Arrange the following behaviours of the child as per Piaget's stages of cognitive development.

A. The child says the volume of water in a long glass is same even when it is poured into flat bowl
B. The child looks for an object in the same place where it was hidden earlier
C. The child says that the clay ball in round shape is smaller than that the one flattened right in front of her
D. The child argues that cycling gives a better exercise to hip muscles than bending exercises by citing reasons

Choose the **correct** answer from the options given below:

1. B, C, A, D 2. B, A, C, D
3. A, C, B, D 4. C, A, B, D

43. Arrange the following cognitive points sequentially to explain helping behaviour as suggested by Darley and Latane:

A. Taking responsibility
B. Defining an emergency
C. Taking Action
D. Noticing
E. Planning a course of Action

Choose the **correct** answer from the options given below:

1. B, D, E, A, C
2. B, E, D, A, C
3. D, A, B, E, C
4. D, B, A, E, C

44. Arrange the following in the sequence of personality development propounded by psychoanalitic theory:

A. Children refuse to defecate in the toilet, while some hold back the feces
B. Children enjoy breast feeding by mother and put everything in mouth
C. Children develop interest in opposite sex
D. Children are found to play with their genital organs

Choose the **correct** answer from the options given below:

1. A, C, D, B 2. B, C, D, A
3. B, A, D, C 4. D, A, B, C

45. Arrange the following behaviours of a University professor in a hierarchical order as per Maslow's theory of motivation:

A. Buys a two-bedroom flat
B. Attends at least one refresher course in his discipline every year
C. Applies regularly for various awards
D. Tries to maintain close relationship with the students

Choose the **correct** answer from the options given below:

1. A, D, C, B 2. D, A, B, C
3. D, C, B, A 4. A, B, D, C

46. Arrange the following stages of therapy advocated by Adler:

A. Building therapeutic relationship
B. Gathering information
C. Developing new skill
D. Gaining insight

Choose the **correct** answer from the options given below:

1. B, A, D, C 2. A, B, D, C
3. B, A, C, D 4. A, C, B, D

47. Arrange the following in a sequence as per the health belief model where an individual:

A. Reads about the various factors related to cancer
B. Stops smoking

C. Feels that since his father died of cancer he is likely to be genetically disposed
D. Understands that if he continues to smoke there is higher possibility of his suffering from cancer

Choose the **correct** answer from the options given below:

1. C, D, A, B 2. D, A, C, B
3. A, C, D, B 4. D, C, A, B

48. Following are the steps that should be followed to enhance critical thinking. Arrange them in sequential order:

A. Adopt the attitude of a critical thinker
B. Evaluate information sources
C. Recognize and avoid critical thinking hindrances
D. Identify and characterize arguments
E. Evaluate arguments

Choose the **correct** answer from the options given below:

1. A, C, D, B, E
2. A, B, C, E, D
3. B, A, C, E, D
4. C, A, B, E, D

49. Cognitive psychologists and survey researchers have acknowledged that answering survey questions can be a complex cognitive task. Research suggests that when people answer survey questions, they go through four stages. Arrange the stages in order:

A. Comprehension
B. Judgement
C. Response communication
D. Retrieval

Choose the **correct** answer from the options given below:

1. A, D, B, C 2. A, B, D, C
3. B, A, D, C 4. B, C, A, D

50. Arrange the early schools of psychology in order:

A. Structuralism B. Functionalism
C. Behaviourism D. Humanistic

Choose the **correct** answer from the options given below:

1. B, A, C, D 2. B, C, A, D
3. A, B, C, D 4. A, C, B, D

51. Read the following situations. Then order them in the sequence of nominal, ordinal, equal interval and ratio.

A. Eggs in the supermarket are graded as small, medium, large and jumbo
B. Employees are assigned identification numbers
C. Achievement motivation of hockey players
D. Players' height

Choose the **correct** answer from the options given below:

1. B, C, D, A 2. B, A, C, D
3. A, B, D, C 4. A, C, B, D

52. One organisational psychologist wanted to verify the efficacy of a group based development intervention. For this purpose he undertook an Action Research. Suggest the correct sequence of the following components of his research.

A. Acting through the intervention
B. Observation
C. Planning about the intervention
D. Reflection

Choose the **correct** answer from the options given below:

1. B, C, D, A 2. C, B, A, D
3. C, A, B, D 4. B, C, A, D

53. One psychologist has developed a tool on Nature connectedness. What would be correct sequence of the following psychometric activities.

A. Carrying out Exploratory Factor Analysis
B. Establishing Percentile Norm
C. Examining Croanbach Alfa
D. Verifying Predictive Validity
E. Establishing Content Validity

Choose the **correct** answer from the options given below:

1. E, C, A, D, B
2. E, C, A, B, D
3. C, A, E, B, D
4. C, E, A, D, B

54. Place the components of 'Broaden-and-Build model of Positive Emotion' in correct sequence:

A. Building Enduring Personal Resources
B. Positive Emotions
C. Enhanced Health Fulfillments
D. Novel Thoughts, Activities, Relationships

Choose the **correct** answer from the options given below:

1. B, D, A, C 2. B, A, D, C
3. D, B, A, C 4. D, A, B, C

55. Arrange the following literary works on different facets of 'Yoga' in chronological order.

A. 'Anasakti Yoga' by Mahatma Gandhi
B. 'Gitarahasya' by B.G. Tilak
C. 'Gatha' by Tukaram
D. 'Upadesha' by Raman Maharshi

Choose the **correct** answer from the options given below:

1. C, D, B, A 2. C, B, D, A
3. B, C, D, A 4. B, C, A, D

56. Which of the following statements are correct?

A. Internal locus of control enhances the perception of stress
B. Stress functions as a motivator
C. The behavioural indicators of stress in children are seen in cognitive abilities, social competence and academic performance
D. In resistance stage of General Adaptation Syndrome (GAS), the physiological arousal peaks upto the all time high
E. Neglect, Victimization, Physical assault constitute toxic stress for children

Choose the **correct** answer from the options given below:

1. A, C, E only 2. B, C, E only
3. A, C, D only 4. C, D, E only

57. Which of the following statements are correct?

A. Emotionally arousing stimuli have also been seen to lead to amnesia
B. Some cognitive processing must occur before an individual can experience an emotional response to an event
C. Repression is a form of motivated forgetting
D. Functional Magnetic Resonance Imaging (fMRI) and Position Emission Topography (PET) are invasive scanning techniques of studying the brain functioning
E. Theories of emotions have not changed much over the years

Choose the **correct** answer from the options given below:

1. A, B, C only
2. A, B, D only
3. B, C, D, E only
4. A, B, D, E only

58. Richardson's Resilience model refers to which of the following?

A. Reintegration with a loss
B. Resistance index
C. Biopsychospiritual homeostasis
D. Disruption
E. Outcome Index

Choose the **correct** answer from the options given below:

1. B, C, E only
2. C, D, E only
3. A, C, D only
4. B, C, D only

59. Pineal Gland:

A. Helps increase the blood calcium level
B. Secretes a hormone called 'melatonin'

C. Is located in epithalamus
D. Secretes hormones called 'parathormone' and 'calcitonin'
E. Is used to be known as the 'Third eye'

Choose the **correct** answer from the options given below:

1. A, D, E only 2. B, C, E only
3. C, D only 4. A, B, C, E only

60. Reality Therapy in counselling:

A. Is based on principles of choice
B. Emphasises self-evaluation
C. Focuses on the way we live and exist
D. Views empowerment from a strength-based perspective
E. Follows the stages of Wants, Direction, Evaluation and Planning (WDEP)

Choose the **correct** answer from the options given below:

1. A, B, E only 2. A, C, E only
3. A, B, D only 4. C, D, E only

61. Five ways to be proactive includes the following:

A. Predict B. Prevent
C. Program D. Plan
E. Participate

Choose the **correct** answer from the options given below:

1. A, B, C, E only
2. B, C, D, E only
3. A, B, D, E only
4. A, B, C, D only

62. Which of the following are included in Bruner's theory of cognitive development?

A. Enactive B. Echoic
C. Iconic D. Symbolic
E. Deontic

Choose the **correct** answer from the options given below:

1. A, B, C only 2. A, C, D only
3. A, C, E only 4. A, B, E only

63. Which of the following are not true about the differences between simple regression and multiple regression?

A. The number of predictors
B. The number of criteria
C. Coefficient of determination
D. Sample size

Choose the **correct** answer from the options given below:

1. A, C, D only 2. A, B, D only
3. B, C, D only 4. A, B, C only

64. Which of the following terms are associated with Gestalt approach?

A. Molar
B. Nativistic
C. Atomistic, Elementistic
D. Cognitive, Phenomenological
E. Objective

Choose the **most appropriate** answer from the options given below:

1. A, C, D only
2. A, B, D, E only
3. B, C, D, E only
4. A, B, D only

65. Which one of the following are the reasons for forgetting?

A. The information is not attended to and fails to be encoded
B. Information accessed repeatedly decays
C. Older information in memory interferes with the learning of new information
D. Newer information interferes with the retrieval of older information
E. Information attended and perception is poor

Choose the **correct** answer from the options given below:

1. A, C, D only
2. A, B, C, D only
3. A, B, D only
4. B, C, D, E only

66. Which of the following are community based protective factors for resilience among children?

A. Ties to pro-social organisations
B. Authoritative parenting
C. Organised home environment
D. Neighbourhood with high collective efficacy
E. Effective schools

Choose the **correct** answer from the options given below:

1. A, C, D only 2. A, D, E only
3. C, D, E only 4. B, C, D only

67. Which of the following methods can be used to determine the number of factors to be extracted in Exploratory Factor Analysis?

A. Liserel Analysis
B. Scree Test
C. Eigenvalue criteria
D. Rotation

Choose the **correct** answer from the options given below:

1. A, B only 2. B, C only
3. C, D only 4. A, D only

68. Which of the following softwares can be more helpful for analysis in qualitative research by a psychologist?

A. SPSS B. AMOS
C. NVivo D. ATLAS
E. R

Choose the **correct** answer from the options given below:

1. A, B only 2. B, D only
3. C, D only 4. B, D, E only

69. Which of the following refer to Advanced Empathy as per the Developmental Model of Counselling?

A. Confrontive challenging
B. Theme identification
C. Connecting islands
D. Making the implicit explicit
E. Fortune telling

Choose the **correct** answer from the options given below:

1. A, B, E only 2. C, D, E only
3. B, C, D only 4. B, D, E only

70. Which of the following are methods used in challenging in counselling as per the Developmental model of Egan?

A. Reviewing better times
B. Asocial response
C. Identification of models
D. Immediacy
E. Self-disclosure

Choose the **correct** answer from the options given below:

1. B, D, E only 2. A, C, D only
3. A, D, E only 4. C, D, E only

71. Which of the following are included in the steps of Eye Movement Desensitization Reprocessing (EMDR) therapy?

A. Assessment
B. Cognitive restructuring
C. Installation
D. Skill Acquisition
E. Body scan

Choose the **correct** answer from the options given below:

1. A, C, D only 2. A, C, E only
3. B, D, E only 4. B, C, D only

72. Which of the following refer to the theories of Health Behaviour?

A. Reflection-Action Theory
B. Protective Motivation Theory
C. Dialectical Behavioural Theory
D. Precaution Adoption Process Model
E. Organismic Integration Theory

Choose the **correct** answer from the options given below:

1. A, C, D only 2. B, C, D only
3. A, C, E only 4. B, D, E only

73. Which of the following are characteristics of a good Hypothesis?

A. Affirmative statement
B. Interrogative statement
C. Falsifiability
D. Conjectural
E. Concludes relationship between variables

Choose the **correct** answer from the options given below:

1. B, D, E only
2. A, C, D only
3. B, C, D only
4. A, C, E only

74. Which of the following are measures of dispersion?

A. Standard Deviation
B. Quartile Deviation
C. Mode
D. Variance
E. Range

Choose the **correct** answer from the options given below:

1. A, B, E only
2. B, C, D only
3. A, B, D, E only
4. A, B, C, D only

75. Advaita Vedanta asserts that sensory knowledge is ....

A. Illusionary
B. Absolutely false
C. Possible in a transcendental state
D. Relatively true, but not absolutely true

Choose the **correct** answer from the options given below:

1. C, D only
2. A, B only
3. A, D only
4. B, C only

76. Match the List-I with List-II.

List-I (Theories of Motivation)	**List-II (Theorists)**
A. Drive-Reduction Theory	I. Yerkes and Dodson
B. Personality and Nach	II. Richard Ryan and Edward Deci
C. Arousal Theory	III. Carol Dweck
D. Self-Determination Theory	IV. Hull

Choose the **correct** answer from the options given below:

1. A-IV, B-I, C-II, D-III
2. A-IV, B-III, C-I, D-II
3. A-II, B-III, C-IV, D-I
4. A-I, B-IV, C-II, D-III

77. Match the List-I with List-II.

List-I (Sage Bharata's Classification of Bhavas)	**List-II (The English Equivalent)**
A. Krodha	I. Disgust
B. Bhaya	II. Wonder/ Astonishment
C. Jugupsa	III. Anger
D. Vismaya	IV. Fear

Choose the **correct** answer from the options given below:

1. A-III, B-IV, C-I, D-II
2. A-I, B-IV, C-II, D-III
3. A-II, B-IV, C-I, D-III
4. A-IV, B-III, C-II, D-I

78. Match the List-I with List-II.

List-I (Parts of Nervous System)	**List-II (Function)**
A. Hypothalamus	I. Fear responses and memory of fear
B. Hippocampus	II. Regulates body temperature, thirst, hunger

C. Amygdala — III. Forms long-term declarative memories

D. Cingulate cortex — IV. Slective attention, working memory

Choose the **correct** answer from the options given below:

1. A-III, B-IV, C-I, D-II
2. A-II, B-I, C-III, D-IV
3. A-II, B-III, C-I, D-IV
4. A-I, B-III, C-IV, D-II

79. Match the List-I with List-II.

List-I	List-II
A. Gestalt Therapy	I. Five universal human needs
B. Reality Therapy	II. You are the architect of your life
C. Existentialism	III. Empty chair technique
D. Solution-focused Therapy	IV. Steve de Shazer and Insoo Kim Berg

Choose the **correct** answer from the options given below:

1. A-II, B-I, C-IV, D-III
2. A-I, B-II, C-III, D-IV
3. A-IV, B-I, C-II, D-III
4. A-III, B-I, C-II, D-IV

80. Match the List-I with List-II.

List-I	List-II
A. Non-maleficence	I. Response to stress
B. HPA Axis	II. Encountering paradoxes of life
C. Art Therapy	III. Counselling ethics
D. Existentialism	IV. Intervention for emotional release

Choose the **correct** answer from the options given below:

1. A-II, B-III, C-I, D-IV
2. A-IV, B-II, C-III, D-I
3. A-III, B-I, C-II, D-IV
4. A-III, B-I, C-IV, D-II

81. Match the List-I with List-II.

List-I	List-II
A. Entropy	I. Comparative assessment of facilitating and restraining forces in the environment
B. Decay Curve	II. A sudden downward drop in the curve of health behaviour
C. Force field Analysis	III. Ginzberg's theory of career development
D. Fantasy, Tentative, Realistic	IV. A gradual progressive decline in the health behaviour curve

Choose the **correct** answer from the options given below:

1. A-II, B-IV, C-I, D-III
2. A-IV, B-III, C-II, D-I
3. A-III, B-II, C-I, D-IV
4. A-I, B-III, C-IV, D-II

82. Match the List-I with List-II.

List-I	List-II
A. Phenomenology	I. Indepth detailed examination of an entity in real world context
B. Case study	II. Application of inductive-reasoning
C. Ethnography	III. Lived experiences
D. Grounded theory	IV. Description of peoples and culture

Choose the **correct** answer from the options given below:

1. A-III, B-II, C-I, D-IV
2. A-II, B-I, C-III, D-IV
3. A-III, B-I, C-IV, D-II
4. A-I, B-III, C-IV, D-II

83. Match the List-I with List-II.

List-I	List-II
A. Tay-Sach disorder	I. The 23rd pair is actually missing an X

B.	Down's syndrome	II.	Fatal neurological disorder
C.	Klinefelter's syndrome	III.	An extra chromosome in what normally be the 21st pair
D.	Turner's syndrome	IV.	The 23rd set of sex chromosomes is XXY

Choose the **correct** answer from the options given below:

1. A-III, B-IV, C-II, D-I
2. A-II, B-III, C-IV, D-I
3. A-IV, B-I, C-III, D-II
4. A-I, B-III, C-II, D-IV

84. Match the List-I with List-II.

List-I	List-II
A. Dukha	I. Suffering is part of life
B. Dukha-Samudaya	II. Suffering has an end
C. Dukha-Nirodha	III. Suffering has a cause
D. Dukha-Nirodha Marga	IV. There is a way to end suffering

Choose the **correct** answer from the options given below:

1. A-I, B-II, C-IV, D-III
2. A-II, B-I, C-III, D-IV
3. A-III, B-I, C-II, D-IV
4. A-I, B-III, C-II, D-IV

85. Match the List-I with List-II.

List-I	List-II
A. Material form	I. Vedana
B. Feeling or sensation	II. Vinnana
C. Perception	III. Rupa
D. Reason or intelligence	IV. Sana

Choose the **correct** answer from the options given below:

1. A-III, B-I, C-IV, D-II
2. A-II, B-I, C-III, D-IV
3. A-I, B-IV, C-II, D-III
4. A-III, B-II, C-I, D-IV

86. Match the List-I with List-II.

List-I	List-II
A. Eros Love	I. Treating love as a game
B. Ludos Love	II. Treating love as friendship
C. Storge Love	III. Loving an ideal person
D. Agape Love	IV. Selfless love

Choose the **correct** answer from the options given below:

1. A-II, B-III, C-I, D-IV
2. A-I, B-II, C-IV, D-III
3. A-III, B-I, C-II, D-IV
4. A-IV, B-I, C-III, D-II

87. Match the List-I with List-II.

List-I	List-II
A. Premak principle	I. The rapid change in performance level as the size of reinforcement is varied
B. Zeigarnik effect	II. Reinforcement strengthens the neighbouring response in addition to the response that it produced
C. Crespi effect	III. The opportunity to engage in a frequently occurring activity can be used to reinforce a less frequently occurring activity
D. Spread of effect	IV. The tendency to remember incomplete tasks longer than complete ones

Choose the **correct** answer from the options given below:

1. A-II, B-I, C-IV, D-III
2. A-I, B-III, C-II, D-IV
3. A-IV, B-III, C-I, D-II
4. A-III, B-IV, C-I, D-II

88. Match the List-I with List-II.

List-I	List-II
A. Principle of closure	I. Tendency to complete incomplete experiences to make them more meaningful
B. Principle of Polarity	II. Learned material is most performed in the same direction in which it was originally learned
C. Principle of Parsimony	III. Choosing the simpler one out of the two equally effective theories
D. Principle of falsification	IV. In order for a theory to be scientific it must make risky prediction if not confirmed, would refute the theory

Choose the **correct** answer from the options given below:

1. A-I, B-II, C-III, D-IV
2. A-II, B-I, C-IV, D-III
3. A-III, B-I, C-II, D-IV
4. A-II, B-III, C-I, D-IV

89. Match the List-I with List-II.

List-I	List-II
A. Standard scores always has a mean of 50 and SD of 10	I. Percentile
B. Standard scores change the unit of measurement	II. Z-Score
C. Standard with a mean of zero and SD of 1	III. T-Score
D. Units in testing that help to evaluate a person's performance in comparison with others who took the same test	IV. Standard Score

Choose the **correct** answer from the options given below:

1. A-III, B-II, C-I, D-IV
2. A-II, B-III, C-I, D-IV
3. A-III, B-I, C-II, D-IV
4. A-IV, B-III, C-I, D-II

90. Match the List-I with List-II.

List-I	List-II
A. Synthetic skill	I. Decisions about how to deploy the skills available to a person
B. Analytic skill	II. To see problems with new points of view and get rid of conventional thinking
C. Practical contextual skill	III. To recognize which ideas are worth pursuing and which are not
D. Thinking styles	IV. To know how to persuade others regarding one's ideas

Choose the **correct** answer from the options given below:

1. A-II, B-IV, C-III, D-I
2. A-II, B-III, C-IV, D-I
3. A-I, B-II, C-IV, D-III
4. A-IV, B-III, C-I, D-II

Directions (Qs. No. 91-95): *Read the paragraph given below and answer the questions.*

The researchers assumed that older adults are different from younger adults in their suicidal ideation and in their reasons for thinking about committing suicide because of differences in life experiences and coping competence. Hence, they used cross-sectional research and recruited 150 older adults (60-95 years) who were matched with 150 younger adult (17-34 years) on gender ethnicity, religion and self reported health status. Beck's scale for suicidal ideation was used to measure suicidal ideation. They used '*t*' test for comparison of variables and found no significant difference. According to Siegler, neither cross-sectional nor longitudinal study provide much information about how those changes occur over time. He discussed a method that involves carefully observing behaviour during periods when rapid change is occurring and collecting both quantitative and qualitative information.

91. A potential problem with cross-sectional research is that there may be other variables that are confounded with age. This problem is called:
1. Habitat effect
2. Cohort effect
3. Interrupted effect
4. Protective effect

92. The combination of cross-sectional and longitudinal research is called:
1. Time series research
2. Correlational research
3. Sequential research
4. Thematic research

93. What is the *df* for the '*t*' test used here
1. 297
2. 296
3. 294
4. 298

94. What is the method Siegler discussed for studying the process of change?
1. Macrogenetic method
2. Exogenetic method
3. Chromogenetic method
4. Microgenetic method

95. When null hypothesis is false and we are accepting it then we make?
1. Type I error
2. Type II error
3. Error of falsifiability
4. Acceptance error

Directions (Qs. No. 96-100): *Read the paragraph given below and answer the questions.*

Motivation is the driving force behind human activities. Researchers identified three components of motivation. Motivation originates externally or internally, are defined by action or non-action and can be categorized as extrinsic, identified, intrinsic, or introjected. One of the causes of flow motivation is "just because an approach or method worked for someone else does not mean that it will work for you". Self-determination theory is built on the idea that people are actively motivated to persue their goals.

96. What are the three components of motivation?
1. Need, persistence and goal
2. Activation, persistence and intensity
3. Intensity, identification and drive
4. Activation, intensity and goal

97. What are the components of intrinsic motivation?
1. Autonomy, Competence, Tendency
2. Competence, Mastery, Purpose
3. Mastery, Tendency, Competence
4. Autonomy, Mastery, Purpose

98. "Just because an approach or method worked for someone else does not mean that it will work for you" refers to:
1. One size fits all
2. Absurd function approach
3. There is no common approach for all
4. The approach will work for me

99. Introjected motivation is:
1. A negative internalized motivation
2. A positive externalized motivation
3. A negative externalized motivation
4. A positive internalized motivation

100. Self-determination theory is developed by:
1. Shelley E Taylor
2. Deci and Ryan
3. Barbara Frederick
4. Seligman and Lubomirsky

EXPLANATORY ANSWERS

1. **(3):** People living on railway platforms, crowded market areas, or on main roads with heavy traffic are subject to anthropogenic stress, which is stress caused by human activities. This includes exposure to noise pollution, air pollution from vehicles, overcrowding, lack of sanitation, and constant social and environmental pressure. The term "anthropogenic" refers to anything originating from human activity, and in this context, such environments cause both physical and psychological stress due to unregulated urbanization and human-induced environmental degradation.

2. **(2):** Pretaxic mode is not a part of Harry Stack Sullivan's interpersonal theory of personality, which outlines three basic modes of experience—Prototaxic, Parataxic, and Syntaxic.
   - **Prototaxic mode:** Found in infancy, where experiences are not connected and have no logical sequence.
   - **Parataxic mode:** Involves illogical connections between events, often based on superstitions or beliefs that are not reality-based.
   - **Syntaxic mode:** Involves logical and rational thinking, which develops through interpersonal experiences and learning.

   There is no such concept as "pretaxic mode" in Sullivan's theory; it does not exist in psychological literature, making it the incorrect one here.

3. **(3):** The Parieto-Frontal Integration Theory (P-FIT) is a leading neuroscience-based theory of intelligence. It suggests that intelligence arises from the integration of information between parietal and frontal brain regions.
   - Proposed by Jung and Haier in 2007.
   - The parietal regions are involved in sensory processing and attention.
   - The frontal lobes handle problem-solving, planning, and reasoning.
   - Neuroimaging studies (such as fMRI) support this theory, showing that individuals with higher intelligence demonstrate more efficient processing in these brain areas.

   Hence, this theory provides a biological and cognitive basis for understanding intelligence.

4. **(1):** The Kruskal-Wallis Test is a non-parametric alternative to the one-way ANOVA. It is used when the assumptions of ANOVA—such as normal distribution of data—are not met.
   - It compares the medians of three or more independent groups.
   - It ranks the data and evaluates whether the mean ranks differ significantly.
   - No assumption of normality or equal variance is required.
   - It is particularly useful when data are ordinal or not interval-scaled.

   The other tests mentioned, like Mann-Whitney and Wilcoxon, are also non-parametric but used for two-group comparisons, while Kruskal-Wallis handles three or more groups, just like ANOVA.

5. **(2):** In the linear regression equation $Y = a + bX$, the term b represents the regression coefficient or slope of the regression line.
   - It quantifies the amount by which Y changes for a one-unit change in X.
   - For example, if $b = 3$, then for every one-unit increase in X, Y increases by 3 units.
   - It indicates the strength and direction of the relationship between the independent variable (X) and the dependent variable (Y).
   - If b is positive, the relationship is direct; if negative, it's inverse.
   - The value of a in the equation is the intercept—i.e., the value of Y when $X = 0$.

   Hence, b is not a constant or intercept, but the regression coefficient.

6. **(3):** In the case of the normal probability curve, the graph is typically plotted with z-scores on the x-axis and the corresponding relative frequencies (or probabilities) on the y-axis.
   - The z-score represents the number of standard deviations a data point is from the mean.
   - The relative frequency indicates the proportion of observations within a certain range.

- The curve is bell-shaped and symmetrical, centered at a z-score of 0 (the mean), with most data falling within ±1, ±2, and ±3 standard deviations.
- This standard normal distribution has mean = 0 and standard deviation = 1, allowing researchers to compare scores across different distributions.

7. (3): Snowball sampling is the most appropriate technique when studying hidden or hard-to-reach populations, such as gamblers, drug users, or sex workers.

- In this method, initially identified participants help in recruiting further participants by referring others in their network.
- It is particularly useful when the population is small, stigmatized, or difficult to access using traditional sampling methods.
- The sample "snowballs" as more people are added through referrals, making it ideal when official records or lists do not exist, as in the case of gamblers.

8. (4): Peterson and Seligman (2004) conducted a major study to classify human strengths and virtues as a counterpart to the DSM, under the banner of Positive Psychology.

- Their work led to the development of the "Values in Action" (VIA) project, which categorized 24 character strengths under six broad virtues (wisdom, courage, humanity, justice, temperance, and transcendence).
- The VIA Classification of Strengths is considered a foundational framework in positive psychology, focusing on what is right with people instead of deficits.
- It promotes well-being and flourishing through the cultivation of strengths.

9. (1): Conflicts over allocation of resources, such as funding distribution, arise due to conflicts of interest.

- These conflicts occur when different groups compete to maximize their own benefit, often at the expense of others.
- Unlike conflicts of values (which are ideological) or demand characteristics (which relate to experimental bias), interest-based conflicts are grounded in practical or material concerns, such as money, power, or resources.
- Such conflicts are common in organizational, political, and social settings.

10. (2): According to both Mahatma Gandhi and Patanjali, Vairagya (detachment or non-attachment) is essential for practicing Ahimsa (non-violence).

- In Patanjali's Yoga Sutras, Vairagya is one of the key requirements for controlling the mind and overcoming desires that lead to violence.
- Mahatma Gandhi, deeply influenced by Indian philosophy, emphasized that true non-violence requires freedom from personal desires and attachments, which can only be achieved through Vairagya.
- This detachment helps in overcoming anger, greed, and hatred—the root causes of violence.

11. (3): Spreading rumours behind someone's back is best described as indirect aggression.

- It refers to actions intended to harm another person without direct confrontation.
- These behaviours are covert, such as gossiping, excluding someone socially, or damaging a person's reputation.
- While physical aggression involves bodily harm and social or relational aggression involves manipulating social relationships, indirect aggression specifically emphasizes non-obvious, behind-the-scenes actions aimed at hurting someone emotionally or socially without open hostility.
- It is commonly observed in both adolescent and adult social dynamics.

12. (4): The PASS model developed by J.P. Das, Jack A. Naglieri, and John R. Kirby stands for:

- **Planning:** Goal-setting, strategy development, and self-monitoring.
- **Attention-Arousal:** The ability to selectively attend to stimuli and maintain alertness.
- **Simultaneous Processing:** Integrating information into a cohesive whole (e.g., visual-spatial tasks).

- **Successive Processing:** Organizing information in sequential order (e.g., language processing).

This model is based on Luria's theory of brain functioning and provides a neurocognitive perspective on intelligence, offering an alternative to traditional IQ-based models.

13. (3): The Item Characteristic Curve (ICC) is the preferred method for determining item bias, especially within the framework of Item Response Theory (IRT).

- It plots the probability of a correct response to an item against the ability level of respondents.
- An item is considered biased if the ICC differs significantly between different groups (e.g., males vs. females), even when the groups have the same ability level.

This method provides a precise graphical and statistical representation of how items function across different subgroups, making it superior to traditional methods like item difficulty or discrimination index alone.

14. (1): The Multitrait-Multimethod (MTMM) design, introduced by Campbell and Fiske (1959), is used to evaluate the construct validity of psychological tests. It assesses two main types of validity:

- **Convergent validity:** When different methods measuring the same trait produce similar results.
- **Discriminant validity:** When different traits measured by the same or different methods remain distinct.

However, MTMM does not provide evidence for predictive validity, which refers to a test's ability to predict future performance or behaviour.

MTMM is a cross-sectional design and does not assess relationships with outcomes over time, which predictive validity requires.

15. (3): A distribution that is skewed to the left, with one high point and many high scores, is known as a negatively skewed distribution. In such a distribution:

- The tail is longer on the left side (towards the lower scores).
- The bulk of the data is concentrated on the higher score side (right side).
- The mean < median < mode, indicating the direction of skewness.

This typically occurs in situations where most participants score high, such as an easy test or performance tasks where most individuals do well.

16. (4): The Standard Error of Measurement (SEM) is essential for interpreting individual test scores and for calculating confidence intervals around those scores.

- SEM indicates the amount of error inherent in an observed test score due to the imperfect reliability of psychological tests.
- A lower SEM implies greater reliability and less fluctuation in repeated measures.
- Confidence intervals (e.g., 95%) are constructed using SEM to provide a range in which the true score is likely to fall.
- Formula: $SEM = SD \times \sqrt{(1 - \text{reliability coefficient})}$

Thus, SEM is a key statistic in score interpretation, far more relevant for this purpose than correlation or variance.

17. (4): In 2011, Baddeley, Allen, and Hitch expanded the working memory model by adding a fourth component called the Episodic Buffer. The original model included:

- Phonological Loop (verbal and auditory information)
- Visuospatial Sketchpad (visual and spatial data)
- Central Executive (attention control and coordination)

The Episodic Buffer was added to integrate information from the subsystems and long-term memory into coherent episodes or chunks. It serves as a multimodal temporary storage system with limited capacity, linking working memory to consciousness and episodic long-term memory.

18. (2): Signal Detection Theory (SDT) is used to analyze how decisions or judgments are made under conditions of uncertainty, such as detecting a faint stimulus or interpreting ambiguous signals.

- It separates sensitivity (true ability to detect) from response bias (tendency to say "yes" or "no").
- Originally developed in psychophysics, SDT is now widely used in perception, memory, diagnostic testing, and decision-making research.

SDT parameters:

- d' (d-prime): Sensitivity index
- β (beta): Response bias

It explains outcomes like hits, misses, false alarms, and correct rejections.

19. (1): Clark L. Hull's approach to theory construction is known as the hypothetico-deductive method.

- He proposed a formalized, mathematical model in which behaviour could be predicted using a set of postulates (assumptions) and deduced theorems.
- Hull used symbolic logic to express psychological laws, making his work resemble that of physics.
- His model included concepts like habit strength, drive, and reinforcement.
- He believed that scientific theories must be tested through logical deductions followed by empirical verification.

20. (2): Edwin Guthrie is not considered as a reinforcement theorist, unlike Thorndike, Hull, and Skinner, who all placed reinforcement theorist at the core of learning.

- Guthrie proposed the contiguity theory of learning, which posited that a stimulus and response connected in time and space becomes associated regardless of reward.
- He believed a single pairing could form a lasting connection without the need for reinforcement.

In contrast,

- Thorndike's Law of Effect,
- Hull's drive-reduction theory, and
- Skinner's operant conditioning,

all emphasized the role of reinforcement in strengthening learning.

21. (2): The Cannon-Bard Theory of Emotion posits that physiological reactions and emotional experiences occur simultaneously, not sequentially. This theory was proposed by Walter Cannon and Philip Bard in the 1920s as a critique of the James-Lange theory.

According to Cannon-Bard:

- A stimulus is perceived → simultaneously triggers activity in the thalamus, which sends signals to both the cortex (producing emotion) and the autonomic nervous system (producing physiological response).
- For example, upon seeing a snake, you feel fear at the same time as your body begins to tremble or your heart rate increases.
- This theory emphasizes the central nervous system's role in processing emotions.

22. (2): Alfred Adler, a personality theorist and founder of Individual Psychology, believed that individuals are always in a process of becoming and that behaviour is goal-directed and shaped by individual striving for superiority or perfection. He rejected deterministic views like those of Freud, emphasizing that nothing is fixed or predetermined. Adler introduced concepts such as:

- Social interest
- Inferiority complex and compensation
- Lifestyle and creative self

His theory focuses on the individual's capacity for growth, choice, and personal responsibility, aligning with the belief in constant psychological evolution.

23. (4): Klinefelter's syndrome is a chromosomal disorder in which a male is born with an extra X chromosome (XXY instead of XY). This leads to physical and developmental differences such as:

- Reduced masculine traits
- Gynecomastia (enlarged breasts)
- Tall stature
- Obesity or poor muscle tone
- Possible learning difficulties and infertility

It is one of the most common chromosomal abnormalities in males, occurring in approximately 1 in 500 to 1,000 male births. Diagnosis often occurs during puberty or adulthood via karyotyping or hormonal tests.

24. (1): In Multiple Sclerosis (MS), the myelin sheath—the protective covering that insulates nerve fibers in the central nervous system—is progressively damaged or destroyed. This damage, known as demyelination, disrupts the transmission of electrical impulses between the brain and the rest of the body. It leads to symptoms such as:

- Muscle weakness or spasms
- Vision problems
- Fatigue
- Loss of coordination or balance

MS is considered an autoimmune disorder, where the body's immune system mistakenly attacks its own nervous tissue. This disease can be relapsing-remitting or progressive in nature.

25. (3): Gamma-Aminobutyric Acid (GABA) is the brain's primary inhibitory neurotransmitter. It plays a major role in:

- Reducing neuronal excitability
- Promoting relaxation and sleep
- Controlling anxiety and muscle tone

By inhibiting overactivity in the brain, GABA helps regulate processes like inhibitory movement, thus maintaining balance between excitation and inhibition. Low levels of GABA are associated with anxiety, insomnia, epilepsy, and other disorders involving over-excitation. Many sedative and anxiolytic drugs (e.g., benzodiazepines) work by enhancing GABA activity.

26. (2): Broca's Area is the region in the frontal lobe of the brain, typically located in the left hemisphere, that is responsible for speech production.

- It interacts with motor areas (for articulation), temporal areas (for language comprehension), and the frontal cortex (for planning and decision making).
- Discovered by Paul Broca in 1861, damage to this area results in Broca's aphasia, where the individual knows what they want to say but has difficulty in speech production (non-fluent, effortful speech).
- Broca's area is crucial in forming grammatically correct sentences and coordinating the muscles involved in speaking.

27. (3): The psychological construct of hardiness, introduced by Suzanne Kobasa in the 1970s, consists of three main components:

- **Control:** Belief that one can influence life events rather than feeling helpless.
- **Commitment:** A sense of purpose and involvement in life's activities.
- **Challenge:** Viewing change and difficulty as opportunities for growth rather than threats.

These components act as buffers against stress, promoting resilience and positive coping mechanisms in high-pressure situations.

28. (3): The best way to establish construct validity of a questionnaire, especially in behavioural research, is through Factor Analysis.

- Construct validity assesses whether a test truly measures the theoretical construct it claims to measure (here, attitude toward workplace support).
- Factor analysis identifies underlying structures (factors) among a large set of variables or items, revealing if the items group together meaningfully.
- It helps confirm whether the questionnaire items align with expected theoretical dimensions.
- Unlike reliability measures (e.g., Cronbach Alpha), factor analysis deals directly with the validity of the construct representation.

29. (2): According to Enright, Freedman, and Rique (1998), the four phases of forgiveness are:

- **Uncovering Phase:** The individual becomes aware of the emotional pain caused by the offense.
- **Decision Phase:** The individual makes a conscious choice to forgive.
- **Work Phase:** Effort is made to understand the offender and begin the process of letting go.
- **Deepening Phase:** There is emotional transformation, often resulting in increased personal growth, meaning, and empathy.

This model provides a structured approach for therapeutic work on interpersonal forgiveness.

30. **(2):** The first psychology department in India was formally established in 1916 at the University of Calcutta by N.N. Sengupta.

- He was a student of Wilhelm Wundt, the founder of experimental psychology, and brought the experimental approach to Indian academia.
- Under his leadership, the department became a center for psychological research and teaching in India.

This marked the beginning of formal academic psychology in the country, laying the foundation for future psychological studies and institutions across India.

31. **(1):** The Mandukya Upanisad, one of the principal Upanishads, describes the four states of consciousness:

- Jagrat (wakefulness)
- Svapna (dream state)
- Sushupti (deep sleep)
- Turiya (the fourth state or transcendental consciousness)

Turiya is beyond the physical and mental planes and represents pure awareness or Atman, untouched by the dualities of waking, dreaming, or sleeping. The Mandukya Upanisad is unique in its concise yet profound treatment of the non-dual philosophy of Advaita Vedanta, focusing exclusively on consciousness and self-realization.

32. **(4):** The Taittiriya Upanisad explains the Pancha Kosas or the five sheaths of human existence, which veil the true self (Atman). These are:

- Annamaya kosha (physical body or food sheath)
- Pranamaya kosha (vital energy sheath)
- Manomaya kosha (mind or mental sheath)
- Vijnanamaya kosha (intellect or wisdom sheath)
- Anandamaya kosha (bliss sheath)

The Upanishad elaborates how spiritual progress involves transcending each sheath to realize the innermost self, which is pure consciousness.

33. **(2):** The Robber's Cave experiment conducted by Muzafer Sherif et al. (1961) demonstrated that intergroup conflict arises from competition over limited resources, but it can be reduced through equal status contact and superordinate goals. In the study, two groups of boys at a summer camp were set against each other, resulting in hostility. However, when they were made to cooperate on common goals (e.g., fixing a broken water supply), intergroup hostility diminished. This led to the development of Realistic Conflict Theory and highlighted the importance of equal status and cooperation in reducing prejudice and promoting harmony.

34. **(1):** According to Tajfel and Turner's Social Identity Theory (1979), the formation of social identity involves a sequential process:

- **Social categorization:** People categorize themselves and others into groups (e.g., by religion, profession).
- **Social identity:** Individuals adopt the identity of the group they belong to, which influences self-concept.
- **Social comparison:** People compare their in-group with out-groups to maintain or enhance self-esteem, often leading to in-group favouritism.

This theory explains how group membership shapes behaviour, attitudes, and intergroup conflict.

35. **(3):** Persuasion is the process through which one person attempts to change another's beliefs, attitudes, intentions, or behaviours using communication, reasoning, and emotional appeal. It involves elements such as:

- Source (credibility and attractiveness of the persuader)
- Message (clarity, logic, and emotional impact)
- Audience (motivation, openness, prior beliefs)

Persuasion plays a major role in areas like marketing, politics, health communication, and social influence, and is studied extensively in social psychology.

36. **(1):** The foot-in-the-door technique is a persuasion strategy where a person is first asked to agree to a small request, which is easy to accept, and once they comply, they are then asked to agree to a larger request.

This technique works based on the principle of commitment and consistency—people who agree to a small action are more likely to remain consistent by agreeing to a larger action. For example, asking someone to sign a petition (small request) and later asking them to donate money to the cause (larger request). It is widely used in sales, advertising, and behavioural change campaigns.

37. **(4):** Verification is not one of the core components of creativity as proposed by E. Paul Torrance, who is well known for developing the Torrance Tests of Creative Thinking (TTCT).

Torrance identified the following major components:

- **Fluency:** Generating many ideas
- **Flexibility:** Producing varied ideas
- **Originality:** Generating novel or unique responses
- **Elaboration:** Adding details to enrich ideas
- **Abstractness of titles:** Creating conceptual or metaphorical titles
- **Resistance to premature closure:** Avoiding rushing to obvious conclusions

Verification, in contrast, refers more to scientific or logical validation, which is part of problem-solving or innovation models but not of Torrance's creativity framework.

38. **(3):** While Carkhuff's model emphasizes communication skills as pre-processing skills (i.e., preparation for therapeutic interaction), Ivey and Ivey introduced the Micro-Skill Approach. This model breaks down complex counseling interactions into basic, teachable units, known as micro-skills, such as:

- Attending behaviour
- Open/closed questions
- Paraphrasing
- Reflection of feeling

The micro-skill training method is widely used in counseling education to build interpersonal competence and effectiveness in a step-by-step way.

39. **(4):** A working alliance is a central element in all therapeutic relationships, regardless of the therapeutic approach.

It refers to the collaborative partnership between therapist and client, consisting of:

- Agreement on therapeutic goals
- Consensus on the tasks of therapy
- Development of a personal bond built on trust and respect

Research consistently shows that a strong working alliance is the best predictor of positive therapeutic outcomes, sometimes even more than the specific technique used.

40. **(2):** Distal risk factors are early-life or distant events or conditions that increase the likelihood of developing a disorder later in life, even though their effects may not be immediately observable.

Examples include:

- Childhood trauma
- Genetic predispositions
- Early neglect or chronic poverty

These are contrasted with proximal risk factors, which are immediate triggers or conditions occurring closer to the onset of a disorder (e.g., recent job loss or divorce).

Distal factors lay the foundation for vulnerability and are often interacted with by proximal factors to result in psychological problems.

41. **(1):** According to Lawrence Kohlberg's theory of moral development, individuals progress through three levels and six stages of moral reasoning. The correct sequence here matches the developmental order of these stages:

C. **Behaves appropriately to avoid punishment:** This corresponds to Stage 1 – Obedience and Punishment Orientation under the Pre-conventional Level.

E. **Makes choices based on what is right-behaviour:** This relates to Stage 2 – Individualism and Exchange, still in the Pre-conventional Level.

A. **Being a moral person in the eyes of others:** This represents Stage 3 – Good Interpersonal Relationships, part of the Conventional Level.

B. **Makes moral choices based on beliefs:** Corresponds to Stage 5 – Social Contract and Individual Rights, part of the Post-conventional Level.

D. **Conflicts with moral principles and individual rights:** This signifies Stage 6 – Universal Ethical Principles, the highest stage of moral reasoning.

42. (1): According to Jean Piaget's stages of cognitive development, children move through a series of stages with distinct cognitive abilities:

B. **The child looks for an object in the same place where it was hidden earlier:** Reflects Sensorimotor stage (birth–2 years) where object permanence begins to develop.

C. **The child says that the clay ball in round shape is smaller than the one flattened:** Reflects Preoperational stage (2–7 years), characterized by centration and lack of conservation.

A. **The child says the volume of water in a long glass is same even when it is poured into a flat bowl:** Signifies entry into the Concrete operational stage (7–11 years), where conservation and logical thinking develop.

D. **The child argues about exercise and muscles citing reasons:** Shows Formal operational stage (12 years and up), marked by abstract and hypothetical reasoning.

43. (4): The cognitive model of helping behaviour proposed by Darley and Latané (1968) outlines five sequential steps:

D. **Noticing:** First, a person must notice that something unusual is happening.

B. **Defining an emergency:** The situation must be interpreted as an emergency.

A. **Taking responsibility:** The bystander must feel responsible to intervene.

E. **Planning a course of action:** They must decide how to help.

C. **Taking action:** Finally, the person acts upon their decision to help.

This model explains the bystander effect, where people are less likely to help when others are present.

44. (3): According to Freud's psychoanalytic theory, personality develops through five psychosexual stages in a specific order:

B. **Children enjoy breast feeding and put everything in mouth:** Represents the Oral stage (0–1.5 years).

A. **Children refuse to defecate or hold feces:** Describes the Anal stage (1.5–3 years), involving toilet training and control.

D. **Children are found to play with their genital organs:** Reflects the Phallic stage (3–6 years), where awareness of gender and genitals emerges.

C. **Children develop interest in opposite sex:** Indicates the Latency and early Genital stages, where the Oedipus complex and mature sexual identity develop.

This sequence explains how early experiences shape adult personality.

45. (1): According to Abraham Maslow's hierarchy of needs, human motivation follows a pyramid-like progression:

A. **Buys a two-bedroom flat:** Addresses Physiological and Safety needs.

D. **Tries to maintain close relationship with the students:** Corresponds to Belongingness and Love needs.

C. **Applies regularly for various awards:** Reflects Esteem needs, seeking recognition and respect.

B. **Attends at least one refresher course in his discipline every year:** Represents Self-actualization, striving to fulfill one's potential and personal growth.

Thus, the hierarchy progresses from basic to higher-order needs, guiding motivated behaviour.

46. (2): According to Alfred Adler's stages of therapy, the therapeutic process follows a structured four-phase model:

A. **Building therapeutic relationship:** The first step involves establishing trust, collaboration, and mutual respect between the therapist and client. Adler emphasized egalitarian partnership.

B. **Gathering information:** This includes understanding the client's family constellation, early recollections, and lifestyle to assess the individual's belief system and life goals.

D. **Gaining insight:** The therapist helps the client interpret their behaviours and belief patterns, leading to self-awareness and deeper understanding of their difficulties.

C. **Developing new skill:** The final stage involves implementing new strategies and behaviours, fostering encouragement, social interest, and constructive life choices.

47. **(3):** As per the Health Belief Model, an individual's behaviour change follows this sequence:

A. **Reads about the various factors related to cancer:** This step involves acquiring knowledge and awareness of health issues, leading to better perceived susceptibility and severity.

C. **Feels that since his father died of cancer he is likely to be genetically disposed:** Here, the individual develops a personalized perception of risk (perceived susceptibility).

D. **Understands that if he continues to smoke there is higher possibility of his suffering from cancer:** This reflects perceived severity and consequences of the behaviour.

B. **Stops smoking:** The final action is behavioural change, influenced by the previous beliefs and risk assessments.

Thus, the model shows how perceived threat, benefits vs. barriers, and cues to action guide health-related behaviour.

48. **(1):** Enhancing critical thinking requires a systematic process:

A. **Adopt the attitude of a critical thinker:** Begin by cultivating open-mindedness, skepticism, and a desire for truth.

C. **Recognize and avoid critical thinking hindrances:** Understand and overcome biases, fallacies, and emotional reasoning.

D. **Identify and characterize arguments:** Learn to break down statements into claims, evidence, and reasoning.

B. **Evaluate information sources:** Check for credibility, bias, and accuracy of sources.

E. **Evaluate arguments:** Finally, assess logic, consistency, and validity of arguments to form well-reasoned judgments.

49. **(1):** When responding to survey questions, people go through the following four cognitive stages:

A. **Comprehension:** Understanding the question being asked.

D. **Retrieval:** Accessing relevant information from memory.

B. **Judgement:** Forming a judgment or estimation based on the retrieved information.

C. **Response communication:** Providing the answer in the form required (e.g., ticking a box or verbalizing).

These stages, identified by Tourangeau and colleagues, highlight the complexity behind what seems like a simple task.

50. **(3):** The chronological order of the early schools of psychology is:

A. **Structuralism:** Initiated by Wilhelm Wundt and further developed by Edward Titchener, it focused on the structure of consciousness using introspection.

B. **Functionalism:** Developed by William James, it emphasized the functions of the mind in adapting to the environment.

C. **Behaviourism:** Introduced by John B. Watson and later advanced by B.F. Skinner, this school focused on observable behaviour and rejected introspection.

D. **Humanistic:** Emerged in the 1950s as a reaction to psychoanalysis and behaviourism, led by Carl Rogers and Abraham Maslow, emphasizing free will, self-actualization, and human potential.

51. **(2):** The correct sequence of measurement scales—Nominal, Ordinal, Interval, and Ratio—is illustrated as follows:

B. **Employees are assigned identification numbers:** This represents Nominal scale, where numbers are just labels and carry no quantitative meaning.

A. **Eggs in the supermarket are graded as small, medium, large and jumbo:** This is an Ordinal scale, indicating order or rank, but not the magnitude of difference between categories.

C. **Achievement motivation of hockey players:** This fits Equal interval scale, where the differences between scores are meaningful, but there is no true zero. Motivation scales typically fall here.

D. **Players' height:** This represents a Ratio scale, as it has all properties of interval scale plus a true zero, allowing for ratios (e.g., someone can be twice as tall as another).

52. (3): In Action Research, the process is cyclical and systematic, usually following these four phases:

C. **Planning about the intervention:** Identify the problem and design the intervention strategy.

A. **Acting through the intervention:** Implement the planned intervention or development program.

B. **Observation:** Collect data during the intervention to monitor changes and outcomes.

D. **Reflection:** Analyze data and reflect on findings to understand effectiveness and guide future actions.

This cycle helps in continuous improvement and is widely used in organizational psychology and education.

53. (4): The sequence of psychometric activities for developing a tool on Nature Connectedness should logically proceed as follows:

C. **Examining Cronbach Alpha:** First, check the internal consistency reliability of items to ensure they measure the same construct.

E. **Establishing Content Validity:** Then, evaluate whether the items represent the entire domain of the construct through expert judgment.

A. **Carrying out Exploratory Factor Analysis (EFA):** Identify the underlying factor structure to validate the construct empirically.

D. **Verifying Predictive Validity:** Check whether the tool predicts related outcomes, supporting its external validity.

B. **Establishing Percentile Norm:** Finally, create norms for interpretation, classifying scores in terms of relative standing in the sample.

54. (1): The Broaden-and-Build Theory of Positive Emotions, proposed by Barbara Fredrickson, progresses through the following stages:

B. **Positive Emotions:** Emotions like joy, gratitude, and love broaden momentary thought–action repertoires.

D. **Novel Thoughts, Activities, Relationships:** These broadened repertoires lead to exploration, creativity, and building of connections.

A. **Building Enduring Personal Resources:** Over time, this results in the development of lasting psychological, social, intellectual, and physical resources.

C. **Enhanced Health Fulfillments:** These resources contribute to better health, resilience, and life satisfaction in the long term.

55. (2): Chronologically, these literary works on different aspects of Yoga and spiritual philosophy follow this order:

C. **'Gatha' by Tukaram:** Written in the 17th century, these are spiritual verses in Marathi emphasizing Bhakti Yoga and devotion.

B. **'Gitarahasya' by B.G. Tilak:** Published in 1915, it provides a nationalist and Karma Yoga interpretation of the Bhagavad Gita.

D. **'Upadesha' by Raman Maharshi:** Composed in the early 20th century, this work offers insights on Jnana Yoga (self-inquiry).

A. **'Anasakti Yoga' by Mahatma Gandhi:** Written in the 1920s, it reflects on detachment and selfless action, interpreting the Gita through the lens of non-violence and duty.

56. (2):

B. **Stress functions as a motivator:** Correct. Stress, particularly eustress (positive stress), can act as a motivator, enhancing focus and performance in challenging tasks.

C. **The behavioural indicators of stress in children are seen in cognitive abilities, social competence and academic performance:** Correct. Stress can negatively affect concentration, memory, peer relationships, and school achievements in children.

E. **Neglect, Victimization, Physical assault constitute toxic stress for children:** Correct. These are examples of toxic stress, which involves strong, frequent, or prolonged adversity without adequate adult support, and can have long-term effects on brain development and health.

A. **Internal locus of control enhances the perception of stress:** Incorrect. An internal locus is associated with better stress management because individuals believe they can control outcomes.

D. **In resistance stage of General Adaptation Syndrome (GAS), the physiological arousal peaks up to an all-time high:** Incorrect. In the resistance stage, the body tries to adapt, and arousal remains elevated but does not peak as it does in the alarm stage.

57. (1):

A. **Emotionally arousing stimuli have also been seen to lead to amnesia:** Correct. High emotional arousal can impair memory consolidation, especially in cases of trauma, leading to dissociative or psychogenic amnesia.

B. **Some cognitive processing must occur before an individual can experience an emotional response to an event:** Correct. This aligns with Lazarus' Cognitive-Mediational Theory, where appraisal precedes emotion.

C. **Repression is a form of motivated forgetting:** Correct. It is a defense mechanism, where distressing memories are unconsciously excluded from awareness.

D. **fMRI and PET are invasive scanning techniques:** Incorrect. These are non-invasive neuroimaging methods used to study brain function and structure.

E. **Theories of emotions have not changed much over the years:** Incorrect. Emotion theories have evolved significantly, from James-Lange and Cannon-Bard to modern cognitive and neurobiological models.

58. (3): Richardson's Resilience Model includes the following concepts:

A. **Reintegration with a loss:** Correct. This refers to how individuals adapt to adversity—they may reintegrate with or without resilience.

C. **Biopsychospiritual homeostasis:** Correct. This model sees resilience as a return to internal balance across biological, psychological, and spiritual domains.

D. **Disruption:** Correct. Adversity disrupts homeostasis, initiating the process of adaptation and growth.

B. **Resistance index and E. Outcome Index:** These terms are not core components of Richardson's model.

59. (2):

B. **Secretes a hormone called 'melatonin':** Correct. The pineal gland produces melatonin, regulating circadian rhythms and sleep-wake cycles.

C. **Is located in epithalamus:** Correct. The pineal gland is anatomically part of the epithalamus, situated near the center of the brain.

E. **Is used to be known as the 'Third eye':** Correct. In spiritual and ancient texts, it was considered the third eye, linked with intuition and consciousness.

A. **Helps increase the blood calcium level:** Incorrect. This is a function of the parathyroid glands via parathormone.

D. **Secretes parathormone and calcitonin:** Incorrect. Parathormone is secreted by parathyroid glands, and calcitonin by the thyroid gland.

60. (1): Reality Therapy, developed by William Glasser, includes the following elements:

A. **Is based on principles of choice:** Correct. It emphasizes Choice Theory, where behaviour is driven by five basic needs (survival, love/belonging, power, freedom, and fun).

B. **Emphasises self-evaluation:** Correct. Clients are encouraged to assess whether their behaviour is helping them meet their needs effectively.

E. **Follows the stages of Wants, Direction, Evaluation and Planning (WDEP):** Correct. The WDEP model is central to Reality Therapy:

- W – Wants and needs
- D – Direction and doing
- E – Evaluation
- P – Planning

C. Focuses on the way we live and exist and D. Views empowerment from a strength-based perspective: These are more aligned with existential or strength-based therapies, not specifically with Reality Therapy.

61. (3): The five ways to be proactive emphasize anticipating and addressing situations before they escalate. These include:

A. **Predict:** Anticipate possible issues before they arise.

B. **Prevent:** Take steps to stop problems from occurring.

D. **Plan:** Strategize and organize resources to handle potential outcomes.

E. **Participate:** Be actively involved in decision-making and solution implementation.

C. Program is not generally listed among the standard proactive behaviours; it relates more to implementation rather than proactive cognitive or behavioural strategy.

62. (2): Jerome Bruner's theory of cognitive development outlines three modes of representation, which are stages of how information is stored and processed:

A. **Enactive (0–1 year):** Learning through actions or motor responses (e.g., grasping, pushing).

C. **Iconic (1–6 years):** Learning through images or visual representations.

D. **Symbolic (7 years and up):** Learning through language, symbols, and abstract thinking.

B. Echoic relates to auditory memory, not Bruner's developmental modes.

E. Deontic refers to duties or obligations in linguistics or logic, unrelated to Bruner's theory.

63. (3): The differences between simple regression and multiple regression are as follows:

B. **The number of criteria:** Incorrect difference. Both types of regression predict a single dependent variable (criterion). So, this is not a difference.

C. **Coefficient of determination:** Incorrect as a differentiating factor. Both simple and multiple regression can compute an R^2 value, so this is not unique to either.

D. **Sample size:** Not a defining difference, but more predictors in multiple regression require larger sample sizes for stability and statistical power. Still, this is not a conceptual distinction.

A. **The number of predictors:** True difference. Simple regression uses one predictor, while multiple regression uses two or more.

Hence, B, C, D are not true differences.

64. (4): The Gestalt approach to psychology is centered on understanding experiences as structured wholes rather than isolated parts. Key associated terms include:

A. **Molar:** Focuses on whole behaviours, not isolated stimuli or responses.

B. **Nativistic:** Gestalt theorists believed that perception is innate, especially in visual organization.

D. **Cognitive, Phenomenological:** Gestalt psychology is cognitive (it considers internal mental processes) and phenomenological (focuses on subjective experience).

C. **Atomistic, Elementistic:** These are rejected by Gestaltists as they break experience into meaningless parts.

E. **Objective:** Not a central theme in Gestalt, which emphasizes subjective experience.

65. (1): Reasons for forgetting in cognitive psychology include:

A. **The information is not attended to and fails to be encoded:** If attention is not given, encoding fails, and the information is not stored.

C. **Older information in memory interferes with the learning of new information:** This is known as proactive interference.

D. **Newer information interferes with the retrieval of older information:** Known as retroactive interference.

B. **Information accessed repeatedly decays:** This is incorrect. Repetition prevents decay; decay occurs when information is not accessed.

E. **Information attended and perception is poor:** This is vague and not a commonly accepted reason in memory theories.

66. (2): Community-based protective factors for resilience in children are those that originate outside the home but strongly influence child development by offering supportive social structures and environments:

A. **Ties to pro-social organisations:** Correct. Involvement in religious groups, sports teams, clubs, etc., provides children with positive social connections and role models.

D. **Neighbourhood with high collective efficacy:** Correct. Collective efficacy refers to social cohesion and mutual trust within a community, which enhances safety and collective child supervision.

E. **Effective schools:** Correct. Schools that foster academic success, emotional support, and inclusive environments serve as major protective factors.

B. Authoritative parenting and C. Organised home environment are family-based factors, not community-based.

67. (2): The number of factors to be extracted in Exploratory Factor Analysis (EFA) is commonly determined using:

B. **Scree Test:** Correct. A graph of eigenvalues is plotted, and the "elbow" point indicates the number of factors to retain.

C. **Eigenvalue criteria:** Correct. A common rule is to retain factors with eigenvalues > 1 (Kaiser's criterion).

A. Liserel Analysis is used for Structural Equation Modeling (SEM), not EFA.

D. Rotation is used to simplify factor loadings after extraction, not to determine the number of factors.

68. (3): For qualitative research, psychologists use specialized software to manage and analyze large volumes of textual data:

C. **NVivo:** Correct. NVivo supports thematic analysis, coding, and content analysis for qualitative data.

D. **ATLAS.ti:** Correct. Similar to NVivo, it is used to organize, code, and interpret qualitative data.

A. SPSS, B. AMOS, and E. R are primarily used for quantitative data analysis, statistical modeling, and SEM.

69. (3): In the Developmental Model of Counselling, Advanced Empathy refers to the therapist's ability to understand and reflect deeper or hidden feelings and meanings that the client may not be fully aware of:

B. **Theme identification:** Correct. Recognizing recurring underlying patterns in the client's narrative.

C. **Connecting islands:** Correct. Linking disparate pieces of client's communication to reveal deeper insights.

D. **Making the implicit explicit:** Correct. Bringing unconscious or vague content to the client's awareness.

A. Confrontive challenging and E. Fortune telling do not fall under advanced empathy; the latter is not part of any valid therapeutic approach.

70. (1): In Gerard Egan's Developmental Model of Counselling, the challenging process involves interventions that push clients to confront discrepancies or change perspectives:

B. **Asocial response:** Correct. Highlighting maladaptive, non-relational patterns to promote awareness.

D. **Immediacy:** Correct. Addressing what is happening in the moment during the client-counselor interaction.

E. **Self-disclosure:** Correct. Counselor shares relevant personal experiences or reactions to promote insight or challenge distortions.

A. Reviewing better times and C. Identification of models are generally used in goal-setting or support-building, not specifically for challenging.

71. (2): Eye Movement Desensitization and Reprocessing (EMDR) is an evidence-based psychotherapy for trauma and PTSD. The standard EMDR protocol includes eight phases, of which the following are core components:

A. **Assessment:** Identification of the traumatic memory and associated negative cognition.

C. **Installation:** Strengthening of positive cognitions that replace the earlier negative ones.

E. **Body scan:** Observing residual physical sensations in the body after processing the memory.

B. Cognitive restructuring and D. Skill acquisition are more associated with Cognitive Behavioural Therapy (CBT), not EMDR.

72. (4): Theories explaining Health Behaviour focus on how individuals make decisions related to health and illness:

B. **Protective Motivation Theory:** Explains how fear appeals and coping appraisals affect health behaviour intentions.

D. **Precaution Adoption Process Model:** Describes the stages of change from unawareness to sustained behaviour change.

E. **Organismic Integration Theory:** A sub-theory of Self-Determination Theory, it addresses the internalization of health-related behaviours.

A. Reflection-Action Theory and C. Dialectical Behavioural Theory are not theories of health behaviour; the former is a learning theory, and the latter is a therapeutic model.

73. **(2):** Characteristics of a good hypothesis include:

A. **Affirmative statement:** A good hypothesis is usually stated as a declarative sentence, not a question.

C. **Falsifiability:** According to Karl Popper, a hypothesis must be testable and refutable.

D. **Conjectural:** It should propose a tentative explanation or prediction subject to empirical testing.

B. Interrogative statement is incorrect because hypotheses are not framed as questions.

E. Concludes relationship between variables is partially true, but more precisely, a hypothesis should propose (not conclude) such a relationship.

74. **(3):** Measures of dispersion describe the spread or variability of a data set:

A. **Standard Deviation:** Measures how much individual scores deviate from the mean.

B. **Quartile Deviation:** Measures variability by using the interquartile range.

D. **Variance:** The square of standard deviation, represents average squared deviations.

E. **Range:** The difference between the highest and lowest values.

C. **Mode** is a measure of central tendency, not of dispersion.

75. **(1):** In Advaita Vedanta (non-dualistic philosophy of Shankaracharya) sensory knowledge is:

C. **Possible in a transcendental state:** Correct. True knowledge (Brahma Jnana) is possible only in a state beyond sensory perception, in Turiya or Atman realization.

D. **Relatively true, but not absolutely true:** Correct. Sensory knowledge is Vyavaharika Satya (empirical truth), which is relatively valid in the practical world, but not the ultimate truth (Paramarthika Satya).

A. Illusionary and B. Absolutely false are more applicable to Maya or delusion, not to all sensory knowledge per se.

76. **(2):**

A. Drive-Reduction Theory – IV. Hull: Proposed by Clark Hull, this theory explains motivation in terms of reducing internal tension caused by unmet biological needs.

B. Personality and Nach – III. Carol Dweck: Carol Dweck is associated with motivation and personality theories, especially regarding Need for Achievement (Nach) and growth vs. fixed mindsets.

C. Arousal Theory – I. Yerkes and Dodson: The Yerkes-Dodson Law suggests that performance is optimal at moderate levels of arousal, forming an inverted U-shaped curve.

D. Self-Determination Theory – II. Richard Ryan and Edward Deci: This theory emphasizes intrinsic motivation, autonomy, competence, and relatedness as core psychological needs.

77. **(1):**

A. Krodha – III. Anger: Krodha directly translates to anger, one of the nine Sthayi Bhavas in Bharata's Natyashastra.

B. Bhaya – IV. Fear: Bhaya is the Sanskrit word for fear, a primal emotion.

C. Jugupsa – I. Disgust: Jugupsa refers to revulsion or disgust, often arising from moral or physical aversion.

D. Vismaya – II. Wonder/Astonishment: Vismaya means amazement or awe, usually a response to the unexpected or extraordinary.

78. **(3):**

A. Hypothalamus – II. Regulates body temperature, thirst, hunger: The hypothalamus controls essential biological drives and homeostasis.

B. Hippocampus – III. Forms long-term declarative memories: The hippocampus is vital for memory consolidation, especially episodic and declarative memory.

C. Amygdala – I. Fear responses and memory of fear: The amygdala is the brain's fear center, processing emotional responses, especially threat-related.

D. Cingulate cortex – IV. Selective attention, working memory: Involved in attention regulation, decision-making, and emotional regulation, part of executive functioning.

79. (4):

A. Gestalt Therapy – III. Empty chair technique: In Gestalt therapy developed by Fritz Perls, the empty chair technique is used for role-play and internal dialogue.

B. Reality Therapy – I. Five universal human needs: Developed by William Glasser, it focuses on meeting five basic needs: survival, love/belonging, power, freedom, and fun.

C. Existentialism – II. You are the architect of your life: Existential therapy, influenced by Viktor Frankl and Rollo May, emphasizes personal responsibility and meaning-making.

D. Solution-focused Therapy – IV. Steve de Shazer and Insoo Kim Berg: This approach emphasizes brief, goal-directed therapy focusing on strengths and solutions.

80. (4):

A. Non-maleficence – III. Counselling ethics: A core ethical principle meaning "do no harm", guiding responsible therapeutic practice.

B. HPA Axis – I. Response to stress: The Hypothalamic-Pituitary-Adrenal axis governs the body's response to stress, releasing cortisol and other hormones.

C. Art Therapy – IV. Intervention for emotional release: Used to promote self-expression, emotional healing, and insight through creative processes.

D. Existentialism – II. Encountering paradoxes of life: Focuses on freedom, isolation, death, and meaning, often involving confronting existential dilemmas.

81. (1):

A. Entropy – II. A sudden downward drop in the curve of health behaviour: In behavioural science, entropy symbolizes disorder or breakdown, often visualized as a sudden drop in compliance or engagement in health behaviours.

B. Decay Curve – IV. A gradual progressive decline in the health behaviour curve: The decay curve reflects a slow decline over time, often seen in health habits when reinforcement or motivation fades.

C. Force field Analysis – I. Comparative assessment of facilitating and restraining forces in the environment: Developed by Kurt Lewin, this technique helps identify driving vs. restraining forces influencing behaviour change.

D. Fantasy, Tentative, Realistic – III. Ginzberg's theory of career development: Eli Ginzberg proposed these three sequential stages in career development from childhood to adulthood.

82. (3):

A. Phenomenology – III. Lived experiences: Phenomenology is a qualitative method focusing on the first-person perspective and understanding conscious experience.

B. Case study – I. In-depth detailed examination of an entity in a real-world context: Case studies offer comprehensive, contextualized understanding of a single case (individual, group, or event).

C. Ethnography – IV. Description of peoples and culture: Ethnography involves immersive study of cultures, emphasizing participant observation.

D. Grounded theory – II. Application of inductive-reasoning: This approach generates theories based on data, collected and analyzed through iterative inductive processes.

83. (2):

A. Tay-Sachs disorder – II. Fatal neurological disorder: This is a genetic disorder leading to the destruction of neurons, causing death in early childhood, especially in Ashkenazi Jewish populations.

B. Down's syndrome – III. An extra chromosome in what normally be the 21st pair: It is caused by trisomy 21, leading to intellectual disability and characteristic physical features.

C. Klinefelter's syndrome – IV. The 23rd set of sex chromosomes is XXY: Males with an extra X chromosome, often have reduced testosterone, infertility, and gynecomastia.

D. Turner's syndrome – I. The 23rd pair is actually missing an X: Females have only one X chromosome (XO), leading to short stature, infertility, and other developmental issues.

84. (4): These are the Four Noble Truths of Buddhism:

A. Dukha – I. Suffering is part of life: The first noble truth, acknowledging that suffering (dukha) is universal.

B. Dukha-Samudaya – III. Suffering has a cause: The second truth, identifying desire (tanha) as the root of suffering.

C. Dukha-Nirodha – II. Suffering has an end: The third truth, explaining that cessation of desire leads to the end of suffering (nirvana).

D. Dukha-Nirodha-Marga – IV. There is a way to end suffering: The fourth truth, prescribing the Eightfold Path as the method to achieve liberation.

85. (1): These terms correspond to the Five Aggregates (Pancha Skandhas) in Buddhist psychology:

A. Material form – III. Rupa: Refers to the physical body and sensory matter.

B. Feeling or sensation – I. Vedana: Covers pleasure, pain, and neutrality arising from contact with stimuli.

C. Perception – IV. Sana: Involves recognition and mental labeling of objects and experiences.

D. Reason or intelligence – II. Vinnana: Represents consciousness, the awareness of mental and sensory inputs.

86. (3):

A. Eros Love – III. Loving an ideal person: Eros is characterized by intense physical attraction and passion. It reflects the desire for a perfect or ideal partner. The person experiencing Eros love tends to idealize their lover and seeks beauty and perfection in them, often experiencing emotional highs and lows.

B. Ludos Love – I. Treating love as a game: Ludos is playful and uncommitted love. The lover enjoys the act of seduction and treats love as entertainment or a conquest, often avoiding deep emotional involvement.

C. Storge Love – II. Treating love as friendship: Storge is a slow-developing love rooted in deep friendship. It is based on mutual trust, respect, and long-term commitment rather than passion or physical attraction.

D. Agape Love – IV. Selfless love: Agape is altruistic, unconditional love that is given selflessly without expecting anything in return. It is often considered spiritual or divine love, focused entirely on the welfare of the beloved.

87. (4):

A. Premack principle – III. The opportunity to engage in a frequently occurring activity can be used to reinforce a less frequently occurring activity: This principle, formulated by David Premack, suggests that a more preferred activity can be used as a reinforcer for a less preferred activity. For example, allowing a child to play video games after finishing homework.

B. Zeigarnik effect – IV. The tendency to remember incomplete tasks longer than complete ones: According to Bluma Zeigarnik, people remember unfinished or interrupted tasks better than those they have completed. This effect is often seen in situations of suspense or pending responsibilities.

C. Crespi effect – I. The rapid change in performance level as the size of reinforcement is varied: The Crespi effect demonstrates how sudden changes in reward magnitude can significantly impact the intensity or speed of a response.

D. Spread of effect – II. Reinforcement strengthens the neighbouring response in addition to the response that it produced: According to Thorndike, reinforcement can generalize to behaviours closely associated with the reinforced behaviour.

88. (1):

A. Principle of closure – I. Tendency to complete incomplete experiences to make them more meaningful: In Gestalt psychology, this principle explains our tendency to mentally fill in gaps to perceive a complete image or experience, even when it is incomplete.

B. Principle of polarity – II. Learned material is most performed in the same direction in which it was originally learned: This principle reflects directional dependency in learning, such as reading or sequencing tasks.

C. Principle of parsimony – III. Choosing the simpler one out of the two equally effective theories: Also known as Occam's Razor, this principle guides researchers to prefer the theory with fewer assumptions when two theories explain the same phenomena.

D. Principle of falsification – IV. In order for a theory to be scientific it must make risky prediction if not confirmed, would refute the theory: Proposed by Karl Popper, falsifiability is essential for a theory to be scientifically valid—it must be testable and refutable.

89. (3):

A. Standard scores always has a mean of 50 and SD of 10 – III. T-Score: A T-score is a type of standard score often used in psychological and educational assessments, where the mean is 50 and standard deviation is 10.

B. Standard scores change the unit of measurement – I. Percentile: Percentile scores rank individuals relative to others, changing raw scores into relative standing, thus altering the original measurement scale.

C. Standard with a mean of zero and SD of 1 – II. Z-Score: Z-scores standardize scores across distributions, making different datasets comparable by converting them into a scale where mean = 0 and SD = 1.

D. Units in testing that help to evaluate a person's performance in comparison with others who took the same test – IV. Standard Score: These scores allow norm-referenced interpretation, helping to understand how a person performed relative to a normative group.

90. (2):

A. Synthetic skill – II. To see problems with new points of view and get rid of conventional thinking: This refers to creativity and innovation—the ability to think in novel ways and generate original ideas.

B. Analytic skill – III. To recognize which ideas are worth pursuing and which are not: Analytical thinkers can evaluate options logically, detect patterns, and identify valid arguments or conclusions.

C. Practical contextual skill – IV. To know how to persuade others regarding one's ideas: These skills are about applying intelligence in real-world contexts, including social and emotional intelligence like persuasion and negotiation.

D. Thinking styles – I. Decisions about how to deploy the skills available to a person: Thinking styles relate to how individuals prefer to use their cognitive abilities, such as being more creative, analytical, or practical in different situations.

91. (2): In cross-sectional research, differences between age groups may not solely reflect aging but instead be influenced by cohort effects—differences due to participants being born and raised during different historical or cultural contexts.

For example, a 70-year-old and a 20-year-old might differ not only in age but also in education system, societal norms, or healthcare access they experienced, which can confound results. This is a well-known limitation in cross-sectional designs, where age is confounded with generational experiences.

92. (3): Sequential research combines both cross-sectional and longitudinal designs to overcome their individual limitations. It tracks multiple cohorts over time, allowing researchers to separate age effects, cohort effects, and time-of-measurement effects. This method provides more robust insights into developmental changes and how they occur over time.

93. (4): The degrees of freedom (df) for an independent samples t-test is calculated as:

$$df = n_1 + n_2 - 2$$
$$= 150 + 150 - 2 = 298$$

This *df* value is used to refer to the appropriate row in the *t*-distribution table to assess the significance of the test result.

94. (4): Robert Siegler proposed the microgenetic method to study processes of change in cognition. This method involves frequent, detailed observation of behaviour over a short period during which rapid change is occurring. It provides both quantitative and qualitative data to understand how and why cognitive changes unfold. It is particularly used in cognitive development research to study how children acquire new skills or strategies.

95. (2): A Type II error occurs when the null hypothesis is false, but the researcher fails to reject it, i.e., accepts it as true. In this case, the study would miss detecting a real effect. For example, concluding no difference between groups when one actually exists is a Type II error, often due to low statistical power or small effect size.

96. (2): These are the three primary components of motivation recognized in psychological theories:

- Activation refers to the decision to initiate a behaviour or action (e.g., enrolling in a course).
- Persistence is the continued effort toward a goal despite obstacles (e.g., studying regularly).
- Intensity is the amount of energy or concentration expended on pursuing the goal.

Together, these components explain how motivation begins, continues, and varies in strength across different activities and individuals.

97. (4): These are the key components associated with intrinsic motivation, particularly in the context of Self-Determination Theory (SDT) and motivational psychology:

- **Autonomy:** The feeling of having choice and control over one's actions.
- **Mastery:** The drive to improve and develop competence in tasks.
- **Purpose:** A sense of meaning and alignment with personal values or broader goals.

These factors fuel self-driven behaviours where the activity itself is rewarding, without the need for external rewards.

98. (3): The statement, "Just because an approach or method worked for someone else does not mean that it will work for you", reflects the idea that individuals vary in terms of what motivates them and how they respond to different strategies.

This corresponds to the notion that "there is no common approach for all", emphasizing the need for personalized motivation strategies.

It rejects a "one-size-fits-all" mindset, which is often ineffective in real-life learning, therapy, and behaviour change contexts.

99. (1): Introjected motivation is a type of internalized motivation that is driven by internal pressures like guilt, obligation, or the need to maintain self-worth. Though internal, it is not fully accepted by the self, and often feels controlling or pressured.

It is considered negative because the individual acts to avoid negative feelings, rather than genuine interest or value in the task.

Example: Studying just to avoid feeling like a failure, not because of love for learning.

100. (2): Self-Determination Theory (SDT) was developed by Edward Deci and Richard Ryan in the 1980s. It is a broad framework of human motivation and personality that emphasizes the importance of humans' evolved inner resources for personality development and behavioural self-regulation.

According to SDT, optimal motivation arises when three basic psychological needs are met:

- Autonomy
- Competence
- Relatedness

SDT differentiates between intrinsic and extrinsic motivation and explains how internalization of values occurs.

Previous Years' Paper

National Testing Agency (NTA)

UGC-NET Junior Research Fellowship & Assistant Professor Eligibility Exam

Psychology, December-2023

(Exam held on 14-12-2023)

PAPER-II

1. According to Piaget's theory a cognitive process in which a schema is modified as a response to feedback from environment.

A. Operation B. Assimilation
C. Conservation D. Accommodation

2. Which of the following is a disease not related to Cardiovascular system?

A. Atherosclerosis B. Angina Pectoris
C. Crohn's Disease D. Aneurysm

3. Zeigarnik effect explains:

A. The translation of learning into behaviour.
B. Behaviour directed toward some goal.
C. The tendency to remember uncompleted tasks longer than completed ones.
D. A number of interrelated individual memory traces.

4. Autoclitic behaviour refers to:

A. A grammatical framework for verbal behaviour
B. A person who works alone
C. Behaviour for the benefit of oneself
D. Behaviour exhibited when one meets a specified objective

5. Statutory rape refers to:

A. The husband forcing the unwilling wife for sexual intercourse
B. Forcibly having sexual intercourse with a resisting minor
C. Forcibly having sexual intercourse with a resisting person from the same gender
D. Violence in sexual intercourse by a husband or wife legally married

6. Name the psychologist who has proposed and suggested that the declarative memory can either be Episodic or Semantic.

A. Tulving B. Lockhart
C. Craik D. Warrington

7. The increased accessibility or retrievability of information stored in memory produced by the prior presentation of relevant cues is called:

A. Priming B. Primacy
C. Cue D. Acquisition

8. One psychologist while collecting data from gamblers, first identified one gambler and from him traced out three more; and through these three further more. He continued like this.

This is an example of ______.

A. Quota sampling
B. Stratified sampling
C. Snowball sampling
D. Accidental sampling

9. Parameter : population : : ______ : sample.

A. Dispersion B. Inference
C. Statistic D. Operation

10. Which of the following is considered to be error component in ANOVA?
A. Between mean square
B. Within mean square
C. Interaction mean square
D. Total mean square

11. Which of the following software is used extensively for analysis of qualitative data by researchers in psychology?
A. SPSS B. AMOS
C. N-VIVO D. LISEREL

12. To calculate the correlation between a genuinely dichotomus variable and a continuous variable we have to use _____.
A. Bi-serial '*r*' B. Point Biserial '*r*'
C. Tetrachoric '*r*' D. Phi coefficient

13. Attitude which is conscious and easy to report is called _______.
A. Implicit attitude
B. Explicit attitude
C. Unconscious attitude
D. Intrinsic attitude

14. A theory which advocates prejudice stems, at least in part, from economic competition between social groups is ______.
A. Contact hypothesis
B. Social identify theory
C. Realistic conflict theory
D. Repulsion hypothesis

15. If members in a group are performing additive tasks, then ______.
A. Social loafing will be less
B. Social loafing will be more
C. Social loafing will not exist
D. Level of social loafing cannot be decided

16. The psychological state characterized by reduced self awareness brought on by external conditions is known as ______.
A. Exhaustion
B. Entitativity
C. Deindividuation
D. Discrimination

17. Although she likes to wear gold ear-ring very much, Tanmaya removed the same when she joined a school where gold ornaments are not allowed.

This social influence is example of _____.
A. Compliance
B. Conformity
C. Symbol influence
D. Pluralistic ignorance

18. The two specific objectives of Watson's Behaviourism are 'NOT':
A. to predict the response by knowing the stimulus and to predict the stimulus by knowing the response
B. to predict the behaviour of the learner and to modify the behaviour
C. to control the behaviour of the learner and vary the experimental condition to bring about the change
D. to study the learner in a controlled laboratory environment and to examine the effect of reinforcement

19. The ability of brain to adopt to the environment and to replace function following damage is known as:
A. Neuroplasticity
B. Accommodation
C. Assimilation
D. Hemespherical coordination

20. Temporal Lobe epilepsy results in:
A. Docile behaviour
B. Aggressive behaviour
C. Antisocial behaviour
D. Prosocial behaviour

21. Socrates questioning is a:
A. Philosophical questioning
B. Technique for self understanding
C. Psychoanalytical technique
D. Technique in which counsellor asks the questions to the client

22. Studies on weight loss programs in a follow up study revealed that:

A. Weight gain was more for those practicing drug therapy
B. Weight gain was more for those practicing behaviour modification therapy
C. Weight loss was less for those practicing drug therapy
D. Those practicing behaviour modification therapy were able to maintain their body weight

23. Homeostatic temperature in the body is regulated by:
A. changes in the external environment
B. drive reduction
C. preoptic region of the hypothalamus
D. electrical activities in the brain

24. Which of the fcllowing is not true of structuralism?
A. it provided strong scientific impetus
B. it provided a thorough test of classical introspective method
C. it emphasised on basic conscious elements
D. it provided a strong and clear orthodoxy against which other schools resisted

25. Which of the following is not a technological system designed to aid, enhance or inspire learning:
A. Python B. Logo
C. Squeak D. Boxer

26. According to Watson, Conscious mentalism refer to :
A. Wakeful state of mind
B. Knowledge about mental activities
C. Reasoning ability
D. Attention to thinking activities

27. A decrease in sensitivity to leptin is found to be a factor contributing to:
A. weight gain
B. weight loss
C. maintaining homeostasis
D. loss of appetite

28. On the basis of which criterion the tests are classified into 'Verbal Tests' and 'Non-verbal Test'.
A. Criterion of purpose
B. Criterion of contents of items
C. Criterion of scoring
D. Criterion of time limits

29. The Bender Visual-Motor Gestalt Test (Bender 1938) has ______.
A. Six Designs B. Seven Designs
C. Eight Designs D. Nine Designs

30. Which one of the following is not intrinsic factor affecting reliability?
A. Group variability
B. Length of the test
C. Range of total scores
D. Homogeneity of items

31. Which scale of measurement has absolute zero?
A. Nominal B. Ordinal
C. Interval D. Ratio

32. Wechsler Adult Intelligence Scale (WAIS) published in 1955 has:
A. 5 Verbal and 5 Performance
B. 5 Verbal and 6 Performance
C. 6 Verbal and 5 Performance
D. 6 Verbal and 6 Performance

33. Sigmund Freud was born on ______.
A. 23-09-1939 B. 06-05-1939
C. 23-09-1856 D. 06-05-1856

34. Which one of the following is NOT among the twenty needs listed by Murray, 1938?
A. Succorance B. Sentience
C. Sex D. Safety

35. "Foreign Hull' is the concept coined by:
A. Kurt Lewin B. Alfred Adler
C. Erik Erikson D. Abraham Maslow

36. Which of the following is 'NOT' source of work related stress?
A. Responsibility for others
B. Lack of support from coworkers

C. Conflict with family members
D. Unpleasant work environment

37. The concept of 'collective unconscious' is one of the most powerful, original and controversial features of:
A. Adler's Personality Theory
B. Jung's Personality Theory
C. Freud's Personality Theory
D. Fromm's Personality Theory

38. Brainstorming is technique in Gerard Egan's problem management approach to helping. Which of the statements given below is NOT a characteristics feature of brainstorming.
A. Develop 'wild' possibilities
B. Suspend judgement
C. Use one idea as a takeoff point for another
D. Set of time frame

39. The number of cases of a disease, injury or disability at a given point of time which can be expressed as the number of new cases or the number of existing cases is called:
A. Mortality B. Prevalence
C. Morbidity D. Incidence

40. 'Miracle Question' is a technique used in:
A. Narrative therapy
B. Solution focused brief therapy
C. Feminist therapy
D. Reality therapy

41. Which of the following comes under divergent thinking?
(*a*) Fluency
(*b*) Flexibility
(*c*) Elaboration
(*d*) Preparation
(*e*) Verification

Choose the correct answer from the options given below:
A. (*b*), (*c*), (*d*) only
B. (*a*), (*c*), (*e*) only
C. (*a*), (*b*), (*c*) only
D. (*b*), (*c*), (*e*) only

42. Which are the major components of Emotional Intelligence by Goleman (1995):
(*a*) Recognizing the purpose in life
(*b*) Knowing our own emotions
(*c*) Recognizing the emotions of others
(*d*) Handling relationship
(*e*) Understanding meaning of life

Choose the correct answer from the options given below:
A. (*a*), (*b*), (*d*) only
B. (*b*), (*c*), (*d*) only
C. (*a*), (*b*), (*c*), (*e*) only
D. (*a*), (*c*), (*d*), (*e*) only

43. The components of 'Type A' Pattern of personality encompasses:
(*a*) Happy-go-Lucky
(*b*) Prosocial
(*c*) Emotion-Focused
(*d*) Competitive Striving for Achievement
(*e*) Sense of Time urgency

Choose the correct answer from the options given below:
A. (*a*), (*b*) only
B. (*c*), (*d*) only
C. (*d*), (*e*) only
D. (*a*), (*c*), (*e*) only

44. Scientifically sound test must possess which of the following:
(*a*) Objectively
(*b*) Norms
(*c*) Time Limit
(*d*) Reliability
(*e*) Validity

Choose the correct answer from the options given below:
A. (*a*), (*b*), (*c*), (*d*) only
B. (*a*), (*b*), (*d*), (*e*) only
C. (*a*), (*b*), (*c*), (*e*) only
D. (*e*), (*d*), (*c*), (*b*) only

45. Study of Values prepared by all port, Vernon and Lindzey has some basic areas, which of the following areas are included in it?

(*a*) Moral
(*b*) Aesthetic
(*c*) Cognitive
(*d*) Religions
(*e*) Economic

Choose the correct answer from the options given below:
A. (*a*), (*b*), (*c*) only
B. (*b*), (*c*), (*d*) only
C. (*b*), (*d*), (*e*) only
D. (*a*), (*d*), (*e*) only

46. Factors covered by the General Aptitude Test Battery (GATB) are:
(*a*) Verbal Aptitude
(*b*) Form Perception
(*c*) Mechanical Reasoning
(*d*) Motor Coordination
(*e*) Clerical Perception

Choose the correct answer from the options given below:
A. (*a*), (*b*), (*c*), (*d*) only
B. (*b*), (*c*), (*d*), (*e*) only
C. (*c*), (*d*), (*e*), (*a*) only
D. (*a*), (*b*), (*d*), (*e*) only

47. What is true about retrospective studies?
(*a*) Data are often collected with the help of narrative methods
(*b*) It is also known as naturalistic inquiry
(*c*) Collected data can be analysed through
(*d*) It is same as quasi-experiment
(*e*) Biographical research is a good example of retrospective study

Choose the correct answer from the options given below:
A. (*a*), (*b*), (*d*) only
B. (*b*), (*c*), (*d*) only
C. (*a*), (*c*), (*e*) only
D. (*b*), (*c*), (*e*) only

48. Which is correct explanation about Rene Descartes:
(*a*) The mind controls the body both in animals and human beings
(*b*) He postulated that the mind and the body were governed by different laws
(*c*) The mind was free and possessed only by humans
(*d*) The duality of mind and body

Choose the correct answer from the options given below:
A. (*a*), (*c*), (*d*) only
B. (*b*), (*c*), (*d*) only
C. (*a*), (*b*), (*c*) only
D. (*a*), (*b*), (*d*) only

49. Which best explains about 'Paradigm'?
(*a*) It is the study of intact, meaningful mental events
(*b*) A viewpoint regarding physical reality as we perceive
(*c*) A point of view shared by a substantial number of scientists that provides a general framework for empirical research
(*d*) It is usually more than just one theory and corresponds more closely to what is called a school of thought

Choose the correct answer from the options given below:
A. (*b*), (*d*) only
B. (*c*), (*d*) only
C. (*a*), (*d*) only
D. (*a*), (*c*) only

50. Egan's developmental model of counselling mentions the following distinct steps in its three stages:
(*a*) Possibilities, Commitment
(*b*) Best fit, Leverage
(*c*) Blindspot, Focusing
(*d*) Leverage, Confronting
(*e*) Agenda, Commitment

Choose the correct answer from the options given below:
A. (*a*), (*b*), (*d*) only
B. (*a*), (*b*), (*e*) only
C. (*a*), (*b*), (*c*) only
D. (*a*), (*b*), (*c*), (*e*) only

51. Which of the following are true of method of Appreciative Inquiry?
(*a*) Inquiry begins with appreciation
(*b*) It is not collaborative
(*c*) It is not proactive
(*d*) Inquiry is applicablc

Choose the correct answer from the options given below:
A. (*a*), (*d*) only B. (*b*), (*c*) only
C. (*c*), (*d*) only D. (*a*), (*b*) only

52. According to psychophysical school which of the following statements are true?
(*a*) Weber's ratio increases as the stimulus intensity increases
(*b*) DL increases proportionately to the changes in the stimulus intensity
(*c*) Limens determines the perception of sensory stimulus
(*d*) Weber's ratio and techner's law are contradictory in nature

Choose the correct answer from the options given below:
A. (*a*), (*b*) only B. (*b*), (*c*) only
C. (*a*), (*d*) only D. (*a*), (*c*) only

53. What is true about multiple regression?
(*a*) There can be more than two criterion
(*b*) There can be more than two predictors
(*c*) It indicates linear relation between one predicator and one criterion
(*d*) The equation for regression line contains partial regression coefficients

Choose the correct answer from the options given below:
A. (*a*), (*b*) only
B. (*b*), (*c*) only
C. (*b*), (*d*) only
D. (*a*), (*d*) only

54. Which of the following can foster prejudice?
(*a*) Threats to self-esteem
(*b*) Competition for resources
(*c*) Social categorization
(*d*) Social recategorization

Choose the correct answer from the options given below :
A. (*a*), (*c*), (*d*) only
B. (*a*), (*b*), (*c*) only
C. (*a*), (*b*), (*d*) only
D. (*b*), (*c*), (*d*) only

55. Resistance to persuasion may be increased:
(*a*) Reactance
(*b*) Emotional appeal
(*c*) Fore warning
(*d*) Selective avoidance

Choose the correct answer from the options given below:
A. (*a*), (*b*) only B. (*b*), (*c*) only
C. (*a*), (*b*), (*d*) only D. (*a*), (*c*), (*d*) only

56. Which of the following are the influencing skills of counselling:
(*a*) Self disclosure
(*b*) Information giving
(*c*) Confrontation
(*d*) Smart-goals

Choose the correct answer from the options given below:
A. (*d*) only
B. (*a*), (*b*), (*d*) only
C. (*b*), (*c*), (*d*) only
D. (*a*). (*b*), (*c*) only

57. Which of the following statements are true for a panic disorder:
(*a*) Recurrent bouts of intense and extreme fear
(*b*) Sensation of shortness of breath or smothering
(*c*) Persistent worry or concern about having additional attacks
(*d*) An episode of panic attack followed by the use of a drug or medication

Choose the correct answer from the options given below:
A. (*a*), (*b*), (*c*) only
B. (*b*), (*c*), (*d*) only
C. (*b*), (*d*) only
D. (*a*), (*c*), (*d*) only

58. Which of the following are the identity statuses of James Marcia's theory:

(*a*) Identity achievement
(*b*) Identity fore closure
(*c*) Identity diffusion
(*d*) Identity crisis
(*e*) Identity moratorium

Choose the correct answer from the options given below:

A. (*a*), (*b*), (*c*), (*e*) only
B. (*a*), (*b*), (*c*), (*d*) only
C. (*b*), (*c*), (*d*), (*e*) only
D. (*c*), (*d*) only

59. Which of the following are the stages in the transtheoretical model of behaviour change:

(*a*) Maintenance
(*b*) Intention
(*c*) Contemplation
(*d*) Action

Choose the correct answer from the options given below:

A. (*a*), (*b*), (*c*) only
B. (*a*), (*c*), (*d*) only
C. (*b*), (*c*), (*d*) only
D. (*b*), (*c*) only

60. Which of the following are not the components of yama as per Astanga Yoga:

(*a*) Ahimsa
(*b*) Shoucha
(*c*) Asteya
(*d*) Tapas

Choose the correct answer from the options given below:

A. (*a*), (*c*) only
B. (*a*), (*b*) only
C. (*b*), (*d*) only
D. (*b*), (*c*) only

61. How type II error can be reduced while testing hypothesis?

(*a*) Decreasing the chosen level of significance
(*b*) Increasing the chosen level of significance
(*c*) Decreasing the sample size
(*d*) Increasing the sample size

Choose the correct answer from the options given below:

A. (*a*), (*d*) only
B. (*b*), (*d*) only
C. (*a*), (*c*) only
D. (*b*), (*c*) only

62. Which of the following statements is correct about 'assimilation':

(*a*) A kind of matching between the cognitive structures and the physical environment
(*b*) Learning that one event leads to another
(*c*) It can be roughly equated with recognition or knowing
(*d*) Studying a phenomenon as 'it occurs naturally in the environment'

Choose the correct answer from the options given below:

A. (*a*), (*b*), (*c*) only
B. (*a*), (*d*) only
C. (*a*), (*c*) only
D. (*a*), (*c*), (*d*) only

63. Which of the following statements is correct about Gestalt psychology?

(*a*) Gestalt approach is dementistic
(*b*) Gestalt psychology has sometimes been called phenomenology
(*c*) Gestalt psychology can be thought of as an attempts to apply field theory from physics
(*d*) Gestalt psychologists believed that whatever happens to a person influences everything else about the person

Choose the correct answer from the options given below:

A. (*a*), (*b*), (*d*) only
B. (*a*), (*c*), (*d*) only
C. (*a*), (*b*), (*c*) only
D. (*b*), (*c*), (*d*) only

64. The theoretical positions about personality whose development have been heavily dependent on factor analysis are:

(*a*) R.B. Cattell (*b*) Spearman
(*c*) H.J. Eysenck (*d*) J.P. Guilford
(*e*) Howard Gardner

Choose the correct answer from the options given below:

A. (*a*), (*c*), (*e*) only
B. (*b*), (*d*), (*e*) only
C. (*a*), (*c*), (*d*) only
D. (*a*), (*c*), (*d*), (*e*) only

65. Freud believed that at times Ego is unable to control impulses of ID so uses various defense mechanism such as:

(*a*) Fixation (*b*) Repression
(*c*) Rationalization (*d*) Displacement
(*e*) Projection

Choose the correct answer from the options given below:

A. (*a*), (*b*), (*c*), (*d*) only
B. (*b*), (*c*), (*d*), (*e*) only
C. (*c*), (*d*), (*e*), (*a*) only
D. (*d*), (*e*), (*a*), (*b*) only

66. Match List-I with List-II.

List-I	List-II
(*a*) Implicit memory	I. The kind of memory that underlies perceptual and cognitive skills
(*b*) Working memory	II. A vivid and relatively permanent record of the circumstances in which one learned of an emotionally charged, significant event
(*c*) Long-term memory	III. Stored for only a few records
(*d*) Flashbulb memory	IV. Semi-permanent memory

Choose the correct answer from the options given below:

	(*a*)	(*b*)	(*c*)	(*d*)
A.	I	III	IV	II
B.	I	II	IV	III
C.	II	III	IV	I
D.	III	IV	II	I

67. Match List-I with List-II.

List-I	List-II
(*a*) Associationism	I. Wundt
(*b*) Structuralism	II. Lashley
(*c*) Functionalism	III. Ebbinghaus
(*d*) Behaviourism	IV. Stanley Hall

Choose the correct answer from the options given below:

	(*a*)	(*b*)	(*c*)	(*d*)
A.	II	III	IV	I
B.	IV	II	I	III
C.	III	I	IV	II
D.	II	IV	III	I

68. Match List-I with List-II.

List-I	List-II
(*a*) Perception	I. Vinnana
(*b*) Consciousness	II. Vedana
(*c*) Feelings	III. Sanna
(*d*) Body	IV. Rupa

Choose the correct answer from the options given below:

	(*a*)	(*b*)	(*c*)	(*d*)
A.	II	I	IV	III
B.	III	I	II	IV
C.	IV	II	III	I
D.	III	IV	II	I

69. Match List-I with List-II.

List-I	List-II
(*a*) Secondary Trait	I. Traits that dominate an individual's entire personality
(*b*) Cardinal Trait	II. Key dimensions of personality that underlie many other traits
(*c*) Central Traits	III. A bunch of traits that best describes an individual's personality
(*d*) Source Traits	IV. Traits that exert relatively specific and weak effects on behaviour

Choose the correct answer from the options given below:

	(a)	(b)	(c)	(d)
A.	I	II	III	IV
B.	II	III	IV	I
C.	III	IV	I	II
D.	IV	I	III	II

70. Match List-I with List-II.

With reference to psychosocial theory of Development (Erikson):

List-I	List-II
(a) Autonomy	I. Guilt
(b) Industry	II. Shame & Doubt
(c) Initiative	III. Stagnation
(d) Generativity	IV. Inferiority

Choose the correct answer from the options given below:

	(a)	(b)	(c)	(d)
A.	II	IV	I	III
B.	II	III	IV	I
C.	I	II	III	IV
D.	III	II	IV	I

71. Match List-I with List-II.

List-I	List-II
(a) Coefficient of Dispersion	I. Standard deviation as a percentage of mean
(b) Standard Deviation	II. Mean of squared deviations of individual scores from mean
(c) Coefficient of variation	III. Variance in terms of mean
(d) Variance	IV. Positive square root of variance

Choose the correct answer from the options given below:

	(a)	(b)	(c)	(d)
A.	IV	III	I	II
B.	III	IV	II	I
C.	III	IV	I	II
D.	IV	II	III	I

72. Match List-I with List-II.

List-I	List-II
(a) Theory of planned behaviour	I. Tajfel and Turner
(b) Theory of causal attribution	II. Pettigrew
(c) Social identity theory	III. Ajzen & Fishbein
(d) Contact hypothesis	IV. Kelley

Choose the correct answer from the options given below:

	(a)	(b)	(c)	(d)
A.	II	I	IV	III
B.	I	II	III	IV
C.	III	IV	I	II
D.	III	IV	II	I

73. Match List-I with List-II.

Match the substages of Kolhberg's Moral Development Theory:

List-I	List-II
(a) Obedience Orientation	I. Moral reasoning based on winning the approval of others
(b) Interpersonal norms	II. Moral reasoning based on moral principles that apply to all
(c) Social contract	III. Moral reasoning based on the belief that adults know what is right or wrong
(d) Universal ethical principles	IV. Moral reasoning is based on the belief that laws are for the good of all members of society

Choose the correct answer from the options given below:

	(a)	(b)	(c)	(d)
A.	III	IV	I	II
B.	III	I	IV	II
C.	I	IV	II	III
D.	I	II	IV	III

74. Match List-I with List-II.

List-I	List-II
(*a*) Passive euthanasia	I. The doctor ends a suffering of a patient's life at his/her request by administering a lethal does of a drug
(*b*) Voluntary active euthanasia	II. The doctor helps the patient take his/her life by enabling the patient swallow or inject a lethal dose of drug
(*c*) Assisted suicide	III. The doctor ends a suffering of a patient by administering a lethal does of drug without the patients consent or permission
(*d*) Involuntary active euthanasia	IV. The doctor withholds or withdraws treatment by permitting the patient to die naturally, on the request of the patient

Choose the correct answer from the options given below:

	(*a*)	(*b*)	(*c*)	(*d*)
A.	IV	I	II	III
B.	IV	II	III	I
C.	I	II	III	IV
D.	I	II	IV	III

75. Match List-I with List-II.

List-I	List-II
(*a*) Gestalt psychology	I. Believing that one has various horrible disease conditions
(*b*) Hypochon-driacal delusions	II. Emphasis on personal growth and self-direc-tion
(*c*) Humanistic existential therapy	III. Whole in more than the sum of its parts
(*d*) Existential neurosis	IV. Feeling of alienation meaninglessness and apathy

Choose the correct answer from the options given below:

	(*a*)	(*b*)	(*c*)	(*d*)
A.	III	IV	I	II
B.	III	I	II	IV
C.	II	I	IV	III
D.	II	I	III	IV

76. Csikszentmihalyi (1996) observed that the creative process normally takes five steps. Arrange those steps in order:

(*a*) Preparation
(*b*) Evaluation
(*c*) Incubation
(*d*) Elaboration
(*e*) Insight

Choose the correct answer from the options given below:

A. (*a*), (*b*), (*d*), (*e*), (*c*)
B. (*a*), (*c*), (*b*), (*d*), (*e*)
C. (*a*), (*c*), (*e*), (*b*), (*d*)
D. (*a*), (*b*), (*e*), (*c*), (*d*)

77. Arrange the following sentences in sequential order according to classical conditioning:

(*a*) A stimulus such as food is presented to an organism which is called unconditioned stimulus (US)
(*b*) The neutral stimulus light alone is provided which makes the organism to salivate
(*c*) A neutral stimulus such as light is presented to the organism just prior to the presentation of US
(*d*) Another neutral stimulus (tone) is provided prior to light
(*e*) The neutral stimulus (tone) above is provided which makes the organism to salivate

Choose the correct answer from the options given below :

A. (*a*), (*c*), (*d*), (*b*), (*e*)
B. (*a*), (*b*), (*d*), (*c*), (*e*)
C. (*a*), (*c*), (*b*), (*d*), (*e*)
D. (*a*), (*c*), (*b*), (*e*), (*d*)

78. Put the following milestones of psychology in ascending chronological order:

(*a*) Intelligence test developed by Binet and Simon in France
(*b*) The first psychology Laboratory in Leipzig by Wundt
(*c*) First psychology course in United States by James
(*d*) American Psychological Association (APA) was founded by Stanley Hall
(*e*) Pavlov wins the Nobel prize for his work on digestive system

Choose the correct answer from the options given below:

A. (*a*), (*b*), (*d*), (*c*), (*e*)
B. (*b*), (*c*), (*d*), (*e*), (*a*)
C. (*c*), (*b*), (*d*), (*e*), (*a*)
D. (*d*), (*b*), (*c*), (*a*), (*e*)

79. According to Astanga yoga arrange the stages in the correct sequence:

(*a*) Dhyana
(*b*) Asana
(*c*) Samadhi
(*d*) Pranayama

Choose the correct answer from the options given below:

A. (*b*), (*d*), (*a*), (*c*)
B. (*a*), (*c*), (*d*), (*b*)
C. (*d*), (*b*), (*c*), (*a*)
D. (*c*), (*a*), (*b*), (*d*)

80. Arrange the following in correct sequence of HPA axis response to stress, and consequences:

(*a*) Adrenal glands get stimulated
(*b*) Release of corticotropin releasing factor
(*c*) Release of cortisol, epinephrine and nor epinephrine
(*d*) Release of glucose from liver and muscle
(*e*) Release of adrenocorticotropic hormone

Choose the correct answer from the options given below:

A. (*a*), (*b*), (*c*), (*e*), (*d*)
B. (*a*), (*c*), (*b*), (*e*), (*d*)
C. (*b*), (*e*), (*a*), (*c*), (*d*)
D. (*e*), (*b*), (*a*), (*c*), (*d*)

81. In one Exploratory sequential design what would be the correct sequence?

(*a*) Quantitative Data Collection
(*b*) Qualitative Data Collection
(*c*) Quantitative Data analysis
(*d*) Qualitative Data Analysis
(*e*) Interpretation

Choose the correct answer from the options given below:

A. (*a*), (*b*), (*c*), (*d*), (*e*)
B. (*b*), (*a*), (*d*), (*c*), (*e*)
C. (*a*), (*c*), (*b*), (*d*), (*e*)
D. (*b*), (*d*), (*a*), (*c*), (*e*)

82. One psychologist developed a questionnaire on employee 'Green behaviour', what would be the correct sequence in the context of this tool development:

(*a*) Identifying the discrimination index of the items
(*b*) Calculation of croan-bach alpha
(*c*) Developing a standard score norm
(*d*) Confirmatory factor analysis
(*e*) Exploratory factor analysis

Choose the correct answer from the options given below:

A. (*c*), (*a*), (*b*), (*d*), (*e*)
B. (*c*), (*b*), (*a*), (*d*), (*e*)
C. (*a*), (*e*), (*b*), (*c*), (*d*)
D. (*a*), (*b*), (*e*), (*d*), (*c*)

83. Arrange the stages of group development as suggested by Tuckman:

(*a*) Storming
(*b*) Performing
(*c*) Forming
(*d*) Adjourning
(*e*) Norming

Choose the correct answer from the options given below:

A. (*c*), (*a*), (*b*), (*e*), (*d*)
B. (*c*), (*a*), (*e*), (*b*), (*d*)
C. (*a*), (*c*), (*e*), (*b*), (*d*)
D. (*a*), (*c*), (*b*), (*e*), (*d*)

84. Development of psychoanalysis is marked by four phases namely antecedent analysis who were associated with each phase sequentially:

(*a*) Breur
(*b*) G.T. Fechner
(*c*) Sullivan
(*d*) Adler

Choose the correct answer from the options given below:

A. (*b*), (*a*), (*d*), (*c*)
B. (*a*), (*b*), (*c*), (*d*)
C. (*c*), (*b*), (*a*), (*d*)
D. (*d*), (*c*), (*b*), (*a*)

85. The program evaluation model of a community health program has 4 steps. Arranged the following in sequences:

(*a*) Outcome evaluation
(*b*) Identifying goals and desired outcomes
(*c*) Process evaluation
(*d*) Impact evaluation

Choose the correct answer from the options given below:

A. (*b*), (*c*), (*a*), (*d*)
B. (*b*), (*c*), (*d*), (*a*)
C. (*c*), (*b*), (*d*), (*a*)
D. (*c*), (*d*), (*b*), (*a*)

86. Given below are two statements : one is labelled as Assertion (A) and the other is labelled as Reason (R).

Assertion (A): One psychometrician used Cronbach's alpha to verify reliability of a general knowledge test with answers, in True/False format.

Reason (B): Cronbach's alpha estimates the internal consistency of a Test.

In the light of the above statements, choose the most appropriate answer from the options given below:

A. Both (A) and (R) are correct and (R) is the correct explanation of (A)
B. Both (A) and (R) are correct, but (R) is not the correct explanation of (A)
C. (A) is correct, but (R) is not correct
D. (A) is not correct, but (R) is correct

87. Given below are two statements : one is labelled as Assertion (A) and the other is labelled as Reason (R).

Assertion (A): Allostasis is a process of adaptation to acute stress by releasing stress hormones in the event of challenge with a goal to restore the homeostasis.

Reason (R): HPA axis gets activated in the event of stress.

In the light of the above statements, choose the most appropriate answer from the options given below:

A. Both (A) and (R) are correct and (R) is the correct explanation of (A)
B. Both (A) and (R) are correct, but (R) is not the correct explanation of (A)
C. (A) is correct, but (R) is not correct
D. (A) is not correct, but (R) is correct

88. Given below are two statements : one is labelled as Assertion (A) and the other is labelled as Reason (R).

Assertion (A): The researcher manipulating one or more variables is called an experiment.

Reason (R): A research design is one in which a variable is manipulated with a goal of identifying the causes of events is called experimental design.

In the light of the above statements, choose the most appropriate answer from the options given below:

A. Both (A) and (R) are correct and (R) is the correct explanation of (A)
B. Both (A) and (R) are correct, but (R) is not the correct explanation of (A)
C. (A) is correct, but (R) is not correct
D. (A) is not correct, but (R) is correct

89. Given below are two statements: one is labelled as Assertion (A) and the other is labelled as Reason (R).

Assertion (A) : Tabooed words are difficult to recognise.

Reason (R): Perception of the tabooed words is dependent or knowledge about socio-cultural factors.

In the light of the above statements, choose the most appropriate answer from the options given below:

A. Both (A) and (R) are correct and (R) is the correct explanation of (A)
B. Both (A) and (R) are correct, but (R) is not the correct explanation of (A)
C. (A) is correct, but (R) is not correct
D. (A) is not correct, but (R) is correct

90. Given below are two statements : one is labelled as Assertion (A) and the other is labelled as Reason (R).

Assertion (A): Sexual drive is one of the physiological need.

Reason (R): Human beings cannot live without gratifying sexual drive.

In the light of the above statements, choose the most appropriate answer from the options given below:

A. Both (A) and (R) are correct and (R) is the correct explanation of (A)
B. Both (A) and (R) are correct, but (R) is not the correct explanation of (A)
C. (A) is correct, but (R) is not correct
D. (A) is not correct, but (R) is correct

Directions (Qs. No. 91-95): *Read the following passage carefully and answer the questions that follow:*

Jeevan, a twelve year old boy was brought to the psychologist because he hated school. When the teacher was contacted she informed that Jeevan was unpopular in the class because of his show-off behaviour that even disrupted the class. Apparently, the parents at home used to find such behavioural entertaining and laughed and enjoyed it. The psychologist drew out a programme to bring a change in Jeevan's behaviour. She first helped the parents to understand what is show off behaviour and what is not. His parents were instructed by the psychologist to avoid paying attention to Jeevans show off behaviour. The teacher was instructed to praise other children whenever anyone helped a classments in any way. The psychologist also added that each time Jeevan manifested show-off behaviour, the loud noise of bore-well digging be played to him by the teacher. In fact, the psychologist used therapeutic interventions.

91. Teaching the parents to understand which is show off behaviours and which is not, is helping them with:

A. Discrimination B. Deactivation
C. Generalization D. Discretion

92. By instructing the parents not to pay attention to Jeevan's show off behaviour at home the psychologist aimed at:

A. Punishment
B. Stimulus discrimination
C. Extinction
D. Stimulus generalization

93. By instructing the teacher to praise those children whenever anyone helped their classmates the psychologist applied the factor of:

A. Positive reinforcement for Jeevan
B. Modelling for Jeevan
C. Reinforcement substitution for Jeevan
D. Classical conditioning for Jeevan

94. By instructing the teacher to play the loud noise of bore-well digging the psychologist introduced:

A. Aversion Therapy
B. Inplosive Therapy
C. Response Shaping
D. Rogerian Therapy

95. The approach of the psychologist in handling the problem of Jeevan can be summarised as:
A. Gestalt Therapy
B. Reality Therapy
C. Behaviour Therapy
D. Client-centered Therapy

Directions (Qs. No. 96-100): *Read the following passage carefully and answer the questions that follow:*

A researcher studied the variables that determined the Post Traumatic Growth (PTG) in the husbands of breastcancer survivors. The existing literature identified a number of factors such as emotionai support, quality of marital relationship, exposure to individual with PTG, as important determinants of PTG in women. No information was available on PTG of the husbands of the patients. The researcher investigated the same factors influencing their husbands.

96. What is the design used by the researcher?
A. Correctional design
B. Quasi experimental design
C. ABBA design
D. Single group pre and post test design

97. What type of statistical analysis should be used by the researcher address his objective?
A. One way ANOVA
B. 't' test
C. Regression Analysis
D. Chi-Square

98. What is the criterion variable in this study?
A. Gender
B. Social context factor
C. Post-traumatic growth
D. Quality of marital relationship

99. There are different domains of PGT. Which one of the following does not come under them?
A. Personal strength
B. Spiritual change
C. Relationship with others
D. Creativity

100. Which of the following will be the correct hypothesis for the study?
A. The emotional support, quality of marital relationship and exposure to individual modelling of PTG will all contribute husband's experience of PTG
B. PTG of the husbands will be different from that of wives
C. The social context factors of husbands and the social context factors of wives will correlate
D. The emotional support, quality of marital relationship and exposure to individuals modelling PTG will correlate

ANSWERS

1. (D): Jean Piaget's theory of cognitive development highlights the role of accommodation as a mechanism through which children adjust their schemas in response to new experiences. Accommodation occurs when existing schemas (cognitive structures) are altered or new schemas are created in response to new information that does not fit into previously held schemas. This process is crucial for cognitive growth, as it enables the individual to handle new challenges and integrate more complex information into their understanding of the world. For example, a child who knows that birds fly might need to accommodate this schema when they learn that not all birds, such as penguins and ostriches, can fly.

2. (C): Crohn's Disease is an inflammatory bowel disease (IBD), primarily affecting the gastrointestinal tract, and is unrelated to the cardiovascular system. In contrast, the other options listed—Atherosclerosis, Angina Pectoris, and Aneurysm—are all directly associated with cardiovascular health. Atherosclerosis involves the buildup of fats, cholesterol, and other substances in and on the artery walls which can lead to severe health issues including heart attacks and strokes. Angina Pectoris is chest pain caused by reduced blood flow to the heart muscles. Aneurysms are an abnormal bulge or ballooning in the wall of a blood vessel, often occurring in the aorta or arteries at the base of the brain.

3. **(C):** The Zeigarnik effect, named after the psychologist Bluma Zeigarnik, describes the psychological phenomenon where people tend to remember uncompleted or interrupted tasks better than tasks that have been completed. This effect is believed to be due to the greater cognitive tension associated with unfinished tasks, which increases their memorability. This principle has been utilized in various fields such as productivity strategies and educational techniques to enhance retention and engagement by structuring activities around the concept of leaving tasks in an incomplete state to boost recall.

4. **(A):** Autoclitic behaviour in behaviour analysis, particularly within the framework of verbal behaviour as outlined by B.F. Skinner, refers to a secondary behaviour that modifies the effects of primary verbal behaviours. It essentially acts as a grammatical framework within which the verbal behaviour is organized to enhance communication and understanding. Autoclitics can provide additional context, clarify meaning, indicate the speaker's attitude, or modify the listener's response to the primary verbal behaviour. For example, the statement "I think it's going to rain" includes "I think," which serves as an autoclitic modifying the assertion about the rain.

5. **(B):** Statutory rape refers to non-consensual sexual intercourse with a minor, where consent is not legally valid due to the minor's age. The law stipulates that minors below a certain age (which varies by jurisdiction) are incapable of giving informed consent. This legal framework is designed to protect young individuals from exploitation and abuse, regardless of the presence or absence of physical resistance by the minor. It emphasizes the power imbalance and the inherent inability of minors to consent, thereby criminalizing such acts irrespective of alleged consent or the nature of the relationship.

6. **(A):** Endel Tulving, a prominent psychologist, significantly contributed to the understanding of human memory with his proposal of the division of declarative memory into two distinct types: episodic and semantic. Episodic memory refers to the ability to recall personal experiences and specific events located in time and place, such as remembering a wedding day. Semantic memory, on the other hand, involves knowledge about the world that is devoid of personal context, such as knowing the capital of a country. Tulving's theory has been influential in shaping research in cognitive psychology and neuroscience, highlighting how different types of memories are encoded and retrieved.

7. **(A):** Priming is a phenomenon in cognitive psychology where exposure to one stimulus influences a response to a subsequent stimulus, without conscious guidance or intention. For instance, if a person reads a list of words including the word "flower,"

they are more likely to spell the stem "fl-" as "flower" than "floor" on a later test. Priming enhances the accessibility of certain information or concepts stored in the memory by previously presented related cues, thus facilitating faster or more accurate responses to related tasks. This process is widely studied for its implications in understanding memory, perception, and interactions within neural networks.

8. **(C):** Snowball sampling is a non-probability sampling technique used in research, particularly useful when members of a population are hard to locate, such as gamblers. It starts with a small group of initial subjects who are part of the target population. These subjects then recruit future subjects from among their acquaintances, thus the sample group grows like a rolling snowball. This method was employed by the psychologist who identified one gambler and then used him to trace further participants, effectively expanding the sample through personal networks.

9. **(C):** The term "statistic" is to a sample what "parameter" is to a population. In statistical analysis, parameters are numerical characteristics that describe an entire population, such as the population mean or standard deviation. Conversely, statistics are similar measures calculated from a sample drawn from the population. These statistical measures, like sample mean or variance, are used to estimate population parameters. This analogy emphasizes the relationship between what is calculated from a sample and how it informs understanding of the broader population.

10. **(B):** Within mean square in Analysis of Variance (ANOVA) represents the variance within each group or condition, essentially measuring how much individual data points deviate from their group mean. This component is considered the error term in ANOVA because it reflects the random variability that cannot be explained by the model's predictors. ANOVA partitions the total variance observed in the data into components attributed to different sources of variation (between-group differences and within-group differences), with the within mean square highlighting the intrinsic error not accounted for by the treatment or condition effects.

11. **(C):** N-VIVO is a software extensively used for analyzing qualitative data in various fields including psychology. Unlike quantitative data analysis tools like SPSS or AMOS, N-VIVO is designed to help researchers organize, analyze, and find insights in unstructured or qualitative data such as interviews, open-ended survey responses, articles, social media, and web content. It facilitates coding, sorting, and linking different types of data, and provides tools for querying, visualizing, and modeling to deepen the understanding of complex phenomena captured in qualitative data.

12. **(B):** The point-biserial correlation coefficient (Point Biserial 'r') is used to measure the strength and direction of the association that exists between one dichotomous variable and one continuous variable. This statistic is appropriate when researchers need to correlate a naturally dichotomous variable (e.g., gender, yes/no decision) with a variable of continuous nature (e.g., test scores, height). It provides a way to understand how presence versus absence in the dichotomous variable relates to variation in the continuous variable.

13. (B): Explicit attitudes are those attitudes that individuals are consciously aware of and can easily report or express when asked. These attitudes are usually formed from direct experiences and are influenced by external information and reflect deliberate judgments. For example, a person may express a favorable explicit attitude toward recycling because of its benefits to the environment, which they can readily communicate in a survey or interview.

14. (C): Realistic conflict theory argues that prejudice and discrimination are likely to arise between groups when they are in competition for limited resources. This theory suggests that such intergroup conflicts can lead to increased prejudice as groups struggle to achieve economic or social goals at the expense of each other. This view is particularly relevant in contexts where economic disparities or competition for jobs, housing, or other resources are prevalent, as it posits that these tensions are a significant source of the negative attitudes between groups.

15. (B): Social loafing describes the phenomenon where individuals exert less effort to achieve a goal when they work in a group than when they work alone. When members in a group perform additive tasks, where the contributions of each member are simply added together to produce a group output, social loafing tends to occur. This is because the individual contributions might not be easily identifiable, and some members might feel their efforts are less essential, leading them to reduce their effort.

16. (C): Deindividuation refers to a psychological state where individuals in a group experience a reduction in self-awareness and a diminished sense of individual identity. This state is often facilitated by external conditions such as large crowd settings or anonymity provided by uniforms or masks. Deindividuation leads to a decrease in the usual social inhibitions and may result in impulsive and deviant acts that a person would not typically engage in if they were alone or easily identifiable. It's a key concept in understanding behaviours observed in riots, aggressive crowd events, and other group situations.

17. (B): Conformity is the social influence involved when an individual changes their behaviour, beliefs, or actions to align with the norms of a group. In Tanmaya's case, although she personally likes to wear gold earrings, she removed them to adhere to the rules of her school where wearing gold ornaments is prohibited. This change in her behaviour to fit in with the school's norms is an example of conformity, reflecting the power of social norms in influencing individual actions, even against personal preferences.

18. (D): John B. Watson's behaviourism focused primarily on observable behaviour, aiming to predict and control behaviour by understanding the stimulus-response associations. Watson's objectives did not inherently include studying the learner in a controlled laboratory environment or examining the effect of reinforcement. Instead, his work emphasized the prediction and control of behaviour through the manipulation of environmental stimuli, without delving into internal mental states or processes. His approach marked a fundamental shift towards the observable and measurable aspects of psychology.

19. (A): Neuroplasticity, also known as brain plasticity, refers to the brain's ability to reorganize itself by forming new neural connections throughout life. This ability allows the neurons (nerve cells) in the brain to compensate for injury and disease and to adjust their activities in response to new situations or changes in their environment. Neuroplasticity can involve the making and breaking of connections between nerve cells, and it is a fundamental aspect of the brain's capacity to recover from brain injuries and to adapt to learning new skills or facing new challenges.

20. **(B):** Temporal lobe epilepsy, a neurological condition where epileptic seizures originate in the temporal lobe of the brain, can lead to various behavioural changes, including increased aggression. Studies and clinical observations have noted that some individuals with temporal lobe epilepsy exhibit aggressive behaviour, which may be due to the effects of seizures on areas of the brain that regulate emotion and behaviour. This form of epilepsy can impact the limbic system, which is involved in controlling emotional responses, potentially leading to heightened aggressive reactions.

21. **(B):** Socratic questioning, named after the classical Greek philosopher Socrates, is a form of disciplined questioning that can be used to pursue thought in many directions and for many purposes, including to explore complex ideas, to uncover underlying assumptions, to differentiate what we know from what we do not know, and to analyze concepts or logical implications. It is a technique for self-understanding and critical thinking that fosters deep insights by challenging individuals to reflect on the validity of their beliefs and knowledge. This method encourages individuals to engage in introspection and continuous inquiry.

22. **(D):** Studies on weight loss programs that included a follow-up typically reveal that those practicing behaviour modification therapy are more likely to maintain their body weight. Behaviour modification therapy in weight management focuses on changing eating habits and lifestyle choices through various techniques like self-monitoring, goal setting, and reinforcement strategies. This approach helps individuals develop lasting habits that support weight maintenance, compared to other methods such as drug therapy, which might not have as sustainable effects once the treatment concludes.

23. **(C):** The homeostatic regulation of body temperature is primarily controlled by the preoptic region of the hypothalamus. This area of the brain acts as a thermostat by receiving input about the body's current temperature and activating mechanisms to either release heat and cool the body or generate heat to warm the body. This regulatory process ensures that the body's core temperature remains within the narrow limits necessary for optimal physiological functioning, regardless of external environmental conditions.

24. **(D):** Structuralism, founded by Wilhelm Wundt and further developed by his student Edward Titchener, emphasized the analysis of the basic elements of consciousness and the study of sensory experiences through introspection. While it did provide a systematic and rigorous approach to understanding the components of human consciousness, it did not establish a strong and clear orthodoxy. Instead, structuralism was criticized for its reliance on introspection, which was seen as subjective and unreliable. This criticism led to resistance from other emerging psychological schools, such as functionalism, which focused on the purpose

of consciousness and behaviour rather than its composition.

25. (A): Python is a high-level programming language known for its clear syntax and readability, which has a wide range of applications in software development, web development, data analysis, artificial intelligence, and more, but it is not specifically designed as a technological system to aid, enhance, or inspire learning in the educational technology sense. Unlike Python, Logo, Squeak, and Boxer are educational technologies developed with the explicit purpose of supporting learning, particularly in areas like mathematics, programming, and problem-solving for children and educational settings.

26. (D): John B. Watson, the founder of behaviourism, criticized the focus on internal mental states, which he termed "conscious mentalism." He believed that psychology should only concern itself with observable behaviours rather than internal thoughts or feelings. By labeling "conscious mentalism" as attention to thinking activities, Watson was emphasizing his viewpoint that traditional psychology's focus on thoughts, introspection, and consciousness was unscientific. Instead, he advocated for a behavioural approach that centered around observable and measurable actions, dismissing any introspective methods as unreliable and subjective.

27. (A): Leptin is a hormone associated with regulating body weight and energy balance by signaling satiety to the brain, helping to suppress appetite and burn stored fat. However, a decrease in sensitivity to leptin, known as leptin resistance, disrupts this signaling, leading to increased food intake and subsequent weight gain. In leptin resistance, even with high levels of leptin typical of individuals with more fat mass, the brain fails to recognize the satiety signal, mistakenly perceiving low energy stores and thus promoting increased food intake and reduced energy expenditure. This miscommunication contributes significantly to obesity and other metabolic issues.

28. (B): Psychological tests are differentiated into 'Verbal Tests' and 'Non-verbal Tests' based on the Criterion of contents of items. Verbal tests involve tasks that require the use of language, including reading comprehension, vocabulary, and other language-based skills. Non-verbal tests rely on the ability to understand and analyze visual information without verbal mediation and may include tasks like pattern recognition, puzzle solving, and spatial reasoning. This classification is crucial because it allows tests to be tailored to different populations, taking into account the subject's language skills or potential cultural biases inherent in language use.

29. (D): The Bender Visual-Motor Gestalt Test, designed by Lauretta Bender in 1938, comprises nine designs. These designs are used to evaluate visual-motor integration skills, which are crucial for coordinating cognitive, visual, and motor abilities. The test is often employed in psychological assessments to identify developmental disorders, neurological impairments, and even certain psychological conditions. The simplicity of the designs allows for a wide range of interpretive possibilities, making it a valuable tool in both clinical and educational settings.

30. (A): Group variability does not affect the intrinsic reliability of a test but rather influences its validity across different groups. Intrinsic factors affecting reliability typically include elements like the length of the test, the homogeneity of its items, and the scoring consistency. Group variability refers to differences in performance among various groups taking the test, which might affect the generalizability or fairness of the test but does not inherently impact the test's reliability. Reliability concerns the consistency and repeatability of the test results, irrespective of who the test takers are.

31. (D): The ratio scale of measurement is characterized by the presence of an absolute zero point, which represents the complete absence of the quantity being measured. This scale allows for the measurement of both the difference between data points and the relative magnitude of differences. For example, weight and height are measured on a ratio scale because they can be quantified starting from zero (e.g., 0 kilograms or 0 meters) and comparisons can be made in terms of ratios (e.g., one object can be twice as heavy as another).

32. (C): The Wechsler Adult Intelligence Scale (WAIS), first published in 1955 by David Wechsler, is structured into two main sections: Verbal and Performance. The original WAIS consisted of 6 Verbal subtests and 5 Performance subtests. The Verbal subtests typically assess aspects such as knowledge, comprehension, and reasoning using language-based materials. The Performance subtests evaluate processing speed, perceptual organization, and nonverbal problem-solving skills through tasks that do not require verbal expression.

33. (D): Sigmund Freud, the founding father of psychoanalysis, was born on May 6, 1856. Freud's contributions to psychology include his theories on the unconscious mind, the structure of personality (id, ego, superego), and the mechanisms of repression. His theories have profoundly influenced the fields of psychiatry, anthropology, literature, and art, despite being controversial and widely debated in contemporary psychology.

34. (D): Among the twenty needs listed by Henry Murray in his theory of personality, "Safety" is not included. Murray's theory, developed in 1938, categorized human needs into primary (viscerogenic) and secondary (psychogenic) types, which include needs like achievement, affiliation, power, and others such as succorance, sentience, and sex. Safety, while a basic human motivation discussed in other psychological theories like Maslow's hierarchy of needs, was not specifically listed by Murray among his set of psychogenic needs.

35. (A): The concept of "Foreign Hull" was coined by Kurt Lewin, a pioneer in social, organizational, and applied psychology. Lewin's metaphor of the "Foreign Hull" describes individuals who, because of migration or displacement, find themselves living in a cultural or social environment that is vastly different from their native or familiar environment. This concept is used to analyze the psychological and social adjustments and tensions experienced by individuals who must navigate and adapt to these new, often challenging environments. Lewin's theories significantly contributed to our understanding of group dynamics and the psychological impacts of environmental changes on individual behaviour.

36. (C): Conflict with family members is not typically considered a direct source of work-related stress. Work-related stress usually arises from factors within the work environment itself, such as responsibility for others, lack of support from coworkers, or an unpleasant work environment. These factors directly impact an individual's performance and psychological state in the workplace. Although family conflict can contribute to overall stress levels, which might affect one's work performance, it is not categorized as a work-related stressor in the typical organizational context.

37. (B): The concept of the 'collective unconscious' is a central element in Carl Jung's personality theory. Unlike Sigmund Freud, who focused on the personal unconscious, Jung introduced the idea of a deeper level of the unconscious shared across humanity, comprising latent memories from our ancestral past. This collective unconscious is thought to be the source of archetypes, which are universal, archaic symbols and images that derive from the collective experience of the human race. These archetypes manifest in cultural creations and psychological experiences across different cultures and societies.

38. (D): Setting a time frame is not typically a characteristic feature of brainstorming in Gerard Egan's problem management approach. Brainstorming is designed to encourage creativity and the generation of a wide range of ideas. The key features of effective brainstorming include developing 'wild' possibilities, suspending judgment to allow free flow of ideas, and using one idea as a springboard for another. These strategies are intended to create an open and uninhibited environment where participants can think creatively without time constraints or premature criticism, which can stifle idea generation.

39. (C): The term "morbidity" refers to the incidence or prevalence of a disease, injury, or disability in a population at a specific time. It is concerned with the effects of illness and can be expressed in terms of both existing cases (prevalence) and new cases (incidence) in the population. Morbidity rates provide valuable information for understanding the impact of various health conditions on a population and for planning public health strategies and interventions to reduce the burden of illness.

40. (B): The 'Miracle Question' is a technique used in Solution-Focused Brief Therapy (SFBT), which was developed by Steve de Shazer and Insoo Kim Berg. This technique involves asking clients to imagine that a miracle has occurred while they were sleeping and that the problems they are facing have been magically solved. The client is then asked to describe the changes they would notice in their life. This question helps clients identify goals and the potential steps they might take toward solving their problems, emphasizing a future-focused, goal-oriented approach to therapy.

41. (C): Divergent thinking is a type of thinking that generates creative ideas by exploring many possible solutions. It involves thinking out of the box and is typically measured by fluency (the ability to generate a large number of ideas), flexibility (the ability to produce a variety of ideas), and elaboration (the ability to flesh out and add details to ideas). Preparation and verification, on the other hand, are more associated with convergent thinking, where the focus is on narrowing down multiple ideas to find the best solution to a given problem.

42. (B): Daniel Goleman's model of Emotional Intelligence, outlined in his 1995 book, emphasizes five main components, but the major ones include knowing our own emotions (self-awareness), recognizing the emotions of others (social awareness), and handling relationships (relationship management). These components are crucial for effective emotional regulation and social interaction, enabling individuals to navigate social complexities and achieve positive outcomes in their interactions with others.

43. (C): The 'Type A' personality pattern is characterized by a continuous struggle for achievement, high competitiveness, impatience, and a sense of urgency. These individuals are typically very driven and can be quite stress-prone due to their high desire to achieve and their constant feeling of being pressed for time. They are known for their ambitious nature and often exhibit behaviours aligned with a strong sense of time urgency and a competitive spirit. This personality type is contrasted with 'Type B,' which is more relaxed and less constantly driven.

44. (B): A scientifically sound test must possess several key qualities: objectivity (the test produces similar results under consistent conditions and is not influenced by the biases of the examiner), norms (standardized data that allows comparison of scores to a representative population), reliability (the test yields consistent results over time and across different populations), and validity (the test accurately measures what it claims to measure). Time limits are often a practical component of test administration but are not required for a test's scientific soundness.

45. (C): The Study of Values by Gordon Allport, Philip E. Vernon, and Gardner Lindzey focuses on six major value types, but the primary ones included in their scale are theoretical (cognitive), economic, aesthetic, social, political (not specifically religious as a separate category), and religious. This assessment measures the relative importance of different values to an individual, helping to identify what drives a person's decisions and actions in various aspects of life, including moral, aesthetic, and economic arenas.

46. (D): The General Aptitude Test Battery (GATB) covers a broad range of aptitudes that are relevant for determining individuals' suitability for various types of jobs. The factors included are Verbal Aptitude, which assesses language abilities; Form Perception, which evaluates the ability to discern and understand visual patterns; Motor Coordination, which measures the ability to coordinate movements efficiently; and Clerical Perception, which focuses on the capability to notice details in written or tabulated material. Mechanical Reasoning, while also an important aptitude, is not specifically listed under these primary factors.

47. (C): Retrospective studies involve looking back at events that have already occurred, often using data that were not originally collected for research purposes. In these studies, data are often collected through narrative methods such as interviews, or by examining records and documents. Biographical research, which involves studying detailed descriptions of individuals' lives, is a good example of a retrospective study. These types of studies allow researchers to analyze past data to identify trends and outcomes but are limited by the reliability and completeness of the available data.

48. (B): René Descartes, a 17th-century French philosopher, is well-known for his concept of dualism, which posited that the mind and body are two fundamentally different things that interact but are governed by different laws. According to Descartes, the mind, which is free and immaterial, is a unique attribute of humans and is distinct from the body, which is material and subject to physical laws. This duality is a core aspect of his philosophy, emphasizing the separation between the mental and physical realms.

49. (B): A 'paradigm' in the context of scientific inquiry and philosophy of science, as described by Thomas Kuhn in his seminal work, represents a framework or set of practices that defines a scientific discipline during a particular period of time. It includes theories, research methods, and standards that are accepted by a substantial number of scientists within a community. A paradigm provides a comprehensive model for understanding and conducting research within a discipline, and it is often broader than just one theory, encompassing what might be referred to as a 'school of thought.'

50. (B): Gerard Egan's developmental model of counseling, known for its structured and phased approach, involves three distinct stages each comprising specific steps that guide the counseling process. The key steps include setting the agenda, exploring possibilities, and committing to action. 'Possibilities' refers to the identification of different options or courses of action; 'Commitment' involves the client committing to certain actions to address their issues; and 'Agenda' involves setting the topics or issues to be addressed in the counseling sessions. These steps are designed to help clients identify and clarify their problems, explore possible solutions, and commit to making changes to improve their situation.

51. (A): Appreciative Inquiry is a method used in organizational change and development that focuses on identifying what is working well in a current setup and building upon it. It is characterized by its collaborative and proactive nature, beginning each process with an appreciation for the current assets and strengths of an organization. Inquiry in this method is indeed applicable as it seeks to leverage positive aspects to drive improvement and transformation.

52. (B): In psychophysics, Weber's Law states that the just noticeable difference (JND), or difference threshold, is proportional to the magnitude of the original stimulus. This means as the stimulus intensity increases, the difference threshold (DL) also increases proportionately. Limens, or thresholds, do indeed play a critical role in the perception of sensory stimuli, determining when a stimulus is perceptible. Weber's Law and Fechner's Law (often described through the psychophysical scale) are not contradictory; rather, Fechner's Law expands on Weber's Law by attempting to explain the relationship between stimulus magnitude and perceived intensity in a logarithmic relationship.

53. (C): In multiple regression, there is typically one criterion variable and multiple predictor variables. The key feature of multiple regression is its ability to use more than two predictors to explain variance in the criterion. The equation for the regression line in multiple regression includes partial regression coefficients, which reflect the unique contribution of each predictor to the criterion, controlling for the influence of other predictors. This setup allows for a detailed analysis of the relationships between variables and provides insights into how various predictors influence the criterion variable.

54. (B): Factors that can foster prejudice include threats to self-esteem, competition for resources, and social categorization. When individuals feel their self-esteem is threatened, they may react defensively and negatively towards outgroups. Competition for scarce resources can also lead to conflicts and prejudice as groups vie for those resources. Social categorization, the process of classifying people into groups, enhances ingroup bias and often leads to negative stereotypes and prejudices against those not belonging to one's own group.

55. (D): Resistance to persuasion can be increased by techniques such as reactance, forewarning, and selective avoidance. Reactance occurs when people perceive their freedom to choose is being restricted, which makes them more likely to resist persuasion. Forewarning involves informing individuals that they will encounter a persuasive message, which can lead them to be more critical of the arguments presented. Selective avoidance refers to the tendency to dodge information or situations that might require changing one's attitudes or beliefs, thereby maintaining existing attitudes. Emotional appeal, conversely, is often used to decrease resistance and increase persuasiveness, not to increase resistance.

56. (D): The influencing skills of counseling that are effective in facilitating change and growth in clients include self-disclosure, information giving, and confrontation. Self-disclosure involves the counselor sharing personal experiences selectively to build empathy and trust. Information giving helps to educate and empower clients by providing necessary knowledge or resources. Confrontation, used carefully, challenges clients to reconsider their behaviours or thoughts in a supportive environment. SMART goals, while useful in planning and goal-setting within counseling, are not considered a direct influencing skill but rather a technique for structuring measurable and specific objectives.

57. (A): Panic disorder is characterized by recurrent bouts of intense and extreme fear or discomfort that peaks within minutes, often accompanied by physical symptoms such as shortness of breath, palpitations, or smothering sensations. Additionally, a significant feature of panic disorder is the persistent worry or concern about the possibility of having more attacks and the implications these attacks could have. This anticipatory anxiety can lead to significant behavioural changes in an effort to avoid future attacks. The statement involving the use of a drug or medication following an episode is not specifically associated with defining panic disorder.

58. (A): James Marcia's theory of identity status involves four statuses that describe the process of identity formation during adolescence and adulthood: identity achievement, identity foreclosure, identity diffusion, and identity moratorium. Identity achievement occurs when an individual has explored various options and committed to a specific identity. Identity foreclosure is when an individual commits to an identity without adequate exploration. Identity diffusion involves lack of both exploration and commitment. Identity moratorium is the state of active exploration without commitment. The option 'identity crisis' is not used by Marcia as a specific status but may describe the general condition of those in the moratorium phase.

59. (B): The transtheoretical model of behaviour change, also known as the stages of change model, includes several key stages through which individuals pass when changing behaviour. These stages are precontemplation, contemplation, preparation, action, maintenance, and termination. The options listed that are stages in this model include maintenance, contemplation, and action. Maintenance involves continuing the new behaviour long-term after successful action, while contemplation is thinking about changing, and action is the stage of actively implementing behaviour change.

60. (C): In the context of Astanga Yoga, Yama refers to ethical disciplines involving behaviours that are abstained from to live a more virtuous life. The components of Yama include Ahimsa (non-violence), Satya (truthfulness), Asteya (non-stealing), Brahmacharya (right use of energy), and Aparigraha (non-greed or non-possessiveness). Shoucha (purity) and Tapas (self-discipline) are not components of Yama; they belong to other limbs of yoga—Shoucha is part of Niyama, and Tapas is also considered a Niyama, reflecting personal observances rather than social restraints.

61. (B): Type II error, or the failure to reject a false null hypothesis, can be reduced by increasing the level of significance and increasing the sample size. Increasing the level of significance (e.g., from 0.05 to 0.10) means you are more willing to reject the null hypothesis, thereby decreasing the risk of missing an effect when there is one (reducing Type II error). Similarly, increasing the sample size enhances the statistical power of the test, making it more likely to detect an effect if one exists, which also contributes to reducing Type II errors.

62. (C): Assimilation in the context of Piaget's theory of cognitive development refers to the process by which new information is incorporated into pre-existing cognitive schemas. It involves matching cognitive structures to the physical environment, allowing an individual to handle new information within the context of existing knowledge. Assimilation can be thought of as the process of recognizing or knowing new information by fitting it into already established categories in the mind, without changing the existing schemas significantly.

63. (D): Gestalt psychology, a theory of mind and brain positing that the operational principle of the brain is holistic, parallel, and analog, with self-organizing tendencies. It is sometimes referred to as phenomenology, which emphasizes the perception of patterns and whole figures, rather than merely summing parts. Gestalt psychology has indeed applied principles similar to field theory from physics to understand perceptual grouping. Gestalt psychologists also believe that the psychological phenomena are deeply interconnected; changes in one aspect of experience or behaviour are reflected throughout the person's psyche.

64. (C): The personalities of Raymond B. Cattell, Hans J. Eysenck, and J.P. Guilford have had their theoretical positions heavily influenced by factor analysis. Cattell used factor analysis to develop a theory of 16 personality factors, Eysenck used it to propose his theory of personality focused on the dimensions of neuroticism, extraversion, and psychoticism, and Guilford applied factor analysis in his model of intelligence, which identified various operations, contents, and products. These psychologists have utilized factor analysis extensively to structure complex traits into more manageable and interpretable components.

65. (B): Sigmund Freud believed that when the ego struggles to control the id's impulses, it employs various defense mechanisms to manage anxiety and conflict. The primary defense mechanisms include repression (pushing unacceptable impulses out of awareness), rationalization (concocting a socially acceptable reason for behaviour that is actually being driven by unconscious impulses), displacement (shifting sexual or aggressive impulses to a more acceptable or less threatening target), and projection (attributing one's own unacceptable desires to others). These mechanisms help the ego reduce stress caused by the conflict between the id's desires and the superego's moral constraints.

66. (A):

(*a*) Implicit memory - I. The kind of memory that underlies perceptual and cognitive skills. Implicit memory refers to the memory system involved in acquired skills and learned habits.

(*b*) Working memory - III. Stored for only a few seconds. Working memory is a short-term system for temporarily holding and processing information necessary for complex tasks such as learning, reasoning, and comprehension.

(*c*) Long-term memory - IV. Semi-permanent memory. Long-term memory refers to the storage of information over extended periods of time, potentially life-long.

(*d*) Flashbulb memory - II. A vivid and relatively permanent record of the circumstances in which one learned of an emotionally charged, significant event. Flashbulb memories are detailed recollections of the circumstances surrounding emotionally significant or shocking events.

67. (C):

(*a*) Associationism - III. Ebbinghaus. Ebbinghaus developed the associationist theory of memory, studying the formation of associations.

(*b*) Structuralism - I. Wundt. Wundt is considered the father of structuralism, emphasizing the analysis of immediate conscious experience.

(*c*) Functionalism - IV. Stanley Hall. Although James is more directly associated with functionalism, Hall was a significant figure in spreading psychology in America, where functionalism flourished.

(*d*) Behaviourism - II. Lashley, among others, contributed to the behaviourist movement, although John B. Watson is more typically credited as a founder.

68. (B): In Buddhist psychology, each term corresponds to a specific aspect of human experience:

- Perception (Sanna) is classified under Option III, as it involves the process of interpreting or making sense of different stimuli based on past conditioning and mental formations.
- Consciousness (Vinnana) aligns with Option I, representing the awareness of sensory and mental events.
- Feelings (Vedana) are captured in Option II, relating to the sensations experienced as pleasant, unpleasant, or neutral, which arise from contact between the senses and their objects.
- Body (Rupa) is accurately described by Option IV, referring to physical forms or material existence, including the body itself as perceived in the physical world.

69. (D):

(*a*) Secondary Trait - IV. Traits that exert relatively specific and weak effects on behaviour. Secondary traits are less consistent or pervasive traits in a person's behaviour.

(*b*) Cardinal Trait - I. Traits that dominate an individual's entire personality. Cardinal traits are those that dominate and shape all of a person's behaviour.

(*c*) Central Traits - III. A bunch of traits that best describes an individual's personality. Central traits are the basic and most useful traits to describe an individual's personality.

(*d*) Source Traits - II. Key dimensions of personality that underlie many other traits. Source traits are basic factors underlying human personality, as identified in factor analyses.

70. (A):

(*a*) Autonomy - II. Shame & Doubt. Autonomy versus shame and doubt is Erikson's second stage of psychosocial development, focusing on children's growing sense of personal control.

(*b*) Industry - IV. Inferiority. Industry versus inferiority is the fourth stage, dealing with mastery of knowledge and intellectual skills.

(*c*) Initiative - I. Guilt. Initiative versus guilt is the third stage, focusing on children beginning to assert control and power over their world through directing play and other social interaction.

(*d*) Generativity - III. Stagnation. Generativity versus stagnation is Erikson's seventh stage, involving the challenge of contributing to the world through family and work and the broader community.

71. (C): The Coefficient of Dispersion, also known as the Coefficient of Variation, is the standard deviation expressed as a percentage of the mean, serving as a measure of relative variability. It illustrates how spread out the distribution of a data set is in relation to its mean. Standard Deviation is the positive square root of the variance and measures the average distance each data point is from the mean. Variance itself is calculated as the mean of the squared deviations of individual scores from the mean, representing the average of the squared differences from the mean.

72. (C): The Theory of Planned Behaviour, developed by Ajzen and Fishbein, emphasizes that behaviour is directly influenced by behavioural intention which is itself determined by an individual's attitude towards the behaviour, subjective norms, and perceived behavioural control.

Theory of Causal Attribution formulated by Kelley, deals with how people interpret events and how this relates to their thinking and behaviour.

Social Identity Theory by Tajfel and Turner describes how people's self-concepts are based on their membership in social groups. The Contact Hypothesis by Pettigrew posits that under appropriate conditions interpersonal contact is one of the most effective ways to reduce prejudice between majority and minority group members.

73. (B): Lawrence Kohlberg's theory of moral development includes various stages of moral reasoning. Obedience Orientation is when morality is externally controlled based on avoiding punishment and obeying authority. Interpersonal Norms describe the stage where individuals behave according to societal norms and expectations, particularly to win approval from others. Social Contract is the stage where individuals believe laws and rules are flexible instruments for improving human purposes. Universal Ethical Principles represent the highest stage of moral development, where moral reasoning is based on universal ethical principles and abstract reasoning.

74. **(A):** Passive Euthanasia (Option IV) occurs when medical treatment is withheld or withdrawn, allowing the patient to die naturally, often at the patient's request. This contrasts with Voluntary Active Euthanasia (Option I), where a physician directly administers a lethal dose to end a patient's life at their request. Assisted Suicide (Option II) is when a doctor provides the means for death, typically medication, allowing the patient to perform the act when they choose. Involuntary Active Euthanasia (Option III) involves ending a patient's life without their consent, often under controversial and ethically complex circumstances.

75. **(B):** Gestalt Psychology (Option III) is centered on the idea that the whole of anything is greater than its parts. This approach to psychology studies the human mind and behaviour as a whole, rather than breaking it down into smaller components. Hypochondriacal Delusions (Option I) involve the belief that one has, or is at high risk of developing, serious diseases. Humanistic Existential Therapy (Option II) emphasizes personal growth and self-direction, focusing on the client's capacity for self-awareness and how they can live authentically. Existential Neurosis (Option IV) reflects a condition of meaninglessness and alienation, often manifesting as a profound existential crisis.

76. **(C):** Csikszentmihalyi identified a multi-step process that typically unfolds during the creative journey. First, there is Preparation, where the individual absorbs information and materials needed for the task. This is followed by Incubation, a period of unconscious or less intense conscious processing of the information. Insight then occurs, which is the moment of "eureka" when a novel idea or solution suddenly comes to mind. After Insight, the Evaluation stage sets in, where the idea is scrutinized and refined. Finally, Elaboration, the last step, involves the detailed working out and application of the idea to produce a finished work or a visible solution.

77. **(C):** Classical conditioning involves the association of a neutral stimulus with an unconditioned stimulus so that the neutral stimulus comes to elicit a response on its own. The sequence begins with presenting the Unconditioned Stimulus (US), which naturally elicits a response. A neutral stimulus, such as light, is then introduced just before the US. Over time, this neutral stimulus alone, initially the light and later another neutral stimulus like a tone introduced prior to the light, begins to elicit the response initially associated only with the US, demonstrating the conditioned response.

78. **(C):** To place these milestones in chronological order, one should start with the earliest event. William James taught the first psychology course in the United States around 1875. Following this, Wilhelm Wundt established the first psychology laboratory in Leipzig in 1879. The founding of the American Psychological Association by G. Stanley Hall occurred in 1892. Ivan Pavlov was awarded the Nobel Prize for his work on the digestive system in 1904, and finally, the intelligence test was developed by Binet and Simon in France in 1905.

79. (A): Astanga yoga, also known as the eight limbs of yoga, outlines a path of practice that starts with ethical and moral standards and ends with the aspirant ready for meditation. Asana, which refers to physical postures, is the third limb and prepares the body for prolonged meditation. Pranayama, the fourth limb, involves breath control exercises that help master the respiratory process while acknowledging the connection between the breath, the mind, and the emotions. Dhyana, or meditation, is the seventh limb, involving profound contemplation of the divine. Samadhi, the eighth limb, is the state of ecstasy achieved when the meditator merges with their point of focus and transcends the Self.

80. (C): The HPA axis (hypothalamic-pituitary-adrenal axis) response to stress starts with the hypothalamus releasing corticotropin-releasing factor (CRF). This triggers the pituitary gland to release adrenocorticotropic hormone (ACTH). ACTH stimulates the adrenal glands to release cortisol, along with epinephrine and norepinephrine. The increase in these hormones leads to various physiological changes, including the release of glucose from the liver and muscles to provide immediate energy necessary to handle the stressor.

81. (D): In an Exploratory Sequential Design, which is a specific type of mixed methods approach, the correct sequence begins with Qualitative Data Collection (*b*) to explore a phenomenon and gather broad data insights without preset categories. This is followed by Qualitative Data Analysis (*d*) to interpret the qualitative data collected and identify patterns or themes. Quantitative Data Collection (*a*) then occurs, typically informed by insights gained from the qualitative phase, aiming to measure the trends identified earlier with a broader sample. Quantitative Data Analysis (*c*) follows, which involves statistical analysis to further explore the qualitative findings. Finally, Interpretation (*e*) integrates all data to form comprehensive conclusions.

82. (D):

83. (B): Tuckman's stages of group development progress in a structured sequence that facilitates group cohesion and effectiveness. It begins with Forming (*c*), where the group meets and begins to understand the tasks and boundaries. Storming (*a*) follows, where conflicts and competition are most likely to surface as group members assert their opinions. Norming (*e*) is next, where consensus develops and norms emerge. Performing (*b*) is when the group fully functions towards goal achievement. Lastly, Adjourning (*d*) marks the conclusion of group tasks and the dissolution of the group structure.

84. (A): The development of psychoanalysis, including its antecedent analysis, involved several key figures in distinct phases. G.T. Fechner (*b*), an early influence, contributed to psychophysical research that indirectly influenced psychoanalytic theory. Breur (*a*) worked directly with Freud on the study of hysteria and developed the talking cure, a precursor to psychoanalytic techniques. Adler (*d*) initially collaborated with Freud but later diverged with his own individual psychology. Finally, Sullivan (*c*) expanded psychoanalytic theory into interpersonal relationships, marking a later phase of psychoanalytic evolution.

85. (A):

86. (D): The Assertion (A) is incorrect, but the Reason (R) is correct. Although Cronbach's alpha is indeed a measure used to estimate the internal consistency of a test, it may not be the most suitable choice for a true/false format test. In cases of dichotomous items like True/False questions, other reliability coefficients like Kuder-Richardson Formula 20 (KR-20) are generally more appropriate because Cronbach's alpha assumes polytomous (multi-level) data and may be biased or inaccurate for dichotomous data.

87. (A): Both the Assertion (A) and the Reason (R) are correct, and (R) provides the correct explanation of (A). Allostasis involves achieving stability through physiological or behavioural change, which is indeed a process of adaptation involving acute stress response, and the activation of the HPA axis is a key component of this process. The release of stress hormones as part of the HPA axis activity is crucial for restoring homeostasis after stress, aligning with the definition of allostasis.

88. (B): Both the Assertion (A) and the Reason (R) are correct, but (R) does not provide the correct explanation of (A). An experiment does involve manipulating one or more variables to determine cause and effect relationships, which is correctly identified in both statements. However, the assertion broadly defines experimentation, while the reason specifically defines experimental design, making the reason correct but not a direct explanation of the assertion.

89. (B): Both the Assertion (A) and the Reason (R) are correct, but (R) is not the correct explanation of (A). Tabooed words are typically recognized more quickly and with greater emotional arousal due to their salient and often socially sensitive nature. However, the reason that perception of tabooed words is dependent on sociocultural knowledge, while true, is not directly explaining the recognition difficulty; rather, it explains the social context in which these words are processed and understood.

90. (C): The Assertion (A) is correct, but the Reason (R) is not correct. Sexual drive is indeed one of the physiological needs according to various psychological theories including Maslow's hierarchy of needs, where it is listed among the basic physiological needs. However, the reason that human beings cannot live without gratifying sexual drive is not accurate. While sexual activity can be important for psychological and physical well-being, humans can survive without fulfilling sexual drives.

91. (A): Teaching the parents to differentiate between show-off behaviour and acceptable behaviour involves helping them recognize the specific characteristics that define each type of behaviour. This is essentially teaching them "discrimination", which in psychological terms means the ability to perceive and respond differently to various stimuli. Discrimination training is a key component in behaviour modification and is used here to help parents identify and subsequently modify their responses to Jeevan's behaviour.

92. (C): By advising the parents not to pay attention to Jeevan's show-off behaviour, the psychologist is using a technique known as "extinction." Extinction in behavioural psychology involves withholding reinforcement that previously maintained a behaviour, which in this case is the parents' attention. By ignoring the show-off behaviour, the psychologist aims to reduce its frequency, as the behaviour no longer produces the reinforcing outcome (parental attention).

93. (B): When the psychologist instructs the teacher to praise children for helping their classmates, it is a strategy to provide a model of desirable behaviour for Jeevan. This approach uses "modeling" where

Jeevan can observe and learn from the positive reinforcement given to his peers for pro-social behaviour. This strategy not only encourages the other students but also serves as a behavioural guide for Jeevan, showing him what behaviour is valued and rewarded in the school setting.

94. (A): The use of loud noise (from bore-well digging) as a response to Jeevan's show-off behaviour is an example of "aversion therapy". Aversion therapy is a form of psychological treatment where negative stimuli are deliberately presented in conjunction with undesirable behaviours to create an unpleasant association. This method aims to reduce the occurrence of the behaviour by associating it with discomfort or an unpleasant experience.

95. (C): The psychologist's overall approach in handling Jeevan's case is an application of "behaviour therapy". Behaviour therapy is a broad term encompassing techniques and interventions that modify observable behaviorus through various methods like reinforcement, punishment, modeling, and aversion therapy. In Jeevan's case, different behavioural techniques are used to both decrease unwanted behaviours and encourage desirable behaviours, all grounded in behavioural principles.

96. (B): The researcher is investigating the same factors influencing Post Traumatic Growth (PTG) among husbands of breast cancer survivors that were identified in previous studies as determinants of PTG in women. The use of a quasi-experimental design is indicated by the lack of random assignment and the systematic investigation of pre-identified variables. This design allows the researcher to examine the influence of variables like emotional support, quality of marital relationship, and exposure to individuals with PTG, without manipulating the environment but rather observing the natural occurrence of these factors and their impact.

97. (C): For analyzing the influence of multiple factors (like emotional support, quality of marital relationship, and exposure to individuals with PTG) on a continuous outcome variable (PTG), regression analysis is appropriate. This statistical method allows the researcher to understand how much each factor predicts the level of PTG, accounting for the influence of other factors simultaneously.

98. (C): In this study, the criterion variable or the dependent variable is Post-Traumatic Growth (PTG). This is the main outcome variable that the researcher aims to explain or predict based on other independent variables such as emotional support, quality of marital relationship, and exposure to individuals with PTG.

99. (D): Common domains of Post-Traumatic Growth (PTG) include personal strength, spiritual change, and relationships with others. These domains reflect typical areas of growth individuals might experience following trauma. "Creativity" is not typically listed as a domain of PTG in the literature; instead, it often focuses on changes in perception of self, changes in relationships, and changes in philosophy of life.

100. (A): A suitable hypothesis for the study given its objectives would be that factors such as emotional support, quality of marital relationship, and exposure to individuals modeling PTG will all contribute to the husbands' experience of PTG. This hypothesis directly relates to the aim of investigating how these specific factors influence PTG in this particular group, aligning well with the goals of the research.

Previous Years' Paper

National Testing Agency (NTA)

UGC-NET Junior Research Fellowship & Assistant Professor Eligibility Exam

Psychology, June-2023

(Exam held on 15-06-2023)

PAPER-II

1. _____Vidya is the disciplined and systematic knowledge of the self and the environment attained through precise observation and critical reasoning.

A. Adhibhautika B. Adhyatmika
C. Bhautika D. Atmika

2. The Bhagvadgita has 18 chapters (Adhyaya) named after some form of Yoga. Which is not the correct adhyaya out of the following?

A. Dhyana Yoga
B. Aksara-Brahma Yoga
C. Purusottama Yoga
D. Jagrata Yoga

3. Paedocentrecism is:

A. Show the path of knowledge and guide the child to get knowledge
B. Centre on child's skill and behaviour
C. Involve child's behaviour with parents and teachers
D. Focus how the child works and the progress he/she makes

4. There are three types of post-modern therapies. Which out of the following is not a part of post-modern therapy?

A. Solution focused therapy
B. Field based therapy
C. Narrative therapy
D. Collaborative therapy

5. To conduct a study on Anganwadi workers, the researcher randomly selected five districts out of 30 districts of a state and collected data from each and every Anganwadi worker from these five districts. This is an example of _____.

A. Stratified sampling
B. Cluster sampling
C. Quota sampling
D. Convenient sampling

6. One sports psychologist wanted to carry out a biographical study by writing and recording the experiences of a hockey legend. This is an example of _____ approach.

A. Phenomenology
B. Ethnography
C. Narrative study
D. Grounded theory approach

7. "The present article describes a qualitative study of the career development of 16 prominent, highly achieving Indian women across six occupational fields. Our overall aim was to explore critical influences on the career development of these women, particularly those related to their attainment of professional success".

The above mentioned purpose statement indicates a _____.

A. Phenomenological study
B. Grounded Theory Study
C. Ethnographic study
D. Case study

8. Standard deviation of sampling distribution is known as ______.
A. Effect size
B. Sampling error
C. Parameter
D. Transitivity

9. The test requires someone to demonstrate his/her tailoring ability is best classified as:
A. Self report test
B. Standardized test
C. Test of maximal performance
D. Objective test

10. A basic set of beliefs that guide action is called:
A. Axiology
B. Paradigm
C. Rhetorical
D. Ontology

11. A researcher carried out an analysis in which he looked for underlying theoretical structures in his construct. Which one of the following design he used?
A. Linear Regression
B. Analysis of variance
C. Exploratory factor analysis
D. Confirmatory factor analysis

12. The formula used to estimate how many homogeneous test questions should be added to a test to raise its reliability to the described level is:
A. Coefficient alpha
B. Spearman Brown formula
C. Pearson product moment correlation
D. KR-20

13. Which parts of the brain are connected by the cerebral Aqueduct?
A. Third and fourth ventricles of the brain
B. Lateral ventricles of the brain
C. Left and right frontal Lobe
D. Frontal and Parietal Lobe

14. A unipolar neuron found in the somatosensory system are sensitive to:
A. Visual sensations
B. Auditory sensations
C. Tactile sensations
D. Olfactory sensations

15. Amygdala, part of the Limbic system, is specifically responsible for one of the following functions:
A. Thinking
B. Learning
C. Memory
D. Emotion

16. Which one of the following areas is not located in the Temporal Lobe?
A. Area for perception of body sensations such as, heat, cold, touch, pressure, and pain
B. Area for perception of movements, and recognition of faces
C. Broca's speech area
D. Primary auditory area

17. What is meant by stroboscopic motion?
A. We perceive an object is in motion whenever its image moves across our retina
B. Loss in sensitivity to motion
C. Tracking objects only in darkness
D. Tracking only the upward motion of objects

18. What is Thorndike's law of effect?
A. Behaviour that operates on the environment producing consequences
B. Behaviours followed by favourable consequences become more likely and that behaviours followed by unfavourable consequences become less likely to occur
C. Learning that certain events occur together
D. Behaviour that occurs as an automatic response to some stimulus.

19. When a lighting flashes nearby, we wince and start to prepare ourselves for the thunder to follow. This response to impending thunder is known as:
A. Unconditioned stimulus
B. Unconditioned response
C. Conditioned stimulus
D. Conditioned response

20. Which among the following is true about process of extinction of behaviour in classical conditioning?
A. Increase in magnitude of CR
B. Gradual diminishing of CR
C. CS and UCS develop strong association
D. UCS follows CS

21. What is meant by stroop effect?
A. The tendency to focus on a superficial feature of the problem at hand.
B. Automaticity of the reading process
C. Planning before acting
D. Role of silence in language

22. Which of the following is not a metacognitive activity?
A. Wondering how one could have been mistaken
B. Reflecting on our own thinking process
C. Theory of mind
D. Communicating one's present postal address

23. Which of the following is true about the concept of heritability?
A. The heritability of a trait refers to differences in percentages of a trait within an individual
B. Heritability refers to a population not to individual
C. The heritability of a trait is a single and fixed number
D. Heritability tells us about the source of mean differences between groups

24. Which of the following is not a chromosomal disorder characterized by subaverage intellectual functioning?
A. Down syndrome
B. Fragile X syndrome
C. Cerebral palsy
D. Trisomy 13

25. As per Values in Action (VIA), classification of character strengths and virtues are as under:
A. Character strengths - 20; Virtues - 06
B. Character strengths - 24; Virtues - 06
C. Character strengths - 18; Virtues - 06
D. Character strengths - 24; Virtues - 04

26. Three stage model of chronic stress formulated by Hans Selye is called:
A. GAS - General Adjustment Syndrome
B. GAS - General Adjustment System
C. GAS - General Adaptation System
D. GAS - General Adaptation Syndrome

27. The emergence of the Oedipus and Castration complexes are the chief events of which stage of development in the Freudian theory.
A. Oral stage B. Anal stage
C. Phallic stage D. Genital stage

28. Who is the author of the book "Escape from Freedom"?
A. Fromm B. Sullivan
C. Adler D. Horney

29. Women are likely to gain more number of valued positions during the time of crisis. This is referred as ______.
A. Glass ceiling effect
B. Glass-cliff effect
C. Tokenism
D. Singlism

30. Efforts to cope with the knowledge that we will die is known as ______.
A. Magical Thinking
B. Terror Management
C. Planning Fallacy
D. Availability Heuristics

31. Which therapeutic approach to counselling is based on the premise 'You are the architect of your life'?
A. Gestalt B. Existential
C. Adlerian D. Reality

32. Late adulthood often involves a gradual withdrawal from the world on physical, psychological and social levels. Which theory supports this?

A. Disengagement theory
B. Activity theory
C. Continuity theory
D. Selective Isolation theory

33. Simple skills develop in infants separately and independently and later develop into more complex skills. Which governing principle of growth is applied here?
A. Proximodistal Principle
B. Cephalocaudal principle
C. Principle of hierarchical integration
D. Principle of independence of the systems

34. Which of the following is not correct about REBT?
A. REBT aims to help individuals think clearly, feel appropriately and act effectively.
B. REBT uses the A-B-C theory of personality to identify client's problems.
C. The focus of the therapist is on the feelings and behaviour of the individual than on the incident that induced the negative feelings
D. REBT aims at a combination of philosophical change with cognitive emotional and behavioural strategies.

35. Which of the following is correct about the impact of stress on immune system of an individual?
A. The immune system is weakened because of an increase in the blood pressure in the face of stress
B. Increased release of glucose from the liver during stress neutralizes the immune functioning of the WBC
C. Increased level of ACTH in blood destroys the T cells
D. Increased level of cortisol in blood destroys the T cells.

36. Which of the following contributes to maintaining a health risk behaviour?
A. Lack of knowledge and the health risk behaviour helping the individual in avoidance of pain
B. The incentive ingrained in health risk behaviour and availability of leisure time
C. Avoidance of pain and need to spend money
D. Avoidance of pain and high self-efficacy

37. Which of the following describes resilience?
A. Individuals at risk whose performance is better than expected
B. Individuals in enriched environment excelling in performance.
C. Individuals with very good performance sliding down following a traumatic experience
D. Individuals who avoid risks and are happy with their average performance

38. Which of the following does not come under Cardiovascular Disease (CVD)?
A. Myocardial Infarction
B. Crohn's disease
C. Angina Pectoris
D. Cardiomyopathy

39. Which one of the following is not a principal characteristic of the REM sleep?
A. EEG desynchrony (Rapid Irregular Waves)
B. Lack of muscle tonus
C. Lack of genital activity
D. Dreams

40. Which of the following behaviours is not a stage of observational learning?
A. Be motivated to reproduce the behaviour
B. Remember what was observed
C. Exploring the environment
D. Pay attention to the model's behaviour

41. The basic aspects of the philosophy of early Buddhism fall into:
(*a*) Theory of Knowledge
(*b*) Theory of Society
(*c*) Theory of Reality
(*d*) Theory of Perception

Choose the most appropriate answer from the options given below:

A. (*a*), (*d*) only
B. (*a*), (*b*), (*c*) only
C. (*a*), (*c*), (*d*) only
D. (*b*), (*d*) only

42. Existentialism is associated with which of the following names.
(*a*) Soren Kierkegaard
(*b*) Vlademier
(*c*) Friedrich Nietzsche
(*d*) Husserl

Choose the most appropriate answer from the options given below:
A. (*a*), (*b*) only
B. (*a*), (*b*), (*c*) only
C. (*a*), (*c*), (*d*) only
D. (*a*), (*b*), (*d*) only

43. Which of the following should be assured before going for parametric analysis of variance?
(*a*) Independence of scores of the subjects
(*b*) Categorical dependent variable
(*c*) Random assignment of subjects to the treatments
(*d*) Homogeneity of variance of the subjects' scores

Choose the most appropriate answer from the options given below:
A. (*a*), (*b*), (*c*), (*d*)
B. (*a*), (*b*), (*c*) only
C. (*a*), (*c*), (*d*) only
D. (*b*), (*c*), (*d*) only

44. Which of the following are true about Multiple Regression?
(*a*) It is linear regression
(*b*) There are more than one criterion.
(*c*) There are more than one predictor
(*d*) It doesn't have intercept constant.

Choose the most appropriate answer from the options given below:
A. (*b*), (*c*) only
B. (*a*), (*c*) only
C. (*a*), (*b*), (*d*) only
D. (*b*), (*c*), (*d*) only

45. Which are correct about Multitrait - Multimethod design?
(*a*) Investigates construct validity
(*b*) Associates with Coombs and Holladay
(*c*) Associates with Campbell and Fiske
(*d*) Investigates Composite reliability

Choose the most appropriate answer from the options given below:
A. (*a*), (*b*) only B. (*a*), (*c*) only
C. (*b*), (*c*) only D. (*b*), (*d*) only

46. In the context of formula for Cohen's Kappa
(*a*) $K = \frac{f_o - f_c}{N - f_c}$

(*b*) f_o = observed frequency
(*c*) f_c = expected frequency
(*d*) N = Overall total of data points in the frequency matrix

Choose the most appropriate answer from the options given below:
A. (*a*), (*b*) only
B. (*a*), (*c*) only
C. (*a*), (*b*), (*c*) only
D. (*a*), (*b*), (*c*), (*d*)

47. A specific brain region can be destroyed by some of the following methods. Choose the correct answer.
(*a*) Immunocytochemical method
(*b*) Radiofrequency lesion method
(*c*) Excitotoxic lesion method
(*d*) Fluorogold method
(*e*) Experimental ablation method.

Choose the most appropriate answer from the options given below:
A. (*b*), (*c*), (*e*) only
B. (*a*), (*b*), (*c*) only
C. (*c*), (*d*), (*e*) only
D. (*a*), (*d*), (*e*) only

48. Which of the following are true about negative reinforcement?

(*a*) It strengthens a response
(*b*) It works by reducing or removing something undesirable or unpleasant
(*c*) Fastening a seatbelt in car to turn off beeping sound is an example of negative reinforcement
(*d*) It weakens a response
(*e*) It works by increasing desirability and pleasantness of a stimulus

Choose the most appropriate answer from the options given below:
A. (*d*), (*b*) only
B. (*a*), (*b*), (*c*) only
C. (*a*), (*e*) only
D. (*d*), (*b*), (*c*) only

49. Which of the following is/are true about perceptual constancy?
(*a*) It applies to perception of size and colour only
(*b*) Many visual illusions may be explained by the various constancies
(*c*) Constancies occur in all sensory modalities
(*d*) It keeps the appearance of objects the same in spite of large variations in the initial representation of the stimuli received by the sense organs that are engendered by various environmental factors.

Choose the most appropriate answer from the options given below:
A. (*a*), (*b*), (*d*) only
B. (*b*), (*c*), (*d*) only
C. (*a*), (*b*) only
D. (*d*) only

50. What is meant by theory of mind?
(*a*) People's idea about feelings perceptions and thoughts of self and others, and the behaviour these might predict
(*b*) A term first coined by Daniel Goleman
(*c*) People's ideas about their own and other's mental states
(*d*) By the age of six months, children worldwide display an advanced level of theory of mind acquisition
(*e*) People with autism are said to have an impaired theory of mind.

Choose the most appropriate answer from the options given below:
A. (*a*), (*c*) only B. (*a*), (*c*), (*e*) only
C. (*a*), (*b*) only D. (*c*), (*e*) only

51. Which of the following is/are true about a Phoneme?
(*a*) It refers to the disrupted language of a patient with aphasia
(*b*) Every language has its own set of phonemes
(*c*) A phoneme is a category of speech sounds
(*d*) It is the smallest unit of language that carries meaning.

Choose the most appropriate answer from the options given below:
A. (*a*) only B. (*b*), (*d*) only
C. (*b*), (*c*) only D. (*d*) only

52. Self-determination theory of Deci and Ryan focused on following basic needs to explain well being:
(*a*) Creativity
(*b*) Engagement
(*c*) Competence
(*d*) Relatedness
(*e*) Autonomy

Choose the most appropriate answer from the options given below:
A. (*a*), (*b*), (*c*) only
B. (*c*), (*d*), (*e*) only
C. (*b*), (*d*), (*e*) only
D. (*a*), (*c*), (*d*) only

53. The structural components of the corrective unconscious (Jung) are called by different names.
(*a*) Archetypes
(*b*) Imagoes

(*c*) Creative ego
(*d*) Libido
(*e*) Dominants

Choose the most appropriate answer from the options given below:
A. (*a*), (*e*), (*c*) only
B. (*b*), (*c*), (*d*) only
C. (*a*), (*b*), (*c*), (*d*) only
D. (*a*), (*b*), (*e*) only

54. In late adulthood, retirement from job follows specific stages, as per Atchley (1982):
(*a*) Honeymoon
(*b*) Disenchantment
(*c*) Craving for money
(*d*) Reorientation
(*e*) Social withdrawal

Choose the most appropriate answer from the options given below:
A. (*a*), (*b*), (*e*) only
B. (*b*), (*c*), (*d*) only
C. (*c*), (*d*), (*e*) only
D. (*a*), (*b*), (*d*) only

55. As indicated by reflexes, a newborn baby responds to touch around the area of:
(*a*) Head, Neck and Mouth
(*b*) Belly, Foot and Neck
(*c*) Mouth, Calf and Head
(*d*) Mouth and Foot
(*e*) Palm

Choose the most appropriate answer from the options given below:
A. (*a*), (*b*) only B. (*b*), (*e*) only
C. (*c*), (*e*) only D. (*d*), (*e*) only

56. Etiological models of psychopathology includes:
(*a*) Nervous system going awry
(*b*) Social conflicts
(*c*) Intrapsychic conflicts
(*d*) Learning dysfunctional behaviour
(*e*) Indulgence in religion.

Choose the most appropriate answer from the options given below:
A. (*a*), (*b*), (*c*) only
B. (*b*), (*c*), (*d*), (*e*) only
C. (*a*), (*c*), (*d*) only
D. (*a*), (*c*), (*d*), (*e*) only

57. Conflicts are readily kindled and fueled by:
(*a*) Competition
(*b*) Conciliation
(*c*) Cooperation
(*d*) Misperception
(*e*) Social Dilemmas

Choose the most appropriate answer from the options given below:
A. (*a*), (*b*), (*c*) only
B. (*b*), (*c*), (*d*) only
C. (*c*), (*d*), (*e*) only
D. (*a*), (*d*), (*e*) only

58. What is meant by bottom-up processing?
(*a*) It always distorts our observations
(*b*) Sensory analysis that starts at the entry level
(*c*) When our experience and expectations guide our perception
(*d*) Higher level mental processes are involved
(*e*) Helps to detect the lines, angles and colours

Choose the most appropriate answer from the options given below:
A. (*a*), (*b*) only B. (*a*), (*c*), (*d*) only
C. (*b*), (*e*) only D. (*c*), (*e*) only

59. Robert Sternberg proposed a triarchic theory of following intelligence types
(*a*) Creative (*b*) Analogical
(*c*) Analytical (*d*) Emotional
(*e*) Practical

Choose the most appropriate answer from the options given below:
A. (*a*), (*c*), (*e*) only
B. (*a*), (*b*), (*d*) only
C. (*a*), (*b*), (*c*) only
D. (*a*), (*c*), (*d*) only

60. Which of the following is/are related to Developmental screening Tests?
(*a*) Gesell Developmental Schedule
(*b*) Denver Developmental Screening Test
(*c*) Holland Developmental Schedule
(*d*) Burner Developmental Screening Test

Choose the most appropriate answer from the options given below:
A. (*a*), (*c*) only B. (*b*), (*d*) only
C. (*a*), (*b*) only D. (*c*), (*d*) only

61. Human personality is analyzed into five factors as viewed by Buddhism. Choose the correct factors included in personality:
(*a*) Material, Perception, Feeling
(*b*) Disposition, Consciousness
(*c*) Thinking, Belief, Intelligence
(*d*) Memory, Attention

Choose the most appropriate answer from the options given below:
A. (*a*), (*b*) only B. (*b*), (*c*) only
C. (*c*), (*d*) only D. (*a*), (*d*) only

62. Which of the following is/are true about stimulus generalization?
(*a*) People's emotional reactions to one stimulus generalize to similar stimuli
(*b*) With repeated exposure and reinforcement dogs can differentiate between types of sounds
(*c*) Normally desirable foods, such as cakes and pastries are unappealing when shaped to resemble dog's feces
(*d*) Sudden appearance of forgotten response.

Choose the most appropriate answer from the options given below:
A. (*a*), (*d*) only B. (*a*), (*c*) only
C. (*a*), (*b*) only D. (*b*), (*d*) only

63. Which of the following does not come under the matrix reasoning subtest of WAIS IV:
(*a*) Visuospatial reasoning
(*b*) Psychomotor speed
(*c*) Abstract reasoning
(*d*) Visual Organization
(*e*) Ability to follow directions.

Choose the most appropriate answer from the options given below:
A. (*a*), (*b*), (*c*) only
B. (*a*), (*c*), (*d*) only
C. (*b*), (*c*), (*d*) only
D. (*a*), (*b*), (*c*), (*d*) only

64. Identify the components of the 'Ethical Decision Making':
(*a*) Moral Awareness
(*b*) Moral Anxiety
(*c*) Moral Intent
(*d*) Moral Judgement
(*e*) Moral Context

Choose the most appropriate answer from the options given below:
A. (*a*), (*b*), (*c*) only
B. (*b*), (*c*), (*d*) only
C. (*c*), (*d*), (*e*) only
D. (*a*), (*c*), (*d*) only

65. Informed consent, as suggested by Diener and Crandall includes the components:
(*a*) Voluntarism
(*b*) Researcher's competence
(*c*) Information
(*d*) Comprehension

Choose the most appropriate answer from the options given below:
A. (*a*), (*c*) only
B. (*a*), (*b*), (*c*) only
C. (*a*), (*c*), (*d*) only
D. (*b*), (*c*), (*d*) only

66. Match List-I with List-II:

List-I	List-II
(*a*) Samacariya	I. Transformation wholeness
(*b*) Tanha	II. Desire
(*c*) Satori	III. Healthy virtuous
(*d*) Sammadithhi	IV. Thinking

Choose the correct answer from the options given below:

	(a)	(b)	(c)	(d)
A.	III	I	II	IV
B.	IV	I	II	III
C.	III	II	I	IV
D.	II	III	I	IV

67. Match List-I with List-II:

List-I	List-II
(a) Grounded Theory	I. Lives of individual studied and retold to develop a chronology
(b) Phenomeno-logical Research	II. Studying intact cultural group in national setting.
(c) Narrative Research	III. Deriving a general abstract theory through views of participants
(d) Ethnography	IV. Understanding lived experiences of a small member of participants

Choose the correct answer from the options given below:

	(a)	(b)	(c)	(d)
A.	III	I	IV	II
B.	II	IV	I	III
C.	II	I	IV	III
D.	III	IV	I	II

68. Match List-I with List-II:

List-I	List-II
(a) Preferred method for determining item bias	I. Slope
(b) Coefficient for correla-ting two absolutely dichotomous variables	II. Intercept
(c) The place where the regression line crosses the *y* axis	III. Phi coefficient
(d) The expected change in Y for every one unit change in X on the regression line	IV. Item characte-ristic curve

Choose the correct answer from the options given below:

	(a)	(b)	(c)	(d)
A.	IV	III	II	I
B.	III	IV	II	I
C.	I	III	II	IV
D.	I	II	IV	III

69. Match List-I with List-II:

List-I	List-II
(a) Effortful processing	I. Associates new and old information and solves problem
(b) Spacing Effect	II. Encoding of space, time and word meanings
(c) Working Memory	III. Remembering the concepts of psychology
(d) Automatic Processing	IV. Better long term reten-tion through distributed practice

Choose the correct answer from the options given below:

	(a)	(b)	(c)	(d)
A.	I	II	III	IV
B.	II	III	I	IV
C.	III	IV	I	II
D.	IV	II	III	I

70. Match List-I with List-II:

List-I	List-II
(a) Young-Helmholtz theory	I. Colour perception
(b) Place theory	II. High pitches
(c) Touch sensations	III. Rubber-hand illu-sion
(d) Gate control theory	IV. Pain

Choose the correct answer from the options given below:

	(a)	(b)	(c)	(d)
A.	IV	III	II	I
B.	I	II	III	IV
C.	II	I	III	IV
D.	III	IV	I	II

71. Match List-I with List-II:

List-I	List-II
(a) Sigmund Freud	I. Genetic view
(b) B.F. Skinner	II. Psychoanalytic view
(c) Carl Rogers	III. Behavioural view
(d) Hans Eysenck	IV. Humanistic view

Choose the correct answer from the options given below:

	(a)	(b)	(c)	(d)
A.	IV	I	II	III
B.	II	III	I	IV
C.	II	III	IV	I
D.	I	II	III	IV

72. Match List-I with List-II:

List-I	List-II
(a) Manic Disorder	I. Frontai-striatal region of the brain implicated
(b) Panic Disorder	II. Elevated expansive mood and increased energy
(c) Schizo-phrenia	III. Heightened awareness of emotion specific stimulus
(d) ADHD	IV. Delusion, Hallucination, incoherent speech

Choose the correct answer from the options given below:

	(a)	(b)	(c)	(d)
A.	II	III	IV	I
B.	I	IV	II	III
C.	III	II	I	IV
D.	IV	III	II	I

73. Match List-I with List-II:

List-I	List-II
(a) Object Perma-nence	I. Pre Operation
(b) Abstract thinking	II. Sensory motor
(c) Ego centrism	III. Concrete operation
(d) Conservation	IV. Formal Operation

Choose the correct answer from the options given below:

	(a)	(b)	(c)	(d)
A.	II	IV	III	I
B.	II	IV	I	III
C.	II	I	IV	III
D.	IV	III	II	I

74. Match List-I with List-II:

List-I	List-II
(a) Rosenstock	I. Protective Motivation Theory
(b) Rogers	II. Health Belief Model
(c) Fishbein	III. Self-Regulation Model
(d) Leventhal	IV. Theory of Reasoned Action

Choose the correct answer from the options given below:

	(a)	(b)	(c)	(d)
A.	II	I	IV	III
B.	II	III	I	IV
C.	II	IV	I	III
D.	II	I	III	IV

75. Match List-I with List-II:

List-I	List-II
(a) Pratyahara	I. Concentration
(b) Dharana	II. Attaining Oneness or Integration
(c) Dhyana	III. Control over thoughts
(d) Samadhi	IV. Meditation

Choose the correct answer from the options given below:

	(a)	(b)	(c)	(d)
A.	II	I	IV	III
B.	III	II	I	IV
C.	III	I	IV	II
D.	II	I	III	IV

76. Arrange Erik Eriksons stages of psychosocial development and basic strengths:

(a) Trust vs mistrust

(b) Initiative vs guilt

(c) Industriousness vs inferiority

(d) Autonomy vs doubt, shame

Choose the correct answer from the options given below:

A. (*a*), (*d*), (*b*), (*c*)
B. (*a*), (*c*), (*b*), (*d*)
C. (*a*), (*b*), (*d*), (*c*)
D. (*b*), (*c*), (*a*), (*d*)

77. Prepare the steps involved in Action Research in correct sequence with reference to behavioural science
(*a*) Action
(*b*) Observation
(*c*) Plan
(*d*) Reflection

Choose the correct answer from the options given below:
A. (*a*), (*b*), (*c*), (*d*)
B. (*b*), (*c*), (*a*), (*d*)
C. (*c*), (*a*), (*b*), (*d*)
D. (*c*), (*b*), (*d*), (*a*)

78. Arrange the following statements in the correct sequence of the movement of ions during the action potential
(*a*) Na^+ channels open, Na^+ begins to enter cell
(*b*) K^+ continues to leave cell, causes membrane potential to return to resting level
(*c*) K^+ channels open, begins to leave cell
(*d*) K^+ channels close, Na^+ channels reset
(*e*) Na^+ channels become refractory, no more Na^+ enters the cell

Choose the correct answer from the options given below:
A. (*a*), (*b*), (*c*), (*d*), (*e*)
B. (*a*), (*c*), (*e*), (*b*), (*d*)
C. (*a*), (*e*), (*c*), (*d*), (*b*)
D. (*d*), (*e*), (*a*), (*c*), (*b*)

79. Correctly arrange the components of emotion as explained in the two-factor theory of Schachter and Singer, 1962.
(*a*) Stimulus
(*b*) Cognitive appraisal of arousal
(*c*) General physiological arousal
(*d*) Subjective experience of emotion

Choose the correct answer from the options given below:
A. (*a*), (*b*), (*c*), (*d*)
B. (*a*), (*c*), (*b*), (*d*)
C. (*d*), (*a*), (*c*), (*b*)
D. (*c*), (*b*), (*d*), (*a*)

80. What would be the correct order of the steps involved in prosocial behaviour?
(*a*) Accept the responsibility for helping
(*b*) Noticing something unusual
(*c*) Decision about possession of required knowledge or skills
(*d*) Interpreting the event as emergency
(*e*) Deciding to actually help

Choose the correct answer from the options given below:
A. (*a*), (*c*), (*b*), (*d*), (*e*)
B. (*b*), (*d*), (*a*), (*c*), (*e*)
C. (*b*), (*d*), (*c*), (*a*), (*e*)
D. (*e*), (*b*), (*d*), (*c*), (*a*)

81. Arrange the following in sequence as per Development model of Counselling:
(*a*) Identification of blind spots
(*b*) Brain storming
(*c*) Developing possibilities
(*d*) Force-field analysis

Choose the correct answer from the options given below:
A. (*a*), (*c*), (*b*), (*d*)
B. (*b*), (*c*), (*a*), (*d*)
C. (*a*), (*c*), (*d*), (*b*)
D. (*a*), (*b*), (*d*), (*c*)

82. Arrange the following physiological response to stress sequentially:
(*a*) Release of Adrenocorticotropin hormone from pituitary gland
(*b*) Release of CRF from hypothalamus
(*c*) Perception of stress
(*d*) Suppression of immune system functioning
(*e*) Glucocorticoid release from Adrenal gland

Choose the correct answer from the options given below:

A. (*b*), (*c*), (*e*), (*a*), (*d*)
B. (*c*), (*b*), (*a*), (*e*), (*d*)
C. (*a*), (*c*), (*d*), (*b*), (*e*)
D. (*e*), (*d*), (*c*), (*a*), (*b*)

83. Arrange 'Pancha Kosha' in order:

(*a*) Annamaya Kosha
(*b*) Maanomaya Kosha
(*c*) Vijnanamaya Kosha
(*d*) Pranainaya Kosha
(*e*) Anandamaya Kosha

Choose the correct answer from the options given below:

A. (*a*), (*e*), (*b*), (*d*), (*c*)
B. (*a*), (*d*), (*b*), (*c*), (*e*)
C. (*a*), (*b*), (*d*), (*c*), (*e*)
D. (*a*), (*c*), (*b*), (*e*), (*d*)

84. Arrange the emergence of following leadership approaches in a chronological order:

(*a*) Behavioural approach
(*b*) Transformational approach
(*c*) Trait approach
(*d*) Contingency Approach

Choose the correct answer from the options given below:

A. (*a*), (*c*), (*b*), (*d*)
B. (*a*), (*c*), (*d*), (*b*)
C. (*c*), (*a*), (*b*), (*d*)
D. (*c*), (*a*), (*d*), (*b*)

85. Sequentially arrange the sections of the vertebrae of the spinal column from top to bottom.

(*a*) Thoracic vertebrae
(*b*) Sacral vertebrae
(*c*) Cemical vertebrae
(*d*) Lumbar vertebrae

Choose the correct answer from the options given below:

A. (*a*), (*d*), (*b*), (*c*) B. (*c*), (*a*), (*d*), (*b*)
C. (*a*), (*c*), (*b*), (*d*) D. (*b*), (*a*), (*d*), (*c*)

86. Given below are two statements : One is labelled as Assertion (A) and the other is labelled as Reason (R).

Assertion (A): There are five universal human needs according to reality therapy.

Reason (R): These needs are - survival, love and belonging, power, freedom and fun.

In the light of the above statements, choose the most appropriate answer from the options given below:

A. Both (A) and (R) are correct and (R) is the correct explanation of (A)
B. Both (A) and (R) are correct but (R) is not the correct explanation of (A)
C. (A) is correct but (R) is not correct
D. (A) is not correct but (R) is correct

87. Given below are two statements: One is labelled as Assertion (A) and the other is labelled as Reason (R).

Assertion (A): To eliminate the impact of an extraneous independent variable, the researcher can choose participants who are homogeneous on that independent variable.

Reason (R): 'Matching' is one of the method to control extraneous variance.

In the light of the above statements, choose the most appropriate answer from the options given below:

A. Both (A) and (R) are correct and (R) is the correct explanation of (A)
B. Both (A) and (R) are correct but (R) is not the correct explanation of (A)
C. (A) is correct but (R) is not correct
D. (A) is not correct but (R) is correct

88. Given below are two statements: One is labelled as Assertion (A) and the other is labelled as Reason (R).

Assertion (A): Monozygotic twins are called fraternal twins, who share half of their genes. Both members of the twins may be males or females.

Reason (R): Dizygotic twins develop from two different eggs and share the genes like a brother and sister. One of the twins may be a male and the other one may be a female.

In the light of the above statements, choose the most appropriate answer from the options given below:

A. Both (A) and (R) are correct and (R) is the correct explanation of (A)
B. Both (A) and (R) are correct but (R) is not the correct explanation of (A)
C. (A) is correct but (R) is not correct
D. (A) is not correct but (R) is correct

89. Given below are two statements: One is labelled as Assertion (A) and the other is labelled as Reason (R).

Assertion (A): Project Head start and other preschool quality programme boost children's chances of success in future by increasing their school readiness.

Reason (R): Genes and experience together determine cognitive and social skills.

In the light of the above statements, choose the most appropriate answer from the options given below:

A. Both (A) and (R) are true and (R) is the correct explanation of (A)
B. Both (A) and (R) are true but (R) is not the correct explanation of (A)
C. (A) is true but (R) is false
D. (A) is false but (R) is true

90. Given below are two statements:

Statement I: Motivation is a condition that energizes behaviour but gives no direction.

Statement II: Motivational States arise only from external incentive factors.

In the light of the above statements, choose the most appropriate answer from the options given below:

A. Both Statement I and Statement II are correct
B. Both Statement I and Statement II are incorrect
C. Statement I is correct but statement II is not correct
D. Statement I is incorrect but Statement II is correct

Directions (Qs. No. 91-95): *Read the following paragraph and answer the five questions that follow:*

A study was conducted to find out whether participation in meditation influences well-being in children. Hence a group of children who have not participated in meditation before but are now planning to begin participating in meditation were given a well-being scale before they began meditation. The children were administered the same test again after 2 months of meditation. The well-being was measured on an internal scale, with higher scores indicating higher well-being. The scores on the scale were normally distributed. The scores are given below.

Before	After
4	6
8	5
10	11
12	10
14	15
16	17
18	16

91. What is the degrees of freedom for the test?

A. 10 B. 11
C. 6 D. 5

92. What statistical test should be used to analyze the data?

A. Mann-Whitney U test
B. Wilcoxon signed Rank test
C. Correlated 't' test
D. Independent 't' test

93. Rejection of null hypothesis indicates:
A. Participation in meditation leads to significant difference in well-being scores
B. Participation in meditation leads to just above the well-being score after meditation
C. Participation in meditation leads to lower well being scores
D. Participation in meditation has no significant effect

94. Which of the following is correct about directional hypothesis?
A. Meditation has effect on well-being
B. Meditation has positive effect on well-being
C. Meditation has both positive and negative effect on well-being
D. Meditation has direction for well-being

95. Which of the following is correct about interval scale?
A. Identity, Magnitude, equal unit size and absolute zero are the properties of this scale
B. Identity and equal unit size are its properties
C. Identity, Magnitude and equal unit size are its properties
D. Identity and magnitude are the properties of this scale

Directions (Qs. No. 96-100): *Read the following paragraph and answer the five questions that follow:*

Lev S. Vygotsky developed a theory of cognitive development. He explained that experienced adults help children with innate basic capabilities to attain more complex and higher order cognitive capabilities. To describe and assess this potential, he proposed the notion of ZPD. Based on Vygotskian thinking, an instructional process was developed in which the more knowledgeable partner adjusts the amount and type of support he offers to fit with the child's learning needs over the course of interaction. According to Vygotsky, psychological tools and signs facilitate and direct thinking process.

96. The theory of Vygotsky is called:
A. Cultural theory of cognitive development
B. Social theory of cognitive development
C. Sociocultural theory of cognitive development
D. Bio-sociocultural theory of cognitive development

97. The ZPD stands for:
A. Zone of postnatal development
B. Zone of proximal development
C. Zone of proximodistal development
D. Zone of proximal distance

98. ZPD is defined by Vygotsky as:
A. The region of sensitivity for learning characterized by the difference between the developmental level when the child is working alone and the level he/she is capable of reaching with the aid of an adult
B. The region of difference between inability to use a known thing and benefit from the use of such a strategy
C. The region of learning what a child has learnt from experience and knows about the world in general
D. The region of ability to fit into change and choose environments that best fulfill the child's needs and desires to learn from society and culture.

99. The instructional process in which the more knowledgeable partner adjusts the amount and type of support he offers to fit with the child's learning needs over the course of interaction is called:
A. Tacit knowledge B. Social referencing
C. Pragmatics D. Scaffolding

100. The psychological tools and signs such as language, counting, mnemonics, algebraic symbols, art and writing that facilitate and direct thinking process is called by Vygotsky as:
A. Moderators B. Mediators
C. Confounders D. Facilitators

ANSWERS

1. **(B):** Adhyatmika Vidya, translated as spiritual or self-knowledge, embodies a disciplined and systematic approach to understanding both oneself and the surrounding environment. Rooted in ancient Indian philosophical traditions, Adhyatmika Vidya delves into the realms of the inner self, exploring the depths of consciousness and spirituality. It emphasizes the importance of precise observation and critical reasoning as essential tools for unraveling the mysteries of one's existence. Practitioners of Adhyatmika Vidya engage in introspection and self-inquiry, seeking profound insights into the nature of the self and its connection to the broader cosmos. This knowledge is not confined to a mere intellectual understanding but strives for a transformative experience that transcends conventional boundaries, leading individuals toward self-realization and a harmonious relationship with the external world. In essence, Adhyatmika Vidya serves as a beacon guiding individuals on a journey of self-discovery, fostering a holistic understanding of life and the interconnectedness of all things.

2. **(D):** The Bhagavad Gita, a sacred Hindu scripture, unfolds its profound teachings across 18 chapters known as Adhyayas, each named after a specific form of Yoga. However, "Jagrata Yoga" is not among the chapters and is therefore not a correct Adhyaya. The chapters that do grace this ancient text include "Dhyana Yoga," emphasizing the path of meditation and concentration; "Aksara-Brahma Yoga," delving into the imperishable and eternal nature of the ultimate reality; and "Purusottama Yoga," exploring the concept of the Supreme Person or the divine within. The Bhagavad Gita serves as a philosophical and spiritual guide, providing insights into duty, righteousness, and the various paths of Yoga, including Bhakti (devotion), Karma (action), and Jnana (knowledge). The absence of "Jagrata Yoga" in the chapter titles underlines the precision with which each Adhyaya is dedicated to elucidating distinct facets of spiritual wisdom and practice, contributing to the Gita's timeless relevance and universal appeal.

3. **(A):** Paedocentrecism is a principle that emphasizes the role of teachers as guides to knowledge. According to Aurobindo, teachers should not spoon-feed information, but instead help children discover their latent abilities. Paedocentrism, is an educational approach that revolves around showing the path of knowledge and guiding the child in their pursuit of learning. This perspective places a strong emphasis on the role of educators and guides in facilitating the child's journey of acquiring knowledge. In a paedocentric framework, educators take on the responsibility of not just imparting information but also actively guiding and nurturing the child's intellectual development. It involves creating an educational environment that is supportive, encouraging, and tailored to the individual needs of each child, recognizing their unique learning styles and preferences. Paedocentrism thus seeks to go beyond a mere transfer of information, focusing on fostering a genuine love for learning and providing the necessary guidance for the child to navigate the path of knowledge acquisition with curiosity and enthusiasm. Aurobindo's philosophy combines idealism, realism, naturalism, and pragmatism. He believed that Jnana (knowledge), Bhakti (devotion), and Karma (work ethics) can lead people to a divine path. He also believed that a sound personality requires a synthesis of spirituality, creativeness, and intellectuality.

4. **(B):** Post-modern therapies represent a departure from traditional psychotherapeutic approaches by embracing a more collaborative, dialogical, and narrative-oriented perspective. Solution-Focused Therapy, one of the post-modern approaches, focuses on clients' strengths and resources, aiming to amplify solutions rather than delving deeply into the analysis of problems. Narrative Therapy, on the other hand, considers individuals as the authors of their own stories, encouraging the exploration and reconstruction of personal narratives to bring about transformative change. Collaborative Therapy places a strong emphasis on the therapeutic relationship, viewing the therapist and client as equal partners working together to co-create new meanings and possibilities. However, "Field-based therapy" is not a standard term associated with post-modern therapy; its absence reflects the diverse and evolving nature of therapeutic practices that fall under the post-modern umbrella. While each approach shares the overarching theme of moving away from rigid structures, "Field-based therapy" does not have widespread recognition in the context of post-modern therapeutic modalities.

5. **(B):** The utilization of cluster sampling in this study involves a systematic approach to selecting a representative subset of the population. In cluster sampling, the population is partitioned into clusters, and a random sample of these clusters is chosen for study inclusion. In this specific case, the state's 30 districts served as the clusters, and the researcher randomly selected five districts to capture a diverse yet manageable representation of the entire population. Once the clusters were identified, the researcher collected data from every Anganwadi worker within these chosen districts. This methodology streamlines the data collection process by focusing efforts on specific geographic or administrative units. Cluster sampling proves advantageous in instances where clusters are heterogeneous internally but share commonalities within each unit. By randomly selecting entire clusters, this method facilitates efficiency in data collection and analysis, providing a practical compromise between comprehensive coverage and resource constraints.

6. **(C):** The psychologist's endeavor to conduct a biographical study by documenting and recording the experiences of a hockey legend reflects a narrative study approach. In narrative studies, researchers delve into the unique stories and lived experiences of individuals to gain a deeper understanding of their lives. By choosing to explore the intricate details and personal narratives of the hockey legend, the psychologist is adopting a qualitative research approach that seeks to unveil the subjective aspects of the athlete's journey. This method typically involves in-depth interviews, written accounts, or other narrative forms to comprehensively capture and interpret the individual's life story. The narrative study approach is particularly well-suited for gaining insight into the personal, emotional, and contextual dimensions of the hockey legend's experiences, contributing to a richer and more nuanced understanding of the psychological aspects of sports achievement.

7. **(B):** Grounded theory is a qualitative research method characterized by its inductive approach to theory development. In this study, the researchers aim to explore the career development of 16 highly achieving Indian women across various occupational fields without imposing preconceived theoretical frameworks. The emphasis is on allowing themes and patterns to emerge organically from the collected data, ultimately leading to the formulation of a grounded theory based on the unique experiences of the participants. This approach is particularly suitable when the goal is to generate a theory that is deeply rooted in the specifics of the studied context, in this case, the career

trajectories and critical influences on success for the selected group of Indian women. The researchers will iteratively analyze and code the data, progressively refining and developing a theory that captures the essential aspects of the women's career development experiences.

8. (B): The standard deviation of the sampling distribution, often referred to as sampling error, represents the variability or spread of sample means around the population mean in repeated sampling. It is a critical concept in statistics that quantifies the extent to which individual sample means may deviate from the true population mean. This measure is essential for assessing the precision and reliability of sample statistics in estimating population parameters. A smaller sampling error implies that sample means are likely to cluster closely around the population mean, indicating greater precision. On the other hand, a larger sampling error suggests more variability among sample means, reflecting less precision in estimating the true population parameter. Understanding and quantifying sampling error is fundamental in inferential statistics, helping researchers make inferences about the broader population based on information derived from finite samples. It is crucial for researchers and analysts to account for sampling error to draw accurate conclusions and make valid statistical inferences.

9. (C): A "Test of maximal performance" involves assessing an individual's ability to showcase their skills or perform a specific task at their highest level of competence. In the case of tailoring ability, this type of test would likely require the person to practically demonstrate their proficiency in various tailoring tasks, such as pattern cutting, sewing, or garment fitting. Unlike self-report tests, which rely on individuals' subjective perceptions, or standardized tests that measure performance against a predetermined norm, a test of maximal performance focuses on the actual, observable demonstration of skills. This approach is particularly beneficial in evaluating practical skills, as it provides a more direct and authentic measure of an individual's abilities. It is often employed in vocational settings or fields where hands-on expertise is crucial, allowing evaluators to witness and assess the individual's tailoring skills in a real-world context.

10. (B): In the realm of research, a basic set of beliefs that fundamentally guides actions and shapes the worldview of the investigator is often referred to as a philosophical worldview or paradigm. This concept is well-explained by the statement provided, emphasizing that these foundational beliefs are brought into the research process by the investigator and are interchangeably known as worldviews. In the context of social research, the term "paradigm" is specifically employed to denote the philosophical assumptions or the essential set of beliefs that not only guide the actions of the researcher but also define their overall worldview. Essentially, the chosen paradigm influences how researchers perceive, interpret, and engage with the subject matter, thereby impacting the entire research process. This highlights the critical role of paradigms in shaping the researcher's approach, methodology, and the interpretation of findings, reinforcing the idea that a basic set of beliefs indeed forms the cornerstone of their investigative endeavors.

11. (C): The researcher's choice of an analysis focused on uncovering underlying theoretical structures in their construct indicates the application of Exploratory Factor Analysis (EFA). EFA is a sophisticated statistical technique employed in the social sciences and other research domains to reveal the latent factors or dimensions that may be operating beneath the surface of observed variables. Unlike methods such as Linear

Regression or Analysis of Variance, which are primarily concerned with relationships between variables, EFA is specifically designed for dimensionality reduction and pattern recognition. In the researcher's case, EFA allows for the systematic exploration of the construct's inherent structure without presupposing the number or nature of latent factors. This open-ended approach is advantageous when dealing with complex constructs where the researcher seeks a deeper understanding of the interrelationships between variables and the emergence of potential underlying constructs. It offers a nuanced perspective, helping to uncover the intricate theoretical structures influencing the observed phenomena and contributing to a more comprehensive understanding of the construct in question.

12. **(D):** The KR-20 formula serves as a pivotal statistical tool for assessing the reliability of a test by calculating the internal consistency among its items. Computed by dividing the sum of variances of all items by the variance of the total test score, the KR-20 coefficient offers a numerical indication of the degree of reliability inherent in the test. Importantly, it is not only a measure of the current reliability but can also be employed to estimate how many homogeneous test questions should be integrated to enhance the test's reliability to a predetermined level. This involves determining the existing KR-20 coefficient, establishing the desired increase, and then utilizing the KR-20 formula to compute the number of homogeneous items necessary for achieving the targeted improvement. It is noteworthy that the KR-20 formula is just one of several methods used to gauge test reliability, and a comprehensive evaluation often involves considering other measures like Cronbach's alpha and test-retest reliability to obtain a more holistic understanding of a test's consistency and dependability.

13. **(A):** The cerebral aqueduct, also known as the Sylvian aqueduct, is a narrow canal-like structure within the brain that plays a crucial role in facilitating the flow of cerebrospinal fluid. Specifically, it serves as the conduit connecting the third ventricle, located at the center of the brain, to the fourth ventricle, situated in the posterior part of the brainstem. This interconnected system of ventricles is essential for maintaining homeostasis within the central nervous system, as cerebrospinal fluid provides buoyancy and protection for the brain while also aiding in the exchange of nutrients and waste removal. Dysfunction or blockages in the cerebral aqueduct can lead to disturbances in the normal flow of cerebrospinal fluid, potentially resulting in conditions such as hydrocephalus. Therefore, the cerebral aqueduct serves as a vital anatomical structure in facilitating the circulation and regulation of cerebrospinal fluid between the third and fourth ventricles, ensuring the overall well-being and functioning of the brain.

14. **(C):** Unipolar neurons, prevalent in the somatosensory system, are particularly sensitive to tactile sensations. These specialized neurons are crucial components of the sensory pathways responsible for transmitting information related to touch, pressure, vibration, and proprioception from the periphery to the central nervous system. Structurally, unipolar neurons have a single process extending from the cell body that branches into two distinct axonal pathways—one leading towards the periphery (often referred to as a sensory receptor) and the other projecting centrally to the spinal cord or brainstem. In the context of the somatosensory system, these neurons play a pivotal role in relaying sensory input from the skin, muscles, and joints, contributing to our ability to perceive and respond to various tactile stimuli. The intricate functioning of unipolar neurons in the somatosensory system underscores their

significance in the complex neural networks that allow us to experience and interpret sensations associated with touch and spatial awareness.

15. (D): The amygdala, situated within the limbic system, plays a crucial role in the processing and regulation of emotions. This almond-shaped cluster of nuclei is intricately involved in emotional responses, fear conditioning, and the formation of emotional memories. It serves as a neural hub where sensory input, particularly related to emotions, converges and is assessed for its emotional significance. The amygdala is instrumental in the initiation and modulation of emotional responses, influencing both the perception of emotional stimuli and the physiological reactions associated with them. Additionally, it contributes to the storage and retrieval of emotionally charged memories, shaping our future responses to similar situations. Dysfunction in the amygdala has been linked to emotional disorders and conditions such as anxiety and post-traumatic stress disorder. In essence, the amygdala is a key component of the intricate neural circuitry that underlies our ability to experience, interpret, and respond to a wide array of emotions in various contexts.

16. (A & C): The area for the perception of body sensations such as heat, cold, touch, pressure, and pain is primarily associated with the parietal lobe rather than the temporal lobe. The parietal lobe plays a crucial role in processing sensory information from the body, enabling individuals to perceive and respond to various sensations related to temperature, touch, and pain. This region integrates input from different sensory modalities to create a comprehensive understanding of the body's interactions with the external environment.

On the other hand, Broca's speech area is traditionally linked to the frontal lobe, not the temporal lobe. Broca's area, specifically located in the left hemisphere for the majority of right-handed individuals, is responsible for language production and speech formation. Damage to Broca's area can result in expressive aphasia, a condition characterized by difficulties in articulating words and constructing grammatically correct sentences. This linguistic function underscores the importance of the frontal lobe, particularly Broca's area, in the intricate processes involved in speech and language production.

Therefore, both the area for the perception of body sensations and Broca's speech area are not primarily located in the temporal lobe but are associated with the parietal and frontal lobes, respectively.

17. (A): Stroboscopic motion, rooted in the persistence of vision, is a visual phenomenon where the human eye perceives continuous motion when presented with a rapid sequence of discrete images. This perceptual illusion hinges on the eye's ability to retain an image briefly after it disappears, blending the individual frames into a coherent and fluid movement. In practical terms, this principle is widely applied in animation, filmmaking, and other visual technologies to create the illusion of dynamic motion. By displaying a succession of static images with minimal time gaps between them, the brain seamlessly connects these frames, producing the perception of motion. Stroboscopic motion not only plays a pivotal role in the creation of animated sequences and special effects in cinema but also extends to various technological applications, including the design of displays, signage, and entertainment devices. Understanding this phenomenon provides insights into how the human visual system processes sequential images, contributing to the immersive and dynamic experiences we encounter in visual media and technological interfaces.

18. (B): Thorndike's Law of Effect, a foundational principle in behavioural psychology, posits that behaviours followed by favourable consequences are more likely to be repeated, while those followed by unfavourable consequences become less likely to occur. This law emphasizes the critical role of consequences in shaping behaviour through a process of learning. If a particular behaviour leads to positive outcomes or rewards, individuals are inclined to exhibit that behaviour more frequently as they associate it with favourable consequences. Conversely, behaviours resulting in negative consequences are discouraged, reducing the likelihood of their repetition. This principle forms the basis of operant conditioning, highlighting the influence of reinforcement and punishment in the acquisition and extinction of behaviours. Thorndike's Law of Effect has far-reaching implications in understanding how organisms learn from their experiences, adapt their behaviours based on consequences, and navigate their environments to achieve desirable outcomes.

19. (D): "Conditioned response (CR)", refers to the learned response in classical conditioning that develops after repeated pairings of a conditioned stimulus (CS) with an unconditioned stimulus (UCS). In the context of the example provided, when a lightning flash (CS) is consistently paired with the impending thunder (UCS), individuals learn to associate the two stimuli. As a result, the wincing and preparatory response to the lightning flash, even before the actual occurrence of thunder, becomes the conditioned response (CR). This learned behaviour is a testament to the process of classical conditioning, where a neutral stimulus gains the ability to evoke a response through its association with a naturally triggering stimulus. The conditioned response demonstrates the adaptability of the organism in anticipating and preparing for an event based on learned associations, showcasing the powerful impact of environmental stimuli on shaping behaviour through the principles of classical conditioning.

20. (B): The process of extinction in classical conditioning involves a systematic reduction in the strength of a conditioned response (CR) that has been previously acquired through the association of a conditioned stimulus (CS) with an unconditioned stimulus (UCS). In classical conditioning, an organism learns to anticipate a specific outcome (UCS) based on the repeated pairing of a neutral stimulus (CS) with that outcome. During extinction, the CS is presented without the UCS, signaling a change in the predictive relationship. The absence of the expected UCS leads to a gradual weakening of the association between the CS and the learned response, resulting in the diminishment of the CR over time. This process reflects the organism's ability to adapt to changing circumstances and adjust its behaviour when anticipated outcomes fail to materialize. Extinction is not erasure of the learned association but rather a form of inhibitory learning, where the conditioned response weakens as the predictive relationship between the CS and UCS is disrupted, providing valuable insights into the flexibility and adaptability of learned behaviours in response to changing environmental contingencies.

21. (B): The Stroop effect is a cognitive phenomenon that reveals the automaticity of the reading process. In tasks associated with the Stroop effect, individuals are presented with words written in different colored inks, and their challenge is to name the ink colour while ignoring the word's semantic meaning. The intriguing aspect of the Stroop effect lies in the interference caused by automatic reading processes. Despite the task requiring attention to the colour of the ink, individuals often find it difficult to suppress the automatic tendency to read the words, leading to slower reaction times and increased errors. This effect underscores the efficiency and automatic nature of word reading, demonstrating the inherent difficulty in overriding automatic cognitive processes even when directed to focus on a different task. The Stroop effect has become a valuable tool in cognitive psychology for studying attention, automaticity, and the complexities of cognitive control.

22. **(D):** "Communicating one's present postal address", represents a practical and straightforward task that doesn't inherently involve metacognitive processes. This activity primarily demands the retrieval of stored information–-namely, one's postal address—and the subsequent effective communication of that information to another party. Unlike the other options, which delve into metacognition by exploring reflective aspects of thought processes, error recognition, and understanding the mental states of oneself and others, this option lacks the depth of cognitive engagement characteristic of metacognitive activities. Metacognition typically involves higher-order thinking, such as pondering potential mistakes, analyzing one's cognitive strategies, and grasping the perspectives of others. In contrast, communicating a postal address is a functional, memory-based action that doesn't inherently require self-reflection or the evaluation of cognitive mechanisms. While valuable in practical situations, this task falls outside the scope of metacognitive activities, highlighting the distinction between routine information retrieval and the more complex realm of thinking about one's own thinking processes.

23. **(B):** The concept of heritability refers to a population-level estimate rather than individual differences. Heritability is a statistical measure used in behavioral genetics to quantify the extent to which genetic factors contribute to the observed variation in a trait within a specific population. It is essential to recognize that heritability does not pertain to differences within an individual but rather assesses the proportion of variability in a trait across a group that can be attributed to genetic factors. In other words, it reflects the degree to which genetic variation influences the phenotypic variation in a population. This understanding underscores the importance of distinguishing between population-level trends and individual-level characteristics when interpreting heritability estimates. Consequently, heritability informs researchers about the relative contributions of genetic and environmental factors to the observed variability in traits across members of a specific population rather than offering insights into the genetic influence on individual differences.

24. **(C):** Cerebral palsy, unlike the other options presented, is not a chromosomal disorder characterized by subaverage intellectual functioning. It is a neurological condition that primarily affects motor function and muscle coordination due to damage to the developing brain during early life. While disorders such as Down syndrome, Fragile X syndrome, and Trisomy 13 involve specific chromosomal abnormalities leading to intellectual disabilities, cerebral palsy's origin lies in disruptions to the brain's development, particularly in areas that control movement. Cerebral palsy is often associated with difficulties in muscle control, balance, and coordination, but it does not necessarily impact intellectual functioning. This distinction is crucial in understanding the diverse etiologies of developmental conditions, emphasizing that not all disorders affecting motor function are directly tied to chromosomal anomalies and intellectual impairments.

25. **(B):** According to the Values in Action (VIA) framework, the accurate classification of character strengths and virtues is reflected in option B: Character strengths - 24: Virtues - 06. The VIA Classification of Character Strengths is a comprehensive model that identifies 24 universal character strengths, each contributing to positive human functioning. These strengths are

further organized under six core virtues: Wisdom, Courage, Humanity, Justice, Temperance, and Transcendence. The virtues serve as broad categories encompassing specific character strengths that align with positive moral traits and behaviours. This classification provides a structured and systematic approach to understanding and cultivating positive aspects of human character, offering a framework that has been widely utilized in the fields of positive psychology and character development. Therefore, option 2 accurately captures the VIA framework's delineation of 24 character strengths and six overarching virtues, reflecting the richness and diversity of positive human attributes.

26. (D): Hans Selye's three-stage model of chronic stress is known as the General Adaptation Syndrome (GAS). This model outlines the physiological responses that organisms undergo when exposed to chronic stressors. The three stages in the GAS are the alarm stage, resistance stage, and exhaustion stage. In the alarm stage, the body reacts to the stressor with the "fight or flight" response, activating the sympathetic nervous system and releasing stress hormones like cortisol. The resistance stage follows, during which the body attempts to adapt to the ongoing stressor, and physiological changes persist to cope with the sustained challenge. If the stressor persists for an extended period, the organism enters the exhaustion stage, characterized by a depletion of resources and increased vulnerability to various health issues. Selye's General Adaptation Syndrome provides a conceptual framework for understanding the body's physiological reactions to chronic stress and emphasizes the importance of adaptive responses and the eventual consequences of prolonged exposure to stressors.

27. (C): In Freudian psychoanalytic theory, the emergence of the Oedipus and Castration complexes marks the chief events of the Phallic stage, which is the third stage in Freud's psychosexual development. This stage typically occurs between the ages of 3 and 6 years. The Oedipus complex involves a child's feelings of desire for his mother and jealousy and rivalry with his father, while the Castration complex involves the child's fear of punishment (castration) by the father as a result of these forbidden desires. The Phallic stage is crucial in the development of psychosexual identity, as children navigate their emotions and conflicts related to gender and sexuality. The resolution of the Oedipus and Castration complexes is considered vital for the child's healthy psychological development, paving the way for the subsequent stages of Freud's theory, namely the Latency stage and the Genital stage.

28. (A): "Escape from Freedom" is a seminal work written by Erich Fromm, a prominent German-American psychologist and social philosopher. Published in 1941, the book delves into the psychological aspects of human behavior, particularly the individual's relationship with freedom and the challenges posed by the modern social and political landscape. Fromm explores the paradoxical nature of freedom, contending that while individuals inherently desire autonomy, they often experience a sense of anxiety and isolation when confronted with the responsibilities and choices that come with true freedom. Fromm delves into the psychological mechanisms people employ to escape from this anxiety, such as conformity, authoritarianism, and embracing destructive ideologies. The book critically examines the impact of social and economic structures on individual psychology, offering profound insights into the complex interplay between human nature and societal dynamics. Fromm's "Escape from Freedom" remains a thought-provoking exploration of the human psyche and a relevant analysis of the challenges posed by the pursuit of individual freedom in the modern world.

29. (B): The concept of the glass-cliff effect pertains to the phenomenon where women are more likely to ascend to leadership positions during times of crisis or organizational turbulence. This contrasts with the glass ceiling effect, which highlights the invisible barriers hindering women's advancement in more stable or prosperous periods. The glass-cliff reflects the tendency for women to be appointed to leadership roles when the risk of failure and potential negative outcomes is high. Organizations may turn to women in crisis situations, perhaps as a strategic response to signal change or as a means to address challenging circumstances. However, this also poses a unique set of challenges, as women leaders may face increased scrutiny and a higher likelihood of failure during such tumultuous periods. The glass-cliff effect underscores the complex interplay between gender dynamics and organizational leadership, emphasizing the need for a nuanced understanding of how gender influences opportunities and challenges in the professional sphere.

30. (B): Terror Management Theory (TMT) is a psychological framework that explores how human beings manage the awareness of their own mortality, often referred to as death anxiety. According to TMT, the acknowledgment of our eventual death creates existential terror, and individuals employ various psychological strategies to cope with this anxiety. These strategies include cultural beliefs, societal norms, self-esteem, and connections with others. By adhering to cultural worldviews, achieving personal goals, and maintaining positive self-esteem, individuals can construct a sense of meaning and significance that helps alleviate the fear of death. TMT posits that much of human behaviour is influenced by these efforts to manage existential terror, impacting everything from personal relationships to cultural and religious beliefs. The theory has been influential in understanding how thoughts of mortality shape human behaviour and the various mechanisms people employ to cope with the existential challenges posed by the inevitability of death.

31. (B): Existential therapy, aligned with the premise "You are the architect of your life", is rooted in existential philosophy and psychology, emphasizing individual agency and responsibility for creating meaning in one's existence. This therapeutic approach recognizes that individuals have the freedom to shape their lives and make choices that align with their authentic selves. Existential therapists guide clients in exploring fundamental aspects of human existence, such as the search for meaning, the experience of freedom, and the confrontation of life's inherent uncertainties. The therapeutic process involves a deep exploration of personal values, beliefs, and existential concerns, encouraging clients to take an active role in shaping their destinies. Existential therapy doesn't provide ready-made answers but instead supports individuals in facing life's inherent challenges with courage and authenticity. It is a profound exploration of the human experience, promoting self-awareness and empowering individuals to construct their lives in alignment with their values and aspirations.

32. (A): The Disengagement Theory, proposed by sociologists Elaine Cumming and William Henry in 1961, posits that late adulthood is characterized by a gradual and mutual withdrawal between the aging individual and society on physical, psychological, and social levels. According to this theory, as individual's age, they naturally disengage from their previous roles and activities, leading to a reduced level of interaction with the external world. This withdrawal is not only physical but also involves a psychological shift in which older adults may reevaluate their priorities, interests, and social connections. The Disengagement

Theory suggests that this process is a normal and adaptive aspect of aging, allowing older individuals to gradually step back from societal responsibilities, make room for younger generations, and focus more on personal reflection and enjoyment. While this theory has faced criticism for potentially reinforcing stereotypes about aging, it remains one of the early and influential perspectives on the social dynamics of late adulthood.

33. (C): The Principle of Hierarchical Integration, as applied in child development, underscores the progression from the development of simple skills to the integration of these skills into more complex abilities. This principle recognizes that infants initially acquire basic motor and cognitive skills independently and gradually integrate them into more sophisticated and coordinated actions. For example, an infant may first learn to grasp objects with individual fingers before refining this skill into a more complex action, such as manipulating objects with purposeful intent. The hierarchical integration process reflects the sequential and organized nature of skill development, where foundational abilities serve as building blocks for higher-order functions. This principle aligns with the idea that the developmental trajectory involves the gradual incorporation and coordination of simpler skills into more advanced and complex behaviours as a child matures and gains mastery over their physical and cognitive capacities.

34. (C): Rational Emotive Behaviour Therapy (REBT) is a cognitive-behavioural approach that aims to help individuals cultivate clear thinking, appropriate emotional responses, and effective behaviours. The therapy employs the A-B-C theory of personality, where A represents the activating event, B signifies the individual's beliefs about the event, and C denotes the emotional and behavioural consequences. REBT focuses on identifying and challenging irrational beliefs that contribute to negative emotions and maladaptive behaviours. The therapy places significant emphasis on the thoughts and beliefs of the individual, understanding that modifying irrational beliefs can lead to more rational thinking and healthier emotional responses. REBT aims for a comprehensive approach, combining philosophical change with cognitive, emotional, and behavioural strategies. The therapeutic process involves helping clients recognize and replace irrational beliefs with more rational alternatives, ultimately fostering psychological well-being and resilience.

35. (D): The impact of stress on the immune system involves a complex interplay of physiological responses, with the release of cortisol being a key factor. Chronic stress triggers the prolonged release of cortisol, a stress hormone, which can have immunosuppressive effects. Elevated cortisol levels can interfere with the normal functioning of the immune system, particularly by impairing the activity of T cells. T cells play a crucial role in orchestrating the body's immune response, identifying and destroying infected or abnormal cells. When cortisol levels remain elevated, it can lead to a reduction in the number and effectiveness of T cells, weakening the immune system's ability to defend against infections. Additionally, stress-induced changes in other aspects of the endocrine system, such as increased release of glucose from the liver, can also contribute to immune system dysregulation. The intricate relationship between stress and the immune system highlights the importance of managing stress for overall health and well-being.

36. (A): Maintaining a health risk behaviour often involves a complex interplay of psychological and situational factors. This emphasizing lack of knowledge and the health risk behaviour serving as a means of avoidance of pain, underscores the importance of understanding the psychological motivations behind such behaviours. The absence of knowledge about potential health consequences can create a barrier to behaviour change, as individuals may not fully comprehend the risks involved. Moreover, when engaging in a health risk behaviour provides immediate relief from emotional or physical pain, individuals might develop a coping mechanism that reinforces the behaviour. This psychological reinforcement can contribute to a cycle of continued engagement in the health risk behaviour, as it becomes a strategy for managing stress, anxiety, or other challenging emotions. Addressing the maintenance of health risk behaviours requires a multifaceted approach, incorporating education, awareness, and targeted interventions to disrupt the patterns of avoidance and encourage healthier alternatives.

37. (A): Resilience, goes beyond mere survival in the face of adversity; it embodies the remarkable ability of individuals to not only endure but to thrive and excel despite being at risk. Resilience encompasses a dynamic process involving psychological, emotional, and social factors that contribute to an individual's capacity to bounce back from setbacks. It involves the cultivation of coping strategies, adaptive thinking, and emotional fortitude, allowing individuals to navigate challenges with resilience. Those at risk, whether due to personal, environmental, or socio-economic factors, may not only demonstrate a surprising resilience in their performance but also showcase a remarkable ability to learn and grow from adverse experiences. Resilience is about harnessing strength from adversity, transforming setbacks into opportunities for personal development, and defying conventional expectations by not just maintaining but often exceeding one's potential despite the odds. It emphasizes the human capacity for strength, adaptability, and flourishing in the face of life's difficulties.

38. (B): Cardiovascular Disease (CVD) constitutes a diverse spectrum of disorders primarily affecting the heart and blood vessels, with options are directly associated with this category. Myocardial Infarction, or heart attack, involves the blockage of blood flow to a part of the heart, leading to tissue damage. Angina Pectoris is characterized by chest pain or discomfort resulting from reduced blood flow to the heart muscle. Cardiomyopathy refers to diseases of the heart muscle that compromise its ability to pump blood effectively. In contrast, Crohn's disease is an inflammatory bowel disease affecting the gastrointestinal tract, with no direct involvement in cardiovascular function. Crohn's disease entails chronic inflammation in various segments of the digestive system, causing symptoms such as abdominal pain, diarrhea, and fatigue. The distinction between Crohn's disease and cardiovascular disorders is crucial for accurate diagnosis and tailored treatment plans, as they target different physiological systems, emphasizing the importance of comprehensive healthcare approaches tailored to specific medical conditions.

39. (C): REM (Rapid Eye Movement) sleep is characterized by several distinct features, integral to its nature. During REM sleep, the electroencephalogram (EEG) shows desynchrony, marked by rapid irregular waves, reflecting heightened brain activity similar to wakefulness. Muscle tonus is significantly reduced during REM sleep, leading to a state of temporary paralysis known as atonia, which prevents individuals from physically acting out their dreams. Dreams are a hallmark of REM sleep, representing vivid and immersive experiences. However, the lack of genital activity is not entirely accurate. But as compare to the given options this point comes as subsidiary characteristics of

REM. Thus, the lack of genital activity is the right choice. Therefore, understanding the multifaceted characteristics of REM sleep is crucial for comprehending the complexities of the sleep cycle and the various physiological processes that occur during different stages of sleep.

40. (C): Observational learning, a cognitive process identified by Albert Bandura, encompasses several stages that contribute to the acquisition of new behaviours through observation of others. The first stage involves the observer being motivated to reproduce the behaviour they have witnessed, emphasizing the importance of internal motivation and personal relevance. The second stage focuses on the retention of the observed behaviour, requiring the individual to remember what was witnessed. This highlights the role of memory and cognitive processes in the learning experience. The third stage, exploring the environment, is not typically considered a distinct component of observational learning. Instead, the primary stages involve attention, motivation, and retention. Lastly, paying attention to the model's behavior is a critical stage, as it ensures that the observer is actively engaged in the learning process, directing their focus towards the model's actions. Understanding these stages provides insights into how individuals acquire new behaviors through observation and how cognitive factors contribute to the learning process.

41. (B): The basic aspects of the philosophy of early Buddhism are as follows:

(*a*) **Theory of Knowledge:** Early Buddhism emphasizes a particular understanding of knowledge. The core teachings, encapsulated in concepts like the Four Noble Truths and the Eight-fold Path, represent a form of knowledge that transcends ordinary, mundane understanding. It involves a profound awareness and insight into the nature of existence, suffering, and the path to liberation.

(*b*) **Theory of Society:** While the primary focus of early Buddhism is on individual liberation and enlightenment, it does provide guidance on ethical living and societal harmony. The Buddha's teachings include principles for ethical conduct, social responsibility, and the alleviation of suffering not only for oneself but also for others in society.

(*c*) **Theory of Reality:** Central to early Buddhist philosophy is the exploration of the nature of reality. The Four Noble Truths articulate the reality of suffering (dukkha), its causes, the possibility of its cessation, and the path leading to that cessation. The emphasis on impermanence (anicca), unsatisfactoriness (dukkha), and non-self (anatta) reflects the understanding of reality in early Buddhism.

42. (C): The laureates associated with existentialism are:

(*a*) **Soren Kierkegaard:** Often considered as "father of existentialism", Kierkegaard's philosophical works laid the groundwork for existentialist thought. His writings, particularly "Fear and Trembling" and "The Sickness Unto Death," explored the concept of individual subjectivity and the leap of faith required to confront the challenges of existence. Kierkegaard emphasized the importance of personal choice, passionate commitment, and the subjective experience of the individual in navigating life's complexities. His ideas influenced later existentialist thinkers, including Jean-Paul Sartre and Albert Camus.

(*c*) **Friedrich Nietzsche:** Nietzsche's impact on existentialism is profound, despite not explicitly identifying as an existentialist. His critiques of traditional morality, rejection of religious values, and the concept of the "will to power" resonated with existentialist themes. Existentialist philosophers drew inspiration from Nietzsche's exploration of individualism, self-overcoming, and the eternal recurrence, finding resonance in his call for the "overman" or "Ubermensch".

(*d*) **Edmund Husserl:** Although Husserl is not strictly an existentialist, his development of phenomenology significantly influenced existentialist thought. Phenomenology, as conceived by Husserl, involves the detailed examination of consciousness and subjective experience. Existentialist thinkers, particularly those associated with the existential phenomenology movement, such as Jean-Paul Sartre and Martin Heidegger, drew upon Husserl's methods to explore the lived experiences of individuals. The focus on the first-person perspective, consciousness, and the subjective nature of reality became central themes in existentialist philosophy.

Soren Kierkegaard's emphasis on individual subjectivity and choice, Friedrich Nietzsche's critiques of traditional values and advocacy for self-affirmation, and Edmund Husserl's development of phenomenology all played crucial roles in shaping the existentialist movement. While each thinker approached existentialist themes from a unique perspective, their ideas collectively contributed to the rich and diverse landscape of existentialist philosophy.

43. **(C):** Before going for parametric analysis of variance we should follow:

(*a*) **Independence of scores of the subjects:** The assumption of independence ensures that the scores of one subject are not influenced by or dependent on the scores of other subjects. This independence is crucial to avoid confounding variables and to maintain the integrity of the statistical analysis. When subjects are independent, the variability in the data can be attributed to the treatment conditions rather than external factors.

(*c*) **Random assignment of subjects to the treatments:** Random assignment involves assigning subjects to different treatment groups in a completely random manner. This helps control for potential confounding variables and ensures that any observed differences between groups can be attributed to the treatment conditions rather than pre-existing differences among subjects. Random assignment enhances the internal validity of the study.

(*d*) **Homogeneity of variance of the subjects' scores:** Homogeneity of variance, also known as homoscedasticity, assumes that the variance (spread) of scores within each treatment group is roughly equal. This assumption is essential for the validity of ANOVA results because the F-ratio, which ANOVA uses to test for differences between group means, is sensitive to differences in variance. Violations of this assumption can lead to increased Type I errors and affect the accuracy of the F-ratio.

44. **(B):** True things about multiple regression are:

(*a*) **It is linear regression:** This statement is correct. Multiple Regressions is a type of linear regression. Linear regression models the relationship between a dependent variable and one or more independent variables by fitting a linear equation to observed data. In Multiple Regression, the linear equation involves multiple independent variables, allowing for a more comprehensive understanding of how these variables collectively influence the dependent variable.

(*c*) **There is more than one predictor:** This statement is also correct. In Multiple

Regression, there are indeed more than one predictor variable. Predictors are the independent variables that are used to predict the value of the dependent variable. The inclusion of multiple predictors enables researchers to assess the unique contribution of each predictor to the variability in the dependent variable, while controlling for the effects of the other predictors.

Multiple Regressions involves linear modeling and incorporates more than one predictor variable, making it a valuable tool for analyzing complex relationships between variables in statistical modeling.

45. (B): Correct statements about Multitrait-Multimethod design are:

(*a*) **Investigates construct validity:** Construct validity is a crucial aspect of measurement validity, ensuring that a test or measurement tool accurately assesses the intended psychological construct. MTMM design, pioneered by Donald T. Campbell and Donald W. Fiske, is a methodology specifically designed to assess construct validity. This design involves measuring multiple traits (multitrait) using multiple methods (multimethod). By doing so, researchers can examine the patterns of correlations between different traits measured by the same method (convergent validity) and between the same trait measured by different methods (discriminant validity). The goal is to provide evidence that the measure is indeed capturing the intended psychological construct and not influenced by irrelevant factors.

(*c*) **Associates with Campbell and Fiske:** Donald T. Campbell and Donald W. Fiske are indeed the prominent psychologists associated with the development of Multitrait-Multimethod design. In their seminal work published in 1959, they introduced this design as a systematic approach to assess the construct validity of psychological measures. Their collaboration laid the foundation for using MTMM design in psychometrics, making significant contributions to the methodology of evaluating the quality of psychological measurement instruments.

46. (D)

47. (A): The methods which can destroy a specific region of brain are:

(*b*) **Radiofrequency lesion method:** This method involves using radiofrequency waves to create lesions or damage specific brain regions. It is a form of neurosurgery where a fine electrode is inserted into the brain, and high-frequency electrical current is applied to generate heat, leading to the targeted destruction of brain tissue. This method is often used in research to investigate the functions of specific brain regions by observing the effects of their damage.

(*c*) **Excitotoxic lesion method:** Excitotoxicity involves the overactivation of receptors for excitatory neurotransmitters, such as glutamate, leading to cell damage or death. In the excitotoxic lesion method, substances that induce excitotoxicity are injected into specific brain regions, resulting in the selective destruction of neurons in those areas. This method allows researchers to study the functions of particular brain regions by observing the behavioural and physiological consequences of their damage.

(*e*) **Experimental ablation method:** Experimental ablation involves surgically removing or damaging specific brain regions to study their functions. This can be achieved through various techniques, including aspiration (suction), knife cuts, or other methods that physically disrupt the targeted brain tissue. Experimental ablation is a classic approach used in neuroscience research to investigate the roles of different brain regions in behaviour, cognition, and other functions.

48. (B): True statements about negative reinforcement are:

(*a*) **It strengthens a response:** Negative reinforcement is a process that strengthens or increases the likelihood of a particular behaviour by removing or avoiding an aversive stimulus. This occurs because the removal of the aversive stimulus serves as a reinforcing consequence, making the behaviour more likely to be repeated in the future. For example, if a person studies hard to avoid the aversive consequence of failing an exam, the act of studying is strengthened through negative reinforcement.

(*b*) **It works by reducing or removing something undesirable or unpleasant:** Negative reinforcement operates by eliminating or reducing the impact of an undesirable or unpleasant stimulus. In the context of negative reinforcement, the focus is on the consequence that follows a behaviour and involves the removal of something unpleasant. For instance, if a child cleans their room to stop their parents from nagging, the removal of the nagging serves as negative reinforcement for the cleaning behaviour.

(*c*) **Fastening a seatbelt in a car to turn off a beeping sound is an example of negative reinforcement:** This real-life example illustrates the principle of negative reinforcement. The beeping sound in the car is an aversive stimulus, and fastening the seatbelt leads to the removal or cessation of the unpleasant noise. As a result, the behaviour of fastening the seatbelt is strengthened because it successfully eliminates the undesirable stimulus, demonstrating the concept of negative reinforcement in everyday situations.

49. (B): True statements about perceptual constancy are:

(*b*) **Many visual illusions may be explained by the various constancies:** Perceptual constancies play a crucial role in understanding and explaining visual illusions. Visual illusions occur when our perception deviates from the physical reality of the stimuli. The constancies, such as size constancy and colour constancy, help us make sense of illusions where the apparent size or colour of an object seems to change under different conditions. For example, the perceived size of an object remains constant even if it appears smaller in the distance, thanks to size constancy.

(*c*) **Constancies occur in all sensory modalities:** While the question specifically mentions size and colour, perceptual constancy extends beyond vision and applies to all sensory modalities. For instance, auditory constancy helps us recognize familiar voices regardless of the pitch or loudness variations. Tactile constancy allows us to identify objects by touch, maintaining a consistent perception despite changes in pressure or texture.

(*d*) **It keeps the appearance of objects the same despite large variations in the initial representation of the stimuli received by the sense organs that are engendered by various environmental factors:** This statement captures the essence of perceptual constancy. Our sensory organs receive varied stimuli influenced by environmental factors like lighting, distance, and angles. Despite these variations, perceptual constancy enables us to perceive objects consistently. For instance, an apple maintains its perceived colour under different lighting conditions due to colour constancy.

Perceptual constancies, including size, colour, and those in other sensory modalities, help us make sense of our perceptual experiences by maintaining stable perceptions despite changes in stimuli and environmental conditions. They play a crucial role in explaining visual illusions and ensuring a coherent and reliable perception of the world around us.

50. (B): Theory of mind is defined as:

(*b*) **People's idea about feelings, perceptions, and thoughts of self and others, and the behaviour these might predict:** This aspect of ToM refers to the ability to understand and attribute mental states such as beliefs, desires, intentions, emotions, and knowledge to oneself and others. It involves recognizing that others can have different thoughts, beliefs, and emotions than one's own.

(*c*) **People's ideas about their own and others' mental states:** This is closely related to self-awareness and the ability to understand that individuals have their own unique thoughts, beliefs, and emotions. It encompasses not only understanding others' mental states but also recognizing and reflecting on one's own mental states.

(*e*) **People with autism are said to have an impaired theory of mind:** Individuals with autism spectrum disorder (ASD) often face challenges in developing a typical Theory of Mind. They may struggle with understanding and predicting the thoughts, feelings, and intentions of others. This can impact their social interactions and communication skills.

Understanding Theory of Mind is crucial for various aspects of social cognition, empathy, and effective communication. It allows individuals to navigate social situations by anticipating others' behaviours and adjusting their own responses accordingly. The development of Theory of Mind typically occurs during early childhood, and by the age of six, most children have a well-established Theory of Mind.

51. (C): True statements about Phoneme are:

(*b*) **Every language has its own set of phonemes:** This statement is accurate. Phonemes are the basic building blocks of spoken language, and each language has its own specific set of phonemes. Different languages may have distinct sounds that are considered phonemic in one language but not in another. For example, the English language has different phonemes than the Japanese language, and what constitutes a unique and meaningful sound in one language may not have the same distinction in another.

(*c*) **A phoneme is a category of speech sounds:** This statement is also correct. A phoneme is indeed a category of speech sounds. Phonemes are groups of sounds that are perceived as the same by speakers of a particular language. They are the abstract representations of the speech sounds that speakers recognize as distinct and meaningful. For example, the /p/ sound in "pat" and the /b/ sound in "bat" are considered different phonemes in English because they can change the meaning of a word.

52. (B): Self-determination theory of Deci and Ryan focused on:

(*c*) **Competence:** In the self-determination theory, competence refers to the need to feel effective and capable in one's activities. It involves experiencing a sense of mastery and accomplishment. When individuals engage in tasks or activities that challenge them at an optimal level (neither too easy nor too difficult), they are more likely to feel competent, which contributes to their overall well-being.

(*d*) **Relatedness:** Relatedness is the need for social connections and positive relationships. Humans are inherently social beings, and forming meaningful connections with others is considered crucial for psychological well-being. Having a sense of belonging, being understood, and experiencing positive interactions with others satisfy the relatedness need.

(*e*) **Autonomy:** Autonomy is a fundamental concept in the self-determination theory, emphasizing the need for individuals to feel a sense of choice and control over their actions. When people perceive that their actions are self-determined rather than externally controlled, they are more likely to experience higher levels of well-being. Autonomy involves making choices that align with one's values and interests, fostering a sense of ownership and responsibility.

53. (D): The structural components of the collective unconscious are also called as:

(*a*) **Archetypes:** Archetypes are fundamental, universal symbols or themes that are present in the collective unconscious, according to Carl Jung. These archetypes represent shared human experiences, patterns, or motifs that transcend cultural and individual differences. Examples of archetypes include the Hero, the Mother, the Shadow, and the Anima/Animus. Archetypes serve as organizing principles that shape human perceptions, behaviours, and narratives.

(*b*) **Imagoes:** In Jungian psychology, the term "imago" is often used to refer to the unconscious image of a significant person, typically from early life, that influences an individual's relationships and perceptions. This concept is particularly relevant in understanding how early experiences and relationships with caregivers or significant figures shape one's psychological patterns and interpersonal dynamics.

(*e*) **Dominants:** The term "dominants" in Jungian psychology refers to the most influential or powerful archetypes within an individual's psyche. These dominant archetypes play a central role in shaping a person's personality, values, and behaviours. Identifying and understanding the dominant archetypes can provide insights into an individual's unique psychological makeup and patterns of relating to the world.

54. (D): According to Atchley, the specific stages of rate adulthood are:

(*a*) **Honeymoon:** The Honeymoon stage represents the initial phase of retirement. During this stage, individuals often experience a sense of excitement, liberation, and positive feelings associated with the newfound freedom and leisure that retirement brings. It's a time when individuals may engage in activities they had longed to do but couldn't while working. The Honeymoon stage is characterized by a sense of adventure and exploration.

(*b*) **Disenchantment:** Disenchantment is the phase that follows the Honeymoon stage. During this stage, the initial excitement and positive feelings may diminish. Individuals may face challenges and disillusionment as they encounter the realities of retirement, such as changes in routines, social dynamics, and a potential loss of identity associated with the work role. It's a period of adjustment and self-reflection.

(*d*) **Reorientation:** The Reorientation stage is a subsequent phase where individuals start to adapt to retirement. During this stage, individuals may actively seek new activities, interests, or roles that provide a sense of purpose and fulfillment. There is a reevaluation of personal goals, and individuals redirect their energy toward meaningful pursuits. This stage involves a positive adjustment and a proactive approach to shaping one's retirement lifestyle.

55. (D): A newborn baby will always respond when we touch his/her:

(*d*) **Mouth and Foot:**

Mouth: Newborns exhibit the sucking reflex in response to anything that touches the roof of their mouth. This reflex is crucial for feeding, as it helps infants latch onto the breast or a bottle. It's an automatic and coordinated response that aids in the intake of nourishment.

Foot: The Babinski reflex is associated with the foot. When the sole of the foot is stroked, the baby's toes spread apart and the big toe turns upward. This reflex is a normal response in newborns, and its part of the assessment of the nervous system's development. The Babinski reflex tends to disappear as the nervous system matures.

(*e*) **Palm:** The grasp reflex is associated with the hands and fingers, not just the palm. When an object or finger is placed in a baby's palm or when the palm is touched, the baby's fingers automatically close around the object. This reflex is important for a baby's ability to grip onto objects and is considered a primitive reflex that typically diminishes as voluntary motor control develops.

56. (C): Etiological models of psychopathology are:

(*a*) **Nervous system going awry:** In the context of psychopathology, the nervous system going awry refers to abnormalities or dysregulation in the functioning of the central nervous system (CNS) and peripheral nervous system (PNS). This could involve disruptions in neurotransmitter systems, irregularities in brain structure or function, and genetic factors that contribute to the development of mental health disorders. For example, imbalances in serotonin, dopamine, or other neurotransmitters are implicated in conditions like depression and schizophrenia.

(*c*) **Intrapsychic conflicts:** Intrapsychic conflicts are conflicts that occur within an individual's own mind. These conflicts often involve unconscious desires, unresolved emotions, and tensions between different aspects of one's personality. Psychodynamic theories, especially those developed by Sigmund Freud, emphasize the role of unconscious processes and how unresolved conflicts from early childhood can influence current thoughts, emotions, and behaviours. For instance, an unresolved Oedipus complex might contribute to relationship difficulties later in life.

(*d*) **Learning dysfunctional behaviour:** Learning models in psychopathology focus on how behaviours are acquired, maintained, and modified thrcugh learning processes. Classical conditioning, operant conditioning, and observational learning play crucial roles. For example, a person may develop anxiety in response to a specific situation if they have learned to associate that situation with a traumatic event. Cognitive-behavioural models also emphasize how dysfunctional thought patterns contribute to maladaptive behaviours and emotions.

57. (D): The factors, which can kindle and fuel the conflicts are:

(*a*) **Competition:** Competition, in the context of conflicts, can arise when individuals or groups vie for the same resources, opportunities, or goals. It is a natural and often healthy aspect of human interaction, fostering innovation and growth. However, conflicts may intensify when competition becomes cutthroat, unfair, or lacks proper regulations. Unethical practices, aggression, or a zero-sum mindset can contribute to heightened conflicts in competitive situations.

(*d*) **Misperception:** Misperceptions refer to the incorrect understanding or interpretation of information, intentions, or actions. In the realm of conflicts, misperceptions can lead to misunderstandings, false assumptions, and biased judgments. These inaccuracies in perception may generate conflict as parties react to perceived threats or provocations. Clear communication, active listening, and efforts to clarify intentions can be crucial in addressing misperceptions and preventing conflicts.

(*e*) **Social Dilemmas:** Social dilemmas involve situations where individual self-interest conflicts with the collective well-being. People facing social dilemmas may prioritize personal gains over the greater good, leading to suboptimal outcomes for the group. Conflicts arise when there is a tension between individual and collective interests. Addressing social dilemmas often requires fostering a sense of shared responsibility, encouraging cooperation, and establishing systems that align individual incentives with collective benefits.

58. **(C):** Bottom-up processing means:

(*b*) **Sensory analysis that starts at the entry level:** Bottom-up processing refers to the analysis of sensory information that begins at the basic or entry level of the sensory system. It involves the processing of elemental features of a stimulus, such as colour, shape, and orientation, by the sensory receptors. These features are then combined to form a more complex perception. Bottom-up processing is data-driven, meaning it relies on the actual sensory input to construct a perceptual experience. This approach is often considered more objective as it is based on the characteristics of the stimulus itself.

(*e*) **Helps to detect the lines, angles, and colours:** This statement aligns with the idea that bottom-up processing helps to detect and analyze the basic features of a stimulus. For example, when you look at an image, bottom-up processing allows your visual system to detect and process the lines, angles, and colours present in the image without relying on prior knowledge or expectations. It involves the building of perception from the ground up, starting with the sensory details.

59. **(A):** According to Robert Sternberg, types of intelligence are:

(*b*) **Creative Intelligence:** Creative intelligence involves the ability to think creatively and generate novel ideas, solutions, or approaches. Individuals with strong creative intelligence can approach problems in innovative ways, think outside conventional boundaries, and engage in original thinking. This type of intelligence is crucial for tasks that require unconventional problem-solving and imaginative thinking.

(*c*) **Analytical Intelligence:** Analytical intelligence focuses on logical reasoning, critical thinking, and problem-solving. Individuals with strong analytical intelligence excel in tasks that require analyzing information, evaluating options, and making reasoned judgments. This type of intelligence is closely associated with academic and cognitive abilities that involve logical and systematic approaches to problem-solving.

(*e*) **Practical Intelligence:** Practical intelligence pertains to the ability to apply knowledge effectively in real-world situations. Individuals with strong practical intelligence can adapt to different environments, navigate everyday challenges, and use their knowledge and skills to achieve goals in practical contexts. This type of intelligence is valuable in situations that demand street smarts, adaptability, and the ability to succeed in various life scenarios.

In Sternberg's triarchic theory, these three types of intelligence are viewed as complementary and essential for a comprehensive understanding of human cognitive abilities. The theory recognizes that intelligence goes beyond traditional measures and encompasses a range of skills and capacities needed for success in diverse aspects of life. It provides a more holistic approach to intelligence that acknowledges the importance of creativity, analytical thinking, and practical problem-solving.

60. (C): The Developmental Screening Tests are related with:

(*a*) **Gesell Developmental Schedule:** The Gesell Developmental Schedule, developed by Arnold Gesell, is a developmental screening tool used to assess the developmental progress of infants and children. It focuses on evaluating a child's developmental milestones in various domains such as motor skills (both fine and gross motor), language development, social skills, and adaptive behavior. The assessment is often structured as a series of age-appropriate activities, and the child's performance is compared to typical developmental norms for their age group. The Gesell Developmental Schedule is commonly used by healthcare professionals, educators, and researchers to identify potential developmental delays or concerns.

(*b*) **Denver Developmental Screening Test:** The Denver Developmental Screening Test (DDST) is a widely used developmental screening tool designed to assess the developmental milestones of children from birth to 6 years old. The test covers four main domains: personal-social, fine motor-adaptive, language, and gross motor skills. It involves a set of age-specific activities and tasks that are administered to the child to observe their performance in each developmental area. The results are then compared to established norms for the child's age group. The Denver Developmental Screening Test is often employed in clinical settings, such as pediatrician offices or early childhood development programs, to identify children who may be at risk for developmental delays or disorders.

Both the Gesell Developmental Schedule and the Denver Developmental Screening Test aim to provide a systematic and standardized approach to assess a child's developmental progress and identify any areas where additional support or intervention may be needed.

61. (A): As per Buddhism, the factors at human personality are:

(*a*) **Material (Rupa), Perception (Sanna), Feeling (Vedana):**

Material (Rupa): Rupa refers to the physical aspect of existence, including the body and the external material world. It encompasses the tangible and visible aspects of reality. In the context of personality, the physical form, health, and bodily experiences are considered within this aggregate.

Perception (Sanna): Perception involves the mental processes of recognizing and interpreting sensory information. It includes the categorization and labeling of sensory input. In terms of personality, perception influences how individuals interpret events, people, and the world, shaping their understanding and responses.

Feeling (Vedana): Vedana is the aspect of experience related to feelings or sensations. It involves the emotional tone or quality of an experience, categorized as pleasant, unpleasant, or neutral. Feelings play a crucial role in shaping emotional responses and contributing to the overall disposition of an individual.

(*b*) **Disposition (Sakhara), Consciousness (Vinnaa):**

Disposition (Sakhara): Sakhara encompasses volitional formations or mental activities. It includes the mental processes related to thoughts, intentions, and habitual tendencies. In terms of personality, dispositions reflect the mental habits, inclinations, and patterns of thinking that influence behaviour and character.

Consciousness (Vinnaa): Viññaa refers to consciousness or awareness. It represents the subjective experience of being aware of sensory input and mental processes. Consciousness is fundamental to perception, cognition, and self-awareness. In the context of personality, consciousness is integral to how individuals perceive and understand themselves and the world.

62. (B): True statements about stimulus generalization are:

(*a*) **People's emotional reactions to one stimulus generalize to similar stimuli:** Stimulus generalization occurs when a conditioned response, which has been learned in response to a specific stimulus, also occurs in the presence of stimuli that are similar to the original stimulus. In the context of emotions, if an emotional response is conditioned to a particular stimulus, similar stimuli may also evoke a similar emotional reaction. For example, if someone develops a fear of a specific type of dog, they might generalize that fear to other dogs that share similar characteristics.

(*c*) **Normally desirable foods, such as cakes and pastries, are unappealing when shaped to resemble dog's feces:** This example illustrates stimulus generalization where a response (appetite or attraction) to normally desirable stimuli (cakes and pastries) is generalized to an undesirable stimulus (dog's feces) when the latter is shaped to resemble the former. The association of the shape with an unpleasant or aversive stimulus leads to a similar response. This demonstrates how a response conditioned to one stimulus (desirable food) can generalize to a similar but different stimulus (undesirable shape).

63. (*)

64. (D): The components of the Ethical Decision Making are:

(*a*) **Moral Awareness:** Moral awareness is the first step in the ethical decision-making process. It involves recognizing that a situation has moral or ethical implications. Individuals need to be aware that there is a moral dimension to consider before proceeding to make a decision. This awareness may involve recognizing potential consequences, considering values, and understanding the impact of actions on stakeholders.

(*c*) **Moral Intent:** After becoming morally aware, individuals move on to forming moral intent. This component involves the commitment to act in a manner consistent with ethical principles. It reflects the individual's genuine desire to make a morally acceptable decision and to follow through with actions that align with their ethical values. Moral intent reflects the internal commitment to doing what is considered right.

(*d*) **Moral Judgment:** Moral judgment is the process of evaluating different courses of action based on ethical principles, values, and relevant considerations. It involves weighing the potential consequences, considering the rights and interests of individuals involved, and applying moral reasoning to arrive at a decision. Moral judgment is central to making ethical decisions that are well-founded and aligned with ethical principles.

The three components—Moral Awareness, Moral Intent, and Moral Judgment—represent key stages in the ethical decision-making process. Individuals first need to recognize the ethical dimension of a situation, and then commit to acting ethically, and finally, make a moral judgment based on careful consideration of relevant factors. These components collectively contribute to ethical decision-making in various personal and professional contexts.

65. (C): Components of Informed Consent are:

(*a*) **Voluntarism:** Voluntarism refers to the principle that participation in research should be entirely voluntary and free from coercion. Participants should have the freedom to decide whether or not to take part in a study without facing any undue pressure or influence. Researchers must ensure that participants are not compelled, coerced, or manipulated into participating and that they can freely withdraw from the study at any time without negative consequences.

(*c*) **Information:** Providing information is a fundamental component of informed consent. Researchers are ethically obligated to furnish participants with comprehensive details about the research study. This information includes the purpose of the study, the procedures involved, potential risks and benefits, confidentiality measures, and any other pertinent details. It is crucial that participants receive enough information to make an informed decision about whether or not to participate.

(*d*) **Comprehension:** Comprehension is the understanding component of informed consent. It emphasizes that participants should not only be given information but should also comprehend that information. Researchers should ensure that the information is presented in a clear and accessible manner, using language and terms that participants can understand. This involves confirming that participants comprehend the purpose of the study, the potential risks and benefits, and any other critical aspects that might influence their decision to participate.

66. (C) **67. (D)** **68. (A)**

69. (C) **70. (B)** **71. (C)**

72. (A) **73. (B)** **74. (A)**

75. (C)

76. (A): The proper sequence of Erik Erikson's stages of psychosocial development are:

(*a*) **Trust vs. Mistrust:** ***Age Range:*** Infancy (0-1 year); ***Basic Strength:*** Hope

Explanation: In the infancy stage, the primary caregiver's consistency in meeting the baby's needs establishes the foundation for trust. When caregivers provide comfort, nourishment, and responsive care, infants develop a sense of security and hope. A trusting attitude toward the world and others is formed, contributing to a positive psychosocial foundation.

(*d*) **Autonomy vs. Doubt, Shame:** ***Age Range:*** Early Childhood (1-3 years); ***Basic Strength:*** Will

Explanation: The autonomy stage involves toddlers exploring their independence. Encouraging autonomy through choices and exploration fosters a sense of will and self-control. However, if caregivers are overly restrictive or critical, it can lead to doubt and shame. Successful resolution of this stage results in a willful and self-assured attitude towards challenges.

(*b*) **Initiative vs. Guilt:** ***Age Range:*** Preschool (3-6 years); ***Basic Strength:*** Purpose

Explanation: During the preschool years, children become more engaged in activities and initiatives. Positive reinforcement and encouragement for their creative endeavors lead to a sense of purpose and initiative. On the other hand, excessive criticism or limitations can result in feelings of guilt. Successful resolution fosters a sense of purposeful action and initiative.

(*c*) **Industriousness vs. Inferiority:** ***Age Range:*** Middle Childhood (6-11 years); ***Basic Strength:*** Competence

Explanation: In middle childhood, children are immersed in learning and mastering new skills. Support and positive reinforcement for their efforts contribute to a sense of industry and competence. Conversely, if experiences are marked by failure or lack of recognition, it can lead to feelings of inferiority. A successfully resolved stage results in a sense of competence and industry.

Erikson's psychosocial stages provide a framework for understanding the challenges and developmental tasks individuals face at different life stages.

77. **(C):** The steps involved in Action Research in correct sequence are:

(*c*) **Plan:** This initial step involves carefully planning the action research process. Researchers define the problem or issue they want to address, set clear objectives, and devise a plan for implementing interventions or changes. Planning is crucial for ensuring that the research is focused, systematic, and aligned with the goals of improving behavioural outcomes.

(*a*) **Action:** Once the plan is in place, researchers move to the action phase. This involves implementing the planned interventions or changes in the real-world setting. The action phase is where the researcher puts their ideas into practice, introducing new strategies or modifying existing ones to address the identified behavioural issues.

(*b*) **Observation:** During the action phase, researchers systematically observe and collect data related to the targeted behaviour or issue. This step involves carefully monitoring the effects of the interventions, collecting relevant information, and documenting observations. The goal is to gather empirical evidence to assess the impact of the implemented actions.

(*d*) **Reflection:** After the data collection, the reflection phase begins. Researchers analyze the data, reflect on the outcomes, and consider the implications of their interventions. This reflection is crucial for drawing insights, identifying what worked or didn't work, and understanding the factors influencing the observed behaviours. Reflection informs future planning and decision-making, creating a continuous cycle of improvement.

78. **(B):** The correct sequence of the movement of action during the action potential is:

(*a*) **Na^+ channels open, Na^+ begins to enter the cell:** At the resting potential, a stimulus triggers the opening of sodium (Na^+) channels. Sodium ions rush into the neuron due to the concentration gradient and electrical forces. This influx of positive ions leads to depolarization, shifting the membrane potential towards a more positive state.

(*c*) **K^+ channels open, K^+ begins to leave the cell:** As the membrane potential becomes more positive, potassium (K^+) channels begin to open. Potassium ions start to leave the neuron, initiating repolarization. This counteracts the sodium influx and helps restore the membrane potential towards its resting state.

(*e*) **Na^+ channels become refractory no more Na^+ enters the cell:** Following the depolarization phase, sodium channels become refractory and close. This prevents further entry of sodium ions into the neuron. The refractory period is essential for regulating the action potential and ensuring a controlled process.

(*b*) **K^+ channels continue to leave the cell, causing the membrane potential to return to the resting level:** Potassium channels remain open, allowing continued efflux of potassium ions. This ongoing movement of potassium ions contributes to repolarization, bringing the membrane potential back towards its resting level. The neuron returns to a negative resting potential.

(*d*) **K^+ channels close, Na^+ channels reset:** Once repolarization is complete, potassium channels close. Sodium channels reset to their original state, becoming capable of responding to new stimuli. The neuron is now in a state ready for another action potential.

79. (B): Correct sequence of the components of emotions in the two-factor theory is:

(*a*) **Stimulus:** The emotional process begins with a stimulus, an external event or situation that triggers a response. This could be anything from encountering a snake, receiving good news, or participating in an exciting event.

(*c*) **General Physiological Arousal:** In response to the stimulus, the body undergoes a general physiological arousal. This arousal is non-specific and includes physiological changes such as increased heart rate, sweating, and heightened alertness. The key point here is that the physiological response is not directly linked to a specific emotion but represents a state of physiological activation.

(*b*) **Cognitive Appraisal of Arousal:** Following the physiological arousal, individuals engage in cognitive appraisal. This involves interpreting and making sense of the arousal. During this stage, individuals consider the context, environmental cues, and their own thoughts to attribute meaning to the physiological response. For example, if the arousal is interpreted as stemming from encountering a snake, the emotion might be fear.

(*d*) **Subjective Experience of Emotion:** The cognitive appraisal leads to the subjective experience of a specific emotion. The individual consciously experiences the emotion based on their interpretation of the physiological arousal and the context. If the cognitive appraisal is one of joy, the person will subjectively feel happy; if it is fear, the person will subjectively feel afraid.

The two-factor theory highlights the importance of both physiological arousal and cognitive interpretation in the experience of emotion. The theory proposes that the same physiological arousal can lead to different emotional experiences depending on how it is cognitively appraised. This cognitive appraisal provides a nuanced and individualized aspect to the emotional experience, acknowledging the role of cognition in shaping our emotional responses to stimuli.

80. (B): Correct sequence at the steps involved in prosocial behaviour is:

(*b*) **Noticing something unusual:** This initial step involves being observant and attentive to the environment. Individuals become aware of a situation that might require help, whether it's a person in distress, an accident, or an opportunity for a simple act of kindness.

(*d*) **Interpreting the event as an emergency:** Once something unusual is noticed, individuals evaluate the situation to determine if it constitutes an emergency. This assessment involves gauging the urgency and potential harm associated with the situation. It sets the stage for understanding the seriousness of the circumstances.

(*a*) **Accepting the responsibility for helping:** If the situation is perceived as an emergency, individuals need to decide whether they are willing to take responsibility and provide help. This decision involves considering their own capabilities, willingness to intervene, and the ethical obligation to assist in the given context.

(*c*) **Deciding about possession of required knowledge or skills:** After accepting the responsibility, individuals assess their own competencies. They consider whether they have the necessary knowledge and skills to offer effective assistance. This step ensures that the help provided is meaningful and doesn't unintentionally escalate the situation.

(*e*) **Deciding to actually help:** The final and crucial step is making the conscious decision to take action. Individuals commit to helping the person in need, overcoming any personal apprehensions or doubts. This decision is driven by a genuine desire to make a positive impact on the situation and contribute to the well-being of others.

81. (A): Steps for the Development Model of counselling are:

(*a*) **Identification of blind spots:** In this initial step, the counselor and client work collaboratively to identify blind spots—unconscious patterns, beliefs, or behaviours that may be impeding the client's personal growth and well-being. This phase involves introspection and gaining awareness of aspects that might not be readily apparent.

(*c*) **Developing possibilities:** After the identification of blind spots, the counseling process moves towards developing possibilities. This phase involves exploring new avenues for growth and change. The client and counselor engage in discussions and reflections to brainstorm alternative ways of thinking, feeling, and behaving. The emphasis is on expanding the client's perspective and envisioning positive possibilities.

(*b*) **Brainstorming:** Brainstorming is a more specific and focused stage that occurs after identifying blind spots and before developing possibilities. During this phase, the client and counselor actively generate ideas and options for overcoming the identified limitations. It is a creative process that encourages free thinking and opens up avenues for potential solutions.

(*d*) **Force-field analysis:** The final step involves a comprehensive analysis of the forces that either support or hinder the desired change. Force-field analysis helps the client and counselor understand the dynamics at play. By identifying and evaluating the driving and restraining forces, they can develop effective strategies to overcome obstacles and strengthen the factors that contribute to positive change.

82. **(B):** Correct sequence of the physiological response to stress is:

(*c*) **Perception of stress:** The stress response begins with the perception of a stressor, which can be a physical or psychological challenge. This perception triggers a cascade of physiological events to prepare the body for a response.

(*b*) **Release of CRF from hypothalamus:** In response to the perception of stress, the hypothalamus, a region in the brain, releases corticotropin-releasing factor (CRF). CRF acts as a signaling molecule to initiate the stress response.

(*a*) **Release of Adrenocorticotropin hormone from pituitary gland (A):** CRF stimulates the pituitary gland to release adrenocorticotropin hormone (ACTH). ACTH then travels through the bloodstream to the adrenal glands, which are situated on top of the kidneys.

(*e*) **Glucocorticoid release from Adrenal gland:** Upon receiving the signal from ACTH, the adrenal glands release glucocorticoids, with cortisol being the primary one. These hormones play a crucial role in various stress responses, including the mobilization of energy stores and anti-inflammatory effects.

(*d*) **Suppression of immune system functioning:** Prolonged exposure to stress, particularly elevated levels of cortisol, can lead to the suppression of the immune system. While this response is adaptive in the short term, as it reallocates resources to address immediate threats, chronic stress can have detrimental effects on immune health over time.

83. **(B):** Proper sequence of Pancha Kosha is:

(*a*) **Annamaya Kosha:** This sheath is the physical body made up of the five elements—earth, water, fire, air, and space. It is the outermost layer and represents the tangible, material aspect of our existence. Annamaya Kosha is sustained through the intake of food, and its health and well-being are crucial for the overall balance of the individual.

(*d*) **Pranamaya Kosha:** This layer encompasses the vital energy or life force known as prana. Pranamaya Kosha is responsible for the dynamic aspects of the body, including breathing, circulation, and the flow of energy. Pranamaya Kosha ensures the continuous vitality and functioning of the physical body. It serves as a bridge between the physical and mental layers.

(*b*) **Manomaya Kosha:** Manomaya Kosha is the mental and emotional sheath, representing thoughts, feelings, desires, and sensory experiences. It is the layer where our mental and emotional responses originate. This sheath plays a crucial role in shaping our perceptions, reactions, and overall psychological well-being. It serves as an intermediary between the physical and intellectual realms.

(*c*) **Vijnanamaya Kosha:** Vijnanamaya Kosha is the intellectual sheath associated with discernment, reasoning, decision-making, and knowledge. It represents the capacity for higher cognitive functions. This sheath allows individuals to engage in intellectual pursuits, make informed choices, and process information at a deeper level. It contributes to the development of wisdom.

(*e*) **Anandamaya Kosha:** Anandamaya Kosha is the innermost layer, representing pure bliss, joy, and peace. It transcends the limitations of the other sheaths and is associated with the spiritual essence of an individual. Anandamaya Kosha is considered the source of deep fulfillment and connection to a higher state of consciousness. It reflects the innate happiness that goes beyond transient worldly experiences.

84. **(D):** Chronological order for the emergence of leadership approaches is:

(*c*) **Trait Approach:** The trait approach emerged in the early 20th century and sought to identify specific personality traits that were believed to be associated with effective leadership. Traits such as confidence, decisiveness, and intelligence were thought to distinguish leaders from non-leaders. This approach assumed that effective leaders possessed a set of inherent qualities. Researchers aimed to identify a universal set of traits that would predict leadership success. However, it faced challenges in establishing a consistent set of traits applicable across various contexts.

(*b*) **Behavioural Approach:** The behavioural approach shifted the focus from inherent traits to observable behaviours. Researchers, including Kurt Lewin and others, conducted studies to identify different leadership styles and behaviours. This approach categorized leadership into autocratic, democratic, and laissez-faire styles. Leadership effectiveness was seen as a result of specific behaviours exhibited by leaders. The focus was on what leaders did rather than who they were. The Ohio State studies and the University of Michigan studies were influential in shaping this approach.

(*d*) **Contingency Approach:** The contingency approach, popularized by Fred Fiedler and others, recognized that effective leadership is contingent on various factors, including the situation, the leader's style, and the relationship between the leader and followers. Fiedler's Contingency Model proposed that different leadership styles are more effective in different situations. Contingency theorists argued that there is no one-size-fits-all leadership style. The effectiveness of a leadership style depends on the specific circumstances and characteristics of the situation. This approach introduced the idea of matching leadership styles to situational factors.

(*b*) **Transformational Approach:** The transformational approach emerged in the late 20th century, notably through the work of James MacGregor Burns and later expanded by Bernard Bass. Transformational leaders are characterized by their ability to inspire and motivate followers, encouraging them to exceed their own expectations. Transformational leaders focus on creating a shared vision, fostering innovation, and promoting positive change within organizations. They emphasize charisma, individualized consideration, intellectual stimulation, and inspirational motivation as key elements of their leadership style.

85. (B): The sections of the vertebrae from top to bottom are:

(*c*) **Cervical Vertebrae:** The cervical vertebrae, denoted by C1 to C7, constitute the uppermost section of the spinal column. These vertebrae are characterized by their relatively small size and light weight. Notably, the first two cervical vertebrae, known as the atlas (C1) and axis (C2), have unique structures. The atlas supports the skull and allows nodding movements, while the axis facilitates rotational movement. Collectively, the cervical vertebrae provide the necessary flexibility for the neck, enabling a range of movements crucial for daily activities.

(*a*) **Thoracic Vertebrae:** Situated below the cervical vertebrae, the thoracic vertebrae span the mid-back region and are labeled T1 to T12. These vertebrae are intricately associated with the ribs, featuring facets that articulate with the rib heads. This connection contributes to the structure of the rib cage, offering protection to vital organs within the chest. The thoracic region plays a pivotal role in providing stability to the spinal column and supporting the upper body's framework.

(*d*) **Lumbar Vertebrae:** The lumbar vertebrae, numbered L1 to L5, represent the lower back and are distinguished by their substantial size and strength. Functionally, the lumbar region bears the majority of the body's weight and is integral for activities such as standing and lifting. Due to the significant load it supports, the lumbar spine is a common site for lower back pain. These vertebrae contribute to the overall stability and mobility of the spine.

(*b*) **Sacral Vertebrae:** At the base of the spinal column, the sacral vertebrae form the sacrum, a triangular bone that connects the spine to the pelvic bones. Comprising five fused vertebrae labeled S1 to S5, the sacrum contributes to the stability of the pelvic girdle. Articulating with the hip bones (ilia), the sacrum forms the posterior part of the pelvis.

This section of the spine plays a crucial role in weight transmission and pelvic support.

86. (A): Assertion (A): "There are five universal human needs according to reality therapy." This assertion is accurate in reflecting the core tenets of reality therapy, a therapeutic approach developed by William Glasser. Reality therapy posits that individuals have five innate and universal psychological needs, which, when satisfied, contribute to mental well-being and effective functioning.

Reason (R): "These needs are - survival, love & belonging, power, freedom, and fun." Reason (R) provides a specific enumeration of the five universal human needs according to reality therapy:

Survival: The basic need for sustaining life and well-being.

Love & Belonging: The need for meaningful connections, relationships, and a sense of belonging.

Power: The need for personal agency, influence, and a sense of control over one's life.

Freedom: The need for autonomy, independence, and the ability to make choices.

Fun: The need for enjoyment, pleasure, and a positive emotional experience.

The Reason directly supports the Assertion by providing a concise and accurate list of the five fundamental human needs recognized in reality therapy. In this context, Reason (R) serves as a correct explanation for Assertion (A).

87. (B): Assertion (A): "To eliminate the impact of an extraneous independent variable, the researcher can choose participants who are homogeneous on that independent variable." This assertion is correct. Researchers often try to control for extraneous variables by selecting participants who are similar or homogeneous in terms of those variables. This helps minimize the impact of these extraneous factors on the study's outcomes.

Reason (R): "'Matching' is one of the methods to control extraneous variance." This reason is also correct. Matching involves pairing participants who are similar on a specific variable, ensuring that the groups being compared are comparable in terms of that variable. It is indeed a method used to control extraneous variance.

However, while both statements are correct, the reason does not directly explain or serve as a justification for the assertion. Therefore, Reason (R) is not the correct explanation of Assertion (A).

88. (D): Assertion (A): "Monozygotic twins are called fraternal twins, who share half of their genes. Both members of the twins may be males or females."

This statement is incorrect. Monozygotic twins, commonly known as identical twins, originate from a single fertilized egg that splits into two embryos. As a result, monozygotic twins are genetically identical, sharing 100% of their genes. The assertion inaccurately refers to monozygotic twins as "fraternal", which is a term typically used for dizygotic twins.

Reason (R): "Dizygotic twins develop from two different eggs and share the genes like a brother and sister. One of the twins may be a male, and the other one may be a female".

This statement is correct. Dizygotic twins, also known as fraternal twins, arise from the fertilization of two separate eggs by two different sperm. As a result, they share approximately 50% of their genetic material, similar to the genetic relationship between siblings born at different times. The reason accurately describes the genetic characteristics of dizygotic twins.

89. (A): Assertion (A): Project Head Start and other preschool quality programs can boost children's chances of success in the future by increasing their school readiness. This assertion is considered true based on the evidence provided, indicating the positive impact of preschool programs on various aspcets of child development and school readiness.

Reason (R): Genes and experience together determine cognitive and social skills: This reason is also considered true. It aligns with established principles in developmental psychology, emphasizing the interplay between genetic factors and environmental experiences in shaping cognitive and social skills.

In this context, Reason R (the interplay between genes and experiences) is considered the correct explanation for why preschool quality programs like Project Head Start contribute to children's success.

Both (A) and (B) are true, and (R) is the correct explanation of (A).

90. (B): Statement I: Motivating factors energize behaviour but give no direction.

This statement doesn't capture the full essence of motivation. Motivation not only provides the energy to engage in a behaviour but also guides the direction of that behaviour. Whether the motivation is intrinsic (internal) or extrinsic (external), it often shapes the goals, choices, and focus of the individual. For example, someone motivated by a passion for art will be energized to create, and this motivation inherently guides the direction of their artistic endeavors.

Statement II: Motivational states arise only from external incentive factors.

This statement overlooks the significant role of intrinsic motivation. Motivational states can certainly be influenced by external factors like rewards or punishments, but they can also emerge from internal sources. Intrinsic motivation arises from personal enjoyment, curiosity, a sense of purpose, or the inherent satisfaction derived from an activity. Individuals can be motivated to engage in activities without relying solely on external incentives.

91. (C) **92. (C)** **93. (A)**

94. (B) **95. (C)**

96. (C): Lev S. Vygotsky's theory, known as the socio-cultural theory of cognitive development, emphasizes the profound impact of social and cultural factors on a child's cognitive growth. According to Vygotsky, the Zone of Proximal Development (ZPD) is a crucial concept, suggesting that children can achieve more advanced cognitive skills with the assistance of a more knowledgeable partner, typically an experienced adult or peer. The instructional process derived from this theory involves the adept partner adjusting their support to align with the child's learning needs during interaction. Vygotsky underscores the role of psychological tools and signs in guiding and enhancing the thinking processes. This socio-cultural perspective places significance on the influence of cultural and social contexts in shaping cognitive development, highlighting the collaborative and dynamic nature of learning.

97. (B): The Zone of Proximal Development (ZPD) is a concept central to Lev Vygotsky's socio-cultural theory of cognitive development. It refers to the range of tasks that a learner can perform with the assistance of a more knowledgeable individual, such as a teacher, mentor, or peer, but cannot yet perform independently. Vygotsky proposed that learning occurs most effectively when a learner is guided through tasks within their ZPD, as this represents the "sweet spot" of challenge and support. The ZPD recognizes the potential for cognitive growth by engaging in activities that are just beyond the learner's current level of capability. This dynamic zone emphasizes the importance of social interaction and collaborative learning, as the assistance provided by a knowledgeable partner facilitates the acquisition of new skills and knowledge, ultimately fostering cognitive development.

98. (A): The Zone of Proximal Development (ZPD), as defined by Vygotsky, represents the realm of learning where a child can benefit significantly from the guidance and support of a more knowledgeable individual, such as a teacher or mentor. It is the gap between what a child can achieve independently and the higher level of development attainable with assistance. This dynamic zone is characterized by the sensitivity to learning, acknowledging that learners are most receptive to acquiring new skills and knowledge when guided within this specific range. The ZPD underscores the importance of social interaction and collaboration, emphasizing that learning is most effective when tailored to the learner's current abilities with the support of a knowledgeable partner, fostering cognitive development in a way that transcends individual capabilities.

99. (D): Scaffolding, in the context of Vygotsky's socio-cultural theory of cognitive development, refers to the instructional process where a more knowledgeable partner, often an experienced adult or peer, provides structured support to a learner. This support is tailored to the learner's specific needs and abilities, allowing them to accomplish tasks within their Zone of Proximal Development (ZPD). The knowledgeable partner adjusts the level and type of support based on the learner's progress, gradually reducing assistance as the learner becomes more proficient. The term "scaffolding" metaphorically captures the idea of providing a temporary framework or support structure that helps the learner reach higher levels of understanding and skill. This dynamic interaction promotes independent learning, as the learner gains the necessary skills and knowledge to perform tasks without assistance over time.

100. (B): According to Vygotsky, psychological tools and signs such as language, counting, mnemonics, algebraic symbols, art, and writing are termed as "mediators". These mediators play a crucial role in facilitating and directing the thinking process. Vygotsky emphasized that these cultural and psychological tools are not just aids but integral components that shape and guide cognitive development. Language, for instance, serves as a powerful mediator by allowing individuals to internalize knowledge, communicate, and engage in complex thought processes. The use of symbols, both linguistic and mathematical, enhances cognitive functions and problem-solving abilities. The concept of mediation underscores the idea that these tools, deeply rooted in cultural and social contexts, mediate the relationship between an individual and their environment, significantly influencing cognitive growth and learning.

YOUR SPACE

Previous Years' Paper (Solved)

National Testing Agency (NTA)

UGC-NET Junior Research Fellowship & Assistant Professor Eligibility Exam

PSYCHOLOGY, March–2023

(Online exam held on 15-03-2023)

PAPER-II

Note: *This paper contains* ***hundred (100)*** *objective type questions of* ***two (2)*** *marks each.* ***All*** *questions are* ***compulsory.***

1. The term 'integral yoga' is popularized by:
A. Panini
B. Patanjali
C. Sri Aurobindo
D. Ramakrishna Paramahansa

2. Which of the following correlation coefficient represents the variables with the weakest degree of relationship?
A. –.84 B. –.56
C. +.75 D. +.08

3. If observers disagree 15 times out of 75, then the inter-rater reliability is:
A. 50% B. 80%
C. 20% D. 60%

4. If a student scored 12 on a test, of which the mean is 16 and the standard deviation is 4, what is his z-score?
A. –1.0 B. +1.0
C. +3.0 D. 0.0

5. Which one is the correct formula for variance?

A. $\text{Variance} = \frac{(\Sigma X - \Sigma \overline{X})^2}{N}$

B. $\text{Variance} = \frac{\Sigma (X - \overline{X})^2}{N}$

C. $\text{Variance} = \frac{(\Sigma X - \overline{X})^2}{N^2}$

D. $\text{Variance} = \frac{(\Sigma X^2 - \overline{X})^2}{N}$

6. A researcher is interested in testing the effectiveness of Pre-post intervention on a single group. The statistical test that could be used is:
A. Correlation B. Chi square
C. ANOVA D. '*t*' test

7. Which of the following is correct?
A. Test-retest reliability is determined by assessing the degree of relationship between scores on one half of a test with scores on the other half of the test.
B. Alternate forms reliability is determined by assessing the degree of relationship between scores on two different equivalent tests.
C. Split-half reliability is determined by assessing the degree of relationship between scores on the same test, administered on two different occasions.
D. Internal reliability is the extent to which the effect of the dependent variable is the result of the independent variable and not some other aspect of the study.

8. CogScreen, a computer assisted tool, has been used in the selection of ______.
A. Human Resource Managers
B. Doctors
C. Airline pilots
D. Electronic Media journalists

9. Utility of Semantic differential scale is not contingent upon:
A. Finding appropriate adjective pairs
B. Meaning of the words
C. Length of the items in the scale
D. Contextual reference of the items

10. Which structure of the Limbic system is mostly responsible for controlling the emotional behaviour of fear?
A. Amygdala
B. Hippocampus
C. Cingulate gyrus
D. Mammilary bodies

11. REM sleep is characterized by one of the following conditions:
A. PGO waves B. ULPA
C. Flip-flop D. Histamine

12. Class is to the ______ property of measurement as time is to the ______ property of measurement.
A. Magnitude. Identity
B. Equal unit size, magnitude
C. Identity, absolute zero
D. Absolute zero, equal unit size

13. A genetic inability to metabolize amino acid phenylalanine leads to one of the following conditions:
A. Down's syndrome
B. Autism
C. Cerebral Palsy
D. PKU

14. A person who had experienced an intensive negative emotion fails to recollect the emotional event. This is known as:
A. Forgetting due to interference
B. Retrieval failure
C. Motivated Forgetting
D. Forgetting due to decay

15. The tendency of a consumer to decide on buying a product that was repeatedly appearing on T.V. screen is attributed to:
A. Effectiveness of the product
B. Price of the product
C. Subliminal perception
D. Utility of the product

16. Brain lesions of subcortical regions produced by passing electrical current through an insulated electrode is called:
A. Excitotoxic lesions
B. Radiofrequency lesions
C. Sham lesions
D. Excitatory lesions

17. A person dressed in a gorilla suit walked unnoticed through a group of students playing basket ball. How can this phenomenon be described?
A. Change of attention
B. Attention loss
C. Inattention blindness
D. Attention lapse

18. The light sensation from the left and right visual field travels to the visual cortex through:
A. Lateral geniculate nucleus
B. Superior colliculus
C. Optic radiations
D. Pulvinar nucleus

19. Step by step interaction of operating a mechanical gadget is an example of:
A. Trouble shooting
B. Algorithm
C. Heuristic approach
D. Means-end analysis

20. Making a reference to a respected person believed to be well informed, when one's own logic or reasoning is weak, is called:
A. Arguing in circles
B. False Analogy
C. Appeal to authority
D. Overgeneralization

21. When a person who needs to use a tool in a novel way but cannot do, it is attributed to:
A. Lack of interest
B. Lack of motor skill
C. Functional fixedness
D. Lack of motivation

22. Which of the following examines information processing approach to intelligence?
A. Overall success in living
B. Structure of intelligence
C. Functions of intelligence
D. Processes underlying intelligent behaviour

23. In the Drive Reduction Theory given by Hull, SHR stands for:
A. Excitatory potential
B. Drive reduction
C. Habit strength
D. Inhibitory potential

24. Which of the following attributions indicate an optimistic explanatory style in the face of stress?
A. Internal cause, specific impact, and unstable outcome
B. External cause, specific impact and unstable outcome
C. Internal cause, global impact and unstable outcome
D. Internal cause, global impact and stable outcome

25. An individual encountering prolonged stress is prone to suffer from skin infection because:
A. Corticotropin Releasing Factor (CRF) flows into the blood causing damage to the skin
B. Adrenalin released into blood absorbs the vitamin B that is necessary for nourishing the skin
C. Cortisol released into blood causes damage to the T and B cells in the WBC
D. Corticosteroids get deposited in the skin due to stress

26. Hardiness is a combination of three cognitive factors involved in the interpretation of life events. Find out from the following which is not correct for hardy personality.
A. Control B. Coping
C. Challenge D. Commitment

27. Cognitive dissonance theory explains that attitude change occurs as a result of:
A. Distance between one's belief and behaviour
B. Reduction of the unpleasant arousal people experience while they engage in a behaviour that conflicts with their attitude
C. A resolution of conflict by a neutral third party who studies both sides and imposes a settlement
D. A strategy in which people create obstacles to success so that potential failure can be blamed on these external factors

28. Social loafing is defined as:
A. Personal characteristics that others view as insurmountable handicaps preventing competent or morally trustworthy behaviour
B. The tendency by group members to slack off and reduce their effort on additive tasks, which cause the group's output to fall short of its potential
C. The set of interpersonal relationships associated with the social position a person occupies
D. Individuals' concept of self in specific social roles

29. Which of the following is a group decision-making technique?
A. Brainstorming
B. Ordinal group technique
C. Risky shift
D. Random shift

30. Which of the following is correct about the result of Milgram's study?
A. In the real word, most people will refuse to follow orders to inflict harm on a stranger
B. Many people will obey an authority figure even if innocent people get hurt
C. Most people are willing to give obviously wrong answers when ordered to do so
D. Most people stick to their own judgement even when group members unanimously disagree

31. Which of the following definitions is not correct according to Gestalt therapy?

A. Introjection refers to the internalized rules governing our thoughts, feelings and behaviour which we absorb from parental and other influences from childhood onwards.

B. Retroflection refers to the process whereby we do to ourselves what we would like to do to someone else.

C. Confluence refers to the style of relating to other people which is based on an absence of conflict and a conviction that everyone should be in agreement

D. Deflection refers to the process of attributing aspects of ourselves to other people

32. The counsellor can use the following formula for a rough assessment of severity of client's problem, prescribed by Mehrabian and Reed (1969).

A. Distress + Uncontrollability + Frequency

B. Distress + Uncontrollability – Frequency

C. Distress × Uncontrollability × Frequency

D. (Distress + Controllability) × Frequency

33. Which of the following name is associated with Play Therapy?

A. Eric Berne

B. Elizabeth Hurlock

C. Gerard Egan

D. Virginia Axline

34. In REBT, treatment is based on:

A. Assessment of goals and activating events only

B. Diagnostic categories, beliefs and consequences

C. Believes and consequences only

D. Assessment of goals, activating events, believes and consequences

35. Transactional analysis is concerned with four major areas of analysis. Which out of the following does not come under this?

A. Structural analysis

B. Hypnotic analysis

C. Ground analysis

D. Game analysis

36. Which of the following is not relevant to a cardiac patient's behaviour of adherence to treatment?

A. Self-efficacy

B. Perception about how serious is the condition

C. Sense of humour

D. Perception of how much control one can exercise on health

37. Which of the following is not a risk factor for hypertension?

A. Obesity

B. Atherosclerosis

C. Multiple Sclerosis

D. Exposure to stress

38. Actions taken to identify and treat an illness or injury early with an aim of stopping or reversing the problem comes under:

A. Primary prevention

B. Secondary prevention

C. Tertiary prevention

D. Protection prevention

39. In the context of health behaviour, Matarazzo (1984) claims:

A. Behaviour that protects health as 'behavioural immunogenes' and that puts health at risk as 'behavioural compromise'

B. Behaviour that protects health as 'behavioural immunogenes' and that puts health at risk as 'Behavioural pathogens'

C. Behaviour that protects health as 'psycho immunogenes' and that puts health at risk is 'Immunocompromisers'

D. Behaviour that protects health as 'Immunological behaviour' and that puts health at risk as 'pathological behaviour'

40. Martin Seligman proposed a theory of authentic happiness and well being which contains five elements. Which of the following does not come under Seligman's theory?

A. Positive emotion
B. Meaning that defines authentic happiness
C. Resilience
D. Accomplishment

41. Which of the following is correct about cognitive perspective?
(*a*) Thinking and understanding about the world
(*b*) Information processing
(*c*) Overt behaviour only
(*d*) Similarity of thinking and working of a computer

Choose the ***most appropriate*** answer from the options given below:
A. (*a*) and (*d*) only
B. (*c*) and (*d*) only
C. (*a*), (*b*) and (*d*) only
D. (*a*) and (*b*) only

42. According to Indian concept of Self, elements of Psychological self include:
(*a*) Manas (*b*) Buddhi
(*c*) Anthakarna (*d*) Dhyana

Choose the ***correct*** answer from the options given below:
A. (*a*), (*b*) and (*d*) only
B. (*b*), (*c*) and (*d*) only
C. (*a*), (*c*) and (*d*) only
D. (*a*), (*b*) and (*c*) only

43. Which of the following can be used to determine the number of factors to be extracted in factor analysis?
(*a*) Scree-plot
(*b*) Orthogonal rotation
(*c*) Eigen value
(*d*) Factor Loading

Choose the ***most appropriate*** answer from the options given below:
A. (*a*) only B. (*b*) and (*c*) only
C. (*c*) only D. (*a*) and (*c*) only

44. Which of the following are the types of probability sample?
(*a*) Simple random sampling
(*b*) Proportionate stratified sampling
(*c*) Disproportionate stratified sampling
(*d*) Saturation sampling

Choose the ***correct*** answer from the options given below:
A. (*a*), (*b*) and (*c*) only
B. (*b*), (*c*) and (*d*) only
C. (*a*), (*c*) and (*d*) only
D. (*a*), (*b*) and (*d*) only

45. Which of the following statements are true of aptitude?
(*a*) They are acquired
(*b*) They are innate
(*c*) Training ensures optimal performance
(*d*) Aptitudes and interests are positively related

Choose the ***most appropriate*** answer from the options given below:
A. (*a*) and (*b*) only
B. (*b*) and (*c*) only
C. (*a*), (*b*) and (*c*) only
D. (*c*) and (*d*) only

46. What is true about norm in Psychological Test?
(*a*) Norm helps as comparative device
(*b*) 'Percentage' is a type of norm used by some psychometricians
(*c*) T-score is a type of standard score norm
(*d*) Raw score is converted to derived score for norm interpretation

Choose the ***most appropriate*** answer from the options given below:
A. (*a*) and (*d*) only
B. (*a*), (*b*) and (*d*) only
C. (*a*), (*c*) and (*d*) only
D. (*a*), (*b*) and (*c*) only

47. True description about Differential Aptitude Test (DAT) are:
(*a*) It has eight sub tests
(*b*) Meant for students from grade 8 to grade 12
(*c*) Meant for students in the age of 8 to 12 years
(*d*) It has also been adapted by Indian Psychologists

Choose the ***most appropriate*** answer from the options given below:

A. (*a*) and (*b*) only
B. (*a*) and (*c*) only
C. (*b*), (*c*) and (*d*) only
D. (*a*), (*b*) and (*d*) only

48. Which of the following domains are assessed by Neuropsychological tests?

(*a*) Language
(*b*) Opinion
(*c*) Memory
(*d*) Executive Functioning
(*e*) Reaction

Choose the ***correct*** answer from the options given below:

A. (*b*), (*c*) and (*e*) only
B. (*a*), (*c*) and (*d*) only
C. (*c*), (*d*) and (*e*) only
D. (*a*), (*b*) and (*d*) only

49. Which of the following statement/s are True of Biofeedback?

(*a*) It is accurate
(*b*) Behaviour can be modified through biofeedback
(*c*) It helps in bringing involuntary actions to voluntary actions
(*d*) It is one of the components of polygraphy

Choose the ***most appropriate*** answer from the options given below:

A. (*a*), (*b*) and (*c*) only
B. (*a*) and (*b*) only
C. (*c*) and (*d*) only
D. (*a*), (*b*) and (*d*) only

50. Which of the following are the motivating factors in learning:

(*a*) Intelligence
(*b*) Nature of task
(*c*) Knowledge of result
(*d*) Reinforcement

Choose the ***most appropriate*** answer from the options given below:

A. (*a*), (*b*) and (*c*) only
B. (*b*), (*c*) and (*d*) only
C. (*b*) and (*c*) only
D. (*a*) and (*c*) only

51. Which one is not correct about classical conditioning:

(*a*) Classical conditioning is also known as respondent conditioning.
(*b*) A previously natural stimulus comes to elicit a response after it is paired with a stimulus that automatically elicits that response.
(*c*) It is based on the fact that certain stimuli automatically elicit certain response without learning.
(*d*) Classical Conditioning is also known as Instrumental Conditioning.
(*e*) In Classical conditioning there is no association between stimulus and response.

Choose the ***correct*** answer from the options given below:

A. (*a*) and (*d*) only
B. (*a*), (*c*) and (*d*) only
C. (*b*), (*c*), (*d*) only
D. (*c*) and (*d*) only

52. Which of the following are true of perceptual constancy?

(*a*) Shape (*b*) Illumination
(*c*) Colour (*d*) Distance

Choose the ***most appropriate*** answer from the options given below:

A. (*a*) and (*c*) only B. (*a*) and (*b*) only
C. (*b*) and (*c*) only D. (*b*) and (*d*) only

53. Which of the following are The types of longterm memory?

(*a*) Declarative memory
(*b*) Flash bulb memory
(*c*) Episodic memory
(*d*) Sensory memory

Choose the ***most appropriate*** answer from the options given below:

A. (*a*), (*b*) and (*c*) only
B. (*b*), (*c*) and (*d*) only
C. (*a*) and (*d*) only
D. (*a*) and (*c*) only

54. Which of the following statements are true?
(*a*) All intelligent persons are creative
(*b*) Creativity is also known as divergent thinking
(*c*) Creativity is genetically determined
(*d*) Research is not conclusive about the relationship between intelligence and creativity

Choose the ***correct*** answer from the options given below:
A. (*a*) and (*b*) only B. (*b*) and (*c*) only
C. (*a*) and (*d*) only D. (*b*) and (*d*) only

55. Which of the following indicate aspects of language development?
(*a*) Pragmatics (*b*) Syntax
(*c*) Imprinting (*d*) Semantics

Choose the ***correct*** answer from the options given below:
A. (*a*), (*b*) and (*c*) only
B. (*a*) and (*b*) only
C. (*a*), (*b*) and (*d*) only
D. (*b*) and (*c*) only

56. Which of the following is true about linguistic-relativity hypothesis?
(*a*) Thought produces language
(*b*) Language shapes perception and understanding
(*c*) Language determines thought
(*d*) Thinking and language interact

Choose the ***most appropriate*** answer from the options given below:
A. (*a*) and (*d*) only
B. (*b*) and (*c*) only
C. (*a*) only
D. (*b*), (*c*) and (*d*) only

57. Which of the following statements related to stress are correct?
(*a*) Anthropogenic stress refers to stressors such as crowding
(*b*) The impact of earth energies on human well being is called 'Geopathic Stress'
(*c*) Stress due to the efforts of the individual to fit oneself into the design of man made objects is called 'Energetic stress'
(*d*) 'Ergonomic Stress' refers to the stress induced due to exposure to radioactive rays

Choose the ***most appropriate*** answer from the options given below:
A. (*a*) and (*b*) only
B. (*b*) and (*c*) only
C. (*c*) and (*d*) only
D. (*a*) and (*d*) only

58. Which of the following is true with reference to psychological stress?
(*a*) Stress is a temporary phenomenon
(*b*) Stress is a subjective perception
(*c*) Personality and stress are not related
(*d*) A certain degree of stress is needed for optimal performance.

Choose the ***correct*** answer from the options given below:
A. (*a*), (*b*) and (*c*) only
B. (*b*), (*c*) and (*d*) only
C. (*a*), (*c*) and (*d*) only
D. (*a*), (*b*) and (*d*) only

59. Which of the following is true about leadership?
(*a*) Leaders influence followers
(*b*) Situation is not important in leadership
(*c*) All managers are leaders
(*d*) Transactional leaders are different from transformational leaders

Choose the ***correct*** answer from the options given below:
A. (*a*) and (*d*) only
B. (*a*), (*b*) and (*d*) only
C. (*a*), (*c*) and (*d*) only
D. (*a*) and (*b*) only

60. Which of the following is applicable to Fiedler's contingency model of leadership effectiveness?
(*a*) The leader's position power
(*b*) The degree of task structure
(*c*) The leader-member relationship
(*d*) The inborn traits of the leader

Choose the ***most appropriate*** answer from the options given below:

A. (*a*) and (*b*) only

B. (*a*), (*b*) and (*c*) only

C. (*d*) only

D. (*a*), (*b*) and (*d*) only

61. Transactional Analysis refers to the ego states such as:

(*a*) Critical Parent, Adult

(*b*) Parent, Child, Adult

(*c*) Nurturant Parent, Little Professor

(*d*) Adapted child, Deviant child

Choose the ***correct*** answer from the options given below:

A. (*a*), (*b*) and (*c*) only

B. (*c*) and (*d*) only

C. (*b*), (*c*) and (*d*) only

D. (*a*) and (*d*) only

62. In force-field analysis the counselee analyses:

(*a*) The force one has to apply in the field to assert oneself

(*b*) The forces that constitute one's resources

(*c*) The force applied by the counsellor in initiating action

(*d*) Facilitating factors and restraining factors in the situation

Choose the ***most appropriate*** answer from the options given below:

A. (*a*) only B. (*a*) and (*c*) only

C. (*b*) and (*d*) only D. (*d*) only

63. In counselling, 'advanced empathy' includes:

(*a*) Connecting islands and identifying themes

(*b*) Identifying themes and brain storming

(*c*) Making the implicit explicit and identifying themes

(*d*) Connecting islands and paraphrasing.

Choose the ***correct*** answer from the options given below:

A. (*a*) and (*b*) only

B. (*a*) and (*c*) only

C. (*a*) and (*d*) only

D. (*a*), (*b*) and (*d*) only

64. The principle of Classical Conditioning is used in:

(*a*) Token economy

(*b*) Systematic desensitization

(*c*) Electroconvulsion therapy

(*d*) Aversion therapy

Choose the ***correct*** answer from the options given below:

A. (*a*) and (*b*) only B. (*a*) and (*c*) only

C. (*b*) and (*c*) only D. (*b*) and (*d*) only

65. In the Transactional Analysis, Ego State Analysis involves analyzing:

(*a*) Id, Ego, Super Ego

(*b*) Alter Ego

(*c*) Parent. Adult, child

(*d*) Voluntary and Involuntary Ego

Choose the ***most appropriate*** answer from the options given below:

A. (*a*) and (*c*) only B. (*b*) only

C. (*c*) only D. (*c*) and (*d*) only

66. Match List I with List II.

List-I	List-II
(*a*) An inferential test used to determine effect size for a chi-square test; the correlation used when both measured variables are dicho-tomous and nominal	I. Point-biserial correlation coefficient
(*b*) The correlation used when one of its variables is measured on a dichotomous nominal scale and the other is measured on an interval or ratio scale	II. Regression analysis
(*c*) A procedure that allows to predict an individual's score on one variable based on knowing one or more variables	III. Partial correlation

(*d*) A correlation technique that involves measuring three variables and then statistically removing the effect of the third variable from the correlation of the remaining two variables	IV. Phi-coefficient

Choose the ***correct*** answer from the options given below:

	(*a*)	(*b*)	(*c*)	(*d*)
A.	IV	II	III	I
B.	III	II	IV	I
C.	II	IV	III	I
D.	IV	I	II	III

67. Match List I with List II.

List-I	**List-II**
(*a*) Phenomenology	I. Constructionist Approach
(*b*) Narrative analysis	II. Social media
(*c*) Grounded theory	III. Eidetic variation
(*d*) Netnographic Analysis	IV. Theoretical coding

Choose the ***correct*** answer from the options given below:

	(*a*)	(*b*)	(*c*)	(*d*)
A.	I	III	IV	II
B.	II	IV	III	I
C.	III	I	IV	II
D.	IV	I	III	II

68. Match List I with List II.

List-I	**List-II**
(*a*) Non-parametric test used to determine difference between three or more groups on a ranked variable for between subjects design	I. Mann Whitney Test
(*b*) Non-parametric test for seeing whether the number of times scores from one sample are ranked significantly higher than scores from another unrelated sample	II. Wilcoxon-Signed Rank Test
(*c*) Non-parametric test for assessing whether the scores from two samples that come from the same or similar cases differ significantly	III. Kruskal Wallis Test
(*d*) Non-parametric test for determining whether the mean ranks of three or more related samples under two factors differ significantly	IV. Friedman's Test

Choose the ***correct*** answer from the options given below:

	(*a*)	(*b*)	(*c*)	(*d*)
A.	III	II	IV	I
B.	III	I	II	IV
C.	IV	II	III	I
D.	I	II	IV	III

69. Match List I with List II.

List-I *(Attitude Scales)*	**List-II** *(Psychologists)*
(*a*) Summated Rating scale	I. Thurstone
(*b*) Semantic differential scale	II. Guttman
(*c*) Equal Appearing Interval scale	III. Likert
(*d*) Cumulative scale	IV. Osgood

Choose the ***correct*** answer from the options given below:

	(*a*)	(*b*)	(*c*)	(*d*)
A.	IV	I	II	III
B.	III	IV	I	II
C.	III	IV	II	I
D.	IV	I	III	II

70. Match List I with List II.

List-I	**List-II**
(*a*) Turner's syndrome	I. An imbalance in X chromosome where two X from the ovam combine with a Y-sperm

(*b*) Fragile-X syndrome — II. An extra 21st chromosome

(*c*) Down's syndrome — III. Ovum containing on X chromosome is fertilized by an 'X' bearing sperm

(*d*) Klinefelter syndrome — IV. The X chromosome is compressed or broken

Choose the ***correct*** answer from the options given below:

	(*a*)	(*b*)	(*c*)	(*d*)
A.	I	III	II	IV
B.	III	IV	II	I
C.	II	III	I	IV
D.	III	II	IV	I

71. Match List I with List II.

List-I	List-II
(*a*) Semantic Memory	I. Memory for general knowledge and facts about the world as well as memory for the rules of logic that are used to deduce other facts
(*b*) Episodic Memory	II. Memory centered on a specific important event that are vivid as if they represented a snapshot of the event
(*c*) Flashbulb Memory	III. Memory for skills and habits
(*d*) Procedural Memory	IV. Memory for events that occur in a particular time, place or context

Choose the ***correct*** answer from the options given below:

	(*a*)	(*b*)	(*c*)	(*d*)
A.	I	II	IV	III
B.	I	II	III	IV
C.	II	III	I	IV
D.	I	IV	II	III

72. Match List I with List II.

List-I	List-II
(*a*) Thurstone	I. Triarchic Theory
(*b*) Gardner	II. Set of seven primary mental abilities
(*c*) Sternberg	III. Multiple intelligence
(*d*) J.P. Das	IV. Pass Model

Choose the ***correct*** answer from the options given below:

	(*a*)	(*b*)	(*c*)	(*d*)
A.	IV	I	II	III
B.	II	I	III	IV
C.	II	III	I	IV
D.	II	III	IV	I

73. Match List I with List II.

List-I	List-II
(*a*) Inductive reasoning	I. Inferring specific instances from general principles or rules
(*b*) Deductive reasoning	II. Cognitive short-cuts that provide adequately accurate inferences for most of the time
(*c*) Heuristics	III. Inferring general principles or rules from specific facts
(*d*) Algorithm	IV. A procedure that consists of a series of steps to solve a problem

Choose the ***correct*** answer from the options given below:

	(*a*)	(*b*)	(*c*)	(*d*)
A.	III	IV	II	I
B.	I	II	IV	III
C.	IV	III	II	I
D.	III	I	II	IV

74. Match List I with List II.

List-I	List-II
(*a*) Emotions are largely innate reactions to certain stimuli	I. Cannon-Bard theory
(*b*) Emotions result from perception of autonomic arousal	II. Schachter's two-factor theory
(*c*) Emotion is inferred from arousal and then labelling it after interpretation	III. Evolutionary theories

(*d*) Emotions originate in sub-cortical areas of the brain	IV.	James-Lange theory

Choose the ***correct*** answer from the options given below:

	(*a*)	(*b*)	(*c*)	(*d*)
A.	II	I	IV	III
B.	III	IV	II	I
C.	I	II	III	IV
D.	IV	II	I	III

75. Match List I with List II.

List-I	List-II
(*a*) Snyder	I. Bottom-up Theories vs Top-down theories of happiness
(*b*) Diener	II. Broaden and Build Model
(*c*) Antonovsky	III. Hope theory
(*d*) Fredrickson	IV. Salutogenic Model

Choose the ***correct*** answer from the options given below:

	(*a*)	(*b*)	(*c*)	(*d*)
A.	III	I	IV	II
B.	III	II	I	IV
C.	II	III	IV	I
D.	I	III	II	IV

76. Arrange in sequence the following scales of measurement Ordinal, Nominal, Ratio and Interval according to properties of scale:
(*a*) Identity
(*b*) Identity and Magnitude
(*c*) Identity, magnitude and equal unit size
(*d*) Identity, magnitude, equal unit size and absolute Zero

Choose the ***correct*** answer from the options given below:
A. (*b*), (*a*), (*d*), (*c*) B. (*b*), (*c*), (*d*), (*a*)
C. (*a*), (*b*), (*d*), (*c*) D. (*c*), (*b*), (*a*), (*d*)

77. What is the correct sequence in development of a psychological tool?
(*a*) Establishing reliability
(*b*) Item analysis
(*c*) Developing norm
(*d*) Establishing validity

Choose the ***correct*** answer from the options given below:
A. (*a*), (*b*), (*d*), (*c*) B. (*b*), (*a*), (*d*), (*c*)
C. (*a*), (*d*), (*c*), (*b*) D. (*b*), (*a*), (*c*), (*d*)

78. What is the sequence of steps involved in conducting Radiofrequency lesion by using stereotoxic apparatus?
(*a*) Drill a hole in the skull of the rat using coordinates from the stereotoxic atlas.
(*b*) Pass on radiofrequency current through the tip of the insulated electrode to the brain area.
(*c*) Close the hole on the skull of the rat and provide appropriate medical treatment.
(*d*) Fix the head of the rat on the stereotoxic apparatus.
(*e*) Push an electrode to the appropriate depth of the brain till it touches the specified brain area.

Choose the ***correct*** answer from the options given below:
A. (*a*), (*b*), (*d*), (*e*), (*c*)
B. (*c*), (*a*), (*b*), (*d*), (*e*)
C. (*d*), (*a*), (*e*), (*b*), (*c*)
D. (*b*), (*d*), (*a*), (*c*), (*e*)

79. Arrange the following in order of their occurrence in observational learning.
(*a*) Retention
(*b*) Attention
(*c*) Reproduction
(*d*) Motivation

Choose the ***correct*** answer from the options given below:
A. (*d*), (*b*), (*a*), (*c*) B. (*a*), (*b*), (*c*), (*d*)
C. (*b*), (*d*), (*a*), (*c*) D. (*b*), (*a*), (*c*), (*d*)

80. Arrange the bodily consequences of stress in the order as proposed by Hans Selye:
(*a*) Exhaustion (*b*) Alarm
(*c*) Resistance (*d*) Hardiness

Choose the ***correct*** answer from the options given below:
A. (*d*), (*b*), (*c*), (*a*) B. (*b*), (*c*), (*a*), (*d*)
C. (*b*), (*c*), (*a*) D. (*b*), (*c*), (*d*)

81. The Four Stage theory of creativity was proposed by Joseph Wallas. Arrange these stages in a sequence.

(*a*) Preparation (*b*) Incubation
(*c*) Illumination (*d*) Verification

Choose the ***correct*** answer from the options given below:

A. (*a*), (*c*), (*b*), (*d*) B. (*a*), (*b*), (*c*), (*d*)
C. (*a*), (*d*), (*b*), (*c*) D. (*a*), (*c*), (*d*), (*b*)

82. Arrange in order the Hierarchy of Needs by Maslow.

(*a*) Physiological (*b*) Esteem
(*c*) Affiliation (*d*) Safety
(*e*) Self-actualization

Choose the ***correct*** answer from the options given below:

A. (*a*), (*e*), (*c*), (*b*), (*d*)
B. (*a*), (*d*), (*c*), (*b*), (*e*)
C. (*a*), (*b*), (*d*), (*c*), (*e*)
D. (*a*), (*c*), (*e*), (*d*), (*b*)

83. The correct sequence of a person who is hungry in terms of motivational cycle is:

(*a*) Disequilibrium
(*b*) Reaching goal
(*c*) Instrumental behaviour
(*d*) Homeostasis
(*e*) Consumption of food

Choose the ***correct*** answer from the options given below:

A. (*a*), (*c*), (*b*), (*e*), (*d*)
B. (*d*), (*a*), (*b*), (*e*), (*c*)
C. (*c*), (*a*), (*b*), (*d*), (*e*)
D. (*e*), (*d*), (*a*), (*c*), (*b*)

84. As per Tuckman's group development model, identify the correct sequence:

(*a*) Norming (*b*) Storming
(*c*) Performing (*d*) Forming
(*e*) Adjourning

Choose the ***correct*** answer from the options given below:

A. (*a*), (*c*), (*b*), (*d*), (*e*)
B. (*a*), (*d*), (*b*), (*c*), (*e*)
C. (*d*), (*b*), (*a*), (*c*), (*e*)
D. (*d*), (*a*), (*b*), (*c*), (*e*)

85. Arrange the following from early to later development:

(*a*) Autonomy versus shame and doubt
(*b*) Identity versus role confusion
(*c*) Industry versus inferiority
(*d*) Initiative versus guilt

Choose the ***correct*** answer from the options given below:

A. (*a*), (*c*), (*d*), (*b*) B. (*d*), (*c*), (*a*), (*b*)
C. (*c*), (*d*), (*a*), (*b*) D. (*a*), (*d*), (*c*), (*b*)

86. Given below are two statements : One is labelled as Assertion (A) and the other is labelled as Reason (R).

Assertion (A): Effectiveness of psychological research increases if multiple methods are used by the researcher.

Reason (R): Triangulation helps in relating information collected from different methods to arrive at meaningful inference.

In the light of the above statements, choose the ***most appropriate*** answer from the options given below:

A. Both (A) and (R) are correct and (R) is the correct explanation of (A)
B. Both (A) and (R) are true, but (R) is not the correct explanation of (A)
C. (A) is true, but (R) is false
D. (A) is false, but (R) is true

87. Given below are two statements:

Statement I: Posterior of pituitary gland secretes antidiuretic hormone which stimulates kidneys to reabsorb water to prevent dehydration.

Statement II: Cortex of adrenal glands located on the top of Kidneys helps in uterine contraction during child birth and release of milk through mammary glands in females and contraction of sperm duct during ejaculation in males.

In the light of the above statements, choose the ***most appropriate*** answer from the options given below:

A. Both Statement I and Statement II are true
B. Both Statement I and Statement II are false
C. Statement I is true, but Statement II is false
D. Statement I is false, but Statement II is true

88. Given below are two statements:

Statement I: In a figure-ground perception, the stimulus with two or more distinct region, the region seen as figure contains the object of interest and the other region is perceived as the background.

Statement II: Figure-ground perception can be ambiguous.

In the light of the above statements, choose the ***most appropriate*** answer from the options given below:

A. Both Statement I and Statement II are correct
B. Both Statement I and Statement II are incorrect
C. Statement I is correct, but Statement II is incorrect
D. Statement I is incorrect, but Statement II is correct

89. Given below are two statements : One is labelled as Assertion (A) and the other is labelled as Reason (R).

Assertion (A): Monthly salary of Government employees can be termed as a reinforcement at workplace.

Reason (R): Variable ratio, as a partial reinforcement schedule, leads to higher rate of responses.

In the light of the above statements, choose the ***most appropriate*** answer from the options given below:

A. Both (A) and (R) are true and (R) is the correct explanation of (A)
B. Both (A) and (R) are true, but (R) is not the correct explanation of (A)
C. (A) is true, but (R) is false
D. (A) is false, but (R) is true

90. Given below are two statements : One is labelled as Assertion (A) and the other is labelled as Reason (R).

Assertion (A): A person who has type A personality experiences high stress.

Reason (R): Research shows evidence for correlation between personality and stress.

In the light of the above statements, choose the ***most appropriate*** answer from the options given below:

A. Both (A) and (R) are true and (R) is the correct explanation of (A)
B. Both (A) and (R) are true, but (R) is not the correct explanation of (A)
C. (A) is true, but (R) is not false
D. (A) is false, but (R) is true

Direction (Qs. No. 91-95) : *Read the given paragraph and answer the questions that follow:*

An experimenter conducted a study on a group of children in order to find out their development level. In his study he provided two clay balls and took their agreement that the two balls are of equal size. Then he changed the shape of one ball to a flat shape in front of the children and asked which out of the two shapes containd more clay. Few children responded that the flat shape contained more clay. Later he asked another question as follows: "If an aeroplane is called an elephant, can it fly?" Few children answered "Yes it can fly".

91. The children who answered the Aeroplane-elephant question correctly come under the stage of:

A. Concrete operational stage
B. Intuitive operational stage
C. Formal operational stage
D. Preoperational stage

92. The clay ball experiment measures children's ability of:

A. Object Permanence
B. Egocentrism
C. Conservation
D. Animism

93. The psychologist associated with the above experiment:

A. Vygotsky
B. Piaget
C. Bruner
D. Bandura

94. In which stage of development are the children who answered that the flattened ball contained more clay?
A. Formal operational stage
B. Preoperational stage
C. Sensori Motor stage
D. Concrete operational stage

95. The theory underlining the above study is:
A. Psychodynamic theory
B. Social observational learning
C. Cognitive development theory
D. Cognitive dynamic behaviour theory

Direction (Qs. No. 96-100) : *Read the following passage and answer the questions.*

An experimenter conducted a study to see the effect of social support on well being. He recruited a group of students from a school where he was working. Later he decided to see the role of gender on the relation between social support and well being. He formulated a hypothesis taking all these variables into account. The hypothesis was that the strength of the relationship between social support and well being would change when the gender variable is included. After collecting the data, normal distribution of scores was confirmed. The result was not in accordance with the hypothesis. Later the experimenter interpreted the result of the study.

96. What design was used in the above experiment?
A. Between group design
B. Within group design
C. Correlational design
D. Factorial design

97. What sampling was used in the study?
A. Quota sampling
B. Purposive sampling
C. Cluster sampling
D. Stratified sampling

98. What type of variable was gender in the study?
A. Predictive variable
B. Criterion variable
C. Mediation variable
D. Moderation variable

99. The interpretation of the result the experiment made was:
A. $P < 0.05$
B. $P < 0.01$
C. $P < 0.001$
D. $P > 0.05$

100. Which type of statistical analysis was used?
A. Simple linear regression
B. Biserial correlation
C. Multiple regression
D. Log linear correlation

ANSWERS

1. (C): Sri Aurobindo popularized the term 'integral yoga.' Sri Aurobindo was an Indian philosopher, yogi, guru, poet, and nationalist who sought to integrate traditional yogic practices with his vision of human evolutionary potential. He believed that the physical, mental, and spiritual dimensions of a person could be developed in tandem, leading to a greater realization of self and unity with the divine. His teachings emphasized an 'integral' approach to yoga, which included elements of karma yoga (the yoga of action), jnana yoga (the yoga of knowledge), and bhakti yoga (the yoga of devotion), along with additional elements unique to his philosophy.

2. (D): A correlation coefficient of +.08 represents the weakest degree of relationship. The correlation coefficient is a measure of the strength and direction of the linear relationship between two variables. It ranges from −1 to +1, with −1 indicating a perfect negative correlation, +1 a perfect positive correlation, and 0 no correlation. The closer the coefficient is to 0, the weaker the relationship, regardless of the sign. Hence, among the given options, +.08 is closest to zero, indicating the weakest relationship.

3. **(B):** The inter-rater reliability in this case would be 80%. Inter-rater reliability is a measure of how consistently different raters or observers evaluate the same thing. If observers disagreed 15 times out of 75, it means they agreed 60 times. To compute the inter-rater reliability, we would divide the number of agreements by the total number of evaluations. So, 60/75 gives us a reliability of 0.80, or 80%.

4. **(A):** The *z*-score in this case is –1.0. The *z*-score is a measure of how many standard deviations a data point is from the mean of the data set. It's calculated using the formula $z = (X - \mu)/\sigma$, where X is the raw score, μ is the mean, and σ is the standard deviation. Here, if a student scored 12 on a test with a mean of 16 and a standard deviation of 4, his *z*-score would be $(12 - 16)/4 = -1.0$.

5. **(B):** Variance is calculated as the average of the squared differences from the Mean. The formula is: variance $= \Sigma((x - \mu)^2)/N$, where *u* represents each value in the dataset, μ is the mean of the dataset, and N is the number of data points. Variance provides a measure of how data points in a set vary from the mean.

6. **(D):** A '*t*' test would be the appropriate statistical test to use if a researcher is interested in testing the effectiveness of pre-post intervention on a single group. The '*t*' test is used to determine whether there is a significant difference between the means of two groups. In this case, it can be used to compare the group's mean score before and after the intervention.

7. **(B):** Alternate forms reliability is determined by assessing the degree of relationship between scores on two different equivalent tests. This form of reliability, also known as parallel-forms reliability, measures the extent to which two measures or tests are equivalent and interchangeable, despite being composed of different items. It's particularly useful in contexts where test takers might become familiar with test items if the same test is administered more than once.

8. **(C):** CogScreen is a computer-assisted tool used in the selection of airline pilots. It is a neuropsychological screening instrument designed to rapidly evaluate cognitive and motor abilities relevant to the operation of an aircraft. The tests assess a variety of cognitive domains, including attention, immediate and delayed recall, spatial processing, mathematical processing, and other cognitive abilities that are crucial for flying an aircraft safely and efficiently.

9. **(C):** The utility of the Semantic Differential Scale is not contingent upon the length of the items in the scale. The Semantic Differential Scale is a type of a rating scale designed to measure the connotative meaning of objects, events, and concepts. It operates on the basis of polar adjectives or adjective phrases. The scale's effectiveness does not depend on the length of the items, but rather on the appropriateness of the adjective pairs, the meaning of the words, and the contextual reference of the items.

10. **(A):** The Amygdala, a part of the Limbic System, is primarily responsible for controlling the emotional behaviour of fear. The amygdala plays a critical role in processing our emotions and is directly involved in fear responses or reactions to threatening situations. Research shows that the amygdala can trigger a response to fearful or emergency events, thereby initiating a protective response.

11. **(A):** REM (Rapid Eye Movement) sleep is characterized by PGO (Ponto-Geniculo-Occipital) waves. PGO waves are electrical waves that originate in the pons, move to the thalamus (specifically, the lateral geniculate nucleus), and then to the occipital cortex.

PGO waves are typically associated with REM sleep, where most vivid dreaming occurs. During REM sleep, our brains are highly active, almost to the level when we are awake. This period is characterized by rapid eye movements, increased respiration rate, and brain temperature.

12. (C): Class relates to the Identity property of measurement as Time relates to the Absolute zero property of measurement. The identity property indicates that each value on the scale has a unique meaning, while the absolute zero property refers to a scale that has a true zero point, which signifies the absence of the attribute being measured. Class, like all categorical variables, can provide identity (distinct categories like freshmen, sophomores, etc.) while Time, being a ratio variable, provides an absolute zero point where time equals zero.

13. (D): A genetic inability to metabolize the amino acid phenylalanine leads to a condition known as PKU, or phenylketonuria. Phenylketonuria is a genetic disorder that's inherited from one's parents. It's characterized by a deficiency in the enzyme needed to process phenylalanine, an essential amino acid. If it goes untreated, it can lead to intellectual disabilities, seizures, behavioural problems, and mental disorders.

14. (C): A person who had experienced an intensive negative emotion and fails to recollect the emotional event is experiencing Motivated Forgetting. Motivated forgetting is a psychological defense mechanism where a person subconsciously suppresses or forgets memories that are threatening, painful, or unpleasant. Freud termed this as 'repression'. The memory is still stored in the unconscious mind but is not readily accessible by the conscious mind.

15. (C): The tendency of a consumer to decide on buying a product that was repeatedly appearing on a T.V. screen is attributed to Subliminal Perception. Subliminal perception refers to the processing of stimuli presented below the level of conscious awareness. The repeated exposure to the product advertisement, even without the viewer's active attention, can influence their purchasing behaviour.

16. (B): Brain lesions of subcortical regions produced by passing electrical current through an insulated electrode is referred to as Radio Frequency lesions. The technique involves destroying a region of brain tissue by heating it using a high-frequency current passed through an electrode. This is typically used in animal studies to study the function of specific brain regions.

17. (C): A person dressed in a gorilla suit walking unnoticed through a group of students playing basketball can be described as a phenomenon called Inattentional blindness. This refers to the failure to notice a fully-visible but unexpected object or event when one is focusing attention on something else. In the famous "invisible gorilla" experiment, observers engrossed in counting basketball passes failed to notice a person in a gorilla suit walking across the scene.

18. (A, C)

19. (B): Step-by-step interaction of operating a mechanical gadget is an example of an Algorithm. An algorithm is a specific procedure for solving a well-defined computational problem. It involves a set of precise steps that are to be executed in a specific order to achieve a goal. In this case, the goal is to operate a mechanical gadget, and the steps are the actions needed to do so.

20. (C): Making a reference to a respected person believed to be well-informed, when one's own logic or reasoning is weak, is called an Appeal to authority. This is a type of logical fallacy where the opinion of an authority on a topic is used as evidence to support an argument. It's considered a fallacy when the authority is not a legitimate expert on the subject matter, or when the reference to the authority is used in lieu of actual evidence to back up the argument.

21. (C): The inability to use a tool in a novel way can be attributed to Functional Fixedness. This cognitive bias limits a person to using an object only in the way it is traditionally used. Functional fixedness may prevent someone from seeing the full range of ways in which a tool or other object could be used, potentially hampering problem-solving and creativity. It is a type of mental set where you cannot see a new function or purpose for a familiar object.

22. (D): The Processes underlying intelligent behaviour are examined in an information processing approach to intelligence. This approach focuses on the mental processes that underlie intelligent behaviour. It investigates how people perceive, remember, think, speak, and solve problems. An individual's intelligence, then, is inferred from behaviours and performances in tests that require these processes.

23. (C): In Hull's Drive Reduction Theory, SHR stands for Habit strength. Habit strength is a concept used to describe the connection between a stimulus and response. Hull's theory proposes that organisms learn to execute behaviours that lead to a reduction in physiological drives, and the strength of a 'habit' depends on how often the behaviour has resulted in drive reduction in the past.

24. (B): An Optimistic explanatory style in the face of stress is indicated by External cause, specific impact, and unstable outcome. This means that a person tends to attribute the causes of negative events to external factors (factors outside of their control), believes the impact of these events is limited or specific (not affecting all areas of their life), and thinks that the outcomes of these events are unstable or temporary (will change over time). This positive outlook can help an individual better manage stress and bounce back from adversities.

25. (C): An individual encountering prolonged stress is prone to suffer from skin infection because Cortisol released into blood causes damage to the T and B cells in the White Blood Cells. Prolonged stress leads to an overproduction of cortisol, a steroid hormone that regulates a wide range of processes throughout the body. This includes suppressing the immune system and reducing inflammation, which can impair the functioning of T and B cells that are essential for the immune response. Consequently, this can increase susceptibility to infections, including those of the skin.

26. (B): Hardy personality is characterized by three cognitive attitudes: Control, Commitment, and Challenge. Therefore, Coping is not correct for hardy personality. Control refers to a person's belief in their ability to influence events; Commitment is a sense of involvement and purpose in life; and Challenge is viewing change and adversity as opportunities for growth rather than threats. These attitudes help individuals resist stress and maintain their health.

27. (B): The Cognitive Dissonance Theory explains that attitude change occurs as a result of the reduction of the unpleasant arousal people experience while they engage in a behaviour that conflicts with their attitude. Cognitive dissonance refers to the discomfort that individuals feel when they hold two or more contradictory beliefs, values, or attitudes, especially in situations where they cannot rationalize the discrepancy. To resolve this discomfort, people may change their attitudes or beliefs to align with their behaviour.

28. (B): Social loafing is defined as the tendency by group members to slack off and reduce their effort on additive tasks, which cause the group's output to fall short of its potential. This phenomenon often occurs when individual performance isn't visible or isn't deemed critical to the group's success.

It's influenced by factors such as cultural norms, task meaningfulness, and individual personality traits.

29. (A): Brainstorming is a group decision-making technique. It is a method designed to generate a large number of ideas for the solution to a problem. The key principle of brainstorming is that it encourages free thinking and open expression of ideas, where criticism or judgment of ideas is withheld until a later point. This encourages creative problem-solving among group members and can yield a wide array of potential solutions.

30. (B): The result of Stanley Milgram's study shows that many people will obey an authority figure even if innocent people get hurt. In his notorious experiment, participants were instructed to administer electric shocks to a 'learner' for wrong answers (although in reality, no shocks were given). Despite the 'learner's' apparent distress, a substantial majority of participants continued to obey the instructions to administer shocks, showing the power of authority and obedience.

31. (D): The incorrect definition according to Gestalt therapy is Deflection. In the context of Gestalt therapy, deflection is a mechanism that individuals use to distract or veer away from their feelings, needs, or issues. It is often used as a means to avoid acknowledging and dealing with painful or uncomfortable emotions or thoughts. It does not refer to the process of attributing aspects of ourselves to other people as stated in the question. Instead, this process of attributing our qualities to others is known as projection.

32. (C): Mehrabian and Reed (1969) proposed that a counsellor can use the formula Distress × Uncontrollability × Frequency for a rough assessment of the severity of a client's problem. In this formula, 'Distress' refers to the level of emotional pain or discomfort the issue causes the client. 'Uncontrollability' refers to the degree to which the client feels they cannot control or manage the problem. 'Frequency' represents how often the problem occurs. When these factors are multiplied together, they provide an estimation of the problem's overall severity.

33. (D): Virginia Axline is associated with Play Therapy. She is recognized as a pioneer in the development of non-directive Play Therapy and she has made fundamental contributions to the principles and practices within the field. Her book "Play Therapy" is considered a seminal work and it details her approach which emphasizes the importance of creating an empathetic, warm and permissive environment where the child can freely express themselves through play.

34. (D): In Rational Emotive Behaviour Therapy (REBT), treatment is based on the assessment of goals, activating events, beliefs, and consequences. REBT is a form of cognitive-behavioural therapy developed by Albert Ellis. The treatment process involves identifying irrational beliefs, understanding the activation events that trigger these beliefs, and understanding the consequences of such beliefs. The client's goals are also taken into account, as the aim is to change irrational beliefs and reactions to healthier ones that align with the client's life goals.

35. (B): Transactional Analysis is not concerned with Hypnotic Analysis. Transactional Analysis is a psychoanalytic theory and method of therapy wherein social transactions are analyzed to determine the ego state of the patient (whether parent-like, child-like, or adult-like) as a basis for understanding behaviour. It mainly focuses on structural analysis, transactional analysis, game analysis, and script analysis, aiming to identify problematic behavioural patterns and devise strategies to change them.

36. (C): Sense of humour is not directly relevant to a cardiac patient's behaviour of adherence to treatment. Factors like self-efficacy (belief in one's ability to execute actions necessary for managing treatment), perceptions about the seriousness of the condition, and perceived control over health are crucial in adherence to treatment. Although having a sense of humour can help manage stress and promote overall well-being, it does not directly impact treatment adherence.

37. (C): Multiple Sclerosis is not a risk factor for hypertension. Hypertension, also known as high blood pressure, is influenced by factors such as obesity, age, family history, tobacco use, physical inactivity, high-salt diet, high alcohol intake, and stress. While Multiple Sclerosis is a disease that affects the central nervous system, there is no established direct link indicating it as a risk factor for hypertension.

38. (B): Secondary prevention is defined as the actions taken to identify and treat an illness or injury early with an aim of stopping or reversing the problem. This stage of prevention happens after an illness or serious risk factors have already been diagnosed. The goal is to halt or slow the progress of disease (if possible) in its earliest stages. This is often accomplished through regular screenings, lifestyle modifications, and prescribed medications.

39. (B): In the context of health behaviour, Matarazzo (1984) refers to behaviour that protects health as 'behavioural immunogenes' and that puts health at risk as 'Behavioural pathogens'. Behavioural immunogenes are activities that strengthen a person's physical health and immunity, such as regular exercise and balanced nutrition. In contrast, behavioural pathogens are activities that can cause disease or compromise health, such as smoking or excessive alcohol consumption.

40. (C): Resilience does not come under Seligman's theory of authentic happiness and well-being. The theory, often referred to as PERMA model, comprises five key elements: Positive Emotion, Engagement, Relationships, Meaning, and Accomplishment. While resilience or the ability to bounce back from adversity contributes to overall well-being and happiness, it is not explicitly defined as a component in Seligman's PERMA model.

41. (C): The cognitive perspective is primarily concerned with how people perceive, process, and retrieve information. It includes both thinking and understanding the world (a) and information processing (b). It compares human cognition to the operations of a computer, with inputs, processing, and outputs (d). The cognitive perspective does not limit itself to overt behaviour only; instead, it delves into internal mental processes such as memory, perception, thinking, and problem-solving.

42. (D): In the Indian concept of self, psychological self is understood to comprise of three key elements - Manas (mind), Buddhi (intellect), and Anthakarana (inner organ). Manas is associated with the processing of thoughts, Buddhi is related to wisdom and decision making, and Anthakarana is the collective term used for mind, intellect, consciousness, and ego. Dhyana, however, refers to meditation, a practice rather than a component of self.

43. (D): The number of factors to be extracted in factor analysis is often determined by the use of a scree plot (a) and eigen values (c). The scree plot helps to visualize the factors and their relative importance. Eigen values represent the amount of variance in the data that is accounted for by a particular factor, and factors with eigen values greater than 1 are often retained. Factor loadings and orthogonal rotations are techniques used after factors have been extracted.

44. (A): Simple random sampling, proportionate stratified sampling, and disproportionate stratified sampling are all types of probability sampling (a, b, c). Probability sampling methods are based on the concept of random selection. In contrast, saturation sampling (d) is a type of non-probability sampling method often used in qualitative research until no new themes or ideas emerge from the data.

45. (B): Aptitudes are typically thought of as innate (b), though they can be honed through education and experience. Training can indeed help optimize performance (c), by developing the skills and knowledge needed to fully utilize one's aptitudes. Aptitudes are individual characteristics that predispose people to perform certain tasks better than others. They are not necessarily acquired (a), and they are not always positively related to interests (d).

46. (C): Norms in psychological testing serve as comparative devices (a) to interpret individual scores within a broader context. T-scores are indeed a type of standard score norm used in psychological testing (c). A raw score often needs to be converted to a derived score (d) to allow for more meaningful interpretations. However, not all psychometricians use 'percentage' as a type of norm (b); this can vary depending on the nature of the test and its intended use.

47. (D): The Differential Aptitude Test (DAT) is a comprehensive, multi-subtest measure that includes eight subtests (a). It is intended for use with students from grade 8 to grade 12 (b), not specifically for the age range of 8 to 12 years (c). The DAT has been adapted and used in various countries, including by psychologists in India (d).

48. (B): Neuropsychological tests evaluate cognitive functioning to identify impairment and guide treatment and recovery. They assess domains such as language (a), memory (c), and executive functioning (d), among others. They do not typically assess opinion (b) or reaction (e), as these do not pertain directly to cognitive functioning.

49. (A): Biofeedback is indeed accurate (a) and can help modify behaviour (b) by giving an individual real-time feedback about their physiological processes. It is used to bring involuntary actions like heart rate and muscle tension into voluntary control (c), aiding in stress management, anxiety reduction, and the treatment of certain health conditions. Biofeedback is not a component of polygraphy (d), which measures physiological responses to determine truthfulness.

50. (B): The nature of the task (b), knowledge of results (c), and reinforcement (d) are all motivating factors in learning. The nature of the task can affect interest and engagement, knowledge of results provides feedback on progress and performance, and reinforcement strengthens the likelihood of a behaviour being repeated. Intelligence (a), while it may impact the speed or ease of learning, is not typically considered a motivating factor.

51. (D): Classical Conditioning is also known as Pavlovian or respondent conditioning but not instrumental conditioning. This term (instrumental conditioning) refers to another learning process known as Operant Conditioning, which was proposed by B.F. Skinner. In Classical Conditioning, a natural (unconditioned) stimulus is paired with a neutral one. After enough repetition, the neutral stimulus triggers the same response as the unconditioned stimulus, making it a conditioned stimulus. This is different from Instrumental Conditioning, where an individual's behaviour is modified by its consequences.

52. (A): Perceptual constancy is our ability to recognize the same object as remaining 'constant' under different conditions. It includes shape and colour constancy. Shape constancy allows us to recognize people and objects from different angles while maintaining their shape, and colour constancy ensures that the perceived colour of an object remains the same under varying illumination conditions. Illumination and distance, however, are not types of perceptual constancy but rather factors that might affect our perception.

53. (A, D)

54. (D): Creativity, or the ability to generate novel and useful ideas, is not necessarily tied to intelligence. Although there may be some correlation, not all intelligent people are creative and not all creative people are high in intelligence. Creativity is indeed also known as divergent thinking, the ability to generate many different ideas. Whether creativity is genetically determined is not fully understood, but it's likely a mix of genetic and environmental influences.

55. (C): Language development involves several aspects. Pragmatics refers to the use of language in different contexts and the way language is affected by the context. Syntax is the set of rules by which we construct sentences, and Semantics involves understanding and interpreting the meaning of words and sentences. Imprinting, however, is a term used in ethology to describe a critical period of learning and bonding in animals, and it's not directly related to language development.

56. (B)

57. (A): Anthropogenic stress refers to human-induced changes that lead to stressful environments, such as overcrowding, noise, or pollution (a). Geopathic stress refers to the impact of Earth's energies on human wellbeing, including harmful effects of certain natural electromagnetic field patterns (b). However, 'Energetic stress' (c) and 'Ergonomic Stress' (d) are not established stress categories in psychology.

58. (D): Psychological stress is indeed subjective - its perception varies from individual to individual based on their coping mechanisms, personality traits, and previous experiences (b). Contrary to statement (a), stress isn't just a temporary phenomenon; chronic stress can last for extended periods. Statement (c) is incorrect as personality and stress are indeed related, with certain traits predisposing to higher stress levels. Lastly, an optimal level of stress, known as eustress, can boost performance and productivity (d).

59. (A)

60. (B): Fiedler's contingency model of leadership effectiveness considers three key situational factors: the leader-member relationship, the degree of task structure, and the leader's position power (b). The model posits that there is no best style of leadership, and the effectiveness of a leader depends on these situational contingencies. The inborn traits of the leader (d), however, are not a part of Fiedler's contingency model, which focuses more on situational elements.

61. (A) **62. (C)**

63. (B): 'Advanced empathy' in counselling is a deeper level of empathy that goes beyond simple acknowledgment of a client's feelings. It involves making connections across various elements of the client's experience (connecting islands) and identifying recurring themes within those experiences. It also involves making the implicit explicit, that is, helping the client become aware of underlying feelings or thoughts they might not have articulated.

64. (D): Classical Conditioning is a learning principle first defined by Ivan Pavlov. It involves learning by association where a neutral stimulus, when repeatedly paired with an unconditioned stimulus, elicits a conditioned response. Systematic desensitization, used for treating phobias, applies this principle by pairing relaxation (conditioned response) with a fear-inducing object or situation (neutral stimulus). Aversion therapy also uses this principle, but instead pairs an undesirable behaviour with an unpleasant stimulus to decrease the behaviour.

65. (C): In Transactional Analysis, Ego State Analysis involves examining the three ego states: Parent, Adult, and Child. These states reflect different aspects of a person's behaviour and thoughts. The Parent state is composed of learned behaviours, attitudes, and beliefs from parental figures. The Adult state relates to behaviours that are direct responses to the here-and-now, using logical thinking and rationality. The Child state is our internal echo of the child we once were, containing our childhood feelings and experiences.

66. (D) **67. (C)** **68. (B)**

69. (B) **70. (B)**

71. (D): Semantic memory is a type of declarative memory that includes general knowledge and facts about the world, as well as the rules of logic that are used to deduce other facts, which corresponds to Option I. Episodic memory refers to memory for events that occur in a particular time, place, or context, matching with Option IV. Flashbulb memory refers to the memory centered on a specific important event that is as vivid as if it represented a snapshot of the event, corresponding to Option II. Lastly, procedural memory is our memory for skills and habits, aligning with Option III.

72. (C): Thurstone proposed the theory of Primary Mental Abilities, which includes seven factors of intelligence, matching Option II. Howard Gardner proposed the theory of Multiple Intelligences, suggesting that intelligence is not a single entity but a combination of various distinct types, corresponding to Option III. Robert Sternberg's Triarchic Theory of Intelligence is identified with Option I. J.P Das's PASS Model, which stands for Planning, Attention, Simultaneous and Successive, is represented by Option IV.

73. (D): Inductive reasoning involves inferring general principles or rules from specific facts, which corresponds to Option III. Deductive reasoning is about inferring specific instances from general principles or rules, which matches Option I. Heuristics are cognitive shortcuts that provide adequately accurate inferences most of the time, represented by Option II. Finally, an algorithm is a step-by-step procedure to solve a problem, which aligns with Option IV.

74. (B)

75. (A): Hope Theory was proposed by Snyder, which corresponds to Option III. Diener is known for his extensive research on subjective well-being and happiness, relating to Option I. Antonovsky is known for his Salutogenic Model, which is focused on factors that support human health and well-being, aligning with Option IV. Fredrickson's Broaden-and-Build theory of positive emotions matches with Option II.

76. (A): Nominal scale represents the property of identity, and this scale just labels and categorizes without any order or priority, hence (a) Identity. The Ordinal scale represents the properties of identity and magnitude, allowing us to rank order the levels of the variable being studied, hence (b) Identity and Magnitude. The Interval scale represents identity, magnitude, and equal unit size, hence (c) Identity, magnitude, and equal unit size. The Ratio scale includes all the properties - identity, magnitude, equal unit size, and absolute zero, hence (d) Identity, magnitude, equal unit size, and absolute Zero.

77. (B): The first step is to create items, followed by an item analysis, which is used to check the quality of the items (b). Once the items are analyzed and selected, the reliability of the tool is established (a). Next, the validity of the tool is determined (d), to ensure that the tool is measuring what it intends to measure. Lastly, norms are developed based on the test scores from the representative sample (c).

78. (C): The first step involves fixing the head of the rat on the stereotoxic apparatus (d). Then a hole is drilled in the skull of the rat using coordinates from the stereotoxic atlas (a). An electrode is pushed to the appropriate depth of the brain till it touches the specified brain area (e). Radiofrequency current is passed through the tip of the insulated electrode to the brain area (b). Finally, the hole on the skull of the rat is closed and appropriate medical treatment is provided (c).

79. (D): Observational learning begins with attention (b), as the learner must first pay attention to the model. Next is retention (a), where the observer must remember the behaviour they have observed. Then comes reproduction (c), which is the actual imitation of the behaviour. Finally, there must be motivation (d) for the observer to repeat the behaviour.

80. (C): Hans Selye proposed the General Adaptation Syndrome model to describe the body's short-term and long-term reaction to stress. The first stage is the Alarm stage (b) where the body reacts to the stressor. Next is the Resistance stage (c) where the body attempts to resist or adapt to the stressor. Finally, if the stressor continues, the body moves into the Exhaustion stage (a), where resources are depleted and the body's ability to resist is reduced.

81. (B): The Four Stage theory of creativity proposed by Wallas comprises four steps: Preparation, Incubation, Illumination, and Verification. In the Preparation stage, one gathers information and experiences about the problem at hand. Following this, Incubation is the process where the unconscious mind takes over, working on the problem while we're engaged in other activities. Illumination is the "eureka" moment when the solution comes to mind. Finally, Verification involves evaluating the solution and checking if it effectively solves the problem.

82. (B): Maslow's Hierarchy of Needs is a five-tier model of human needs, often depicted as hierarchical levels within a pyramid. From bottom to top, the sequence is Physiological, Safety, Affiliation (also referred to as Love/ Belonging), Esteem, and Self-actualization. Physiological needs are basic life necessities, Safety needs focus on security and stability, Affiliation needs emphasize interpersonal relationships, Esteem needs involve the need for respect and recognition, and self-actualization refers to the pursuit of personal growth and fulfillment.

83. (A): The motivational cycle starts with Disequilibrium, where a need or desire creates a state of tension. This leads to Instrumental Behaviour, where one engages in actions that are believed to satisfy the need. Reaching the Goal is the next step, where the successful actions lead to the desired outcome. Consumption of Food refers to the act of satisfying the specific need. Finally, Homeostasis refers to a state of balance or equilibrium, which is achieved once the need or desire is fulfilled.

84. (C): Tuckman's model of group development consists of five stages: Forming, Storming, Norming, Performing, and Adjourning. Forming is when the group is just starting to come together and is characterized by dependence and politeness. Storming involves conflict and competition as individual personalities and roles emerge. Norming is when rules and values are established, leading to more cooperation among members. Performing is when the group starts to get work done effectively. Finally, Adjourning (or Mourning) is the stage of breaking up the group after the task is accomplished.

85. (D): The correct sequence of Erik Erikson's stages of psychosocial development is: Autonomy versus Shame and Doubt (toddlers, 1-3 years), Initiative versus Guilt (preschool, 3-6 years), Industry versus Inferiority (school age, 6-12 years), and Identity versus Role Confusion (adolescence, 12-18 years). Each stage involves a crisis of two conflicting forces, and successful resolution of the crisis leads to the development of a virtue or a key strength.

86. (A) **87. (C)** **88. (A)**
89. (B) **90. (B)**

91. (C): The children who correctly answered the Aeroplane-elephant question are in the Formal Operational Stage, according to Piaget's theory of cognitive development. This stage typically begins around age 11 and lasts into adulthood. During this stage, children are able to think abstractly and understand metaphorical or hypothetical questions, like the Aeroplane-elephant question. They can comprehend that changing the name of an object doesn't change its inherent properties, so an aeroplane called an elephant can still fly.

92. (C): The clay ball experiment measures children's understanding of conservation. Conservation is the realization that quantity or amount does not change if the shape or arrangement changes, as long as nothing is added or taken away. Some children believed the flattened ball had more clay because its shape was larger, which indicates they are not yet able to grasp the principle of conservation.

93. (B): The psychologist associated with the experiments described above is Jean Piaget. Piaget's work centered around the cognitive development of children. He designed numerous experiments, including the clay ball task and questions about the characteristics of objects when their names are changed, to understand the stages of cognitive development.

94. (B): The children who answered that the flattened ball contained more clay are in the Preoperational Stage according to Piaget's theory. This stage typically includes children aged 2-7 years. These children have difficulty understanding the principle of conservation and may believe that changing the shape of an object changes its volume or quantity.

95. (C): The theory underlining the experiments in the question is the Cognitive Development Theory, proposed by Jean Piaget. This theory focuses on how our cognitive abilities develop as we grow, describing different stages of cognitive development. These stages are the sensorimotor stage, preoperational stage, concrete operational stage, and formal operational stage. Each stage involves different abilities and understanding, demonstrated through tasks like the clay ball experiment.

96. (C): The design used in this experiment is the Correlational Design. This is because the study examines the relationships between different variables - in this case, social support, well-being, and gender. The experimenter hypothesized a change in the strength of the relationship between social support and well-being, dependent on the gender variable. Correlational designs can show if a relationship exists, but they do not prove causality.

97. (B): Purposive Sampling was used in this study. The researcher deliberately chose a group of students from the school where he was working. This type of non-probability sampling method involves the researcher using their judgment to select participants who are most representative of the population being studied.

98. (D): In this study, Gender acts as a Moderation Variable. This is because the experimenter was testing whether the relationship between social support and well-being was different for different genders. Moderating variables are those which affect the direction and/or strength of the relation between dependent and independent variables.

99. (D): The interpretation of the result the experimenter made is "$P > .05$". A P-value greater than 0.05 suggests that the results are not statistically significant. In this study, it means that the hypothesis that the strength of the relationship between social support and well-being changes when gender is included was not supported.

100. (C): Multiple Regression is likely to have been used in this study. As the experimenter was studying the relationship of well-being with two other variables (social support and gender), multiple regression would allow for the analysis of the effect of these variables simultaneously. It helps to understand how much the dependent variable changes when we change the independent variables.

Previous Years' Paper (Solved)

National Testing Agency (NTA)

UGC-NET Junior Research Fellowship & Assistant Professor Eligibility Exam

PSYCHOLOGY, June–2022

(Online exam held on 12-07-2022)

PAPER-II

Note: *This paper contains* ***hundred (100)*** *objective type questions of* ***two (2)*** *marks each.* ***All questions are compulsory.***

1. Computer assisted testing is principally based on ________.

A. Item response theory
B. Efficiency of modern computers
C. Emphasis on internal consistency
D. Compatibility between manual and computerised scoring

2. Identify the plausible logic for the introduction of deviation IQ.

A. Level of ratio IQ varies with age
B. Ratio IQ is not measured on interval scale
C. SD of ratio IQ varies scale-to-scale
D. Comparison of ratio IQ at different age levels is not possible as SD of IQ is not constant over age

3. At which difficulty level (pass proportion) the item can make highest differentiation?

A. 0.35 B. 0.50
C. 0.75 D. 0.25

4. Which components of psychoneuro immunological system is not effected by glucocorticoids?

A. Posterior pituitary
B. T-cells
C. B-cells
D. Hippocampal neurons

5. When an experimenter wishes to ensure equal representation of a highly correlated variable with dependent variable at all levels of independent variable, he/she should use ______ design.

A. Repeated measures
B. Randomized groups
C. Latin Square
D. Randomized block

6. The type of psychological tests in which validation criterion is the performance in specialized training is _______.

A. Achievement B. Attitude
C. Aptitude D. Intelligence

7. Identify the theorist who has stated the following:

"When we have passed beyond individualising, then we shall be real persons. Ego was the helpler, Ego is the bar".

A. Carl Rogers B. Abraham Maslow
C. Sri Aurobindo D. Carl G. Jung

8. Indigenization of research was proposed for:

A. The promotion of native culture
B. Overcoming difficulty in establishing reliability
C. Overcoming difficulty in explaining phenomena in a given culture
D. Ensuring objectivity in research

9. Myelin sheath which insulates most axons in CNS is produced by ________.

A. Oligodendrocytes
B. Schwann cells
C. Microglia
D. Astrocytes

10. The largest structure in the Limbic System is the ________.
A. Hippocampus B. Cingulate gyrus
C. Fornix D. Amygdala

11. The human retina contains approximately ________.
A. Six million rods
B. One hundred twenty million cones
C. Six million cones and 120 million rods
D. Six million rods and 120 million cones

12. An EEG record during NREM sleep shows _______ waves.
A. Delta B. Alpha
C. Theta D. Beta

13. One of the primary objectives for developing first Wechsler Intelligence Scales was to:
A. Meet the need of an effective adult scale
B. Provide a test with increased face validity
C. Develop widely acceptable scale for children
D. Have scale with emphasis on speed component

14. A researcher interested to verify the effect of three independent variables on two dependant variables, shall use ______ for data analysis.
A. ANOVA B. ANCOVA
C. MANCOVA D. MANOVA

15. The process by which we translate sensory information into a meaningful representation that we process is known as________ .
A. Semantic encoding
B. Episodic decoding
C. Propositional representation
D. Pragmatic representation

16. Which of these is not one of the Gestalt principle of visual organization?
A. Similarity B. Proximity
C. Lateralization D. Common fate

17. The somatic nervous system functions with the help of _______ nerves.
A. Cranial
B. Spinal
C. Cranial and Spinal
D. Ganglionic neurons and cranial

18. Positivist paradigm subscribes to:
A. Social construction of reality
B. Observer independent reality
C. Phenomenological analysis of reality
D. Maintaining positivity in research

19. Social constructionist approach would allow cultural ______ .
A. Invariance B. Homogeniety
C. Hegemony D. Diversity

20. Sensation seeking among adolescents is best described by ______.
A. Low self regulation
B. Looking for noval experiences
C. Risk taking
D. Socializing

21. What type of question the following is in a questionnaire?
"Why did you go to cinema last night?"
A. Knowledge B. Motivation
C. Factual D. Opinion

22. The critical perspective on research does not subscribe to the view that:
A. Research has to smash myths and empower people to change society.
B. Reality is stable and subject to natural laws.
C. Research has to be informed by a theory that unveils illusion.
D. Research must expose false beliefs that hide power and objective conditions.

23. A researcher using a group of ten subjects under four conditions repeatedly, what will be degree of freedom for the error terms?
A. 9 B. 27
C. 36 D. 39

24. Psychological research does not allow one of the following activities:
A. Debriefing the participants
B. Maintaining confidentiality
C. Non granting permission to withdraw from research process
D. Obtaining consent to conduct the research

25. In a normally distributed group, an examinee scores one SD above the mean. What shall be her/his percentile score?

A. 34 B. 68
C. 84 D. 51

26. Which one of the following statements does not apply to normal probability curve?
A. It is bilaterally symmetrical
B. It is bell shaped
C. It's skewness is zero
D. It's kurtosis is zero

27. Qualitative research can follow several approaches to knowledge. Identify one which is contrary to the assumptions of qualitative research.
A. Realist
B. Positivist
C. Social Constructionist
D. Phenomenological

28. _______ is a measure of dispersion that considers all the scores.
A. Range B. Quartile deviation
C. Average deviation D. Inter quartile range

29. By what symbol the standardized regression coefficient is usually depicted?
A. β B. b
C. R D. K

30. As per threshold hypothesis there exists:
A. Modest positive relationship between intelligence and creativity when IQ is above the threshold.
B. Modest positive relationship between intelligence and creativity when IQ is below the threshold.
C. Weak positive relationship between intelligence and creativity when IQ is below the threshold.
D. Weak positive relationship between intelligence and creativity when IQ is above the threshold.

31. Gardner's theory of intelligence posits that a person who is introspective, self reflective, understands the strengths and weaknesses tends to have higher level of _______.
A. Intrapersonal intelligence
B. Naturalist intelligence
C. Interpersonal intelligence
D. Linguistic intelligence

32. Crystallized intelligence includes _______.
A. Learned knowledge and skills
B. Novel ideas
C. Divergent thinking
D. Emotional Skills

33. The 'Product' approach to creativity primarily focuses on:
A. What type of people are creative?
B. How does environment shape creativity?
C. How do people arrive at creative ideas?
D. What is considered to be creative?

34. A bell was sounded by Pavlov and then two minutes later a plate of meat powder was presented to the dog. We would term this arrangement as ______ conditioning.
A. Delay B. Trace
C. Backward D. Forward

35. Emotionally arousing stimuli have also found to lead to amnesia, even though no physical damage to brain structure related to memory have occurred. This refers to ______ .
A. Non verbal cue-utilization
B. Retrograde amnesia
C. Confabulations
D. Flashbulb memory repression

36. The process of Chunking permits us to:
A. Extend the duration of sensory memory
B. Transfer information into LTM
C. Expand the capacity of our STM
D. Expand the capacity of our LTM

37. Psychologists define _______ as a long lasting change in behaviour induced by experience.
A. Education B. Maturation
C. Learning D. Creativity

38. Today employees are required to work in teams as it is believed that performance will be better in teams. This is because in a team:
A. Social facilitation occurs
B. Social loafing occurs
C. Motivation loss is low
D. People are more attentive

39. Which of the following statements reflects the argument made by cognitive social learning theory?
A. Self regulation is more important than advanced reasoning
B. Social construction is the way children learn morality
C. Humans since long had capacity to develop moral behaviour
D. Humans are born with innate disposition shaped by our genes

40. The 'Robber's Cave' experiment by Sherif showed the value of ________ in reducing prejudice.
A. Contact
B. Superordinate goals
C. Subordinate goals
D. Stereotypes

41. Group think may occur when:
(*a*) Members feel they cannot fail.
(*b*) Members' motivation is low.
(*c*) Members do not express opinions that differ from own group members.
(*d*) Members stereotype their enemy as weak, stupid or unreasonable.

Choose the ***correct*** answer from the options given below:
A. (*a*), (*c*) and (*d*) only
B. (*a*), (*b*) and (*c*) only
C. (*b*), (*c*) and (*d*) only
D. (*a*), (*b*) and (*d*) only

42. Which of the following are major/sources of stressors linked to Coronary Heart Disease?
(*a*) Catastrophes (*b*) Hassles
(*c*) Major life events (*d*) Type A personality
(*e*) Low Motivation

Choose the ***correct*** answer from the options given below:
A. (*a*), (*b*), (*c*) and (*d*) only
B. (*a*), (*b*), (*c*) and (*e*), only
C. (*b*), (*c*) and (*d*) only
D. (*a*), (*b*) and (*e*), only

43. Choose the health promoting life style factors from the given list.
(*a*) Exercising occasionally
(*b*) Engaging only in protected and safe sex
(*c*) Maintaining weight
(*d*) Eating balanced meals
(*e*) Wearing seat belts and helmets

Choose the ***correct*** answer from the options given below:
A. (*a*), (*c*) and (*d*) only
B. (*b*), (*d*) and (*e*) only
C. (*c*) and (*d*) only
D. (*a*) and (*d*) only

44. Which of the following are NOT the attributes of mindfulness?
(*a*) Patience (*b*) Judging
(*c*) Trust (*d*) Acceptance
(*e*) Attachment

Choose the ***correct*** answer from the options given below:
A. (*a*) and (*b*) only B. (*c*) and (*e*) only
C. (*b*) and (*e*) only D. (*b*) and (*c*) only

45. Which of the following about acculturation is NOT correct?
(*a*) It includes sticking to one's cultural beliefs
(*b*) It involves displaying prejudice toward people from different cultures
(*c*) It involves adopting new ways of behaving
(*d*) It involves balancing between values of two different cultures

Choose the ***correct*** answer from the options given below:
A. (*c*) only
B. (*a*) and (*b*) only
C. (*a*), (*b*) and (*c*) only
D. (*d*) only

46. Diffusion of responsibility is a hypothesized cause of:
(*a*) Identity formation
(*b*) Prosocial behaviour
(*c*) By Stander effect
(*d*) Compliance
(*e*) Sharing behaviour

Choose the ***correct*** answer from the options given below:
A. (*b*) and (*c*) only B. (*a*) and (*b*) only
C. (*c*) and (*d*) only D. (*a*) and (*e*) only

47. Systematic desensitization involves:
(*a*) Aversion therapy
(*b*) Reciprocal inhibition
(*c*) Anxiety hierarchy
(*d*) Time out

Choose the ***correct*** answer from the options given below:
A. (*a*) and (*b*) only B. (*b*) and (*d*) only
C. (*b*) and (*c*) only D. (*a*) and (*d*) only

48. What are the purposes of research?
(*a*) Explaining a phenomenon
(*b*) Making a discovery
(*c*) Fulfilling a gap in knowledge
(*d*) Attempt to resolve contradictory findings
(*e*) Making an invention

Choose the ***correct*** answer from the options given below:
A. (*a*) and (*c*) only
B. (*a*), (*b*) and (*c*) only
C. (*a*), (*c*) and (*d*) only
D. (*b*), (*c*) and (*e*) only

49. The mean can be misleading if a distribution has _______.
(*a*) Marked skewness
(*b*) Large number of scores
(*c*) Few extremely high valued scores
(*d*) Small number of scores
(*e*) Few extremely low valued scores

Choose the ***correct*** answer from the options given below:
A. (*a*), (*b*) and (*d*) only
B. (*c*), (*d*) and (*e*) only
C. (*a*), (*c*) and (*e*) only
D. (*b*), (*c*) and (*d*) only

50. The ***central*** aspect of rational thinking involves:
(*a*) Deduction
(*b*) Induction
(*c*) Conduction logic
(*d*) Reduction approach
(*e*) Paradigm

Choose the ***correct*** answer from the options given below:
A. (*a*) and (*d*) only B. (*a*) and (*b*) only
C. (*b*) and (*d*) only D. (*d*) and (*e*) only

51. Which of the following hypothalamic nuclei were considered as hunger regulator?
(*a*) Supra optic nucleus
(*b*) Ventromedial hypothalamus
(*c*) Medial
(*d*) Lateral
(*e*) Paraventricular

Choose the ***correct*** answer from the options given below:
A. (*d*) only B. (*b*) and (*c*) only
C. (*b*) and (*d*) only D. (*a*) and (*e*) only

52. Identify the posterior pituitary hormones
(*a*) Thyrotropin
(*b*) Follicle Stimulating Hormone
(*c*) Oxytocin
(*d*) Luteinizing Hormone
(*e*) Vasopressin

Choose the ***correct*** answer from the options given below:
A. (*c*) only B. (*b*) only
C. (*a*) and (*b*) only D. (*c*) and (*e*) only

53. Identify the indices of item validity:
(*a*) Item-inter correlation
(*b*) Item-total correlation
(*c*) Item-pass proportion
(*d*) Item-criterion correlation

Choose the ***correct*** answer from the options given below:
A. (*a*) and (*d*) only
B. (*a*) and (*c*) only
C. (*b*) and (*d*) only
D. (*b*), (*c*) and (*d*) only

54. Victor Frankl stated that the survivors of Nazi concentration camps could do so because they hanged on to a sense of meaning and purpose in their life. Which psychotherapy is based on this?
A. Well-being therapy
B. Logo therapy
C. Positive psychotherapy
D. Acceptance and Commitment therapy

55. _______ refers to the capacity of the nervous system to perceive a stimulus presented at an intensity that is below threshold.

A. Unconscious processing
B. Stimulus adaption
C. Subliminal perception
D. Supraliminal sensation

56. What is the median of the scores given below?

15, 8, 30, 12, 5, 40, 30, 20

A. 8.50 B. 17.50
C. 20 D. 15

57. Name the test that can verify the hypothesis that two related groups have been drawn from the same population.
A. Wilcoxon signed rank test
B. Mann-Whitney U-test
C. Kruskal-Wallis test
D. Friedman's test

58. The fourth force in counselling is indicated by which approach?
A. Humanistic B. Solution focussed
C. Multicultural D. Indian

59. The phenomenon of object permanence occurs in which stage of cognitive development?
A. Sensori-Motor
B. Preoperational
C. Concrete operational
D. Formal operational

60. The linguistic relativity hypothesis states that:
A. Language depends on thought processes.
B. Thinking is shaped by language.
C. Language and thought follow independent pathways of development.
D. Language and thought are related in an interdependent fashion.

61. Which one of the following does not describe the state of flow?
A. Loss of self B. Internal talk
C. Oneness D. Clarity of action

62. ______ does not explain our obeying unjust commands of authority.
A. Genetic endowment to obedience
B. Ingrained habit
C. Normative influence
D. Informational influence

63. ________ is an impairment of language functioning caused by damage to the brain.
A. Agraphia B. Amnesia
C. Aphasia D. Autism

64. Which theory includes environmental mastery as one of the dimensions of well being?
A. Keyes' mental health continuum
B. PERMA model of well being
C. Ryff's theory of psychological well being
D. Eudaimonic theory of happiness

65. The first response that people typically express when frustrated is to:
A. Try again B. Get angry
C. Give up D. Be creative

66. Match List-I with List-II.

List-I	List-II
(*a*) Actualizing tendency	I. Organism continuously weighs the experiences in terms of its ability to satisfy
(*b*) Subjective frame of reference	II. Organism attempts to fulfil the inherent potentials
(*c*) Experiencing	III. Perceptual frame of reference of the organism
(*d*) Organismic valuing process	IV. Receiving the impact of external and internal sensations at the moment

Choose the ***correct*** answer from the options given below:

	(*a*)	(*b*)	(*c*)	(*d*)
A.	IV	III	I	II
B.	II	III	IV	I
C.	III	I	II	IV
D.	I	III	II	IV

67. Match List-I with List-II.

List-I (Neurotransmitters)	List-II (Type)
(*a*) Glutamate	I. Catecholamine
(*b*) Dopamine	II. Amino acid
(*c*) Acetylcholine	III. Indoleamine
(*d*) Serotonin	IV. Quaternary amine

Choose the ***correct*** answer from the options given below:

	(*a*)	(*b*)	(*c*)	(*d*)
A.	IV	III	II	I
B.	III	IV	I	II
C.	I	II	III	IV
D.	II	I	IV	III

68. Match List-I with List-II.

List-I (Theory of Attention)	**List-II (Researchers)**
(*a*) Early Selection	I. Deutsch & Deutsch
(*b*) Attenuation	II. Cherry
(*c*) Late selection	III. Johnston & Heinz
(*d*) Multi model	IV. Triesman

Choose the ***correct*** answer from the options given below:

	(*a*)	(*b*)	(*c*)	(*d*)
A.	II	I	IV	III
B.	II	IV	I	III
C.	I	IV	II	III
D.	IV	I	III	II

69. Match List-I with List-II.

List-I (Process)	**List-II (Description)**
(*a*) Flourishing	I. Capacity to appreciate and enhance positive experiences
(*b*) Savouring	II. Preventing stress from happening in the first place
(*c*) Proactive coping	III. A state of optimal human functioning
(*d*) Languishing	IV. A state of feeling emptiness

Choose the ***correct*** answer from the options given below:

	(*a*)	(*b*)	(*c*)	(*d*)
A.	I	III	II	IV
B.	III	I	II	IV
C.	I	II	IV	III
D.	II	I	III	IV

70. Match List-I with List-II.

List-I (Type of cell)	**List-II (Function)**
(*a*) Antigen	I. Cell mediated immunity
(*b*) Phagocytes	II. Consume and destroy microorganism
(*c*) T-cells	III. Antibody mediated immunity
(*d*) B-cells	IV. Distinguishes foreign cell

Choose the ***correct*** answer from the options given below:

	(*a*)	(*b*)	(*c*)	(*d*)
A.	IV	I	II	III
B.	IV	II	I	III
C.	II	IV	I	III
D.	IV	III	II	I

71. Match List-I with List-II.

List-I (Concepts)	**List-II (Process)**
(*a*) Heuristics	I. Breaking whole into manageable part
(*b*) Analysis	II. An existing model for representing a problem
(*c*) Synthesis	III. Mean-end analysis
(*d*) Mental Set	IV. Putting together elements into a useful whole

Choose the ***correct*** answer from the options given below:

	(*a*)	(*b*)	(*c*)	(*d*)
A.	II	III	IV	I
B.	III	I	IV	II
C.	IV	II	III	I
D.	III	I	II	IV

72. Match List-I with List-II.

List-I (Approaches to personality)	**List-II (Key feature)**
(*a*) Psychodynamic	I. Learned drives
(*b*) Humanistic	II. Social learning
(*c*) Cognitive	III. Inner forces
(*d*) Behaviouristic	IV. Self actualization

Choose the ***correct*** answer from the options given below:

	(*a*)	(*b*)	(*c*)	(*d*)
A.	III	I	II	IV
B.	I	II	III	IV
C.	III	IV	II	I
D.	II	IV	III	I

73. Match List-I with List-II.

List-I (Theories)	List-II (Propositions)
(*a*) Realistic Conflict	I. Identity is formed by social comparison, categorization and construction of self identity.
(*b*) Relative Deprivation	II. Competition for scarce resources results in intergroup tensions.
(*c*) Social Identity	III. Comparison of one self to others in ways that raise one's self esteem.
(*d*) Social Comparison	IV. Feeling of getting less than what one is entitled to.

Choose the ***correct*** answer from the options given below:

	(*a*)	(*b*)	(*c*)	(*d*)
A.	II	IV	I	III
B.	I	II	III	IV
C.	I	III	II	IV
D.	IV	II	I	III

74. Match List-I with List-II.

List-I (Name of the disorder)	List-II (Category of the disorder)
(*a*) Autism	I. Neurocognitive
(*b*) Alzheimer	II. Elimination
(*c*) Bulimia nervosa	III. Neuro-developmental
(*d*) Encopresis	IV. Eating

Choose the ***correct*** answer from the options given below:

	(*a*)	(*b*)	(*c*)	(*d*)
A.	III	I	IV	II
B.	I	III	II	IV
C.	I	II	IV	III
D.	III	II	IV	I

75. Match List-I with List-II.

List-I (Psychologists)	List-II (Key concept)
(*a*) C.L. Hull	I. Need
(*b*) S. Freud	II. Drive
(*c*) H. Murray	III. Instinct
(*d*) D.C. McClelland	IV. Fantasy

Choose the ***correct*** answer from the options given below:

	(*a*)	(*b*)	(*c*)	(*d*)
A.	II	III	I	IV
B.	III	II	IV	I
C.	I	IV	III	II
D.	IV	I	II	III

76. Match List-I with List-II.

List-I	List-II
(*a*) Self determination	I. D.O. Hebb
(*b*) Contact Comfort	II. Hans Selye
(*c*) Cell assembly	III. Edward Deci
(*d*) General Adaptation Syndrome	IV. Harry Harlow

Choose the ***correct*** answer from the options given below:

	(*a*)	(*b*)	(*c*)	(*d*)
A.	III	IV	II	I
B.	III	IV	I	II
C.	II	I	III	IV
D.	I	II	IV	III

77. Match List-I with List-II.

List-I (Issue Addressed)	List-II (Perspective)
(*a*) Changes in thoughts over the life span	I. Cognitive perspective
(*b*) Personality and hidden motives of person	II. Psychodynamic perspective
(*c*) Brain function as mediating behaviour	III. Developmental perspective
(*d*) Thoughts of a person in a given situation	IV. Biological Perspective

Choose the ***correct*** answer from the options given below:

	(*a*)	(*b*)	(*c*)	(*d*)
A.	I	IV	III	II
B.	III	II	IV	I
C.	II	III	I	IV
D.	IV	I	II	III

78. Match List-I with List-II.

List-I (Concept)	List-II (Term)
(*a*) A health strategy that focuses on providing education materials people	I. Social support
(*b*) Having a group of friends can buffer the risks posed by chronic stress	II. Hassles
(*c*) A person exposed to a severe stressor may experience that event	III. Primary prevention
(*d*) Minor annoying events that can add to diminish health	IV. Post traumatic stress disorder

Choose the ***correct*** answer from the options given below:

	(*a*)	(*b*)	(*c*)	(*d*)
A.	II	III	IV	I
B.	III	I	IV	II
C.	I	III	II	IV
D.	IV	II	III	I

79. Match List-I with List-II.

List-I	List-II
(*a*) Z Score	I. $\bar{X} = 50, \sigma = 10$
(*b*) Stanine	II. $\bar{X} = 5.5, \sigma = 2$
(*c*) T Score	III. $\bar{X} = 5, \sigma = 2$ (approx)
(*d*) Sten	IV. $\bar{X} = 0, \sigma = 1$

Choose the ***correct*** answer from the options given below:

	(*a*)	(*b*)	(*c*)	(*d*)
A.	IV	III	I	II
B.	IV	I	III	II
C.	I	II	IV	III
D.	II	III	I	IV

80. Trace the sequence of events followed by the exposure to prolonged stress:

(*a*) Glucocorticoids are released by adrenal cortex

(*b*) Lymphocytes are activated

(*c*) Hippocampal Cells get degenerated

(*d*) Anterior pituitary releases ACTH

(*e*) T-cells and B-cells get activated

Choose the ***correct*** answer from the options given below:

A. (*a*), (*d*), (*e*), (*b*), (*c*)

B. (*b*), (*c*), (*d*), (*e*), (*a*)

C. (*d*), (*a*), (*b*), (*e*), (*c*)

D. (*c*), (*b*), (*a*), (*e*), (*d*)

81. Trace the correct sequence of the components of auditory information processing

(*a*) The inferior colliculus receives the information

(*b*) Cochlear nucleus and olivary nuclei receive the information

(*c*) The medial geniculate nucleus receives the information

(*d*) The organ of corti sands information to the brain

(*e*) Primary auditory cortex receives the information

Choose the ***correct*** answer from the options given below:

A. (*d*), (*a*), (*c*), (*b*), (*e*)

B. (*e*), (*c*), (*a*), (*b*), (*d*)

C. (*d*), (*b*), (*a*), (*c*), (*e*)

D. (*e*), (*a*), (*b*), (*c*), (*d*)

82. Trace the pathway of visual information processing:

(*a*) Geniculate nuclei send information to striate cortex.

(*b*) Information reaches to extrastriata cortex.

(*c*) Retina sends to lateral geniculate nucleus.

(*d*) Information reaches to inferior temporal cortex and parietal cortex.

(*e*) Stimulation of visual receptor.

Choose the ***correct*** answer from the options given below:

A. (*c*), (*d*), (*e*), (*a*), (*b*)

B. (*e*), (*c*), (*a*), (*b*), (*d*)

C. (*d*), (*b*), (*a*), (*c*), (*e*)

D. (*e*), (*a*), (*c*), (*b*), (*d*)

83. According to Bhagvad Gita the spiritual journey towards self realization and attainment of peace involves movement across several stages. Identify the correct order:

(*a*) Tyaga (*b*) Dhyana

(*c*) Abhyasa (*d*) Gyana

(*e*) Shanti

Choose the ***correct*** answer from the options given below:

A. (*d*), (*b*), (*a*), (*c*), (*e*)
B. (*c*), (*d*), (*b*), (*a*), (*e*)
C. (*c*), (*b*), (*d*), (*a*), (*e*)
D. (*b*), (*c*), (*a*), (*d*), (*e*)

84. Arrange the following tests in the increasing order of structuredness:

(*a*) WAT (*b*) TAT
(*c*) Rorschach (*d*) MMPI

Choose the ***correct*** answer from the options given below

A. (*b*), (*c*), (*a*), (*d*) B. (*d*), (*a*), (*b*), (*c*)
C. (*c*), (*a*), (*b*), (*d*) D. (*c*), (*b*), (*a*), (*d*)

85. Find the correct sequence of events in reference to James-Lange theory of emotions

(*a*) The feedback received constitutes feeling of emotions
(*b*) The emotion producing situation is interpreted by the cortex
(*c*) The brain receives sensory feedback of responses occuring in the body
(*d*) The cortex triggers changes in peripheral nervous system
(*e*) The muscular and visceral changes occur in the body

Choose the ***correct*** answer from the options given below:

A. (*b*), (*d*), (*e*), (*c*), (*a*)
B. (*a*), (*d*), (*c*), (*e*), (*b*)
C. (*d*), (*b*), (*e*), (*c*), (*a*)
D. (*b*), (*d*), (*c*), (*e*), (*a*)

86. Given below are two statements.

Statement I : Life - course - persistent anti-social behaviour occurs during adulthood.

Statement II : Adolescence - limited anti-social behaviour occurs due to maturity gap.

In light of the above statements, choose the ***most appropriate*** answer from the options given below:

A. Both Statement I and Statement II are correct
B. Both Statement I and Statement II are incorrect
C. Statement I is correct, but Statement II is incorrect
D. Statement I is incorrect, but Statement II is correct

87. Given below are two statements.

Statement I : Stress is experienced in relatively ordinary life conditions.

Statement II : Any life event that requires people to change, adapt or adjust can result in stress.

In light of the above statements, choose the ***correct*** answer from the options given below:

A. Both Statement I and Statement II are true
B. Both Statement I and Statement II are false
C. Statement I is true, but Statement II is false
D. Statement I is false, but Statement II is true

88. Given below are two statements.

Statement I : Being marginalized also means you are discriminated.

Statement II : Marginalization and discriminations are not related.

In light of the above statements, choose the ***most appropriate*** answer from the options given below:

A. Both Statement I and Statement II are correct
B. Both Statement I and Statement II are incorrect
C. Statement I is correct, but Statement II is incorrect
D. Statement I is incorrect, but Statement II is correct

89. Given below are two statements, one is labelled as Assertion (A) and the other is labelled as Reason (R).

Assertion (A) : Counsellors generally follow eclectic approach to counselling suitable to specific context.

Reason (R) : When counsellor and client differ in their cutural background, it requires multicultural counselling skills.

In light of the above statements, choose the correct answer from the options given below:

A. Both (A) and (R) are true and (R) is the correct explanation of (A)
B. Both (A) and (R) are true, but (R) is NOT the correct explanation of (A)
C. (A) is true, but (R) is false
D. (A) is false, but (R) is true

90. Given below are two statements, one is labelled as Assertion (A) and the other is labelled as Reason (R).

Assertion (A) : Drive reduction was proposed to explain the actions of people taken to reduce tension created by needs.

Reason (R) : Human body maintains balance in its physical status. This is called homeostasis.

In light of the above statements, choose the ***correct*** answer from the options given below:

A. Both (A) and (R) are true and (R) is the correct explanation of (A)
B. Both (A) and (R) are true, but (R) is NOT the correct explanation of (A)
C. (A) is true, but (R) is false
D. (A) is false, but (R) is true

Directions (Qs. No. 91-95): *Read the following passage carefully and answer the five questions that follows.*

An investigator designs an experiment to see the effect of illumination level and duration of visual signal on detectability of change in illumination in a dark room on 120 randomly selected sample of college going male students. She decided to use low and high levels of illumination and three levels of duration of stimulus as 30, 50 and 70 milliseconds through an electric chronoscopic instrument. The investigator used separate group design for various combination of treatments. These participants were required to press a 'Yes' button if they detect the signal or 'No' button if they do not. Each participant was given a total of 50 trials within which 10 signals were randomly presented. Proportions of hits and false alarms was computed for each participant and were analysed to get answers to research questions.

91. Identify the experimental design used:

A. Randomized group
B. Single factor
C. Multifactor
D. Repeated Measures

92. What type of independent variables were included?

A. Both were fixed factors.
B. Both were random factors.
C. Illumination level was a fixed factor while the duration was a random factor.
D. Illumination level was a random factor while the duration was a fixed factor.

93. How many hypotheses the used design will allow to be verified?

A. One
B. Three
C. Four
D. Seven

94. Find the degree of freedom for the error term:

A. 119
B. 117
C. 2
D. 114

95. Identify the variables that were controlled by the experimenter.

A. Ambient illumination and duration of signal
B. Gender and level of illumination of the signal
C. Gender and ambient illumination
D. Frequency of signal and level of illumination

Directions (Qs. No. 96-100): *Read the following paragraph and answer the five questions that follows.*

A group of researchers were curious to understand the behaviour of guards in prisons and wanted to know whether it was due to dispositional (personality) or environment dependent (situational) factors. To study the roles of guards and prisoners they created a mock prison. 23 men unfamiliar with each other volunteered to participate in the study and were assigned the role of prisoners and guards. Both adopted to their new roles. A rebellion on the second day led to harsh retaliation by the guards. Ruthless retributive action was taken to punish the prisoners. The researchers intended to run the experiment for 2 weeks. It was however, terminated on the sixth day due to the emotional breakdown of prisoners and excessive aggression by the guards. The experiment revealed how people confirm to the social roles they are expected to play.

96. Name the Psychologist who led this research:
A. Milgram B. Zimbardo
C. Asch D. Sherif

97. What went wrong with the experiment because of which it was terminated on the 6th day?
A. The experiment was boring
B. The university administration asked the researchers to stop the study
C. The prisoners felt upset and humiliated
D. The prisoners and guards became friends

98. The experiment:
A. Was highly appreciated
B. Was highly criticized
C. Resulted in the development and recognition of ethical guidelines
D. Resulted in the study of behaviour of guards

99. This study shows that we behave according to our:
A. beliefs B. attitudes
C. roles D. background

100. This experiment is known as:
A. Obedience experiment
B. Stanford prison experiment
C. False memory experiment
D. Michigan experiment

ANSWERS

1	2	3	4	5	6	7	8	9	10
A	D	B	A	D	C	C	C	A	B
11	**12**	**13**	**14**	**15**	**16**	**17**	**18**	**19**	**20**
C	A	A	D	A	C	C	B	D	B
21	**22**	**23**	**24**	**25**	**26**	**27**	**28**	**29**	**30**
B	B	B	C	C	D	B	C	A	B
31	**32**	**33**	**34**	**35**	**36**	**37**	**38**	**39**	**40**
A	A	D	B	B	C	C	A	A	B
41	**42**	**43**	**44**	**45**	**46**	**47**	**48**	**49**	**50**
A	A	B	C	B	A	C	C	C	B
51	**52**	**53**	**54**	**55**	**56**	**57**	**58**	**59**	**60**
C	D	C	B	C	B	A	C	A	B
61	**62**	**63**	**64**	**65**	**66**	**67**	**68**	**69**	**70**
B	A	C	C	B	B	D	B	B	B
71	**72**	**73**	**74**	**75**	**76**	**77**	**78**	**79**	**80**
B	C	A	A	A	B	B	B	A	C
81	**82**	**83**	**84**	**85**	**86**	**87**	**88**	**89**	**90**
C	B	B	D	A	D	A	B	B	B
91	**92**	**93**	**94**	**95**	**96**	**97**	**98**	**99**	**100**
C	A	B	D	C	B	C	C	C	B

Previous Years' Paper (Solved)

National Testing Agency (NTA)

UGC-NET Junior Research Fellowship & Assistant Professor Eligibility Exam

PSYCHOLOGY, June–2021

(Online exam held on 21-11-2021)

PAPER-II

Note: *This paper contains* ***hundred*** (**100**) *objective type questions of* ***two*** (2) *marks each.* ***All*** *questions are* ***compulsory***.

1. Which of the following nerves carry the sensory messages from skin, eyes and ears to Central Nervous System?

A. Efferent B. Afferent
C. Cranial D. Peripheral

2. A Woman who learns that she has been deprived of promotion to a higher job in a company, may storm into her boss's office and have temper tentrum. It exemplifies:

A. Sublimation
B. Rationalization
C. Reaction Formation
D. Regression

3. Which of the following is correct for the Pheromones?

A. Biochemicals found within the brain which effect a person's behaviour
B. Biochemicals which play an important role in transmitting information from neuron to neuron
C. Chemical messengers found in the Central Nervous System
D. Chemical substances emitted by the person into the environment affecting the behaviour of others

4. Which of the following describes the enduring facilitation of synaptic transmission that occurs following activation of synapses by high intensity and high frequency stimulation of pre-synaptic neurons?

A. Action potential
B. Absolute refractory period
C. Relative refractory period
D. Long term potentiation

5. If a person's distinctive social category makes him or her vulnerable to stereotyping, it is referred to as:

A. Token integration B. Neosexism
C. Ingratiation D. Token bias

6. Which of the following statements is wrong?

A. Body's requirement of sleep varies with age
B. Tertiary prevention is action taken to identify and treat an illness or injury early with an aim of stopping or reversing the problem
C. Endorphins are released during exercise
D. Excessive alcohol consumption leads to shrinking of frontal lobe of the brain

7. Which of the following is involved in Type 'a' processes of thinking as described by Wertheimer?

A. Grouping and reorganization
B. Assimilation and conditioning
C. Blind trial and error
D. Partially productive methods

8. A person's chronological Age is 20 years, and mental age is 16 years. What would be his IQ?

A. 120 B. 100
C. 80 D. 110

9. "When individuals believe that moral choices are not dependent on close ties to others and that rules must be enforced in the same manner for everyone and each person should uphold them".

The following statement is characteristic of which stage of Moral Development according to Kohlberg?

A. Social contract orientation
B. Morality of Interpersonal Cooperation
C. Social order maintaining orientation
D. Universal Ethical principle orientation

10. Which of the following statements describe the term 'Diffusion of Responsibility?

A. People help others in order to reduce their emotional discomfort
B. Greater the number of witnesses to an emergency, the less likely the victims are to receive help
C. Helping others is a means of increasing one's own status and reputation
D. Prosocial acts are motivated solely by the desire to help someone in need

11. Cattell proposed his theory of fluid and crystallized intelligences on the basis of which of the following?

A. First order factors of abilities
B. Second order factors of abilities
C. Third order factors of abilities
D. Higher order factors of abilities

12. Behaviour is a direct result of behavioral intentions, this is explained by which of the following?

A. Theory of reasoned action
B. Theory of social impact
C. Equity theory
D. Correspondent inference theory

13. As per Socrates' Greek Philosophy, which of the following is NOT true about eudaemonia?

A. It means living well or flourishing
B It is more than merely attaining pleasure
C. Being virtuous is almost identical to eudaemonia
D. Being virtuous does not guarantee eudaemonia

14. Multivariate Analysis of Variance (MANOVA) is best suited for making groupwise comparisons for several dependent variables. Which of the following are these?

A. Uncorrelated
B. Moderately correlated
C. Very highly correlated
D. Either uncorrelated or have small negative correlations

15. Who among the following proposed that different emotional stimuli induce different patterns of ANS activity and that these different patterns produce different emotional experiences?

A. James–Lange
B. Cannon–Bard
C. Singer–Schachter
D. Plutchik

16. The tendency to believe that a task will take less time than it really will, is known as:

A. Magical thinking
B. Planning Fallacy
C. Optimistic Bias
D. Fundamental Attribution Error

17. Which of the following are the correct differences between Parkinson's disease and Huntington's disease?

(*a*) Parkinson's disease is a disorder of middle and old age while Huntington's disease is a disorder of young.
(*b*) Parkinson's disease is a movement disorder while Huntington's disease is an emotional disorder.
(*c*) Unlike Parkinson's disease, Huntington's disease has a strong genetic base.
(*d*) Parkinson's disease is not associated with severe dementia while Huntington's disease is.

Choose the ***correct*** answer from the options given below:
A. (*a*) and (*b*) only
B. (*c*) and (*d*) only
C. (*a*), (*c*) and (*d*) only
D. (*b*), (*c*) and (*d*) only

18. Memory that is thought to contain knowledge, facts, information, ideas that can be recalled or described in words, pictures, or symbols is called:
A. Procedural memory
B. Episodic memory
C. Semantic memory
D. Declarative memory

19. Young adults who return after leaving home for some period, to live in their middle aged parents home are known as:
A. Sandwich children
B. Benevolent children
C. Boomerang children
D. Compliant children

20. Integration of cognitive aspects of learning with the emotional aspects of experience and learning is known as:
A. Integrated approach to learning
B. Confluent education
C. Feeling class approach to education
D. Motivational approach to learning

21. Which one of the following is usually not considered an example of the evaluative dimension of the Osgood Semantic Differential?
A. Clean — Dirty
B. Slow — Fast
C. Good — Bad
D. Kind — Cruel

22. In which schools of Indian thought about yoga, 'Prakrti' remains isolated as a principle of ultimate reality into self and is active only in the presence and service of 'Purusa'?
A. Integral yoga philosophy
B. Vedanta
C. Samkhya
D. Sahaj yoga

23. Pattern of familial transmission of intelligence from one generation to other is investigated in which of the following?
A. Linkage analysis studies
B. Adoption studies
C. Association studies
D. Segregation analysis studies

24. Persons inclined to be verbally aggressive have:
A. low threshold for Behaviour Activation system
B. low threshold for Flight–Fight system
C. high threshold for Behaviour Inhibition system
D. high threshold for Behaviour Activation system

25. The person's failure to respond to the second stimulus while continuing to respond to the first stimulus is because of:
A. Event Related Potential (ERP)
B. Psychological Refractory Period (PRP)
C. Priming effect
D. Excessive mental effort

26. Some people are able to draw an object, match similar objects and describe the component parts but they fail to recognize the objects that they had just seen or drawn. Which of the following describes this phenomena?
A. Associative Agnosia
B. Apperceptive Agnosia
C. Visual Neglect
D. Form Agnosia

27. Discovery and understanding of our own abilities brings happiness but also brings fear of new responsibilities and duties. It is called:
A. Fear of failure B. Jonah complex
C. Motives conflict D. Fear of success

28. Qualities such as calmness, tolerance, sociability, love of comfort and easy goingness depict, which of the following?
A. Viscertonia
B. Somatotonia
C. Cerebrotonia
D. Ectomorphia

29. In which phase of Enright's model of psychological forgiveness, individual gains a cognitive understanding of the offender in a new light that brings a positive change in view about the offender, self and the relationship?

A. Uncovering phase B. Decision phase
C. Work phase D. Deepening phase

30. It is possible to accept the world as it is, without experiencing dissatisfaction. This is related to which of the following in Buddhism?

A. Right thought in eight-fold path
B. Right mindfulness in eight-fold path
C. Elimination of craving
D. Existence of satisfaction/dissatisfaction

31. Which one of the following is considered as a culture-fair test?

A. Bhatia's Battery of Intelligence
B. Kaufman's Intelligence Tests
C. Wechsler's Adult Intelligence scale
D. Naglieri Nonverbal Ability Test

32. Projective measures, particularly inkblot tests, index which of the following?

A. Novelty context of creativity
B. Meaning context of creativity
C. Domain specific creativity
D. General creative potential

33. When a target is defined by just one distinctive feature which is available on its feature map and it calls attention to itself is known as:

A. Binding effect
B. Pop-out effect
C. Conjunction effect
D. Orienting effect

34. Which one of the following is a nearest parametric alternative to Kruskal–Wallis test?

A. Independent samples t test
B. Paired samples t test
C. One–way ANOVA for independent groups
D. One–way ANOVA for repeated measures

35. Which theory determines poverty as a psychological problem of separated classes in society?

A. Attribution theory
B. Depletable self-control theory
C. Distancing theory
D. Multiple factor theory of poverty

36. Visuospatial sketch pad is a component of which of the following?

A. Long-term memory
B. Short-term memory
C. Working memory
D. Sensory memory

37. Who of the following emphasised nomothetic approach in personality research?

A. Allport B. Eysenk
C. Jung D. Galton

38. After being robbed by a boy recently the shopkeeper says "beware of teenagers in our community".

Which of the following explains his reactions?

A. Algorithm
B. Availability Heuristic
C. Representative Heuristic
D. Gambler's fallacy

39. Communication of the understanding of the 'internal frame of reference' to client by a therapist pertains to which type of counseling skills?

A. Reflection B. Focusing
C. Empathy D. Social influencer

40. Vouyerstic and exhibitionistic disorders are included in which of the following in DSM-5?

A. Sexual dysfunctions
B. Paraphillic disorders
C. Other conditions that focus on clinical attention
D. Disruptive impulse control and conduct disorders

41. Which of the following are true regarding Broca's area?

(*a*) It is located in the frontal lobe.
(*b*) Its function is speech production.
(*c*) Understanding and processing aspects of language are associated with it.
(*d*) It helps people using sign language.

Choose the ***correct*** answer from the options given below:

A. (*a*) and (*b*) only
B. (*c*) and (*d*) only
C. (*a*), (*b*) and (*c*) only
D. (*a*), (*b*), (*c*) and (*d*)

42. Which of the following is/are correctly associated with Plato's idea of 'Chariot that is pulled by two horses'?

(*a*) Desiring soul is the charioteer.
(*b*) Rational soul is located in the head.
(*c*) Rational soul is governed by restraint and modesty.
(*d*) Spirited soul knows the honour.

Choose the ***correct*** answer from the options given below:

A. (*c*) only
B. (*a*) and (*b*) only
C. (*b*) and (*d*) only
D. (*a*), (*c*) and (*d*) only

43. Ethological approach to motivation mainly explains:

(*a*) biological aspects of behaviour.
(*b*) evolutionary history of behaviour.
(*c*) causation of behaviour in terms of stimulus, hormonal and neurobiological events.
(*d*) proximal determinants of behaviour.

Choose the ***most appropriate*** answer from the options given below:

A. (*a*) and (*b*) only
B. (*c*) and (*d*) only
C. (*a*), (*b*) and (*c*) only
D. (*b*), (*c*) and (*d*) only

44. Loftus and Pickrell (1995) asked people to read and think about events which had happened to them in childhood and also instructed to write a description of one event which was actually fictitious. About one third of the participants described the fictitious events as having really happened to them. This is called:

(*a*) Eyewitness memory
(*b*) False memory
(*c*) Flash bulb memory
(*d*) Autobiographical memory

Choose the ***correct*** answer from the options given below:

A. (*a*) and (*b*) only B. (*b*) only
C. (*b*) and (*c*) only D. (*a*) only

45. Which of the following characteristics are applicable to emotions that are considered to occur as a result of interaction among subjective and environmental factors and neural and hormonal processes?

(*a*) Emotions give rise to hedonic experiences.
(*b*) Emotions stimulate to generate cognitive explanations.
(*c*) Emotions trigger variety of internal neuro-biological changes.
(*d*) Emotions always elicit rewarding behaviour.

Choose the ***most appropriate*** answer from the options given below:

A. (*a*) and (*b*) only
B. (*b*) and (*c*) only
C. (*a*), (*b*) and (*c*) only
D. (*b*), (*c*) and (*d*) only

46. In the two group design with a continuous dependent variable, which of the following measures of effect size can be employed?

(*a*) Cohen's d
(*b*) Point biserial correlation
(*c*) Eta square
(*d*) Partial eta square

Choose the ***most appropriate*** answer from the options given below:

A. (*a*) only
B. (*b*) and (*c*) only
C. (*a*), (*b*) and (*c*) only
D. (*a*), (*b*) and (*d*) only

47. Which of the following are considered as projective tests of personality?

(*a*) Thematic Apperception Test (TAT)
(*b*) Rotter's Incomplete Sentences Blank (RISB)

(*c*) Guttman's Scalogram Analysis
(*d*) Kent-Rosenoff Free Association Test

Choose the ***correct*** answer from the options given below:
A. (*a*) and (*d*) only
B. (*a*), (*b*) and (*c*) only
C. (*a*), (*b*) and (*d*) only
D. (*a*), (*b*), (*c*) and (*d*)

48. Which of the following are correctly described influences of Behaviourism?
(*a*) Watson's scientific psychology was designed to predict and control human behaviour
(*b*) Mary Cover Jones studied the effectiveness of counter conditioning
(*c*) Skinner claimed to have introduced the term 'Behaviour therapy' and is also credited for it
(*d*) Lazarus emphasised the extension of Thorndike's Law of effect

Choose the ***correct*** answer from the options given below:
A. (*a*) and (*d*) only
B. (*b*) and (*c*) only
C. (*a*) and (*b*) only
D. (*c*) and (*d*) only

49. Interscorer reliability is relevant in:
(*a*) projective tests of personality
(*b*) achievement tests with short answers
(*c*) achievement tests with essay type questions
(*d*) self-report personality inventories

Choose the ***correct*** answer from the options given below:
A. (*a*) and (*b*) only
B. (*a*) and (*c*) only
C. (*a*), (*b*) and (*c*) only
D. (*b*), (*c*) and (*d*) only

50. Which of the following tactics for gaining compliance are based on reciprocity?
(*a*) The Door-in-the – face technique
(*b*) "That's – Not-All" Approach
(*c*) Playing hard to get
(*d*) Foot-in-the Door Technique

Choose the ***correct*** answer from the options given below:
A. (*a*) and (*b*) only B. (*a*) and (*c*) only
C. (*b*) and (*d*) only D. (*c*) and (*d*) only

51. Which of the following type of inversion is observed in reaction formation?
(*a*) Implicit (*b*) Explicit
(*c*) Conscious (*d*) Unconscious

Choose the ***correct*** answer from the options given below:
A. (*a*) and (*d*) only
B. (*b*) and (*c*) only
C. (*b*) and (*d*) only
D. (*a*) and (*c*) only

52. Attitudes can be classically conditioned even without our awareness by which of the following?
(*a*) Subliminal conditioning
(*b*) Observational learning
(*c*) Mere exposure
(*d*) Social networks

Choose the ***correct*** answer from the options given below:
A. (*a*) and (*b*) only B. (*b*) and (*c*) only
C (*a*) and (*c*) only D. (*b*) and (*d*) only

53. Which among these is correct for Cyber bullying?
(*a*) It involves disinhibition
(*b*) Lesser role of Bystanders
(*c*) Ability of targets to retaliate is more
(*d*) No evidence left behind

Choose the ***correct*** answer from the options given below:
A. (*a*) and (*b*) only
B. (*a*), (*b*) and (*c*) only
C. (*b*), (*c*) and (*d*) only
D. (*a*), (*b*) and (*d*) only

54. Which of the following in learning environment are considered to be true about school success?
(*a*) The self image is vital to learning
(*b*) Very high goal setting is necessary to motivate and study

(*c*) Success experience is a function of challenge more than repetition

(*d*) Child's spiritual identity is vital to learning

Choose the ***correct*** answer from the options given below:

A. (*a*) and (*d*) only

B. (*b*) and (*c*) only

C. (*a*), (*c*) and (*d*) only

D. (*b*), (*c*) and (*d*) only

55. Which of the following are the performance subtests of WAIS?

(*a*) Digit span

(*b*) Similarities

(*c*) Digit symbol

(*d*) Object assembly

Choose the ***correct*** answer from the options given below:

A. (*a*) and (*c*) only

B. (*c*) and (*d*) only

C. (*b*), (*c*) and (*d*) only

D. (*a*), (*c*) and (*d*) only

56. Which of the following categories were given by Skinner for different verbal responses in terms of how they are reinforced?

(*a*) Mand

(*b*) Tact

(*c*) Echoic Behaviour

(*d*) Autoclitic Behaviour

Choose the ***correct*** answer from the options given below:

A. (*a*) and (*b*) only

B. (*c*) and (*d*) only

C. (*a*), (*b*) and (*c*) only

D. (*a*), (*b*), (*c*) and (*d*) only

57. Which among the following does not refer to Social Referencing?

(*a*) Intentional search for information about others' feelings, to help explain the meaning of uncertain circumstances and events

(*b*) It occurs around the age of 2 – 3 years

(*c*) Infants make use of facial expressions in social referencing

(*d*) Infants need to understand the significance of other's behaviour within the context of a specific situation

Choose the ***most appropriate*** answer from the options given below:

A. (*b*) only
B. (*a*) and (*c*) only

C. (*b*) and (*c*) only
D. (*a*) and (*d*) only

58. Which of the following characterizes Cognitive Dissonance?

(*a*) Dissonance often occurs in situations involving forced compliance

(*b*) Attempts to resolve dissonance are reflected in increased cortical activity

(*c*) Dissonance cannot be reduced directly but only by adding cognitions that justify our behaviours

(*d*) Dissonance is stronger when we have little justification for our attitude – inconsistent behaviour

Choose the ***correct*** answer from the options given below:

A. (*a*), (*b*) and (*c*) only

B. (*a*), (*b*) and (*d*) only

C. (*b*), (*c*) and (*d*) only

D. (*a*), (*b*), (*c*) and (*d*) only

59. New Mood Therapy:

(*a*) is a cognitive therapy

(*b*) is meant for treatment of depression

(*c*) involves many behavioural interventions

(*d*) was originated by Ellis

(*e*) is action commitment therapy

Choose the ***correct*** answer from the options given below:

A. (*a*), (*b*) and (*d*) only

B. (*a*), (*b*) and (*c*) only

C. (*b*) and (*e*) only

D. (*b*), (*c*) and (*d*) only

60. The components of 'Working Memory' are:

(*a*) Acoustic unit
(*b*) Semantic unit

(*c*) Central executive
(*d*) Episodic buffer

Choose the correct answer from the options given below:

A. (*a*) and (*b*) only B. (*a*) and (*c*) only
C. (*b*) and (*d*) only D. (*c*) and (*d*) only

61. Mayer-Salovey-Caruso Emotional Intelligence Test (MSCEIT) measures:

(*a*) Perceiving emotions
(*b*) Using emotions to facilitate thought
(*c*) Understanding emotions
(*d*) Implicit motivation

Choose the ***correct*** answer from the options given below:

A. (*a*) and (*b*) only
B. (*c*) and (*d*) only
C. (*a*), (*b*) and (*c*) only
D. (*b*), (*c*) and (*d*) only

62. Which of the following are features of Meta-cognition?

(*a*) Encoding (*b*) Regulation
(*c*) Monitoring (*d*) Evaluation

Choose the ***most appropriate*** answer from the options given below:

A. (*a*), (*b*) and (*c*) only
B. (*a*) and (*b*) only
C. (*c*) and (*b*) only
D. (*b*), (*c*) and (*d*) only

63. Jensen's Level I and Level II abilities can be best understood in terms of which of the following?

(*a*) Difficulty and complexity of tasks
(*b*) SES Differences
(*c*) Racial Differences
(*d*) Gender Differences

Choose the ***most appropriate*** answer from the options given below:

A. (*a*) and (*b*) only
B. (*c*) and (*d*) only
C. (*a*), (*b*) and (*c*) only
D. (*b*), (*c*) and (*d*) only

64. What are the characteristics of 'Emerging persons' in Rogerian approach?

(*a*) Honest and open
(*b*) Indifferent to material comforts and rewards
(*c*) Caring
(*d*) Having profound trust in authority

Choose the ***most appropriate*** answer from the options given below:

A. (*a*) and (*b*) only
B. (*c*) and (*d*) only
C. (*a*), (*b*) and (*c*) only
D. (*b*), (*c*) and (*d*) only

65. Which of the following are correct for the Biopsychosocial Model of health?

(*a*) Close interaction between body and mind, though they are separate entities
(*b*) Active participation of the patient
(*c*) Health and illness are on the same continuum
(*d*) Treatment process involves medication, surgery and radiation

Choose the ***most appropriate*** answer from the options given below:

A. (*a*), (*b*) and (*c*) only
B. (*a*), (*b*) and (*d*) only
C. (*b*), (*c*) and (*d*) only
D. (*a*), (*b*), (*c*) and (*d*)

66. Match List-I with List-II.

List-I (Concept)	***List-II (Description)***
(*a*) Turiyavastha	(*i*) Transcognitive realisation
(*b*) Aparvidya	(*ii*) Highest state of consciousness
(*c*) Paravidya	(*iii*) Transcendental knowledge
(*d*) Nididhasan	(*iv*) Empirical knowledge

Choose the ***correct*** answer from the options given below:

	(*a*)	(*b*)	(*c*)	(*d*)
A.	(*i*)	(*iii*)	(*ii*)	(*iv*)
B.	(*ii*)	(*iii*)	(*iv*)	(*i*)
C.	(*ii*)	(*i*)	(*iii*)	(*iv*)
D.	(*iii*)	(*ii*)	(*iv*)	(*i*)

67. Match List-I with List-II.

List-I (Variable type)	***List-II (Examples)***
(*a*) Artificially discrete variable	(*i*) Reaction time
(*b*) Continuous behavioural variable	(*ii*) Gender
(*c*) Continuous organismic variable	(*iii*) Selection test result interms of selected, Not selected, On waiting lise
(*d*) Dummy variable	(*iv*) Height

Choose the ***correct*** answer from the options given below:

	(*a*)	(*b*)	(*c*)	(*d*)
A.	(*iii*)	(*i*)	(*iv*)	(*ii*)
B.	(*iii*)	(*iv*)	(*i*)	(*ii*)
C.	(*ii*)	(*iv*)	(*i*)	(*iii*)
D.	(*i*)	(*iii*)	(*ii*)	(*iv*)

68. Match List-I with List-II.

List-I (Depth Cues)	***List-II (Explanations)***
(*a*) Motion Parallax	(*i*) Both eyes fixate on the same point in space
(*b*) Texture Gradient	(*ii*) Partial occlusion of a far object by a near object
(*c*) Interposition	(*iii*) Graded variation in the shape, size and density of the surface elements
(*d*) Convergence	(*iv*) Movement in one part of the image relative to another

Choose the ***correct*** answer from the options given below:

	(*a*)	(*b*)	(*c*)	(*d*)
A.	(*iii*)	(*ii*)	(*iv*)	(*i*)
B.	(*iiv*)	(*iii*)	(*ii*)	(*i*)
C.	(*i*)	(*iv*)	(*iii*)	(*ii*)
D.	(*ii*)	(*i*)	(*iii*)	(*iv*)

69. Match List-I with List-II.

List-I (Tests)	***List-II (Psychologists)***
(*a*) Creative Achievement Questionnaire	(*i*) Carson-Peterson-Higgins
(*b*) Ideational Behaviour Scale	(*ii*) Runco
(*c*) Preference for Active Divergence Scale	(*iii*) Basadur
(*d*) Consensual Assesment Technique	(*iv*) Amabile

Choose the ***correct*** answer from the options given below:

	(*a*)	(*b*)	(*c*)	(*d*)
A.	(*i*)	(*ii*)	(*iii*)	(*iv*)
B.	(*ii*)	(*i*)	(*iv*)	(*iii*)
C.	(*iii*)	(*iv*)	(*i*)	(*ii*)
D.	(*iv*)	(*iii*)	(*ii*)	(*i*)

70. Match List-I with List-II.

List-I (Indices)	***List-II (Test)***
(*a*) Universal Index	(*i*) OATB
(*b*) Disclosure Index	(*ii*) MCMI
(*c*) True Response Inconsistency	(*iii*) MMPI
(*d*) Coping Deficit Index	(*iv*) Rorschach Inkblot Test

Choose the ***correct*** answer from the options given below:

	(*a*)	(*b*)	(*c*)	(*d*)
A.	(*i*)	(*ii*)	(*iii*)	(*iv*)
B.	(*ii*)	(*i*)	(*iv*)	(*iii*)
C.	(*iii*)	(*iv*)	(*i*)	(*ii*)
D.	(*iv*)	(*iii*)	(*ii*)	(*i*)

71. Match List-I with List-II.

List-I (Social Concepts)	***List-II (Explanations)***
(*a*) Elaboration Likelihood Model	(*i*) Gender stereotypes
(*b*) Realistic Conflict Theory	(*ii*) Central and peripheral route to persuasion

(*c*) Glass Cliff	(*iii*)	Idealogical change in core aspect of a group
(*d*) Schism	(*iv*)	Intergroup competition as a source of prejudice

Choose the ***correct*** answer from the options given below:

	(*a*)	(*b*)	(*c*)	(*d*)
A.	(*i*)	(*iii*)	(*ii*)	(*iv*)
B.	(*iii*)	(*iv*)	(*i*)	(*ii*)
C.	(*ii*)	(*i*)	(*iv*)	(*iii*)
D.	(*ii*)	(*iv*)	(*i*)	(*iii*)

72. Match List-I with List-II.

List-I (Type of communication in family therapy)		***List-II (Description)***
(*a*) Congruent	(*i*)	Carries an air of self importance
(*b*) Placating	(*ii*)	Placing others above oneself
(*c*) Blaming	(*iii*)	Seeing the world with a lens of objectivity and coolness
(*d*) Super reasonable	(*iv*)	Reasonably flexible with a sense of connection

Choose the ***correct*** answer from the options given below:

	(*a*)	(*b*)	(*c*)	(*d*)
A.	(*iii*)	(*i*)	(*ii*)	(*iv*)
B.	(*ii*)	(*iii*)	(*i*)	(*iv*)
C.	(*iv*)	(*ii*)	(*i*)	(*iii*)
D.	(*iv*)	(*i*)	(*ii*)	(*iii*)

73. Match List-I with List-II.

List-I (Concept)		***List-II (Description)***
(*a*) Situational Poverty	(*i*)	Not equipped with tools to move out
(*b*) Generational Poverty	(*ii*)	Not able to meet the average standard of society
(*c*) Relative Poverty	(*iii*)	Scarcity of necessities like shelter, running water and food
(*d*) Absolute Poverty	(*iv*)	Caused by environmental disasters, divorce and other issues like poor health etc

Choose the ***correct*** answer from the options given below:

	(*a*)	(*b*)	(*c*)	(*d*)
A.	(*i*)	(*iii*)	(*iv*)	(*ii*)
B.	(*iii*)	(*i*)	(*iv*)	(*ii*)
C.	(*iv*)	(*i*)	(*ii*)	(*iii*)
D.	(*iv*)	(*ii*)	(*i*)	(*iii*)

74. Match List-I with List-II.

List-I (Theoretical Perspective)		***List-II (Explanation)***
(*a*) Encoding Specificity Hypothesis	(*i*)	Does not endorse different memory storage
(*b*) Retrival Induced Forgetting	(*ii*)	Suppress unwanted memories
(*c*) Schema Theory of Memory	(*iii*)	Superiority of recognition over recall
(*d*) Level of Processing Theory	(*iv*)	Effect of meaning and knowledge on memory

Choose the ***correct*** answer from the options given below:

	(*a*)	(*b*)	(*c*)	(*d*)
A.	(*ii*)	(*iv*)	(*i*)	(*iii*)
B.	(*iii*)	(*ii*)	(*iv*)	(*i*)
C.	(*i*)	(*ii*)	(*iii*)	(*iv*)
D.	(*iv*)	(*i*)	(*ii*)	(*iii*)

75. Match List-I with List-II.

List-I		***List-II***
(*a*) Cognitive Assessment System	(*i*)	Dass
(*b*) Hold and Don't Hold Test	(*ii*)	Wechsler

(*c*) Cognitive Assessment Battery (*iii*) Cattell
(*d*) Differential Ability Test (*iv*) Elliot

Choose the ***correct*** answer from the options given below:

	(*a*)	(*b*)	(*c*)	(*d*)
A.	(*i*)	(*ii*)	(*iii*)	(*iv*)
B.	(*ii*)	(*i*)	(*iv*)	(*iii*)
C.	(*iii*)	(*iv*)	(*i*)	(*ii*)
D.	(*iv*)	(*iii*)	(*ii*)	(*i*)

76. Arrange the first five elements of 'Flow' in correct sequence:
(*a*) Clarity of Goals
(*b*) Immediate Feedback of Actions
(*c*) Balance between challenges and skills
(*d*) Merger of awareness and actions
(*e*) Exclusion of distractions from consciousness

Choose the ***correct*** answer from the options given below:
A. (*a*), (*b*), (*c*), (*d*), (*e*)
B. (*a*), (*c*), (*b*), (*d*), (*e*)
C. (*b*), (*c*), (*a*), (*e*), (*d*)
D. (*c*), (*b*), (*a*), (*d*), (*e*)

77. Arrange the following as per the Yogic Concept of Cognition.
(*a*) Sensorial transformation is attended by manas
(*b*) Reaction by budhi to the object of cognition
(*c*) Registration of external object on mind
(*d*) Assimilation and discrimination by manas
(*e*) Information to Ahamkara

Choose the ***correct*** answer from the options given below:
A. (*c*), (*a*), (*e*), (*b*), (*d*)
B. (*c*), (*a*), (*d*), (*e*), (*b*)
C. (*a*), (*c*), (*d*), (*e*), (*b*)
D. (*c*), (*a*), (*b*), (*d*), (*e*)

78. Arrange the following correlations in ascending order in terms of their strength of relationship:
(*a*) –0.75 (*b*) –0.30
(*c*) 0.40 (*d*) 0.68

Choose the ***correct*** answer from the options given below:
A. (*b*), (*c*), (*d*), (*a*) B. (*b*), (*a*), (*c*), (*d*)
C. (*a*), (*b*), (*c*), (*d*) D. (*d*), (*c*), (*b*), (*a*)

79. The evolution of the various explanations or models of memory occur in the following sequence:
(*a*) Multistore
(*b*) Working memory
(*c*) Level of processing
(*d*) Interference

Choose the ***correct*** answer from the options given below:
A. (*d*), (*a*), (*c*), (*b*) B. (*d*), (*c*), (*b*), (*a*)
C. (*a*), (*b*), (*c*), (*d*) D. (*b*), (*c*), (*d*), (*a*)

80. Arrange in correct sequence, the first five intelligences given by Gardner:
(*a*) Linguistic Intelligence
(*b*) Logico-mathematical Intelligence
(*c*) Spatial Intelligence
(*d*) Kinesthetic Intelligence
(*e*) Natural Intelligence

Choose the ***correct*** answer from the options given below:
A. (*a*), (*b*), (*c*), (*d*), (*e*)
B. (*b*), (*a*), (*c*), (*e*), (*d*)
C. (*c*), (*b*), (*a*), (*d*), (*e*)
D. (*d*), (*c*), (*e*), (*b*), (*a*)

81. Arrange the Nafs (Self in Sufism) from lower to higher self:
(*a*) The self pleasing to God
(*b*) The pure self
(*c*) Inspired self
(*d*) Serene self
(*e*) The pleased self

Choose the ***correct*** answer from the options given below:
A. (*e*), (*c*), (*a*), (*b*), (*d*)
B. (*c*), (*d*), (*e*), (*a*), (*b*)
C. (*c*), (*e*), (*a*), (*d*), (*b*)
D. (*b*), (*c*), (*e*), (*d*), (*a*)

82. According to Master and Johnson, which of the following is correct sequence of Sexual Response?

(*a*) Excitement (*b*) Desire
(*c*) Plateau (*d*) Orgasm
(*e*) Resolution

Choose the ***correct*** answer from the options given below:

A. (*a*), (*c*), (*d*), (*e*) B. (*b*), (*a*), (*d*), (*e*)
C. (*b*), (*a*), (*c*), (*d*) D. (*a*), (*b*), (*c*), (*d*)

83. Give the correct sequence of stages in the relationship maintenance as suggested by Thibaut and Kelly (1959) in their Social Exchange Theory:

(*a*) Bargaining
(*b*) Commitment
(*c*) Sampling
(*d*) Institutionalization

Choose the ***correct*** answer from the options given below:

A. (*a*), (*c*), (*b*), (*d*) B. (*c*), (*a*), (*b*), (*d*)
C. (*b*), (*d*), (*a*), (*c*) D. (*c*), (*b*), (*d*), (*a*)

84. Give the sequence of Identity Formation in Adolescents.

(*a*) Consolidation (*b*) Exploration
(*c*) Rapprochement (*d*) Differentiation

Choose the ***correct*** answer from the options given below:

A. (*b*), (*d*), (*c*), (*a*) B. (*d*), (*b*), (*a*), (*c*)
C. (*d*), (*b*), (*c*), (*a*) D. (*c*), (*a*), (*b*), (*d*)

85. Arrange in a sequence the Stop-start Relapse Cycle of Internet Addiction:

(*a*) Regret (*b*) Rationalization
(*c*) Relapse (*d*) Abstinence

Choose the ***correct*** answer from the options given below:

A. (*a*), (*d*), (*b*), (*c*) B. (*b*), (*a*), (*d*), (*c*)
C. (*d*), (*a*), (*c*), (*b*) D. (*a*), (*b*), (*d*), (*c*)

86. Given below are two statements : One is labelled as Assertion (A) and the other is labelled as Reason (R):

Assertion (A) : Chances of inheriting the dominant genes are twice in females as compared to males.

Reason (R) : Females in comparison to males have two 'X' chromosomes.

In the light of the above statements, choose the ***most appropriate*** answer from the options given below:

A. Both (A) and (R) are correct and (R) is the correct explanation of (A)
B. Both (A) and (R) are correct, but (R) is not the correct explanation of (A)
C. (A) is correct, but (R) is not correct
D. (A) is not correct, but (R) is correct

87. Given below are two statements:

Statement (I) : Edwards Personality Preference Schedule (EPPS) uses forced choice format.

Statement (II) : The forced choice format is presumed to prevent socially desirable responding.

In the light of the above statements, choose the ***most appropriate*** answer from the options given below:

A. Both Statement (I) and Statement (II) are correct
B. Both Statement (I) and Statement (II) are incorrect
C. Statement (I) is correct, but Statement (II) is incorrect
D. Statement (I) is incorrect, but Statement (II) is correct

88. Given below are two statements : One is labelled as Assertion (A) and the other is labelled as Reason (R):

Assertion (A) : In fixed interval schedule of reinforcement behaviour is reinforced in a fixed time period.

Reason (R) : When students get feedback intermittently their level of performance increases.

In the light of the above statements, choose the ***most appropriate*** answer from the options given below:

A. Both (A) and (R) are correct and (R) is the correct explanation of (A)
B. Both (A) and (R) are correct, but (R) is Not the correct explanation of (A)
C. (A) is correct, but (R) is not correct
D. (A) is not correct, but (R) is correct

89. Given below are two statements : One is labelled as Assertion (A) and the other is labelled as Reason (R):

Assertion (A) : Cattell incorporated factors Q_1, Q_2, Q_3 and Q_4 in 16 PF.

Reason (R) : Some factors appeared only in L-data not in Q and T-data.

In the light of the above statements, choose the ***most appropriate*** answer from the options given below:

A. Both (A) and (R) are correct and (R) is the correct explanation of (A)
B. Both (A) and (R) are correct, but (R) is Not the correct explanation of (A)
C. (A) is correct, but (R) is not correct
D. (A) is not correct, but (R) is correct

90. Given below are two statements : One is labelled as Assertion (A) and the other is labelled as Reason (R):

Assertion (A) : Lewin asserted that avoidance – avoidance conflicts are relatively more stable.

Reason (R) : Opposing forces tend to remain in a state of disequilibrium.

In the light of the above statements, choose the ***most appropriate*** answer from the options given below:

A. Both (A) and (R) are correct and (R) is the correct explanation of (A)
B. Both (A) and (R) are correct, but (R) is Not the correct explanation of (A)
C. (A) is correct, but (R) is not correct
D. (A) is not correct, but (R) is correct

Directions (Q.No. 91 to 95): *Read the following paragraph and answer the five questions that follow:*

A psychologist was interested in developing English Language Usage test for HSSC students. She wrote 120 questions trying to cover several areas of the language usage. Each question had five alternatives, out of which only one was right. The draft version of the test was given to a sample of 200 students. The test items were analyzed in two ways – carrying out item-remainder correlation and discrimination index for each item. For the purpose of computing item discrimination index, she labelled those who had a total score below P_{27} as low scorers, and those who had a total score above P_{73} as high scorers. (Assume that P_{27} and P_{73} had non-fractional, i.e., full integer values). The statistical significance of the discrimination index of each item was evaluated by appropriate test. Ninety items were retained in item analysis. The Ninety-item version was administered to a fresh sample of 400 subjects. Cronbach alpha was computed. The psychologist also wondered if she could compute Kuder-Richardson (K-R) reliability for her test. Since the Cronbach alpha was pretty high, i.e., .947, and the test was quite long, she decided to develop the two parallel forms, each of 45 items. She randomly assigned the items to two halves, labelling them as Form A and Form B. For each Form, she assessed average inter-item correlation, mean, standard deviation and Cronbach alpha. The two forms satisfied the criteria for parallel forms.

91. Item I was passed by 30 subjects in Low scoring group and by 56 subjects in High scoring group. What would be the discrimination index for item I?

A. 0.241 B. 0.481
C. 0.556 D. 0.796

92. Which one of the following test can be used for evaluating statistical significance of the discrimination index?

A. Chi-square test
B. *t* test
C. F test
D. Mann-Whitney U test

93. What is the expected Cronbach alpha for the Form A?

A. .474 B. .899

C. .913 D. .947

94. Give below are two statements : One is labelled as Assertion (A) and the other is labelled as Reason (R):

Assertion (A) : It is not possible to compute K-R reliability for the above test, since each item has five alternatives

Reason (R) : K-R reliability can be computed, when the items can be dichotomously scored.

In the light of the above statements, choose the ***most appropriate*** answer from the options given below:

A. Both (A) and (R) are correct and (R) is the correct explanation of (A)

B. Both (A) and (R) are correct, but (R) is Not the correct explanation of (A)

C. (A) is correct, but (R) is not correct

D. (A) is not correct, but (R) is correct

95. For computing inter-item correlations, which one of the following is suitable?

A. Point biserial correlation

B. Biserial correlation

C. Rank difference correlation

D. Phi-coefficient

Directions (Q.No. 96 to 100): *Read the following paragraph and answer the five questions that follow:*

An experimental psychologist wanted to test two hypotheses. The first hypothesis proposed that stress would adversely affect the rate of serial learning. The second hypothesis proposed that the type of material (meaningless vs. meaningful) would moderate the effect of stress. The psychologist formed six groups by manipulating stress (A) at three levels — Low, Moderate and High and Type of material (B) at two levels. The subjects were randomly assigned to these groups from an initial pool of subjects. The list of 15 CVC trigrams constituted meaningless material and the list of 15 three-lettered meaningful words constituted meaningful material. The number of trials required to learn the list was the dependent variable. The data were analysed by suitable analysis of variance. Following are the selected findings.

1. The ratio of largest to smallest standard deviations for the six groups was reasonably close to one.
2. The degrees of freedom for error variance was 135.
3. The F ratio for the effect of stress was 0.95.
4. The effect sizes for each effect were calculated both by obtaining *eta* square and partial *eta* square.

96. The above design can best be labelled as:

A. Randomized 3 × 2 balanced factorial design

B. Randomized 3 × 2 balanced factorial design with a covariate

C. Randomized 3 × 2 unbalanced factorial design

D. Randomized block design

97. The above data indicates:

A. that the assumption of homogeneity of variance is satisfied

B. that the assumption of homogeneity of variance is not satisfied

C. the absence of information related to the assumption of homogeneity of variance

D. the formal test of homogeneity of variance needs to be carried out

98. The above results indicate that:

A. the first hypothesis is verified

B. the first hypothesis is rejected

C. the first hypothesis is partially verified

D. the inadequate information for evaluating the first hypothesis

99. Which one of the following F ratio would be used to evaluate second hypothesis?

A. $F = MS_A/MS_E$

B. $F = MS_B/MS_E$

C. $F = MS_{A \times B}/MS_E$

D. $F = MS_A/(MS_{A \times B} + MS_E)$

100. The above findings indicate that the post-hoc comparisons are:

A. Necessary for the effect of stress

B. Necessary for the effect of type of material

C. Necessary both for the effect of stress and type of material

D. Neither necessary for the effect of stress nor the type of material

ANSWERS

1	2	3	4	5	6	7	8	9	10
B	D	D	D	A	B	A	B	C	B
11	**12**	**13**	**14**	**15**	**16**	**17**	**18**	**19**	**20**
B	A	D	B	A	B	B	D	C	B
21	**22**	**23**	**24**	**25**	**26**	**27**	**28**	**29**	**30**
B	C	A	A, B, C	B	A	B	A	C	C
31	**32**	**33**	**34**	**35**	**36**	**37**	**38**	**39**	**40**
D	B	B	C	C	C	B	C	A	B
41	**42**	**43**	**44**	**45**	**46**	**47**	**48**	**49**	**50**
A	C	C	B	C	C	C	C	C	A
51	**52**	**53**	**54**	**55**	**56**	**57**	**58**	**59**	**60**
C	C	B	C	B	D	A	B	B	D
61	**62**	**63**	**64**	**65**	**66**	**67**	**68**	**69**	**70**
C	D	C	C	D	*	A	B	A	A
71	**72**	**73**	**74**	**75**	**76**	**77**	**78**	**79**	**80**
D	C	C	B	A	A	B	A	A	A
81	**82**	**83**	**84**	**85**	**86**	**87**	**88**	**89**	**90**
B	A	B	C	B	A	A	B	B	C
91	**92**	**93**	**94**	**95**	**96**	**97**	**98**	**99**	**100**
B	A	B	D	D	C	A	B	C	D

** No option is correct or the question is wrong.*

YOUR SPACE

UGC-NET JRF
PSYCHOLOGY
PART-A

CHAPTER 1

Perceptual Process

GESTALT APPROACH TO PERCEPTION

The word gestalt (configuration) is to be described as a psychological structure based on the formula that the whole is something more than the additive aggregate of its elements (parts and relations). The main trait of perceptual gestalt is that it possesses at least one property which is not possessed distributively by its parts and relations. The process of perceptual gestalt-formation is generally regulated by the principle of figural organization *i.e.,* the principle of proximity, similarity, continuity and frame of reference.

According to the gestalt theory, since the gestalt formation consists of a psychological transformation of sensation into perception, the essential factor is the 'synthetic relationship' which constitutes the determining principle of the combinatorial possibilities of the elements and their elementary relations. The result of this synthetic transformation is the emergence of a gestalt quality not possessed by the elements analytically considered.

The gestalt psychologists incorporated the postulate of isomorphism and field effect as a basic part of their physiological explanation of perception. According to Kohler, the tendency of electrostatic charges always distribute or 'shape' in a way that would product an equilibrium over the surface of a conductor. It had been proved earlier that as impulses reach autonomic nerve endings a chemical substance is secreted into the surrounding medium between the end of the nerve fibre and the muscle fibre which it activates. It has been found in the case of a white square seen on a gray background, that the activity will be more intense in that cortical area represented by the square than in the part represented by the ground. Since ions are involved in chemical process, it is assumed to have concentration of ions inside the figure different from that in the ground outside, as these parts are represented in the cortex. Since ions diffuse from regions of higher concentration into those of lower, one of these areas will become electrostatic potential, which constitutes an electromotive force, a current is set up. The current passes circularly from the cortical region of the figure through that of the ground in the surrounding tissues, and back into the figure again. The self-distribution of electrostatic potential in the field, arising originally from the optical sources and neural transmission to the brain, thus 'segregates' the figure from its ground and give it unity and homogeneity.

PERCEPTUAL ORGANIZATION

Gestalt Psychology was founded by Max Wertheimer(1923), Wolfgang Kohler (1947) and Kurt Koffka (1935) and they focused on how people interpret the world. According to Gestalt psychology "the whole is greater than the sum of its parts". Based upon this belief, Gestalt psychologists developed a set of principles to explain perceptual organization, or how smaller objects are grouped to form larger ones. These principles are often referred to as the "laws of perceptual organization."

According to Stephen Palmer, 1999 [The process by which the] bits and pieces of visual information are structured into the larger units of perceived objects and their interrelations are referred to as perceptual organization.

Law of Proximity: One of the most important factors determining the perceptual organization of a scene is proximity of the elements within it. Things that are close together are grouped together.

Law of Similarity: Items or things that look 'similar' are grouped together.

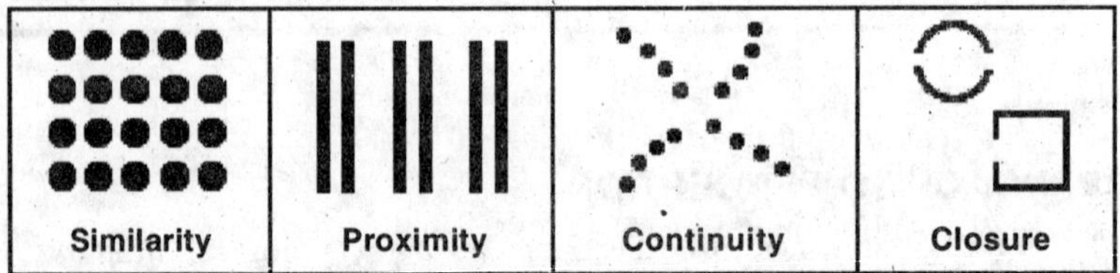

Law of Continuity: The law of continuity holds the point that quite dissimilar objects may be perceived as "belonging together" by virtue of a combination of proximity and good continuity. The Gestalt psychologists argued that perceptual organization will tend to preserve smooth continuity rather than yielding abrupt changes.

Law of Closure: According to the law of Closure, things are grouped together if they seem to complete some entity. Our brains often ignore contradictory information and fill in gaps in information.

Law of Common Fate: According to this law things that appear to move together are grouped together. For example, think of a flock of birds. A camouflaged animal will remain well hidden only if it remains stationary. As soon as it moves it is easier to see.

Common Fate

Law of Pragnanz: The law of Pragnanz is sometimes referred to as the law of good figure or the law of simplicity. This law holds that objects in the environment are seen in a way that makes them appear as simple as possible.

Pragnanz

Figure-Ground

Law of Figure-Ground: The concept of figure-ground perception is often illustrated with the classic "faces or vases" illusion, also known as the Rubin vase. Depending upon whether you see the black or the white as the figure, you may see either two faces in profile (meaning you perceive the black colour as the figure) or a vase in the center (meaning you see the white colour as the figure). In simpler term the gestalt notion "figure - ground phenomenon" refers to the characteristic organization of perception into a figure that 'stands out' against an undifferentiated background.

PERCEPTUAL CONSTANCY

Perceptual constancy, also called **Object Constancy, or Constancy Phenomenon,** is the tendency of animals and humans to see familiar objects as having standard shape, size, colour, or location regardless of changes in the angle of perspective, distance, or lighting.

Size Constancy: The perceived size of an object can be based on its retinal (or proximal) size or on an inferred physical (or distal) size. The phenomenon known as size constancy has been defined as "the tendency for objects to appear much the same size over a wide range of distances in spite of the changes of the retinal images associated with distance of the object" (Gregory, 1963)

Shape Constancy: Shape constancy refers to the fact that the percept of the shape of a given object remains constant despite changes in the shape of the retinal image. The retinal image may change because of changes in the orientation of the object relative to the observer (Pizlo, 1994).

Brightness Constancy: Refers to the tendency to perceive brightness as remaining the same in changing illumination. Our perception of the brightness (or colour) of a part of a image is strongly influenced by the brightness (colour) values of the neighbouring parts.

ILLUSION

A perception, as of visual stimuli (optical illusion) that represents what is perceived in a way different from the way it is in reality is termed as illusion. "Illusions are essentially phenomena of perception. They cannot be phenomena of the physical object world for they are systematic deviations from physical fact," (Gregory, 1979). Although it is hard to give any satisfactory definition of illusion, it may be considered as the departure from reality, or from truth. There are three main types of illusion which include optical illusions, auditory illusions, and tactile illusions.

Optical Illusions: Optical illusions, more appropriately known as visual illusions, involve visual deception. It can also be defined as something that deceives or misleads intellectually. Optical illusions teach us about how the eye and brain work together to create vision. In our everyday three-dimensional (3-D) world, our brain gets clues about depth, shading, lighting, and position to help us interpret what our eyes see. But when we look at two-dimensional (2-D) images that lack some of these clues, the brain can be misleading, causing errors in perception.

Auditory Illusions: An auditory illusion is an illusion of hearing, in which the listener hears those sounds that are either not present in the stimulus, or "impossible" sounds.

Tactile Illusion: The wrong perception of touch receptors. A person's false perception that is made by touching the thing but he cannot identify it properly. To perceive something different from the one that is actually exists. The phantom limb is a tactile illusion wherein the patient still 'feels' pain on the leg, arm or other area that has already been removed.

DEPTH PERCEPTION

Monocular and binocular vision both contribute to our perception of distance—that is, depth perception. Distance perception may be categorized into absolute and relative depth perception.

- Absolute depth perception (distance perception) is an estimate of the physical distance, in units such as meters, to an object. It is based primarily on monocular depth cues.
- Relative depth perception (depth perception) estimates the location of objects in relation to other objects, rather than in terms of physical distances. It is based on monocular and binocular depth cues.

Monocular Depth Cues

Monocular cues are the ones that are obtained from the 2D image of only one eye. These include the following:

Occlusion: When one object is hidden fully or partially, this hidden (occluded) object is considered to be farther away, behind object which is covering it (occluding object).

Relative Size: Another interesting monocular cue. Our learning contributes heavily to this cue. When the image of an object gets larger on the retina, we interpret that as a distance cue (closer). Conversely, when the image on the retina gets smaller, we interpret that as the object becoming farther away.

Shadow: The shadow monocular depth cue has several rules: If an object is solid, it will cast a shadow. If there is only one light source, then all shadows will fall in the same direction and the shadow will be opposite from the source of light. Objects with shadows falling on them are farther away than objects casting the shadow. If the object is lower than the "ground plane" (like a well), the shadow will appear on the same side as the source of light.

Linear perspective: Parallel lines appear to meet as they travel into the distance. For example, Imagine that you were standing at the head of the railroad tracks. The railroad tracks start as two perfectly parallel lines. You notice that the further away from you the tracks are, the closer they get to each other. It appears as if they meet each other in the distance. The point where the parallel lines appear to meet is called the vanishing point.

Interposition: Objects that are in front of other objects may partially block our view of the rearmost object or when one object overlaps another, the object that is partially obscured is perceived as being farther away.

Gradients of Texture: It is the monocular cue provided by our proximity to an object. The closer one is to something, the more detail or texture one can see. For example, while looking at a grassy field, the texture becomes less and less apparent the farther it goes into the distance.

Aerial Perspective: Aerial perspective acts as a depth cue over long distances when we are outside. Objects that are farther away seem to be blurred or slightly hazy due to atmosphere.

Movement or Motion Parallax: As our eyes are constantly moving. Also, our head movements allow us to change our viewpoints of the environment very frequently. These movements cause motion parallax by which nearby objects tend to cross the retinal image lane faster than the distant objects which serve as an important depth cue. This is the same phenomenon that makes nearby objects from a train speedily pass by in a blur, but distant objects move slightly.

Binocular Depth Perception

Binocular cues depend on the images from both the eyes. Our eyes are placed about 6 cm apart and hence they get a different view of the objects in the environment that appear in both the eyes. Thus the way retina receive slightly different or disparate views of the world, is known as retinal disparity. For example. Try holding up two fingers one in front of the other. Focus on the front one. Now move the back one away from, the back towards you, while still focusing on the front one. What happens to the two images you see as the back finger moves?

Another binocular cue is convergence. Because of two eyes converge on an object when we are viewing it, the brain can use the angle of convergence as a cue to how far away that object is. The angle of convergence is smaller when the eye is fixating on far away objects. Convergence is effective for distances less than 10 meters.

MOVEMENT PERCEPTION

The perceptual experience of movement is analogous to other qualities of sensory experience such as colour or size—we perceive movement as a property of the object. Movement is an "either-or" experience. An object either appears to be moving or it appears to be stationary (although of course its perceived speed may vary). There is no middle ground.

Various kinds of conditions lead to movement perception. When we perceive movement where something is actually moving this is referred to as *real movement perception.* But often we perceive movement where nothing in the real world is in motion. There are several kinds of such illusory impressions of movements, some of which are mentioned below:

Stroboscopic Motion: The illusion of motion that occurs when a stationary object is first seen briefly in one location and, following a short interval, is seen in another location. Stroboscopic motion is seen in movies and on television, is a common example of apparent motion.

Autokinetic Effect or Movement: It is another example of apparent motion. Autokinetic effect is a phenomenon that takes place when the eye looks at a stationary, bright light in the dark for a long time. After a period of time, the light appears to move. This is due to the fact that as one stares at a fixed point of light; one's eye muscles become fatigued, causing a slight eye movement. Without the usual reference points available in the everyday environment, the movement of the image on the retina is perceived as its actual movement in space.

Induced Motion: It involves the perception of motion - ours or that of another body—when in reality there is none. This can arise as the result of a comparison of one thing with another. For example, the moon is often perceived as "racing" through a thin layer of clouds. The movement of the framework of clouds "induces" movement in the relatively stationary moon.

ROLE OF MOTIVATION IN PERCEPTION

There exist some indirect hints that the motives underlying wishful thinking have an impact on visual perception. For example, Changizi and Hall (2001) demonstrated that participants who were thirsty perceived more transparency in ambiguous visual stimuli than did those who were not thirsty, presumably because transparency is a characteristic associated with water. This example suggests an enhanced perceptual sensitivity for features in visual stimuli that are relevant to biological drives or desires.

According to New Look theorists, perception was an active and constructive process influenced by many top-down factors. One class of such factors was the needs and values of the perceiver. For example, Haigh (1948) asked 4-8 year olds to draw pictures of Father Christmas at intervals during the month before Christmas and the two weeks after Christmas. They found that as Christmas approached the pictures became larger and so did Santa's sack of toys! After Christmas, however, the toys shrank and so did Santa! This suggests that motivation (higher before Christmas than after) influenced the child's perception of Santa and his toys making them more salient before Christmas and less salient after.

In another similar study, Bruner and Goodman (1947) asked children in diverse social economic conditions to estimate the size of monetary coins by manipulating the diameter of a beam of light. Poorer children, for whom the value of money was greater, over-estimated the size of the coins compared with more affluent children, who were presumed to place less value on the same coins.

Perception of an object is importantly influenced by the perceiver's expectations as well as the context surrounding that object (Biederman, Mezzanotte, Rabi Nowitz, 1982; Boyce and Pollatsek, 1992; Li and Warren, 2004; Long and Toppino, 2004).

However, the specific New Look assertion that motivational states influence perception did not achieve the same stature and longevity as the other insights. Critics pointed out that poorer children might misjudge the size of coins because they were not as familiar with them, or that their misjudgements might involve problems of memory rather than perception (McCurdy, 1956).

According to Balcetis and Dunning (2006) people's motivational states—their wishes and preferences—influence their processing of visual stimuli. In 5 studies, participants shown an ambiguous figure (*e.g.*, one that could be seen either as the letter B or the number 13) tended to report seeing the interpretation that assigned them to outcomes they favoured. This finding was affirmed by unobtrusive and implicit measures of perception (*e.g.*, eye tracking, lexical decision tasks) and by experimental procedures demonstrating that participants were aware only of the single (usually favoured) interpretation they saw at the time they viewed the stimulus. These studies suggest that the impact of motivation on information processing extends down into preconscious processing of stimuli in the visual environment and thus guides what the visual system presents to conscious awareness.

MULTIPLE CHOICE QUESTIONS

1. Which school of psychology was originally developed by Max Wertheimer, Kurt Koffka and Wolfgang Kohler?
   A. Developmental Psychology
   B. Humanistic Psychology
   C. Gestalt Psychology
   D. Industrial psychology
2. According to which law a person's mind can perceive objects as a whole, even when they're not complete in front of them.
   A. Law of Closure
   B. Law of Thorndike
   C. Law of Movement
   D. Law of Texture Gradients
3. Which law is sometimes referred to as the law of good figure?
   A. Law of Proximity
   B. Law of Continuity
   C. Law of Closure
   D. Law of Pragnanz
4. The concept of figure-ground perception is often illustrated with the classic "faces or vases" illusion, also known as :
   A. Two face man theory
   B. Rubin vase
   C. White figure
   D. Ground black
5. .... Constancy is the tendency to perceive an object as being the same size regardless of whether it is close or far away.
   A. Size B. Shape
   C. Colour D. Motion
6. .... is the perception of an object or quality as constant even though our sensation of the object changes.
   A. Size constancy
   B. Colour constancy
   C. Brightness constancy
   D. Perceptual constancy
7. Which principle states that elements that move in the same direction will be perceived as belonging together and forming a figure.
   A. Principle of figure-ground
   B. Principle of proximity
   C. Principle of common fate
   D. Principle of texture gradient
8. .... refers to the use of contextual information-to the use of the 'big picture'.
   A. Top-down processing
   B. Bottom-up processing
   C. Lateral processing
   D. Complex processing
9. .... is the difference in the images falling on the retina of the two eyes.
   A. Size disparity
   B. Retinal disparity
   C. Shape disparity
   D. Brightness disparity
10. The cues that can be processed by just one eye, is often referred to as:
    A. Monocular cues B. Perceptual cues
    C. Sensation cues D. Binocular cues
11. The two eyes of humans are separated from each other by about .... millimetres.
    A. 95 B. 75
    C. 65 D. 55
12. When you are looking at an object that extends into the distance, such as a grassy field, the texture becomes less and less apparent the farther it goes into the distance is an example of which type of monocular cue?
    A. Relative size B. Motion parallax
    C. Ariel perspective D. Texture gradient
13. .... is characterized by visually perceived images that are deceptive or misleading.
    A. Auditory illusion
    B. Tactile illusion
    C. Optical illusion
    D. Both A & B
14. Phantom limb, the Thermal grill illusion, and the Cutaneous rabbit illusion is an example of which type of illusion?
    A. Tactile illusions B. Auditory illusion
    C. Optical illusion D. None of the above

15. In which type of illusion the listener hears either sounds which are not present in the stimulus, or "impossible" sounds?
A. Optical illusion
B. Auditory illusion
C. Tactile illusions
D. All of the above

16. Figure-ground relationship was first established by:
A. Gestalt Psychologists
B. Behaviourists
C. Structuralists
D. Functionalists

17. The .... is the optical illusion of perceiving continuous motion between separate objects viewed rapidly in succession.
A. Hallucination
B. Purkinje Effect
C. Perceptual Defence
D. Phi-phenomenon

18. Perceiving a rope as a snake in darkness is an example of ....
A. Hallucination B. Phi-phenomenon
C. Illusion D. Misinterpretation

19. A white piece of paper indoors reflects considerably less light than does a black lump of coal outside on a bright, sunny day. Yet the paper looks white, and the coal black is an example of:
A. Size constancy
B. Perceptual constancy
C. Brightness constancy
D. None of the above

20. The rails appear to be meeting at a distance, even though it is parallel. This is an example of :
A. Aerial Perspective
B. Linear Perspective
C. Texture Gradient
D. Principle of Closure

21. ...., the kind is seen in movies and on television, is a common example of apparent motion.
A. Stroboscopic motion
B. Illusion
C. Autokinetic effect
D. Real motion

22. In visual perception, the part that seems to stand out in front is called:
A. Figure B. Ground
C. Contour D. Icon

23. What does this statement "We perceive things as we are and not as they are" means?
A. Our perception is misinterpreted
B. Our perception is influenced by our emotions
C. Our perception is influenced by our motives
D. None of the above

24. Which combination of sense organ and their function is wrong?
A. Olfactory — Smell
B. Auditory — Hearing
C. Cutaneous — Feeling of pain, pressure, cold and warmth.
D. Gustatory — Vision

25. Who was the first psychologist to study figure-ground relationship in 1915?
A. Skinner B. Rubin
C. Kohler D. Koffka

26. A sense organ that detects information used in the perceptual process is:
A. the eyes B. the ear
C. the skin D. All of the above

27. Our tendency to perceive objects as unchanging despite changes in sensory input is an illustration of:
A. Figure-Ground relationship
B. Perceptual constancy
C. Binocular cues
D. Linear perspective

28. The idea that we may be 'ready' and 'primed for' certain kinds of sensory input is known as:
A. Set B. Mood
C. Sensory process D. None of the above

29. Read each of the following two statements—Assertion (A) and Reason (R) and indicate your answer using the codes given below:

Assertion (A): We are able to recognize the similarity and differences of two objects.

Reason (R): Dissociable subsystems operate simultaneously in each cerebral hemisphere.

Codes:

A. Both (A) and (R) are true and (R) is the correct explanation of (A).
B. Both (A) and (R) are true, but (R) is not the correct explanation of (A).
C. (A) is true, but (R) is false.
D. Both (A) and (R) are false.

30. Which of the following is true about the perception of an object?

A. Objects are usually considered in isolation.
B. As someone walks towards us, we tend to perceive that he/she increases in size.
C. We infer the object's identity on the basis of incomplete information.
D. The context in which an object appears has no influence on its identification.

31. The phi-phenomenon, stroboscopic motion, induced motion and autokinetic motion are all

A. Pictorial cues
B. Apparent motion
C. Double images
D. Non-verbal cues

32. When we perceive an apple from a distance of 6 or 16 feet, it makes no difference in our perception. Choose the correct reason from the following options.

A. Perceptual assimilation
B. Perceptual contract
C. Perceptual constancy
D. Perceptual vigilance

33. Match the monocular cues with their explanations and select the correct answer using the code given below:

List-I (Cues)	List-II (Explanation)
(*a*) Relative size	1. Straight lines seem to join together as they become more distant.
(*b*) Linear perspective	2. An object changes position on the retina as the head moves.
(*c*) Motion Parallax	3. If two objects are of same size, the one producing the smaller retinal image is farther away.
(*d*) Texture gradient	4. The texture of a surface appears smoother as distance increases.

Codes:

	(*a*)	(*b*)	(*c*)	(*d*)
A.	3	1	2	4
B.	1	3	4	2
C.	4	2	3	1
D.	2	4	1	3

34. Match each of the following organizational laws with its meaning. Select the correct answer using the code given below :

List-I (Law)	List-II (Explanation)
(*a*) Closure	1. Elements close together are grouped together.
(*b*) Proximity	2. Patterns are perceived in the most basic, direct manner possible.
(*c*) Similarity	3. Groupings are made in terms of complete figures.
(*d*) Simplicity	4. Elements similar in appearance are grouped together.

Codes:

	(*a*)	(*b*)	(*c*)	(*d*)
A.	1	4	2	3
B.	2	3	1	4
C.	4	2	3	1
D.	3	1	4	2

35. A .... is a perception in the absence of external stimulus that has qualities of real perception.
A. Illusion B. Phi-phenomenon
C. Hallucination D. Perceptual Defence

36. The fact that a nearer object may obscure a more distant object from the view is due to:
A. Figure and ground
B. Proximity
C. Interposition
D. Closure

37. Which of the following is a top-down factor that affects attention and selection?
A. Personality B. Novelty
C. Familiarity D. Colour

38. As we enter a movie theatre from bright light the visual sensitivity increases and within 5-10 minutes we are able to see under low levels of illumination. This is due to
A. Visual acuity B. Dark adaptation
C. Saturation D. Transduction

39. Perceiving one thing in relation to another when both are presented simultaneously is called:
A. Simultaneous perception
B. Figure-Ground perception
C. Consecutive perception
D. Successive perception

40. When we look at a waterfall for about a minute and then looks at the stationary rocks at the side of the waterfall, these rocks appear to be moving upwards slightly, this type of perception is referred to as:
A. Motion after effect
B. Illusion
C. The figural and ground effect
D. Distorted perception

41. Which of the following do not belong to laws of perceptual grouping?
I. Law of figure and ground
II. Law of good continuation
III. Law of common fate
IV. Law of closure
V. Law of proximity

Codes:
A. I and V B. II and IV
C. III and V D. I and III

42. The occurrence of phi-phenomenon is observed in:
A. Meditation B. Piece of music
C. Violent mob D. Cinema

43. While travelling in a train, nearby objects appears to move faster in the opposite direction than do far away objects, this phenomenon is called:
A. Phi-phenomenon
B. Motion parallax
C. Autokinetic movement
D. Perception of movement

44. Similarity, contrast and contiguity are the laws of:
A. Learning B. Psychophysics
C. Emotion D. Reasoning

45. Read each of the following two statements—Assertion (A) and Reason (R) and indicate your answer using the codes given below:

Assertion (A): Retinal disparity is an important monocuiar cue in depth perception.

Reason (R): Convergence is a muscular cue in depth perception.

Codes:
A. Both (A) and (R) are true and (R) is the correct explanation of (A)
B. Both (A) and (R) are true, but (R) is not the correct explanation of (A)
C. (A) is true, but (R) is false
D. (A) is false, but (R) is true

46. Psychophysics is the scientific discipline that
A. Relates the activity of sensory nerve fibers to perception.
B. Characterizes the physical nature of sensory stimulation.
C. Compares human perceivers to a computer-generated model.
D. Relates a sensory stimulus to a perceptual event.

47. Visual cliff is a laboratory method for testing depth perception in:
A. Infants
B. Children
C. Adults
D. Old people

48. When infants are placed in the middle of a visual cliff, they usually
A. Remain still
B. Move to the shallow side of the apparatus
C. Move to the deep side of the apparatus
D. Approach their mother when called, whether that requires moving to the shallow or deep side.

49. Read each of the following two statements—Assertion (A) and Reason (R) and indicate your answer using the codes given below:

Assertion (A): A building shall appear in same perceived size whether one views it from near or far point.

Reason (R): The size of retinal image remains invariant.

Codes:
A. Both (A) and (R) are true and (R) is the correct explanation of (A)
B. Both (A) and (R) are true, but (R) is not the correct explanation of (A)
C. (A) is true, but (R) is false
D. (A) is false, but (R) is true

50. The tendency to fill in gaps in the perception of a figure is called
A. Sensory completion B. Closure
C. Figure-ground D. Proximity

ANSWERS

1	2	3	4	5	6	7	8	9	10
C	A	D	B	A	D	C	A	B	A
11	**12**	**13**	**14**	**15**	**16**	**17**	**18**	**19**	**20**
C	D	C	A	B	A	D	C	C	B
21	**22**	**23**	**24**	**25**	**26**	**27**	**28**	**29**	**30**
A	A	C	D	B	D	B	A	A	C
31	**32**	**33**	**34**	**35**	**36**	**37**	**38**	**39**	**40**
B	C	A	D	C	C	A	B	B	A
41	**42**	**43**	**44**	**45**	**46**	**47**	**48**	**49**	**50**
D	D	B	B	D	D	A	B	C	B

❑❑❑

CHAPTER 2

Learning Process

CLASSICAL CONDITIONING

Ideas of classical conditioning originate from old philosophical theories. However, it was the Russian Physiologist Ivan Pavlov who elucidated classical conditioning. His work provided a basis for later behaviourists like John Watson and B.F. Skinner.

The defining procedure for classical conditioning is that of establishing a stimulus contingency or if-then relationship between two stimuli which are used as independent variables in the conditioning process. Critical to this definition is the fact that one stimulus at the beginning of the procedure is neutral in function (NS/CS). That is, it does not elicit the reflexive response being investigated for conditioning. The other stimulus, both from the beginning and throughout the procedure, is an effective elicitor (UCS) for the reflexive response (UCR) being conditioned.

Classical conditioning begins with any stimulus which naturally produces a response. For example, food naturally and reliably produces the response of salivation. In this example, the food is the unconditioned stimulus (UCS) and the response of salivation is the unconditioned response (UCR). Learning occurs when a neutral stimulus (one that would not normally produce a reliable response) is paired with the UCS and, as a result of this pairing, it acquires the ability to produce the UCR. Because the neutral stimulus becomes effective through the conditioning process, it is called the conditioned stimulus (CS). The response produced by the CS, although technically almost the same as the UCR, becomes a conditioned response (CR) because it is produced through the conditioning process. For example:

Stage-1 (Before learning)

Food (UCS) ⟶ Salivation (UCR)

Stage-2 (During the learning process)

Bell (CS) + Food (UCS) ⟶ Salivation (UCR)

Stage-3 (After learning)

Bell (CS) ⟶ Salivation (UCR)

Extinction and Spontaneous Recovery in Classical Conditioning

According to Pavlov, when the US (unconditioned stimulus: food) does not follow the CS (conditioned stimulus: tone), the CR (conditioned response: salivation) begins to decrease and eventually causes ***extinction.*** He also found that, following apparently complete extinction of a CR, if the UCS is paired with the CS again that CS quickly (often after only one pairing) regains its ability to elicit the CR again. The reappearance of a CR to the testing presentation of a CS would occasionally occur even without reconditioning, thus appearing to be a spontaneous recovery of the prior conditioning effect. It is from this reappearance that the phenomenon is called spontaneous recovery.

Stimulus Generalization and Discrimination in Classical Conditioning

Tendency to respond to stimuli similar to the CS is called ***generalization***. Pavlov conditioned the dog's salivation (CR) by using miniature vibrators (CS) on the thigh. When he subsequently stimulated other parts of the dog's body, salivation dropped. However ***discrimination*** is the learned ability to distinguish between a conditioned stimulus and other stimuli that do not signal an unconditioned stimulus.

Applications of Classical Conditioning

Watson used classical conditioning procedures to develop advertising campaigns for a number of organizations, where he used his knowledge of classical conditioning to change consumer attitudes and purchasing behaviours through stimulus contingencies that appear in various forms of advertising. Thus advertising—where instead of fears, highly positive feelings toward a product or brand are conditioned—has become one of the most pervasive classical conditioning applications in modern societies around the world (Watson, 1936).

Other classical conditioning applications have focused on preventing coyotes from killing livestock. Farmers have used basic laboratory work by John Garcia on conditioned food aversion (Garcia, Kimeldorf, Hunt, Davies, 1956).

Classical conditioning procedures have psychotherapeutic value as well. Phobias are often treated with a process stemming from classical conditioning called systematic desensitization (Wolpe, 1958). Alcoholism and other addictions are also treated using a form of classical conditioning (Forrest, 1985).

INSTRUMENTAL LEARNING

Instrumental conditioning is sometimes also known as operant conditioning. Operant conditioning describes how we develop behaviours that "operate upon the environment" to bring about behavioural consequences in that environment. Operant conditioning applies many techniques and procedures first investigated by E.L. Thorndike (1898) but later refined and extended by B.F. Skinner (Skinner, 1938).

Reinforcers and Punishers in Instrumental Conditioning

Reinforcers are the responses from the environment that increase the probability of a behaviour being repeated. Reinforcers can be either positive or negative. Punisher on the other hand is the responses from the environment that decrease the likelihood of a behaviour being repeated. Punishment weakens behaviour.

There are two kinds of positively reinforcing stimuli (stimuli that are generally reinforcing when presented to an individual) known as primary reinforcers and secondary (or conditioned) reinforcers. Both types can be delivered following various rules for delivery, thus defining various schedules of reinforcement.

A primary reinforcer is anything that has the power to increase behavioural probabilities because it is involved with a biological need of the organism. Food, sex and temperature stabilities are often used as reinforcement because we need them as a species. A conditioned or secondary reinforcer is anything that can increase the probability of behaviour because of its reliable association with primary reinforcers.

Another way to positively reinforce behaviour is to rely upon Premack's Principle (Premack, 1959, 1971). According to the Premack Principle, a normally higher frequency behaviour can be used to positively reinforce a desired behaviour that is normally lower in frequency. A parent is more likely to positively reinforce a child for studying (a low frequency behaviour without intervention) by allowing the child to watch TV (a high frequency behaviour without intervention) after studying for some specified time. In this case, allowing the consequential behaviour of watching TV causes the probability of studying to increase.

Skinner (1938) also found that consequences resulting in the removing an aversive (painful, uncomfortable, or undesired) stimulus that was already present could also increase the probability that a certain behaviour would occur. He called this process negative reinforcement.

Escape and Avoidance Learning

Frequent use of negative reinforcement will lead to what is often referred to as escape and/or avoidance behaviour. Escape learning occurs to terminate an unpleasant stimulus such as annoyance or pain, thereby negatively reinforcing the behaviour. Avoidance learning on the other hand is the process by which an individual learns a behaviour or response to avoid a stressful or unpleasant situation or noxious stimulus. The behaviour is to avoid, or to remove oneself from, the situation. You can transform escape learning into avoidance learning if you give a signal, such as a tone, before the unwanted stimulus.

Punishment in Operant Conditioning

Punishment refers to the use of punishers to suppress or stop a response from occurring in the future. According to Skinner (1938) positive punishment involves a decrease in the probability of a behaviour through presentation of (addition of, and thus the term ''positive'') an aversive stimulus as a behavioural consequence. Negative punishment describes the removal of a positive stimulus as a behavioural consequence. A stimulus cannot be considered a ''punisher'' if it's presentation (positive punishment) or removal (negative punishment) does not decrease the likelihood of a behaviour.(Skinner, 1938).

In an attempt to decrease the likelihood of a behaviour occurring in the future, an operant response is followed by the presentation of an aversive stimulus. This is positive punishment. However in an attempt to decrease the likelihood of a behaviour occurring in the future, an operant response is followed by the removal of an appetitive stimulus. This is negative punishment.

Skinner's operant conditioning procedures introduce alternative manipulations of operant conditioning variables, such as antecedent stimuli and reinforcement contingency rules. These various operant procedures include extinction, generalization, discrimination, shaping, chaining, and a variety of different schedules of reinforcement.

Extinction in Operant Conditioning

In operant conditioning, extinction can occur if the trained behaviour is no longer reinforced or in the type of reinforcement used is no longer rewarding.

Generalization in Operant Conditioning

In conditioning, stimulus generalization is the tendency for the conditioned stimulus to evoke similar responses after the response has been conditioned.

Discrimination in Operant Conditioning

In instrumental conditioning, discrimination is a process of learning to make response to one stimulus and another response or no response to another stimulus.

Chaining in Operant Conditioning

It involves reinforcing individual responses occurring in a sequence to form a complex behaviour. It is frequently used for training behavioural sequences (or "chains") that are beyond the current repertoire of the learner.

Different Schedules of Reinforcement in Operant Conditioning

A schedule of reinforcement is basically a rule stating which instances of a behaviour will be reinforced. There are four schedules of partial reinforcement:

Fixed-ratio schedules are those where a response is reinforced only after a specified number of responses.

Variable-ratio schedules occur when a response is reinforced after an unpredictable number of responses.

Fixed-interval schedules are those where the first response is rewarded only after a specified amount of time has elapsed.

Variable-interval schedules occur when a response is rewarded after an unpredictable amount of time has passed.

VERBAL LEARNING

The language we speak, the communication devices we use are the result of verbal learning. The signs, pictures, figures, sounds and voice are some essential instruments used in verbal learning. In simpler words, the acquisition and retention of verbal information is often referred to as verbal learning. In the study of verbal learning, psychologists use a variety of materials including nonsense syllables, familiar words, unfamiliar words, sentences and paragraphs.

Methods of Verbal Learning

1. Method of Paired Association: This method is similar to S-S conditioning and S-R learning. The president of the American Psychological Association, Mary Whiton Calkins (1905) invented this technique. The paired associate's method requires a subject to learn pairs of items by forming associations between them. First a list of paired-associates is prepared. The first word of the pair is used as the stimulus, and the second word as the response. For example:

Stimulus	–	Response
RUL	–	TIME
JAX	–	GOLD
HMW	–	COAL
REK	–	DEER

Paired-associate learning (PAL) as it is frequently studied involves two, at least conceptually, distinct processes: the learning of relevant responses to the general situation (*e.g.*, as in nonsense syllable-syllable pairs), and the associative "hook-up" of these relevant responses to their appropriate stimulus members.

2. Method of Serial Learning: Hermann Ebbinghaus is credited with conducting the first studies of verbal memory involving serial learning. In this method the participant is presented the entire list of verbal items, *i.e.*, nonsense syllables, most familiar or least familiar words and is required to produce the items in the same serial order as in the list.

One important procedure in serial learning, known as serial anticipation is used most commonly. In this one stimulus is presented at a time and the learner uses that word as a cue for the next word. The second word then serves as a cue for the third one, and third word becomes a cue for the fourth one and so on. Learning trials continue until the participants correctly anticipates all the items in the given order.

It has been found through various studies of serial learning, that the participants usually tend to remember the first few and last few words better and are more likely to forget those in the middle of the list. This type of learning curve is called serial position effect. Also the tendency to recall earlier words is called the primary effect; the tendency to recall the later words is called the recency effect.

3. Method of Free Recall: In this method the participants are presented a list of words, which is shown only for a fixed interval or duration and thus immediately after the presentation of material or list the participants are required to recall the items or words in any order they like. One of the basic measures of performance in the free recall paradigm is simply the number of words recalled from a list, which varies with a number of factors, including the list length, the type of material studied, and any task used to process the words (*e.g.*, a simple judgement).

MULTIPLE CHOICE QUESTIONS

1. What does the 'Bell' denotes in Pavlov's Classical conditioning experiment.
A. Unconditional Stimulus (UCS)
B. Conditioned Stimulus (CS)
C. Unconditional Response (UCR)
D. Conditioned Response (CR)

2. Operant conditioning is also known as:
A. Classical Conditioning
B. Instrumental conditioning
C. Backward conditioning
D. Forward conditioning

3. .... is a chamber that contains a bar or key that an animal can press or manipulate in order to obtain food or water as a type of reinforcement.
A. Skinner Box
B. Thorndike puzzle box
C. Pavlov's Box
D. Both B and C

4. Reconditioning is .... original learning.
A. Slower than
B. Equal to
C. Different
D. More rapid than

5. Who wrote the book "Beyond Freedom and Dignity"?
A. Pavlov B. Thorndike
C. Hull D. Skinner

6. .... refers to a procedure whereby an unconditioned stimulus is consistently presented before a neutral stimulus.
A. Forward conditioning
B. Instrumental conditioning
C. Backward conditioning
D. Emotional conditioning

7. A dog conditioned to salivate to a tone of a particular pitch and loudness will also salivate with considerable regularity in response to tones of higher and lower pitch is an example of:
A. Generalization
B. Discrimination
C. Spontaneous recovery
D. Chaining

8. In classical conditioning, ... is the ability to differentiate between a conditioned stimulus and other stimuli that have not been paired with an unconditioned stimulus.

A. Discrimination
B. Generalization
C. Spontaneous recovery
D. Chaining

9. In classical conditioning, ... refers to the re-emergence of a previously extinguished conditioned response after a delay.
A. Chaining
B. Spontaneous recovery
C. Discrimination
D. Generalization

10. .... is any event that strengthens or increases the behaviour it follows.
A. Reinforcement B. Punishment
C. Fear D. Phobias

11. The presentation of an adverse event or outcome that causes a decrease in the behaviour it follows is known as:
A. Reinforcement
B. Behaviour modification
C. Backward conditioning
D. Punishment

12. Which process involves reinforcing individual responses occurring in a sequence to form a complex behaviour.
A. Extinction B. Discrimination
C. Chaining D. Generalization

13. In which paradigm, participants study a list of items on each trial, and then are prompted to recall the items in any order.
A. Serial learning
B. Paired association
C. Free recall
D. None of the above

14. .... is the tendency of a person to recall the first and last items in a series best, and the middle items worst.
A. Serial position effect
B. Thorndike law of effect
C. Average memory effect
D. Middle forgetting effect

15. When asked to recall a list of items in any order (free recall), people tend to begin recall with the end of the list, recalling those items best. This is called:
A. Primacy effect B. Recency effect
C. Delayed process D. None of the above

16. Positive and negative punishment tends to:
A. Strengthen behaviour
B. Weaken behaviour
C. Make child stubborn
D. Diminish personality

17. According to Skinner .... are those behaviour or responses, which are emitted by animals and human beings voluntarily and are under their control.
A. Operants
B. Flooding
C. Schedule
D. Learning diability

18. A schedule of reinforcement in which a specific interval of time must elapse before a response will yield reinforcement is known as:
A. Continuous reinforcement schedule
B. Fixed ratio schedule
C. Variable ratio schedule
D. Fixed interval schedule

19. In operant conditioning, ... refers to a situation in which a stimulus reinforces a behaviour after it has been associated with a primary reinforcer.
A. Primary reinforcement
B. Negative reinforcement
C. Secondary reinforcement
D. Positive reinforcement

20. A schedule of reinforcement in which reinforcement occurs only after a variable number of responses have been performed is known as:
A. Variable interval schedule
B. Variable ratio schedule
C. Fixed ratio schedule
D. Fixed interval schedule

21. .... is an experimental process used in operant conditioning by which successive approximations of a target behaviour are reinforced.
A. Shaping
B. Chaining
C. Emotional conditioning
D. Sign learning

22. In which type of conditioning the organism learns to avoid punishment by making an appropriate anticipatory response?
A. Escape conditioning
B. Avoidance conditioning
C. Emotional conditioning
D. None of the above

23. .... occurs when the animal learns to perform an operant to terminate an ongoing, aversive stimulus.
A. Emotional conditioning
B. Avoidance conditioning
C. Escape conditioning
D. None of the above

24. .... is a form of forward conditioning in which the onset of the CS precedes the onset of the UCS and the CS and UCS do not overlap.
A. Trace conditioning
B. Applied operant conditioning
C. Blind conditioning
D. Differential conditioning

25. When a behaviour occurs consistently in the presence of a discriminative stimulus, it is said to be under ....
A. Third party control
B. Loose control
C. Environmental control
D. Stimulus control

26. A series of responses that gradually approach a desired pattern of behaviour are called:
A. Adaptations
B. Gradients
C. Successive approximations
D. Conditioning trials

27. Which of the following is correct while comparing classical and operant conditioning?
A. Operant conditioning takes place before reinforcement while classical conditioning takes place after reinforcement.
B. Operant conditioning takes place as a result of some voluntary action while classical conditioning takes place without choice.
C. In operant conditioning, response is elicited while in classical conditioning it is emitted.
D. In operant conditioning magnitude of the response is the index of conditioning while in classical conditioning it is the rate of response.

28. In Thorndike's law of effect, events critical for conditioning
A. occur after the response.
B. occur before the response.
C. occur simultaneously with the response.
D. are unrelated to the response except during extinction.

29. Read each of the following two statements—Assertion (A) and Reason (R) and indicate your answer using the codes given below:

Assertion (A): A desirable behaviour of an individual can be effectively used as a reference for another less desirable activity.

Reason (R): Premack has suggested that all responses should be thought of as potential reinforcers.

Codes:
A. Both (A) and (R) are true and (R) is the correct explanation of (A).
B. Both (A) and (R) are true, but (R) is not the correct explanation of (A).
C. (A) is true, but (R) is false.
D. (A) is false, but (R) is true.

30. Given below are two statements, one labelled as Assertion (A) and the other labelled as Reason (R). Indicate your answer using the codes given below:

Assertion (A): If your teacher embarrasses you for asking a question in class, it is less likely that you would ask questions in class in future.

Reason (R): Negative reinforcement reduces the occurrence of a behaviour.

Codes:

A. Both (A) and (R) are true, and (R) is the correct explanation of (A).
B. Both (A) and (R) are true but (R) is not the correct explanation of (A).
C. (A) is true, but (R) is false.
D. (A) is false, but (R) is true.

31. Punishment is most effective in suppressing behaviour when it is:
A. immediate, consistent, and intense.
B. delayed, consistent, and mild.
C. immediate, consistent, and mild.
D. delayed, inconsistent, and intense.

32. An oil painting itself can include all of the following cues to depth perception except :
A. Linear Perspective
B. Retinal Disparity
C. Texture Gradient
D. Relative Image Size

33. The presentation of an aversive stimulus or the removal of a positive stimulus are both examples of:
A. Negative reinforcement
B. Punishment
C. Positive reinforcement
D. Secondary reinforcement

34. Backward conditioning occurs when:
A. CS and US are presented simultaneously
B. CS is presented first and US is presented before the termination of CS
C. CS is presented first and US is presented after the termination of CS
D. US is presented first and CS is presented after the termination of US

35. Some factors that influence the effectiveness of rewards are
1. Magnitude of the reward
2. Reward delay
3. Successive approximation
4. Need

Codes:

A. 1, 2 and 4
B. 2 and 4
C. 1 and 2
D. 2, 3 and 4

36. Which of the following are problems with punishment?
1. The effect of punishment is often temporary.
2. Severe punishment creates fear and anxiety.
3. Mild punishment is paired with reinforcement of the correct behaviour.
4. Aggressive punishment can model aggressive behaviour.

Codes:

A. 1 and 4 B. 2 and 3
C. 2, 3 and 4 D. 1, 2 and 4

37. The greatest degree of resistance to extinction is typically caused by a .... schedule of reinforcement.
A. variable interval B. variable ratio
C. fixed interval D. fixed ratio

38. Match List-I with List-II and indicate your answer using the codes given below :

List-I (Presentation of reinforcement)	List-II (Type of reinforcement)
(*a*) An unpleasant stimulus is presented to decrease behaviour	1. Positive reinforcement
(*b*) An unpleasant stimulus is removed to increase behaviour	2. Negative reinforcement
(*c*) A pleasant stimulus is presented to increase behaviour	3. Positive punishment
(*d*) A pleasant stimulus is removed to decrease behaviour	4. Negative punishment

Codes:

	(*a*)	(*b*)	(*c*)	(*d*)
A.	1	2	3	4
B.	2	3	4	1
C.	4	1	3	2
D.	3	2	1	4

39. In operant conditioning, the reinforcer occurs .... the response, and in classical conditioning, it occurs ....

A. after; before
B. before; after
C. before; before
D. after; after

40. Learning of fears is best explained by :

A. Operant conditioning
B. Classical conditioning
C. Observational learning
D. Latent learning

41. Learning by imitating others' behaviour is called .... learning. The researcher best known for studying this type of learning is ....

A. Observational ; Bandura
B. Secondary ; Pavlov
C. Observational ; Watson
D. Secondary ; Skinner

42. Two schedules of reinforcement that produce the highest rates of response are:

A. Continuous and fixed interval.
B. Fixed interval and variable interval.
C. Variable interval and variable ratio.
D. Fixed ratio and variable ratio.

43. Match List-I with List-II and indicate your answer using the codes given below:

List-I (Brief description)	**List-II (Type of reinforcement)**
(*a*) reinforcement occurs after a set time period	1. fixed ratio
(*b*) reinforcement occurs after a set number of responses	2. variable interval
(*c*) reinforcement occurs after a varying time period	3. fixed interval
(*d*) reinforcement occurs after a varying number of responses	4. variable ratio

Codes:

	(*a*)	(*b*)	(*c*)	(*d*)
A.	3	1	2	4
B.	1	4	3	2
C.	4	3	1	2
D.	2	4	3	1

44. The technique of using desensitization involves:

A. flooding the person with images of the feared stimulus.
B. gradually exposing the person to the feared stimulus.
C. gradually exposing the person to the feared stimulus only when they are fully relaxed.
D. systematically increasing the stimulus intensity up to the breaking point.

45. Which set of processes is involved in storing of information in long-term memory?

1. Chunking
2. Long term potentiation
3. Consolidation
4. Monitoring

Codes:

A. 2 and 3
B. 1, 2 and 4
C. 3 and 4
D. 1, 3 and 4

46. Read each of the following two statements—Assertion (A) and Reason (R) and indicate your answer using the codes given below:

Assertion (A): People who learn more and more lists of words on successive days have more and more difficulty learning each new list next day.

Reason (R): People have limited capacity to learn verbal material.

Codes:

A. Both (A) and (R) are true and (R) is the correct explanation of (A).
B. Both (A) and (R) are true, but (R) is not the correct explanation of (A).

C. (A) is true, but (R) is false.
D. (A) is false, but (R) is true.

47. Reinforcement in operant conditioning is most effective when it is:
A. Response contingent.
B. Stimulus contingent.
C. US-CS contingent.
D. NS-CS contingent.

48. Put the steps involved in observational learning in sequence of its occurrence:
I. Reproduction
II. Attention
III. Motivation for later use
IV. Retention

Codes:
A. IV, II, I, III
B. I, IV, III, II
C. II, IV, I, III
D. III, I, II, IV

49. Organizing items into familiar, manageable units, often automatically, is termed:
A. Priming B. Chunking
C. Shaping D. Encoding

50. Which of the following statements concerning reinforcement is correct?
A. Learning is most rapid with partial reinforcement, but continuous reinforcement produces the greatest resistance to extinction.
B. Learning is most rapid with continuous reinforcement but partial reinforcement produces the greatest resistance to extinction.
C. Learning is the fastest and resistance to extinction is the greatest after continuous reinforcement.
D. Learning is the fastest and resistance to extinction is the greatest following partial reinforcement.

ANSWERS

1	2	3	4	5	6	7	8	9	10
B	B	A	D	D	C	A	A	B	A
11	**12**	**13**	**14**	**15**	**16**	**17**	**18**	**19**	**20**
D	C	C	A	B	B	A	D	C	B
21	**22**	**23**	**24**	**25**	**26**	**27**	**28**	**29**	**30**
A	B	C	A	D	C	B	A	A	C
31	**32**	**33**	**34**	**35**	**36**	**37**	**38**	**39**	**40**
A	B	B	D	A	D	A	D	A	B
41	**42**	**43**	**44**	**45**	**46**	**47**	**48**	**49**	**50**
A	D	A	C	A	C	A	C	B	B

❑❑❑

CHAPTER 3

Memory and Forgetting

MEMORY

"Memory is the means by which we draw on our past experiences in order to use this information in the present' (Sternberg, 1999). In simpler words memory is essential to all our lives. Without a memory of the past we cannot operate in the present or think about the future. Memory is conceptualised as a process consisting of three independent, though interrelated stages. These are **encoding, storage and retrieval**.

1. **Encoding:** "Encoding" refers to the processes involved in the transformation of an event in the world into a representation in your mind/brain. It is the first stage which refers to a process by which information is recorded and registered for the first time so that it becomes usable by our memory system. There are three main ways in which information can be encoded (changed) - Visual (picture), Acoustic (sound) and Semantic (meaning). A considerable amount of memory research has examined ways that events are encoded by manipulating the way people process materials during study episodes. Generally speaking, the encoding of an event can be relatively impoverished or enriched (Craik 2002, Craik and Tulving 1975), and memory scientists have identified several encoding factors that tend to promote good memory performance.

   Attention is critical to the encoding of memories, but attention comes in many forms. According to some theorists, these qualitative differences in how people attend to information are the main factors influencing how much they remember. For example, Craik and Lockhart (1972) argues that different rate of forgetting occur because some methods of encoding create more durable memory codes than others.

2. **Storage:** It is the second stage of memory and "storage" refers to the process through which information is retained and held over a period of time. Storage is the more or less passive process of retaining information in the brain, whether in the sensory memory, the short-term memory or the more permanent long-term memory.

3. **Retrieval:** It is the third stage of memory and "retrieval" refers to processes involved in reconstructing what occurred at a particular place and time. In other word retrieval refers to bringing the stored information to his/her awareness so that it can be used for performing various cognitive tasks such as problem-solving and decision making. Memory scientists assume that retrieval processes are always initiated by retrieval cues, identifiable triggers for retrieval processes, and that the experience of remembering occurs when retrieval cues interact with information in memory traces.

STAGES OF MEMORY

Numerous theories (began in earnest by Atkinson & Shiffrin in 1968) seem to suggest that our memories can be divided into three stores or stages. These are the sensory memory, short-term memory (STM) and long-term memory (LTM). Each of these systems has different features and performs different functions with respect to the sensory inputs.

Sensory Memory: Our sensory memory briefly stores information from our senses (eyes and ears for example) and this enters the Sensory Information Store. Sensory memory has a large capacity. However it is of very short duration *i.e.,* less than a second. Incoming sensory information is stored in separate sub systems called sensory registers. Psychologists believe there are separate sensory registers for each of the senses. ***Iconic Memory*** (from the Greek word icon, which means image) is the name given to visual sensory memory, or the memory of visual sensory information. Visual images in their original form are usually retained in iconic memory for about one-third (1/3) of a second or about 0.2-0.4 seconds, but they last just long enough for identification of the stimulus to begin. On the other hand ***Echoic memory*** (from the word echo) is the name given to auditory sensory memory, or the memory of auditory sensory information. Echoic memory processes all kinds of sounds, such as speech, the barking of dog, and the horns of the vehicles. Echoic memory stores information for longer periods than does iconic memory, typically 3-4 seconds.

Short-Term Memory: Information that is attended to enter the second stage called the short tem memory or STM. It also sometimes called working memory. STM term storage is estimated to last anywhere between 20 and 30 seconds if the new information is not rehearsed. If the information is rehearsed, the information will last as long as the rehearsal process continues. The amount of information that can be stored in short-term memory can vary. According to George Miller, people can store between five and nine items in short-term memory. More recent research suggests that people are capable of storing approximately four chunks or pieces of information in short-term memory. 'Chunk' refers to any discrete unit of information. For example, if you read letter BARNDARTAINH once it will be possible to remember about seven of them. However, if the same letter is regrouped to spell RABINDRANATH, it would be easier to remember the entire group of letter. Thus Rabindranath is a chunk. The information is now one unit of information. Through chunking it is possible to expand the capacity of STM which is otherwise 7 + or –2.

Information encoding in short term memory is acoustic in nature *i.e.,* it consists of speech, sounds, visual images and words. It is also semantic in nature which means meaningful words may be stored easily than meaningless words.

Long-Term Memory: Through the process of association and rehearsal, the content of short-term memory can become long-term memory. It is a permanent storehouse of all information and stores a large amount of information over a long period of days, months, years or even a lifetime. Long-term memory is divided into two separate sections: **Declarative memory** and **Procedural memory.**

Procedural memory involves memories of body movement and how to use objects in the environment. How to drive a car or use a computer are examples of procedural memories. However Declarative includes all of the memories that are available in consciousness. It can be further divided into ***episodic memory*** (specific events) and ***semantic memory*** (knowledge about the world).

Episodic memory records an individual's past experiences and the episodes of one's daily life. Episodic memory is both specific and autobiographical. For example one remembers a birthday party, attended yesterday means that the event is stored in episodic memory. Semantic memory on the other hand involves the abstract knowledge and meaning of words, symbols, ideas and rules for relating them. For example, you read an article about mouth cancer resulting in death of many persons. Sometimes later the episode may be forgotten but the knowledge of the fact that smoking causes mouth cancer, which lead to death remains in memory. This knowledge is a part of semantic memory. Episodic memory is more susceptible to forgetting as compared to semantic memory.

THEORIES OF FORGETTING

Forgetting

Forgetting (retention loss) refers to apparent loss of information already encoded and stored in an individual's long term memory. It is a spontaneous or gradual process in which old memories are unable to be recalled from memory storage. Forgetting was first studied in detail by **Hermann Ebbinghaus** (1885/1913). In experiments where is used himself as the subject, Ebbinghaus tested his memory using three-letter nonsense syllables. These consist of a sequence of consonant, vowel, and consonant (CVC) that does not spell anything in one's language — in English, CAJ would be an example. Ebbinghause constructed lists of perhaps 20 of these items and then proceded to memorize these lists systematically. After some number of repetitions, Ebbinghaus would attempt to recall the items on the list. It turned out that his ability to recall the items improved as the number of repetitions went up, rapidly at first and then more slowly, until finally the list was mastered. This was the world's first **learning curve.**

Ebbinghaus, using the savings measure of memory, discovered that the greatest amount of forgetting occurred soon after learning the list. Then the memory slowly weakened with time. The curve Ebbinghaus discovered is called the **forgetting curve.**

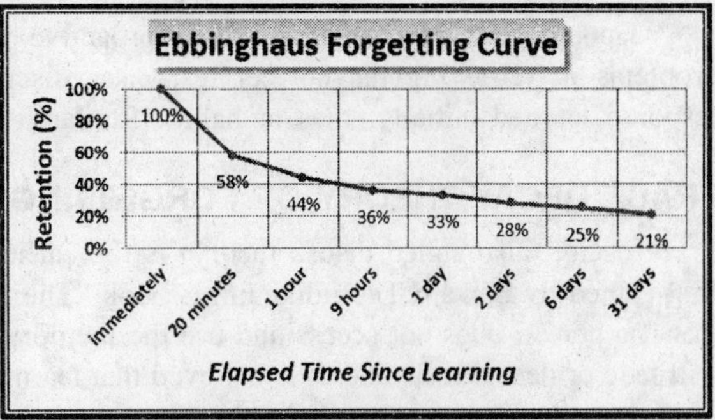

Ebbinghaus also studied how repetition or what he called "**over learning**" affects memory retention. He defined over learning as the number of repetitions of material after that material can be 100% recalled.

Ebbinghaus was the first to discover the **serial position curve**, the relation between the serial position of an item (its place in the list) and the ability to recall it. Items near the beginning of the list are easier to recall than those in the middle (the primacy effect). Those near the end of the list are also easier to recall than those in the middle (the recency effect.) These two effects together yield a curve that is roughly U-shaped.

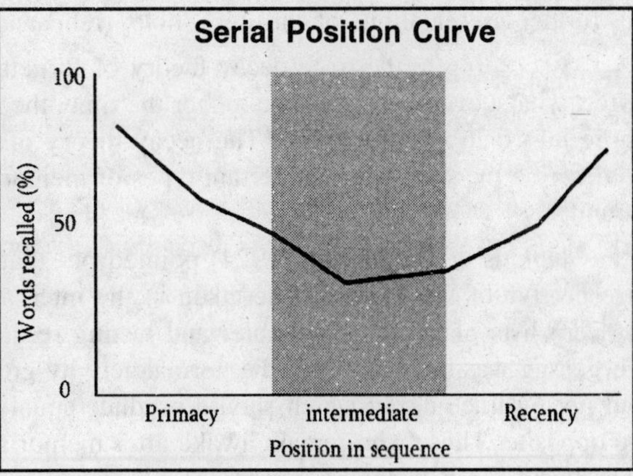

INTERFERENCE THEORY OF FORGETTING

Interference theory refers to the idea that forgetting occurs because the recall of certain items interferes with the recall of other items. According to (Baddeley, 1999), Interference theory states that forgetting occurs because memories interfere with and disrupt one another. In other words forgetting occurs because of interference from other memories. Interference by previous memories is proactive interference. Interference by later learning is retroactive interference. Underwood and Postman (1960) showed that interference is:

- Maximal when two different responses have been associated with the same stimulus.
- Intermediate when two similar responses have been associated with the same stimulus.
- Minimal when two different stimuli are involved.

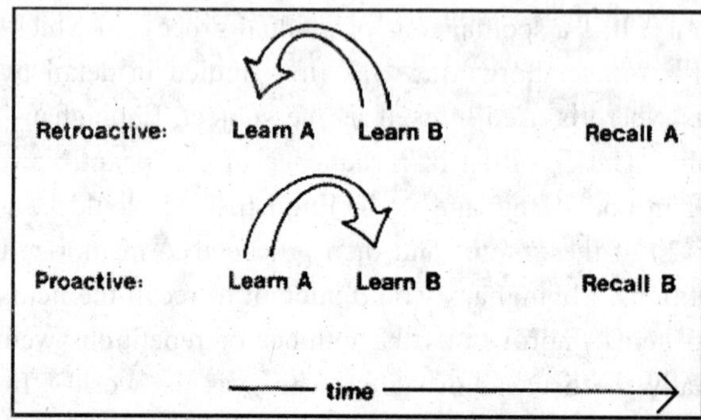

Jacoby et al. (2001) argued that proactive interference might occur for two reasons: Due to problems in retrieving the correct response (discriminability); Due to the strength of the incorrect response learned initially (bias or habit). Research shows the latter to be the case.

TRACE DECAY THEORY OF FORGETTING

Trace decay (also called disuse theory) is the earliest theory of forgetting. The term decay theory was first coined by Edward Thorndike in his book "The Psychology of Learning" in 1914. This simply states that if a person does not access and use the memory representation they have formed, the memory trace will fade or decay over time. It is believed that learning leaves a trace in the brain as a result of excitation of nerve cells. The trace may take the form of neural activity which gradually dies away unless activated by further presentations of the item, or by rehearsal.

According to the trace decay theory of forgetting, the events between learning and recall have no affect whatsoever on recall. The longer the time, the more the memory trace decays and as a consequence more information is forgotten. The decay theory of forgetting has an intuitive appeal about it. It seems to describe the way in which certain types of memory fade away like the feeling of touch, or an auditory sound.

Jenkins & Dallenbach (1924) pointed out that decay theory predicts a constant rate of forgetting irrespective of the activity undertaken in the interval. They tested this prediction by asking participants to learn lists of nonsense syllables and testing recall after various intervals of sleep or normal activity. Forgetting was most rapid for the normal activity group and this can be explained by interference theory, but not by trace decay which should produce equal forgetting rates. In this way the results came out to be opposite. Those who remain awake after memorising (waking condition) show greater forgetting than those who sleep (sleeping condition).

The theory of trace decay has been criticized on several grounds. First, this theory fails to explain why some memories fade and others are maintained for life. Secondly, decay theory has difficulty dealing with situations where items which cannot be remembered at one time can be remembered as a future time even though no additional presentations have been made. Third, Solso (1995) has concluded that there is no evidence that the major cause for forgetting from long term memory is neurological decay.

RETRIEVAL FAILURE THEORY

The retrieval failure theory says that often, memories can't be recalled because there are certain retrieval cues that are absent. For example, you are trying hard to recall a person whom you met at a party whose name or face you do not remember. Just than your sister describe the dress of that person. You realise that you are now able to recall that person. Thus the dress of the person acted as a cue which helped you to retrieve the information. This is referred to as cue-dependent forgetting. There are two different types of cue-dependent forgetting:

1. **Context-Dependent Forgetting:** It occurs if the environmental cues that were present when learning took place, are absent when the information has to be recalled. In other words it refers to improved recall of specific episodes or information when the context present at encoding and retrieval are the same.
2. **State-Dependent Forgetting:** It is the phenomenon through which memory retrieval is most efficient when an individual is in the same state of consciousness as they were when the memory was formed. In other words, if we are very happy when we learn information, we may remember it better if we are very happy at the time of recall. This was investigated in a study by Bower et al, where he manipulated the mood of his participants while they were under hypnosis.

There is considerable evidence that information is more likely to be retrieved from long-term memory if appropriate retrieval cues are present. This evidence comes from both laboratory experiments and everyday experience. A retrieval cue can be a variety of things: Categories; Context; Physical State; Underwater etc. *e.g.* a teacher giving clues when trying to illicit an answer from students.

MULTIPLE CHOICE QUESTIONS

1. Which theory proposes that memory fades due to the mere passage of time?
   A. Motivated forgetting theory
   B. Retrieval failure theory
   C. Interference theory
   D. Trace decay theory
2. When new learning is disturbed by previous learning it s called:
   A. Distortion of memory
   B. Retroactive inhibition
   C. Reconstruction of memory
   D. Proactive inhibition
3. When the first learning is disturbed by the new learning it is called:
   A. Retroactive inhibition
   B. Proactive inhibition
   C. Distortion of memory
   D. Reconstruction of memory
4. Which memory system is also sometimes known as working memory?
   A. Sensory memory
   B. Short-term memory
   C. Long term memory
   D. Flashbulb memory

5. Damage to thalamus and hypothalamus structures of brain plays a role in amnesia observed in which type of disease?
   A. Alzheimer's disease
   B. Depression
   C. Korsakoff's syndrome
   D. None of the above

6. .... refers to the process through which information is retained and held over a period of time.
   A. Storage B. Encoding
   C. Retrieval D. Memory

7. Answering a question on a fill-in-the-blank test is a good example of which type of memory retrieval?
   A. Recognition B. Recollection
   C. Recall D. None of the above

8. Which type of memory retrieval involves reconstructing memory, often utilizing logical structures, partial memories, narratives or clues ?
   A. Recognition B. Recall
   C. Relearning D. Recollection

9. Taking a multiple-choice quiz requires that you recognize the correct answer out of a group of available answers, is an example of which type of memory retrieval?
   A. Relearning B. Recognition
   C. Recall D. Recollection

10. Who define chunking in his paper "The Magical Number Seven, Plus or Minus Two: Some Limits on our Capacity for Processing Information".
    A. Ebbinghaus B. Thorndike
    C. Miller D. Burttlet

11. .... is seen as consisting of three interrelated processes of encoding, storage and retrieval.
    A. Memory B. Forgetting
    C. Remembering D. Relearning

12. .... refers to loss of stored information over a period of time.
    A. Level of processing
    B. Memory
    C. Retrieval
    D. Forgetting

13. .... is the memory of autobiographical events (times, places, associated emotions, and other contextual knowledge) that can be explicitly stated.
    A. Semantic memory
    B. Episodic memory
    C. Sensory memory
    D. Long term memory

14. Which type memory involves memories of body movement and how to use objects in the environment?
    A. Declarative memory
    B. Procedural memory
    C. Episodic memory
    D. Semantic memory

15. Which type of memory involves the abstract knowledge and meaning of words, symbols, ideas and rules for relating them?
    A. Semantic memory
    B. Episodic memory
    C. Procedural memory
    D. Declarative memory

16. .... is derived from the Greek word icon, which means image, is the name given to visual sensory memory, or the memory of visual sensory information.
    A. Episodic memory
    B. Semantic memory
    C. Echoic memory
    D. Iconic Memory

17. .... is a permanent storehouse of all information and stores a large amount of information over a long period of days, months, years or even a lifetime.
    A. Sensory memory
    B. Short term memory
    C. Long term memory
    D. Episodic memory

18. Items near the beginning of the list are easier to recall than those in the middle, is called:
A. Primacy effect B. Recency effect
C. After effects D. Word length effect

19. Items near the end of the list are also easier to recall than those in the middle is called:
A. Recency effect B. Primacy effect
C. Word length effect D. After effects

20. .... are strategies for improving memory.
A. Mind games B. Mnemonics
C. Relearning D. None of the above

21. The process through which information stored in memory is located is called:
A. Encoding B. Storage
C. Retrieval D. None of the above

22. Who first to discover the serial position curve?
A. Thorndike B. Burttlet
C. Watson D. Ebbinghaus

23. .... refers to improved recall of specific episodes or information when the context present at encoding and retrieval are the same.
A. Context-Dependent Forgetting
B. State-Dependent Forgetting
C. Motivated Forgetting
D. None of the above

24. .... is the phenomenon through which memory retrieval is most efficient when an individual is in the same state of consciousness as they were when the memory was formed.
A. State-Dependent Forgetting
B. Context-Dependent Forgetting
C. Motivated Forgetting
D. None of the above

25. Most of the information kept in short-term memory will be stored for approximately ....
A. 15-25 seconds
B. 10-20 seconds
C. 20 to 30 seconds
D. 1 minute

26. The sensory register has all of the following characteristics, except:
A. Visual information lasts about a quarter of a second.
B. It holds an exact image of each sensory experience.
C. Auditory information lasts about 4 seconds.
D. The capacity is 7 ± 2 bits of information.

27. Which of the following best describes the serial position curve?
A. Greater accuracy of recall of words in the beginning of the list and in the middle of the list.
B. Greater accuracy of recall of words in the beginning of the list and gradual diminished accuracy by the end of the list.
C. Greater accuracy of recall of words in beginning and at end of the list.
D. Greater accuracy of recall of words in the middle and at the end of the list.

28. The graphic representation of learning which shows that the strength of response gradually increases with more and more learning trials is called:
A. Acquisition Curve
B. Forgetting Curve
C. Retention Curve
D. Plateau

29. Match List-I with List-II and indicate your answer with the help of the codes given below:

List-I (Definition)	**List-II (Memory system)**
(*a*) Memory for factual information that we acquire at a specific time	1. Procedural memory
(*b*) Memory for general, abstract knowledge that we cannot remember acquiring at a specific time	2. Episodic memory
(*c*) Memory for information necessary to perform skilled motor activity	3. Autobiographical memory
(*d*) Memory for events in our own life	4. Semantic memory

Codes:

	(a)	(b)	(c)	(d)
A.	2	4	1	3
B.	2	1	3	4
C.	3	2	4	1
D.	1	3	2	4

30. .... is the process of putting more than one bit of information into a unit, thereby expanding the capacity of STM.
A. Semantic codes
B. Chunking
C. Rehearsal
D. Working memory

31. One type of rehearsal in which items in short-term store are simply repeated over and over is called:
A. Elaborative Rehearsal
B. Sensory Register
C. Maintenance Rehearsal
D. Rehearsal Buffer

32. Each of the following is true regarding differences between STM and LTM, except:
A. information in STM is stored in terms of physical qualities
B. information in LTM may be permanent
C. information in LTM is primarily stored in the frontal lobes of the cortex
D. information in LTM is indexed

33. Rhyming is a:
A. Matrix
B. Mnemonic Device
C. Cue
D. Sign

34. The theory of forgetting that suggests that the conscious mind pushes information into the unconscious is called:
A. Repression B. Interference
C. Sublimation D. Decay

35. A process following learning during which a memory becomes more firmly established is called:
A. Over-learning
B. Consolidation
C. Transfer period
D. Constructive processing

36. Although short-term memory stores information in terms of physical qualities, long-term memory stores information in terms of;
A. acoustic codes
B. matrix
C. semantic codes
D. chunks

37. Amnesia is considered to be an extreme case of:
A. Regression B. Rationalization
C. Displacement D. Repression

38. Glanzer and Cunitz (1966) identified which effects?
A. Primary and recency
B. Retrospective interference
C. Proactive interference
D. Maintenance rehearsal

39. The memory we merely remember as long as it is in our eyes, casting an image in our retina, is:
A. Sensory Memory
B. Iconic Memory
C. Episodic Memory
D. Semantic Memory

40. According to the interference theory, which one of the following causes forgetting?
A. Failure of storage
B. Failure of encoding
C. Failure of retrieval
D. Response competition

41. The "Decay Theory" is sometimes called:
A. Over-learning theory
B. Interference Theory
C. Leaky-bucket Theory
D. Levels-of-processing Theory

42. Which of the following is a way of testing retrieval of long-term memories?
A. Relearning B. Recognition
C. Recall D. All of the above

43. Which type of memory has a biographical reference?
A. Semantic Memory
B. Iconic Memory
C. Episodic Memory
D. Levels-of-processing

44. A process following learning during which a memory becomes more firmly established is called:
A. Over-learning
B. Consolidation
C. Transfer period
D. Constructive processing

45. Which structure of the working memory model was responsible for storing speech sounds for a limited duration?
A. Phonological loop
B. Short-term memory
C. Episodic memory
D. Long-term memory

46. Which characteristic of long-term memory facilitates the retrieval of information?
A. The chunking of information
B. The organization of material
C. Unlimited capacity
D. All of the above

47. Short term memory is capable of holding approximately how many items of unrelated information?
A. one
B. two to four
C. five to nine
D. ten to twelve

48. Which type of memory results from conditioning of forced associations?
A. Semantic Memory
B. Iconic Memory
C. Rote Memory
D. Episodic Memory

49. Peterson and Peterson (1959) observed that which of the following factors resulted in forgetting?
A. Non-availability of cues
B. Lack of attention
C. Due to interference
D. The time between learning and recall

50. Retroactive Inhibition—the interference of interpolated activity—is like:
A. Negative transfer effect
B. Positive transfer effect
C. Zero transfer effect
D. Bilateral transfer effect

ANSWERS

1	2	3	4	5	6	7	8	9	10
D	D	A	B	C	A	C	D	B	C
11	**12**	**13**	**14**	**15**	**16**	**17**	**18**	**19**	**20**
A	D	B	B	A	D	C	A	A	B
21	**22**	**23**	**24**	**25**	**26**	**27**	**28**	**29**	**30**
C	D	A	A	C	D	C	A	A	B
31	**32**	**33**	**34**	**35**	**36**	**37**	**38**	**39**	**40**
C	C	B	A	B	C	D	A	A	D
41	**42**	**43**	**44**	**45**	**46**	**47**	**48**	**49**	**50**
C	D	C	B	A	B	C	C	D	A

❑❑❑

CHAPTER 4

Thinking and Problem Solving

THEORIES OF THOUGHT PROCESSES: ASSOCIATIONISM

The philosophical tradition of associationism can be traced back to Aristotle, but it developed mainly from the 17-19th century through the effort of scholars, mostly who were interested in the origins and nature of human knowledge (Warren 1921). Associationism is a theory about how items combine in the mind to produce thought and learning. Important exponents of associationism include Thomas Hobbes (1588–1679), David Hartley (1705–1757), E´tienne Bonnot de Condillac (1715–1780), James Mill (1773–1836), Thomas Brown (1778–1820), John Stuart Mill (1806–1873), Alexander Bain (1818–1903), and Herbert Spencer (1820–1903). Associationism also can be found in the philosophical works of John Locke (1632–1704), George Berkeley (1685–1753), and David Hume (1711–1776).

Current forms of associationism assume that complex psychological units are built from simpler elements on the basis of experience and through a process ("association") that is both general across domains and structure-independent. This process is typically sensitive to coincidences, correlations, or statistical dependencies among events, and the psychological units formed on its basis come to reflect such dependencies.

To uncover the psychological principles, the associationist philosophers used the introspective method and the phenomenological investigation of thought sequences. Anderson and Bower (1973), define "associationism" in terms of four basic assumptions:

1. Psychological units are connected by experience.
2. Complex units can be reduced to a limited stock of primitive units.
3. These primitive units consist of sensations.
4. Units combine through simple additive rules.

According to Fodor (1983), associationism includes: A set of basic elements out of which more complex structures are built, a relation of association defined over these elements and structures, principles of association whereby experience determines which structures are built and theoretical parameters of the associative relation and its terms.

The basic tenants of Associationism are quite easy to understand: items are associated in the mind through experience. These items are derived from experience, and combine to form thought. For example, a small child learns not to touch an electric wire because that child associates the wire with electric shock, the electric shock coming from past experience. Each item can combine with other items to form a more complex idea.

There are four typical principles of associationism, and three main processes. The principles state that items that are contiguous in time or space are lined by association, that items that are similar are linked by association, that items that contrast are linked and that items that have a cause/effect relationship are also linked. These linking are all occurring through the three processes of sequencing, compounding and deco positioning. Sequencing refers to a type of chronological pattern, where as compounding refer to the building up and breaking down of items, respectively.

INFORMATION PROCESSING

While cognitive psychology is the dominant school of thought today, the information processing approach is the dominant view within this area. The information-processing theory is associated with the development of high-speed computers in the 1950s. Researchers—most notably Herbert Simon and his colleagues—demonstrated that computer-oriented information-processing models could provide new insight into how the human mind receives, stores, retrieves and uses information.

Information processing approach is an approach to the study of cognitive development which focuses on how information is encoded from the environment cast into a symbolic form which the mind can process, and processed through a variety of mental operations to create useful output, such as solution to a problem.

In general there are four major theories of how we humans process information:

(*a*) Stage approach

(*b*) Levels-of-processing theory

(*c*) Parallel distributed processing theory

(*d*) Connectionistic models

The stage model focuses on how information is stored in memory. According to Atkinson and Shriffin (1968) information is processed and stored in three stages: Sensory memory, Short-term memory and Long term memory. However the major proposition in ***the level of processing theory*** proposed by Craik and Lockhart (1972), is that all stimuli that activate a sensory receptor cell are permanently stored in memory. According to these researchers, the issue is not storage, but retrieval.

The parallel-distributed processing model states that information is processed simultaneously by several different parts of the memory system, rather than sequentially as hypothesized by Atkinson-Shiffrin. ***The connectionistic model***, on the other hand proposed by Rumelhart and McClelland (1986) states that information is stored in multiple locations throughout the brain in the form of networks of connections. It is consistent with the levels-of-processing approach in that the more connections to a single idea or concept (*i.e.*, the more extensively elaboration is used), the more likely it is to be remembered.

According to Siegler (1998) while there are a large number of information-processing theories, all approaches share three basic assumptions.

1. Thinking is information processing, that is, any thought process such as remembering or perceiving involves the processing of information.
2. It emphasizes the need to study the change mechanisms that move development from one state to the next.
3. It includes self-modification, that is, earlier knowledge and strategies can modify thinking and thus lead to higher levels of development.

According to Siegler (1998), information processing theories focuses on the organization of the information–processing system, or what he calls the structural characteristics, and the processes that provide the means for cognition to adapt to the changing demands of the environment.

CONCEPT FORMATION

Concepts are mental categories used to group objects, events, information, etc or we can say that concepts are mental representations that can be expressed by a single word or set of ideas described by a few words such as plant or animal, table or chair, apple or mango. Through the use of language individual concepts can then be connected to build more complex concepts, for example,'birds fly' and 'humans walk'. There are many theoretical views of concepts, concept formation and learning. The classical view treats concepts as entities with well-defined borderlines and describable by sets of singly necessary and jointly sufficient conditions. Other view includes the prototype view, the exemplar view, the frame view, and the theory view. Each view captures specific aspects of concepts, and has a different implication for concept formation and learning.

In the classical view, every concept is understood as a unit of thought that consists of two parts, ***the intension and the extension*** of the concept. The intension of a concept is an abstract description of common feature or properties shared by elements in the extension, and the extension consists of concrete examples of the concept. A concept is thus described jointly by its intension and extension. The classical model clearly defines a triangle as a geometric shape with three sides and 180 degrees interior angles.

Grotzer (1999) coined the term ***'deep understanding***" which means that the concepts are well represented and connected. At the neural level it implies that concepts consists of webs of interconnected neurons that then get connected to even larger systems in the case of models or in more abstract situations. Whereas ***deep understanding*** involves the ability to recall many connected concepts at once, where every single concept has a deep meaning in itself. ***Deep thinking*** involves the construction of new concepts and is almost always based on what student already knows. When a learner makes sense of new material he is able to make connections between different concepts.

Two things that are important in concept formation are ***context and hierarchy***. A context in which concepts are formed provides meaningful interpretations of the concepts. Whereas hierarchy is organized in a tower or the partial ordering, in which higher level concepts depend on lower-level concepts. The first-level concept is formed directly from the perceptual data. The higher-level concepts, representing a relatively advanced state of knowledge, are formed by a process of abstracting from abstractions.

Previous research in machine learning suggests that the processes of concept formation can be divided into three distinct components—***aggregation, characterization and utilization.***

Aggregation is a process of collection, in which instances of experience are grouped together into a set. An aggregate represents an important collection of experience. ***Characterization*** is a process which involves constructing a description for an aggregate of experience, based on individual descriptions of each member of the aggregate. Thus, while aggregation identifies important experience, characterization attempts to explicitly represent what is important about the experience. ***The utilization process*** on the other hand integrates the characterization or concept description with the performance element of the system. Infact it tries to evoke the important property of the aggregate through the use of characterization, and so it serves as a test of the efficacy of the characterization process in capturing the important aspects of aggregate.

REASONING

Reasoning may be defined as the set of mental processes used to derive inferences or conclusions from premises. There are two ways of arriving at a conclusion: deductive reasoning and inductive reasoning.

Deductive Reasoning and Inductive Reasoning

Deductive reasoning also sometimes called "top-down" approach works from the more general information to the more specific. The brain systems that implement deductive reasoning depend on whether the reasoning problem consists of familiar versus unfamiliar semantic content. It also depends on whether a reasoning problem produces correct versus incorrect conclusions. In other words deductive reasoning links premises with conclusions. If all premises are true, the terms are clear, and the rules of deductive logic are followed, then the conclusion reached is necessarily true. When a lawyer uses evidence (premises) to prove his/her case (conclusion), he/she is using deductive reasoning. Another example of a deductive argument goes like this: It is Friday, Kunal always wears jeans on a Friday, and therefore Kunal is wearing jeans.

Inductive reasoning also sometimes called "bottom-up" approach works the opposite way, moving from specific observations to broader generalizations and theories. Inductive reasoning is the process of observing data, recognizing patterns, and making generalizations from your observations. It is reasoning in which the premises seek to supply strong evidence for (not absolute proof of) the truth of the conclusion. While the conclusion of a deductive argument is supposed to be certain, the truth of the conclusion of an inductive argument is supposed to be probable, based upon the evidence given. Much of geometry uses inductive reasoning. Discovering that the sum of the measures of the interior angles of a triangle is 180° by tearing the angles of different triangles and observing that the sum of their measures is 180° for each of the triangles is an example of inductive reasoning. Other example of inductive reasoning include: Swati is a doctor. Doctors are smart. Swati is assumed to be smart.

Although inductive reasoning can sometimes lead to false conclusions, it can often be a useful first step in the process of applying deductive reasoning to determine whether a conclusion is true.

Deductive and Inductive Arguments

1. Induction is usually described as moving from the specific to the general, while deduction begins with the general and ends with the specific.
2. Arguments based on laws, rules and accepted principles are generally used for deductive reasoning. Observations tend to be used for inductive arguments.
3. In a deductive argument, the premises are intended to provide support for the conclusion that is so strong that, if the premises are true, it would be impossible for the conclusion to be false. However, in an inductive argument, the premises are intended only to be so strong that, if they are true, then it is unlikely that the conclusion is false or the truth of the premises, at best, only makes the conclusion possible.

PROBLEM SOLVING

Problem can generally be defined as an obstacle that remains perplexing until solved. Researchers have distinguished between two main types of problems; well defined and ill defined. Well defined problems have a definite initial state and the goals and operators are known. Whereas ill defined problems are ones in which the solver does not know the operators, the goal, or even the current state.

Newell and Simon (1972) proposed that problem solving consists of a search in a problem space. A problem space has an initial state, a goal state, and a set of operators that can be applied that will move the solver from one state to another.

One of the most important aspects of problem solving becomes one of searching for a path through the problem space that will lead to the goal state. Problem solvers will use strategies or heuristics that allow them to move through a problem space. In problem solving research, ***a heuristic*** is a rule of thumb that will generally get one at the correct solution, but does not guarantee the correct solution. Heuristics can be contrasted with ***algorithms***, where application of the algorithm always guarantees the correct answer (*e.g.*, the rules of addition).

A slightly more complex strategy known as ***"hill climbing technique"*** is an optimization technique for solving computationally hard problems or is used to that state that looks most like the goal state. In this situation, the solver just looks one move ahead and chooses the state that most closely approximates the goal state. This strategy can be useful if it is impossible to look more than one move ahead, but can lead subjects astray.

Another strategy is ***means-ends-analysis***. Using this strategy, a solver looks at what the goal state is and sees what the difference is between the current state and the goal state. In case of any blockage while execution, the solver sets a sub goal of removing the block. It means the problem solver then decomposes the difference between the current state and the goal state into another sub problem and sets a goal of solving that problem. In this situation, removing the blocked state becomes the new goal. If that sub problem cannot be solved using the current operators, the problem is further decomposed until an operator can be applied. This strategy can be applied recursively until the problem is solved.

OBSTACLES TO PROBLEM SOLVING

When referencing an old technique that may have worked on a similar problem, one may not realize that it's not applicable. A ***mental set*** is created in which a tendency to respond to a new problem is similar to the approach to a previous problem.

Another obstacle while dealing with a problem situation is ***functional fixedness.*** Functional fixedness is a type of cognitive bias that involves a tendency to see objects as only working in a particular way. However, it is not always a bad technique. In many cases, it can act as a mental shortcut allowing us to quickly and efficiently determine a practical use for an object. Other obstacles to problem solving may be lack of specific knowledge, lack of interest, low self-esteem, fatigue, and/or drugs.

ROLE OF CONCEPTS IN THINKING

Concepts are one of the key elements of thinking. Concepts represent objects, activities, ideas, or living organisms. They also represent properties (such as "sour" or "brave"), abstractions (such as "anger" or "fear"), and relations (such as "smaller than" or "more intelligent than"). Concepts enable us to organize knowledge in systematic ways. We cannot observe them directly, but we can infer them from behaviour.

Concepts are the bodies of knowledge that are stored in long-term memory and are used by default in the higher cognitive processes (categorization, inductive and deductive reasoning, analogy making, language understanding, etc.). Concepts constitute ***a natural kind***, which may develop out of our everyday experiences in the world. You may possess a natural concept of a "animal" based on your experiences with animals. While these may involve words, they also involve visual images, emotions and nonverbal memories. Although a growing amount of evidence suggests that concepts do not constitute a natural kind. Not all concepts are natural; however, some are drawn from our experiences. These concepts are referred to as ***artificial concepts*** which are defined by rules, such as word definitions and mathematical formulas. Artificial concepts are categorised by our brains in this way when they have defining features. For example a 'square' is a concept and this is used to describe objects which have four right angles and four equal sides. If an object does not meet these exact requirements then it is not a square. This is an artificial concept and is one of the easiest concepts to learn. These concepts vary in generality, thus creating concept hierarchies, which organize concepts from the most general to the most specific. The ability to assimilate experiences into familiar mental categories and take the same action toward them or give them the same label is regarded as one of the most basic attributes of thinking organisms.

MULTIPLE CHOICE QUESTIONS

1. John B. Watson in his book on behaviourism (1952) define, '............ is largely sub vocal talking'.
A. Memory B. Language
C. Speech D. Thinking

2. In which type of thinking, concepts are the mediating processes?
A. Conceptual thinking
B. Verbal thinking
C. Non-verbal learning
D. None of the above

3. .... is associated with thinking, cognition, and intellect.
A. Emotion B. Learning
C. Reasoning D. Entertainment

4. The .... characterizes thinking as the environment providing input of data, which is then transformed by our senses.
A. Information processing approach
B. Concept formation approach
C. Learning approach
D. None of the above

5. A concept defined by the simultaneous possession or presence of two or more attributes of objects is known as:
A. Verbal Concepts
B. Conjunctive concept
C. Disjunctive concepts
D. Non-verbal concepts

6. A bike that has many attributes but can still be a bike without one of the attributes, is an example of:
A. Verbal Concepts
B. Non-verbal concepts
C. Conjunctive concept
D. Disjunctive concepts

7. .... is a process of collection, in which instances of experience are grouped together into a set.
A. Characterization
B. Utilization process
C. Aggregation
D. None of the above

8. The tendency to solve certain problems in a fixed way based on previous solutions to similar problems is known as:
A. Mental set
B. Heuristic behaviour
C. Autistic
D. Habitual

9. Who was the first articulated the term 'mental set' in the 1940s and demonstrated this in his well-known water jug experiments.
A. Thorndike B. Watson
C. Pavlov D. Luchins

10. .... is a cognitive bias that limits a person to using an object only in the way it is traditionally used
A. Computer modeling
B. Functional fixedness
C. Simulation
D. None of the above

11. .... gives problem solving a direction.
A. Mental set
B. Motivation
C. Functional fixedness
D. Focusing

12. A group or individual creativity technique by which efforts are made to find a conclusion for a specific problem by gathering a list of ideas spontaneously contributed by its member(s) is known as:
A. Brainstorming B. Abstractions
C. Analogy plays D. Heuristics

13. .... are the rules of thumb that permit us to make decisions and judgements in a rapid and efficient manner.
A. Heuristics
B. Algorithms
C. Means-end analysis
D. Brainstorming

14. What involves an effort to develop or choose amongst the various responses in order to attain desired goal?
A. Creative thinking
B. Divergent thinking
C. Problem solving
D. Cognition

15. .... is a problem solving technique in which the overall problem is divided into parts and efforts are made to solve each part in turn.
A. Heuristic
B. Hill climbing technique
C. Algorithm
D. Means-end analysis

16. A type of concept that can be clearly defined by a set of rules is called:
A. Natural concepts
B. Artificial concepts
C. Prototype concepts
D. None of the above

17. The tendency to become increasingly committed to bad decisions even when the losses associated with them increases is known as:
A. Risk prone
B. Mental set
C. Problem solving strategy
D. Escalation of commitment

18. .... are those concepts which may develop out of our everyday experiences in the world.
A. Natural concepts
B. Artificial concepts
C. Prototype concepts
D. None of the above

19. An abstract or general idea inferred or derived from specific instances is called:
A. Thinking B. Concepts
C. Remembering D. Problem

20. An egocentric thought processes that have little or no relation to reality, and focus largely on self-absorption is called:
A. Escalation of commitment
B. Imagination
C. Autistic thinking
D. Fantasy

21. .... is a logical process of an inductive or deductive nature used to draw a conclusion from fact or premise.
A. Thinking B. Learning
C. Concept formation D. Reasoning

22. The ultimate goal of .... is to overcome obstacles and find a solution that best resolves the issue.
A. Reasoning
B. Concept formation
C. Problem solving
D. Learning

23. Mental set and .... are two elementary processes within problem solving.
A. Insight
B. Concept formation
C. Thinking
D. Reasoning

24. When a problem cannot be solved using conventional stepwise methods, ... is used, which is often described as a sudden, unconscious and unintended process.
A. Reasoning B. Learning
C. Insight D. Recall method

25. .... increases the likelihood of a procedure being selected because it has repeatedly been successful in the immediate past.
A. Reasoning B. Mental set
C. Learning D. Insight

26. What among the following define a problem space?
1. An initial state
2. A goal state
3. A set of operations

Codes:
A. 1, 3 B. 1, 2
C. 2, 3 D. 1, 2, 3

27. .... is the process of classifying information into meaningful categories.
A. Concept
B. Conjunctive concept
C. Relational concept
D. Concept formation

28. Which stage of cognitive development, according to Piaget, is the best period of problem solving behaviour for children?
A. Secondary Circular Reaction
B. Tertiary Reaction
C. Primary Circular Reaction
D. Reflex

29. Read each of the following two statements—Assertion (A) and Reason (R) and indicate your answer using the codes given below:

Assertion (A): We use mental short-cuts to solve problems.
Reason (R): Problem solving includes thinking.
Codes:
A. Both (A) and (R) are true and (R) is correct explanation of (A).
B. Both (A) and (R) are true, but (R) is not the correct explanation of (A).
C. (A) is true, but (R) is false.
D. (A) is false, but (R) is true.

30. Which is not the obstacle to problem solving?
A. Confirmation bias B. Fixation
C. Mental Set D. Heuristics

31. A disjunctive concept separates objects into a class by reason of their possession of:
A. Any two characteristics
B. Any one characteristic
C. Any three characteristics
D. Any four characteristics

32. Problem solving comprises of four stages. Choose the correct sequence of stages:
A. Incubation, preparation, verification, illumination
B. Preparation, incubation, illumination, verification
C. Incubation, preparation, illumination, verification
D. Preparation, illumination, incubation, verification

33. Match the following lists according to the types and characteristics of thinking:

List-I (Types of Thinking)	List-II (Characteristics)
(*a*) Autistic thinking	1. Reasoning
(*b*) Realistic thinking	2. Drawing facts
(*c*) Convergent thinking	3. Unusual uses
(*d*) Creative thinking	4. Fantasy

Codes:

	(*a*)	(*b*)	(*c*)	(*d*)
A.	1	3	4	2
B.	3	1	2	4
C.	2	1	3	4
D.	4	1	2	3

34. Experimental results received by Luchins indicated that set can be controlled by controliing the Subjects:
A. Present Experience
B. Future Experience
C. Behaviour
D. Past Experience

35. The "Information Processing Theory" explains language learning by analogy with:
A. EEG model B. Computer model
C. Both A & B D. Polygraph model

36. Thinking consists of the cognitive rearrangement or manipulation of both information from the environment and the symbols stored in:
A. Short-term memory
B. Long-term memory
C. Unconscious
D. Subconscious

37. A German Psychologist, Karl Duncker, first proposed the concept of:
A. Subvocal Talking
B. Functional Fixity
C. Realistic Thinking
D. Implicit Speech

38. Creativity makes use of, ... which is solving problems with many possible solutions, as opposed to ...., which is solving problems with a single, correct answer.
A. Divergent thinking, convergent thinking
B. Convergent thinking, divergent thinking
C. Divergent thinking, hill climbing technique
D. Means end analysis, convergent thinking

39. J. B. Watson, the founding father of Behaviorism, held that thinking is nothing but:
A. Subvocal talking
B. Silent talking
C. Silent meditation
D. Relaxation technique

40. Given below are two statements, one labelled as Assertion (A), and the other labelled as Reason (R). Indicate your answer using the codes given below:
Assertion (A): Algorithm is a logical rule that guarantees solving a particular problem.

Reason (R): One can find the solution even to complex problems by following step by step procedure.

Codes:

A. Both (A) and (R) are true, but (R) is not the correct explanation of (A).
B. Both (A) and (R) are true and (R) is the correct explanation of (A).
C. (A) is true, but (R) is false.
D. (A) is false, but (R) is true.

41. First step in process of problem solving is to
A. design a solution B. define a problem
C. practicing solution D. organizing data

42. The thinking of the scientists or inventors is an example of:
A. Creative Thinking
B. Logical Thinking
C. Scientific Thinking
D. Abstract Thinking

43. Natural concepts are based on:
A. A set of rules B. Prototypes
C. Schemas D. Propositions

44. Reasoning is the stepwise thinking along with:
A. purpose or goal B. creativity
C. imagination D. set of rules

45. The images used in thinking are abstractions and constructions based on information stored in:
A. Short-term memory
B. Unconscious
C. Long-term memory
D. Conscious

46. The most important mental activity in the reasoning process is:
A. Thinking
B. Imagination
C. Recognition
D. Free association of ideas

47. Deductive reasoning involves....
A. Reasoning from the particular to the general
B. Reasoning from the general to the particular
C. Generalization of result from the population
D. None of the above

48. Which of the following methods are used by Graham Wallas to study steps involved in the creative thinkers thinking?
A. Interviews B. Reminiscences
C. Questionnaires D. All of the above

49. We sometimes attempt to solve problems by applying the technique that worked in similar situations in past. What type of method are we using?
A. Algorithm B. Heuristic
C. Analogy D. None of the above

50. Which of the following factors influence problem solving behaviour?
A. Motivation B. Past experience
C. Mental Set D. All of the above

ANSWERS

1	2	3	4	5	6	7	8	9	10
D	A	C	A	B	D	C	A	D	B
11	**12**	**13**	**14**	**15**	**16**	**17**	**18**	**19**	**20**
B	A	A	C	D	B	D	A	B	C
21	**22**	**23**	**24**	**25**	**26**	**27**	**28**	**29**	**30**
D	C	A	C	B	D	D	B	B	D
31	**32**	**33**	**34**	**35**	**36**	**37**	**38**	**39**	**40**
B	B	D	D	B	B	B	A	A	B
41	**42**	**43**	**44**	**45**	**46**	**47**	**48**	**49**	**50**
B	A	B	A	C	A	B	D	C	D

❑❑❑

CHAPTER 5

Motivation and Emotion

BASIC MOTIVATIONAL CONCEPTS

Motivation is the process that account for an individual's intensity, direction, and persistence of effort toward attaining a goal. In other words motivation is a need or desire that energizes behaviour and directs it towards a goal. There are two types of motivation: ***Extrinsic and Intrinsic motivation***.

Extrinsic motivation is something outside the person that energizes behaviour. For *e.g.* Money, fame, power. The intrinsic motivation on the other hand is something within the person that energizes behaviour. Interest, curiosity, personal challenge and improvement are the intrinsic motivators.

Instincts

In animals, instincts are inherent tendencies to spontaneously engage in a specific pattern of behaviour. On the other hand, in humans, many reflexes are examples of instinctive behaviours. The most important of these include sucking, swallowing, coughing, blinking. According to Tinbergen, (1951), instincts are complex behaviours that have fixed patterns throughout different species and are not learned.

According to the instinct theory of motivation, all organisms are born with innate biological tendencies that help them survive. These instincts provide the energy that channels behaviour in appropriate directions. In other words instinct refers to the inborn patterns of behaviour that are biologically determined rather than learned. Some common human instincts include curiosity, fight, repulsion, reproduction etc. William McDougall (1908), suggested that there are 18 instincts that included curiosity, the maternal instinct, laughter, comfort, sex, and hunger etc. Other theorists (Bernard, 1924) came up with claiming that there are exactly 5,759 distinct instincts! The term instinct most approximately refers to an urge to do something. An instinct has an 'impetus' which drives the organism to do something to reduce that impetus.

Needs

Need refers to a condition or state of our mind that prompts or persuades us to act or behave in a specific way. Abraham Maslow developed a theory of hierarchy of needs and suggests that before more sophisticated, higher-order needs can be met, certain primary needs must be satisfied (Maslow, 1970, 1987). In the levels of the five basic needs, the person does not feel the second need until the demands of the first have been satisfied or the third until the second has been satisfied, and so on. Maslow's basic needs are as follows:

Physiological Needs: These are biological needs. They consist of needs for oxygen, food, water, and a relatively constant body temperature.

Safety Needs: This includes protection from elements, security, order, law, stability, freedom from fear.

Needs of Love, Affection and Belongingness: Maslow states that the people seek to overcome feelings of loneliness and alienation and thus involve both giving and receiving love, affection and the sense of belonging.

Needs for Esteem: When the first three classes of needs are satisfied, the needs for esteem can become dominant. This includes achievement, mastery, independence, status, dominance, prestige, self-respect, and respect from others.

Needs for Self-Actualization: Maslow describes self-actualization as a person's need to be and do that, for which the person was "born to do." "A musician must make music, an artist must paint, and a poet must write." In other words it includes realizing personal potential, self-fulfilment, seeking personal growth and peak experiences.

Drive

A drive is motivational tension, or arousal, that energizes behaviour in order to fulfil some need. In his theory, Hull used the term drive to refer to the state of tension or arousal caused by biological or physiological needs. Thirst, hunger and the need for warmth are all examples of drives. A drive creates an unpleasant state; a tension that needs to be reduced. Drive reduction theories of motivation suggest that people act in order to reduce needs and maintain a constant physiological state. For example, people eat in order to reduce their need for food. The idea of homeostasis is central to drive reduction theories. Homeostasis is the maintenance of a state of physiological equilibrium. There are two types of drive namely, primary and secondary drive.

The primary drive includes many basic kinds of drives, such as hunger, thirst, sleepiness, and sex, which are related to biological needs of the body. Secondary drives are drives that are associated with the primary drives. The needs involved in secondary drives are created by prior experience and learning.

Incentives

An incentive is an environmental stimulus that pulls people to act in a particular way. Incentive approaches to motivation suggest that motivation stems from the desire to obtain valued external goals, or incentives. In this view, the desirable properties of external stimuli—it be the grades or marks in any subject, money, affection, food, or sex—account for a person's motivation. Incentives can be used to get people to engage in certain behaviours, but they can also be used to get people to stop performing certain actions.

It can only become powerful if the individual places importance on the reward.

Motivational Cycle

The individual always tries to satisfy his wishes or desires following in a cycle around need, drive, incentive and reward.

Need is the physical or psychological deficiency in the body. For example, a thirsty person may need something to drink. Drive is a motivational state created by the need. For example, a thirsty person may seek water to satisfy the drive for thirst which is his need. The third component incentive is something that motivates an individual to perform an action. If a person is thirsty, then water will be incentive for him. Incentive can be anything. For example, food, water, wealth, promotion, recognition etc. When an individual achieves his or her incentive and drives satisfaction from it he enjoys the reward. Reward is the last component of the motivational cycle.

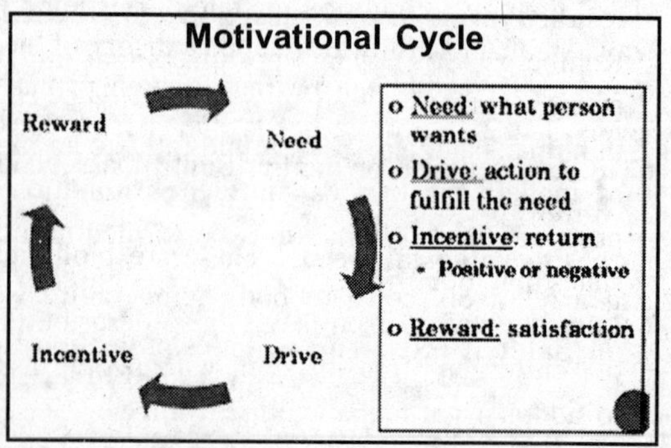

APPROACHES TO THE STUDY OF MOTIVATION: PSYCHOANALYTICAL

Much of psychoanalytic theory was derived from Freud's clinical experience in treating neurotic patients. Freud recognized two fundamental motivating forces. The first one is the constructive one called the ***Eros or life urges*** and the other is the destructive one called the ***Thanatos or the death urges***. Eros finds its output through drives known as ***self-preservation*** drive or ego drive and sex drive which play a significant role in Freudian psychoanalysis. ***Self-destructive*** behaviour, he believed, was one expression of the death drive. However, he believed that these death instincts were largely tempered by the life instincts.

The motivating principle in life is the ***pleasure principle***, which according to psychoanalysis, is the tendency to avoid pain and to seek pleasure. This dominates in sex drive. As one attains maturity, this is supplemented by the ***reality principle.***

Freud introduced the threefold division of mind into ***conscious mind, pre-conscious mind and unconscious mind.*** Our behaviour and feelings are powerfully affected by unconscious motives and the problems we face as adults (including psychological problems) are rooted in our childhood experiences. One basic assumption of psychoanalytical approach is that our personality is made up of three parts (*i.e.*, tripartite): ***the id, ego and super-ego*** and parts of the unconscious mind (the id and superego) are in constant conflict with the conscious part of the mind (the ego). This conflict creates anxiety, which could be dealt with by the ego's use of defence mechanisms and the personality is shaped as the drives are modified by different conflicts at different times in childhood (during psychosexual development).

ETHOLOGICAL APPROACH

Human ethology can be defined as the biology of human behaviour. Human ethology focuses on the evolutionary and adaptive significance of human behaviour (frequently comparing it to other species' behaviour). The fixed-action pattern (inherited movement coordination) is a fundamental ethological concept (Eibl-Eibesfeldt 1989). An important aspect for the survival of organisms is behaviour actualized on the basis-innate releasing mechanisms (Tinbergen 1951), some of them having the nature of a so-called "key stimuli," e.g. baby-scheme, etc. (Lorenz 1943). In the majority of cases, topical behaviour of the organism results from certain kinds of motivational states and its intensity and a specific external stimulus. The searching of organisms with a high inner motivational state for such an adequate stimulus situation is called appetitive behaviour.

Pullian and Dunford (1980) describe social learning as a shortcut for obtaining adaptive behaviour, since it need not rely on individual trial and error learning. They propose primary reinforcers which have resulted from natural selection which facilitate this process. The cognitive development theory of Kohlberg (1969), which postulates that imitation is intrinsically motivated, is compatible with this point of view. Imitation and identification since long has been given importance in behavioural development in humans and also been found to have an important effect on human adaptiveness. The observable result of modelled action can influence imitation is well established. With regards to this Gewirtz (1969) proposes that all imitation is performed ultimately because of external reinforcement and Bandura (1969) states that identificatory responses are greatly influenced by reinforcing the consequences of the behaviour. Lumsden and Wilson (1981) also describe imitation and vicarious learning as one of the primary means of "culturgen" transmission, with people assessing the costs and benefits of an action before deciding to adopt a particular culture choice.

SELF-REGULATION (S-R) APPROACH

According to Zimmerman and Schunk (2008), self-regulation is "the control of one's present conduct based on motives related to a subsequent goal or ideal that an individual has set for him—or herself". In other words self-regulation involves controlling one's behaviour in order to achieve a goal.

Behavioural self-regulation, also known as executive functioning, has three central components: working memory, attention control, and response inhibition (Cameron et al., 2008; McClelland et al., 2007). **Attention control** is a central component because it allows children to carry out behaviours, focus on a task or problem, access working memory, and complete tasks. It is also important for learning correct behaviour from models.

Working memory allows children to remember and follow directions and helps them plan solutions to problems (McClelland et al., 2007), and it may be involved as the child compares the behaviour he produced with that modelled earlier.

Inhibitory control develops rapidly during early childhood (Diamond, 2002) and helps children control behaviour by stopping incorrect solutions to a problem or incorrect behaviours and carrying out more adaptive responses or behaviours (McClelland et al., 2007).

Another term in self regulation *i.e.,* ***Effortful control,*** on the other hand is defined as "the ability to suppress a dominant response to perform a subdominant response" (Kochanska, Murray, & Harlan, 2000).

According to Bandura's social-cognitive theory (1997), self-evaluation plays a central role in the development of self-regulation. Children learn about which behaviours are rewarded and punished in the environment through action and observing the actions of others and evaluating the effects of these actions. These evaluations lead to the development of expectations for the outcomes of future behaviours and the establishment of internal criteria for judging the adequacy of the behaviours. Children then use these criteria to evaluate and regulate their own behaviour and evaluate their effectiveness.

Bronson (2000) argues that motivation and self-regulation are intertwined in two ways: first, people are innately rewarded by competence and control (*e.g.*, White, 1959), and second, people need self-regulated control to reach other goals. Children take pleasure in controlling their own activities and producing effects in the environment, and this can lead to feelings of competence (White, 1959). People are also motivated to reach specific goals and earn rewards such as social approval or material gain, and self-regulation is usually required to achieve these goals and rewards. Whether the activity is intrinsically or extrinsically motivated, it is self-regulation that enables goal attainment and motivation that facilitates self- regulation. Simply put, we are motivated to self-regulate.

COGNITIVE APPROACH

The cognitive theories of motivation include the Expectancy-Value theory, Goal-Setting theory and the Attribution theory. ***The expectancy-value theory***, stresses that the probability of occurrence of behaviour depends upon individuals' perception of the value of a goal as well as their expectation of reaching it. Expectancy-value theories hold that people are goal-oriented beings. The behaviours they perform in response to their beliefs and values are undertaken to achieve some end. Utilizing this approach, behaviour, behavioural intentions, or attitudes are seen as a function of "(1) expectancy (or belief) – the perceived probability that an object possesses a particular attribute or that a behaviour will have a particular consequence; and (2) evaluation – the degree of affect, positive or negative, toward an attribute or behavioural outcome" (Palmgreen, 1984).

The goal-setting theory was proposed by Edwin Locke in the 1960s. This theory proposes that the goal setting has an influence on task performance. Specific and challenging goals are more likely to motivate a person and lead to a better execution of tasks, whereas vague and easy goals may result to poor task performance.

According to ***attribution theory***, humans naturally seek to understand why events have occurred, especially when the outcome is important or unexpected (Moeller & Koeller, 1999; Weiner, 1992). We all try to explain our performance through causal attributions, interpretations of events based on past performance and social norms (Weiner, 2000). Attribution theory rests on three basic assumptions. First, it assumes that we do attempt to determine the causes of both our own behaviour and that of others. Secondly, the assignment of causes to behaviour is not done randomly; that is rules exist that can explain how we come to the conclusions we do about the cause of behaviour. Lastly, the causes attributed to particular behaviours will influence subsequent emotional and non-emotional behaviours. The attributions we make, then, may activate other motives.

HUMANISTIC APPROACH

Humanistic Psychology was developed primarily by Carl Rogers and Abraham Maslow and came into prominence in the 1950s and 60s. According to Cartwright (1979), humanistic psychology "is concerned with topics that are meaningful to human beings, focusing especially upon subjective experience and the unique, unpredictable events in individual human lives". More specifically, humanistic psychologists argue that psychology should be based on phenomenolology.

According to Maslow humans are innately good and have an innate capacity for constructive growth, honesty, generosity and love. He believed that our actions are motivated in order achieve certain hierarchy of needs which is a combination of ***deficiency needs*** (need for survival, need for safety) and ***growth needs*** (need for love and belonging, need for esteem, need for self-actualisation). This hierarchy suggests that people are motivated to fulfil basic needs before moving on to other, more advanced needs. The five different levels in Maslow's hierarchy of needs include-the ***physiological need,*** such as the need for water, air, food, and sleep. These needs are the most basic and instinctive needs in the hierarchy because all needs become secondary until these physiological needs are met. Second, is the ***security need***, which are important for survival, but they are not as demanding as the physiological needs. Third, is the ***social needs,*** which include needs for belonging, love, and affection. Fourth, is the ***esteem needs,*** which includes the need for things that reflect on self-esteem, personal worth, social recognition, and accomplishment. Lastly, is the highest level need termed as ***self-actualizing needs.*** According to Maslow (1954), self-actualisation can be described in the following way:" A musician must make music, an artist must paint, a poet must write, if he is to be ultimately at peace with himself. What a man can be, he must be.

Self-actualised people are characterised by an acceptance of themselves, spontaneity, the need for privacy, resistance to cultural influences, empathy, profound interpersonal relations, a democratic character structure, creativeness, and a philosophical sense of humour. According to Maslow, Abraham Lincoln, Eleanor Roosevelt, and Albert Einstein were identified as self-actualisers.

Carl Rogers (1902-1987) was another humanistic psychologist who agreed with the main assumptions of Abraham Maslow, but added that for a person to "grow", they need an environment that provides them with genuineness (openness and self-disclosure), acceptance (being seen with unconditional positive regard), and empathy (being listened to and understood).

SOCIAL MOTIVE

Social motives are also called as learned motives or secondary motives. They are called social because they are learned in "social groups", especially in the family. Murray described a needs as a, "potentiality or readiness to respond in a certain way under certain given circumstances" (1938). He identified needs as one of two types: Primary needs and Secondary needs. The primary needs are biological in nature and includes the need for oxygen, food and water. Secondary needs on the other hand are psychological in nature. For example, need for nurturing, independence and achievement.

Need for Achievement (N-Arc)

The need to achieve is basically defined as a need to be successful "in competition with some standard of excellence," wherein "doing as well as or better than someone is a primary concern". Behavioural manifestations of N-Achievement occur as an effective response "in connection with evaluated performance." Thus the elements of success, standard of excellence, competition, and evaluated performance are all elements related to the conception of the achievement motive.

Researches on N-Achievement had found that N-Achievement is developed in early childhood within the dynamics of the mother-child interaction. Besides that other researchers has found that individuals who have high need to achieve and low anxiety scores show preference for tasks with intermediate probability of success. Such individuals also maintain a generally high performance level and are persistent in problem solving tasks. Whereas, individuals who are low in N-Achievement and high in anxiety scores tend to choose tasks with probabilities for success at either extreme-that is, they tend to select unrealistic levels of aspiration. Such individuals are also less effective in their performance and less persistent in problem solving situations.

According to Daft (2008) the Need for Achievement is "the desire to accomplish something difficult, attain a high standard of success, master complex tasks, and surpass others". Individuals who exhibit the Need for Achievement seek to accomplish realistic but challenging goals.

Need for Affiliation (n-Affiliation)

According to McClelland (1961), "Affiliation refers to establishing, maintaining, or restoring a positive affective relationship with another person. This relationship is most adequately described by the word friendship" Daft (2008), on the other hand defined the need for Affiliation as "the desire to form close personal relationships, avoid conflict, and establish warm friendships".

There is an essential need for human beings to establish and maintain affinitive relationships with others. This need is called the affiliation need. The affiliation need is important when we consider human relations or group formation. People who want to establish and maintain a friendly relationship with another person are apt to follow or sympathize with this person.

Those with a high need for affiliation (nAff) need maintain harmonious relationships with other people and need to feel accepted by other people. They tend to conform to the norms of their work group. High nAff individuals prefer work that provides significant personal interaction. For example, In a setting like an office, need for affiliation might include joining office organizations, making friends with co workers, and creating a sense of belonging within the company. A low need of affiliation can be part of a more independent personality. People who do not feel a strong desire to affiliate with others may be viewed as loners, and could have difficulty finding support.

Need for Approval

According to Horney, people who do not have their needs for love and affection satisfied during childhood develop basic hostility toward their parents and, as a consequence, suffer from basic anxiety. Horney theorized that people combat basic anxiety by adopting one of three fundamental styles of relating to others.

- moving toward people
- moving against people
- moving away from people

In her book ***Self-Analysis* (1942),** Horney outlined the 10 neurotic needs she had identified. Among these one need is need for Affection and Approval. This needs include the desires to be liked, to please other people, and meet the expectations of others. People with this type of need are extremely sensitive to rejection and criticism and fear the anger or hostility of others.

THEORIES OF EMOTIONS: JAMES-LANGE THEORY

The James–Lange theory was developed independently by two 19th-century scholars, ***William James and Carl Lange***. According to this theory environmental stimuli triggers physiological responses and bodily movements, and emotion occurs when the individual interprets his or her visceral and muscular responses. For example, You see a beer while walking on the road. You might begin to tremble and your heart begins to race. This theory states that all emotion is derived from the presence of a stimulus, which evokes a physiological response, such as muscular tension, a rise in heart rate, perspiration, and dryness of mouth. This physical arousal makes a person feel a specific emotion. According to this theory, emotion is a secondary feeling, indirectly caused by the primary feeling, which the physiological response is caused by the presence of a stimulus.

Perceived Stimulus → Physiological Responses → Experience Emotions
(Different for different emotions)

Cannon-Bard Theory

The Cannon-Bard theory of emotion was developed by Walter Cannon and Philip Bard. According to the Cannon-Bard Theory of emotion, emotions and bodily changes do not share a cause-and-effect relationship. Rather, they occur simultaneously, following a stimulating event. In other words it states that we feel emotions and experience physiological reactions such as sweating, trembling and muscle tension simultaneously. For example, If someone dies, the reactions of crying and feeling sad occur at the same time. Even if a person sees a bear, he feels afraid and his muscles get tensed at the same time, preparing to run away from the dangerous animal.

Stimulus → Physiological & Behavioural changes + Emotions

Schachter and Singer Theory

The Schachter and Singer theory of emotion, also known as "Two-Factor Theory of Emotion", suggests that emotions comes from a combination of a state of arousal and a cognition that makes best sense of the situation the person is in. It is the cognition which determines whether the state of physiological arousal will be labelled as joy, fear etc.

For example, the two-factor theory of emotion argues that when people become aroused they look for cues as to why they feel the way they do. Both cognition and arousal are considered necessary conditions for the occurrence of an emotional state. According to Schachter's (1964), if either of them is missing, no emotion will be experienced.

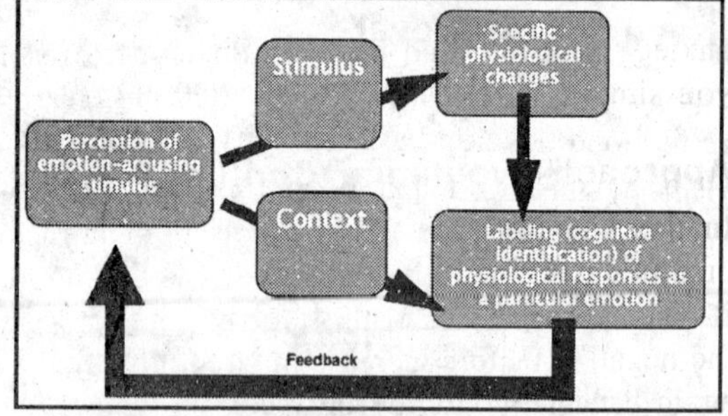

When an individual encounters a stimulating event, perception and interpretation of the stimulus follows. After this, the processed information is divided into two: stimulus and the context of the event, which is a specific cognitive label. The information about the stimulus triggers a general autonomic arousal or we can say certain specific physiological changes takes place. In addition to the general autonomic arousal, the cognitive label causes a particular emotion to be experienced. Once an emotion is experienced, feedback occurs.

CONFLICT

A conflict has generally been defined as a situation in which two or more parties strive to acquire the same scarce resources at the same time. Conflict by itself is neither good nor bad. However, the manner in which conflict is handled determines whether it is constructive or destructive (Deutsch & Coleman, 2000).

According to Fisher (1990), "Conflict is defined as an incompatibility of goals or values between two or more parties in a relationship, combined with attempts to control each other and antagonistic feelings toward each other".

There are three types of conflicts: **approach-approach, avoidance-avoidance, and approach-avoidance.**

Approach-Approach Conflicts

It is a psychological conflict that results when a choice must be made between two desirable alternatives. An example of an approach-approach conflict would be where you have to decide between two appealing destinations for your vacation, for example, Singapore vs Australia. The approach-approach conflict is the one that is the least stressful, although in situations where you need to make important decisions (e.g. deciding between two good career opportunities), it can result in some increased stress. It typically results from limitations on one's time, space, energy and personal and financial resources.

Research suggests that approach-approach conflicts are easier to resolve than any other type. As you tentatively near one goal (say, commerce stream, while choosing between humanities and commerce), its attractiveness increases. As you emphasize the advantages (it has many future prospects), you are closer to your choice. At the same time, the appeal of the other goal decrease and the conflict ends. People generally resolve approach-approach conflicts easily because they always result in something pleasant. Moreover, the alternatives can be achieved in turn.

Avoidance-Avoidance Conflict.

This type of conflict occurs when a person has to make a choice between two unattractive options. For example, Choosing one amongst the two situations where you have to decide between cleaning kitchen (avoidance) or chopping vegetables (avoidance). Research shows that as organisms approach an unattractive choice, it becomes more repellent. Avoidance-avoidance conflicts arouse a great deal of anxiety typically, and they are difficult to resolve. Whatever choice is made will not be satisfying, so you simply have to decide which is the "lesser of two evils", or least stressful.

Approach-Avoidance Conflict

In this situation, the individual is both attracted and repelled by the same goal. The same goal has qualities that make the individual want to approach it and other qualities that make him want to avoid it. The approach side of this type of conflict is easy to start toward the goal, but as the goal is approached the negative factors increase in strength which causes indecision. For example,You may want to exercise again because you know it will make you feel better, but are also afraid of exercising because you are worried you could get injured. In this manner the person is brought back to the original point of equilibrium.

Double-Approach-Avoidance

An individual frequently might face the situation wherein he/she has to choose between two (or more) goals, each of which has both attracting and repelling aspects. Since the tendency is to approach and avoid each of the goals, this pattern is called double approach-avoidance. For example, the only available job is not my cup of tea but will provide income. Or getting to watch the late night 9-12 movie show but not getting enough sleep for school the next day. Double approach-avoidance conflicts are anxiety-provoking and hard to resolve.

MULTIPLE CHOICE QUESTIONS

1. According to which theory of motivation, all organisms are born with innate biological tendencies that help them survive.
A. Instinct theory
B. ERG theory
C. Two Factor theory
D. Need Achievement theory

2. According to which theory of motivation, needs are exist in hierarchy and higher needs can't be achieved until the lower needs are satisfied.
A. Herzberg two factor theory
B. Maslow need hierarchy theory
C. Equity theory
D. None of the above

3. Maslow describes .... as a person's need to be and do that which the person was "born to do."
A. Safety Needs
B. Self-actualization
C. Esteem needs
D. Physiological needs

4. Motivation which is a part of the organism's biological inheritance, such as the need for food, water, sex etc is known as:
A. Extrinsic motive
B. Acquired motives
C. Inborn motives
D. None of the above

5. .... is something outside the person that energizes behaviour.
A. Extrinsic motivation
B. Intrinsic motivation
C. Inborn motive
D. Need achievement motive

6. Maslow refers self-actualization need as ....
A. Deficiency needs B. Basic needs
C. Specific needs D. Growth needs

7. Maslow refers physiological need as ....
A. Deficiency needs
B. Basic needs
C. Specific needs
D. Growth needs

8. .... is motivational tension, or arousal, that energizes behaviour in order to fulfil some need.
A. Incentive B. Drive
C. Motive D. Instincts

9. Who introduced the threefold division of mind into ***conscious mind, pre-conscious mind and unconscious mind.***
A. Maslow B. Freud
C. Herzberg D. McDougall

10. Among these which involves controlling one's behaviour in order to achieve a goal.
A. Attribution B. Attention control
C. Self-regulation D. Instincts

11. According to which need an individual desires to accomplish something difficult, attain a high standard of success, master complex tasks, and surpass others?
A. Need for affiliation
B. Need for power
C. Need for approval
D. Need for achievement

12. .... is a complex psychological state that involves three distinct components: a subjective experience, a physiological response, and a behavioural or expressive response.
A. An emotion B. A motive
C. An instinct D. A desire

13. What includes the desire to form close personal relationships, avoid conflict and establish warm friendships"?
A. Need for achievement
B. Need for affiliation
C. Need for power
D. Need for approval

14. We meet a bear, get frightened, and run is an example of which particular theory of emotion?
A. James-Lange theory of emotion
B. Cannon-Bard theory of emotion
C. Schachter and Singer Theory
D. None of the above

15. .... is the process by which the body regulates its internal conditions to achieve equilibrium and maintain proper bodily functions.
A. Instinct B. Homeostasis
C. Balancing D. Heterostasis

16. According to which theory, emotions and bodily changes do not share a cause-and-effect relationship. Rather, they occur simultaneously, following a stimulating event.
A. Schachter and Singer Theory
B. Expectancy theory
C. James-Lange theory
D. Cannon-Bard theory

17. .... is a personality trait characterized by the desire to want to belong to social groups and the tendency to enjoy group activities and working in groups and teams.
A. Self-preservation
B. Dependency
C. Gregariousness
D. Identification

18. .... is also known as parapraxes, are speech errors that are believed to reveal what is in a person's unconscious mind.
A. Aphasia B. Stuttering
C. Freudian slips D. Apraxia

19. Among these which is a type of psychological conflict that results when a choice must be made between two desirable alternatives?
A. Avoidance-avoidance
B. Approach-approach
C. Approach-avoidance
D. None of the above

20. Which type of conflict occurs when a person has to make a choice between two unattractive options.
A. Avoidance-avoidance
B. Approach-approach
C. Approach-avoidance
D. Double- Approach-Avoidance

21. .... is a situation, in which an individual is both attracted and repelled by the same goal.
A. Avoidance-avoidance
B. Approach-approach
C. Approach-avoidance
D. Double-approach-avoidance

22. .... indicates that, facial expressions can influence as well reflect emotional states.
A. Frustration-Aggression hypothesis
B. James-Lange theory
C. Facial feedback hypothesis
D. Cannon-Bard theory

23. .... is a situation when the interests, needs, goals or values of involved parties interfere with one another.
A. Aggression
B. Frustration
C. Stress
D. Conflict

24. According to Maslow, which need reflects, the need for self-esteem, personal worth, social recognition, and accomplishment.
A. Physiological needs
B. Esteem needs
C. Safety needs
D. Self actualization need

25. Which theory was proposed by Edwin Locke in the 1960's?
A. The goal-setting theory
B. Attribution theory
C. The expectancy-value theory
D. None of the above

26. Why do individuals with high need for achievement quit early when faced by very difficult task?
A. Get tired easily
B. Have poor perseverance
C. Have high anxiety
D. Have high need for efficiency

27. According to Maslow, the self-actualizing tendency is a/an:
A. Instinct
B. Imprinting
C. Growth motivation
D. Deficiency motivation

28. The "need for success", "expectancy for success" and the "incentive value of success" are three motivational factors which determine the strength of:
A. Social Motives
B. Biological Motives
C. Personal Motives
D. Achievement Need

29. What is true of drives?
1. Internal states
2. Aroused by tension
3. Underlying need
4. Guided by external stimuli

Codes:
A. 1, 2 and 4 B. 1, 2 and 3
C. 2, 3 and 4 D. 1, 2, 3 and 4

30. Gregariousness is a:
A. Social motive
B. Biological motive
C. Psychological motive
D. Personal motive

31. Byrne believed sexual motivation results from the inter-play of ...., environment and ....
A. genes; experience
B. genes; imagination
C. physiology; imagination
D. physiology; lust

32. When progress towards a goal is blocked and underlying tension is unresolved, we speak of:
A. Frustration B. Critical Period
C. Problem D. Restriction

33. Choose the correct sequence of emergence of the following theories of emotion:
1. James-Lange
2. Cannon-Bard
3. Schachter and Singer
4. Darwin

Codes:
A. 1 3 2 4 B. 4 3 2 1
C. 4 1 2 3 D. 1 2 3 4

34. .... motives emphasize the individual as striving to maintain equilibrium.

A. Cognitive
B. Affective
C. Preservation-oriented
D. Growth

35. Match List-I with List-II and mark your answer using the codes given below:

List-I (Theory)	**List-II (Description)**
(*a*) James-Lange	1. Triggering the feeling of pleasure and pain simultaneously.
(*b*) Cannon-Bard	2. Emotional experience comprise of the physiological arousal and its cognitive labelling.
(*c*) Opponent-process	3. Emotion arising stimulus simultaneously triggers physiological responses and the subjective experience of emotion.
(*d*) Two-factor	4. Emotional experience refers to our awareness of our physiological responses to emotion arousing stimuli.

Codes:

	(*a*)	(*b*)	(*c*)	(*d*)
A.	4	3	2	1
B.	4	2	3	1
C.	3	2	4	1
D.	3	4	1	2

36. Read the following two statements, Assertion (A) and Reason (R) and indicate your answer using the codes given below:

Assertion (A): The high achievement motivation displayed by children has emotional roots.

Reason (R): Highly motivated children often have parents who encourage their independence from an early age and praise and reward them for their successes.

Codes:

A. Both (A) and (R) are true and (R) is the correct explanation of (A).
B. Both (A) and (R) are true and (R) is not the correct explanation of (A).
C. (A) is true, but (R) is false.
D. (A) is false, but (R) is true.

37. Strong, relatively uncontrollable feelings that affect our behaviour are known as:
A. motivations B. personality
C. emotions D. perceptions

38. Persons high in achievement motivation tend to prefer tasks that are:
A. very easy
B. extremely difficult
C. moderately difficult
D. all types of task

39. A motivated behaviour is directed towards:
A. Situation B. Object
C. Goal D. Group

40. According to ethological theory, species-specific behaviour has following characteristics:
1. Fixed-action pattern
2. Instinctive
3. Unlearned
4. Innate

Codes:
A. 1, 3 and 4 B. 2, 3 and 4
C. 1, 2 and 3 D. 1, 2, 3 and 4

41. Which of the following structures appears to be selectively involved in the recognition of fear stimuli?
A. Amygdala B. Hippocampus
C. Thalamus D. Frontal lobe

42. Choose the odd one for pattern of sympathetic activation during emotions:
A. Increased heart rate
B. Pupil constriction
C. Lowered skin resistance
D. Increased breathing rate

43. As per Schachter and Singer's theory of emotions, one shall experience emotions based on situational clues when:
I. there is a physiological arousal
II. there are cognitions/explanations available for arousal

III. there is no physiological arousal
IV. there are no proper explanations available for one's arousal

Choose the correct codes:

A. I & II B. I & IV
C. II & III D. III & IV

44. Based on cross-cultural research, Ekman and colleagues concluded that there are .... basic emotions.

A. Four B. Five
C. Six D. Eight

45. What is the correct sequence of events for hunger motivation? Indicate your answer using the codes given below:

1. Energy level to its set point
2. A bout of eating
3. Presence of an energy deficit
4. Satiation
5. Hunger

Codes:

A. 1, 2, 3, 4, 5 B. 3, 5, 2, 1, 4
C. 2, 1, 3, 5, 4 D. 5, 4, 3, 1, 2

46. Motives are never observed directly; but they are inferred from:

A. Stimulus B. Conflict
C. Tension D. Behaviour

47. In avoidance-avoidance conflict, the individual is compelled to choose between:

A. One positive and one negative alternative
B. Two negative alternatives
C. Two positive alternatives
D. Two negative alternatives and two positive alternatives

48. Which of the following is an example of an intrinsic motivator?

A. A pay increase
B. Promotion
C. Good working conditions
D. Satisfaction in a job well done

49. Read the following two statements, Assertion (A) and Reason (R) and indicate your answer using the codes given below:

Assertion (A): According to Maslow, after gratification of basic needs we move in positive direction, but it is not automatic.

Reason (R): We often fear our best side, our talents, our finest impulses, our creativeness.

Codes:

A. Both (A) and (R) are true and (R) is the correct explanation of (A).
B. Both (A) and (R) are true and (R) is not the correct explanation of (A).
C. (A) is true, but (R) is false.
D. (A) is false, but (R) is true.

50. Need for achievement can be measured by:

A. Binnet's scale
B. Thurstone's scale
C. TAT (Thematic Apperception Test)
D. Semantic Differential scale

ANSWERS

1	2	3	4	5	6	7	8	9	10
A	B	B	C	A	D	A	B	B	C
11	**12**	**13**	**14**	**15**	**16**	**17**	**18**	**19**	**20**
D	A	B	A	B	D	C	C	B	A
21	**22**	**23**	**24**	**25**	**26**	**27**	**28**	**29**	**30**
C	C	D	B	A	D	C	D	B	A
31	**32**	**33**	**34**	**35**	**36**	**37**	**38**	**39**	**40**
C	A	C	C	A	A	C	C	C	D
41	**42**	**43**	**44**	**45**	**46**	**47**	**48**	**49**	**50**
A	B	B	C	B	D	B	D	A	C

❑❑❑

CHAPTER 6

Human Abilities

INTELLIGENCE

Intelligence (in all cultures) is the ability to learn from experience, solve problems, and use our knowledge to adapt to new situations. Binet and Simon (1905) define intelligence as the "ability to judge well, to understand well, and to reason well"

According to H. Gardner-"An intelligence is the ability to solve problems, or to create products, that are valued within one or more cultural settings."

Wechsler defined intelligence as "the aggregate or global capacity of the individual to act purposefully, to think rationally, and to deal effectively with the environment".

The idea that general intelligence (g) exists comes from the work of Charles Spearman (1863-1945) who helped develop the factor analysis approach in statistics. He proposed the idea that intelligent behaviour is generated by a single, unitary quality within the human mind or brain. Whereas L.L. Thurstone, a critic of Spearman, analyzed his subjects not on a single scale of general intelligence, but on seven clusters of primary mental abilities, including: word fluency, verbal comprehension, spatial ability, perceptual speed, numerical ability, inductive reasoning and memory. Thurstone's work in factor analysis led him to formulate a model of intelligence centered around "Primary Mental Abilities" (PMAs), which were independent group factors of intelligence that different individuals possessed in varying degrees.

Biological Determinants

In the past years, genetics were able to persuade most psychologists that heredity plays an effective role in influencing intelligence (Plomin & DeFries, 1998). However, a high degree of heredity does not mean that the environment has no influence on the development of any trait (Neisser et al, 1995).

The concept of heritability has its origins in animal breeding where variation in genotype and environment is under the control of the experimenter, and under these conditions the concept has some real-world applications. In human, however variability is uncontrolled, there is no "true" degree of variation to estimate, and heritability can take practically any value for any trait depending on the relative variability of genetic endowment and environment in the population being studied.

According to Scott (1998)- "there is no single gene for intelligence, personality, behaviour, or even height". For example, a specific chromosome is responsible for eye colour, and another one is responsible for hair colour. So environment has nothing at all to do in such traits. However, it is important to clarify that environment can be divided into categories. These categories are Shared Environment and Non-Shared Environment (Hughes & Cutting, 1999). Each category may or may not have effects on individual's intelligence.

Numerous studies have used monozygotic (identical) twins and dizygotic (fraternal) twins to get a sense of how strongly heredity affects IQ. Since monozygotic is derived from one fertilized zygote, in the case of identical twins, it is anticipated that the twins will obtain very close IQ scores, even if they are raised in different environment. Furthermore, Dizygotic is derived from two fertilized zygotes. Therefore, in the case of fraternal twins, it is expected that the twins will obtain close IQ scores but not as close as the identical twins because they are not identically heredity. The result of one study conducted on twins by Bouchard and McGue (1981) based on data obtained has found that the data for identical twins that reared together and apart indicates a ***strong influence of heredity*** on intelligence. However the adoption studies, too, indicate that intelligence is not determined entirely by heredity (Capron & Duyme, 1989; Devlin, Fienberg, Resnick, & Roeder, 1995; Waldman, Weinberg, & Scarr, 1994).The ***distinct environments that different families provide*** do have some influence on intellectual development.

Socio-Economic and Cultural Determinants

The evidence from adoption studies that social class greatly affects the IQ of children raises questions about exactly what correlates of socio-economic status (SES) affect IQ. Many researchers have found the socioeconomic status of children to be strongly correlated with both performance and intelligence scores (Molfese, Modglin, & Molfese, 2003). In one study, psychologists used the Wechsler Intelligence Scale for Children as a measure of intelligence. They found that heritability of IQ was much higher in children of above-average SES than it was for children living in poverty.

Linda Gottfredson claimed that low g is actually the "Fundamental Cause" of inequalities both among and within social classes (2004). She has found that 30% of young white adults with IQs of 75 or less live in poverty, while only 2% with IQs higher than 125 live in poverty (Gottfredson, 2004).

The Hart and Risley (1995) findings are amplified by studies using the HOME (Home Observation for Measurement of the Environment) technique. HOME researchers assess family environments for the amount of intellectual stimulation that is present, as indicated by how much the parent talks to the child; how much access there is to books, magazines, newspapers, and computers; how much the parents read to the child; how many learning experiences outside the home (trips to museums, visits to friends) there are; the degree of warmth versus punitiveness of parents' behaviour toward the child; and so on, (Bradley et al., 1993; Phillips et al., 1998). These studies find marked differences between the social classes, and they find that the association between HOME scores and IQ scores is very substantial.

Sternberg (2007) with regards to cultural difference in intelligence said that—people that are considered intelligent may vary from one culture to another, along with the acts that constitute intelligent behaviour. It has been shown, for example, that tests which are highly novel in one culture or subculture may be quite familiar in the next (Valsiner, 2000), so that, for instance, unschooled subjects may fail at classification tasks characteristic of school learning contexts and succeed with classification relevant to their own everyday practical experiences (Cole, 1990; Cole et al. 1971). In other words, people will be good at doing those things that are important to them and that they have opportunities to do often.

In another study, Sternberg and his collaborators found that children who score highly on a test of knowledge about medicinal herbs—a measure of practical intelligence—tend to score poorly on tests of academic intelligence. The results, suggest that practical and academic intelligence can develop independently or even in conflict with each other, and that the values of a culture may shape the direction in which a child develops.

THEORIES OF INTELLIGENCE

Spearman's Two-factor theory

Spearman proposed his two factor theory of intelligence in 1904. According to him intellectual abilities were comprised of two factors: one ***general ability or common ability known as 'G'*** factor and the other a group of ***specific abilities known as 'S'*** factor. 'G' factor is largely innate and accounts for success in all activities. 'S' factor is acquired from the environment and success in any specialized field very much depends on the concerned specific factor which is essentially learnt. It varies from activity to activity in the same individual.

Thurstone's Group-factor Theory

L.L. Thurstone while working on a test of primary mental abilities, came to the conclusion that certain mental operations have in common a 'primary' factor, which, gives them psychological and function unity and which differentiates them from other mental operation. These mental operations, then, constitute a group. A second of mental operations has its own unifying 'Primary factor'; a third group has a third, and so on each of these primary factors giving the group a functional unity and cohesiveness and is said to be relatively independent of others. Thurstone has given the following six primary factors:

1. **The Number Factor (N):** The ability to quickly and accurately solve numerical calculations.
2. **The Verbal Factor (V):** The ability to understand the meaning and relationship of words.
3. **The Space Factor (S):** The ability to do any task in which the subject manipulates the imaginary object in space.
4. **Memory (M):** The ability to memorize quickly.
5. **Word fluency factor (W):** The Ability to think and use many isolated words at a rapid rate.
6. **The Reasoning Factor (R):** Ability to see relationships in situations described in symbols.

Based on these factors Thurstone constructed a new test of intelligence known as ''Test of Primary Mental Abilities (PMA).''

Guilford Structure of Intellect

Guilford (1967, 1985, 1988) proposed a three dimensional structure of intellect model. His "Structure of Intellect" model organized the various abilities along three dimensions: ***content, product, and operations.***

He further classified ***content*** into five categories, namely:

1. Visual—information perceived through seeing.
2. Auditory—information perceived through hearing.
3. Symbolic—items such as words and symbols which generally convey some meaning.
4. Semantic—concerned with verbal meaning and ideas.
5. Behavioural—information perceived as observed behaviour of individual.

The product dimension contains results of applying particular operations to specific contents. Guilford classified ***products*** into six categories, namely:

1. Units—This includes symbolic units such as words and visual units such as shapes, or behavioural units such as facial expressions.
2. Classes—sets of units sharing common attributes.
3. Relations—ability to find out the relationships between pairs of units.
4. Systems—multiple relations interrelated to comprise structures or networks.
5. Transformations—ability to sense changes, perspectives, conversions, or mutations to knowledge.
6. Implications—ability to make predictions, inferences, consequences, or anticipations of knowledge.

Guilford classified ***operations*** into five categories, namely:

1. Cognition—the ability to perceive the various items in terms of understanding, comprehending, discovering information.
2. Memory—the ability to store and retrieve various kinds of information.
3. Divergent production—the ability to generate multiple sclutions to a problem. It includes creativity.
4. Convergent Production—the ability to deduce a single solution to a problem. This area includes most areas of logic type problem solving.
5. Evaluation—the ability to make judgements about information to check whether it is accurate, consistent, or valid.

Since each of these dimensions is independent, there are theoretically 150 different components of intelligence.

MEASUREMENT OF INTELLIGENCE

There is a variety of psychometric tests for measuring intelligence. Two of the most commonly used individual tests are the Standard-Binet Intelligence Scales and the Wechsler Intelligence Scales.

The Standard-Binet Intelligence Scales was originally developed by Alfred Binet in 1905. It was later revised by Lewis Terman and has been revised several times since then. The most revised version of this test (SB-V) measures five weighted factors and consists of both verbal and nonverbal subtests. The five factors being tested are knowledge, quantitative reasoning, visual-spatial processing, working memory, and fluid reasoning. The fifth edition incorporated a new scoring system, which can provide a wide range of information such as four intelligence score composites, five factor indices, and ten subtest scores. Additional scoring information includes percentile ranks, age equivalents, and a change-sensitive score (Janzen, Obrzut, & Marusiak, 2003). Extended IQ scores and gifted composite scores are available with the SB5 in order to optimize the assessment for gifted programs (Ruf, 2003).

The Wechsler Intelligence Scales were developed by Dr. David Wechsler, a clinical psychologist in 1939. Since then, three scales have been developed and subsequently revised, to measure intellectual functioning of children and adults. The Wechsler Adult Intelligence Scale-III (WAIS-III) is intended for use with adults. The Wechsler Intelligence Scale for Children-III (WISC-III) is designed for children ages 6 - 16, while the Wechsler Preschool and Primary Scale of Intelligence-R (WPPSI-R) is designed for children age 4 - 6 1/2 years.

The revised version of the WAIS (2008) includes ten core subtests as well as five supplemental subtests. The test provides four major scores: Verbal comprehension, Perceptual reasoning, Working memory and Processing speed. Additionally, the WAIS-IV provides two overall summary scores: Full scale IQ and General ability index.

Another tool to measure intelligence is Culture-fair tests. These tests is also known as culture-free tests, are designed to assess intelligence (or other attributes) irrespective of environmental factors. Raymond Cattell developed his Culture Fair test in the 1940s to study intelligence across the cultures of "civilized countries." The Cattell scales are intended to assess intelligence independent of cultural experience, verbal ability, or educational level. They are used for special education placement and college and vocational counseling. The tests consist mostly of paper-and-pencil questions involving the relationships between figures and shapes. The Cattell Culture Fair test is now little used because it did not achieve the goal of being free from the influence of culture on learners.

MULTIPLE CHOICE QUESTIONS

1. .... is "the aggregate or global capacity of the individual to act purposefully, to think rationally, and to deal effectively with the environment".
A. Thinking B. Learning
C. Remembering D. Intelligence

2. The formula for calculating IQ is:
A. $\frac{MA}{CA} \times 100$ B. $\frac{CA}{MA} \times 100$
C. $\frac{MA}{CA} \div 100$ D. $\frac{CA}{MA} \div 100$

3. The famous book 'Emotional Intelligence' was written by whom?
A. Spearman B. Galton
C. Goleman D. Thurstone

4. Who proposed the two factor theory of intelligence in 1904?
A. Spearman B. Thurstone
C. Goleman D. None of the above

5. Which factor according to Spearman is largely innate and accounts for success in all activities?
A. Specific ability B. General ability
C. Verbal ability D. Numerical ability

6. Who gave the group factor theory of Intelligence?
A. Wechsler B. Sternberg
C. Thurstone D. Jensen

7. Who coined the term fluid and crystallised intelligence?
A. Galton B. Wechsler
C. Binet D. Cattell

8. When the Mental Age (MA) and Chronological Age (CA) of a person is same, then the IQ of that person will be:
A. 100 B. 50
C. 75 D. 120

9. .... is a type of retardation that appears in infancy due to the insufficient supply of thyroid hormone.
A. Cretinism
B. Down syndrome
C. Fragile X syndrome
D. Phenylketonuria

10. Among these who gave the concept of IQ?
A. Alfred Binet B. Lewis Terman
C. William Stern D. None of the above

11. Who proposed a three dimensional structure of intellect model?
A. Spearman B. Guilford
C. Thurstone D. None of the above

12. The original Guilford's structure of intellect model suggests:
A. 100 identifiable abilities
B. 120 identifiable abilities
C. 125 identifiable abilities
D. 150 identifiable abilities

13. .... includes those aspects of intelligence that involve drawing on previously learned information to make decisions or solve problems.
A. Fluid intelligence
B. Emotional intelligence
C. Artificial intelligence
D. Crystallized intelligence

14. A superior ability in any worthwhile line of human endeavour *i.e.*, physical, emotional, intellectual life is known as:
A. Giftedness B. Retardation
C. General ability D. None of these

15. Who originally developed the Standard-Binet Intelligence Scales in 1905?
A. J.P. Guilford B. Lewis Terman
C. Alfred Binet D. L.L Thurstone

16. Wechsler intelligence test consists of:
A. Performance items
B. Non-verbal items
C. Verbal items
D. Both verbal and performance items

17. Who developed the 'culture-free' test of intelligence?

A. Wechsler B. Cattel
C. Binet D. Thurstone

18. Guilford in his three dimensional structure of intellect model classified operations into how many categories?

A. 3 B. 4
C. 5 D. 6

19. According to Sternberg, the ability to analyze and evaluate ideas, solve problems, and make decisions is known as:

A. Analytical intelligence.
B. Practical intelligence
C. Fluid intelligence
D. Giftedness

20. According to whom the 'g' factor represents the highest-order common factor among individual differences in IQ?

A. Spearman B. Gardner
C. Cattell D. None of the above

21. In the normal distribution curve of intelligence test scores, the mean IQ score is set at:

A. 60 B. 70
C. 90 D. 100

22. Spearman's two-factor theory of intelligence contains the following abilities and/or factors:

A. Crystallised and fluid
B. General and specific
C. Product and operations
D. None of the above

23. .... intelligence is the ability to use skills, knowledge and experience.

A. Crystallized B. Fluid
C. General D. Specific

24. .... intelligence is our ability to call upon existing knowledge and skills to effectively handle new and unusual situations.

A. Analytical B. Creative
C. Practical D. Fluid

25. .... also called componential intelligence, refers to your ability to problem-solve, process information effectively, and complete academic tasks.

A. Analytical intelligence
B. Creative intelligence
C. Practical intelligence
D. Crystallized

26. Raven's Standard Progressive Matrices is presumed to measure

A. Crystallized Intelligence
B. Convergent Thinking
C. General Intelligence
D. Fluid Inteligence

27. Match List-I with List-II and select the correct answer by choosing from the codes given below:

List-I (Authors)	List-II (Concepts)
(*a*) Cattell	1. General and Specific factors
(*b*) Spearman	2. Fluid and Crystallized intelligence
(*c*) Gardner	3. Triarchic theory of intelligence
(*d*) Sternberg	4. Multiple Intellegence theory

Codes:

	(*a*)	(*b*)	(*c*)	(*d*)
A.	1	3	4	2
B.	2	1	4	3
C.	3	4	2	1
D.	4	3	2	1

28. The deviation I.Q. expresses a person's relative intellectual status within his or her age group by a measure derived from:

A. F-Scores
B. T-Scores
C. Z-Scores
D. Standard Deviation (SD)

29. Intellectual functioning is mainly in the domain of which lobe of the Cortex?
A. Occipital lobe
B. Frontal lobe
C. Parietal lobe
D. Temporal lobe

30. Who suggested that superior intelligence was associated with good health, social adaptability and leadership?
A. Binet B. Spearman
C. Terman D. Guilford

31. Read each of the following two statements—Assertion (A) and Reason (R) and indicate your answer using the codes given below:

Assertion (A): Females score higher than males with respect to verbal activities, while males tend to score higher on visual-spatial abilities.

Reason (R): Gender differences in different abilities are due to interplay of heredity and environment.

Codes:
A. Both (A) and (R) are true and (R) is correct explanation of (A).
B. Both (A) and (R) are true, but (R) is not the correct explanation of (A).
C. (A) is true, but (R) is false.
D. (A) is false, but (R) is true

32. According to Thurstone, how many primary mental abilities are there?
A. 6 B. 7
C. 9 D. 12

33. Which one of the following is a product in Guilford's model?
A. Evaluation
B. Cognition
C. Transformation
D. Symbols

34. E.L. Thorndike held that intelligence is a combination of different abilities and functions at:
A. Three different levels
B. Four different levels
C. Five different levels
D. Six different levels

35. Substantially higher performance scores than verbal scores on the subtests of Wechsler Adult Intelligence Scale (WAIS) indicates:
A. Gender differences
B. Learning difficulties
C. Genetic influences
D. Cultural biases

36. Who held the view that mental functioning involves two types of abilities—an associative ability and a cognitive ability?
A. L.L. Thurstone B. Alfred Binet
C. R.B. Cattell D. A.R. Jensen

37. Continuum of "Birth Weight" is the basis of studying:
A. the effect of biological factors on intellectual development
B. the effect of genetics on intellectual development
C. the effect of genetic and socio-cultural factors on intellectual development
D. the effect of biological and socio-cultural factors on intellectual development.

38. Bhatia's test of intelligence is basically designed:
A. To test the rural illiterate population of India
B. To test the urban illiterate population of India
C. To test the urban literate population of India
D. To test the rural literate population of India

39. Major criticisms of Thurston's theory of intelligence are based on
I. Use of subjective measures
II. Restricted heterogeneity in sample
III. Method of factor analysis

Codes:
A. I and II are correct.
B. I and III are correct.
C. II and III are correct.
D. I, II and III are correct.

40. Guilford's concept of intelligence includes what he calls?
A. Creative Thinking
B. Divergent Thinking
C. Abstract Thinking
D. Convergent Thinking

41. Given below are two statements, one labelled as Assertion (A) and the other labelled as Reason (R). Indicate your answer using the codes given below:

Assertion (A): Heritability of intelligence explains variations due to genetics for individuals within a given population.

Reason (R): Earlier the children from deprived families were adopted, the higher their intelligence score will be.

Codes:
A. Both (A) and (R) are true and (R) is the correct explanation of (A).
B. Both (A) and (R) are true, but (R) is not the correct explanation of (A).
C. (A) is true, but (R) is false.
D. (A) is false, but (R) is true.

42. Which of the following is not a subtest used by Wechsler to measure intelligence?
A. Object assembly
B. Comprehension
C. Visual discourse
D. Digit symbol

43. Deterioration Quotient (DQ) was first used in which intelligence tests?
A. Binet-Simon Test
B. Galton-Cattell Test
C. Raven Progressive Matrices
D. Wechsler Adult Intelligence Test

44. Wechsler Adult Intelligence Scale has eleven subtests out of which:
A. Five are verbal and six are performance.
B. Six are verbal and five are performance.
C. Seven are verbal and four are performance.
D. Four are verbal and seven are performance.

45. Children of affluent and educated parents tend to score higher on tests of ability than children of parents living in poverty and who are not well educated. This relationship between socio-economic status and scores on ability tests is because of:
1. genetic differences in ability between different social classes.
2. differences in the adequacy of the biological and environmental factors in nutrition and health care.
3. differences in the cultural and learning experiences provided for children from different social classes.

Codes:
A. 1 and 3 B. 2 and 3
C. 1 and 2 D. 1, 2 and 3

46. Who viewed that intelligence is an adaptive process that involves an interplay of biological maturation and interaction with the environment?
A. David Wechsler B. Jean Piaget
C. Lewis Terman D. None of the above

47. Spearman Inferred General Intelligence on the basis of:
1. Positive manifold in intercorrelation matrix
2. Tetrad differences in equation
3. Unequal scores of same subjects on intelligence tests
4. Reports from the subjects

Codes:
A. 1 & 3 B. 2 & 4
C. 1 & 2 D. 3 & 4

48. Which is the correct order of 'Products' given by Guilford?
   A. Units, Relations, Classes, Systems, Implications, Transformations
   B. Units, Classes, Systems, Relations, Implications, Transformations
   C. Units, Classes, Relations, Systems, Transformations, Implications
   D. Units, Classes, Systems, Relations, Transformations, Implications

49. For an intelligence test, while computing item-remainder correlations for item analysis, we compute
   A. Phi-coefficient
   B. Spearman rho
   C. Tetrachoric correlation
   D. Point-biserial correlation

50. The chronological age that most typically corresponds to a given level of performance is called:
   A. Intelligence Quotient
   B. Maturation
   C. Mental age
   D. None of the above

ANSWERS

1	2	3	4	5	6	7	8	9	10
D	A	C	A	B	C	D	A	A	C
11	**12**	**13**	**14**	**15**	**16**	**17**	**18**	**19**	**20**
B	B	D	A	C	D	B	C	A	A
21	**22**	**23**	**24**	**25**	**26**	**27**	**28**	**29**	**30**
D	B	A	B	A	C	B	C	B	C
31	**32**	**33**	**34**	**35**	**36**	**37**	**38**	**39**	**40**
A	B	C	A	B	D	A	A	C	D
41	**42**	**43**	**44**	**45**	**46**	**47**	**48**	**49**	**50**
B	C	D	B	D	B	C	C	D	C

❑❑❑

CHAPTER 7

Research Methodology

GOALS OF SCIENTIFIC RESEARCH

Scientific research in psychology has four interrelated goals: (1) Description (2) Prediction (3) Explanation/ Understanding (4) Application

Description

The first goal of scientific research is to carefully observe and identify regularly occurring sequences of events, including both stimuli or environmental events and responses or behavioural events. Researchers are often interested in describing the ways in which events are systematically related to one another. For example, Do the height of the kids who play outdoor games increase more than those who play indoor games or do not play any outdoor games? Providing a clear, accurate description is an essential first step in any scientific endeavour; without it, predictions cannot be made and explanations are meaningless.

Prediction

Descriptions of events often provide a basis for prediction. The strength of the relationships allows predictions to be made with some degree of confidence. More formal and systematic predictions can be made by the testing of formal hypotheses using statistical methods. Hypotheses are frequently derived from theories, or interrelated sets of concepts that explain a body of data and make predictions.

Explanation/Understanding

Another goal of scientific research is explanation. Explanation is achieved when the cause or causes of a phenomenon are identified. Cook and Campbell (1979) describe three types of evidence (drawn from the work of philosopher John Stuart Mill) used to identify the cause of a behaviour.

1. **Covariation:** Changes in the presumed cause must be related to changes in the presumed effect. When the cause is present, the effect occurs; when the cause is not present, the effect does not occur. Thus, the researcher introduces, remove, or change the level of a treatment or program, to observe some change in the outcome measures.
2. **Temporal Precedence:** The presumed cause must occur prior to the presumed effect.
   For example, we need to know whether inflation cause unemployment?
3. **Elimination of alternative explanations:** The presumed cause must be the only reasonable explanation for changes in the outcome measures. But sometimes, it's possible that there is some other variable or factor that is causing the outcome. Thus in that we can say that the presumed cause-effect relationship is not correct. Any number of factors other than the treatment or program

could cause changes in outcome measures. Campbell and Stanley (1966) and later, Cook and Campbell (1979) list a number of common plausible alternative explanations (or, threats to internal validity).

Thus, the third goal of scientific research is to ***explain*** the events that have been described. The researcher seeks to understand ***why*** the behaviour occurs.

Application

This final goal of scientific research is application. It involves the various ways of applying those principles of behaviour learned through research, For example, the research on the factors influencing depression enables therapists to help people diagnosed with depression and so on.

RESEARCH PROBLEM

Leedy (1989) defines research problem as a procedure by which we attempt to find systematically, and with the support of demonstrable fact, the answer to a question or the resolution of a problem. According to Kerlinger (1970) a research problem is the systematic, controlled, empirical and critical investigation of hypothetical propositions about presumed relations among natural phenomena.

There are **two ways of stating the problem:** (1) **Research problems**: typically a rather general overview of the problem with just enough information about the scope and purpose of the study to provide an initial understanding of the research. (2) **Research statements and/or questions:** more specific, focused statements and questions that communicate in greater detail the nature of the study.

In quantitative research, research problems tend to emphasize the need to explain, predict, or describe something. In qualitative research, the purpose focuses on exploring or understanding a phenomenon.

Characteristics of Good Research Questions

1. Research questions should be feasible—that is, capable of being investigated with available resources.
2. It should be clear and specific.
3. It should be significant or worthy of investigation.
4. It should refer to the problem or phenomenon.
5. It often (although not always) suggest a relationship to be investigated.
6. It addresses directly or indirectly some real problem in the world.
7. It is not biased in terminology or position.
8. It has multiple possible answers.
9. It takes ethical issues into consideration.
10. It offers something new to, previous research and has the potential to suggest directions for future research.

Sources of Research Problem

Research ideas and research problems originate from many sources. This includes—the casual observation of everyday life experiences or practical issues of life. **Past research** or related literature review can be an excellent source of research ideas. **Theory** (*i.e.,* explanations of phenomena) can also be a source of research ideas. Besides that personal interests and experiences can also be one the source of research problem.

HYPOTHESIS

According to Kerlinger (1956), a hypothesis is a conjectural statement of the relation between two or more variables or a hypothesis may be precisely defined as a tentative proposition suggested as a solution to a problem or as an explanation of some phenomenon. (Ary, Jacobs and Razavieh, 1984).

Any useful hypothesis will enable predictions by reasoning (including deductive reasoning). It might predict the outcome of an experiment in a laboratory setting or the observation of a phenomenon in nature. The prediction may also invoke statistics and only talk about probabilities. This usually involves proposing a possible relationship between two variables: the independent variable (what the researcher changes) and the dependant variable (what the research measures). A hypothesis should be: stated clearly using appropriate terminology; testable; state relationships between variables; limited in scope (focused).

TYPES OF HYPOTHESIS

There are different types of hypothesis:

1. **Null hypothesis:** It states that there is no relationship between the two variables being studied (one variable does not affect the other). In other words, the null hypothesis states that there is no change or difference as a result of the independent variable. In statistical significance, the null hypothesis is often denoted H0 (read "H-nought") and is generally assumed true until evidence indicates otherwise.
2. **Alternative hypothesis:** It states that there is a relationship between the two variables being studied (one variable has an effect on the other). In other words the alternative hypothesis states that there is a change or difference as a result of the independent variable. The alternative hypothesis, denoted by H1 or Ha, is the hypothesis which states that sample observations are influenced by some non-random cause.
3. **One-tailed directional:** A one-tailed directional hypothesis predicts the nature of the effect of the independent variable on the dependent variable. In other words a one tailed hypothesis specifies a directional relationship between groups. For example, 'Girls are more intelligent than boys'.
4. **Two-tailed directional:** A two tailed hypothesis would predict that there was a difference between groups, but, would make no reference to the direction of the effect. For example, 'There will be a significant difference between the intelligence level of girls and boys'.
5. **Non-directional alternative hypothesis:** A non-directional hypothesis is a type of alternative hypothesis used in statistical significance testing. Sometimes called a two-tailed test, a test of a non-directional alternative hypothesis does not state the direction of the difference, it indicates only that a difference exists. In other words a non-directional alternative hypothesis is only concerned that null hypothesis is not true.

VARIABLES

A variable is a concept or abstract idea that can be described in measurable terms. In research, this term refers to the measurable characteristics, qualities, traits, or attributes of a particular individual, object, or situation being studied. Variables are generally used in psychology experiments to determine if changes to one thing result in changes to another.

Types of Variables

1. **Independent Variable (IV):** Those Variables which the experimenter manipulates (*i.e.,* changes) to see its direct effect on the dependent variable. For example, In an experiment looking at the effects of stress on health, stress would be the independent variable. Researchers are trying to determine if changes to the independent variable (stress level) result in significant changes to the dependent variable (the health).
2. **Dependent Variable (DV):** Those variables which are measured by the experimenter after making changes to the independent variable that are assumed to affect the dependent variable. For example, in a study looking at how stress level impacts the health, the dependent variable would be the participant's health score.
3. **Extraneous variables:** Extraneous Variables are undesirable variables that influence the relationship between independent and dependent variables. Thus, the researcher try to control all the other variables that could affect the DV. There are two basic types of extraneous variables:

A. **Participant Variables:** These factors can include background differences, mood, anxiety, intelligence, awareness and other characteristics that are unique to each person.

B. **Situational Variables:** These extraneous variables are related to things in the environment that may impact how each participant responds. Noise, pollution, temperature etc. If, however, a variable cannot be controlled for, it becomes what is known as a confounding variable. This type of variable can have an impact on the dependent variable or can hamper the actual result of the study.

METHODS OF PSYCHOLOGICAL RESEARCH

Experimental Method

In experimental method the researcher or experimenter studies the effect of independent variable (which is controlled and manipulated by the experimenter) on dependent variable (the change in behaviour measured by the researcher.). In an experimental study following characteristics should be included in the study:

1. The independent variable must be completely controlled.
2. The sample of research participants (subjects) must be randomly chosen.
3. The subjects must be assigned randomly to conditions. A condition refers to the groups of subjects who receive different values of independent variable.

There are three types of experiments: ***Laboratory/controlled experiments, Field experiments and Quasi or Natural experiment.***

I. **Laboratory/controlled experiments:** A laboratory experiment is an experiment conducted under highly controlled conditions and therefore accurate measurements are possible. The researcher decides the place, time, and circumstances under which research study will take place using a standardised procedure. Laboratory experiments allow for precise control of variables, however it is not always possible to control all the variables. There may be other variables at work which the experimenter is unaware of. The purpose of control is to enable the experimenter to isolate the independent variable to observe its effect on the dependent variable. The advantage of experimental method is that it can be easily replicated because a standardized procedure is used in this. The other advantage is that it allows establishing a cause and effect relationship because this involves the deliberate manipulation of one variable, while trying to keep all other variables constant. As far as limitation is concerned the artificiality of the setting may produce unnatural behaviour that does not reflect real life. This means it would not be possible to generalize the findings to a real life setting. A further difficulty with the experimental method is demand characteristics. It means if a participant knows they are in an experiment they may seek cues about how they think they are expected to behave.

II. Field experiments: A field experiment is the one that is conducted in the real life environment of the participants. In field experiments the participants are not usually aware that that they are participating in an experiment. The experimenter still manipulates the independent variable, but in a real-life setting (so cannot really control extraneous variables). The advantage of this type of study is that it has higher ecological validity than a lab experiment as because of its natural setting, the behaviour in the field experiment is more likely to reflect the real life. Other advantage is that there is less likelihood of demand characteristics affecting the results, as participants may not know they are being studied. The disadvantage on the other hand is that there is less control over extraneous variables that might bias the results. Other limitation is that in field experiments it is not usually possible to gain informed consent from the participants and it is difficult to debrief the participants.

III. Quasi or natural experiments: A quasi experiment is the one which is conducted in the everyday (*i.e.,* real life) environment of the participants but here the experimenter has no control over the independent variable (IV) as it occurs naturally in real life. These experiments are often called natural experiments. One of the strength of quasi or natural experiment is that because of it natural setting, the behaviour in a natural experiment is more likely to reflect life real *i.e.,* very high ecological validity. In a quasi experiment the researcher takes advantage of pre-existing conditions such as age, sex or an event that the researcher has no control over such as a participant's occupation. As disadvantage these types of experiments are more expensive and time consuming than the lab experiments. Also as there is no control of experimenter over the extraneous variables it might bias the results. Hence replication also becomes difficult.

Case Study Method

The case study method involves an in-depth study of an individual or group of individuals. It often involves simply observing what happens to, or reconstructing 'the case history' of a single participant or group of individuals. In this method almost every aspect of an individual or subject's life and previous happenings or history is taken into account to determine the patterns and causes of the behaviour. The researcher collects data about the subject through interviews, direct observation, psychological testing, or examination of documents and archival records about the subject. There are usually two types of case study methods: Prospective and retrospective.

Prospective: A type of case study in which a participant or group of participants is observed in order to determine outcomes, such as the development of a disease, during the study period and relates this to other factors such as suspected risk or protection factor(s). In this type of case study some criteria's are established and cases fitting the criteria are included as they become available. In a study on a group of smokers and non-smokers over a time, determining or finding out which ones eventually develop cancer and which do not is an example of prospective study or method.

Retrospective: A type of case study which looks backwards and examines exposures to suspected risk or protection factors in relation to an outcome that is established at the start of the study. In other words it involves looking at historical information or establishing criteria for selecting cases from historical records for inclusion in the study. Many valuable case-control studies are good examples of retrospective method. A study is called case-control when 'cases' or diseased subjects and 'controls' or comparable non-diseased subjects are sampled from respective populations and then assessed on their risk-factor exposure status. In case where we first locate a group of participants with cancer and identify which are smokers and which are not is an example of retrospective study or method.

As an advantage, case study method provides detailed or qualitative information about the participant. Also it Provides insight for further research. Case studies tend to be conducted on rare cases where large samples of similar participants are not available. The disadvantage of case study method is that the data collected cannot necessarily be generalised to the wider population. Some case studies are not scientific and it is also very difficult to draw a definite cause/effect from these types of studies.

METHODS OF DATA COLLECTION

Observation

According to Wieck (1968) observation involves broadly selecting, recording and encoding behaviour for empirical aims of description and development of theory. In terms of scientific observation, it is the systematic process of recording the behavioural patterns of people, objects, and occurrences as they are witnessed. In psychology, observation particularly participant observation has been used as a tool for collecting data about people, processes, and cultures in qualitative research.

The qualitative approaches to observation can provide rich, detailed description, unconstrained by predetermined concepts and categories. They are therefore particularly useful for describing the complexity of what is observed, and for generating hypotheses about it and about relationships between different factors or elements. On the other hand in quantitative observational studies, the researcher typically spends time in the same situation as the person or persons they are observing, recording what that person does and what happens to them.

Types of Observation

1. **Covert observation:** Covert observations involve the researcher not informing members of the group the reason for their presence; keeping their true intentions secret. There could be ethical problems or deception and consent with this particular method of observation.
2. **Overt observation:** In this type of observation, the participants are aware that they being a part of research study and they know they are being observed. An advantage of this type of observation is that it allows the researcher to bc honest with the participants, thus avoiding problematic ethical issues such as deception or lack of informed consent.
3. **Naturalistic observation:** This type of observation allows the researcher to observe and record the behaviour exactly as it occurs in the real world. In other words the behaviour is being observed in a more or less natural setting without any intervention. It means the investigator does not manipulate or control the situation or the situation has not been initiated or created by the investigator. Naturalistic observation helps to establish the external validity of research findings.
4. **Controlled observation:** In this behaviour is observed under controlled laboratory conditions. Controlled observation allowed the researches to obtain a base value that could be trusted with regard to the experiment.
5. **Participant observation:** In participant observation the researcher or investigator actively participates in the activities of the group to be observed. The procedure of participant observation is often unstructured and the identity of the observer is often not known to the other members of the group. It allows researchers to observe behaviours and situations that are not usually open to scientific observation. However participant observers may sometimes lose their objectivity or may unduly influence the individuals whose behaviour they are recording.

6. **Non-participant observation:** Non-participant observation is usually structured and the investigator observes the behaviour of the participants in a natural setting but does not remain a participant or member of the group being observed. The data obtained by this type of observation are more reliable and representative. However the non-participant observation fails to record natural context of social settings the way participant observation does.

INTERVIEW

An interview is a data-collection technique that involves oral questioning of respondents, either individually or as a group. In simple word interviews are usually one-on-one between the interviewer and participant, meant to gather information on a specific set of topics using oral questions. Interviews can give us both quantitative and qualitative data about participant's thoughts, feelings and behaviours. Quantitative data can obtained by asking close ended questions which have specific answers to choose among and can be categorized and numerically analyzed. However while obtaining qualitative data, the interviewer asks open-ended questions to respondents and in return he/she answers to these questions in his or her own words.

Types on Interview

There are usually two types of interview, namely formal interview and informal interview.

1. **Formal interview:** Also called ***structured interview*** include pre-planned set of question written down on a piece of paper and the interviewer ask those questions verbally and note down the answers given by the respondents. Infact each candidate is asked similar questions in a predetermined format and thus generalization can be done on the basis of the result obtained from the population or sample population. Structured interview can be conducted through various modes like face-to face interview, over the telephone, videophone and the internet. As an advantage formal or structured interview are fairly quick to conduct and is also easy to replicate as same set of closed questions are used, which are easy to quantify. On the other hand the limitation of these types of test is that they are not flexible and are expensive and time-consuming.
2. **Informal interview:** Also known as ***unstructured interview*** are much more casual and unrehearsed. In this type of interview there is no predetermined set of questions nor is there any present order of questions to be asked by the interviewer. Unplanned spontaneous questions are a key feature of the unstructured interview. For example the media interview with celebrities is a common example of unstructured interview. The advantage of unstructured interview is that it is more flexible and generates qualitative data through the use of open questions. As a limitation there is scope for personal bias of the interviewer in this type of interview. Also the data obtained from informal interview are difficult to quantify and analyze.

QUESTIONNAIRE

A questionnaire is a data collection technique for collecting and recording information about a particular issue of interest. It consists of a predetermined set of questions with clear instruction for administration. It can be administered through mails, telephone, using face to face interviews, postal and electronic mediums. Postal and electronic questionnaires are known as self completion questionnaires, *i.e.*, respondents complete them by themselves in their own time. Face-to-face (F2F) and telephone questionnaires are used by interviewers to ask a standard set of questions and record the participant's responses. Questionnaires that are used by interviewers in this way are sometimes known as interview schedules.

Types of Questionnaire

The commonly used questionnaires in behavioural researches are:

1. **Fixed-response questionnaire:** This type of questionnaire includes those statements of questions which have fixed number of options or choice of response like "yes" or "no". An example of this category includes the statement like- Do you feel there is a need of strict laws against the sexual harassment cases in India? Yes/No. The respondent is asked to choose one option that best suits his or her. These test can also be used in scale format, where respondent should decide to rate the situation in along the scale continuum, similar to Likert questions. Such type of questionnaire is also known as closed form questionnaire or pre-coded type of questionnaire. One advantage of fixed response questionnaire is that it is easy to administer and can be easily scored and coded. It is less time consuming. As a disadvantage, due to restriction of answering question in yes or no format, sometimes the respondent becomes biased in answering the questions.
2. **Open-ended questionnaire:** This type of questionnaire cannot be answered with a simple "yes" or "no". Infact the questions are sometimes phrased as a statement which requires a response or it consists of questions that require short or lengthy answers by the participants. For example,Tell me something about yourself? How would you like to suggest the ways to improve the education system of India? An advantage of open ended questionnaire is that the respondent is free to express his/her ideas or views and thus helps in avoiding the bias that may result from suggesting responses to individuals, a bias which may occur in the case of close-ended questions. Open-ended questions can be also be proved useful if you do not know the possible answers to questions or for gathering insightful or unexpected information. However, the limitation of these types of questionnaire is that it is time consuming and difficult to analyze and interpret the responses of the participants.

TESTS

A psychological test is a standardized procedure to measure quantitatively and qualitatively one or more aspect of human traits or attributes including achievement and ability, personality, and neurological functioning etc. Mostly these tests are objective in nature, however for the some subjective interpretation; the projective tests are widely used. Psychological tests are administered in a variety of settings, including preschools, primary and secondary schools, colleges and universities, hospitals, outpatient healthcare settings, and social agencies. They come in a variety of formats, including written, verbal or non verbal and computer administered.

Types of tests

1. **Individual vs Group tests:** Individual test are those types of tests which are administered on a single person at a time. These types are usually preferred by psychologists in clinics, hospitals and other school and college settings. A common example of individual test is Kohs Block Design Test.

   Group tests on the other hand are those tests that can be administered on more than one person or in a group at a time. Most testing today is administered as group tests considering the many benefits that are associated with these tests. Bell adjustment inventory is an example of group test.
2. **Power vs Speed tests:** A power test is the one which allows the participants to complete the test or answer the items without any time boundation or deadline. Usually, in such type of test the item difficulty level increases item by item. Power tests tend to be demonstrating that how much

the knowledge or information the participant actually has. Intelligence test and aptitude belongs to the power test category.

Speed test on the other hand have time limit boundation and the participants has to complete the items as soon as possible within the limited time frame only. Items are comparatively easy in these type of tests and the item difficulty level are more or less of the same degree. The primary objective of speed tests is to measure the person's ability to process information quickly and accurately, within a set period of time. Speed tests are suitable for testing visual perception, numerical facility, and other abilities related to vocational success. Tests of psychomotor abilities (*e.g.*, eye–hand coordination) often involve speed.

3. **Verbal vs Non-verbal:** Verbal tests are those tests which entirely contains verbal material dealing with vocabulary, general information, reading or writing. These types of tests is also called paper-pencil test because the participant has to write down on a piece of paper while answering the items of the tests. Binet test (1905), Stanford-Binet test, Otis test, etc are example of verbal tests. As far as non-verbal test are concerned, the items in these types of tests involves no language. The items in the test however present the problem with the help of pictures, drawing, block patterns, etc. Raven progressive matrices are a good example of non-verbal test.

Characteristics of a Good Test

A good scientific test should be objective in nature *i.e.,* the items of the test and its scoring system should be objective. Besides that a test should be reliable and valid too and should be guided by certain norms. Above all it should be practicable in use.

MULTIPLE CHOICE QUESTIONS

1. The .... is part of the first stages of any study and is used to apply for ethical approval and to gain permission to access participants or sources of data.
A. Research proposal
B. Hypothesis
C. Objectives
D. Methodology

2. A good research question should be:
A. Feasible, clear, significant, and ethical.
B. Clear, measurable, significant.
C. Significant, subjective, selective.
D. Ethical, measurable, clear.

3. The four interrelated goals of scientific research in psychology are:
A. Objectives, function, description, application
B. Description, prediction, explanation, application
C. Description, formulation, planning, prediction
D. None of the above

4. The .... is a tentative explanation for an observation, phenomenon or scientific problem that can be tested by further investigation.
A. Objective B. Literature review
C. Hypothesis D. Research design

5. Which type of hypothesis states that there is no relationship between the two variables being studied (one variable does not affect the other).
A. Alternative B. Null
C. One-tailed D. None of the above

6. A .... hypothesis specifies a directional relationship between groups.
A. Alternative B. Null
C. Two tailed D. One tailed

7. .... can be defined as those attributes of objects, events, things and beings which can be measured or something which varies.
A. Variable B. Problem
C. Hypothesis D. Objectives

8. In an experiment, the .... is the variable that is varied or manipulated by the researcher, and the .... is the response that is measured.
A. Dependent variable, Independent variable
B. Independent variable, Dependent variable
C. Extraneous variable, Independent variable
D. Independent variable, Extraneous variable

9. .... are undesirable variables that influence the relationship between the variables that an experimenter is examining.
A. Extraneous variables
B. Independent variable
C. Dependent variable
D. Categorical variables

10. Which type of variable can include factors like background differences, mood, anxiety, intelligence, awareness and other characteristics that are unique to each person?
A. Independent variable
B. Dependent variable
C. Extraneous variable
D. Participant Variables

11. A .... is an experiment conducted under highly controlled conditions and therefore accurate measurements are possible.
A. Quasi experiment
B. Field study
C. Laboratory experiment
D. Case study

12. .... are conducted in the everyday (*i.e.*, real life) environment of the participants where the experimenter has no control over the IV as it occurs naturally in real life.
A. Laboratory experiment
B. Field study
C. Natural Experiments
D. Case study

13. A variable that varies along with the independent variable is called:
A. Secondary variable
B. Confounding variable
C. Dependent variable
D. None of the above

14. In which type of research method almost every aspect of an individual or subject's life and previous happenings or history is taken into account to determine the patterns and causes of the behaviour?
A. Case study method
B. Field study
C. Experimental method
D. Quasi experimental

15. The cause-and-effect inferences can be made in which type of research method?
A. Case study B. Experimental
C. Field study D. None of the above

16. Which type of research study divides the population into subgroups according to certain criteria and then make comparisons between these subgroups?
A. Cross-sectional study
B. Field study
C. Case study
D. None of the above

17. .... is the systematic process of recording the behavioural patterns of people, objects, and occurrences as they are witnessed.
A. Interview B. Questionnaire
C. Observation D. Test

18. In which type of observation, the participants are aware that they being a part of research study and they know they are being observed?
A. Covert observation
B. Overt observation
C. Naturalistic observation
D. None of the above

19. .... observation allows the researcher to observe and record the behaviour exactly as it occurs in the real world.
A. Covert observation
B. Overt observation
C. Naturalistic observation
D. Controlled observation

20. In which type of observation method the researcher or investigator actively participates in the activities of the group to be observed?
A. Naturalistic observation
B. Controlled observation
C. Non-participant observation
D. Participant observation

21. Among these which is a data-collection technique that involves oral questioning of respondents, either individually or as a group?
A. Observation B. Interview
C. Questionnaire D. Test

22. .... is also called structured interview include pre-planned set of question written down on a piece of paper and the interviewer ask those questions verbally and note down the answers given by the respondents.
A. Formal interview
B. Informal interview
C. General interview
D. Specific interview

23. A .... consists of a predetermined set of questions with clear instruction for administration which can be administered through mails, telephone, using face to face interviews, postal and electronic medium.
A. Case study B. Test
C. Scale D. Questionnaire

24. .... is a type of questionnaire cannot be answered with a simple "yes" or "no". Infact it consists of questions that require short or lengthy answers by the participants.
A. Close-ended questionnaire
B. Open-ended questionnaire
C. Simple questionnaire
D. Complex questionnaire

25. .... is a standardized procedure to measure quantitatively and qualitatively one or more aspect of human traits or attributes including achievement and ability, personality, and neurological functioning etc.
A. A case study B. An interview
C. A test D. An experiment

26. 'Males are more extroverted than females' is an example of
A. Null hypothesis
B. Non-directional hypothesis
C. Directional hypothesis
D. Unverifiable hypothesis

27. The most frequently used quasi-experimental design is the .... design.
A. Non-equivalent comparison-group
B. Interrupted time-series
C. Changing-criterion
D. Regression discontinuity

28. Which one of the following test is closest to independent samples t test from power-consideration point of view?
A. Mann-Whitney U test
B. Signed rank test
C. Chi-square test
D. Kolmogorov-Smirnov test

29. Given below are the two statements, the first labelled as Assertion (A) and the other labelled as Reason (R). Indicate your answer using the codes given below:

Assertion (A): Naturalistic observation is the highly preferred method in ethological research.

Reason (R): Naturalistic observation is free from observer-bias.

Codes:
A. Both (A) and (R) are true and (R) is the correct explanation of (A).
B. Both (A) and (R) are true, but (R) is not the correct explanation.
C. (A) is true, but (R) is false.
D. (A) is false, but (R) is true.

30. The difference between a speed test and power test is based on:
A. Whether or not the range has been restricted.
B. The time limit allotted for completion of the items.
C. Whether or not the variance has been restricted.
D. All of the above

31. What would be the degrees of freedom for a chi-square based on 4 × 5 contingency table?
A. 7 B. 19
C. 12 D. 20

32. The degree of freedom for paired t-test based on n pairs of observations is:
A. $2n - 1$ B. $n - 2$
C. $2(n - 1)$ D. $n - 1$

33. Which of the following is a limitation of case study?
A. It does not provide indepth information of the subjects.
B. It is difficult to generalize from the case study.
C. It is useful only in clinical and counselling psychology.
D. It uses diverse methods and sources to collect data about the subjects.

34. Researchers use both open-ended and closed-ended questions to collect data. Which of the following statements is true?
A. Open-ended questions directly provide quantitative data based on the researcher's predetermined response categories.
B. Closed-ended questions provide quantitative data in the participant's own words.
C. Open-ended questions provide qualitative data in the participant's own words.
D. Closed-ended questions directly provide qualitative data in the participant's own words.

35. After the recent Earthquake in Nepal, a psychologist interviewed 120 participants to understand the psychological consequence of the event. This is an example of:
A. Ex post facto field research
B. Field experiment
C. Controlled experiment
D. Psychometric research

36. Qualitative observation is usually done for exploratory purposes; it is also called .... observation.
A. Participant B. Naturalistic
C. Covert D. Structured

37. Which of the following are considered as quasi-experimental designs?
1. Time series design
2. Regression-discontinuity design
3. Survey
4. Non-equivalent control group design

Codes:
A. (4) only
B. (1) & (4) only
C. (1), (2) & (4) only
D. (2), (3) & (4) only

38. Rejection of the null hypothesis is a conclusive proof that the alternative hypothesis is:
A. True
B. False
C. Neither true nor false
D. Partially true

39. What is an Ipsative test?
A. For an individual examinee, the high scores on some sub-scales are accompanied by low scores on other sub-scales.
B. A test that measures one or more clearly defined but relatively heterogeneous segments of ability.
C. A test in which the average of the sub-scales is always the same for every examinee.
D. A test which gives an estimate of how much of the total variance in a given trait is due to genuine factors.

40. The chance of rejecting a true hypothesis decreases when sample size is:

A. Decreased
B. Increased
C. Constant
D. Both A and B

41. Given below are the two statements, the first labelled as Assertion (A) and the other labelled as Reason (R). Indicate your answer using the codes given below:

Assertion (A): Experimental method, as compared to other methods, is more suitable for studying cause-and-effect relationship.

Reason (R): As compared to other methods, experimental methods permits more efficient control of extraneous variance.

Codes:

A. Both (A) and (R) are true and (R) is the correct explanation of (A).
B. Both (A) and (R) are true, but (R) is not the correct explanation.
C. (A) is true, but (R) is false.
D. (A) is false, but (R) is true.

42. Two types of errors associated with hypothesis testing are Type I and Type II. Type II error is committed when:

A. We reject a null hypothesis when it is true
B. We accept a null hypothesis when it is not true
C. We reject the null hypothesis whilst the alternative hypothesis is true
D. None of the above

43. The chi-square, computed for a contingency table, was based on six degrees of freedom. If the contingency table had three rows, how many columns would it have?

A. 2 B. 3
C. 4 D. 6

44. In single-case research, "baseline" refers to ....

A. The beginning point of the treatment condition.
B. The end point of the treatment condition.
C. The rate of response established prior to the experimental intervention.
D. The time during which a treatment condition is administered.

45. Which of the following hypothesis are non-directional hypothesis?

1. Males and females differ on anxiety.
2. Intelligence and academic achievement are negatively related.
3. Anxiety disrupts academic performance of the students.
4. Stress and work output are related.

Codes:

A. 2 only B. 1 and 3 only
C. 3 and 4 only D. 1 and 4 only

46. Any statement whose validity is tested on the basis of a sample is called:

A. Null hypothesis
B. Alternative hypothesis
C. Statistical hypothesis
D. Simple hypothesis

47. Which one of the following cannot be employed as the dependent variable in a psychological experiment?

1. Heart rate
2. Learning rate
3. Reaction time
4. Age

Codes:

A. 4 only
B. 1 and 2 only
C. 3 and 4 only
D. 1, 2 and 4 only

48. Parametric methods make assumptions about the .... from which sample populations are selected.

A. underlying distribution
B. sample size
C. population size
D. subject characteristics

49. Given below are the three types psychological investigations:

1. Field experiments,
2. Laboratory experiments, and
3. Ex post facto field studies.

If the above investigations are arranged in descending order in terms of researcher's ability to control secondary variance, the typical order would be:

A. 2, 1, 3
B. 3, 1, 2
C. 2, 3, 1
D. 3, 2, 1

50. What is the non-parametric alternative to one-way ANOVA?
A. Friedman's test
B. Kruskall-Wallis H test
C. Mann-Whitney U test
D. None of the above

ANSWERS

1	2	3	4	5	6	7	8	9	10
A	A	B	C	B	D	A	B	A	D
11	**12**	**13**	**14**	**15**	**16**	**17**	**18**	**19**	**20**
C	C	B	A	B	A	C	B	C	D
21	**22**	**23**	**24**	**25**	**26**	**27**	**28**	**29**	**30**
B	A	D	B	C	C	A	A	C	B
31	**32**	**33**	**34**	**35**	**36**	**37**	**38**	**39**	**40**
C	D	B	C	A	B	C	C	C	B
41	**42**	**43**	**44**	**45**	**46**	**47**	**48**	**49**	**50**
A	B	C	C	D	C	A	A	A	B

❑❑❑

CHAPTER 8

Measurement and Testing

TEST CONSTRUCTION: ITEM WRITING, ITEM ANALYSIS

ITEM WRITING

Whether its psychology, sociology or other educational research, writing test items is a matter of precision and is solely based on certain common or general guidelines for all test types. These are:

1. The test item should measures the intended learning outcome.
2. The test item should be written in such a way that the performance it elicits matches the performance in the learning task.
3. The main requirement for an item to be considered good is that the test items should be clear and definite.
4. The test item should be free from non-functional material as it tends to lower the validity of the item.
5. The test item should not include irrelevant factors as it prevents an informed participant from responding correctly.
6. The test item should not be too easy or too difficult to answer at.
7. The irrelevant cues in the test items should be avoided as it decrease the difficulty level of the item and make it easy for participant to answer correctly.
8. The test items shouldn't include any stereotyped word either in stem or in the alternative responses as it facilitates rote learners in guessing the correct choice or answer.
9. The test item should be written in such a way that there is no disagreement concerning the answer.
10. The test item should be written far enough in advance as whenever required it can be reviewed and modified as needed in future.

As far as multiple choice items are concerned it consists of a problem, known as the stem, and a list of suggested solutions, known as alternatives. The alternatives consist of one correct or best alternative, which is the answer, and incorrect or inferior alternatives, known as distracters. The basic rules for writing multiple choice items are as follows:

1. Each item of the test should be designed in such a way that it measures an important learning outcome.
2. The stem should be meaningful by itself and should present a definite problem.
3. State the stem of the item in simple, clear language.
4. The stem should not contain irrelevant material, which can decrease the reliability and the validity of the test scores.

5. State the stem of the item in positive form, whenever possible.
6. The stem should be negatively stated only when significant learning outcomes require it.
7. The stem should be a question or a partial sentence.
8. Make certain that the intended answer is correct or clearly best.
9. Make all alternatives grammatically consistent with the stem of the item and parallel in form.
10. Alternatives should be mutually exclusive.
11. Make the distracters plausible and attractive to the uninformed.
12. Alternatives should be stated clearly and concisely.
13. Alternatives should be homogenous in content.
14. Avoid verbal clues that might enable student to select the correct answer or to eliminate an incorrect alternative.
15. Avoid using the alternative "all of the above", and use "none of the above" with extreme caution.
16. The alternatives should be presented in a logical order (*e.g.,* alphabetical or numerical) to avoid a bias toward certain positions.
17. Control the difficulty of the item either by varying the problem in the stem or by changing the alternatives.
18. Keep the specific content of items independent of one another.
19. Use an efficient item format.
20. Break (or bend) any of these rules if it will improve the effectiveness of the item.

ITEM ANALYSIS

Item analysis is a set of procedure used to identify the effectiveness of the test items. It is basically applied to know the validity of the items. The items which are valid and fulfil the purpose of the test are selected and rest are either modified or eliminated to match the purpose. The validity of the whole test is dependent upon the validity of the individual items.

Item Difficulty

The first step in item analysis is to find out the difficulty value of the item or the index of difficulty (p) of an item. This index is determined by calculating the proportion of examinees that answer the item correctly. A high percentage indicates an easy item/question and a low percentage indicates a difficult item. In general, items should have values of difficulty no less than 20% correct and no greater than 80%.

Discrimination Index

The item-discrimination index (d), also known as the item validity index is another important aspect in item analysis. For this calculation, we divide the test takers into three groups according to their scores on the test as a whole: an upper group consisting of the 27% who make the highest scores, a lower group consisting of the 27% who make the lowest scores, and a middle group consisting of the remaining 46%. The discrimination index range is between -1 and +1. The closer the index is to +1, the more effectively the item distinguishes between the two groups of students. When 'd' is 1.00, all test takers in the upper group and no test takers in the lower group answered the item correctly. Conversely, if none of the upper group but all of the lower group answered an item correctly; the 'd' value would be –1.00. Both of these circumstances are rare, and we will probably never see a value of -1.00.

Item Characteristic Curve (ICC)

This is a graphical or pictorial depiction of the probability of giving the correct answer to an item as a function of the level of the attribute assessed by the test. In the item characteristic curve the total test score is represented on the horizontal axis and the proportion of test takers passing the item within that range of test scores is scaled along the vertical axis. The probability of correct response is near zero at the lowest levels of ability. It increases until at the highest levels of ability, the probability of correct response approaches 1. This S-shaped curve describes the relationship between the probability of correct response to an item and the ability scale. In item response theory, it is known as the item characteristic curve. Each item in a test will have its own item characteristic curve.

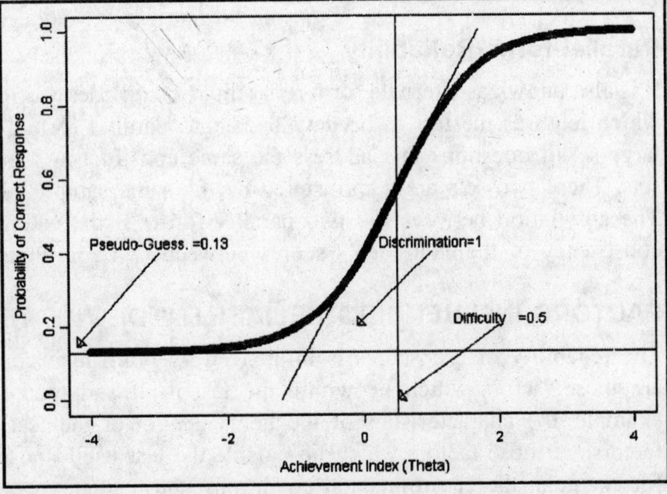

There are two technical properties of an item characteristic curve that are used to describe it. The first is the difficulty of the item and the second is discrimination. The steepness or slope of the ICC conveys about the discriminating power of the item. The steeper the curve, the better the item can discriminate. The flatter the curve, the less the item is able to discriminate since the probability of correct response at low ability levels is nearly the same as it is at high ability levels. Using these two descriptors, one can describe the general form of the item characteristic curve.

TEST STANDARDIZATION: RELIABILITY, VALIDITY AND NORMS

RELIABILITY

In the psychometrics, reliability is the overall consistency of a measure. According to Anastasi (1968), reliability refers to "the consistency of scores obtained by the same individuals when re-examined with test on different occasions, or with different sets of equivalent items, or under other variable examining conditions."

For estimating the reliability coefficient of test scores, the three most common methods are- (1) Test-retest reliability, (2) Internal consistency reliability, (3) Parallel-form reliability or Alternate-forms reliability.

Test-retest Reliability

In test-retest reliability the same test is administered to the same sample on two different occasions with a reasonable time gap, which yields two independent sets of scores. When correlated, these two sets give the value of the reliability coefficient, which is also known as the temporal stability coefficient and thus indicates the extent to which the examinee retain their relative position as measured in terms of the test scores over a given time period. The amount of time allowed between measures is critical. The shorter the time gap, the higher the correlation; the longer the time gap, the lower the correlation.

Internal-consistency Reliability

While estimating the internal consistency reliability a single measurement instrument is used or administered on a group of people on one occasion to estimate reliability. Infact internal consistency reliability indicates the homogeneity of the test. A test is said to homogeneous and holds high internal consistency reliability, when all the items of the test measure the same trait or function. The split-half method, in which the test is divided into two equal or nearly equal halves, is the most common method of estimating the internal consistency reliability.

Parallel-form Reliability

It is also known as alternate form reliability or equivalent form reliability and comparable form reliability, which requires the test to be developed into parallel forms. One way to accomplish this is to create a large set of questions that address the same construct and then randomly divide the questions into two sets. These two sets are administered on the same sample with the time interval of usually a fortnight. The correlation between the two parallel forms is the estimate of reliability. Actually it measures the consistency of the examinee's scores between two administrations of parallel-forms of a single test.

FACTORS INFLUENCING RELIABILITY OF THE TEST SCORES

The reliability of test scores is influenced by both intrinsic and extrinsic factors. The intrinsic factors are those factors which lie within the test itself and tend to influence the reliability of the test, for example, the characteristics of the items, length of the test etc. However on the other hand extrinsic factors are those factors which lie outside the test itself and tend to make the test reliable or unreliable, for example, the environmental conditions, the tendency of guessing by the examinee and momentary fluctuation or distraction while answering the test etc.

VALIDITY

According to Anastasi (1968), "The validity of a test concerns what the test measures and how well it does so." In short validity is defined as the extent or the degree to which a test measures what it claims to measure. For example, a test that is used to screen applicants for a job is valid if its scores are directly related to future job performance. The correlation coefficient computed between the test and the ideal measures or criteria is known as the validity coefficient.

The different types of validity are (1) Content or curricular validity (2) Face validity (3) Construct validity (4) Criterion related validity

Content Validity

Content validity is also known by other terms such as intrinsic validity, relevance, circular validity and representativeness. According to Anastasi & Urbina (1997) content validity is a non-statistical type of validity that involves "the systematic examination of the test content to determine whether it covers a representative sample of the behaviour domain to be measured". In simple words content validity pertains to the degree to which the instrument fully assesses or measures the construct of interest. For example, does an Aptitude test have items covering all areas of aptitude discussed in the scientific literature?

Face Validity

Face validity is a component of content validity and is established when an individual reviewing the instrument concludes that it measures the characteristic or trait of interest. For example, on a measure of stress, the test would be said to have face validity if it appeared to actually measure levels of stress.

Infact face validity is an estimate of whether a test appears to measure a certain criterion; it does not guarantee that the test actually measures phenomena in that domain. Measures may have high validity, but when the test does not appear to be measuring what it is, it has low face validity.

Criterion Related Validity

Criterion-related validity is assessed when one is interested in determining the relationship of scores on a test to a specific criterion. In other words criterion related validity is one which is obtained by comparing (or correlating) the test scores with scores obtained on a criterion available at present or to be available in the future. For example, employee selection tests are often validated against measures of job performance (the criterion), and IQ tests are often validated against measures of academic performance (the criterion). There are two subtypes of criterion related validity- (1) predictive validity and (2) concurrent validity.

Construct Validity

According to Anastasi (1968) construct validity is "the extent to which the test may be said to measure a theoretical construct or trait'. A construct is a non-observable trait such as intelligence which explains our behaviour. For example, to what extent is a questionnaire actually measuring "intelligence"? Construct validity evidence involves the empirical and theoretical support for the interpretation of the construct. Such lines of evidence include statistical analyses of the internal structure of the test including the relationships between responses to different test items. They also include relationships between the test and measures of other constructs. Construct validity is computed only when the scope for investigating criterion-related validity or content validity is bleak.

NORMS

Test norms consist of data that make it possible to determine the relative standing of an individual who has taken a test. In simple words norms are statistical representations of a population. The scores obtained after administration of a test is called raw score however all these raw scores convey no meaning in themselves. Almost always, a test score must be interpreted as indicating the subject's position relative to others in some group. Norms provide a basis for comparing the individual with a group. Usually there are two reference points that are applied in interpreting the test scores. The first is called norm-referencing and the second is criterion referencing.

Norm-referenced tests are designed to examine individual performance in relation to the performance of a representative group. Criterion-referenced tests document individual performance in relation to a domain of information or specific set of skills.

The norm-referenced tests for example, are used to rank each participant with respect to the achievement of others in broad areas of knowledge and to discriminate between high and low achievers. Whereas the criterion-referenced tests are used to determine whether each participant has achieved specific skills or concepts and is also used to find out how much participants know before instruction begins and after it has finished.

Criterion-referenced tests are related directly to instructional objectives, are based on task analysis, and are designed to measure changes in successive performances of an individual. Criterion-referenced tests, therefore, are sensitive to and can be used to measure the effects of instruction. Conversely, norm-referenced tests generally are not related to instructional objectives, do not use task analysis, and are designed to delineate differences among individuals. Norm-referenced tests, therefore, are not sensitive to and should not be used to evaluate the effects of instruction.

Types of Norms

Age equivalent norms: According to Cohen & Swerdlik (2002) age equivalent norms are those norms which indicate the average performance of different samples of test takers who were at various ages at the time the test was administered. These types of norms are best suited to those traits or abilities which increase systematically with age. For example, weight, height etc.

Grade equivalent norms: These norms are used to indicate the average test performance of test takers in a specific grade. It is usually a number that describes a student's location on an achievement continuum. The Grade equivalent corresponding to a given score on any test indicates the grade level at which the typical student obtains this score.

Percentile norms: Percentiles refer to the score at or below which a specific percentage of scores fall. A percentile norm indicates, for each raw score, percentage of standardization sample that falls below that raw score. For example, suppose Neha has a score of 35 on the numerical reasoning test and if 45% of the standardization sample secure below the score of 35 then Neha has a percentile rank of 45 and percentile score of 35.

Standard score norms: A standard score (or scaled score) is calculated by taking the raw score and transforming it to a common scale. A standard score is based on a normal distribution with a mean and a standard deviation. Standard scores estimate whether a student's scores are above average, average, or below average compared to peers. There are several types of standard scores, such as Z score, T score, Stanine score, deviation IQ, etc.

TYPES OF TESTS

INTELLIGENCE

The term "intelligence quotient," or IQ, was first coined in the early twentieth century by a German psychologist named William Stern. This first intelligence test, referred today as the Binet-Simon scale, became the basis for the intelligence tests. In terms of administration, intelligence test is broadly divided into 2 categories-Individual and group intelligence test.

An individual test is one which can be administered on a single person at a time. The Binet-Simon Scale is the first individual intelligence test. The two very important individual intelligence scales of intelligence are Stanford-Binet Scale and Wechsler Scales. The group intelligence test on the other hand is one which can be administered to more than one person at a time in a group. The Army Alpha and the Army Beta test was the first group test. Examples of group tests are-Multidimensional Aptitude Battery, the Cognitive Abilities test and the Scholastic Assessment Tests.

Intelligence tests can be classified on the basis of the nature of items used in tests, such as the verbal (paper-pencil test) and the performance test.

A verbal test is one in which the items or the questions of the test are in written language form and the respondent has to answer them with the help of a pen or pencil on a piece of paper. Such tests are also called paper-pencil test. The verbal test can be administered on a group of participants, but only literate people can take up these type of tests because it involve the use of paper and pencil to answer those questions, which can only be understood by a literate person.

A performance test on the other is the one where there is little or no use of language, the test materials being designed to elicit manual or behavioural responses rather than verbal ones. These types of tests can be administered both on literates and illiterates, as well as on preschool children's, culturally deprived and speech defective people.

The other category of intelligence test also includes the non-verbal or non-language test and culture-free tests.

APTITUDE

Aptitude tests indicate performance that is the product of multiplicity of experiences of everyday life and therefore, indicate the effect of learning under unknown and relatively uncontrolled conditions. In simple words, an aptitude test represents a person's level of competency to perform a certain type of task or it attempts to determine and measure a person's ability to acquire, through future training, some specific set of skills (intellectual, motor, and so on). Aptitude tests are broadly divided into 2 categories- multiple aptitude tests and special aptitude tests.

Multiple aptitude tests are often referred to as batteries instead of tests because it tends to measure several aptitudes, each by an independent subtest. The Differential Aptitude Test or DAT is one of the most common multiple aptitude test. The battery has been developed by Benett, Seashore and Wesman and comprises eight subtests including, Verbal reasoning, numerical ability, abstract reasoning, mechanical reasoning, clerical, speed and accuracy, space relations, spelling and language usage.

Special aptitude tests on the other hand are those tests which intend to measure special abilities at a time such as mechanical aptitude test, musical aptitude test, clerical aptitude test and creativity test etc.

PERSONALITY

A personality test is a questionnaire or other standardized instrument designed to reveal aspects of an individual's character or psychological makeup. The three most common method of personality assessment are- self report inventories, observational methods including situational test and projective techniques.

Self-report Inventories

A self-report inventory, also known as personality inventories is a type of psychological test often used in personality assessment. It is a self rating questionnaire that asks participants to indicate the extent to which sets of statements or adjectives accurately describe their own feelings, environment, and reactions of others towards himself or herself. Some of the examples of self-report inventories include, Minnesota Multiphasic Personality Inventory (MMPI), The 16 Personality Factor Questionnaire, California Personality Inventory etc.

Observational Method

Observational method can be used either in the natural setting (such as a classroom), an experimental setting, or during an interview. Behavioural observations are used to get information that cannot be obtained by other means. The value of behavioural assessment depends on the behaviours selected for observation. The observation becomes the basis for assessing the personality traits. As far as observation in interview is concerned the expectations of the observer, conveyed directly or through body language and other subtle cues, may influence how the interviewee performs and how the observer records and interprets his or her observations.

Projective Techniques

Projective techniques are the most common and popular method of assessing the personality of an individual. In projective test the participant has to respond to some unstructured situations which later on reveals his/her latent or unconscious feelings, needs, emotions, motives etc. Thus this technique gives the participants the ample opportunity to project his/her own personality attributes that are latent or unconscious in the interpretation of an unstructured situation. The best known projective test is the Rorschach Psycho diagnostic Test, or inkblot, test first devised by the Swiss psychologist Hermann Rorschach in the 1920s. Another widely used projective test is the Thematic Apperception Test (TAT), developed at Harvard University in the 1930s.

ATTITUDE SCALES

Attitude scale are the self report inventories underlying a large number of statements, which directly asked the participants what their attitudes are towards certain things, objects or other situations. Some of the common attitude scales are the Thurstone scale, Likert scale, Guttman scale etc.

INTEREST INVENTORIES

An interest inventory is a self assessment tool, used in career planning that assesses one's likes and dislikes of a variety of activities, objects, and types of persons. As such inventories, measures only a limited sample or sets on interests, the interests assessed by such inventories are called inventoried interests. One of the most popular interest inventories is the Strong Vocational interest Blank (SVIB). The other important instrument for measuring interest is Kuder Interest Inventories.

MULTIPLE CHOICE QUESTIONS

1. Which type of test items is most appropriate for measuring higher mental processes which involve the process of synthesis, analysis, evaluation, organization and criticism of the events of the past?
A. Objective type
B. Essay type
C. Two alternative type
D. Multiple Choice

2. Which type of test item is one wherein there is only one fixed correct answer, which the participant gives on his own or selects from a few given ?
A. Objective type B. Essay type
C. Verbal type D. Unstructured type

3. .... is a type of item which consist of two columns-right and left, wherein the left items constitutes a set of related stems called premises and the right side items constitutes options or responses of the items.
A. Two-alternative item
B. Matching items
C. Multiple choice items
D. Essay type items

4. Among these which is a set of procedure, applied to know the indices for the truthfulness (or validity) of items?
A. Item writing B. Reliability
C. Norms D. Item analysis

5. In which type of test the participant is allowed sufficient time for answering all items of the test?
A. Psychological tests
B. Speed test
C. Power test
D. Clinical test

6. Which type of test provide a limited time limit to participants to complete all the item of test?
A. Psychological tests
B. Speed test
C. Power test
D. Clinical test

7. .... refers to the consistency of the scores obtained by the same individual when re-examined on different occasions.
A. Reliability
B. Validity
C. Norms
D. Standard error of measurement

8. Among the options given below which is a type of reliability, in which the single form of the test is administered twice on the same sample with a reasonable time gap?
A. Test-retest reliability
B. Internal consistency reliability
C. Alternate form reliability
D. None of the above

9. Which type of reliability is typically a measure based on the correlations between different items on the same test?
A. Test-retest reliability
B. Internal consistency reliability
C. Alternate form reliability
D. None of the above

10. .... is the extent to which a test accurately measures what it purports to measure.
A. Reliability
B. Norms
C. Validity
D. Standard error of measurement

11. Which type of norms is best suited to those traits or abilities which increase systematically with age, for example weight, height etc.
A. Grade equivalent norms
B. Age equivalent norms
C. Percentile norms
D. Standard score norms

12. The Army alpha test and the Army beta test is an example of which type of test?
A. Personality test B. Aptitude test
C. Interest test D. Intelligence test

13. Among these who first time introduce the intelligence quotient (IQ) in 1916 for the American revision of the Binet-Simon scale done at Stanford University?
A. Terman B. Binet
C. Wechsler D. Ebbinghaus

14. A .... test is one in which the items or the questions of the test are in written language form and the respondent has to answer them with the help of a pen or pencil on a piece of paper.
A. performance B. verbal
C. non-verbal D. culture-free tests

15. Which type of test attempts to determine and measure a person's ability to acquire, through future training, some specific set of skills (intellectual, motor, and so on)?
A. Interest B. Intelligence
C. Personality D. Aptitude

16. Among these which is one of the most common multiple aptitude test consists of 8 subtests- Verbal reasoning, numerical ability, abstract reasoning, mechanical reasoning, clerical, speed and accuracy, space relations, spelling and language usage.
A. General Aptitude test battery (GATB)
B. Flanagan aptitude classification test (FACT)
C. Differential Aptitude test (DAT)
D. Artistic aptitude test

17. A .... test is a questionnaire or other standardized instrument designed to reveal aspects of an individual's character or psychological makeup.
A. Personality
B. Aptitude
C. Interest
D. Intelligence

18. .... are the self-rating questionnaires, wherein the participants describes his own feelings, environment, and reactions of others towards himself.
A. Projective techniques
B. Self-report inventories
C. Paper-pencil techniques
D. Observational techniques

19. The Minnesota Multiphasic Personality Inventory (MMPI), The 16 Personality Factor Questionnaire, California Personality Inventory is an example of:
A. Self-report inventories
B. Observational method
C. Projective techniques
D. Paper-pencil technique

20. Among these which technique gives the participants the ample opportunity to project his/her own personality attributes that are latent or unconscious in the interpretation of an unstructured situation.
A. Interview
B. Observational method
C. Self-report inventories
D. Projective techniques

21. The Rorschach Inkblot Test and the Thematic Apperception Test (TAT) is an example of which technique?
A. Projective techniques
B. Self-report inventories
C. Observational method
D. None of the above

22. The scales such as the Thurstone scale, Likert scale, Guttman scale measures which attribute of an individual?
A. Interest B. Personality
C. Attitude D. Aptitude

23. Among these which is a projective personality test consisting of 30 black and white pictures of people in vague or ambiguous situations?
A. The Thematic Apperception test
B. The Children's Apperception test
C. The Blacky Pictures
D. Pickford Projective Picture

24. Rorschach's projective test is basically designed to measure:
A. Conscious desires
B. Unconscious thoughts
C. Dream types
D. Sexual desires

25. Among these which intelligence test contains scales that measure vocabulary, arithmetic ability, digit span, information comprehension, letter-number sequencing, picture completion ability, reasoning ability, symbol search and object assembly ability in order to assess whether an individual is eligible for special educational needs.
A. The Weschler adult intelligence scale
B. Standford-Binet Scale
C. Culture-fair test
D. Lorge-Thorndike intelligence test

26. A measure of the level of agreement between two or more rater's judgements is known as:
A. Intra-rater reliability
B. Inter-rater reliability
C. Internal reliability
D. Test-retest reliability

27. Some steps in test construction are listed below:
1. Internal consistency assessment
2. Item analysis
3. Test-retest reliability
4. Item writing

Usually, the above steps are carried out in the following sequence.
A. 4, 2, 1, 3 B. 4, 1, 3, 2
C. 2, 4, 1, 3 D. 4, 3, 2, 1

28. Campbell and Fiske devised the multitrait-multimethod matrix to assist in the analysis of
A. Convergent and discriminant validity
B. Concurrent and predictive validity
C. Content and face validity
D. None of the above

29. For which of the following types of tests interscorer reliability is relevant?
1. Objective personality inventories
2. Projective tests
3. Achievement tests with descriptive items
4. Intelligence tests

Codes:
A. 1 and 2 only B. 2 and 4 only
C. 1 and 3 only D. 2 and 3 only

30. The notion that an assessment method may appear to be valid simply because it has questions which intuitively seem relevant to the trait or characteristic being measured is known as:
A. Construct validity
B. Content validity
C. Face validity
D. Criterion validity

31. In the regression approach to predictive validity the estimate of error is referred to as the:
A. Standard error of the mean
B. Standard error of estimate
C. Standard error of measurement
D. Standard error of criterion

32. If a measure correlates highly with other established measures of the same thing, it is said to have high....
A. Construct validity B. Criterion validity
C. Content validity D. Face validity

33. Which of the following statements is true for tests with dichotomous items?
A. Chronbach Alpha is greater than Kuder-Richardson reliability.
B. Chronbach Alpha is smaller than Kuder-Richardson reliability.
C. Chronbach Alpha and Kuder-Richardson reliability are equal.
D. Chronbach Alpha may be greater or smaller than Kuder-Richardson reliability.

34. Comparing Z scores for two different individuals from the same cultural background on a test with norms from a different culture:
A. is indefensible
B. is meaningful
C. can only be done if the norms are without errors
D. can only be done if the sample size on which the norms are based is adequate

35. Cronbach alpha is:
1. larger than split half reliability coefficient
2. smaller than reliability coefficient
3. average of all possible split-half reliability coefficients
4. equal to Kuder-Richardson reliability for dichotomous items

Codes:
A. 1 only B. 2 only
C. 3 and 4 only D. 1 and 4 only

36. According to Classical test score theory, a test score is made up of:
A. true score variance and non-systematic variance
B. observed score variance and true score variance
C. observed score variance and error variance
D. observed score variance and systematic variance

37. If two groups are administered the same test with a time gap of eight weeks, we would be able to compute:
A. Test-retest reliability
B. Parallel form reliability
C. Interscorer reliability
D. None of the above reliabilities can be computed

38. The standard method for fitting a regression line to a set of data is referred to as:
A. An approximation
B. Regression to the mean
C. The least square method
D. The procrustes method

39. Reliability can be defined as
A. $\frac{\text{True score variance}}{\text{Total variance}}$
B. $\frac{\text{Error variance}}{\text{Total variance}}$
C. $\frac{\text{True score variance}}{\text{Error variance}}$
D. $\frac{\text{Error variance}}{\text{True score variance}}$

40. Transforming scores on psychological test is done primarily to:
A. Protect the privacy of the test taker
B. Aid interpretation of the scores
C. Make the scores more manageable
D. Make the scores available for research

41. Alternate-form reliability is also known as...
A. Test-retest reliability
B. Parallel form reliability
C. Split-half reliability
D. Interscorer reliability

42. Reliability of a test can be improved within limits by:
A. Increasing its length (using more items)
B. Decreasing its length
C. Decreasing the time taken to administer it
D. Increasing the time taken to administer it

43. Which of the following is assessed by Chronbachs alpha?
A. Concurrent validity
B. Inter-rater reliability
C. Test-retest reliability
D. Internal consistency

44. Normalised standard scores:
A. are based on percentiles
B. are T scores under another name
C. are based on sten scores
D. have a mean of 100 and a standard deviation of 15

45. The extent that a test will produce roughly similar results when the test is given to the same person several weeks or even months apart (as long as no treatments or interventions have occurred in between) is known as:
A. Test-retest reliability
B. Split-half reliability
C. Inter-rater reliability
D. Parallel form reliability

46. For a newly developed test, the scores on odd and even part correlated by 0.4. After applying Spearman-Brown formula:
A. The corrected reliability would by 0.8.
B. The corrected reliability would be 0.4.
C. The corrected reliability would be greater than 0.4 and lesser than 0.8.
D. The corrected reliability would be lesser than 0.4.

47. What are intraclass-correlations typically used to measure?
A. Intra-rater reliability
B. Test-retest reliability
C. Inter-rater reliability
D. Split-half reliability

48. 'Ethics' can be defined as the formulation of principles to
A. Reduce inappropriate behaviour
B. Punish inappropriate behaviour
C. Reinforce inappropriate behaviour
D. Guide behaviour

49. Empirical keying refers to:
A. Scoring a test based on its ability to discriminate between certain identifiable groups of people.
B. Scoring a test based on the theory of what is being measured.
C. Scoring a test using a scoring key or stencils.
D. Empirically validating test scores via research.

50. The correlation between scores on two variables varies:
A. directly with the product of their reliabilities.
B. directly with the square root of the product of their reliabilities.
C. inversely with the sum of their reliabilities.
D. inversely with the square root of the lower of the reliabilities.

ANSWERS

1	2	3	4	5	6	7	8	9	10
B	A	B	D	C	B	A	A	B	C
11	**12**	**13**	**14**	**15**	**16**	**17**	**18**	**19**	**20**
B	D	A	B	D	C	A	B	A	D
21	**22**	**23**	**24**	**25**	**26**	**27**	**28**	**29**	**30**
A	C	A	B	A	A	A	A	D	C
31	**32**	**33**	**34**	**35**	**36**	**37**	**38**	**39**	**40**
B	B	C	B	C	B	D	C	A	B
41	**42**	**43**	**44**	**45**	**46**	**47**	**48**	**49**	**50**
B	A	D	A	A	C	A	D	A	A

❑❑❑

UGC-NET / JRF

PSYCHOLOGY

PART-B

CHAPTER 1

Perception

SIGNAL DETECTION THEORY

Detection theory, or signal detection theory, is a means to quantify the ability to discern between signal and noise. According to the theory, there are a number of psychological determiners of how we will detect a signal, and where our threshold levels will be. The factors that affect threshold include experience, expectations and physiological state (*e.g.*, fatigue) etc. For instance, a soldier in wartime will likely detect fainter stimuli than the same soldier the in peace time.

According to Tanner & Sweet, (1954), Signal detection theory, has developed into one of the most dominant influence in psychophysics just after few years of its application. To apply signal detection theory to a data set where stimuli were either present or absent and the observer categorized each trial as having the stimulus present or absent, the trials are sorted into one of the 4 categories:

	Respond "Absent"	Respond "Present"
Stimulus Present	Miss	Hit
Stimulus Absent	Correct Rejection	False Alarm

Sensitivity V/S Response Criterion

Sensitivity refers to how hard or easy it is to detect that a target stimuli is present from background events. The assumption in this criterion is that, although the physical stimuli in the situation, the noise (N) and the signal plus noise (SN) are nominally constant, their sensory effects vary from presentation to presentation in a way that is adequately represented by the normal distribution. Most commonly used statistics for computing sensitivity is sensitivity index.

In response criterion, a particular magnitude of central neural effect-is selected by S, who then responds "signal" whenever the central neural effect equals or exceeds the criterion and "no-signal" whenever it is less.

Bias

Bias is the extent to which one response is more probable than another. It means that a receiver may be more likely to respond that a stimulus is present or more likely to respond that a stimulus is not present.

Four Possible Outcomes

	RESPONSE	
	S (Signal)	n (no noise)
SN	"Hit" $P(S/SN) = \frac{\text{No. of hits}}{\text{No. of SN trials}}$	"False alarm" $P(n/SN) = \frac{\text{No. of false rejection}}{\text{No. of SN trials}}$
N	"False alarm" $P(S/SN) = \frac{\text{No. of false alarm}}{\text{No. of N trials}}$	"Correct rejection" $P(n/SN) = \frac{\text{No. of correct rejection}}{\text{No. of N trials}}$

An example from everyday life illustrates this point. Suppose a mother is expecting her son visi from abroad after so many years, which she had awaited since so long. As time goes on, the mother begin to "hear" the son footsteps and may open the door, only to find that nobody is there. The mother i "detecting" a stimulus, or signal, that is not there because she is in hurry and is excited to meet her sor which she don't want to miss and thus check again and again to see if the son is there, only to find tha the son has not yet arrived.

SUBLIMINAL PERCEPTION

Subliminal perception occurs whenever stimuli presented below the threshold or limens for awareness are found to influence thoughts, feelings, or actions. The term subliminal perception was originally usec to describe situations in which weak stimuli were perceived without awareness.

Subliminal perception has been demonstrated in controlled laboratory studies by showing tha stimuii can be perceived even when they are presented under conditions that make it difficult if no impossible to distinguish one stimulus from another stimulus. The classic studies were conducted in the 1970's by the British Psychologist Anthony Marcel. These experiments were based on previous finding indicating that a decision regarding a stimulus is facilitated or primed when the stimulus follows a relate stimulus. For example, if an observer is asked to classify a letter string as either a word (*e.g.*, mother table) or a non-word (*e.g.*, rothem, labte), a letter string such as the word mother will be classified as word faster when it follows a semantically related words (*e.g.*, father) than when it follows a semantically non-related words (*e.g.*, chair).

Examples of subliminal perception are found in studies of patients with neurological damage. In a syndrome called blind-sight, patients with blindsight have damage to the primary visual cortex. As result of this damage, they are often unaware of perceiving stimuli within a restricted area of their visua field. For example, if the visual field is thought of as consisting of four quadrants, a blind sight patien may have normal vision for stimuli presented in three of the quadrants but be completely unaware o stimuli presented in the fourth quadrant. However, even though these patients may claim not to se stimuli located within the "blind" quadrant, they are still able to guess the size, shape or orientatio of the stimuli that hey claim not to see. Another neurological syndrome in which subliminal perceptio occurs is prosopagnosia or face agnosia.

Subliminal perceptions has great practical importance in advertising. James Vicary (1957), a marke researcher claimed that over a six-week period, 45,699 patrons at a movie theatre in Fort Lee, New Jerse were shown two advertising messages, Eat popcorn and drink coca-cola & were flashed for 3/1000 o a second one every five seconds, while they watched the film picnic. Despite the fact that the custome were not aware of perceiving the messages, Vicary claimed that over the six –week period the sales o popcorn rose 57.7% and the sales of coca-cola rose to 18.1%. Vicary's claims are often accepted a established facts.

INFORMATION PROCESSING APPROACH TO PERCEPTION

Generally the understanding of information that plays the greatest role in psychology is due to James J. Gibson. Although most psychologists are unwilling to buy into Gibson's full theory of perception (1966, 1979). They typically agree with him about what information is. Indeed, even Marr (1982) who criticizes Gibson's approach explicitly and lays out a striking non-Gibsonian view of what visual perception is, one that is the model for all cognitive science, seems to agree with Gibson's views of the nature of information. It is information processing, he says, that Gibson doesn't get (1982). There are many other's like Evans (1982), Barwise and Perry (1981), Millikan (2000) and Dretske (1981) who were influenced by Gibson's view.

There are 2 main points to Gibson's theory of perception-

1. Gibson disagreed with the tradition that took the purpose of visual perception to be the internal re-construction of the three dimensional environment from two dimensional inputs. Instead, the function of perception is the guidance of adaptive action.
2. Gibson (1966, 1979) rejected classical views of perception in which perception results from the addition of information in the mind to physically caused sensation.

This information processing way of understanding perception Gibson thought, puts an unbridgeable gap in place between the mind(where the information is added, and the perception happens) and the world (where the merely physical light causally interacts with the retina). Instead, Gibson argued, perception is a direct-non-inferential, non-computational-process, in which information is gathered or picked up from the environment.

Combined, these two give rise to Gibson's most well known contribution, his theory of affordances (1979). If perception is direct, no information is added in the mind; if perception also guides behaviour, the environment must contain sufficient information for the animals to guide its behaviour. In other words, the environment must contain information specifying affordances. These views place significant constraints on the theory of information that Gibson can offer. First, because it is used in non-inferential perception, information must be both ubiquitous in the environment and largely unambiguous; Second, because perception also guides behaviour, the information in the environment must specify opportunities for behaviour, which is to say it must specify affordances.

The following are the key points of this brief description of Gibson's theory of the information available in the environment for perception.

1. Information for perception is not Shannon-Weaver information.
2. Ontologically speaking, information is a relation between energy in the environment (light, vibrations etc. and the substances and surfaces in the environment.
3. Along with the substances and surfaces of the environment the energy in the environment also contains information specifying affordances.
4. Because of (3), information can be used by animals to guide behaviour directly. That is, information about affordances can guide behaviour without intervening inferences or computations.

CULTURE AND PERCEPTION

The human perception is culturally influenced has long been a proposition entertained by many social scientists. The plausibility of this proposition is high, based as it is upon certain contemporary philosophical and social scientific concepts, such as that of cultural relativism.

Cultural influences play a vital part in perception. For example, members of the early tribal communities often develop different perceptual capacities compared to members who live in cities. Research studies on perception have shown that American children who live in cities could discriminate various geometrical design and different shades of colours. On the other hand, tribal children who live in wideness showed a greater capacity for discrimination of different sounds and smell which appeared indistinguishable to children living in big cities.

An interesting observation recorded by C.M. Turnbull in this connection was about the Bambuti pygmies of Congo who rarely venture out of the forest and are, therefore, not used to looking at far off objects. Turnbull observed that from a distance, one of the pygmies could not recognize a herd of buffaloes. On getting closer to the animals, he believed that they were getting magically larger in size. He was unable to grasp the fact that the buffaloes had actually remained constant in size. His eyes transmitted the same message to his brain as those of people who were brought up in other cultures. The only difference was in the way the pygmy interpreted the messages. The perception of the situation was different from Turnbull's.

Nisbett, who argues that there is a difference between how people perceive objects and situations related to the region from which they originate. Nisbett argues that Easterners (Chinese, Koreans, and Japanese) tend to think holistic, are more likely to attend to backgrounds, are more likely to expect change, and group objects in thematic relations, and deal with contradictions, finding truth in both the sides. Westerners (Europeans & Americans) on the other hand think analytic, are more likely to attend to objects, group according to taxonomies, and tend to reject one side of contradictions. More recently, researchers like Berry, Dasen and others have found cultural differences in perceptual skills related to the field independence-dependence dimension. It was found that the more complex and 'differentiated' the physical and social environment in which an individual grows up, the more sophisticated and field independent is that individual likely to be—both in relation to the physical environment and the people.

ECOLOGICAL PERSPECTIVE ON PERCEPTION

For human organism the marked-up world include libraries, maps, price lists, traffic sign, science text, border posts, restaurant menus, fences. We can now rephrase our formulation of the views developed by Gibson in his Ecological approach to visual perception as follows: We are like multi-layered tuning forks-tuned to the environment which surrounds us. We have evolved in such a way as to be attended to our environment on multiple levels, in part because we ourselves have created this world via what Lewontin calls "ecosystem engineering". This means that we have evolved to resonate automatically and directly, not only to those features of our environment which are relevant for survival, but also to new features-of language, culture of externalized memory, which we ourselves have put there.

Unlike Gregory and the Gestalt theorist, Gibson sees real movement as a vital part of perception. Gibson developed his theory into a general theory of visual perception which has 3 key ideas:

1. **Optic Array:** The patterns of light reaching the eye can be thought of as an optic array containing all the visual information available at the retina. This optic array provides unambiguous information about the layout of objects in space.
2. **Textured Gradient:** As the optic array flows around you the viewer, the textured gradient of what you perceive gives information about distance, speed etc. This perception involves almost little or no information processing by the cognitive system.

   For this to happen Gibson's theory on action, or movement. Two constants are important: the pole (or the point to which someone is moving) and the horizon in relation to the height of the person. These invariants helps to maintain size constancy. Gibson further explained an ability to filter the optic array as the potential to filter information through resonance. This is rather like radio waves and the radio, which can pick up frequencies that broadcast music etc, distinguished them from other 'noise'. People are able to 'tune into' their environments fairly automatically.

3. **Affordances:** This means attaching particular meaning to visual information. Gibson rejected the theory that long term memory provides meaning. Rather, he argued that the potential use of an object is directly, perceivable—a ladder 'affords' climbing up or down, a chair 'afford' sitting.

STYLES OF PERCEPTION

There are numerous styles of perception. Some of the major well known styles of perception are:

1. Amodal perception
2. Colour perception
3. Depth perception
4. Form perception
5. Haptic perception
6. Speech perception
7. Pitch perception
8. Harmonic perception
9. Rhythmic perception

1. **Amodal Perception:** Amodal (meaning "without" modality) perception is perception of information that is common or redundant across multiple senses (*e.g.,* auditory, visual, tactile). Amodal information includes changes along three basic parameters of stimulation—time, space and intensity. Properties of objects and events such as temporal synchrony, rhythm, tempo, duration, intensity and co-location are common across auditory, visual and proprioceptive stimulation. Properties such as shape, substance, and texture are common across visual and tactile stimulation. For example, the same rhythm and tempo can be detected by seeing or hearing the pianist strike the notes of the keyboard, and the same size, shape, and texture can be detected by seeing or feeling an apple.

   The term amodal has also been used in a different sense—to refer to perception in the absence of direct information from a specific sense modality, For example, in visual perception, amodal completion describes how we perceive a unitary shape (*e.g.,* a ball), even when part of the object or shape is occluded (hidden) behind another object (*e.g.,* a block).

2. **Colour Perception:** Is the capacity of an organism to distinguish objects based on the wavelengths (or frequencies) of the light they: reflect, emit, and transmit. An apple is perceived to be red only because the human eye can distinguish between different wavelengths. In some dichromatic substances (e.g. pumpkin seed oil) the colour hue depends not only on the spectral properties of the substance, but also on its concentration and the depth or thickness.

3. **Depth Perception:** Is the visual ability to perceive the world in three dimensions (3D). It arises from a variety of depth cues. These are typically classified into binocular cues that require input from both eyes and monocular cues that require the input from just one eye.

Monocular Cues

A. **Interposition:** In this the stimulus at the back which is interposed seems to be at distance and the stimulus in front/ahead seems to be closer.

B. **Proximal size:** The size of the image on the retina decreases with the increase in the distance. Thus the image formed is called proximal size image.

C. **Shadow and Light:** Every stimulus has 3 dimensions-length, breadth and depth. The light falling on the stimulus is not evenly distributed due to these dimensions. The light falling on the stimulus and its shadow also work as cues for the perception of stimulus.

D. **Linear perspective:** If two stimuli are in a form of line or queue and they are parallel to each other, then as their length increases the distance between them decreases. These lines seem to meet at a longer distance. For ex- Railway lines.

E. **Aerial perspective:** Due to light scattering by the atmosphere, objects that are at great distance away have lower luminance contrast and lower colour saturation. The foreground has high contrast; the background has low contrast.

F. **Movement parallax:** The relative speed of the stimuli also works as a cue for perception. For ex-the trees just near the railway line when perceived from a fast moving train, these trees at a distance seems to run comparatively with a slow speed.

G. **Texture gradient:** The experimental study of this factor was done by Gibson (1950) for the first time. Gibson thinks that by increase in distance the density of the surface structure appears to be changed. When the grass, flowers etc in a garden observed closely they appear to be a bit scattered. But when observed from a distance they appear to be densely situated.

Types of Binocular Cues

A. **Binocular disparity:** There is a distance of 2.5 inches between both the human eyes. When a person pay attention on a stimulus then two different images are formed in the two eyes. It is seen if left eye is closed and object is perceived only by the right eye then a little more part of right side of the object is perceived, similarly the left eye perceive some more part of the left side. Therefore the visual area of both eyes differs or that both eyes have different visual areas. This difference is called difference of 2 axis.

B. **Conversion:** When the stimulus is at distance from the subject the lines of focus are parallel. But when the stimulus is close both the focal lines (of both the eyes) unite with each other at the stimulus, this is known as conversion.

C. **Double images:** Double images work as cue because when double image are formed they overlap each other. The stimulus is situated at a distance in this condition, but when the images do not overlap each other, it indicates the proximity of stimulus.

4. **Gestalt Principles of Form Perception:** Gestalt psychology attempts to understand psychological phenomena by viewing them as organised and structured whole rather than the sum of their constituent parts.

   Mostly notably the Max Wertheimer, Wolfgang Kohler, and Kurt Koffka who founded the Gestalt approaches to form perception, more specifically tried to explain human perception of groups of objects and how we perceive parts of objects and form whole objects on the basis of these.

Some of the main laws, are as follows—

Proximity: This law points that when we perceive a collection of objects, we will see objects close to each other as forming group. The proximity can be of time, space or of any other type. Fig-1 gives an example of this.

Fig. 1
Proximity

Similarity: According to this law the stimulus which have similarity, get grouped or organized from point of view. This similarity can be of any dimension like colour, brightness, quality etc.

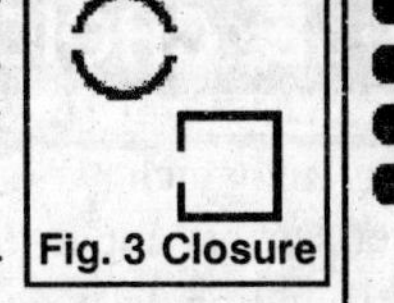
Fig. 3 Closure

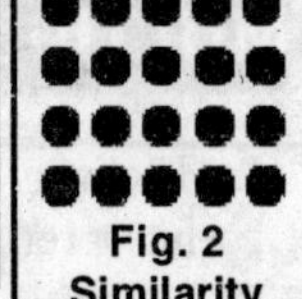
Fig. 2 Similarity

Closure: The components of perception if are clouded or components are grouped or organized, then they are perceived as a whole figure.

Law of Prgnanz (Figure-Ground): This phenomenon captures the idea that in perceiving a visual field, some object take a prominent role (the figure) while others recede into the background (the ground).

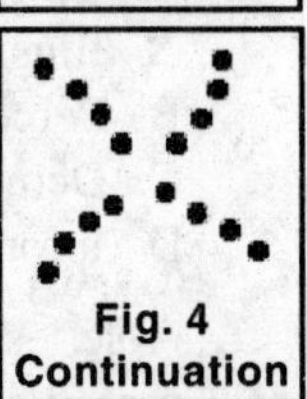
Fig. 4 Continuation

Continuation: The components of stimulus which have continuity are ground or organized due to this continuity, and they are perceived in the form of a stimulus.

Symmetry: It is seen that when there is symmetry in the components of stimulus they organize soon.

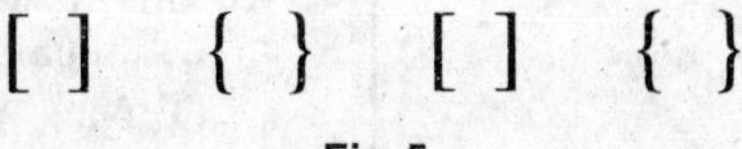

Fig-5

5. **Haptic Perception:** Haptics is commonly viewed as a perceptual system, mediated by two afferent subsystems, cutaneous and kinesthetic, that most typically involves active manual exploration (Lederman & Klatzky, 2009). Whereas vision and audition are recognized for providing highly precise spatial and temporal information, respectively, the haptic system is especially effective at processing the material characteristics of surfaces and objects.

6. **Speech Perception:** Speech perception is the process by which the sounds of language are heard, interpreted and understood. In other words *Speech perception* (SP) is most commonly referred to the perceptual mapping from the highly variable acoustic speech signal to a linguistic representation, whether it be phonemes, diphones, syllables, or words. This is an example of *categorization*, in that potentially discriminable speech sounds are assigned to functionally equivalent classes.

   Most of the research in the field of SP has focused on the mapping from the acoustic speech signal to phonemes, the smallest linguistic unit that changes meaning within a particular language (*e.g.*, /r/ and /l/ as in *rake* vs. *lake*), with the often implicit assumption that phoneme representations are a necessary step in the comprehension of spoken language. The transformation from acoustics to phonemes occurs so rapidly and automatically that it mostly escapes our noticc (Naatanen & Winkler, 1999).

7. **Pitch Perception:** Where auditory communication is concerned it was of course throughout acknowledged that in music pitch is the most important "Carrier of information". However, little attention was paid to the possibility that also in "ordinary life", *i.e.*, in speech communication, and in auditory analysis and recognition of the huge variety of sounds impinging on our ears in daily life; pitch could be a key element. While it is apparent that in speech communication pitch might be involved far beyond that aspect. Although it has been known since centuries (at least) that the ear segregates any complex sound into simple tone pitches (spectral pitches), this phenomenon was more or less regarded as a kind of curiosity which was of interest only to theorists of music (such as, Tartini and Helmholtz).

MULTIPLE CHOICE QUESTIONS

1. The way in which we select, organize and interpret sensory input to achieve a grasp of our surrounding is called:
A. Illusion
B. Perception
C. Delusion
D. Information processing.

2. A series of activities by which stimuli are perceived, transformed into information, and stored is called:
A. Attention
B. Selection
C. Perception
D. Information processing

3. The absolute threshold is the smallest magnitude of a stimuli that can be detected:
A. 30 percent of the time
B. 40 percent of the time
C. 50 percent of the time
D. 60 percent of the time

4. Which of the following stages of the information processing model constitute perception?
A. Exposure and attention
B. Exposure, attention and interpretation
C. Exposure, attention, interpretation and memory
D. Exposure, attention, interpretation, memory and action

5. Who among the following is not a Gestalt psychologist:
A. Kohler B. Koffka
C. Pavlov D. Wertheimer

6. .... occurs whenever stimuli presented below the threshold or limen for awareness are found to influence thoughts, feelings, or actions.
A. Signal detection
B. Depth perception
C. Colour perception
D. Subliminal perception

7. According to which law a stimuli will be perceived as belonging together if they occur together in space or time:
A. Law of Similarity
B. Law of Closure
C. Law of Proximity
D. Law of Figure-Ground

8. Experiments on cultural influences on perception have been conducted by:
A. Bruner and Goodman
B. Rubin
C. Segall, Campbell and Herskovits
D. Max Wertheimer

9. Among these which type of processing happens when we work from the general to the specific; the big picture to the tiny details.
A. Bottom- up B. Top-down
C. Parallel D. Figure-ground

10. The moon is often seen as moving behind the clouds. This is an example of:
A. Induced motion
B. Stroboscopic motion
C. Autokinetic motion
D. Phi-phenomenon

11. We can hear frequencies that range from about
A. 20,000 to 80,000 Hz
B. 2000 to 20,000 Hz
C. 200 to 2000 Hz
D. 20 to 20,000 Hz

12. A .... is a depth perception cue that can be perceived with only one eye.
A. Conversion
B. Binocular cues
C. Monocular cues
D. None of the above

13. Who amongst the following is nativist?
A. Locke B. Descartes
C. Spinoza D. Berkeley

14. What does Gibson's theory of affordances emphasized?
A. Principles of perceptual organization
B. Subliminal perception
C. Past experiences
D. What objects in the environment have to offer the person?

15. In depth perception retinal disparity represents a:
A. Monocular cues
B. Binocular cues
C. External cue
D. None of the above

16. The sensations of colour are dependent upon which three basic factors:
A. size, contrast, and hue
B. frequency, intensity, and hue
C. brightness, hue, and saturation
D. None of the above

17. Which combination of sense organs and their process is wrong?
A. Visual - Eyes
B. Auditory - Ears
C. Olfactory - Nose
D. Cutaneous - Tongue

18. Which type of sensation is responsible for maintaining the equilibrium of the body?
A. Kinesthesis B. Vestibular
C. Gustatory D. Auditory

19. In prosopagnosia disorder a person is not able to :
A. Perceive colour B. Perceive size
C. Perceive shape D. Perceive faces

20. The presumed ability to perceive a stimulus that is below the threshold for conscious experience is called:
A. Perception
B. Subliminal perception
C. Sensation
D. Transduction

21. Negative thinking in pain can increase the perceived intensity of pain is referred to as:
A. Catastrophizing
B. Clairvoyance
C. Delusion
D. None of the above

22. The amount of change in a stimulus required before a person can detect the shift is known as:
A. Difference threshold
B. Just noticeable difference
C. Absolute threshold
D. Subliminal perception

23. According to which law a figure appears nearer to the observer than does the Ground?
A. Weber Law B. Fetcher Law
C. Gestalt Law D. All of the above

24. The Gestalt perceptual law of common fate is associated with which one of these stimulus properties?
A. Size B. Colour
C. Motion D. Contrast

25. The information surrounding a stimulus is known as the
A. Adaptation level
B. Context
C. Aura
D. Internal frame of reference

26. Our expectancies, learning, past experiences and cultural factors play a critical role in shaping our perception. This is well explained by:
A. Information processing approach
B. Bottom-up processing approach
C. Top-down processing approach
D. Hierarchical processing approach

27. In humans, which sensory signals do not go via the thalamus, en route from receptor cells to cortex?
A. Auditory B. Vestibular
C. Visual D. Olfactory

28. The ability to see three-dimensional space and to accurately judge distances is called:
A. Size constancy
B. Shape constancy
C. Depth perception
D. Perceptual organization

29. People who do well on embedded figure tests are characterized to have .... perceptual cognitive style.
A. Constricted
B. Flexible
C. Field-independent
D. Field-dependent

30. The entire range of wavelengths is called the:
A. Electromagnetic Spectrum
B. Visible Spectrum
C. Blind Spot
D. None of the above

31. Which of the following is considered a monocular cue for depth?
A. Convergence
B. Accommodation
C. Depth perspective
D. Singularity

32. Read each of the following two statements—Assertion (A) and Reason (R) and indicate your answer using the codes given below:

Assertion (A): Signal detection theory measures two components of a person's ability to detect signals-perceptual sensitivity and decision criterion.

Reason (R): Studies of vigilance have revealed that the ability to detect an event is dependent on various factors such as training and expectations.

Codes:
A. Both (A) and (R) are true and (R) is the correct explanation of (A).
B. Both (A) and (R) are true, but (R) is not the correct explanation of (A).
C. (A) is true, but (R) is false.
D. (A) is false, but (R) is true.

33. The 'Law of Closure' reflects the idea of striving for:
A. Good figure
B. Continuity
C. Completion
D. Good Contour

34. Misinterpretation of perceptions or experiences in Schizophrenia are known as:
A. Hallucinations
B. Misperceptions
C. Delusions
D. Illusion

35. In which case the sensitivity "d" shall be high in a signal detection task?
A. When proportion of hit responses exceeds the proportion of false alarm responses a lot.
B. When proportion of false alarm responses exceeds the proportion of hit responses a lot.
C. When proportion of hit responses and the proportion of false alarm responses are equal.
D. When proportion of hit responses exceeds the proportion of false alarm responses a little.

36. The perception of a stimulus that is below the threshold for conscious experience is termed as:
A. Just noticeable difference
B. Differential threshold
C. Signal detection
D. Subliminal perception

37. Internal standards used to judge stimuli are referred to as:
A. Adaptation level
B. Context
C. Signal detection
D. Frames of reference

38. Match the items of List-I (Theory) with List-II (Description) and mark your answer with the help of the codes given below:

List-I (Theory)	List-II (Description)
(*a*) Theory of Signal Detection	1. Sensory subjective magnitude grows in proportion to the intensity of the stimulus raised to a power.
(*b*) The Fechner Law	2. The minimal amount of stimulus energy required for a detection of a stimulus.

(c) Absolute Threshold	3. Evaluation of the separate effects of the observer's sensory capacity and response bias.
(d) Stevens Power Law	4. Larger and larger inputs in stimulus energy are required to obtain a corresponding sensory effect.

Codes:

	(a)	(b)	(c)	(d)
A.	1	2	3	4
B.	1	2	4	3
C.	3	4	2	1
D.	3	2	1	4

39. The structure through which all ascending projections in the auditory system are relayed immediately before they reach primary auditory cortex is the:
A. Inferior colliculus
B. Cochlear nucleus
C. Lateral geniculate nucleus
D. Medial geniculate nucleus

40. The law of Pragnanz or law of good figure refers to:
A. Tendency to read an ambiguous stimulus in accordance with an expectation.
B. Viewing under suboptimal conditions such as an object is shaded or overlapped.
C. The tendency to perceive the simplest and most stable figure of all possible perceptual alternatives.
D. The ability to recognise and identify common objects.

41. Closure, nearness, similarity, and continuation are categories of:
A. Perceptual (Gestalt) organization.
B. Cognitive style.
C. Cognitive organization.
D. Perceptual integration.

42. Who developed the 'Retinex Theory' of colour perception?
A. Thomas Young
B. Hermann Von Helmholtz
C. Edward Herring
D. Edwin Land

43. Read each of the following two statements Assertion (A) and Reason (R) and indicate your answer using the codes given below:

Assertion (A): Subliminal perception implies detection of a stimulus with a magnitude for below the absolute threshold.

Reason (R): Receptors always receive information and that is always perceived.

Codes:
A. Both (A) and (R) are true, and (R) is correct explanation of (A).
B. Both (A) and (R) are true, but (R) is not the correct explanation of (A).
C. (A) is true, but (R) is false.
D. (A) is false, but (R) is true.

44. The underlying mechanism for perceptual expectancies is:
A. A misleading perception that distorts or misjudges a stimulus.
B. Top-down processing.
C. The organization of perception by beginning with low-level features.
D. Bottom-up processing.

45. Read the following two statements : Assertion (A) and Reason (R) and indicate your answer using the codes given below:

Assertion (A): A major function of the perceptual system is to keep the appearance of objects the same inspite of change in the stimuli.

Reason (R): The posterior brain system selects objects on the basis of location, shape or colour and the anterior system is responsible for guiding the process.

Codes:
A. Both (A) and (R) are true and (R) is correct explanation of (A).
B. Both (A) and (R) are true, but (R) is not the correct explanation of (A).
C. (A) is true, but (R) is false.
D. (A) is false, but (R) is true.

46. Decreased perceptual response to a repeated stimulus is called:
A. Habituation
B. Selective attention
C. Divided attention
D. Illusion

47. Perceptive auditory receptors in the cochlea are identified as:
A. Basilar cells
B. Hair cells
C. Malleus cells
D. Glial cells

48. Sensations are organized into meaningful perceptions by:
A. Perceptual constancies
B. Meaning
C. Perceptual grouping (Gestalt) principles
D. Sensory adaptation

49. Given below are two statements are labelled as Assertion (A) and the other labelled as Reason (R). Indicate your answer using the code given below:

Assertion (A): Subliminal or below threshold perception exerts an observable influence on various response parameters is not a controversial question.

Reason (R): Subliminally presented emotional stimuli activate cortical areas that mediate emotional experiences.

Codes:
A. Both (A) and (R) are true and (R) is the correct explanation of (A).
B. Both (A) and (R) are true, but (R) is not the correct explanation of (A).
C. (A) is true, but (R) is false.
D. (A) is false, but (R) is true.

50. Read each of the following two statements—Assertion (A) and Reason (R) and indicate your answer using the codes given below:

Assertion (A): Vigilance refers to a person attending to a field of stimulation over a prolonged period of time in which the person seeks to detect the appearance of a particular target stimulus.

Reason (R): Signal Detection Theory suggests that detection of stimuli depends on their physical energy and on internal factors.

Codes:
A. Both (A) and (R) are true and (R) is the correct explanation of (A).
B. Both (A) and (R) are true, but (R) is not the correct explanation of (A).
C. (A) is true, but (R) is false.
D. (A) is false, but (R) is true

ANSWERS

1	2	3	4	5	6	7	8	9	10
B	D	C	B	C	D	C	C	B	A
11	**12**	**13**	**14**	**15**	**16**	**17**	**18**	**19**	**20**
D	C	B	D	B	C	D	B	D	B
21	**22**	**23**	**24**	**25**	**26**	**27**	**28**	**29**	**30**
A	A	C	C	B	C	D	C	C	A
31	**32**	**33**	**34**	**35**	**36**	**37**	**38**	**39**	**40**
A	A	C	C	A	D	D	C	D	C
41	**42**	**43**	**44**	**45**	**46**	**47**	**48**	**49**	**50**
A	D	C	B	B	A	B	C	D	B

CHAPTER 2

Learning Theory

HULL LEARNING THEORY

Hull theories were first presented in Mathematico-dedudctive theory of Rote learning (1940), and Principles of Behaviour (1943), which established his analysis of animal learning and conditioning as the dominant learning theory of its time. Hull had set his theory of learning in terms of 17 postulates and 15 corollaries. They may be briefly discussed as under:

- The postulate first deals with the external stimulation which triggers a sensory impulse that continues for a few seconds after the stimulating event has terminated. This impulse is the stimulus trace.
- The second postulate includes trace interaction. As each organism is bombarded by many stimuli and thus many sensory traces are generated. These traces interact with one another, and represent complexity of stimulation.
- Third postulate deals with the role of reinforcement in learning. Unlearnt behaviours are triggered first when the need arises. If these behaviours fail organism learns new behaviours to reduce the need.
- Fourth postulate dealt with habit formation of what Hull called as habit strength. As the association between stimulus and the response strengthens, Hull says that the "habit" of giving that response to that stimulus increases. This habit strength is represented as:

  $$SHR = 1 - 10(-0.0305\ N) \text{ or}$$

  $$SHR = 1 - 1/100.0305\ N$$

  Where, N is the number of successive reinforcements strengthening stimulus and response.
- Fifth postulate dealt with primary drive (D). Primary drive is also a kind of intervening variable which was very important in Hull's theory. Drive is a temporary state of the organism that is produced by something our body needs or by painful stimulation.
- Sixth and Seventh postulate were also important in explanation of learning. The sixth postulate is concerned with stimulus intensity (V) and the seventh is concerned with incentive motivation (K). The stimulus intensity (V) refers to the fact that the probability of a response to occur increases as the intensity of the stimulus increases. Incentive motivation (K) is a 'pull' factor and refers to the motivating effect of the incentive provided for making a response. It is measured in terms of both quality and quantity.

- Eighth postulate dealt with reaction potential (SER). The probability of a learned response occurring at a particular moment is called reaction potential (SER), and is the product of habit strength and drive. If habit strength or drive equals zero, reaction potential equals zero.

$$_{S}E_{R} = {_{S}H_{R}} \times D$$

- The ninth postulate dealt with inhibition (I) or inhibitory potential. Hull divided inhibition into 2 parts. Reactive inhibition refers to a tendency of not repeating a response that has just been made. Therefore, it is a kind of negative drive and second is conditional inhibition, which is a kind of habit of no responding produced by reactive inhibition.
- Other postulates dealt with those phenomenons which are related to the learning phenomenon. For example tenth postulate was concerned with stimulus generalization, eleventh with stimulus interaction, twelfth with behavioural oscillation, thirteen with reception potential related to threshold, fourteen with reaction potential related to reaction latency, fifteen with reaction potential related to reaction amplitude and sixteenth with reaction potential related to total response to extinction.
- Postulate seventeenth dealt with the problem of individual differences.

In the nutshell, it can be said that the Hull's system of learning comprises a series of postulates and corollaries that mainly centred on drive, reinforcement and response strength.

E. TOLMAN (EDWARD CHACE TOLMAN) LEARNING THEORY

Tolman was an influential early learning theorist who introduced a number of new concepts and vocabulary to the field of learning psychology. Tolman considered behaviour in terms of means-end-relationship. In other words, behaviour , for him, is goal directed, that is, purposive. Due to this reason he has named his system as "an objective behaviouristic purposivism". According to Tolman's theory of sign learning, an organism learns by pursuing signs to a goal, *i.e.,* learning is acquired through meaningful behaviour. Tolman emphasized the organized aspect of learning. "The stimuli which are allowed in are not connected by just simple one to one switches to the outgoing responses. Rather the incoming impulses are usually worked over and elaborated in the central control room into a tentative cognitive like map of the environment. And it is this tentative map, indicating routes and paths and environmental relationships, which finally determines what responses, if any, the animal will finally make."(Tolman, 1948).

Tolman (1932) proposed 5 types of learning: (1) Approach learning, (2) Escape learning, (3) Avoidance learning, (4) Choice point learning, (5) Latent learning. All forms of learning depends upon means-end readiness *i.e.,* goal oriented behaviour, mediated by expectations, perceptions, representations, and other internal or environmental variables.

Tolman's version of behaviourism emphasized the relationship between stimuli rather than stimulus-response (Tolman, 1922). According to Tolman, a new stimulus (the sign) becomes associated with already meaningful stimulus (the significate) through a series of pairings; there was no need for reinforcement in order to establish learning.

Scope/Application

Although Tolman intended his theory to apply to human learning, almost all of his research was done with rats and mazes. Tolman (1942) examines motivation towards war, but this work is not directly related to his learning theory.

Principles

1. Learning is always purposive and goal directed.
2. Learning often involves the use of environmental factors to achieve a goal (*e.g.*, means end analysis).
3. Organisms will select the shortest or easiest path to achieve a goal.

BURRHUS FREDERIK SKINNER (B.F. SKINNER) LEARNING THEORY

The theory of B.F. Skinner is based upon the idea the best way to understand behaviour is to look at the cause of an action and its consequences. He called this approach operant conditioning which was based on the work of Thorndike (1905).

Reinforcement is the key element in Skinner's S-R theory. Behaviour which is reinforced tends to be repeated (strengthens) and the behaviour which is not reinforced tends to be extinguished (weakened). A reinforcer is anything that strengthens the desired response. It could be verbal praise, a good grade or a feeling of increased accomplishment or satisfaction. Positive reinforcement strengthen a behaviour by providing a consequence an individual finds rewarding. For example,if your teacher gives you a chocolate (reward) you like the most every time you complete your assignment or project, you are most likely to repeat this behaviour in the future, thus strengthening the behaviour of completing your assignment or project. Negative reinforcement on the other hand also tends to strengthen behaviour as it stops or removes an unpleasant experience. For example, if you do not complete your assignment or project on time, every time your teacher punishes you by ordering you to take 10 rounds of the school playground, which is really big and its hard for you to run in the scorching heat of the summer. So to avoid those ten rounds of the playground you always complete your project on time, thus strengthening the behaviour of completing you project on time. In operant conditioning the other phenomena like secondary reinforcement, extinction, discrimination, differentiation and aversive conditioning have also been examined.

One of the distinctive aspect of skinner's theory is that it attempted to provide behavioural explanations for a broad range of cognitive phenomenon . For example, skinner explained drive (motivation) in terms of deprivation and reinforcement schedules. Skinner (1975) tried to account for verbal learning and language within the operant conditioning paradigm, although this effort was strongly rejected by linguistic and psycholinguists. Skinner (1971) deals with the issue of free will and social control.

Scope/Application

Operant conditioning has been widely applied in clinical settings widely applied in clinical settings (*i.e.*, behaviour modification) as well as teaching (*i.e.*, classroom management) and instructional development (*e.g.*, programmed instruction).

COGNITIVE APPROACHES IN LEARNING: LATENT & OBSERVATIONAL LEARNING

Place Learning and Latent Learning

A psychologist operating from the cognitive perspective during the middle 20th century was Edward Tolman. Tolman (1930) focused his studies on how rats learn to navigate through mazes. Tolman believed that learning occurred (in animals as well as humans) through mental activity such as insight and the formation of mental representations of the environment he referred to as cognitive maps. Tolman thus believed that animals learn more about "place" rather than how to engage in "habits". Cognitive maps, or mental representations of the spatial layout of the environment, from the critical element in Tolman's theory of place learning.

Taking the cognitive concept of place learning into consideration, Tolman wanted to show that animals could learn to navigate their environment without receiving any reinforcement. Tolman used a complex maze and three groups of rats in what he referred to as latent learning research. The first group, after running, was given no reward at all in the goal box. The second group was given food in the goal box after completion of each run. The third group ran the maze without food or reward for the first 10 days. From 11th day and onwards they were given food in the goal box after each run.

The results supported Tolman's theory. Rats who never received rewards for completing the maze improved only slightly (improvement was measured in number of errors) over the course of 11 days. The rats that were consistently rewarded improved quickly until they reached a maximum efficiency towards the end of the study. The results of the third group of rats (those that had been rewarded only on the 11th day) were the most striking. After the initial reward trial, these rats were just as efficient at completing the maze as those rats that had been rewarded the entire time.

Tolman explained these results as latent learning. The rats had learned to navigate their environment all along, but this learning did not emerge until it was reinforced. It took only one reinforcement for the rats to reach maximum efficiency. The learning was latent or hidden from view until reinforcement brought it out. It did not take reinforcement to learn the behaviour; the behaviour was simply observed and strengthened with reinforcement.

Observational Learning

In social learning theory Albert Bandura (1977) states that behaviour is learned from the environment through the process of observational learning. An illustration of Bandura's concept of observational learning is one of his studies he conducted using Kindergarten age children. All the children in one study watched a film portraying an adult engaged in aggressive behaviour. The adult serves as a simple model for such behaviour, in that this adult was in a room full of toys and was seen verbally insulting, hitting, kicking, throwing and hammering a large plastic inflatable bobo doll. For one group of children, the model was reinforced for the assaults with candy and soda. For the second group, the model was punished verbally and the received a "spanking". The third group of children viewed the aggressive model where no consequences were given. The results demonstrated that humans could learn by simply witnessing the consequences of others.

When left in the room alone with a similar bobo doll, those children in the first group (where the model was rewarded for aggression) displayed much aggressive behaviour by imitating what the model had done as well as showing novel aggressive actions. Those in the group witnessing the model being punished for aggressive behaviour were much more gentle with doll and display few, if any, aggressive acts towards it. Children in the group who witnessed the model receiving no consequences for aggression where more ambiguous in their behaviour, showing some aggressive and some gentle behaviours.

Bandura emphasized the role of observation, attention, imitation and expectations in the process.

EXPERIMENTAL ANALYSIS OF BEHAVIOUR: BEHAVIOUR MODIFICATION, SHAPING

Behaviour Modification

It is derived from psychological treatment approaches based on the tenets of operant conditioning proposed by B.F. Skinner. The theories of operant conditioning state that behaviour can be shaped by reinforcement or lack of it. As a treatment technique, behaviour modification is used to address many problems in both adults and children. Behaviour modification has been successfully used to treat attention deficit hyperactivity disorder (ADHD), obsessive compulsive disorder (OCD), phobias, enuresis (bed wetting), separation anxiety disorder and others.

Stages of Behaviour Modification

Behaviour modification is based on two types of theories. One involves antecedents *i.e.,* events which occur before a particular behaviour is demonstrated and the other is observable behaviour *i.e.,* those events that occur after a particular behaviour has been occurred. A behaviour modification technique is applicable only after a series of changes. An inappropriate behaviour is observed, identified, targeted and stopped. Meanwhile, a new appropriate behaviour must be identified, developed, strengthened and maintained.

Reinforcements and Punishments

Positive reinforcement is the ways in which you encourage the desired behaviour. It increases the future frequency of the desired behaviour. Patting the back, passing a smile, or sometimes even giving a chocolate, reward etc when a person behaves properly is called positive reinforcement. Negative reinforcement on the other hand, increases the likelihood that a particular negative behaviour would not happen in the future. It is often confused with punishment, while punishment is negative, negative reinforcement is positive. It is a positive way of reducing a particular behaviour.

Behaviour Modification Techniques

1. Classroom Monitoring: Effective teaching practices, frequent monitoring, strict rules and regulations, social appraisal etc.
2. Pro-Social Behaviour: Positive and negative reinforcements, modelling of pro-social behaviour, verbal instruction, role playing etc.
3. Moral Education: Moral science classes on real life situations, imaginary situations and literature. Let students play different roles as a teacher, principle, parents etc and participate in school administration.
4. Social Problem Solving (SPS): Direct teaching of SPS skills (example, alternative thinking, means end thinking), dialoguing, self instruction training etc.
5. Effective Communication Models: Values explanation activities, active listening, importance of communication and interpersonal skills, training for students and teachers.

Shaping

The differential reinforcement of successive approximations, or more commonly, shaping is a conditioned procedure used primarily in the experimental analysis of behaviour. It was introduced by B.F. Skinner with pigeons and extended to dogs, dolphins, humans and other species. In shaping, the form of an existing response is gradually changed across successive trials towards a desired target behaviour using differential reinforcement. The principles of shaping are present in everyday interactions with the environment.

Successive Approximations

The successive approximations reinforced are increasingly accurate approximations of a response desired by a trainer. As training progress the trainer stops reinforcing the less accurate approximations. For example, in training a rat to press a lever, the following successive approximations might be reinforced.

To start, the trainer may reward the rat when it makes any movement at all in the direction of the lever. Then, the rat has to actually take a step toward the lever to get rewarded. Then, it has to go over to the lever to get rewarded and so on until only pressing the lever will produce reward.

The trainer would start by reinforcing all behaviours in the first category then restrict reinforcement to responses in the second category, and then progressively restrict reinforcement to each successive, more accurate approximation. As training progresses, the response reinforced becomes progressively more like the desired behaviour. The culmination of the process is that the strength of the response measured here as the frequency of lever pressing increases. In the beginning, there is little probability that the rat would depress the lever, the only possibility being that it would depress the lever by accident. Through training the rat can be brought to depress the lever frequently.

Practical Applications

Shaping is used in two areas in psychology: training operant responses in lab animals, and in applied behaviour analysis or behaviour modification to change human or animal behaviours considered to be maladaptive or dysfunctional. It also plays an important role in commercial animal training. Shaping assist in discrimination and in generalization as well.

DISCRIMINATION LEARNING

In Psychology, discrimination learning is the process by which animals or people learn to make different responses to different stimuli: In more general terms, discrimination is the process of learning to make one response to one stimulus and a different response, or no response to another stimulus.

The term discrimination learning-learning to respond differentially to different stimuli encompasses a diverse range of different types of learning, such as perceptual learning, concept learning, and language learning. Learning to discriminate often involves a process of differentiation and unitization. Differentiation involves learning to separate similar stimuli into different categories (*e.g.*, ravens versus crows); unitization involves learning to group stimuli into larger units and to discriminate based on the unit (*e.g.*, seeing a whole face instead of separate facial features).

In classical conditioning, discrimination occurs when one stimulus triggers a conditional response but another does not. To set up discrimination in the laboratory, a researcher creates a situation in which the two stimuli predict different things. For example, a green light is followed by food, but a red light follows nothing. After a number of repeated trials the dog learns to discriminate between green and red lights. It salivates to the green light but not to the red light.

MULTIPLE CHOICE QUESTIONS

1. Who first presented the Mathematico-Deductive Theory of Rote learning?
A. Tolman B. Hull
C. Pavlov D. Skinner

2. Who emphasized the "purposive" element of animal behaviour?
A. Hull B. Skinner
C. Tolman D. Kohler

3. Operant conditioning is associated with whom?
A. Watson B. Pavlov
C. Kohler D. Skinner

4. The concept of programme learning was introduced by:
A. Hull B. Tolman
C. Skinner D. Thorndike

5. Which theory formed the basis for most of Hull's work?
A. The reinforcement theory
B. The sign learning theory
C. The classical conditioning theory
D. The two factor theory of conditioning

6. Much learning in human being takes place by:
A. Imitation and insight
B. Insight and conditioning
C. Conditioning and imitation
D. Trial and error

7. Who conducted research in all the three of the following areas: hypnosis, aptitude testing, behaviour?
A. Hull B. Tolman
C. Watson D. Skinner

8. Walden Two is .... book about ....
A. Watson; a parenting technique
B. Watson; a Utopian society
C. Skinner's; a parenting technique
D. Skinner's; a Utopian society

9. The rate of response in operant conditioning is usually portrayed by a :
A. Serial learning curve
B. Cumulative curve
C. Both A & B
D. None of the above

10. Latent learning is said to occur :
A. In the absence of punishment
B. In the absence of shock
C. In the absence of reward
D. All of the above

11. Which neurotransmitter has been shown to be most closely associated with reinforcement of behaviour?
A. Acetylcholine B. Epinephrine
C. Dopamine D. Serotonin

12. Who has written the book "Beyond Freedom and Dignity"?
A. Hull B. Tolman
C. Skinner D. Guthrie

13. What was Project Orcon?
A. This was Pavlov's Research on "Classical Conditioning".
B. This was Skinner's Pigeon-training work
C. This was Thorndike Trail & Error work
D. None of the above

14. The Classic bobo doll study, where a child punched a doll after seeing an adult do the same, was a demonstration of:
A. Classical conditioning
B. Operant conditioning
C. Trial and error learning
D. Observational learning

15. Tacit knowledge is mainly acquired through:
A. Lectures and reading
B. Trial and error
C. Observation and experience
D. All of the above

16. A pattern of sign gestalt was called Cognitive map by:
A. Tolman B. Pavlov
C. Guthrie D. Skinner

17. Who coined the concept "habit strength"?
A. Thorndike B. Hull
C. Guthrie D. Skinner

18. 18 postulates and 12 corollaries in learning are related to:
A. Hull B. Tolman
C. Pavlov D. Thorndike

19. Who gave the concept of need reduction theory?
A. Pavlov B. Thorndike
C. Hull D. Skinner

20. Social learning theory explicitly includes which of the following concepts?
A. Sign learning
B. Behavioural modelling
C. Action learning
D. None of the above

21. Whose system is presented in terms of corollaries expressed in verbal and mathematical form?
A. Guthrie B. Pavlov
C. Thorndike D. Hull

22. Behaviour modification mainly focuses on:
A. The process of sign learning
B. The ways to increase intelligence
C. The environmental contingencies that precede and follow behaviour
D. The ways to increase tacit knowledge

23. In Classical conditioning, when the UCS occurs before the CS, this is called:
A. Backward conditioning
B. Forward conditioning
C. Spontaneous recovery
D. None of the above

24. Which of the following reinforcement schedules provides a reward at the end of a particular amount of time, regardless of the number of responses made during that time?
A. Variable interval
B. Fixed ratio
C. Fixed interval
D. Variable ratio

25. A technique in which closer and closer approximations of desired behaviour are required for the delivery of positive reinforcement is known as:
A. Shaping B. Modelling
C. Conditioning D. All of the above

26. Experiments on "Latent Learning" reveal that learning can occur:
A. Without reinforcement
B. With reinforcement
C. Without response
D. Without Stimulus

27. A parent deliberately ignores a child's temper tantrums in an attempt to discourage them. The parent's strategy is in accordance with
A. Negative reinforcement
B. Extinction
C. Operant escape
D. Operant avoidance

28. Latent-learning studies established that .... is/are not always necessary for learning to occur.
A. experience
B. fixed action patterns
C. reward
D. motivation

29. When information currently being learned adversely affects the retention of information acquired previously, the phenomena is referred to as:
A. Distortion
B. Retroactive interference
C. Proactive interference
D. Retrieval failure

30. If positive reinforcement is not given within a short time following the response, learning will proceed slowly. This phenomenon is called:
A. delayed reinforcement
B. extinction
C. conditioned response
D. consistency

31. In an experiment if a light is repeatedly presented just before the electric shock is given the animal learns:
A. Operant escape and then operant avoidance
B. Operant avoidance and then operant escape
C. Only operant escape
D. Only operant avoidance

32. Which of the following is not a Behaviour Therapy Technique?
A. Flooding
B. Counter transference
C. Counter conditioning
D. Systematic desensitisation

33. Which of the following is NOT an assumption of behavioural theories?
A. Focus on overt behaviours rather than unconscious motivations.
B. Action changes brain patterns.
C. Reliance on empirical data and scientific methods.
D. A valuing of an active, directive, prescriptive role for helpers.

34. Children learn to add new words through a process called:
A. Fast mapping B. New mapping
C. Extensions D. Inspiration

35. Client centred therapy is a type of:
A. Humanistic therapy
B. Psychodynamic therapy
C. Cognitive therapy
D. Behavioural therapy

36. Most human habits are resistant to extinction because these are reinforced:
A. In a constant fashion
B. All the times
C. Every now and then
D. In a variable fashion

37. Some people believe that certain objects bring luck and help them in being successful. Such superstitions may be the result of:
A. insight
B. a program of behaviour modification
C. autoshaping
D. token economy systems

38. Bandura felt that .... was/were an effective treatment for phobias.
A. Modelling
B. Electroconvulsive shock therapy
C. Anti-depressant drugs
D. Dream interpretation

39. In Bandura's original experiments on aggression and observational learning, he found that the number of aggressive acts displayed was at its highest when observing:
A. a model act aggressively
B. a model act pleasantly
C. a model watching action movie
D. All of the above

40. Read the following two statements—Assertion (A) and Reason (R) and indicate your answer using the codes given below:

Assertion (A): Research suggests that delay conditioning is generally the most effective method for establishing a conditioned response.

Reason (R): Conditioned stimulus helps predict forthcoming presentation of the unconditioned stimulus.

Codes:
A. Both (A) and (R) are true and (R) is the correct explanation of (A).
B. Both (A) and (R) are true, but (R) is not the correct explanation of (A).
C. (A) is true, but (R) is false.
D. Both (A) and (R) are false.

41. Aversion is one of the conditioning procedures used in:
A. Non-directive therapy
B. Psychoanalytic therapy
C. Behaviour therapy
D. Client-centred therapy

42. Match List-I with List-II and indicate your answer using codes given below:

List-I (Concept)	**List-II (Theorists)**
(*a*) Shaping and chaining	1. Tolman
(*b*) Law of effect	2. Skinner
(*c*) Cognitive map	3. Bandura
(*d*) Modelling	4. Thorndike

Codes:

	(*a*)	(*b*)	(*c*)	(*d*)
A.	1	3	4	2
B.	2	3	1	4
C.	2	4	1	3
D.	3	4	2	1

43. A positive or negative environmental stimulus that motivates behaviour is known as:
A. Reinforcement
B. Punishment
C. Incentive
D. Learning

44. Read each of the following two statements—Assertion (A) and Reason (R) and indicate your answer using the codes given below:

Assertion (A): Children with learning disability are allowed to type or tape record their assignments.

Reason (R): Omitting handwriting as a criterion for evaluating reports/copies is a way of helping children with learning disability.

Codes:

A. Both (A) and (R) are true and (R) is correct explanation of (A).
B. Both (A) and (R) are true, but (R) is not the correct explanation of (A).
C. (A) is true, but (R) is false.
D. (A) is false, but (R) is true.

45. Behaviour analysis is based upon the principles of:
A. Classical conditioning
B. Operant conditioning
C. Dream analysis
D. All of the above

46. Principle stating that a more preferred activity can be used to reinforce a less preferred activity is referred to as:
A. Trace conditioning
B. Hull's principle
C. Principle of stimulus generalization
D. Premack principle

47. Behavioural symptoms of learned helplessness include emotional disturbance, cognitive deficits, and:
A. hallucinations
B. suicidal ideation
C. motivational deficits
D. dissociative personalities

48. Which of the following clinical procedure/s is/are not based on classical conditioning?
1. Flooding
2. Transference
3. Client centered therapy
4. Systematic desensitization

Codes:

A. 1 only B. 2 and 3 only
C. 1, 2 and 3 only D. 1, 3 and 4 only

49. Irrational fears that are thought to be caused by classical conditioning are called:
A. psychosomatic illness
B. avoidance behaviour
C. phobias
D. stimulus discrimation

50. Who elucidates the contiguity theory of reinforcement in the most pronounced and consistent manner?
A. Clark Hull B. Guthrie
C. Tolman D. Mc Dougall

ANSWERS

1	2	3	4	5	6	7	8	9	10
B	C	D	C	A	C	D	D	B	C
11	**12**	**13**	**14**	**15**	**16**	**17**	**18**	**19**	**20**
C	C	B	D	C	A	B	A	C	B
21	**22**	**23**	**24**	**25**	**26**	**27**	**28**	**29**	**30**
D	C	A	C	A	A	B	C	B	A
31	**32**	**33**	**34**	**35**	**36**	**37**	**38**	**39**	**40**
C	B	B	A	A	D	C	A	A	A
41	**42**	**43**	**44**	**45**	**46**	**47**	**48**	**49**	**50**
C	C	A	A	B	D	C	B	C	B

❑❑❑

CHAPTER 3

Models of Memory

ATKINSON SHIFFRIN MEMORY MODEL

The Atkinson Shiffrin model (also known as Multi store model, Multi memory model and the Modal model) is a psychological model proposed in 1968 by Richard Atkinson and Richard Shiffrin as a proposal for the structure of memory. It proposed that human memory involves a sequence of 3 stages:

1. Sensory Memory
2. Short Term Memory (STM)
3. Long Term Memory (LTM)

The multi store model of memory is an explanation of how memory processes work. You hear, see and feel many things, but only a small number are remembered.

1. **Sensory Memory:** Sensory memory has a large capacity. However, it is of very short duration. All the incoming information first enters the sensory memory, where information is registered from each sense organ with reasonable accuracy. The visual system possesses iconic memory for visual stimuli such as shape, size, colour and location (but not meaning), whereas the hearing system has echoic memory for auditory stimuli.

2. **Short Term Memory (STM) or Working Memory:** Information that is attended to and recognized enters the short term memory (STM), where it is held for perhaps 20 to 30 seconds. Some of the information reaching short term memory is processed by being rehearsed- that is, by having attention focused on it, perhaps by being repeated over and over, or perhaps by being processed in some other way that will link it up with other information already stored in memory. Miller (1956) has found that STM has a limited capacity of around 7 + or – 2 'Chunks' of information.

3. **Long Term Memory (LTM):** LTM has a vast capacity and provides the lasting retention of information, from minutes to a life time. Information that once enters the long term memory store is never forgotten because it gets encoded semantically. (Mainly in terms of meaning). It also retains procedural skills and imagery.

Memory may also be transported directly from sensory memory to LTM if it receives instant attention, example, witnessing a fire in your house. This is also known as a "Flashbulb Memory". Also if information in the LTM is not rehearsed it can be forgotten through trace decay.

Criticism

1. **Linearity:** Some agree that the Multi store model is too linear, *i.e.,* it cannot accommodate sub divisions of STM and LTM memory stores.

2. The Atkinson Shiffrin Model distinguishes different form of memory, but it does not take into account what information is presented, nor does it take into account individual differences in subject's performance including a cognitive ability or previous experience with learning techniques.

F.I.M Craik and R.S. Lockhart, Level of Processing Model of Memory

According to Craik & Lockhart, memory was enhanced more by depth of processing than by how long information was rehearsed. They suggested that rehearsal was mainly effective if the rehearsal was done in a deep and meaningful way.

The levels of processing model of memory (Craik and Lockhart, 1972) were put forward partly as a result of the criticism levelled at the multi-store model. This popular model postulated only two levels of memory i.e. Short term memory (STM) and Long term memory (LTM) and suggested that characteristics of a memory are determined by its "location". Instead of concentrating on the stores/structures involved (i.e. short term memory & long term memory), this theory concentrates on the processes involved in memory.

Craick and Lockhart proposed that memory occurs on a continuum from shallow to deep. The shallow processing takes two forms (a) Structural processing, which only encoded the physical qualities of something (b) Phonemic processing, encode the sounds. The shallow level involves analysis in terms of physical and sensory characteristics, such as brightness or pitch. The intermediate level of memory relates to recognition and labelling. The deep processing involves semantic processing, which when encoded, describes the meaning of a word and relate it to similar words with similar meaning which results in more elaborate, longer lasting, and stronger memory traces. Factors which influence the depth of perceptual processing includes attention paid to the stimulus, its compatibility with existing memory structures in the learner's brain, and the amount of processing time available. In addition, the "self-reference effect" in which learner relates to oneself in comparison to material that has less personal relevance takes learning to deeper levels and therefore promotes long term memory.

Craick and Lockhart proposed two kinds of rehearsal

1. **Maintenance Rehearsal:** It involves rote repetition of an item's auditory representation without taking into account its meaning or relation to other items, which leads to fairly short-term retention of information. Example: Repeating the phone number your friend just gave you over and over again so you won't forget it.
2. **Elaborate rehearsal:** It involves meaning-based analysis (e.g. images, thinking, associations etc.) of information and leads to better recall. For example, giving words a meaning or linking them with previous knowledge.

Scope/ Application

The primary application of the levels of processing framework was to verbal learning settings (i.e. memorization of words lists); however, it has been applied to reading and language learning (*e.g.*, Cermak & Craik, 1979).

ENDEL TULVING MEMORY MODEL

Endel Tulving is a Canadian neuroscientist born in Estonia, who researches memory with a speciality in episodic memory. One of his main contributions in his theory is of "Encoding-Specificity". The theory emphasized the fact that memories are retrieved from LTM by means of retrieval cues. For example, a very large number of memories stored in one brain are not currently active, but the word "Disneyland" might instantly call to mind a trip to that amusement park. The theory of encoding specificity states that the most effective retrieval cues are those that were stored along with the memory of the experience itself. Thus, the words "amusement park" might not serve to retrieve the memory of a trip to Disneyland because, while there, the park was not specifically thought of as an "amusement park". Instead, it was thought of as Disneyland. As such, that is the cue that retrieves the appropriate memory from the vast ocean of memories that are stored in one's brain.

His work about episodic memory used the amnesic patient, who had intact semantic memory but no episodic memory. Tulving special interest was focused on episodic memory-the kind of memory that allows us to "mentally travel" in time, and thus recollect our own past experiences, events we have observed and participated in.

One feature that distinguishes episodic from other forms of memory is what Tulving called "autonoetic" (Self knowing) consciousness, which corresponds to a form of consciousness that is most like episodic memory. Tulving (1985) suggested that there is a correspondence between three different types of consciousness and three different memory systems. In addition to autonoetic consciousness, Tulving suggested that that noetic consciousness corresponds to semantic memory and anoetic consciousness corresponds to procedural memory.

Another distinguishing feature of episodic memory is "Chronesthesia", the subjective sense of time, which is also critical for locating memories in the personal past and re-experiencing them as a part of that past. According to Tulving (2002), the awareness of the past, present and future is chronesthesia. Whereas chronesthesia emphasizes the awareness of subjective time, autonoetic consciousness emphasizes the specific role of the experience of self in subjective time. It is theorized that both autonoetic consciousness and chronesthesia allow us to mentally time-travel to re-experience past events and project ourself into the future. (Tulving, 2002; Wheeler, Stuss & Tulving, 1997).

A third (hypothetical) feature of episodic memory which makes it distinguishable from another is that, it exists in human beings only. Many animals-mammals as well as most if not all birds-have excellent "semantic" memory. However, there exists no evidence that they can mentally travel in the same way as humans do, to remember the past and to envision the future. It is the unique ability that only humans are bestowed with.

Semantic Memory

Much of what is in our long term memory consists of knowledge about what words mean, about the ways they are related to one another, and about the rules for using them in communication and thinking. In short, it is the kind of memory which makes our use of language possible. It is called semantic memory. Semantic memory is considered to be very stable; there is little forgetting of the meanings of the words of our language and the rules for their use. In other words, it is the memory of general awareness and knowledge. All the concepts, ideas and rules of logic are stored in semantic memory.

Information seems to be stored in semantic memory in a highly organized way. For instance, some experiments (Collins & Quillian, 1969) have indicated that information is stored in logical hierarchy that go from general categories to specific ones. Such organization makes it possible for us to make logical inferences from the information stored in semantic memory. Other experiments (Rips et . al., 1937) have led to the idea that semantic memory is organized into cluster of words with related meanings, very much as the TOT observations indicated.

Episodic memory (Tulvin, 1972) consists of long term memories of specific things that happened to us at particular times and places. Thus episodic memories are memories of episodes, long or short, in our own lives; they are dated and have a biographical reference. In other words our "remembrances of things past" make up our episodic memory.

Unlike semantic memory, with its network of meanings, episodic memory seems to be organized with respect to when certain events happened in our lives. The episodes do not have to have a logical organization. Thus episodic memory is a record of what has happened to us and does not lend itself to the drawing of inferences. In addition, perhaps because it is less highly organized, episodic memory seems more susceptible to being forgotten than does semantic memory.

Episodic memory is thought of as being a "one-shot" learning mechanism; you only need one exposure to an episode to remember it. Semantic memory, on the other hand, can take into consideration multiple exposures to each referent-the semantic representation is updated on each exposure. Episodic memory can be thought of as a "map" that ties together items in semantic memory.

Off course, episodic and semantic memory is related. For example, episodic memories may be incorporated in our network of general knowledge about the world and thus become a part of our semantic memories; we drive our knowledge about the world from specific things that have happened to us. Any items in semantic memory can become a part of our episodic memory. For instance, you might remember that at a certain time, you used some information from semantic memory.

LONG-TERM MEMORY

Long term memory (LTM) is memory that can last as little as a few days or as long as decades. It is a permanent storehouse of all information that may be as recent as today and as old as decades. Human long term memory is not an untidy jumble of unrelated information; we keep our memory store in order. We organize, categorize, and classify information in a number of ways. Long term memory is a bit like a library with a good gross indexing system.

The Tip Of The Tongue (TOT) Phenomenon

Phenomenon of the tip of the tongue is a feeling of knowing but not remembering the word he/she was asked to describe the characteristics of the elusive words like its first letter, number of syllables it had, words that sounded like it and so on. The tip of the tongue phenomenon supports the fact that information in LTM is organized.

Semantic and Episodic Memory

Two types of information are stored in LTM-semantic and episodic. Episodic memory records an individual's past experiences and the episodes of ones daily life. Episodic memory is both specific and autobiographical. For example,one remember a party one attended yesterday. It means that the event is stored in episodic memory. Semantic memory involves the abstract knowledge and meaning of words, symbols, ideas and rules for relating them. For example,you read an article about the adverse affect of smoking, resulting in death of many persons due to cancer. Sometimes later the episode may be forgotten but the knowledge of the fact that smoking can cause cancer and death remains in memory. This knowledge is a part of semantic memory. Episodic memory is more susceptible to forgetting as compared to semantic.

Encoding and Storing Long Term Memory

Encoding for long term storage requires special attention or strategies of some sort:

1. **The role of organization:** One strategy in remembering things well is to organize, or arrange, the input so that its fits into existing long term memory categories, is grouped in some logical manner, or is arranged in some way that makes "sense".
2. **The role of imagery:** The organization and meaning given to verbal information are as we have seen, quite influential in promoting long term retention. Another factor is whether the incoming information is encoded by forming images of it. Visual images are the one that have been most suited.

3. **The role of construction process:** Certain details are accentuated, the material may be simplified, or it may be changed in many other ways so that what is encoded and stored is far from a literal copy of the input. These modifications are called constructive process.

Retrieval from Long Term Memory

1. **Retrieval Cues:** Finding information in the organized long term memory stored is aided by retrieval cues, or reminders, which direct the memory search to the appropriate part of the long term memory library.
2. **Reconstructive Process:** Reconstructive process are modifications of already stored input. Reconstruction is sometimes called confabulation in the case of people with memory disorders who have stored very little and who then try to fill in the memory gaps during retrieval.

However if items is not recognised then there is failure to recall the item *i.e.,* forgetting occurs.

Retrieval Cues

Most researchers since 1960's, in their researches concludes that information is not lost from long term memory. Instead, they view forgetting primarily as a problem of retrieval. Infact, it has been found that information can be more easily retrieved when the proper retrieval cues are used and some evidence for this lies in what has been called TOT (Tip Of The Tongue Phenomenon), which refers to a state which involves a failure to recall a word of which one has knowledge. People experiencing the tip-of-the-tongue phenomenon can often recall one or more features of the target word, such as the first letter, its syllabic stress, and words similar in sound and/or meaning.

Tulving and Pearlstone (1966, in Willingham, 2001) argued that TOT is a common occurrence, and furthermore that it is a fundamental aspect of memory. There are four basic ways in which information can be pulled from long-term memory. The type of retrieval cues that are available can have an impact on how information is retrieved.

1. **Recall:** Retrieval cues can facilitate recall when there is a strong link between two pieces of information. Cues are thought to be most effective when two items have a strong, complex link. Cued Recall is used when a person is given a list of items to remember and is then tested with cues to remember material. Answering a question on a fill-in-the-blank test is a good example of recall.
2. **Reconstructive memory:** Refers to the idea that recollection of memories involves a process of trying to reconstruct (rather than replay) past events. Although the reconstruction can be quite accurate, the processes responsible can also introduce errors during retrieval. In fact, systematic errors in memory are the primary evidence for its reconstructive nature.
3. **Recognition:** It refers to the retrieval of details associated with the previously experienced event. Recognition memory can be subdivided into two component processes: recollection and familiarity, sometimes referred to as "remembering" and "knowing", respectively. For example, taking a multiple-choice quiz where you have to recognize the correct answer out of other available options.
4. **Relearning:** According to Ebbinghaus, (1885), Relearning is supposedly the most efficient way of remembering information. It is a way of measuring retention by measuring how fast one relearns material that has been learned previously. It makes it easier to remember and retrieve information in the future.

According to Tulving (1974, in Willingham, 2001) Encoding Specificity Principle is another variable that affects cued recall. Other way to cue retrieval is called priming. Priming is the process of presenting an event, episode, stimulus, etc., that prepares a system for functioning.

Flashbulb Memory

Flashbulb memories are distinctly vivid, precise, concrete, long lasting memories of a personal circumstance surrounding a person's discovery of shocking events. Flashbulb memories have six different features that people remember: who told you the news, what you were doing when you heard the news, where you were, how you felt when you heard the news, other's emotional impact, and what happened afterwards.

It is possible for both positive and negative events to produce flashbulb memories. However positive events are pleasant to remember, the negative flashbulb memories are more highly unpleasant causing a person to avoid reliving the negative event. With regards to this, Matlin and Stang (1978) found that people tend to be better at recalling pleasant life experiences and that people rehearse pleasant items more often than unpleasant items. Furthermore, people judge events as more pleasant with the passage of time.

When compared to other researches on memory, the flashbulb memories forgetting curve is far less affected by time than is the case for other types of memories. The flashbulb memories are stored on one occasion and retained for a lifetime. These memories are associated with important historical or autobiographical events. Such events could include Mumbai terrorist attacks or the terrorist attack on September 11, 2001, etc.

In another research study with regards to positive and negative events associated with flashbulb memories it has been found that consequential negative events may be remembered more accurately than highly positive events. At the same time, people do not indulge in their negative flashbulb memories, as they do in their positive flashbulb memories, by making them central to their life stories and frequently sharing them with others. As a consequence, reliving qualities and sensory imagery may be maintained better for highly positive than for highly negative memories. From an evolutionary standpoint, this seems to be a sensible and adaptive behaviour, since, on the one hand, it is important to remember (potentially dangerous) negative situations accurately, whereas, on the other hand, having highly negative memories central to one's life story and identity has been shown to be dysfunctional (Berntsen & Rubin, 2006; Berntsen et al., 2003). At the same time, remembering and reliving positive events may be adaptive. Pleasant memories help to support our personal and social identities and may form reference points for generating optimistic expectations. A positive outlook on life makes it possible to think about and plan for the future without being paralyzed by having to think about all the bad things that have happened, or could happen, in our lives and in the historical reality of our time.

What makes the flashbulb memory special is the emotional arousal at the moment that the event was registered to the memory. It is the emotions elicited by a flashbulb memory event that increase the ability to recall the details of the event.

Criticism

Despite the great vividness of such memories, some research suggests that flashbulb memories are no more likely to be remembered than ordinary memories, as if the ordinary memories are consistently returned to in a similar way. The most pronounced difference between ordinary and flashbulb memory is that people believe flashbulb memories to be more accurately and vividly remembered. Part of the reason for this may be that people discuss such significant events frequently, and the after the fact discussion can modify what people believe they remember about the event. Neisser believes that flashbulb memories are enduring because they are constantly being reinforced by, for example, the media.

Constructive Process In Memory

During encoding, the to be remembered information, especially if it is a complex life events or something you have read, is modified. Certain details are accentuated, the material may be simplified, or it may be changed in many other ways so that what is encoded and stored is far from a literal copy of the input. These modifications are called constructive process.

One important constructive process is encoding only the gist, or meaning of complex information, such as what we have read in a newspaper, magazine, or books. For example, many years ago the British Psychologist, Sir Frederick Bartlet (1932) did some classic experiments in which people were asked to read a rather bizarre folktale. He then obtained successive recalls of the story several hours or days after the reading. He found that the story was shortened and simplified, and details were omitted, so that only the general outline, or gist, was left in many cases. Furthermore, the changes made in the story indicated that the subjects were using inferences in their encoding of the story.

The other experiments have focussed on the use of inferences in the constructive process (Bransford et al., 1972). Suppose you read, "The driver of the car was seen drinking before he was involved in an accident." You would probably infer that drinking caused the accident and remember the sentences as stating causation, although it not. Thus we tend to remember what was inferred at the time of encoding and storage.

Inferences are also made on the basis of the memory organizations, or schemata, that we have in semantic memory. We have all sorts of information about things, events, and their relationships stored in our semantic memories.

Eyewitness Testimony

Eyewitness testimony is an important area of research in cognitive psychology and human memory. Reports from eyewitnesses play an important role in the development and propagation of beliefs. People are often ready to believe the personal reports of what others say that they have seen and experienced. Thus it becomes very important to find out how reliable is person memory and their testimony can be.

Prosecutors recognize that eyewitness testimony, even when given in all honesty and sincerity isn't necessarily credible. It doesn't guarantee that whatever the eye witness is stating has really happened the way he is saying, or he hasn't forget or miss anything happened at that time. There can be discrepancy in seeing and stating, which is one possible reason why not all eyewitnesses are the same. A competent witness, is the one who has adequate powers of perception, ability to remember and report well, and has the ability and willingness to tell the truth.

Even though the testimony is being considered the most reliable form of evidence available, researches into this area has found that eyewitness testimony can be affected by many physical and psychological factors which may includes- age, health, personal bias and expectations, viewing conditions, perception problems, later discussions with other witnesses, stress etc.

Thus, such testimony can be critiqued on several grounds, having impaired perception, having impaired memory, having inconsistent testimony, having bias or prejudice, and not having a reputation for telling the truth. If any of those characteristics can be demonstrated, the competency of the witness is questionable.

Bartlett's theory of reconstructive memory is crucial to an understanding of the reliability of eyewitness testimony as he suggested that recall is subject to personal interpretation dependent on our learnt or cultural norms and values, and the way we make sense of our world. He illustrate that memory is an active process and subject to individual interpretation or construction.

Autobiographical Memory

Memories of events that have occurred during the course of our lifetime are tended to form our autobiographical memories. In other words an autobiographical memory is a personal representation of general or specific events and personal facts. It can be divided into episodic and semantic memories.

Autobiographical memory is generally considered a subset of episodic memory. Episodic memory refers to the conscious recollection of specific events that took place at a particular point in time in the past, involving such information as what, where, and when. It supports the mental time travel of the self to relive previous experiences. Not all episodic memories become part of one's autobiographical history, however, only those that are highly significant to the individual constitute autobiographical memories. A person's autobiographical memory is fairly reliable, although, the reliability of autobiographical memories is questionable because of memory distortions.

Autobiographical memory types can be divided into four distinct categories: Biographical or Personal, Reconstructions vs. Copies, Generic vs. Specific, and Observer vs. Field.

Autobiographical memory serves three broad functions: directive, social, and self-representative. A fourth function, adaptive, was proposed by Williams, Conway and Cohen (2008). The directive function of autobiographical memory uses past experiences as a reference for solving current problems and a guide for our actions in the present and the future. The social function of autobiographical memory develops and maintains social bonds by providing material for people to converse about. Sharing personal memories with others is a way to facilitate social interaction. Autobiographical memory performs a self-representative function by using personal memories to create and maintain a coherent self-identity over time. Finally, autobiographical memory serves an adaptive function. Recalling positive personal experiences can be used to maintain desirable moods or alter undesirable moods.

Autobiographical memories can differ for special periods of life. When people are asked to recall events from their childhood, they usually cannot recall events prior to age three. Not only are they unable to recall memories before age three, but the number of memories retrieved between ages three and six is also markedly below the number available after that period. The loss of these first events is called childhood or infantile amnesia. People tend to recall many personal events from adolescence and early adulthood. This is called the reminiscence bump. Finally, people recall many personal events from the last few years. This is called the recency effect. For adolescents and young adults the reminiscence bump and the recency effect coincide.

THE BIOLOGICAL BASIS OF MEMORY

Most of what we know about the biological basis of memory comes from research in 2 areas:

1. Neuropsychological studies of human brain damaged patients
2. Psycho physiological studies with animals.

Neuropsychological studies: There are generally 2 types of memory impairments that can occur as a result of brain damage:

1. **Retrograde Amnesia:** refers to the condition where patients cannot remember events that occurred prior to the head trauma. Most recent events are the most likely to be lost, and the amount of loss can be from minutes to years.
2. **Anterograde Amnesia:** is a condition wherein patients can remember past events just fine, but they having an inability to form new long-term memories, some types at least.

Patients with Anterograde amnesia do have memory for events that occurred prior to the trauma, so clearly they have an intact memory retrieval system.

Thus it seems their real problem is in storing new memories, but not all kinds of new memories, just episodic memories it seems. Thus the hippocampus appears critical for the formation of episodic memories.

Psycho physiological studies: Critters also appears to form episodic memories which help them to do things like remember locations where they have already searched for food. If their hippocampus is destroyed they also appear to suffer from the loss of episodic memory.

So in summary, we know that there are number of ways things can get into long term memory, and various strategies can be used to facilitate this process. We also know that there at least seems to be different types of long term memory and episodic memory seems to be the most fragile of these.

Finally, we also know that the hippocampus appears critical for the formation of new long term episodic memories, with destruction of the hippocampus leading to Anterograde amnesia.

The Search For Engram

The term engram was coined by the little known but influential memory researcher Richard Semon. Karl Lashley (1929) began the modern search for the underlying neurophysiological mechanisms of learning & memory. Lashley sought to provide evidence for the existence of specific, localized, cortical connections, formed during conditioning. In Lashley's experiments (1929, 1950), rats were trained to run a maze. Tissue was removed from their cerebral cortices, before reintroducing them to the maze, to see how their memory was affected. Increasingly, the amount of tissue removed degraded memory, but more remarkably where the tissue was removed from made no difference. Because of this he formulated the equipotentiality hypothesis in which he suggested that all parts of the cortex have equal potential to produce learning. One possible explanation for Lashley's failure to locate the engram is that many types of memory (e-g, visual-spatial, smell etc) are used in the processing of complex tasks, such as rats running mazes.

Richard F. Thompson and his colleagues used a simpler task than Lashley and sought the engram of memory in the cerebellum. They studied the classical conditioning of eyelid response in the rabbits. They presented first, the tone (CS) and than a puff of air (UCS) to the cornea of the rabbit eye. At first, the rabbit blink at the air puff but not to the tone; however after a number of experiences associating it with a tone, the rabbits became conditioned to blink when they heard the tone, even without a puff. The experiment monitored several brain regions, trying to locate the engram.

One region that Thompson's group studied was the lateral interpositus nucleus (LIP). When it was deactivated chemically, the rabbits lost the conditioning; when re-activated, they responded again, demonstrating that the LIP is a key element of the engram for this response.

Pet Scan

A positron emission tomography (PET) scan is an imaging test that uses a radioactive substance called a tracer to look for disease in the body. In other words it is a method for providing images of the brain via sophisticated computer analysis. However PET images detail brain function rather than structure. The role of PET scan is to measures emissions from radioactively labelled metabolically active chemicals that have been injected into the bloodstream. A compound, called radiotracer, is injected into the bloodstream and eventually makes its way to the brain. Sensors in the PET scanner detect the radioactivity as the compound accumulates in various regions of the brain.

The information is relayed to a computer which create multicoloured 2- or 3-dimensional images or reconstructs an image displaying coloured patches, where accumulated radiations is highest (usually coloured red) and lowest (usually coloured blue). Such an image is called a PET scan. The greatest benefit of PET scanning is that different compounds can show blood flow and oxygen and glucose metabolism in the tissues of the working brain. These measurements reflect the amount of brain activity in the various regions of the brain and allow to learn more about how the brain works.

A PET scan can reveal the size, shape, position, and some function of organs. This test can be used to check brain function, diagnose cancer, heart problems, and brain disorders, it also help to find out how far cancer has spread, and can also show areas in which there is poor blood flow to the heart. PET is also useful in the study of brain abnormalities and various psychiatric disorders such as schizophrenia and manic depression which usually found to have altered PET activity, as transient Ischemic attacks, Parkinson's disease, Multiple sclerosis, Epilepsy, Cerebrovascular disorder & Alzheimer's disease.

IMPROVING MEMORY: STRATEGIES

Mnemonics: This word comes from the Greek word for 'memory' and refers to specific memory-improvement techniques. Mnemonic systems are special techniques or strategies consciously used to improve memory, it helps employ information already stored in long-term memory to make memorisation an easier task. Most mnemonics techniques rely on the linking, or association, of to be remembered material with a systematic and organized set of images or words that are already firmly established in long term memory and can therefore serve as reminder cues.

Method of Loci : The word loci means "places". The method of loci uses locations of a familiar place (imagined in memory) as a framework for memory retrieval. The memory pegs in this system are parts of your image of a scene. The scene can be a street, a hospital building, the layout of a college campus, a temple, or just about anything that can be visualized clearly and contains a number of discrete items in specific locations to serve as memory pegs.

Number and Letter Peg Systems: In number system, you form an image with each number. For instance, a rhyming system can be used for the number 1 through 10. Think of words that rhyme with the numbers—1 is a sun, 2 is a moon, 3 is a star, 4 is a universe, and so on. Now when you have a list to remember, you can associate the items on the list with your images of the numbers.

Letter Systems are Similar: You can establish mnemonic pegs by forming strong, distinctive images of words that start with the sounds of the letter to the alphabet. This will give you 26 pegs for association with what you want to remember.

Stories You Tell Yourself: If you have a list of unrelated items to remember, a useful mnemonic device is to relate the items in a made up story. The story starts with the first item on the list, and, in order, each succeeding item is worked in. Doing this gives coherence and meaning to otherwise unrelated items; it is a form of elaborative encoding.

Remembering Names And Faces: First steps in establishing a good memory for names and faces, we should -(1) be sure we hear the name clearly when introduced, (2) repeat the name when acknowledging the introduction, and (3) if the name is unusual, we can ask the new acquaintance to spell it. While we are making sure we have heard and rehearsed the name, we should be paying close attention to the individual's face. The shape and size of the head and individual characteristics of the hair, forehead, eyebrows, eyelashes, eyes, cheekbones, nose, ears, lips, chin and skin, should all be focal points of attention. Voice quality may also be important. Almost everybody we meet will have one or several features that can be elaborated, exaggerated, or perhaps even caricatured as in a cartoon to form a distinctive memory image that can be related to the person's name.

Chunking: A limited amount of information can be held in STM. STM can hold about five to nine chunks of information. Chunks refer to any discrete unit of information. For example, if you read letters DARZISWTELN once it will be possible to remember about seven of them. However if the same letters are regrouped the spell SWITZERLAND it would be easier to remember the entire group of letters. Thus Switzerland is a chunk. The information is now one unit of information.

MULTIPLE CHOICE QUESTIONS

1. What is too painful to remember, we simply choose to forget is related to which theory?
A. Emotion theory
B. The trace decay hypothesis
C. Motivated forgetting
D. None of the above

2. Which of the following types of memory requires the process, Tulving calls "mental time travel"?
A. Semantic B. Episodic
C. Implicit D. Explicit

3. Who among the following gave the concept of motivated forgetting?
A. Ebbinghaus B. Thorndike
C. Freud D. Jung

4. For the formation of new long term memories which brain structure is responsible?
A. Hypothalamus B. Thalamus
C. Hippocampus D. None of the above

5. Which part of the brain plays an important role in transfer of information from STM to LTM:
A. Thalamus
B. Hypothalamus
C. Temporal lobes, Hippocampus
D. Occipital lobe

6. The Atkinson-Shiffrin model of memory includes:
A. Episodic memory, Semantic memory and Implicit memory
B. Sensory memory, Short term memory and Long term memory
C. Attention, Processing and Elaboration
D. None of the above

7. When new learning is interfered by previous learning it is called:
A. Proactive inhibition
B. Retroactive inhibition
C. Repression
D. Suppression

8. When previous learning is interfered by new learning it is called:
A. Proactive inhibition
B. Retroactive inhibition
C. Repression
D. Suppression

9. .... is the sensory store for vision.
A. Echoic memory
B. Short-term memory
C. Iconic memory
D. Sensory memory

10. The concept of "Leaky bucket hypothesis" is related to:
A. Trace theory
B. Interference theory
C. Motivated forgetting
D. Decay theory

11. Which type of memory is a category of long-term memory that involves the recollection of specific events, situations and experiences?
A. Episodic memory
B. Semantic memory
C. Long term memory
D. None of the above

12. Which law suggests that there is a relationship between performance and arousal?
A. Pavlow of Conditioning
B. Thorndike Law of effect
C. Gestalt Law of Perception
D. Yerkes Dodson Law

13. The capacity for short term memory is:
A. 6 chunks of information
B. 5 + or – 2 chunks of information
C. 8 chunks of information
D. 7 + or – 2 chunks of information

14. .... involves failure to recall a word of which one has knowledge.
A. Tip of tongue phenomenon (TOT)
B. Forgetting
C. Proactive interference
D. None of the above

15. The general abstract knowledge about the world is called:
A. Sensory memory
B. Semantic memory
C. Episodic memory
D. Long term memory

16. Which memory system is called the storehouse of consciousness?
A. Long term memory
B. Short term memory
C. Sensory memory
D. Episodic memory

17. A person who found difficulty in creating new memories has:
A. Hallucination
B. Anterograde amnesia
C. Retrograde amnesia
D. None of the above

18. Memory is better when encoding happens at which level of processing?
A. Deepest level
B. Shallow level
C. Intermediate level
D. Elaboration level

19. The retroactive interference theory was given by:
A. Watson B. Muller and Pilzekar
C. Ebbinghaus D. Thorndike

20. Damage to thalamus and hypothalamus structure of brain plays a role in amnesia is observed in:
A. Alzheimer's disease
B. Depression
C. Korsakoff's syndrome
D. None of the above

21. What type of information is stored in the phonological loop?
A. Visual B. Spatial
C. Auditory D. Speech based

22. .... are means by which memory traces are stored as biophysical or biochemical changes in the brain (and other neural tissue) in response to external stimuli.
A. Engram
B. Axon
C. Phoneme
D. None of the above

23. Which of the following is not a type of long term memory?
A. Semantic memory
B. Episodic memory
C. Acoustic memory
D. Procedural memory

24. TOT phenomenon indicates that information is :
A. Organized in long term memory
B. Organized in short term memory
C. Organized in semantic memory
D. Organized in episodic memory

25. Techniques that are used to improve memory is known as:
A. Confabulation technique
B. Consolidation technique
C. Mnemonic devices
D. All of the above

26. What is the correct name for memories about categories, objects, concepts and meanings?
A. Semantic memory
B. Episodic memory
C. Flashbulb memory
D. Long-term memory

27. Match List-I with List-II and indicate your answer with the help of given codes.

List-I (Task)	List-II (Type of memory)
(*a*) Free recall and recognition	1. semantic memory
(*b*) Sentence verification task	2. sensory memory
(*c*) Priming	3. episodic memory
(*d*) Scanning task	4. implicit memory

Codes:

	(*a*)	(*b*)	(*c*)	(*d*)
A.	4	2	1	3
B.	2	1	3	4
C.	1	4	2	3
D.	3	1	4	2

28. Consolidation of memory is influenced by:
A. Hormones
B. Retroactive interference
C. Electro-convulsive therapy
D. All of the above

29. Which of the following strategies do not help improve memory?
A. Use of Mnemonics
B. Minimize interference
C. Mass learning
D. Elaborative rehearsal

30. Memories outside of conscious awareness are called:
A. Episodic memories
B. Semantic memories
C. Explicit memories
D. Implicit memories

31. Memory can be distorted by being influenced by the individual's expectations rather than what has actually happened. This is termed as:
A. Mood dependent memory
B. Mood congruence effect
C. Flash bulb memory
D. Confirmation bias

32. Reconstructive memory is stored as a series of discrete elements associated with which of the following elements of the experience?
A. Context B. Emotional state
C. Sensory D. All of the above

33. Which of the following is not a cause of forgetting?
A. Interference
B. Decay
C. Selective attention
D. Retrieval inhibition

34. Research indicates that having eyewitnesses rehearse their answers to questions before taking the witness stands:
A. increases uncertainty in the minds of eyewitnesses as to what they actually saw.
B. increases their confidence about what they saw, even if they were wrong.
C. increases their confidence but also raises their anxiety about appearing in court.
D. increases chances of giving a much more detailed and accurate account of what they saw.

35. Match List-I with List-II and indicate your answer using the codes given below:

List-I (Psychologists)	**List-II (Memory Concepts)**
(*a*) George Miller	1. Three memory system
(*b*) Atkinson and Shiffrin	2. Working memory
(*c*) Bartlett	3. Magical number > ± 2
(*d*) Alan Badley	4. Constructive memory

Codes:

	(*a*)	(*b*)	(*c*)	(*d*)
A.	1	2	3	4
B.	2	3	1	4
C.	4	2	1	3
D.	3	1	4	2

36. The memory process includes five steps:
A. intention, attention, association, application, retention.
B. intention, attention, association, retention, recall.
C. attention, association, application, repetition, retention.
D. attention, association, application, retention, recall.

37. Atkinson and Shiffrin proposed the so-called .... model of memory in 1968, which assumed multiple memory structures.
A. Modular
B. Modal
C. Level of processing
D. Encoding-specificity

38. The structure most greatly implicated in Long-term potentiation (LTP) is the:
A. Hypothalamus B. Hippocampus
C. Amygdala D. None of the above

39. Explicit or Declarative memory consist of which of the following types of memories?
1. Procedural memory
2. Episodic memory
3. Semantic memory
4. Autobiographical memory

Codes:
A. 1 and 2
B. 2 and 4
C. 2, 3 and 4
D. 1, 2 and 4

40. Research has shown that people who serve as eyewitnesses to a crime
A. have a vivid memory for trivial details.
B. remember the event perfectly.
C. do not necessarily have a good memory for trivial details.
D. have had their memories refreshed through hypnosis.

41. Match List-I with List-II and indicate your answer with the help of the given codes:

List-I (Type of Memory)	List-II (Type of Information)
(*a*) echoic memory	1. episodic information
(*b*) iconic memory	2. auditory information
(*c*) auto biographical memory	3. visual information
(*d*) implicit memory	4. priming

Codes:

	(*a*)	(*b*)	(*c*)	(*d*)
A.	4	1	3	2
B.	2	3	1	4
C.	3	4	2	1
D.	4	2	1	3

42. Research suggests that eyewitnesses who correctly remember trivial details surrounding a crime
A. also have a better memory for the culprit's face
B. have a poorer memory for the culprit's face
C. are less susceptible to misleading questions
D. are more susceptible to misleading questions

43. The process Tulving calls "mental time travel" is required for which of the following types of memory?
A. Flashbulb
B. Semantic
C. Episodic
D. Implicit

44. Which of the following is not a stage in the information-processing model of memory?
A. short-term memory
B. long-term memory
C. episodic memory
D. sensory register

45. Match List-I with List-II and indicate your answer with the help of given codes:

List-I	List-II
(*a*) Converting information from temporary to more permanent memory and spatial memory	1. Temporal lobes
(*b*) Working memory	2. Hippocampus
(*c*) Semantic memory	3. Neurofibrillary tangles
(*d*) Alzheimer's disease	4. Frontal lobes

Codes:

	(*a*)	(*b*)	(*c*)	(*d*)
A.	2	4	1	3
B.	1	2	3	4
C.	4	3	2	1
D.	3	1	4	2

46. Which researchers' findings suggested that confident witnesses are not much better in general than non-confident ones in their identifications?
A. Sporer (1993)
B. Cutler and Penrod (1989)
C. Bartlet (1932)
D. Tulving and Pearlstone (1966)

47. Which of the following are not the function of working memory?

1. Storing declarative memories
2. Executive functions
3. Sensory register
4. Constructive processes
5. Chunking

Codes:

A. 2, 4 and 5 B. 1 and 3
C. 2 and 5 D. 1, 3 and 4

48. Craik and Tulving's (1975) levels-of-processing hypothesis holds that those items receiving the deepest level of processing are more easily recognized later. According to this model which one among these options represents the deepest level of processing?

A. Semantic B. Phonological
C. Acoustic D. Physical abilities

49. Read each of the following two statements—Assertion (A) and Reason (R) and indicate your answer using the codes given below:

Assertion (A): Information reaching the meaning level of processing and elaboration has the best chance of being retained.

Reason (R): According to information processing theories of memory, information is transferred from stage to stage until some of it is finally lodged in long-term memory.

Codes:

A. Both (A) and (R) are true and (R) is correct explanation of (A).
B. Both (A) and (R) are true, but (R) is not the correct explanation of (A).
C. (A) is true, but (R) is false.
D. (A) is false, but (R) is true.

50. Which of the following tasks is not an example of implicit memory?

A. Free recall B. Walking
C. Swimming D. Riding a bike

ANSWERS

1	2	3	4	5	6	7	8	9	10
C	B	C	C	C	B	A	B	C	A
11	**12**	**13**	**14**	**15**	**16**	**17**	**18**	**19**	**20**
A	D	D	A	B	A	B	B	B	C
21	**22**	**23**	**24**	**25**	**26**	**27**	**28**	**29**	**30**
D	A	C	B	C	A	D	D	C	D
31	**32**	**33**	**34**	**35**	**36**	**37**	**38**	**39**	**40**
D	D	C	B	D	B	B	B	C	C
41	**42**	**43**	**44**	**45**	**46**	**47**	**48**	**49**	**50**
B	B	C	C	A	B	D	A	B	A

❑❑❑

CHAPTER 4

Cognitive Strategies, Convergent & Divergent Thinking and Decision Making

COGNITIVE STRATEGIES: ALGORITHMS AND HEURISTICS

An algorithm is a procedure or formula for solving a problem. Some problems can be successfully solved by following specific, step-by-step instructions, that is, by using an algorithm. If the instructions are followed correctly, there is a guarantee that you will arrive at a correct solution. In mathematics and computer science, an algorithm usually means a small procedure that solves a recurrent problem. In psychology, algorithms are frequently contrasted with heuristics, which is a technique designed for solving a problem more quickly that may or may not yield a successful outcome. Heuristics are "rules of thumb", educated guesses, intuitive judgements or simply common sense. A heuristic is a general way of solving problems. Algorithms can be expressed in many kinds of notation, including natural languages, pseudocode, flowcharts, drakon-charts, programming languages or control tables (processed by interpreters).

In problem solving, heuristics play a major role in the solution process. According to the handbook for Teachers 'A problem is "a situation, quantitative or otherwise, that confronts an individual or group of individuals, that requires resolution, and for which the individual sees no apparent or obvious means or path to obtaining a solution". Heuristics exist because more often than not, they aid in finding an easy path to the answer in complex problems (Renkl, Hilbert, & Schworm, 2008). However, there are instances when heuristics can be misleading and may even hinder solution (Öllinger, Jones, & Knöblich, 2006).

The definition of a problem, implies that one must have some knowledge of the problem to solve it. So the first two steps of the heuristic imply that one needs a great deal of knowledge about the problem to be an effective problem solver. Secondly, problem solving, also implies a connection between thinking and knowledge. It says that problem solving is essentially applying old knowledge to a new situation (Krulik & Rudnick, 1987). However, if knowledge or a problem is genuinely new, then the old knowledge would not apply to it in any way. The third and fourth elements are algorithms and heuristics. Krulik and Rudnick (1980) distinguish between algorithms and heuristics. Unlike employing an algorithm, using a heuristic requires the problem solver to think on the highest level and fully understand the problem. Krulik and Rudnick also prefer heuristics to algorithms because the latter only applies to specific situations, whereas a heuristic applies to many as yet undiscovered problems. However, an algorithm requires more than mere memorization; it requires deep thinking too.

First, in order to apply an algorithm, the student must have sufficient information about the problem to know which algorithm to apply. This would only be possible if the student possessed a conceptual understanding of the subject matter. Further, even if a student could somehow memorize when to apply certain algorithms, it does not follow that he or she would also be able to memorize how to apply it (Hu, 2006; Hundhausen & Brown, 2008; Johanning, 2006; Rusch, 2005).

Second, algorithms and problem solving are related to one another. Algorithms are the product of successful problem solving and to be a successful problem solver one often must have knowledge of algorithms (Hu, 2006; Hundhausen & Brown, 2008; Johanning, 2006; Rusch, 2005).

CONVERGENT AND DIVERGENT THINKING

Convergent and Divergent thinking skills are both important aspects of intelligence, problem solving and critical thinking.

According to Guilford (1950, 1967), the main ingredients of creativity are divergent and convergent thinking, even though we do not claim that these are the only processes involved in creative acts. Divergent thinking is taken to represent a style of thinking that allows many new ideas being generated, in a context where more than one solution is correct. The probably best example is a brainstorming session, which has the aim of generating as many ideas on a particular issue as possible. In contrast, convergent thinking is considered a process of generating one possible solution to a particular problem. It emphasizes speed and relies on high accuracy and logic.

The deductive logic that the fictional character Sherlock Homes is used a good convergent thinking example. Gathering various titbits of facts and data he was able to put the pieces of a puzzle together and come up with a logical answer to the question: Who did it? Einstein on the other hand was a strong divergent thinker. He asked simple questions and then did mental exercises to solve problems.

Convergent thinking would seem to benefit from a strong degree of goal-directedness that is steering and efficiently constraining the search for the right concept or idea. However, efficient divergent thinking would seem to require jumping from one option to another, which suggests that the mutual inhibition between alternative thoughts should be weak.

It has been found through researches that the convergent-and divergent-thinking components of human creativity imply two different, to at least some degree opposite cognitive-control states that facilitate or even generate the respective thinking style. In particular, convergent thinking seems to require either strong top-down control or strong local competition, or both, whereas divergent thinking seems to call for weak top-down control and/or weak local competition.

Standard IQ tests gauge convergent thinking. Pattern recognition, testing knowledge, logic thought flow and the ability to solve problems can all be tested and graded. However, there are no accurate tests able to measure divergent thinking skills.

Divergent and Convergent thinking skills are both important to critical thinking. Not only that, they are interrelated. Deductive reasoning looks inward to find a solution, while divergent reasoning looks outward for a solution.

Techniques to stimulate divergent thinking:

1. **Brainstorming:** Is a technique which involves generating a list of ideas in a creative, unstructured manner. The goal of 'brainstorming' is to generate as many ideas as possible in a short period of time. The key tool in brainstorming is "piggybacking" or using one idea to stimulate other ideas.
2. **Keeping a Journal:** Journals are an effective way to record ideas that one thinks of spontaneously. By keeping a journal, one can capture these ideas and use them later when developing and organizing materials in the pre writing stage.
3. **Free writing:** While free writing, a person focuses on one particular topic and write non-stop about it for a short period of time. This can help generate a variety of thoughts about a topic which can later be restructured or organized following some pattern of arrangement.
4. **Mind or Subject Mapping:** Mind or subject mapping involves putting brainstormed ideas in the form of a visual map or picture that shows the relationships among these ideas.

DECISION-MAKING; IMPEDIMENTS TO PROBLEM-SOLVING

Decision-making is part of problem solving, and decision-making occurs at every step of the problem-solving process. Problem solving is a set of activities designed to analyze a situation systematically and generate, implement, and evaluate solutions. On the other hand-Decision making is a mechanism for making choices at each step of the problem-solving process.

The Decision-Making Process

Step 1. Identify the Problem

Problem identification is undoubtedly the most important and the most difficult step in the process. All subsequent steps will be based on how you define and assess the problem at hand. In carrying out Step 1, you must distinguish between a problem and its solution.

Step 2. Explore Alternatives

The second step in the decision-making process is to explore alternative solutions to the problem identified in Step 1. This step really consists of two parts: Generating alternatives and Evaluating alternatives.

There are three ways to generate alternatives. These are Brainstorming, Surveys and Discussion groups.

Step 3. Select an Alternative

The third step in the problem-solving model is to select one of the alternatives explored in Step 2 for implementation. After you have evaluated each alternative, one should stand out as coming closest to solving the problem with the most advantages and fewest disadvantages.

When selecting an alternative, you will encounter factors that affect your decision-making. These factors may include: Political factors, Safety factors, Financial factors, Environmental considerations, Ethical factors.

Step 4. Implement the Solution

The fourth step involves five subparts:

(*i*) Develop an action plan.

(*ii*) Determine objectives.

(*iii*) Identify needed resources

(*iv*) Build a plan

(*v*) Implement the plan

CREATIVE THINKING AND PROBLEM SOLVING

Creativity is

An Ability: A simple definition is that creativity is the ability to imagine or invent something new.

An Attitude: Creativity is also an attitude, the ability to accept change and newness, a willingness to play with ideas and possibilities, a flexibility of outlook, the habit of enjoying the good, while looking for ways to improve it.

A Process: Creative people work hard and continually, to improve ideas and solutions, by making gradual alterations and refinements to their works.

Creative Methods

1. **Evolution:** This is the method of incremental improvement. This method of creativity also reminds us of that critical principle: Every problem that has been solved can be solved again in a better way.
2. **Synthesis:** With this, two or more existing ideas are combined into a third new idea.
3. **Revolution:** Sometimes the best new idea is a completely different one, and marked change from the previous ones.
4. **Reapplication:** Look at something old in a new way.
5. **Changing Direction:** Many creative break through occurs when attention is shifted from one angle of a problem to another. This is sometimes called creative insight.

Myths about creative thinking and problem solving

1. **Every problem has only one solution (or one right answer):** The goal of problem solving is to speak the problem, and most problems can be solved in any number of ways.
2. **The best answer/solution/method has already been found:** Look at the history of any solution set and you will see that improvements, new solutions, new right answers, are always being found.
3. **Creative answer are complex technologically:** Only a few problems require complex technological solutions. Most problems meet with requires only a thoughtful solution requiring personal action and perhaps a few simple tools. Even many problems that seems to require a technological solution can be addressed in other ways.

Mental blocks to creative thinking and problem solving

1. Prejudice
2. Functional fixation
3. Learned Helplessness
4. Psychological blocks
5. Premature Judgments
6. Habit Transfer
7. Lack of Disciplined Effort
8. Poor Language Skills

Positive attitude for creativity

1. Curiosity
2. Challenge
3. Constructive discontent
4. A belief that most problems can be solved
5. The ability to suspend judgement and criticism
6. Seeing the good in bad
7. Problems lead to improvements
8. A problem can also be a solution
9. Problems are interesting and emotionally acceptable

Miscellaneous good attitudes

1. Perseverance: Most people fail because they spend only 9 minutes on a problem that requires 10 minutes to solve. Creativity and problem solving are hard work and require fierce application of time and energy.
2. A flexible imagination: Creative people are comfortable with imagination and with thinking so called weird, wild or unthinkable thoughts, just for the sake of stimulation.
3. A belief that mistakes are welcome: Failure is an opportunity; mistakes show that something is being done. So creative people have come to realize and accept emotionally that making mistakes is no negative biggie.

Characteristics of the Creative Person

1. Creative individuals have a great deal of physical energy, but they are often quiet and at rest.
2. Creative individuals tend to be smart, yet also naïve at the same time.
3. A third trait is the combination of playfulness and discipline, or responsibility and irresponsibility.
4. Creative individuals alternate between imagination and fantasy at one end, and a rooted sense of reality at the other.
5. Creative individuals seem to harbour opposite tendencies on the continuum between extroversion and introversion.
6. Creative individuals are also remarkably humble and proud at the same time.
7. Creative individuals to a certain extent escape the rigid gender role stereotyping.
8. Creative individuals are generally thought to be rebellious and independent.
9. Most creative persons are very passionate about their work, yet they can be extremely objective about it as well.
10. Lastly, the openness and sensitivity of creative individuals often expose them to sufferings and pain yet also a great deal of enjoyment.

LANGUAGE AND THOUGHT

The connection between language and thought is profound. The majority of our everyday life involves the use of language. We tell our ideas to others with language. We "read" their responses and understand their meanings with language, and often, we "speak" internally to ourselves, when we process this information and make logical conclusions. It seems that rational thinking unavoidably involves certain degree of the use of language.

During the early and mid-20th century, however, several linguistic anthropologists, most notably Benjamin Whorf and Eric Sapir, proposed that language is not merely an interface but also plays a formative role in shaping thought itself. At its strongest, this view is that language "becomes" thought or becomes isomorphic to it.

Some theorists take a more extreme view of the role of language in thinking; they claim that language can actually determine the thoughts we are capable of having. But this linguistic relativity hypothesis, as it is called, has been under increasing attack in recent years.

Because so much thinking involves language, the idea rose in psychology that thinking was actually a kind of inner speech, a kind of "talking to yourself under your breath". According to this idea, people make small movements of the vocal apparatus when they think and carry on their thinking by talking to themselves. Number of experiments has indicated that movements of the vocal apparatus may indeed accompany thoughts, but other experiments have made it clear that such movements are not necessary for thinking.

The discussion so far has been about the use of vocal speech symbols, or verbal language in thinking. Can other language systems be used as tools of thoughts? Studies of the deaf provide an approach to this question. Deaf children with little verbal language ability score in the normal range on standardized tests of cognitive performance (Vernon, 1967), and their cognitive and thinking abilities develop relatively normally. Such findings have been interpreted as indicating that language plays little or no role in the thinking or cognitive development of the deaf. But many of the deaf are taught sign language and even if they are not explicitly taught such a language it has been found that deaf children will develop their own (Goldin-Meadow & Feldman,1977). This may indicate that there is an innate human program for language, be it verbal or gestural.

Evidences in psycholinguistics have shown that thought can exist without the presence of language. What this mean is that language cannot be equated to thought. In addition, language is neural to the thought which it conveys; it is merely a medium for transporting thought from one person to another, or as a tool for organizing and manipulating our rational thought. Language merely assists thoughts, just like a computer does to its user, and it can hardly be argued that they are interdependent, This is not to say thought is entirely independent of language, but its dependence seems trivial when we take other social and cultural factors into consideration.

MULTIPLE CHOICE QUESTIONS

1. .... is a mental process that involves discovering, analyzing and solving problems.
A. Reasoning
B. Experience
C. Problem solving
D. None of the above

2. The essence of decision making is:
A. Choosing between alternatives
B. Finding the course of action to be taken
C. Observation
D. Facing a great deal of problems

3. According to which psychologist 'thinking is largely sub-vocal talking'.
A. Pavlov B. Thorndike
C. Watson D. Hull

4. Motivation gives problem solving a:
A. Mental set B. Scope
C. Direction D. Thinking

5. .... is the term used to describe the way information is processes and manipulated in remembering, thinking and knowing:
A. Cognition B. Mental set
C. Problem solving D. Decision making

6. Arriving at many possible solutions to a problem is called?
A. Heuristic
B. Divergent thinking
C. Convergent thinking
D. None of the above

7. The rules or guidelines that suggest a solution to a problem, but do not guarantee a solution is called:
A. Heuristic
B. Algorithm
C. Divergent thinking
D. Sub goaling

8. ____________ is what you engage in when you answer a multiple choice question?
A. Heuristic
B. Sub goaling
C. Divergent thinking
D. Convergent thinking

9. .... involves the analysis of a finite set of alternatives described in terms of evaluative criteria.
A. Problem solving
B. Concept formation
C. Deductive reasoning
D. Decision making

10. .... is a type of fixation in which an individual tries to solve a problem in a particular way that has worked in the past.
A. A mental set
B. Functional fixedness
C. Inductive reasoning
D. Confirmation bias

11. In which cognitive process technique, the participants are asked to talk aloud while making a decision or solving a problem?
A. Creative thinking
B. Problem solving
C. Verbal protocol analysis
D. All of the above

12. Some people prefer avoiding unnecessary risks while taking decisions, they are called:
A. Risk averse
B. Risk prone
C. Convergent thinker
D. Divergent thinker

13. While taking decision some people prefer taking risk they are called:
A. Risk averse
B. Risk prone
C. Convergent thinker
D. Divergent thinker

14. Moving from specific observations to broader generalizations and theories is called?
A. Inductive reasoning
B. Deductive reasoning
C. Problem solving
D. Decision making

15. After an event people often believe that they knew the outcome of the event before it actually happened is often termed as:
A. Mental set
B. Decision making
C. Hind sight bias
D. None of the above

16. .... is a language's sound system and .... includes the rules for word formation in a language.
A. Morphology, Semantics
B. Phonology, Morphology
C. Semantics, Phonology
D. None of the above

17. Rules that are used to describe how the phrases and the words should be used in a language so that they can make a grammatically acceptable sentence.
A. Semantics
A. Syntax
C. Phonemes
D. Morphemes

18. .... is the study of the meaning of linguistic expressions.
A. Semantics
B. Syntax
C. Phonology
D. Morphology

19. .... is understood as the ability of a computer or other machine to perform those activities that are normally thought to require intelligence.
A. Sub goaling
B. Algorithms
C. Heuristics
D. Artificial intelligence

20. In which stage of creative thinking, ideas come together to form a possible solution?
A. Incubation
B. Preparedness
C. Illumination
D. None of the above

21. The tendency to become trapped in bad decisions, even when losses associated with them increases are known as:
A. Algorithm
B. Incubation
C. Escalation of commitment
D. Heuristic

22. Whom among the following is known for his nativist theory of language development?
A. B.F. Skinner B. Pavlov
C. Hull D. Naom Chomsky

23. During which stage most of the creative thinking occurs?
A. Incubation B. Illumination
C. Preparation D. Evaluation

24. The concept of "Larngeal Habits" is related to:
A. Memory
B. Thinking
C. Decision-making
D. Problem solving

25. .... is a group or individual creativity technique by which efforts are made to find a conclusion for a specific problem by gathering a list of ideas spontaneously contributed by its members.
A. Brainstorming
B. Free writing
C. Mind or Subject mapping
D. Problem solving

26. What does reduce the problem distance between starting point and the goal?
A. Normative-utilitarian
B. Means-end analysis
C. Normative-logical
D. Heuristic short cuts

27. Which of the following strategies facilitate problem solving?
1. Algorithms
2. Mental set
3. Planning fallacy
4. Heuristics
5. Analogy

Codes:
A. 1, 2 and 4 B. 2, 3 and 4
C. 1 and 5 D. 1, 4 and 5

28. Which among these is not a mental block to creative thinking and problem solving?
A. Prejudice
B. Learned helplessness
C. Functional fixation
D. Curiosity

29. The final decisions reached by groups can often be predicted quite accurately by relatively simple rules. What these rules are known as?
A. Thumb rules
B. Logistic rules
C. Cognitive decision schemas
D. Social decision schemas

30. The two most basic units of speech are
A. Words and rules of grammar
B. Ideas and concepts
C. Morphemes and phonemes
D. Connotative and denotative meaning

31. Awareness of one's own thought processes enabling effective learning through correction is called:
A. Algorithm
B. Analogies
C. Meta cognition
D. Constructive process

32. Building on J.P. Guilford's work and created by Ellis Paul Torrance, the Torrance Tests of Creative Thinking (TTCT), a test of creativity, originally involved simple tests of divergent thinking and other problem-solving skills, which were scored on four scales. Choose the correct names of scale:
A. Fluency, Flexibility, Originality, Elaboration
B. Originality, Practicality, Novelty, Elaboration
C. Elaboration, Flexibility, Practicality, Novelty
D. Practicality, Fluency, Flexibility, Emotionality

33. Match List-I with List-II and use the following code for your answer:

List-I	List-II
(*a*) Meaning of words	1. Morpheme
(*b*) Rules that govern the order of words	2. Phoneme
(*c*) Smallest unit of sound	3. Semantics
(*d*) Smallest unit of meaning	4. Syntax

Codes:

	(*a*)	(*b*)	(*c*)	(*d*)
A.	4	3	2	1
B.	1	2	3	4
C.	1	3	4	2
D.	4	2	3	1

34. The rules for ordering words in sentences are called

A. Grammar B. Syllables
C. Syntax D. Semantics

35. Arrange different types of 'Play' in an increasing order of cognitive complexity:

1. Constructive
2. Dramatic
3. Functional
4. Games

Codes:

A. 2 1 3 4 B. 2 3 1 4
C. 1 2 3 4 D. 1 3 2 4

36. In which type of thinking an individual freely considers a variety of potential solutions to artistic, literary, scientific, or practical problems?

A. Convergent thinking
B. Divergent thinking
C. Creative thinking
D. Autistic thinking

37. **Convergent thinking** is a term coined by:

A. Raymond Cattell
B. Joy Paul Guilford
C. Arthur Jensen
D. Ellis Paul Torrance

38. Match List-I with List-II and indicate your answer with the help of given codes:

List-I (Route)	List-II (Processing)
(*a*) Central route to persuasion	1. heuristic processing
(*b*) Peripheral route to persuasion	2. elaboration-likelihood processing
(*c*) Distinct routes to persuasion	3. cognitive dissonance
(*d*) Attitude-behaviour discrepancies	4. systematic processing

Codes:

	(*a*)	(*b*)	(*c*)	(*d*)
A.	4	1	2	3
B.	3	2	4	1
C.	1	2	4	3
D.	2	4	3	1

39. The process of working together spontaneously to generate new ideas is called:

A. Means-end analysis
B. Trial and error
C. Brainstorming
D. All of the above

40. Read each of the following two statements—Assertion (A) and Reason (R) and indicate your answer using the codes given below:

Assertion (A): Researchers have shown that language may play an important role in shaping important aspects of cognition.

Reason (R): 'Linguistic Relativity' hypothesis suggests that language shapes or determines our thoughts and the way we think.

Codes:

A. Both (A) and (R) are true and (R) is correct explanation of (A).
B. Both (A) and (R) are true, but (R) is not the correct explanation of (A).
C. (A) is true, but (R) is false.
D. (A) is false, but (R) is true.

41. Understanding about one's own use of language systematically is referred as:
A. Metalinguistic awareness
B. Pragmatics
C. Pronunciation
D. Syntax

42. What is intuitive decision making based on?
A. Instinct
B. Gambling
C. Reasoning
D. Logic

43. I imagine becoming a renowned dancer some day. I am engaging in:
A. Divergent Thinking
B. Prospective Thinking
C. Creative Thinking
D. Autistic Thinking

44. Match List-I with List-II and indicate your answer with the help of codes given below:

List-I (Author)	List-II (Statement)
(*a*) Carol Gilliyan	1. Decisions are based on morality of carrying and a concern with justice.
(*b*) Kohlberg	2. Decisions of females are preferably based on care orientation.
(*c*) Skoe	3. Decisions are based on commitment to specific individuals and relationship.
(*d*) Walker	4. Decisions are based on universal principles of justice and fairness.

Codes:

	(*a*)	(*b*)	(*c*)	(*d*)
A.	3	4	2	1
B.	2	3	4	1
C.	3	1	2	4
D.	2	3	1	4

45. The four useful decision-making and problem-solving techniques are:
A. Case-based reasoning, nominal group technique, brainstorming, and reflective thinking.
B. Reflective thinking, flexibility, elaboration technique, means-end analysis.
C. Reasoning, questioning, flexibility, brainstorming.
D. Brain storming, case-based reasoning, questioning, elaboration technique.

46. Match List-I with List-II and indicate your answer with the help of the given codes:

List-I (Styles)	List-II (Descriptions)
(*a*) Impulsive cognitive style	1. Responding slowly, carefully and accurately
(*b*) Reflective cognitive style	2. Memorizing but not understanding the learning material
(*c*) Deep processing learning style	3. Responding quickly but often inaccurately
(*d*) Surface processing learning style	4. Understanding the underlying concepts and meaning of learning material

Codes:

	(*a*)	(*b*)	(*c*)	(*d*)
A.	1	2	3	4
B.	3	1	4	2
C.	2	4	1	3
D.	4	3	2	1

47. What is not an assumption underpinning the rational decision making model?
A. High level of certainty regarding the environment
B. Incomplete information
C. Goal setting
D. A structured problem

48. Match List-I with List-II and indicate your answer with the help of codes given below:

List-I (Type of Bias)	List-II (Decision)
(*a*) Anchoring	1. Making estimates from an initial value

(*b*) Hind sight	2. Adjusting past events by current knowledge
(*c*) Framing	3. Phrasing of situation guides biased decision
(*d*) Representativeness	4. Most stereo typical exemplars are selected

Codes:

	(*a*)	(*b*)	(*c*)	(*d*)
A.	2	1	4	3
B.	1	3	2	4
C.	2	3	4	1
D.	1	2	3	4

49. A problem-solving rule or procedure that, when followed step by step, assures that a correct solution will be found is known as:

A. Heuristic

B. Algorithm

C. Sub-goaling

D. Trial and error

50. Ideas interfering with the correct solution of a problem fade during this stage of creative thinking. This stage is:

A. Evaluation

B. Revision

C. Illumination

D. Incubation

ANSWERS

1	2	3	4	5	6	7	8	9	10
C	A	C	C	A	B	A	D	D	A
11	**12**	**13**	**14**	**15**	**16**	**17**	**18**	**19**	**20**
C	A	B	A	C	B	B	A	D	C
21	**22**	**23**	**24**	**25**	**26**	**27**	**28**	**29**	**30**
C	D	A	B	A	B	D	D	D	C
31	**32**	**33**	**34**	**35**	**36**	**37**	**38**	**39**	**40**
C	A	A	C	B	B	B	A	C	B
41	**42**	**43**	**44**	**45**	**46**	**47**	**48**	**49**	**50**
A	A	D	A	A	B	B	D	B	D

❑❑❑

CHAPTER 5

Intelligence & Creativity

THEORIES OF INTELLIGENCE

Raymond Cattell

In psychology, fluid and crystallized intelligence (abbreviated-Gf and Gc, respectively) are factors of general intelligence (g) originally identified by Raymond Cattell. Cattell's doctoral student John Horn was also actively involved in refining and empirically testing Gf-Gc theory and in recognition of his efforts the theory is now referred to as the Cattell-Horn theory of intelligence.

Fluid v/s Crystallized

According to the theory, fluid intelligence represents novel or abstract problem solving capability and is believed to have a physiological basis. According to Cattell (1987), the label reflects the construct's fluid quality of being directable to almost any problem. Gf is typically assessed with items of a nonverbal or graphical format using tests such as Raven's Progressive Matrices. However, verbal items (such as analogies) can also be used to assess Gf if the word pairs contain simple words that are familiar to the population of test takers (Cattell, 1987; Jensen, 1998). Fluid intelligence includes such abilities as problem solving, learning & pattern recognition. Evidence is consistent with the view that Gf is more affected by brain injury.

Crystallized intelligence is associated with learned or acculturated knowledge. That is, Gc is a result of learning and knowledge acquired over one's lifetime. According to Gf-Gc theory, fluid intelligence causes crystallized intelligence. More specifically, Cattell's (1971, 1987) Investment Theory proposes that individuals have a fixed amount of Gf which they can choose to invest in, or apply to, learning in specific crystallized skills or domains. Researchers have found that criminals have disproportionately low levels of crystallized intelligence. Gc is typically measured with verbal items, particularly those assessing vocabulary. Vocabulary tests and the verbal subscales of WAIS are considered good measuring of Gc.

According to Carroll (1993), Gf and Gc are in fact correlated. Also some other researchers have linked the theory of fluid and crystallized intelligence to Piaget's conception operative intelligence and learning. Fluid ability and Piaget's operative intelligence both concern logical thinking and the education of relations. Crystallized ability and Piaget's treatment of everyday learning reflect the impress of experience. Like fluid ability's relation to crystallized intelligence, Piaget's operativity is considered to be prior to, and ultimately provides the foundation for everyday learning.

Fluid intelligence peaks in young adulthood and then steadily declines. The reason behind this decline is related to the local atrophy of the brain in the right cerebellum. Other researchers have suggested that a lack of practice, along with the age related changes in the brain may also contribute to the decline. However Crystallized intelligence increases gradually and stays relatively stable across most of adulthood, and then begins to decline after the age of 65.

Arthur Jensen

Arthur Jensen has systematically researched and extended Charles Spearman's (1927) seminal concept of g, the general factor of intelligence.

The g Factor does not draw back from its most controversial conclusions-that the average differences in IQ found between Blacks and Whites has a substantial hereditary component, and that this difference has important societal consequences. Among biological variables, g loads on heritability coefficients determined from twin studies and inbreeding depression scores calculated in children born from cousin marriages. g is also related to brain size measured by Magnetic Resonance Imaging (MRI), brain evoked potentials, and intracellular brain pH levels. It (g) is a product of human evolution and is also found in nonhuman animals.

The Bell Curve affair in the g Factor's coverage of race fully documents that, on average, the American Black population scores below the White population by about 1.2 standard deviations, equivalent to 18 IQ points. (This magnitude of difference gives a median overlap of less than 15%, meaning that less than 15% of the Black population exceeds the White average of 50%).

The difference between Blacks and Whites in average IQ scores has scarcely changed over the past 80 years (despite some claims that the gap is narrowing) and can be observed as early as three years of age.

Jensen believes only an empirical measure can establish the presence of intelligence scientifically. That measure must be a reliable index of the general factor "g," common to all mental tests. Mental activities that draw heavily upon this general factor, that is, those "heavily loaded with g," are those involving abstract reasoning and problem solving. And the more heavily a test summons forth these kinds of mental activities, the more reliable an index the test is of intelligence. Since IQ tests rely on these kinds of mental activities so demandingly, they are reliable indicators of intelligence. Therefore, intelligence is not an entity but a construct- something which is intended to explain the observed phenomenon, that there is a common denominator or "positive inter-correlation" among all mental tests regardless of their apparently great variety." Jensen conceives intelligence to be a kind of calculative mechanism, a problem-solving apparatus completely open to whatever problems are presented, free of prejudgments, totally objective.

Robert J. Sternberg

Sternberg's definition of human intelligence is "a mental activity directed toward purposive adaptation to, selection and shaping of, real world environments relevant to one's life", which means that intelligence is how well an individual deals with environmental changes throughout their lifespan.

According to the proposed theory of human intelligence and its development (Sternberg, 1980b, 1984, 1985, 1990, 1997, 1999a, 2003b, 2004), a common set of processes underlies all aspects of intelligence. These processes are hypothesized to be universal. For example, although the solutions to problems that are considered intelligent in one culture may be different from the solutions considered to be intelligent in another culture, the need to define problems and translate strategies to solve these problems exists in any culture.

Metacomponents, or executive processes, plan what to do, monitor things as they are being done, and evaluate things after they are done. Performance components execute the instructions of the metacomponents. Whereas Knowledge-acquisition components are used to learn how to solve problems or simply to acquire declarative knowledge in the first place (Sternberg, 1985). Selective encoding is used to decide what information is relevant in the context of one's learning.

Although the same processes are used for all three aspects of intelligence universally, these processes are applied to different kinds of tasks and situations depending on whether a given problem requires analytical thinking, creative thinking, practical thinking, or a combination of these kinds of thinking.

The theory of successful intelligence comprises three sub theories: a componential sub theory dealing with the components of intelligence, an experiential sub theory dealing with the importance of coping with relative novelty and of automatization of information processing, and a contextual sub theory dealing with processes of adaptation, shaping, and selection, the theory has been referred to from time to time as Triarchic.

1. Componential Sub theory

The componential sub theory specifies the potential set of mental processes that underlies behaviour (*i.e.*, how the behaviour is generated). It outlines the structures and mechanisms that underlie intelligent behaviour categorized as metacognitive, performance, or knowledge acquisition components.

2. Experiential Sub theory

Sternberg's II stage of his theory is his experiential sub theory. This theory proposes intelligent behaviour be interpreted along a continuum of experience from novel to highly familiar tasks/situations. Sternberg splits the role of experience into two parts: novelty and automation.

A novel situation is one that you have never experienced before. A process that has been automated has been performed multiple times and can now be done with little or no extra thought. Once a process is automatized, it can be run in parallel with the same or other processes: The problem with novelty and automation is that being skilled in one component does not ensure that you are skilled in the other.

3. Practical theory

This Sub-theory specifies that intelligent behaviour is defined by the sociocultural context in which it takes place and involves adaptation to the environment, selection of better environments, and shaping of the present environment. In general it deals with the mental activity involved in attaining fit to context". This type of intelligence is often referred to as "street smarts". The effectiveness with which an individual fits to his/her environment & contends with daily situations reflects degree of intelligence.

Goleman Emotional Intelligence Theory (EQ-Emotional Quotient)

According to Mayer & Salovey, Emotional Intelligence is "The ability to monitor one's own and others' feelings and emotions, to discriminate among them and to use this information to guide one's thinking and actions."

The Emotional Intelligence Model of Goleman is made up of four Domains, which provide a framework for looking at how aware we are of emotions and how we manage emotions, in ourselves and in others. Each of the four Domains are made up of a number of competencies. Competencies are a set of behaviours that can be developed to create success in a given situation. The first component of emotional intelligence is Emotional Self-Awareness, knowing what one feels. It enables us to understand our own behaviour and to sustain it over time despite setbacks.

The second component of EI, Emotional Self-Management, is the ability to regulate distressing affects like anxiety and anger and to inhibit emotional impulsivity.

The third EI component, Social Awareness encompasses the competency of Empathy, also involves the amygdala. Studies of patients with discrete lesions to the amygdala show impairment of their ability to read nonverbal cues for negative emotions, particularly anger and fear, and to judge the trustworthiness of other people (Davidson, Jackson, & Kalin, 2000).

Finally, Relationship Management, or Social Skill, the fourth EI component, is concerned with how we manage the emotions of other people. It allows us to be aware of other people's feelings, needs and concerns. Being attuned to other people's emotions is the key to building rapport. If we cannot control our emotional outbursts or impulses and lack Empathy, there is less chance we will be effective in our relationships.

In Emotional Intelligence, Goleman explains that some people are "naturals" at high levels of emotional functioning. For most of us, deficits can result in limitations in performance and satisfaction in one or more parts of our life. For the "naturals", as with people who have a high IQ, a natural athlete, artist, or musician, appropriate emotional responses come easily without thinking. As we work to strengthen our emotional functioning, the new behaviour is learned and so must be applied consciously until it is mastered. Studies of "expert" behaviour describe four levels of functioning: unconscious incompetence, conscious incompetence, conscious competence and, at the highest level, unconscious competence. At the lowest level, a person is not aware of his inability to perform a particular task. When he becomes aware of the limitation and chooses to learn the skill required to complete the task, he is at level two. After study and practice, he achieves conscious mastery. With continued practice, he eventually reaches a point where he can perform the desired task without thinking about it.

CREATIVITY : VIEWS OF TORRANCE, GETZELS, GUILFORD

Creativity refers to the phenomenon whereby a person creates something new (a product, a solution, a work of art etc.) that has some kind of value. Torrance is best known for his research in Creativity. His major accomplishments include 1,871 publications: 88 books; 256 parts of books or cooperative volumes; 408 journal articles; 538 reports, manuals, tests, etc.; 162 articles in popular journals or magazines; 355 conference papers; and 64 forewords or prefaces. In 1966 he developed a benchmark method for quantifying creativity with his Torrance tests of creative thinking. Building on J. P. Guilford's work, they involved simple tests of divergent thinking and other problem solving skills, which were scored on four scales.

1. **Fluency:** The total number of interpretable meaningful and relevant ideas generated in response to the stimulus.
2. **Flexibility:** The number of different categories of relevant responses.
3. **Originality:** The statistical rarity of the responses or the ability to produce new original ideas.
4. **Elaboration:** The amount of detail in the response.

The third edition of the TTCT in 1984 eliminated the Flexibility scale from the figural test, but added Resistance to Premature Closure (based on Gestålt Psychology) and Abstractness of Titles as two new criterion referenced scores on the figural. Torrance called the new scoring procedure Streamlined Scoring. He incorporated 5 norm referenced measures and 13 criterion referenced measures in his conceptual framework of creativity. The five norm referenced measures include: fluency, originality, abstractness of titles, elaboration and resistance to premature closure. The criterion referenced measures include: emotional expressiveness, story-telling articulateness, movement or actions, expressiveness of titles, synthesis of incomplete figures, synthesis of lines or circles, unusual visualization, extending or breaking boundaries, humor, richness of imagery, colourfulness of imagery, and fantasy.

According to Arasteh and Arasteh (1976) the most systematic assessment of creativity in elementary school children has been conducted by Torrance & his associates (1960a, 1960b, 1960c, 1961, 1962, 1962a, 1963a, 1964), who have developed and administered the Minnesota tests of creativity thinking (MTCT) to several thousands of school children.

Torrance (1962) grouped the different subtests of the Minnesota test of creative thinking (MTCT) into 3 categories:-

1. Verbal tasks using verbal stimuli
2. Verbal tasks using non verbal stimuli
3. Non-Verbal tasks.

Threshold Hypothesis

There has been debate in the psychological literature about whether intelligence and creativity are part of the same process (the conjoint hypothesis) or represent distinct mental processes (the disjoint hypothesis).

Some researchers believe that creativity is the outcome of the same cognitive processes as intelligence, and is only judged as creativity in terms of its consequences, *i.e.*, when the outcome of cognitive processes happens to produce something novel, a view which Perkins has termed the "nothing special" hypothesis.

A very popular model is what has come to be known as "the threshold hypothesis" proposed by Ellis Paul Torrance. The threshold hypothesis (TH), classic in the psychology of creativity (Guilford, 1967), assumes positive relations between creative abilities and intelligence, but only in the case of people whose intelligence quotient (IQ) is below 120 points. Above that level, the correlation weakens and/or becomes statistically insignificant. Results of several studies (Cho, Nijenhuis, van Vianen, Kim, & Lee, 2010; Fuchs-Beauchamp, Karnes, & Johnson, 1993; Guilford, 1967) confirmed the TH, yet many also lead to its rejection (Kim, 2005; Preckel, Holling, & Wiese, 2006; Runco & Albert, 1986; Runco, Millar, Acar, & Cramond, 2010; Sligh, Conners, & Roskos-Ewoldsen, 2005).

Jacob. W. Getzels

The study which had a great impact on psychologists in the field of education and which had set off a boom in research into the area of creativity was the study of 449 high school children in Chicago, published by J.W. Getzels and P.W. Jackson in 1962. They compared a group of middle-class adolescent pupils who had scored well on intelligence tests with pupils who scored well on creativity tests designed by Guilford. They found that highly creative children were superior in scholastic achievement to pupils with high I.Q., although the high creatives had 20 I.Q. points lower than the high I.Q. students - indicating a positive relationship between creativity and academic ability. The high creatives, although having an average I.Q. 5 points less than their school population taken as a whole performed better in school achievement.

Getzels and Jackson's (1962) study drew criticisms as to its design and the sampling procedures employed. But the educational implications of Getzels and Jackson's study were undeniable. Several research studies replicated the study on other samples.

Researchers like Ahrens (1962), Jacobson (1966), Lucht (1963), Feldhusen, Treffinger and Elias (1970) have come out in support of the Getzels and Jackson phenomenon. Researchers who used the Grade Point Average as a measure of academic achievement, namely, Taylor (1958), Nuss (1961), Parker (1979), Wilson (1968) and Cline, Richards and Needham (1963) have also reported results consistent with the findings of Getzels and Jackson.

However, there are studies that did not support the Getzels and Jackson phenomenon of equivalent achievement of the high creative and the high I.Q groups. Among the earliest were the discrepant studies reported by Torrance (1962) based on his replications of the Getzels and Jackson's study. Many reasons were put forward to explain this. Among them were the lower levels of intelligence among the subjects studied, the different kinds of academic ability measured and to the presence of an I.Q. threshold in the relationship between creativity and academic achievement.

J.P. Guilford

Guilford performed important work in the field of creativity, drawing a distinction between convergent and divergent production (commonly renamed convergent and divergent thinking). Convergent thinking involves aiming for a single correct solution to a problem, whereas divergent thinking involves creative generation of multiple answers to a set problem. Divergent thinking is sometimes used as a synonym for creativity in psychology literature.

Guilford was an early proponent of the idea that intelligence is not a unitary concept. Based on his interest in individual differences, he explored the multidimensional aspects of the human mind, describing the structure of the human intellect based on a number of different abilities. His work emphasized that scores on intelligence tests cannot be taken as unidimensional ranking that some researchers have argued indicates the superiority of some people, or groups of people, over others. In particular, Guilford showed that the most creative people may score lower on a standard IQ test due to their approach to the problem, which generates a larger number of possible solutions, some of which are original. Guilford work, thus allows for greater appreciation of the diversity of human thinking and abilities, without attributing different values to different people.

Guilford developed a theory of creativity, in which he described creativity as sensitivity to problems (1950); as divergent thinking and ability to generate multiple ideas (1959), creation of new patterns, a transformation of knowledge and meaning or use the functions of objects in a new way (1962, 1967). He first proposed the concept of divergent thinking in the 1950's when he noticed that creative people tend to exhibit this type of thinking more than others. He thus associated divergent thinking with creativity, appointing it several characteristics:

1. **Fluency:** The ability to produce great number of ideas or problem solutions in a short period of time.

   OR

   The number of interpretable, meaningful & relevant ideas in response to the stimulus.
2. **Flexibility:** The ability to simultaneously propose a variety of approaches to a specific problem.
3. **Originality:** The ability to produce new original ideas. OR Statistical rarity of the responses.
4. **Elaboration:** The ability to systematize and organize the details of an idea in a head and carry it out.

RELATIONSHIP BETWEEN INTELLIGENCE AND CREATIVITY

There has been debate in the psychological literature about whether intelligence and creativity are part of the same process (The conjoint hypothesis) or represent distinct mental processes (the disjoint hypothesis). Hayes (1989, cited in Sternberg, 2000) states that creativity and intelligence are not fundamentally related but that intelligence may be needed in order to display creativity. Guilford (1950, 1967, 1970, 1975, cited in Sternberg, 2000), theorized that intellect is comprised of 120 different factors, with divergent production being the most relevant to creativity. Divergent production is the generalized gathering of knowledge and use of this knowledge to produce many different ideas in response to problems.

A very popular model is what has come to be known as "the threshold hypothesis", proposed by Ellis Paul Torrance, which holds that a high degree of intelligence appears to be a necessary but not sufficient condition for high creativity. An alternative perspective, Renzulli's three rings hypothesis, sees giftedness as based on both intelligence and creativity.

In contrast, Sternberg and Lubart's (1995) theory, as cited in Sternberg (2000), considers intelligence to be a subset of creativity. They posit that creativity is comprised of six different elements: intelligence, knowledge, thinking styles, personality, motivation, and the environment. Intelligence is comprised of three constructs: synthetic, analytical and practical abilities. All of these specific abilities are needed in order to exhibit creativity.

Other theorists have said that intelligence and creativity are related up to a certain IQ level and then unrelated among individuals with very high IQs (Preckel, Holling, & Wiese 2005). This hypothesis, known as the threshold hypothesis, states that creativity and intelligence are positively correlated up to a certain cut-off point (*e.g.,* 120), beyond which there is no significant correlation.

All individuals having healthy brain have some level of creativity in them. The average person has an IQ of about 100. The mind of a creative person spontaneously generates a large number of random combinations of ideas, and a few chosen combinations become expressed in behaviour. There is no relationship between measured intelligence and creative accomplishment but there is however a measured relationship between intelligence and creative accomplishment for groups of people.

IQ and creativity are two different sides of the same coin. A person having extremely low IQ that is an IQ below 70 will not be having a creative mind, also he will have problems in interaction with people. This shows an extremely low IQ is responsible for lack of creativeness in a person. Creativity is indeed a powerful and yet somewhat mystical ability that brings with a vast array of opportunities and skills that enhance and better our lives. With it, we can move mountains and reach the heights of success.

Techniques to boost up creativity are- Challenge assumptions, let ideas run wild. Similarly there are ways to increase IQ too. The best ways are—Deep breathing, meditation & self hypnosis. Whether IQ tests are the best way to measure intelligence is debatable but some studies do show a correlation between high IQ and creativity. Such studies conclude that the two increase together up to a score of 120. Beyond that level, little increase in creativity has been found.

ABILITIES AND ACHIEVEMENT: CONCEPT AND ROLE OF EMOTIONAL INTELLIGENCE

Emotional Intelligence (EI) refers to the ability to perceive, control and evaluate emotions. Some researchers suggest that emotional intelligence can be learned and strengthened while other claim it is an inborn characteristics.

Salovey and Mayer defined emotional intelligence as the: "Ability to monitor one's own and other's feelings and emotions, to discriminate among them and to use this information to guide one's thinking and actions." (1990).

It has been found that those with high level of EI tend to experience a healthy balance of feelings like: Motivation, friendship, focus fulfilment, peace of mind, awareness freedom, autonomy, contentment etc. Whereas those with lower level of EI tend to feel more loneliness, fear, frustration, guilt, depression instability, disappointment, resentment, anger, failure etc.

Salovey and Mayer proposed a model that identified 4 different factors of emotional intelligence: Perceive emotions, use emotions to facilitate thoughts, understand emotion and manage emotions.

The order of branches, from perception to management, represents the degree to which the ability is integrated within the rest of an individual's major psychological subsystems-that is within his or her overall personality (Mayer, 1998, 2001). Thus the perception and expression of emotion (Branch 1), and the capacity of emotion to enhance thought (Branch 2) are relatively discrete areas of information processing that we expect to be modularized or bound within the emotion system. By contrast, emotion management (Branch 4) must be integrated within an individual's overall plans and goals. Within each branch there also is a developmental progression of skills from the more basic to the more sophisticated (Mayer & Salovey, 1997).

Key Components of EQ

There are 5 components to emotional intelligence.

1. **Self-Awareness:** Means "having a deep understanding of one's emotions, strengths, weaknesses, needs & drives" (Goleman, 1995). People who have a high level of self awareness are very honest with themselves & others. They avoid the extremes of being overly critical & unrealistically hopeful. Furthermore, these people know how their feelings affect them & others.
2. **Self-Regulation:** The ability to control or redirect disruptive impulses and moods, and the propensity to suspend judgment and to think before acting. People with high degree of self regulation are more capable of facing ambiguities & have the potential to stay in control of their feelings and make thoughtful decisions.
3. **Motivation:** Motivated individuals want to achieve beyond their and everyone else's expectations. Motivation extends to deep inner desire to achieve for the sake of achievement. Hallmarks include a strong drive to achieve, optimism even in the face of failure, and organizational commitment.
4. **Empathy:** When an individual shows empathy, he/she is aware and considerate of other's feelings. The empathic person combines other feelings & other factors in order to make decisions.
5. **Social Skills:** Individuals use their friendliness in order to have people do what they want. Social leaders are able to build a rapport easily by finding some type of common ground with everyone, thus establishing a broad circle of acquaintances. (Goleman, 1995). Hallmarks of social skills include effectiveness in leading change, persuasiveness, and expertise building and leading teams.

EQ Training Technique in Classroom

There are 4 stages of training. These are preparation, training, transfer and maintenance & evaluating change (Tucker, Sojka, Barone, Mc. Carthy,2000).

MULTIPLE CHOICE QUESTIONS

1. The term IQ was coined by whom?
A. Terman B. Binet
C. William Stern D. Guilford

2. Who constructed the 'Culture-free' test of intelligence?
A. Spearman B. Terman
C. Binet D. Cattell

3. .... is the ability to think abstractly and to learn readily from experience.
A. Intelligence
B. Memory
C. Learning
D. Concept formation

4. According to Sternberg, ... is the ability to analyze and evaluate ideas, solve problems and make decisions.
A. Creative intelligence
B. Analytical intelligence
C. Fluid intelligence
D. None of the above

5. The original multifactor theory which includes 5 operations, 6 products and 4 contents was given by
A. Guilford B. Spearman
C. Thrustone D. Cattell

6. Who wrote 'Emotional Intelligence' in 1995?
A. Terman B. Goleman
C. Cattell D. Sternberg

7. The first intelligence test was invented by?
A. Skinner B. Chomsky
C. Binet D. Spearman

8. Who first defined the concept of Emotional intelligence in 1990 which emphasises on intermingling of cognition with emotions?
A. Wechsler
B. Terman
C. Salovey and Mayer
D. Noam Chomsky

9. The group factor theory of intelligence was given by whom?
A. Kelly B. Spearman
C. Wechsler D. None of the above

10. According to whom there are 3 basic kinds of intelligence: componential, experiential and contextual.
A. Cattell B. Sternberg
C. Jensen D. Goleman

11. Who gave the theory of 2 levels of intelligence: Level I and Level II?
A. Cattell B. Sternberg
C. Goleman D. Jensen

12. .... is the ability to reason and solve problems in novel or unfamiliar situations:
A. Fluid intelligence
B. Crystallized intelligence
C. General intelligence
D. Common sense

13. Human intelligence is affected by which factor?
A. Heredity
B. Environment
C. Both A & B
D. None of the above

14. According to whose model of intelligence there are 120 identifiable abilities.
A. Guilford B. Torrance
C. Jensen D. Getzel

15. Cretinism disorder that leads to retardation and characteristic physical symptoms is because of:
A. Iodine deficiency
B. Iron deficiency
C. Protein deficiency
D. Thyroxin deficiency

16. Who coined the term mental test?
A. Jensen B. Sternberg
C. Goleman D. Cattell

17. Who proposed that the 'g' factor represents the highest order common factor among individual differences in IQ:
A. Spearman B. Guilford
C. Cattell D. None of the above

18. With the help of which test mentally retarded children can be identified?
A. Personality test
B. Aptitude Test
C. Intelligence test
D. None of the above

19. .... intelligence includes those aspects of intelligence that use previously learned information to solve problems or make decisions.
A. Crystallized B. Fluid
C. General D. Both (A) & (B)

20. Who gave the concept of fluid and crystallised intelligence?
A. Binet B. Jensen
C. Goleman D. Cattell

21. Who proposed that the "g" factor represents the highest order common factor among individual differences in IQ?
A. Binet B. Chomsky
C. Spearman D. None of the above

22. Restriction of amino acids is used in the treatment of which disorder?
A. Down syndrome
B. Phenylketonuria
C. Intellectual deficiency
D. None of the above

23. Self-awareness, self-regulation, motivation, empathy and social skills are the major 5 components of which theory ?
A. Socialization
B. Attitude formation
C. Personality
D. Emotional Intelligence

24. A very popular model is what has come to be known as "the threshold hypothesis", proposed by:
A. Ellis Paul Torrance
B. Getzels
C. Guilford
D. None of the above

25. Who wrote the book "creativity and Intelligence" in 1962 with his Chicago colleague Phillip Jackson?
A. Getzels B. Guilford
C. Torrance D. Jensen

26. According to which one component of Goleman emotional intelligence, we regulate distressing affects like anxiety & anger and inhibit emotional impulsivity?
A. Self-awareness
B. Self-management
C. Social awareness
D. Relationship management

27. The concept of 'creative intelligence' was given by:
A. Gardner B. Guilford
C. Torrance D. Sternberg

28. Some Psychologist stated that the relationship between intelligence and creativity is not the same throughout the range of intelligence (I.Q). Which out of following is appropriate explanation of the relationship between these at different levels of I.Q.
A. Below that critical level of I.Q. the relationship is negative and above that it is positive.
B. Below that critical level of I.Q. it is zero and above that it is positive.
C. Below that critical level of I.Q. the relationship is positive and above that it is negative.
D. Below that critical level of I.Q. the relationship is positive and above that level zero relationship.

29. According to Torrance test of creative thinking, the statistical rarity of the responses or the ability to produce new original ideas is known as:
A. Fluency B. Flexibility
C. Originality D. Elaboration

30. Gardner's theory of multiple intelligence refers to an individual's eight separate abilities, logical mathematical, verbal, ..., spatial, ..., interpersonal, ... and naturalistic.

Codes:

A. Bodily-kinesthetic, mechanical, intra-personal
B. Mechanical, bodily-kinesthetic, intra-personal
C. Mental, bodily-kinesthetic, cognitive
D. Musical, bodily-kinesthetic, intrapersonal

31. Which one of the following can be primarily employed to assess creativity?

A. Convergent thinking
B. Divergent thinking
C. Symbolic thinking
D. Abstract thinking

32. Read each of the following two statements—Assertion (A) and Reason (R) and indicate your answer using the codes given below:

Assertion (A): Environments that affect educational and cultural opportunities influence crystallised intelligence directly and fluid intelligence indirectly.

Reason (R): Crystallised intelligence is developed through the investment of fluid intelligence in cultural settings.

Codes:

A. Both (A) and (R) are true and (R) is correct explanation of (A).
B. Both (A) and (R) are true, but (R) is not the correct explanation of (A).
C. (A) is true, but (R) is false.
D. (A) is false, but (R) is true.

33. In 1987 Cattell added a third ability to his model of intelligence, labelled as Gsar. What did this label represent?

A. Social adjustment abilities
B. Short-term memory abilities
C. Standard ability to maintain relationships
D. None of the above

34. Threshold hypothesis indicates:

A. positive correlation between intelligence and creativity upto a particular level of intelligence.
B. negative correlation between intelligence and creativity upto a particular level of intelligence.
C. curvilinear relationship between intelligence and creativity after a particular level of intelligence.
D. negative correlation between intelligence and creativity after a particular level of intelligence.

35. Which of the following dimension/s given by Guilford in his structure of Intellect model explains the concept of creativity:

(*i*) Operations
(*ii*) Contents
(*iii*) Products

A. (*i*) only B. (*ii*) only
C. (*i*) and (*ii*) D. (*ii*) and (*iii*)

36. Scientific measurement of intelligence was started by:

A. L.L. Thurstone B. Lewin Terman
C. Alfred Binet D. A.R. Jensen

37. Read each of the following two statements: Assertion (A) and Reason (R) and indicate your answer using the codes given below:

Assertion (A): Gf and Gc correlate positively with each other across the age levels but with moderate magnitude.

Reason (R): Gf and Gc have different growth patterns. Gc grows rapidly in childhood and adolescene whereas Gf grows rapidly during adulthood.

Codes:

A. Both (A) and (R) are true and (R) is correct explanation of (A).
B. Both (A) and (R) are true, but (R) is not the correct explanation of (A).
C. (A) is true, but (R) is false.
D. (A) is false, but (R) is true.

38. Which of the following are the characteristics of Cattell's Culture Fair Intelligence Test?
1. Speed
2. Power
3. Non-verbal
4. Performance

Codes:

A. 1 and 3 B. 1, 2 and 3
C. 1, 2 and 4 D. 1 and 2

39. Jensen uses Regression argument to Jensen uses Regression argument to account for:
A. Genetic contribution in abilities
B. Context specific abilities
C. Group differences in intelligence
D. Age related changes in intelligence

40. According to whom intelligence is a capacity of the organism to adjust itself to an increasingly complex environment?
A. Guilford B. Jensen
C. Spencer D. Getzels

41. In Jensen's distinction between level-I and level-II abilities, which one of the following is not a characteristic of Level-I ability?
A. It involves neural registration and consolidation of stimulus inputs.
B. It involves relatively little transformation of input.
C. It is abstract and is measured by tests which are "culture reduced".
D. It is relatively homogeneously distributed among different racial group.

42. Spearman has developed the:
A. Theory of Mental Ability
B. Concept of Abstract level of intelligence
C. Two-type ability theory
D. Two-factor theory of intelligence

43. Which of the following is not a component of Emotional Intelligence as described by Mayer and Salovey?
1. The ability to use emotions to facilitate thinking.
2. The ability to perceive, appraise and express emotions accurately.
3. The ability to perceive, appraise and express emotions appropriately.
4. The ability to adapt to new and different contexts, select appropriate contexts and effectively shape one's environment to suit one's needs.

Codes:

A. 4 only B. 1 and 4
C. 1, 2 and 4 D. 1, 3 and 4

44. Which are the concepts mainly used by Sternberg in his theory of intelligence?
1. Meta components
2. Performance components
3. Factor Analysis
4. Selective encoding

Codes:

A. 1, 2 and 3 B. 2, 3 and 4
C. 1, 2 and 4 D. 1, 3 and 4

45. What is the name of the intelligence quotient which replaced the original quotient developed by Stern (1912)?
A. Standard IQ B. Deviation IQ
C. Multiple IQ D. Average IQ

46. Using Sternberg's theory as the reference, match List-I with List-II.

List-I (Components)	List-II (Type)
(*a*) Experiential	1. Analytic
(*b*) Contextual	2. Creative
(*c*) Componential	3. Practical

Codes:

	(*a*)	(*b*)	(*c*)
A.	3	1	2
B.	2	3	1
C.	4	2	3
D.	2	1	3

47. Out of the following who has not explained intelligence in terms of Psychometric Approach?
A. Jensen B. Cattell
C. Sternberg D. Thurstone

48. Match List-I with List-II and indicate your answer with the help of code given below:

List-I (Phenomenon)	List-II (Psychologist)
(*a*) Explanation of creativity in terms of product	1. Getzels and Jackson
(*b*) Explanation of creativity in terms of process	2. Gordon
(*c*) Explanation of creativity in terms of personality characteristics	3. Torrance
(*d*) Explanation of creativity in terms of motivational factors	4. Rogers

Codes:

	(*a*)	(*b*)	(*c*)	(*d*)
A.	1	2	3	4
B.	3	4	2	1
C.	4	2	3	1
D.	4	3	1	2

49. Match List-I with List-II and indicate your answer using the codes given below:

List-I	List-II
(*a*) Mixed Model	1. Creativity
(*b*) Regression	2. Type I and II intelligence
(*c*) Elaboration	3. Structure of intellect
(*d*) Divergent thinking	4. Emotional intelligence

Codes:

	(*a*)	(*b*)	(*c*)	(*d*)
A.	2	1	4	3
B.	1	2	4	3
C.	4	2	1	3
D.	3	2	4	1

50. Which of the following explains the typical intelligence-creativity relationship?

A. U-shaped relationship
B. Inverted U-shaped relationship
C. Linear negative relationship
D. None of the above

ANSWERS

1	2	3	4	5	6	7	8	9	10
C	D	A	B	A	B	C	C	A	B
11	**12**	**13**	**14**	**15**	**16**	**17**	**18**	**19**	**20**
D	A	C	A	D	D	A	C	A	D
21	**22**	**23**	**24**	**25**	**26**	**27**	**28**	**29**	**30**
C	B	D	A	A	B	D	D	C	D
31	**32**	**33**	**34**	**35**	**36**	**37**	**38**	**39**	**40**
B	D	B	A	A	C	A	B	C	C
41	**42**	**43**	**44**	**45**	**46**	**47**	**48**	**49**	**50**
C	D	A	C	B	B	C	D	C	D

❑❑❑

CHAPTER 6

Personality

CLINICAL & GROWTH APPROACHES TO PERSONALITY

These approaches mainly focus on Carl Rogers Self Centred & Abraham Maslow Self Actualization theory. As these theories basically revolves around self & actualizing self which is basically a growth force that is a part of person's heredity, is also well known as clinical and growth approach, because it not only includes biological potentials but also involves a psychological growth & a moving towards maintaining & enhancing the organism.

Rogers along with Abraham Maslow established the self-growth theories of personality. Client-centered therapy, also known as person-centered therapy, is a non-directive form of talk therapy that was developed by humanist psychologist Carl Rogers during the 1940s and 1950s. Based on his experience as a psychotherapist, Rogers postulated that persons possess resources of self-knowledge and self-healing, and that personality change and development are possible if a definable climate of facilitative conditions is present (Rogers, 1957; Rogers, 1980a).

Two aspects of the person are essential to understanding Rogers' theory: the organism and the self.

1. **Organism:** For Rogers organism is considered as a locus of all experiences varying from our own perception of events that occur within our body to our perception of events that occur in the external world. The total of this experience is called the phenomenal field.
2. **Self:** As a person grows from infancy to adulthood and gains experience, what eventually emerges, as part of the phenomenal field which becomes personalized and differentiated as, "I" or "Me" experiences, the self is said to have formed. For Rogers, the self is a fluid, changing gestalt and it may be either in awareness or out of awareness with the development of self, the infant begins to understand good or bad as well as it tries to evaluate the experiences as positive or negative.

There are 2 sub systems of self-

- Self Concept-consists of all those aspects of experiences which are perceived by person in awareness.
- Ideal Self-consists of experiences relating to what one thinks one ought to be and would like to be.

Rogers assumes we each possess an inherited urge or need for self-actualization. This is thought to be a tendency to develop and utilize all of our potential. Self-actualization is a single goal toward which we all strive. He claimed that self-actualization is a growth force that is part of person's heredity. This not only includes biological potentials but also involves a psychological growth and a moving towards maintaining & enhancing the organism.

Rogers recognized two basic needs that are related to self actualization. They are-

1. Need for positive rewards for others.
2. Need for self regard.

According to Rogers, unconditional positive regard, or acceptance causes us to seek acceptance, warmth and love from the valued people in our life. If we don't get it, we are not advancing. The organism needs positive regard not only from those around it, but also from the self. Both these needs are learnt during infancy when the infant is loved & cared by his/her mother. Rogers self theory has been criticized. It is said that his theory has ignored the unconscious which plays a very important role in controlling behaviour. Despite some criticism Rogers's emphasis upon self has encouraged a lot of researchers and empirical findings. However, not all researchers & findings are in favour.

Maslow Self Actualization Theory

On of the main contribution to Humanistic theory from Maslow is the concept of self-actualization. According to Maslow (1954), self-actualisation can be described in the following way: "A musician must make music, an artist must paint, a poet must write, if he is to be ultimately at peace with himself. What a man can be, he must be. This need we may call self-actualisation".

In his view, we all have higher level growth needs, such as the need for self actualization & understanding of our selves but that these higher needs only assume a dominant role in our lives after our more primitive needs (Physiological needs, safety, need for love and belongingness & self esteem needs) are satisfied. The growth need Maslow believed, help make us distinctly human. Maslow stressed that man has a higher and transcendent nature.

To understand this transcendent nature, Maslow studied models of self actualized people-people who appeared to have fulfilled their basic potentialities. He found some of his subjects in history (Lincoln, Jefferson, and Beethoven) and others from among his contemporaries (Roosevelt, Einstein etc). Maslow (1976) found that this group of "optimal" people shared some distinguishing characteristics.

1. They were reality-centred, problem centred and they had a different perception of means & ends.
2. They enjoyed solitude and were comfortable being alone.
3. They enjoyed autonomy & they resisted enculturation, that is, they were not susceptible to social pressure to be "well-adjusted" or to "fit-in" they were infact nonconformist in the best sense.
4. They had an unhostile sense of humour & also had a quality called acceptance of self and others as they are. Along with this comes spontaneity and simplicity. They preferred being themselves rather than being pretentious or artificial.
5. They had sense of humility & respect towards others.
6. They devoted total efforts to their goals, wanting to be first-rate, or at least as good as they could be.
7. They were dedicated fully & creatively to some cause outside themselves.
8. They had a certain freshness of appreciation along with their ability to be creative, inventive & original.
9. Finally, these people tended to have more peak experiences than the average person. A peak experience is one that takes you out of yourself, that makes you feel very tiny, or very large, to some extent one with life or nature or God.

It is not necessary to display all these characteristics in order to be self-actualised, and not only self-actualised people display them. However, Maslow considered that those individuals that he had identified as self-actualised people displayed these characteristics more. Self-actualisers are people who fulfil their own potential, not perfect human beings. There were several flaws or imperfections he discovered along the way as well. They often suffered considerable anxiety and guilt, but realistic anxiety and guilt, rather than misplaced or neurotic versions.

Two other points he makes about these self actualizers. Their values were "natural" and seemed to flow effortlessly from their personalities, and they appear to transcend many of the dichotomies, such as the difference between the spiritual & the physical, the selfish and the unselfish & the masculine and the feminine.

Existential and Humanistic Theories of Personality

Victor Frankl

Through his experiences in Nazi death camps during the Second World War, Victor Frankl developed his theories and therapies. During the war watching who did and did not survive (given an opportunity to survive) he conclude that people who had hopes of being reunited with loved ones or who had projects they felt a need to complete, or who had great faith, tended to have better chances than those who had lost all hopes. It is from these experiences that Frankl wrote his most significant contribution, Man's Search for Meaning (1984). The first part of this book gives a first hand account of his experience in the concentration camps and his interpretation of these events. The second half of Man's Search for Meaning is an introduction to Frankl's (1984) Logotherapy. The term "logotherapy' is based on the Greek word 'logos', denoting meaning (Frankl, 1984). A literal translation of logotherapy, Frankl (1978) contended, would be 'therapy through meaning'.

Frankl's view of human beings is classified as a Schichthentheorie, or layer theory. He distinguished between three 'layers' that define human beings, namely the physical, psychological and spiritual dimensions (Hutchinson & Chapman, 2005).

According to Frankl (1988), logotherapy is based on three triads. The first consists of the freedom, the will to meaning, and the meaning of life which latter encapsulates the second triad, consists of creative, experiential and attitudinal values. Finally, attitudinal values are related to the third triad: meaningful attitudes towards the 'tragic triad'-suffering, guilt and transitoriness.

It is apparent through his theory that meaning is central to one's existence which is found through one's freedom and responsibleness, and is motivated by the will to meaning. However, often the will to meaning is frustrated, resulting in people being unable to find meaning in their lives. Frankl (1984, 1988) called this condition 'existential frustration'.

In logotherapy, the term 'existential' may be used to refer to three things, namely: (1) existence itself, *i.e.*,, the specifically human mode of being, (2) the meaning of existence; and (3) the striving to find a concrete meaning in personal existence, that is to say, the will to meaning.

The result of this inability to find meaning—existential frustration—is what Frankl called 'existential Vacuum' which is characterized by the will to pleasure or the will to power being dominant in the person's life. In other words, individual try to compensate for their lack of meaning by surrendering to their will to power, as manifested in work holism or an obsessive striving for money, or their will to pleasure, which is embodied in mostly sexual compulsions. Moreover, the existential vacuum 'affects life satisfaction and fulfilment; this condition hinders the internalization and constructive response to stressors'.

According to Frankl existential vacuum is not pathological, however, if prolonged; this vacuum may eventuate in a neurotic disorder for which he coined the term noogenic neurosis.

At the end note it can be concluded that meaning is central to successful functioning, and the attainment of meaning is associated with positive mental health status, whereas meaninglessness is associated with pathological outcomes.

Rollo May

Rollo May is the best known American existential psychologist. According to Rollo May, existential psychology strives to understand human beings in their world and the capacities they bring to therapy. The personal responsibility of existential therapists is to understand their clients' anxieties and experiences and to guide them through their struggles (May, 1996b). Essentially, therapists guide clients to become larger in their use of their capacities and aid them to discover newer approaches for engaging life problems (May, Angel, & Ellenberger, 1958). Rollo May is the only existential psychologist who discusses certain stages (not in the strict Freudian sense, of course) of development, which are mentioned below:-

1. **Innocence:** The pre-egoic, pre-self-conscious stage of the infant. The innocent is premoral *i.e.*, is neither bad nor good. But an innocent does have a degree of will in the sense of a drive to fulfil their needs.
2. **Rebellion:** The childhood and adulthood stage of developing one's ego or self consciousness by means of contrast with adults, from the "no" of the 2 year old to the "no way" of the teenager. The rebellious person wants freedom, but has as yet no full understanding of the responsibility that goes with it.
3. **Ordinary:** The normal adult ego, conventional and little boring, perhaps. They have learned responsibility, but find it too demanding, and so seek refuge in conformity and traditional values.
4. **Creative:** The authentic adult, the existential stage, beyond ego and self actualizing. This is the person who, accepting destiny, faces anxiety with courage.

These are not stages in the traditional sense. A child may certainly be innocent, ordinary or creative at times. An adult may be rebellious. The only attachments to certain ages are in terms of Salience: Rebelliousness stands out in the two year old and the teenager!

Rollo May is every bit as interested in anxiety as an existentialist. He discovered from his studies that anxiety is connected to a threat that occurs toward an individual's values and sense of security. The main idea in this work is that the anxiety resulting from threats motivates people to cut themselves off from their feelings. However, people can consciously confront and incorporate their experiences and feelings and continue to grow or they can choose to avoid facing them and become overwhelmed (Bilmes, 1978; May, 1996a). May believed that any issue that has provoked anxiety is a sign of an individual's being alive.

May asserted that two major types of anxiety can be experienced, not only with regard to many life issues but also regarding the concept of death and the loss of feeling whole (*e.g.*, an individual's sense of self): normal and neurotic or paralyzing anxiety (May, 1996a, 1996b). May believed that normal anxiety was that which affects individuals in situations that do not require them to repress or defend the self (May, 1996a, 1999). An example of normal anxiety could be when a student begins a new class and knows no one in the class. He or she begins to experience the anxiety (*e.g.*, rapid heart rate, sweating, confused thoughts) associated with being in a new setting. The student can then choose to branch out and engage socially in an attempt to alleviate the anxiety, or he or she can repress and avoid the anxiety symptoms and attempt to move on with the class.

Neurotic anxiety manifests in forms of panic or other intense reactions to situations that could otherwise be encountered through more constructive matters of integration (*e.g.*, as with normal anxiety situations). The neurotic anxiety associated with death, for example, can be exhibited through extreme behaviour and physical reactions (*e.g.*, isolation, avoidance of meaningful activities, and loss of appetite, extreme nervousness).

Many of May's unique ideas can be found in the book—"Love & Will". His basic motivational construct is the daimonic. The daimonic is the entire system of motives, different for each individual. It is composed of a collection of specific motives called daimons. Daimons include lower needs, such as food and sex, as well as higher needs, such as love. For May, one of the most important daimons is Eros. Eros is love (not sex). Another important concept for May is will: The ability to organize oneself in order to achieve one's goal.

Abraham Maslow

Abraham Maslow developed a theory of personality that has influenced a number of different fields, including education. Maslow was a humanistic psychologist. Humanists do not believe that human beings are pushed and pulled by mechanical forces, either of stimuli or reinforcements (behaviourism) or of unconscious instinctual impulses (psychoanalysis). Humanists focus upon potentials. Humanists believe that humans strive for a upper level of capabilities.

Maslow has set up a hierarchy of 5 levels of basic needs. Beyond these needs, higher level of needs exists. These include needs for understanding, aesthetic appreciation and purely spiritual needs. In the level of the 5 basic needs, the person does not feel the second until the demands of the first have been satisfied, nor the third until the second has been satisfied, and so on. Maslow basic needs are as follows:

1. **Physiological Needs:** These are biological needs. They consist of needs for oxygen, food, water and a relatively constant body temperature.
2. **Safety Needs:** When the physiological needs are largely taken care of, this second layer of needs comes into play. Adults have little awareness of their security needs except in times of emergency or periods of disorganization in the social structure. Children often display the signs of insecurity & the need to be safe.
3. **Need of Love, Affection & Belongingness:** When physiological needs and safety needs are, by and large, taken care of, a third layer starts to show up. Maslow states that people seek to overcome feelings of loneliness and alienation. This involves both giving and receiving love, affection and the sense of belonging.
4. **Need for Esteem:** Maslow noted two versions of esteem needs, a lower one and a higher one. The lower one is the need for the respect of others, the need for status, fame, glory, recognition, attention, reputation, appreciation, dignity, even dominance. The higher form involves the need for self-respect, including such feelings as confidence, competence, achievement, mastery, independence, and freedom.
5. **Need for Self Actualization:** When all of the foregoing needs are satisfied, then and only then are the needs for self actualization activated. Maslow has used a variety of terms to refer to this level: He has called it growth motivation (in contrast to deficit motivation), being needs (or B-needs, in contrast to D-needs), and self-actualization. He describes self actualization as a person's need to be and do that which the person was "born to do". A musician must make music, an artist must paint & a poet must write.

The hierarchic theory is often represented as a pyramid, with the larger, lower levels representing the lower needs, and the upper point representing the need for self actualization.

PERSONALITY ASSESSMENT: PROJECTIVE, PSYCHOMETRIC & BEHAVIOURAL MEASURES

Personality Assessment Tools

Personality measurement and assessment procedures are useful in understanding the person. Some of the common tools are mentioned below:-

1. **Self Report Inventories:** Also known as personality inventories are the self rating questionnaires, where the individual describes his own feelings, environment and reactions of others towards himself. This type of test is often presented in a paper-and-pencil format or may even be administered on a computer. A typical self report inventory presents a number of questions or statements that may or may not describe certain qualities or characteristics of the test subject. Self report inventories are further classified into the following 5 types:-
   (*a*) Inventories that attempt to measure social and certain other specified traits such as self confidence, dominance, ego strength, extroversion, responsibility, etc. The Bernreuter Personality Inventory, the Eysenck Personality Questionnaire, the Differential Personality Scale are some of the examples of this category.
   (*b*) Inventories that attempt to evaluate the adjustment of the persons to different aspects of the environment such as school, home, health etc. The Bell Adjustment Inventory is the best example.
   (*c*) Inventories that attempt to evaluate pathological traits such as hysteria, paranoia, hypomania, depression, schizophrenia etc. The Minnesota Multiphasic Personality Inventory (MMPI) is the best example.
   (*d*) Inventories that attempt to screen individuals into two or three groups. The Cornell Index is the best example of such an inventory.
   (*e*) Inventories that attempt to measure attitudes, interests and values of persons. The Kuder inventories (vocational, occupational & personal), the strong vocational interest blank etc are the best examples of this category.
2. **Observational Methods:** Observational methods provide either a structured or unstructured situation. A structured situation is a controlled situation whereas an unstructured situation is an uncontrolled situation. Observation procedure may be either informal or formal. Informal observations are primarily qualitative. Although observations are often conducted in the natural environment, there are times when it is useful to observe the person's behaviour in a situation that the psychologist can arrange and control.
3. **Interview:** Interviews have both verbal and nonverbal (*e.g.*, gestural) components. The aim of the interview is to gather information, and the adequacy of the data gathered depends in large part on the questions asked by the interviewer.
4. **Rating Scales:** The rating scale is one of the oldest and most versatile of assessment techniques. Rating scales present users with an item and ask them to select from a number of choices.
5. **Cognitive Assessment:** The types of thoughts experienced by individuals are reflective of their personalities. Cognitive assessment provides information about thoughts that precede, accompany, and follow maladaptive behaviour. It also provides information about the effects of procedures that are intended to modify both how subjects think about a problem and how they behave.

6. **Projective Techniques:** Projective techniques are the most popular method of assessing the personality of the individual. In this technique a person is shown ambiguous stimuli (such as shapes or pictures) and asked to interpret them in some way. Through his responses, his needs, drives, motives, fears etc are revealed. Projective techniques are believed to be sensitive to unconscious dimensions of personality. Defense mechanisms, latent impulses, and anxieties have all been inferred from data gathered in projective situations.

Projective Techniques

Lawrence Kelso Frank is known as the originator of "projection techniques". He defined a projection method as one that, "(...) allows individuals to reveal their way of organising an experience, thanks to providing them with objects, materials and experiences with a relatively low structure and weak cultural pattern so that onto this formable field they can project their own way of perceiving life, their senses, their values and, especially, their own emotions. In this way a projection of the private world of an individual personality is evoked".

In his later work Frank defined the projective technique as, "(...) a method of assessing personality by placing those being assessed in situations where they want to talk about what the situation means to them and how they feel when reacting to it".

In general projective technique can be defined as an unstructured and indirect form of questioning that encourages respondents to project their underlying motivations, beliefs, attitudes or feelings regarding the issue of concern. Since, the individual is not aware of these revelations; he doesn't resort to any defensive reactions. Thus in a projective test the individual has ample opportunity to project his own personality attributes that are mostly latent & unconscious in the interpretation of an unstructured situation.

Classification of Projective Techniques

The earliest classification of projective techniques was done by Frank (1939). He classified projective techniques into 5 categories:

1. Constitutive: This includes all those projective tests which require imposition of structure upon relatively unstructured material. Example—Rorschach, finger painting & drawing completion.
2. Constructive: This includes all those test situations where the examinee is required to arrange material into pattern as in mosaic's test.
3. Interpretative: This includes all those test situations where the testee has to interpret the test situation presented to him as in TAT & Word association test.
4. Refractive: This includes all those techniques through which the examinee is given an opportunity to express his personality in the form of painting, drawing, handwriting etc.
5. Cathartic: This includes those situations whereby the examinee is given opportunity to release pent-up emotional feeling as doll play.

The more convincing classification of projective techniques has been provided by Lindzey (1959). He has divided projective techniques into the following 5 categories:

1. **Association Techniques:** In this technique the respondents are presented with lists of words or images and would be asked to respond with the first thing that comes to their minds. Example,Rorschach test, the Holtzman Inkblot Test & Word Association Test.
2. **Constructive Techniques:** This category includes all those situations where the examinee is required to construct a story after seeing the stimulus materials (usually the picture) within a

certain specific time. No record is generally kept of time but the examinee's themes & modes of responding are considered relevant. Example,TAT, CAT, the Blacky Pictures etc.

3. **Completion Techniques:** This includes those situations where the examinee is asked to complete a sentence, paragraph or a story which is incomplete. Example,The Madeleine Thomas Completion Stories, Rotters Sentence Completion Test.
4. **Role Playing:** The technique requires the examinee to act out a specific role or to assume someone else behaviour. His saying while enacting reveals the underlying motives, needs, attitudes etc.
5. **Pictorial:** The techniques include all those situations where the unstructured situation consists of vague and ambiguous pictures and the examinee is to respond towards those pictures. His response may be in terms of a few words as it is done in Rorschach test & Holtzman Inkblot test or in terms of a series of sentences as it is done in the TAT, the CAT, Rosenzweig Picture Frustration Test, etc.

MULTIPLE CHOICE QUESTIONS

1. Client centred therapy is associated with whom?
A. Rollo May B. Victor Frankl
C. Carl Rogers D. Abhram Maslow

2. According to whom we can discover life's meaning by doing a deed, experiencing a value and suffering?
A. Victor Frankl B. Rollo May
C. Carl Rogers D. Abhram Maslow

3. Who developed word association test as a therapeutic and diagnostic tool?
A. Adler B. Horney
C. Jung D. None of the above

4. Who introduced the concept "collective unconscious"?
A. Horney B. Jung
C. Adler D. Maslow

5. According to Roger .... refers to the person's organismic experiences.
A. Actualizing tendency
B. Ideal self
C. Enhancement needs
D. Safety needs

6. According to Rogers when a conflict exists between the self-actualizing tendency and the organismic self .... arises.
A. Inner tension B. Incongruence
C. Both A & B D. None of the above

7. When a discrepancy exists between the self-concept and the ideal self .... arises.
A. Incongruence
B. Inner tension
C. Actualizing tendency
D. None of the above

8. The concept unconditional positive regard was used by:
A. Maslow B. Jung
C. Allport D. Rogers

9. The humanistic theory of personality was proposed by:
A. Jung B. Allport
C. Maslow D. Frankl

10. According to Rogers, the process of perceiving stimuli without an awareness of the perception is referred to as ....
A. Incongruence
B. Subception
C. Enhancement
D. Maintenance

11. According to whom maintenance and enhancement are two of our basic needs?
A. Rollo May B. Maslow
C. Frankl D. Rogers

12. What are the two primary defensive strategies according to Rogers?
A. Denial and distortion
B. Subception and denial
C. Denial and repression
D. Denial and reaction formation

13. The concept of Masculine protest was given by:
A. Adler B. Jung
C. Frankl D. Rollo May

14. According to Jung the inherited tendencies in the collective unconscious is termed as ....
A. Psyche B. Psychic energy
C. Arche types D. None of the above

15. Who believes that each person has a natural tendency towards growth and self actualization?
A. Rollo May B. Rogers
C. Frankl D. Both A & B

16. Which technique has been adopted by Rogers to measure client self-concepts?
A. Q-Sort B. Q-List
C. Both A & B D. None of the above

17. Who said that by expanding self awareness people can acquire freedom of action?
A. Rogers B. Maslow
C. Rollo May D. Frankl

18. May regarded care as the source of:
A. Philia and will
B. Eros and Philia
C. Love and will
D. None of the above

19. According to whom, an authentic person must unite love with will?
A. Rollo may B. Maslow
C. Rogers D. Both B & C

20. According to Jung the feminine characteristics in man is known as:
A. Shadow B. Anima
C. Animus D. None of the above

21. According to Jung the masculine characteristic in woman is called:
A. Shadow B. Anima
C. Animus D. Persona

22. .... is defined as an intimate, non sexual friendship.
A. Philia B. Eros
C. Care D. None of the above

23. Which existential theorist used the term logo therapy in formulating his existential approach to therapy?
A. Rollo May B. Abraham Maslow
C. Carl Rogers D. Victor Frankl

24. According to whom, the meaning goes beyond self actualization and exists at each of the three levels of meanings (ultimate meaning, meaning of the moment and common day to day meaning).
A. Rollo May B. Victor Frankl
C. Abraham Maslow D. Carl Rogers

25. According to Jung, ... archetype is the inferior, animal like part of the personality.
A. The persona
B. The self
C. The shadow
D. The anima and animus

26. One of the Neo-Freudian psychologists combines the humanistic, existential and psychoanalytic perspectives in which of the following concepts?
A. Personality Development
B. Positive Psychology
C. Theory of Love
D. None of these

27. According to Rogers, the primary goal of life is to ....
A. Successfully overcome developmental challenges.
B. Reach the highest level of need *i.e.*, self actualization.
C. Fulfil one's inborn capacities and potentialities.
D. All of the above

28. Which of the following is most appropriate for the assessment of Self-actualization?
A. Myers-Briggs Type Indicator
B. Personal Orientation Inventory
C. Rosenberg Self-esteem Inventory
D. Edwards Personal Preference Scale

29. The Big five personality dimensions appear to be essentially fixed, and unlikely to change by age:
A. 30 B. 40
C. 45 D. 15

30. Read each of the following two statements: Assertion (A) and Reason (R) and indicate your answer using the codes given below:

Assertion (A): Projective testing would be of the greatest interest to psychodynamic personality psychologist.

Reason (R): Projective testing is designed to uncover unconscious thoughts, feelings, and conflicts.

Codes:
A. Both (A) and (R) are true and (R) is the correct explanation of (A).
B. Both (A) and (R) are true, but (R) is not the correct explanation of (A).
C. (A) is true, but (R) is false.
D. (A) is false, but (R) is true.

31. How many pictures of human figures does TAT contain?
A. 10 B. 20
C. 25 D. 30

32. Match List-I with List-II and indicate your answer with the help of codes given below:

List-I (Personality Approaches)	List-II (Phenomenon)
(*a*) Analytical Psychology	1. Peak experience
(*b*) Individual Psychology	2. Transference neurosis
(*c*) Humanistic Psychology	3. Will to Power
(*d*) Psychoanalysis	4. Archetypes

Codes:

	(*a*)	(*b*)	(*c*)	(*d*)
A.	2	4	1	3
B.	4	3	1	2
C.	1	3	4	2
D.	4	2	3	1

33. From the Big Five personality dimensions, behaviours such as speaking fluently, displaying ambition, and exhibiting a high degree of intelligence is:
A. Agreeableness
B. Openness
C. Extraversion
D. Conscientiousness

34. Arrange the following tests in decreasing order of their projective ability:
1. Rorschach's Ink Blot Test
2. Thematic Apperception Test
3. Rosenzweig's Picture Frustration Scale
4. Sack's Sentence Completion Test

Codes:
A. 1, 2, 3, 4 B. 4, 3, 2, 1
C. 3, 2, 1, 4 D. 2, 3, 1, 4

35. Which personality test relies on the interpretation of inkblots to understand personality?
A. MMPI-2 B. TAT
C. 16 PF D. Rorschach

36. Who among the following is credited with developing Logo therapy?
A. Abraham Maslow
B. Rogers
C. Victor Frankel
D. Rollo May

37. People who score high on the psychoticism (P) scale are:
A. Emotionally over-reactive
B. Empathetic, caring, and cooperative
C. Egocentric, aggressive, and hostile
D. Obsessive-compulsive, egocentric, emotionally over-reactive

38. Match List-I with List-II and indicate your answer with the help of given codes:

List-I (Type of Love)	List-II (Explanation)
(a) Eros	1. A type of unselfish love characterised by devotion to the welfare of others
(b) Agape	2. A type of love that incorporates all other types of love
(c) Authentic love	3. A type of procreative love that is savouring and experiential
(d) Philia	4. Brotherly love

Codes:

	(a)	(b)	(c)	(d)
A.	3	1	2	4
B.	3	4	2	1
C.	4	1	3	2
D.	2	4	1	3

39. Which of the following is NOT one of the four basic types of tools used by psychologists to measure personality?
A. Projective tests
B. Personal interview
C. Aptitude test
D. Self-report inventories

40. Which of the following is correct of the Rorschach Ink Blot Cards?
A. Five chromatic and five achromatic
B. Two chromatic and eight achromatic
C. Three chromatic and seven achromatic
D. Three chromatic, five achromatic and two unstructured

41. The accuracy and usefulness of projective tests depends largely on:
A. The age of the client.
B. The mental state of the client.
C. The understanding and cooperation of the client.
D. The skill of the examiner.

42. Among the following descriptions of major defense mechanisms, which one describes 'projection'?
A. Assigning logical or socially desirable motives to that we do.
B. Directing a motive that cannot be gratified in one form into another channel.
C. Denying that an unpleasant reality exists.
D. Assigning our own undesirable qualities to others.

43. Down syndrome is associated with which of the causal factor?
A. Trisomy 18 B. Trisomy 12
C. Trisomy 21 D. Trisomy 14

44. Behaviour of individuals with Anti-social Personality Disorder often appears impulsive and unpredictable due to switching quickly and unpredictably between:
A. Dysfunctional memories
B. Dysfunctional schemas
C. Dysfunctional thinking
D. Dysfunctional listening

45. Arrange the following treatment methodology in order to which they got known:
1. Client Centered Therapy
2. Psychoanalytic Therapy
3. Reciprocal Inhibition Technique
4. Reinforcement Contingency

Codes:
A. 1, 2, 3, 4 B. 2, 1, 3, 4
C. 2, 1, 4, 3 D. 3, 4, 1, 2

46. Which personality measuring instrument uses four scales and is derived from the work of Jung?
A. Myers-Briggs Type Indicator
B. Big five personality factors
C. Cattell's 16PF traits
D. None of the above

47. Which is the one that is not a "Big Five" factor of personality?
A. Extraversion
B. Psychoticism
C. Conscientiousness
D. Agreeableness

48. Which of the following are features of Borderline Personality Disorder?
1. Affective instability
2. Lack of remorse
3. Impulsivity
4. Self-mutilation
5. Over concern with order and rules.

Codes:
A. 1, 2 and 3 B. 1, 3 and 4
C. 1, 2, 4 and 5 D. 2, 3, 4 and 5

49. Rogers in his Person Centred Counselling approach emphasizes .... and ....
A. Empathy; Sympathy
B. Experiential focussing; Unconditional positive regard
C. Congruence; Sympathy
D. Unconditional Positive Regard; Empathy

50. Among these, which personality disorder is characterised by 'eccentric' behaviour marked by odd patterns of thinking and communication.
A. Borderline Personality Disorder
B. Associative Personality Disorder
C. Dissociative Personality Disorder
D. Schizotypal Personality Disorder

ANSWERS

1	2	3	4	5	6	7	8	9	10
C	A	C	B	A	A	A	D	C	B
11	**12**	**13**	**14**	**15**	**16**	**17**	**18**	**19**	**20**
D	A	B	C	B	A	C	C	A	B
21	**22**	**23**	**24**	**25**	**26**	**27**	**28**	**29**	**30**
C	A	D	B	C	C	C	B	A	A
31	**32**	**33**	**34**	**35**	**36**	**37**	**38**	**39**	**40**
B	B	D	A	D	C	C	A	C	A
41	**42**	**43**	**44**	**45**	**46**	**47**	**48**	**49**	**50**
D	D	C	B	C	A	B	B	D	D

❑❑❑

CHAPTER 7

Scaling & Testing

PSYCHOLOGICAL SCALING: PURPOSE & METHODS

Scaling consists of measuring and comparing objects in some meaningful way. Some social science researchers are continually trying to measure and compare human perceptions. They (a) create scales by assigning psychological objects to numbers and then (b) locate individuals on the scale they have created. Besides being tangible at certain instances, psychological objects can also be perceived through senses which results in some attitudinal response. Psychological objects can be colours, words, tones, and sentences as well as houses, gold stars and names or pictures of television stars. Psychological objects are most often presented as sentences or statements such as "There is no one in this world to trust" or "I hate all". With young children, the objects are often pictures.

Psychological (psychometric) scaling methods are an outgrowth of the psychophysical tradition just described. Although their purpose is to locate stimuli on a linear (straight-line) scale, no quantitative physical values (*e.g.*, loudness or weight) for stimuli are involved. The linear scale may represent an individual's attitude toward a political party, his judgement of the quality of an glossary product, the degree to which he exhibits a personality characteristic, or his preference for different foods. Psychological scales thus are used for having a person rate his own characteristics as well as those of other individuals in terms of such attributes, for example, as leadership potential or initiative. In addition to locating individuals on a scale, psychological scaling can also be used to scale objects and various kinds of characteristics: finding where different foods fall on a group's preference scale; or determining the relative positions of various job characteristics in the view of those holding that job. Reported degrees of similarities between pairs of objects are used to identify scales or dimensions on which people perceive the objects.

Comparative and non-comparative scaling

Comparative scaling involves the direct comparison of stimulus objects. Comparative scale data must be interpreted in relative terms and have only ordinal or rank order properties. (Example: Do you prefer vegetarian or non-vegetarian?). In non-comparative scaling each item is scaled independently of the others (example: How do you feel about non-vegetarian?). The resulting data are generally assumed to be interval or ratio scaled.

Composite Measures

Composite measures of variables are created by combining two or more separate empirical indicators into a single measure, often too complex to measure simply or with one item. Scales and indexes are both composite measures. Self esteem, intelligence, satisfaction with service etc are some concepts that often use composite measure.

TYPES OF DATA & MEASUREMENT SCALES

There are four measurement scales (or types of data): nominal, ordinal, interval and ratio. These are simply ways to categorize different types of variables.

Nominal

Nominal scales are used for labelling variables, without any quantitative value. Nominal scales could simply be called "labels." For example:

What is the colour of your hair?

1. Black 2. Brown 3. Gray 4. Other

Ordinal

With ordinal scales, it is the order of the values which is important and significant, but the differences between each one is not really known. Take an example in terms of ABC, in which we know that (a) is better than (b) or (c), but we don't know-and cannot quantify-how much better it is. Ordinal scales are typically measures of non-numeric concepts like satisfaction, happiness, discomfort, etc.

How satisfied you are with your job?

(*a*) Very satisfied (*b*) Somewhat satisfied
(*c*) Neutral (*d*) Somewhat unsatisfied
(*e*) Very unsatisfied

Interval

Interval scales are numeric scales in which we know not only the order, but also the exact differences between the values. For example, the Fahrenheit scale is an interval scale, since each degree is equal but there is no absolute zero point. This means that although we can add and subtract degrees (100° is 10° warmer than 90°), we cannot multiply values or create ratios (100° is not twice as warm as 50°). Time is another good example of an interval scale in which the increments are known, consistent, and measurable.

Ratio

"A ratio scale is an interval scale in which distances are stated with respect to a rational zero rather than with respect to, for example, the mean" (Nunnally, 1967). If we ask respondents their ages, the difference between any two years would always be the same, and 'zero' signifies the absence of age or birth. Hence, a 100-year old person is indeed twice as old as a 50-year old one. Sales figures, quantities purchased and market share are all expressed on a ratio scale. Ratio scales are the most sophisticated of scales, since it incorporates all the characteristics of nominal, ordinal and interval scales. As a result, a large number of descriptive calculations are applicable.

PSYCHOLOGICAL SCALING METHODS

Comparative scaling techniques

- **Rank-order scale:** A respondent is presented with several items simultaneously and asked to rank them (example: Rate the following bollywood stars from 1 to 10.). This is an ordinal level technique.
- **Bogardus social distance scale:** A scaling technique for measuring social distance, pioneered by Emory S. Bogardus in the 1930s, usually applied to the study of ethnic relations, social classes, and social values generally. The scale attempts to measure respondents' degree of warmth, intimacy, indifference, or hostility to particular social relationships, by having them indicate agreement or

disagreement with a series of statements about particular (say) religious groups. The results are reduced to a single score on a scale. There are also non-comparative versions of this scale.

- **Q-Sort scale:** The Q-sort method was originally developed by Stephenson (1953) in his research on Q factor analysis, in which persons as opposed to scales serve as variables. The technique consists of arranging items into categories to describe an individual. Items uncharacteristic of the individual are given low values, items characteristics of the individual are given high values, neutral items are placed in middle categories. For example, respondents are given hundred attitude statements on individual cards and are asked to place them into eleven piles ranging from "most highly agreed with" to "least highly agreed with".
- **Guttman scale:** Guttman scaling is also sometimes known as cumulative scaling or scalogram analysis. The purpose of Guttman scaling is to establish a one-dimensional continuum for a concept you wish to measure. It utilizes the intensity structure among several indicators of a given variable. Statements are listed in order of importance. The rating is scaled by summing all responses until the first negative response in the list.
- **Constant sum scale:** A respondent is given a constant sum of money, script, credits, or points and asked to allocate these to various items (example : If you had 100 Yen to spend on food products, how much would you spend on product A, on product B, on product C, etc.). This is an ordinal level technique.
- **Pair wise comparison scale:** For the Method of Pairwise Comparisons, each candidate (or alternative) is matched head-to-head (one-on-one) with each of the other candidates. Each candidate (alternative) gets 1 point for a one-on-one win and a half a point for a tie. The candidate (alternative) with the most total points is the winner. For instance, in a 4 sports person competition, suppose participant A beats participant B and D head-to-head, participant B beats participant D and ties participant C head-to-head, participant C beats participant A and ties participant B head-to-head, and participant D beats participant C head-to-head. Participant A would get 2 points (1 each for beating B and D), participant B would get 1.5 points (1 point for beating D and half a point for the tie with C), participant would get 1.5 points (1 point for beating A and half a point for the tie with B), and participant D would get 1 point (for beating C). Since participant A has the highest point total, participant A is the winner by the Method of Pairwise Comparisons.

Non-comparative Scaling Techniques

- **Continuous rating scale (also called the graphic rating scale):** A graphic rating scale is a commonly used scale system for performance appraisals. The scale typically features a Likert scale from 1-3, 1-5, and so on. An example of a 1-3 rating could include responses such as: 1: Poor, 2: Average, and 3: Excellent. The scale that is used for a specific performance appraisal can vary by the dimensions each organization chooses to use. For instance, there may be dimensions such as accountability, customer service, and financial records. The organization has control over how the items measure employee performance. Respondents rate items by placing a mark on a line. The line is usually labelled at each end. There are sometimes a series of numbers, called scale points, (say, from zero to 100) under the line. Scoring and codification is difficult.
- **Likert scale:** Likert-type or frequency scales use fixed choice response formats and are designed to measure attitudes or opinions (Bowling 1997, Burns & Grove 1997). These ordinal scales measure levels of agreement/disagreement.

A Likert-type scale assumes that the strength/intensity of experience is linear, i.e. on a continuum from strongly agree to strongly disagree, and makes the assumption that attitudes can be measured. In it final form, the Likert Scale is a five (or seven) point scale which is used to allow the individual to express how much they agree or disagree with a particular statement.

- **Phrase completion scales:** Respondents are asked to complete a phrase on an 11-point response scale in which 0 represents the absence of the theoretical construct and 10 represents the theorized maximum amount of the construct being measured. The same basic format is used for multiple questions.
- **Semantic differential scale:** The semantic differential is a scale used for measuring the meaning of things and concepts. There are two aspects of meaning: denotative and connotative. The semantic differential measures connotative meaning.
  - **Denotation:** what a name or concept refers to (denote - to mark out plainly, to indicate)
  - **Connotation:** the suggestive significance of a word, apart from its explicit and recognized meaning Respondents are asked to rate on a 7 point scale an item on various attributes. Each attribute requires a scale with bipolar terminal labels.
- **Thurstone scale:** Thurstone was one of the first and most productive scaling theorists. He actually invented three different methods for developing a unidimensional scale: the method of equal-appearing intervals; the method of successive intervals; and, the method of paired comparisons. The three methods differed in how the scale values for items were constructed, but in all three cases, the resulting scale was rated the same way by respondents.

SOURCES OF BIAS IN PSYCHOLOGICAL TESTING

As Jensen (1980) has pointed out in a huge book devoted to the topic of test bias, there are certain fallacies concerning the definition of test bias which must be immediately dismissed.

1. **The Egalitarian Fallacy:** This assumes that if any mean difference occurs between groups on a test, the test is de facto biased.
2. **The Culture Bound Fallacy:** This assumes that group differences on a test are due to the culture bound nature of items.
3. **The Standardisation Fallacy:** It is often assumed that if a test is standardised on one population, it is necessarily biased if it is used on another. Again this is not necessarily so other evidence would be needed to decide if the test was biased in a different population.

Given that we cannot assume test bias on any of the 3 grounds discussed above, it is necessary to examine the data which would constitute test bias in any group.

(*a*) **Predictive test bias:** As Jensen (1980) argues the most important indicator of bias is the regression equation between a test and its criterion. If for any group there is significant difference in the slopes or the intercepts, or in the standard errors of the estimates of the regression lines, then the test is biased. This is the statistical definition of the test bias.

(*b*) **Internal evidence of test bias:** It is possible to examine the characteristics of the test themselves to investigate test bias.

(*i*) The construct validity of the test should be the same for both groups. Construct validity, defined by the patterns of correlations of a test with other variables, should not differ in the groups. The variable can hardly be said to be the same if the correlations with other variables are different *i.e.,* the test is biased.

(*ii*) Test retest reliability should be he same for both groups in an unbiased test, for obvious reasons.

(*iii*) Internal consistency reliability should be the same for both groups. If it is not this may be due to differences in item difficulty. If after this has been allowed for the average correlation between the items is different in the two groups this is evidence of item bias.

(*iv*) If we carry out an analysis of variance of item scores there should be no group X item interactions. If there is then this is evidence of item bias, and the relevant items can be changed or removed.

(*v*) In standard item analysis correlations between items and total score should be the same for the two groups although p values may vary. However large differences in p values should be investigated.

(*vi*) In factor analysis of the items the factor loadings of the items should be the same for both groups, within the limits of the standard errors. Biased items will differ.

(*vii*) The item characteristics curves of the items will be the same for the two groups. Details of the detection of bias by these methods can be found in Mellenbergh (1983).

ETHICAL ISSUES IN PSYCHOLOGICAL TESTING

There are many issues of concern when it comes to ethics, one such issue being the right to privacy. The concepts of individual rights and privacy are an essential part of our society and must be taken seriously when students are involved. The ethical principle asserts individual rights to privacy and confidentiality as well as self determination. The term confidentiality indicated that individuals are guaranteed privacy in term of all personal information that is disclosed and that no information will then be disclosed without the individual's direct permission. There are times however, that confidentiality is breached because managers for example, will seek out psychological information about their employees. Another example is that teachers may seek test scores for students, however with the good intention of understanding issues of performance (McIntire & Miller, 2007).

Another ethical concern is the right to informed consent, Self determination is a right to every individual which means that individuals are entitled to receive complete explanations in regards to why exactly they are being tested as well as how the results of the test will be used and what their results mean. These complete explanations are commonly known as informed consent and should be conveyed in such a way that is straight forward and easy for students to understand. In situations involving minors or those with limited cognitive abilities, informed consent needs to come from both the student themselves as well as their parents or guardian. However, parental permission should not be confused with informed consent. Educators have a responsibility to ensure that the student as well as their parents or guardian understand all implications and requirement that will be involved in any test before it is even administered (McIntire & Miller, 2007).

In addition to the ethics of informed consent, students are also entitled to be prompted with an explanation, as non technical as it may be, of the test results. However due to the fact that some test results may influence the student's self esteem as well as behaviour, it is necessary that the educator explain the result to the student in a sensitive manner (McIntire & Miller, 2007).

Another issue that involves the need for educators to follow the ethical guidelines is the right to protection from stigma. In conjunction with the student's right to know and understand their results, researchers need to be careful not to use any stigmatizing labels when describing the results in terms of the student. Educators need to refrain from using terms such as "feebleminded" and "pathetic". Therefore, the results that the student receives, along with their families, or guardians, should bring upon positive growth and development on part of the student. Educators should be focussed on benefiting their students and should constantly maintain equal respect for each student and should be sure not to discriminate in any way in terms of gender or ethnicity, etc (McIntire & Miller, 2007).

MULTIPLE CHOICE QUESTIONS

1. Under which measurement scale is data categorized, but not ranked?
   A. An ordinal B. A nominal
   C. An interval scale D. Both (a) & (b)

2. Under which measurement scale is data ranked?
   A. An ordinal
   B. A nominal
   C. An interval scale
   D. None of the above

3. Under which measurement scale is data ranked and separated by equal intervals?
   A. An ordinal
   B. A nominal
   C. An interval scale
   D. Both (a) & (b)

4. Who introduced the theory of measurement and scales of measurement into psychology?
   A. Schlosberg B. Stevens
   C. Bogardus D. Guttman

5. The scale in which the response options to a question are "yes" or "no" / "true" or "false" is known as:
   A. Continuous scale
   B. Unforced choice
   C. Dichotmous scale
   D. None of the above

6. Which type of scale measures the connotative meanings of objects, events and concepts.
   A. Semantic differential scale
   B. Likert scale
   C. Graphic rating scale
   D. Summated rating

7. .... may be defined as the act of assigning numbers or symbols to characteristics of objects (as well as people, events or other things) according to rules.
   A. Measurement
   B. Questionnaire
   C. Assessment
   D. None of the above

8. A type of scale with a true zero point is;
   A. An ordinal scale
   B. A nominal scale
   C. A ratio scale
   D. None of the above

9. Who developed a social distance scale as a technique to measure the willingness of people to participate in social relations with other kinds of people.
   A. Bogardus B. Thurstone
   C. Likert D. Guttman

10. .... scale measures to what degree a person has a positive or negative attitude to something.
    A. Constant sum
    B. Pairwise comparison
    C. Rank order
    D. Guttman

11. Which technique requires a large number of judges to assess each item in terms of its degree of favourability towards the object:
    A. The Guttman technique
    B. The Thurstone technique
    C. The Semantic differential technique
    D. Both B & C

12. The advantage of the Likert technique over the Thurstone technique is that:
    A. It has higher content validity
    B. It is easier to assess reliability
    C. It is cost effective
    D. None of the above

13. Thurstone, Likert and the Semantic differential techniques all produce:
    A. Ratio measures
    B. Interval measures
    C. Ordinal measures
    D. Nominal measures

14. .... scale has two aspects of meaning: denotative and connotative.
    A. Nominal
    B. Semantic differential
    C. Likert
    D. Thurstone

15. Likert scales are criticised because:
A. They are too tough to complete
B. They restrict participant answers
C. They cannot be analyzed
D. They are too simple to complete

16. Which type of scale is used to measure attitudes of people and is also known a equal appearing intervals?
A. The Thurstone scale
B. The Guttman scale
C. The Semantic differential scale
D. The Likert scale

17. Rating scales are used to record judgements about:
A. Oneself B. Objects
C. Others D. All of the above

18. A Likert scale is a:
A. Guttman scale B. Summative scale
C. Rank-order scale D. Preference scale

19. The levels of nominal scale variables are simply ....
A. rank order items
B. numbers
C. different categories or groups
D. physical measures

20. .... scaling is also sometimes known as cumulative scaling or scalogram analysis.
A. Likert B. Thurstone
C. Guttman D. Bogardus

21. Ratio scales are like:
A. Ordinal scales with ratio added
B. Interval scales with a true zero points
C. Nominal scales with the brackets
D. Both A & B

22. In .... scale, items are arranged in an order so that an individual who agrees with a particular item also agrees with items of lower rank-order.
A. Guttman scale B. Thurstone scale
C. Likert scale D. Bogardus scale

23. .... is a five or seven point scale, used to allow the individual to express how much they agree or disagree with a particular statement.
A. Guttman scale B. Thurstone scale
C. Likert scale D. Bogardus scale

24. Who introduced the term "absolute scaling" in his paper entitled "A method of scaling psychological and educational tests".
A. Guttman B. Thurstone
C. Bogardus D. Likert

25. Which two scales of measurement have equal distances among the scores they yield?
A. Interval and ratio
B. Ordinal and ratio
C. Nominal and ratio
D. Ordinal and Nominal

26. Which of the following is the correct order of Steven's four levels of measurement?
A. Ordinal, nominal, ratio, interval
B. Nominal, ordinal, interval, ratio
C. Interval, nominal, ordinal, ratio
D. Ratio, interval, nominal, ordinal

27. Read the following two statements—Assertion (A) and Reason (R) and indicate your answer using the codes given below:

Assertion (A): Median is used as a measure of scale value in method of equal appearing intervals.

Reason (R): In normal distribution mean, median and mode are identical.

Codes:
A. Both (A) and (R) are true and (R) is the correct explanation of (A).
B. Both (A) and (R) are true, but (R) is not the correct explanation of (A).
C. (A) is true, (R) is false.
D. (A) is false, (R) is true.

28. Categories are exhaustive when:
A. There is a meaningful zero point
B. Cannot assume negative values.
C. Each object must appear in at least one category.
D. Both A & C

29. Given below are two statements, the first labelled as Assertion (A) and the other labelled as Reason (R). Indicate your answer using the codes given below:

Assertion (A): Total variance of test score is the sum of True Variance and Error Variance.

Reason (R): True score and error score are independent of each other.

Codes:

A. Both (A) and (R) are true and (R) is the correct explanation of (A).
B. Both (A) and (R) are true, but (R) is not the correct explanation of (A).
C. (A) is true, but (R) is false.
D. (A) is false, but (R) is true.

30. In which of the scaling method, item-remainder correlations are frequently calculated?

A. Equal appearing interval
B. Paired comparison
C. Successive intervals
D. Summated ratings

31. Below are two statements, the first labelled as Assertion (A) and the other labelled as Reason (R). Indicate your answer using the codes given below:

Assertion (A): If higher order factor analysis is to be carried out, first order factors should not be subjected to varimax rotation.

Reason (R): Varimax rotation provides oblique factors.

Codes:

A. Both (A) and (R) are true and (R) is the correct explanation of (A).
B. Both (A) and (R) are true, but (R) is not the correct explanation of (A).
C. (A) is true, but (R) is false.
D. (A) is false, but (R) is true.

32. Which of the following techniques is/are well known for being associated with cumulative scales?

1. Bogardus Social Distance Scale
2. Likert's summated ratings
3. Guttman's scalogram analysis
4. Osgood's semantic differential

Codes:

A. 1 only
B. 1 and 2 only
C. 1 and 3 only
D. 1, 3 and 4 only

33. Match List-I with List-II and select the correct answer using the codes given below:

List-I (Attitude scaling technique)	**List-II (Feature)**
(*a*) Equal appearing intervals	1. Checks unidimensionality of the scale
(*b*) Paired comparison	2. Employs 'Z' as a measure of scale value
(*c*) Scalogram	3. Can assess multi-dimensional attitudes
(*d*) Summated ratings	4. Suitable for scaling large number of items

Codes:

	(*a*)	(*b*)	(*c*)	(*d*)
A.	4	2	1	3
B.	2	4	1	3
C.	4	2	3	1
D.	3	1	4	2

34. What is Cronbach's alpha a measure of?

A. Length of a questionnaire
B. Internal consistency of a questionnaire
C. The validity of an observational study's coding scheme
D. Difficulty of a questionnaire

35. Which of the following technique usually yields multidimensional attitude scales?

A. Summated rating
B. Paired comparison
C. Equal appearing interval
D. Scalogram

36. Which of the following statements would be false about multiple correlation?

1. It ranges from –1.00 to 1.00 only
2. It ranges from 0 to 1.00 only
3. It ranges from $-\infty$ to $+\infty$
4. It ranges from –1.00 to 0 only

Codes:

A. 1 only B. 2 only
C. 3 and 4 only D. 1, 3 and 4 only

37. Which is NOT one of the 12 assumptions about testing and assessment?

A. Psychological traits and states can be quantified and measured.
B. Test-related behaviour predicts non-test-related behaviour.
C. Sources of error can be eliminated from the assessment process.
D. Assessment can be conducted in a fair and unbiased manner.

38. Cattell's scree is a

A. plot displaying variables using the first two factors as axes.
B. plot of the order of unrotated factors on X axis and eigen values on Y axis.
C. plot of the order of unrotated factors on X axis and the communalities on the Y axis.
D. eigen values on X axis and communalities on Y axis.

39. How many interactions can be studied in a 2 × 3 × 5 factorial design?

A. 4 B. 5
C. 29 D. 30

40. Read each of the following two statements Assertion (A) and Reason (R) and indicate your answer using the codes given below:

Assertion (A): In method of equal appearing interval, median is often used as a measure of scale value.

Reason (R): In normal distribution mean, median and mode are equal.

Codes:

A. Both (A) and (R) are true and (R) is the correct explanation of (A).
B. Both (A) and (R) are true, but (R) is not the correct explanation of (A).
C. (A) is true, but (R) is false.
D. (A) is false, but (R) is true.

41. Which one of the following pairs is NOT correctly matched?

	Term in factor analysis		Meaning/ Example
A.	Factor extraction method	–	Principal axes
B.	Factor rotation method	–	Promax
C.	Inter factor correlation	–	Correlation between orthogonal factors
D.	Cattell's scree	–	Plot to decide number of factors retain for interpretation

42. If a cricket coach calculates batting averages, what scale would be used?

A. Interval scale B. Ratio scale
C. Nominal scale D. Ordinal scale

43. What is the difference between data measured on an interval scale and data measured on a ratio scale?

A. An interval scale has a true zero point, so zero on the scale corresponds to zero of the concept being measured.
B. A ratio scale has a true zero point, so zero on the scale corresponds to zero of the concept being measured.
C. A ratio scale puts scores into categories, while an interval scale measures on a continuous scale.
D. None of the above

44. .... is a rank order procedure where respondents are asked to sort a given number of items or statements and classify them into a pre-determined number of sets (usually 11) according to some criterion such as preference, attitude, or behavioural intent.

A. Bogardus Social Distance Scale
B. Guttman Scaling
C. Q-Sort Scaling
D. Paired Comparison Scale

45. A nominal scale variable

A. usually the result of counting something.
B. usually involves ranking.
C. is usually based on counting.
D. has a meaningful zero point.

46. Read each of the following two statements—Assertion (A) and Reason (R) and indicate your answer using the codes given below:

Assertion (A): A person's responses on MMPI were disregarded because he has scored very high on frequency sub-scale.

Reason (R): Frequency sub-scale indicates the style of an individual to respond in a typical way.

Codes:

A. Both (A) and (R) are true and (R) is the correct explanation of (A).
B. Both (A) and (R) are true, but (R) is not the correct explanation of (A).
C. (A) is true, but (R) is false.
D. (A) is false, but (R) is true.

47. If eleven attitude statements are to be scaled by the method of paired comparison, what would be the number of pairs?

A. 11 B. 55
C. 22 D. 44

48. What type of error does the process of scaling (converting psychological phenomena into numbers) contain?

A. Random & systematic
B. Random
C. Systematic
D. Standard

49. Interval Scales have:

A. Equal appearing units
B. No equal appearing units
C. No statistical value
D. None of the above

50. An ordinal scale is:

A. The simplest form of measurement
B. A rank-order scale of measurement
C. A scale with equal intervals between adjacent numbers
D. A scale with an absolute zero point

ANSWERS

1	2	3	4	5	6	7	8	9	10
B	A	C	B	C	A	A	C	A	D
11	**12**	**13**	**14**	**15**	**16**	**17**	**18**	**19**	**20**
B	C	C	B	B	A	D	B	C	C
21	**22**	**23**	**24**	**25**	**26**	**27**	**28**	**29**	**30**
B	A	C	B	A	B	B	C	A	D
31	**32**	**33**	**34**	**35**	**36**	**37**	**38**	**39**	**40**
C	C	A	B	A	D	C	B	A	B
41	**42**	**43**	**44**	**45**	**46**	**47**	**48**	**49**	**50**
C	B	B	C	A	A	B	A	A	B

❑❑❑

CHAPTER 8

Physiological Mechanisms

STAGES OF SLEEP

Usually people pass through 5 stages of sleep: 1, 2, 3, 4 and REM (Rapid Eye Movement) sleep. These stages progress cyclically from 1 through REM then begin again with stage 1. A complete sleep cycle takes an average of 90 to 110 minutes. The first sleep cycle each night have relatively short REM sleeps and long periods of deep sleep but later in the night, REM periods lengthen and deep sleep time decreases.

Stage 1: This is light sleep where you drift in and out of sleep and can be awakened easily. In this stage, the eye move slowly and muscle activity slows. During this stage many people also experience sudden muscle contractions called hypnic myoclonia, often preceded by a sensation of starting to fall. This sleep lasts only a brief time (5-10 minutes).

Stage 2: This stage lasts for approximately 20 minutes. During this stage eye movement stop and our brain waves become slower, with occasional bursts of rapid waves called sleep spindles.

Stage 3: When a person enters stage 3, extremely slow brain waves called delta waves are interspersed with smaller, faster waves.

Stage 4: The brain produces delta waves almost exclusively and sleep lasts for approximately 30 minutes. Stage 3 and 4 are referred to as deep sleep, and it is very difficult to wake someone from them. In deep sleep, there is no eye movement or muscle activity. This is when some children experience bedwetting, sleepwalking and night terrors.

REM Sleep: In REM period, breathing becomes more rapid, irregular and shallow, eyes jerk rapidly and limb muscles are temporarily paralyzed. Brain waves during this stage increase to levels experienced when a person is awake. Also, heart rate increases, blood pressure rises, males develop penile erections and body loses some of the ability to regulate its temperature. This is the time when most dreams occur and if awoken during REM sleep, a person can remember the dreams. Most people experience 3 to 5 intervals of REM sleep each night.

Infants spend almost 50% of their time in REM sleep. Adults spend nearly half of sleep time in stage 2, about 20% in REM and the other 30% is divided between the other 3 stages. Older adults spend progressively less time in REM sleep.

DISORDERS OF SLEEP

A sleep disorder (somnipathy) is a medical disorder of the sleep patterns of a person or animal. Some sleep disorders are serious enough to interfere with normal physical, mental and emotional functioning. A test commonly ordered for some sleep disorders is the polysomnogram.

Common Sleep Disorders

1. **Primary Insomnia:** chronic difficulties in falling asleep and/or maintaining sleep that cannot be attributed to a medical, psychiatric, or environmental cause (such as drug abuse or medications).
2. **Bruxism:** Involuntarily grinding or clenching of the teeth while sleeping. Bruxism can occur during the day or night. Generally, patients clench their teeth throughout the day and gnash and clench them during sleep.
3. **Delayed Sleep Phase Syndrome (DPSP):** Inability to awaken and fall asleep at socially acceptable times but no problem with sleep maintenance, a disorder of circadian rhythms. Children and adolescents with DSPS may experience depression and other psychiatric problems including behavioural problems as a result of daytime drowsiness and missing school.
4. **Hypopnea:** Abnormally shallow breathing or slow respiratory rate while sleeping. Hypopnea is distinct from apnea in which there is no breathing.
5. **Narcolepsy:** Excessive daytime sleepiness (EDS) often culminates in falling asleep spontaneously but unwillingly at inappropriate times. The daytime sleep attacks may occur with or without warning, and can occur repeatedly in a single day. Persons with narcolepsy often have fragmented night time sleep with frequent brief awakenings.
6. **Cataplexy:** A sudden weakness in the motor muscles that can result in collapse to the floor at times of strong emotion such as during laughter, anger, fear, or surprise. In so collapsing, people with cataplexy may injure themselves.
7. **Night Terror:** Abrupt awakening from sleep with behaviour consistent with terror. Night terrors occur during the transition from stage 3 non-REM sleep to stage 4 non-REM sleep, beginning approximately 90 minutes after the child falls asleep. The sleep disorder of night terrors typically occurs in children aged 3-12 years, with a peak onset in children aged 3½ years.
8. **Parasomnias:** Disruptive sleep related events involving inappropriate actions during sleep stages, sleep walking and night terrors are examples.
9. **Periodic Limb Movement Disorder (PLMD):** Sudden involuntary movement or jerking of arms and/or legs during sleep, for example kicking the legs. It is the only movement disorder that occurs only during sleep, and it is sometimes called periodic leg (or limb) movements during sleep.
10. **Rapid Eye Movement Behaviour Disorder:** People who suffer from REM behaviour disorder (RBD) act out their dreams. They physically move limbs or even get up and engage in activities associated with waking. Some engage in sleep talking, shouting, screaming, hitting or punching.
11. **Sleep Paralysis:** This is characterized by temporary paralysis of the body shortly before or after sleep.
12. **Sleep Walking or Somnambulism:** Is characterized by walking or other activity while seemingly still asleep. Some types of sleep walking are related to seizure disorders, bipolar disorders, or other neurological conditions, but most cases are transitory and due to unknown causes.
13. **Nocturia:** A frequent need to get up and go to the bathroom to urinate at night. It can be troublesome in itself, by disturbing sleep, and can have a significant impact on quality of sleep and quality of life.
14. **Sleep Apnea:** This disorder is potentially very serious and even life threatening. During the episodes of apnea, the person wakes up to breathe again, disrupting sleep, and also suffer from a brief lack of oxygen or a complete stop of breathing during sleep. There are two main types of sleep apnea; obstructive sleep apnea (OSA) and central sleep apnea (CSA). Mixed sleep apnea refers to the combination of both central and obstructive sleep apnea.

PHYSIOLOGICAL MECHANISM OF SLEEP & WAKING

Neural control of arousal/waking

1. **Acetylcholine:** One of the most important neurotransmitters involved in arousal. Two groups of acetycholinergic neurons located in the pons and basal forebrain, produce activation & cortical de-synchrony when they are stimulated.
2. **Norepinephrine:** Norepinephrine is an excitatory neurotransmitter, and it regulates mood and physical and mental arousal..
3. **Serotonin (5-HT):** It is an important inhibitory neurotransmitter, which can have a profound effect on emotion, mood, and anxiety. It is involved in regulating sleep, wakefulness, and eating. It plays a role in perception as well.
4. **Histamine:** A neurotransmitter implicated in control of wakefulness and arousal; a compound synthesized from histidine, an amino acid.
5. **Tuberomammillary nucleus:** A nucleus in the ventral posterior hypothalamus, just rostral to the mammillary bodies consists of, largely, histaminergic neurons (*i.e.,* neurones releasing histamine) and is involved with the control of arousal, sleep and circadian rhythm.
6. **Hypocretin:** Orexin, also called hypocretin, is a neurotransmitter that regulates arousal, wakefulness, and appetite. It is basically Involved in regulating the sleep on/off cells in the ventro lateral preoptic area (VLPA).

Neural Control of Slow Wave Sleep

Ventrolateral Preoptic Area (VLPA): The VLPO is active during sleep, primarily during non-rapid eye movement sleep (NREM sleep), and releases inhibitory neurotransmitters, mainly GABA and galanin, which inhibit neurons that are involved in wakefulness and arousal.

Lesions of the preoptic area produce total insomnia, leading to death, whereas electrical stimulation of the preoptic area induces signs of drowsiness.

Neural Control of REM Sleep

PGO Wave (Pons, Geniculate, Occipital) are most prominent in the period right before rapid eye movement sleep (or REM sleep), and are theorized to be intricately involved with eye movement of both wake and sleep cycles in many different animals.

INGESTIVE BEHAVIOUR: DRINKING AND ITS NEURAL MECHANISM; HUNGER AND ITS NEURAL MECHANISM.

Neural mechanism in eating & hunger

Neural mechanism in eating and satiation hunger = the body signalling need for nutrients and energy satiation = body signalling satisfaction of need for nutrients and energy.

The hypothalamus has long been considered important in the regulation of hunger motivation. Two significant eating control centres are in the hypothalamus. One is in the lateral hypothalamus (or LH), also know as the "start" switch, the other is in the ventro-medial hypothalamus (or VMH), also known as the "stop" switch. The parietal and temporal cortex are also involved with hunger and the prefrontal cortex is involved with satiety.

Research from the 1940s onwards showed that lesioning (i.e. destroying) tiny areas in the LH in rats, dogs, and other mammals led to a loss of interest in food and eating, the animals seemingly unaware that they were starving themselves. Whereas the opposite happened with lesions to the VMH as this led to the animals concerned eating voraciously, so they became obese. This suggested that the LH initiates eating behaviour (hence the "start" switch) and the VMH stops this behaviour (hence the "stop" switch).

In has also been found that humans with brain tumours or other conditions that have damaged the VMH area overeat and become obese. However, VHM damage is not a common cause of obesity.

Neural control of cognitive factors, Amygdala and inferior prefrontal cortex are involved in our thoughts about food, hence the reason why when we think of food, we want to eat it. The amygdala helps us select our food on the basis of previous experience. Rolls & Rolls: If we remove this in rats, they consume both old and new foods indiscriminately, whereas rats whose amygdala wasn't removed, choose only familiar foods. Inferior frontal cortex, receives message from olfactory bulb (smell area in brain)-smell is connected to taste buds. If damaged, results in less eating because less taste (Kold & Whishaw).

Neural mechanism in drinking

What drives us to drink (Water)? Stimulus factors play a very large role in initiating drinking. We drink to wet a dry mouth or to taste a good beverage. Pulled by these stimuli and incentives, we tend to drink more than the body needs, but it is easy for the kidneys to get rid of the excess fluid.

Since maintaining its water level is essential for life itself, the body has a set of complicated internal homeostatic processes to regulate its fluid level and drinking behaviour. The body's water level is maintained by physiological events in which several hormones play a vital role. One of these is the antidiuretic hormone (ADH), which regulates the loss of water through kidneys.

Research aimed at understanding the cause behind drinking is largely concerned with the associated physiological changes. According to Cannon (1932) 'local body signs' plays a role in thirst. Based on the experiments conducted on himself, Cannon found an association between the sensation of dry mouth and the experience of thirst. However later researches showed that a dry mouth is not primary stimulus for thirst. Thus wetting of mouth does not by itself reduce thirst (Bellows, 1939). Instead thirst is also an outcome of general (instead of local) dehydration. That is, intracellular dehydration (e.g caused by salt-intake), in which body fluid is lost from the cells, leads to thirst. Also extracellular dehydration (e.g due to loss of blood), in which fluid is lost from the compartments outside the cells, triggers thirst (Gilman,1937; Stricker,1966). Dehydration excites a complex pattern of neural activity in the hypothalamus and higher regions in the cortex (Grossma, 1979; Stellar, 1990) which in turn, leading to drinking and, in humans, reported thirst.

On the basis of several year researches, clues emerged as to the crucial role of a region in the anterior wall of the third ventricle in thirst mechanisms when it was shown that ablation of tissue in the anteroventral third ventricle wall (AV3V region) of goats and rats caused either temporary or permanent adipsia. In those animals with lesions that did recover spontaneous water drinking, loss of dipsogenic responsiveness to osmotic and ANG stimuli was evident. Another clue to the location of cerebral osmoreceptors subserving thirst came from studies in sheep suggesting that the cerebral osmoreceptors subserving thirst and vasopressin secretion were, at least in part, located in brain regions lacking a blood-brain barrier. In subsequent years, evidence from the study of lesions, electrophysiological recordings, and the expression of the immediate early gene c-fos in rats have confirmed that neurons in both the organum vasculosum of the lamina terminalis (OVLT) and the subfornical organ (SFO) are most likely the sites of very sensitive osmoreceptors.

Lesion studies in rats have shown that the MnPO (median preoptic nucleus) which is situated in the lamina terminalis longitudinally between the two circumventricular organs and is an integral part of the AV3V region, may play a crucial role in the generation of thirst in response to both osmotic and hormonal signals being relayed to this nucleus by neural inputs from the SFO and possibly the OVLT.

ENDOCRINE SYSTEM: CHEMICAL AND GLANDULAR

The endocrine system is a control system of ductless glands that secrete hormones within specific organs. Hormones act as "messengers," and are carried by the bloodstream to different cells in the body, which interpret these messages and act on them. Although many different hormones circulate throughout the bloodstream, each one affects only the cells that are genetically programmed to receive and respond to its message. Hormone levels can be influenced by factors such as stress, infection and changes in the balance of fluid and minerals in blood.

The endocrine system provides an electrochemical connection from the hypothalamus of the brain to all the organs that control the body metabolism, growth and development, and reproduction. There are two types of hormones secreted in the endocrine system: Steroidal and non-steroidal, (or protein based) hormones.

A gland is a group of cells that produce and secrets, or gives off chemicals. A gland selects and removes materials from the blood, processes them and secrets the finished chemical product for use somewhere in the body. There are two types of glands—Exocrine Glands and Endocrine Glands.

Exocrine Glands are those which release their cellular secretions through a duct which empties to the outside or into the lumen (empty internal space) of an organ. These include certain sweat glands, salivary and pancreatic glands, and mammary glands. They are not considered a part of the endocrine system. On the other hand Endocrine Glands are those glands which have no duct and release their secretions directly into the intercellular fluid or into the blood. The collection of endocrine glands makes up the endocrine system.

The major glands that make up the human endocrine system are:

The Hypothalamus: The hypothalamus, a collection of specialized cells that is located in the lower central part of the brain, is the primary link between the endocrine and nervous systems. Nerve cells in the hypothalamus control the pituitary gland by producing chemicals that either stimulate or suppress hormone secretion from the pituitary.

1. **Pituitary gland:** This is situated at the ventral side of the brain. There are 2 parts—
   (a) **Anterior lobe:** The hormone secreted from this part of gland control the secretion secreted by various gland.
   (b) **Posterior lobe:** Stimulates the pituterin muscle. Along with it stimulates the heart. Pituitary gland is also known as Master gland.
2. **Thyroid gland:** The thyroid located in the front part of the lower neck, is shaped like a bow tie or butterfly and produces the thyroid hormones thyroxin, which effects the physical growth. For instance if the secretion of this gland is not proper in the child his physical growth will be effected or he may remain dwarf. By thyroxin deficiency memory and thought process weakens, span of attention decreases, and other mental abilities also become weaker. When the activity of this gland increases the height increases fast. As a result the person becomes worried, unstable and irritable etc.
3. **Parathyroid gland:** This gland is found inside the thyroid gland and is like the size & shape of a pea. The main function of this gland is to control the quantity of calcium. The development of bones & teeth is smooth with the smooth secretion of this gland. Our peacefulness and emotional behaviour is also affected by this gland. When secretion of this gland is abnormal than contraction is found in the muscles, on the other hand when it functions normally the body is balanced and relaxed.

4. **Pancreas gland:** This gland is related to the tubes of duodenum. The first construction of this gland is secretion of digestive juices. If this gland stops its secretion the digestive system gets upset. The second construction of this gland is Islet tissue. These cells are found all over the gland. Insulin is secreted in the blood by these cells.
5. **Adrenal gland:** This gland is situated inward the kidney. Every kidney has a gland which has two parts. The outer part, the adrenal cortex produces hormones called corticosteroids that influence or regulate salt and water balance in the body, the body's response to stress, metabolism, the immune system & sexual development & function. The inner part, the adrenal medulla produce epinephrine, increases blood pressure & heart rate when the body experience stress.
6. **Gonad glands:** Ovaries in females and testis in males are the gonad glands. The secretion from them is called gonadal hormones. They are 3 in number- Progestin, Androgens, Estrogens. All these secretions affect the personality. Due to these secretions males have the masculine traits like-beard, moustaches, voice etc and females have feminine qualities like breast growth, accumulation of body fat around the hips & thighs, growth spurt that occurs during puberty etc.

MULTIPLE CHOICE QUESTIONS

1. Arousal is linked to which brain structure?
   A. The Amygdala
   B. The Reticular activating system
   C. The Sympathetic nervous system
   D. Both (B) & (C)
2. .... activity characterizes slow-wave sleep.
   A. Delta activity B. Beta waves
   C. Alpha waves D. Theta waves
3. What can be used to record eye movement during sleep?
   A. EOG B. EGG
   C. EEG D. ECG
4. .... is the duration of healthy stages of sleep.
   A. 20-50 minutes B. 90-110 minutes
   C. 110-120 minutes D. 85-110 minutes
5. Increased parasympathetic activity is a characteristic of ....?
   A. Slow wave sleep B. REM sleep
   C. Both (a) & (b) D. None of the above
6. When we are awake and very alert, the EEG normally shows:
   A. Theta waves B. Delta waves
   C. Beta waves D. Alpha waves
7. The presence of beta-wave activity in the EEG of an awake person implies that the person is:
   A. About to enter the first stage of sleep
   B. Drowsy
   C. Alert and attentive
   D. None of the above
8. An effective performance is more likely if the level of arousal is suitable for the activity, according to the-
   A. Performance arousal model
   B. Yerkes Dodson law
   C. James Lange theory of motivation
   D. None of the above
9. The non-REM sleep is commonly associated with:
   A. Night terrors
   B. Increased blood pressure
   C. Frequent dreaming
   D. All of the above
10. Nightmares occur in:
    A. REM sleep B. NREM-I sleep
    C. NREM-II sleep D. NREM-III sleep
11. The .... regulates the sleep wake homeostasis.
    A. The circadian clock
    B. The hippocampus
    C. Temporal lobe
    D. Hypothalamus

12. Narcolepsey includes all the symptoms except:
A. Cataplexy B. Sleep attacks
C. Sleep paralysis D. Sleep walking

13. Homeostatic mechanisms are involved in:
A. Drinking
B. Eating
C. Maintaining body temperature
D. All of the above

14. Each of the following is a cue in regulating drinking except;
A. Mouth dryness
B. Cell fluid level
C. Blood sugar level
D. Total blood volume

15. Cataplexy is seen in:
A. Depression B. Schizophrenia
C. Narcolepsy D. None of the above

16. In which stage of sleep are sleep spindles and K complexes first observed?
A. Stage 3 B. Stage 2
C. Stage 1 D. Stage 4

17. .... is involved with the digestion system and the circulatory system; helps to maintain blood sugar levels
A. Pancreas B. Hormone
C. Proteins D. Polypeptide

18. Non-REM sleep consists of how many stages?
A. 4 B. 3
C. 1 D. 5

19. .... is a control system of ductless glands that secrete chemical messengers called hormones.
A. Testosterone B. Thyroxine
C. Thyroid Gland D. Endocrine System

20. Problems of sleep that occurs during slow-wave sleep (stage-4) includes:
A. Urinating while asleep
B. Talking while asleep
C. Walking while asleep
D. All of the above

21. The giant sloth sleeps for about .... each day.
A. 20 hours B. 12 hours
C. 02 hours D. 00 hours

22. The REM phase of sleep is characterized by:
A. A silent EMG record.
B. The presence of gross eye movements
C. An EEG that appears to be of an awake person.
D. All of the above.

23. Which gland is one of the largest endocrine glands in the body and is involved in the production of the hormones T3 (triiodothyronine) and T4 (thyroxine).
A. The Thyroid gland
B. Pineal gland
C. Pituitary gland
D. Gonad glands

24. .... acts to lower blood sugar levels by allowing the sugar to flow into cells.
A. The pancreas B. Insulin
C. Islet cells D. Glucagon

25. .... is classified as a steroid and is responsible for many of the physical characteristics in males like broad shoulders, muscular body and hair.
A. Testosterone B. Estrogen
C. Progesterone D. Amino Acid

26. Among the options given below, which one of the following locations is for the mechanism that triggers REM-sleep?
A. Amygdala
B. Lateral Hypothalamus
C. Midbrain
D. Pontine reticular formation

27. The pancreas gland has a duct which opens into the:
A. Duodenum B. Kidney
C. Liver D. Large intestine

28. Which gland produces melatonin, a serotonin derived hormone, which affects the modulation of sleep patterns in both seasonal and circadian rhythms?
A. Thyroid gland
B. Adrenal gland
C. Pineal gland
D. Parathyroid gland

29. Hypnogogic images occur during drowsy state *i.e.*, between .... and ...., whereas hypnopompic images occur between .... and ....

A. waking, sleeping; waking, sleeping
B. sleeping, waking; waking, sleeping
C. waking, sleeping; sleeping, waking
D. sleeping, waking; sleeping, waking

30. The highest release of .... normally occurs just after waking.

A. growth hormone
B. cortisol
C. testosterone
D. melatonin

31. Which among these is correct about Insulin?

A. Is secreted by beta cells of pancreas.
B. Increase protein and lipid synthesis.
C. Promotes glycogenesis in liver & muscles.
D. All are correct.

32. Which antidiuretic hormone (ADH) mainly targets kidneys & arterioles, stimulates water retention; raises blood pressure by contracting arterioles?

A. Vasopressin B. Estrogen
C. Oxytocin D. Thyroxine

33. Hunger is caused by

I. Expectation of food
II. Deficiency of energy
III. Homeostatic disturbance
IV. Deficiency of Oxygen

Codes:

A. I B. I, II
C. I, II, III D. I, II, III, IV

34. Antidiuretic hormone acts on the .... and helps regulate ....

A. Liver, blood sugar
B. Kidneys, body water
C. Pancreas, proteins
D. Stomach, body weight

35. The parasomnias include:

A. Somnambulism B. Sleep apnoea
C. Narcolepsy D. Depression

36. Damage to which portion of brain is known to cause insomnia.

A. Preoptic-anterior region of the hypothalamus
B. Posterior hypothalamus
C. Posterior segment of the diencephalons
D. None of the above

37. Insufficiency of thyroxin can lead to:

A. Cretinism B. Myxedema
C. Down syndrome D. Goiter

38. Hormones are chemical messengers secreted by the:

A. Endocrine organs
B. Exocrine organs.
C. Both A and B
D. Digestive system

39. Which of the following is a characteristic of slow wave sleep?

A. Increased parasympathetic activity
B. Decreased parasympathetic activity
C. Increased sympathetic activity
D. Decreased sympathetic activity

40. Antidiuretic hormone is synthesized in the:

A. Anterior pituitary
B. Posterior pituitary
C. Thalamus
D. Hypothalamus

41. Which among these options is incorrect about Narcolepsy?

A. There are less hypocretin secreting cells in the body of those with narcolepsy
B. Cause is due to a loss of REM inhibiting mechanism
C. Begins during the middle ages and worsens as the person gets older
D. Shows familial incidence

42. In which of the following pairs, endocrine glands and its primary action is correct?

A. Thyroid - controls physical growth
B. Parathyroid - controls the quantity of calcium
C. Gonad - affects the personality
D. All of the above are correct

43. The hypothalamus regulates ________
A. heart rate B. body temperature
C. water balance D. All of the above

44. Which of the following signs or symptoms are seen in both primary and secondary adrenal insufficiency?
A. Hyperpigmentation
B. Weakness
C. Chronic headache
D. Both A and C

45. Among these which of the following conditions increase the likelihood of having obstructive sleep apnoea?
A. Obesity B. Hypothyroidism
C. Small airways D. All of the above

46. Each of the following is a cue that helps the hypothalamus regulate eating except:
A. stomach contractions
B. blood sugar levels
C. body fat levels
D. red blood cell levels

47. Which of the following are associated with sleep?
A. GABA B. Raphe nuclei
C. Acetylcholine D. Both A & B

48. The main function of insulin is to:
A. Break down protein
B. Enable glucose to enter body cells
C. To provide sugar free diet to the body
D. Absorb all essential nutrients

49. Which among these is true about Somnambulism?
A. Occurs during REM sleep
B. Is commonly seen between the ages of 5 and 12
C. Is associated with enuresis
D. Both B & C Correct

50. Which one of the followings are male sex hormones?
A. Androgens B. Progesterone
C. Estrogen D. Aldosterones

ANSWERS

1	2	3	4	5	6	7	8	9	10
D	A	A	B	A	B	C	B	A	A
11	**12**	**13**	**14**	**15**	**16**	**17**	**18**	**19**	**20**
A	D	D	C	C	B	A	A	D	D
21	**22**	**23**	**24**	**25**	**26**	**27**	**28**	**29**	**30**
A	D	A	B	A	D	A	C	B	B
31	**32**	**33**	**34**	**35**	**36**	**37**	**38**	**39**	**40**
D	A	C	B	A	A	B	A	A	A
41	**42**	**43**	**44**	**45**	**46**	**47**	**48**	**49**	**50**
C	D	D	B	D	D	D	B	D	A

❑❑❑

CHAPTER 9

Social Psychology

In psychology, social psychology is the scientific study of how people's thoughts, feelings, and behaviours are influenced by the actual, imagined, or implied presence of others. Social psychology is about understanding individual behaviour in a social context. Social psychologists therefore deal with the factors that lead us to behave in a given way in the presence of others, and look at the conditions under which certain behaviour/actions and feelings occur. Social psychology is to do with the way these feelings, thoughts, beliefs, intentions and goals are constructed and how such psychological factors, in turn, influence our interactions with others.

According to Gordon Allport (1954) social psychology is best defined as the discipline that uses scientific methods in "an attempt to understand and explain how the thought, feeling and behaviour of individuals are influenced by the actual, imagined, or implied presence of other human beings".

Myers and Spencer (2006) define social psychology as the "scientific study of how people think about, influence, and relate to one another".

Barron and Byrne (2007) defined social psychology as "the scientific field that seeks to understand the nature and cause of individual behaviour and thought in social situations".

SOCIAL COGNITION

Social cognition is a sub-topic of social psychology that focuses on the way perceivers encode, process, remember, and use information in social contexts in order to make sense of other people's behaviour. It focuses on the role that cognitive processes play in our social interactions. The way we think about others plays a major role in how we think, feel, and interact with the world around us. In other words social cognition is the encoding, storage, retrieval, and processing of information in the brain, which relates to conspecifics (members of the same species).

Social cognition came to prominence with the rise of cognitive psychology in the late 1960s and early 1970s and is now the dominant model and approach in mainstream social psychology. "One of the cornerstones of social cognition theory and research is that different individuals may understand the same situation quite differently, if they view it through the lenses of different knowledge structures, goals, and feelings". Social cognition can loosely be broken down into two main elements: the mental structures that are used to represent social information, and the processes that operate on these representations. Social representations have frequently been assumed to take the form of schemata, associative networks, or prototypes.

Social Cognitive Theory (SCT)

Social Cognitive Theory (SCT) started as the Social Learning Theory (SLT) in the 1960s by Albert Bandura. It developed into the SCT in 1986 and posits that social cognitive theory favours a model of causation involving triadic reciprocal determinism. In this model of reciprocal causation, behaviour, cognition and other personal factors, and environmental influences all operate as interacting determinants that influence each other bidirectionally. The unique feature of SCT is the emphasis on social influence and its emphasis on external and internal social reinforcement.

SCT rests on several basic assumptions about learning and behaviour. One assumption concerns triadic reciprocality or the reciprocal causation is that it reflects the interaction between thought, affect and action. Expectations, beliefs, self perceptions, goals and intentions give shape and direction to behaviour. What people think, believe, and feel, affects how they behave (Bandura, 1986; Bower,1975; Neisser, 1976). The natural and extrinsic effects of their actions, in turn, partly determine their thought patterns and emotional reactions.

The second assumption is concerned with the interactive relation between personal characteristics and environmental influences. Human expectations, beliefs, emotional bents and cognitive competencies are developed and modified by social influences that convey information and activate emotional reactions through modelling, instruction and social persuasion (Bandura, 1986). According to Lerner (1982), the physical characteristics of an individual like their age, size, race, sex etc also evoke different reactions from their social environment.

A third assumption within SCT is the two-way influence between behaviour and the environment, which shows that the people are both products and producers of their environment. They affect the nature of their experienced environment through selection and creation of situations. People tend to select activities and associates from the vast range of possibilities in terms of their acquired preferences and competencies (Bandura & Walters, 1959; Bullock & Merrill, 1980; Emmons & Diener, 1986). Through their actions, people create as well as select environments. Aggressive persons produce hostile environments wherever they go, whereas those who act in a friendlier manner generate an amiable social milieu (Raush, 1965). Thus, behaviour determines which of the many potential environmental influences will come into play and what forms they will take. Environmental influences, in turn, partly determine which forms of behaviour are developed and activated.

Important Aspects of Social Cognitive Theory

- **Observational Learning/Modelling:** One important aspect of SCT is observation. This process is also described as vicarious learning or modelling because learning is a result of watching the behaviour and consequences of models in the environment. According to SCT, observational learning of novel behaviours or skills is dependent on four inter-related processes involving attention, retention, production, and motivation.
- **Outcome Expectations:** "An outcome expectancy is defined as a person's estimate that a given behaviour will lead to certain outcomes" (Bandura, 1977). Outcome expectations are important in SCT because they shape the decisions people make about what actions to take and which behaviours to suppress. The frequency of a behaviour should increase when the outcomes expected are valued, whereas behaviours associated with unfavourable or irrelevant outcomes will be avoided.
- **Perceived Self-efficacy:** Self-efficacy also has emerged as a prominent and influential concept within SCT. It focuses on the interrelationships among self-efficacy, outcome expectancies, and behaviour. Self-efficacy involves people's perceptions that they are capable of successfully

performing a behaviour (Bandura, 1977, 1986c, 1997). Students with greater self-efficacy are more confident in their abilities to be successful when compared to their peers with lower self-efficacy. Consistent with the tenets of SCT, self-efficacy is viewed as a product of individuals' own past performances, the observation and verbal persuasion of others in the environment, and individuals' on-going physiological state (Bandura, 1997).

- **Goal Setting:** Goal setting is another central process within SCT (Bandura, 1986; Schunk, 1990). Goals reflect cognitive representations of anticipated, desired, or preferred outcomes. Hence, goals exemplify the agency view within SCT that people not only learn, they use forethought to envision the future, identify desired outcomes, and generate plans of action.
- **Self-regulation:** The major self regulative mechanism operates through three principle sub functions. These includes self monitoring of one's behaviour, its determinants, and its effects; judgement of one's behaviour in relation to personal standards and environmental circumstances; and effective self-reaction. Self-regulation is a prominent and increasing aspect of SCT that exemplifies the underlying assumptions regarding agency and the influence of personal factors on behaviour and the environment.

Limitation of Social Cognitive Theory

There are several limitations of SCT, which should be considered when using this theory in public health. Limitations of the model include the following:

- The theory is loosely organized, based solely on the dynamic interplay between person, behaviour, and environment. It is unclear the extent to which each of these factors into actual behaviour and if one is more influential than another.
- The theory largely ignores the influence of hormones on one's behaviour as well as also ignores the genetic differences that could lead to disparities between people's cognitive abilities and behaviour.
- The theory didn't pay much attention to motivation, conflict, and emotion.
- The theory relies on self-efficacy excessively, however it failed to answer few of the question related to it, for example why are some self-efficacy expectancies stable and others susceptible to rapid change? Or if self-efficacy expectancies are situation specific how do they relate to broader personality?

SOCIAL INFLUENCE

Social influence is a major topic in social psychology and looks at how individual thoughts, actions and feelings are influenced by social groups. In other words social influence is the effect that people have upon the beliefs or behaviours of others (Aaronson, 2004).Various types of social influence also include peer pressure, obedience, leadership, conformity and persuasion.

Three Aspects of Social Influence Are:

- Social influence in which individuals change their attitudes or behaviour in order to adhere to existing social norms.
- A form of social influence involving direct request from one person to another.
- A form of social influence in which one person obeys direct orders from another to perform some action(s).

Social Influence Strategies

One social influence strategy is the foot-in-the-door technique. Three other strategies include manipulating the reciprocity norm, the lowball technique, and feigned scarcity.

1. **Foot-in-the-door technique:** The foot-in-the-door technique is a persuasion strategy that can be used to gain compliance and get someone to agree to a request. For instance your friend asked you to complete his one subject project, which you agreed, because she has to visit doctor immediately. Once you agree to the smaller request, she then asks if you can complete two more subject's projects for her. Once you agreed to the smaller request, you might feel a sense of obligation to also agree to the larger request. This is a great example of what psychologists refer to as the rule of commitment, and marketers often use this strategy to encourage consumers to buy products and services.
2. **Reciprocity Norm:** This rule operates on a simple principle: We tend to feel obligated to return favors after people do favours for us. When your neighbour presents some gift on your birthday or anniversary, you might feel obligated to return the favor when their birthday or anniversary comes.
3. **The Lowball Technique:** The low-ball is a persuasion and selling technique in which an item or service is offered at a lower price than is actually intended to be charged, after which the price is raised to increase profits. For example a car salesperson tells Varun that a car he is interested in buying costs 5 lakhs. After he has committed to buying the car, the salesperson points out that adding a stereo, an air conditioner, will cost an extra ₹40,000.
4. **Feigned Scarcity:** Feigned scarcity is another social influence method that is widely employed. People tend to desire items that are less available, and the market can draw consumers towards specific items by making the supply of that item appear more limited.

Social Influence Through Persuasion

Persuasion is a form of social influence in which an audience is intentionally encouraged to adopt an idea, attitude, or course of action by symbolic means. We investigate communication's critical role in persuasion and social influence processes. People often try to change other's attitudes through persuasion. There are four elements involved in persuasion: the source, the receiver, the message, and the channel.

The Source: The source of a persuasive message is the communicator who is presenting it. Persuasion is most successful when a source is both likable and credible. Credible sources are those that are trustworthy or that have expertise.

The Message: A message is the content of a piece of communication. Some messages are more persuasive than others. Messages that are both-sided are more persuasive than one-sided messages. Also those messages which arouse fear are likely to be persuasive if people think that by rejecting the message they will have to face dire consequence and that accepting the message will prevent a highly undesirable consequence.

The Receiver: The target of a persuasive message is called a receiver. Some people are more easily persuaded than others. Individuals with low self-esteem are more likely to change their attitudes in response to persuasion than are individuals with high self-esteem. Individuals who hold very extreme attitudes are more resistant to persuasion, and people who are in a good mood are easier to persuade.

The Channel: The channel is the medium used to send the message. Newspapers, television, the internet, radio, movies, direct mail, word of mouth, magazines, and billboard advertisements are just a few of the different media through which people might encounter a persuasive message. The medium can influence the persuasiveness of the message.

PROSOCIAL BEHAVIOUR

The term prosocial behaviour means positive actions that benefit others, prompted by empathy, moral values, and a sense of personal responsibility rather than a desire for personal gain or we can say that prosocial behaviours are those intended to help other people. Prosocial behaviour is characterized by a concern about the rights, feelings and welfare of other people.

Prosocial behaviour is defined as actions that benefit other people or society as a whole (Twenge, Ciarocco, Baumeister, & Bartels, 2007). It is characterized by helping that does not benefit the helper; in fact, prosocial behaviour is often accompanied by costs. Psychologists suggest that one way this behaviour may outweigh the associated costs concerns the human desire to belong to a group. Helping facilitates group work and in turn, provides individuals with immense benefits for the long run (Twenge et al., 2007).

Historical evidence indicates that voluntary action which benefits others has biological roots, observable in both humans and animals (Knickerbocker 2003). The evolutionary psychologists believe that people help others because of three factors that have become ingrained in our genes: kin selection, the norm of reciprocity, and the ability to learn and follow social norms.

The kin selection factor is based on the idea that behaviours that help a genetic relative are favored by natural selection (Hamilton, 1964, Myer, 1999). The kin selection model predicts that individuals engage in altruistic sacrifices on behalf of close relatives, such as off-spring, more than distant relatives, such as cousins, and more toward distant relatives than toward genetic strangers. Hamilton showed the general importance of relatedness in evolution and his theory takes its most accessible form in the inequality known as Hamilton's rule, which predicts that altruistic action will be favoured when $br > c$, where c and b are the cost and benefit to actor and recipient, respectively, and r is their relatedness. Hamilton called his new and general principle of natural selection 'inclusive fitness theory', but it is often known by the term 'kin selection', coined by Maynard Smith.

The norm of reciprocity, according to the evolutionary psychologists is the expectations that helping others will increase the likelihood that they will help us in the future. The reciprocity thus calls for positive reactions to favourable treatment and for negative reactions to unfavourable treatment.

Learning social norms states that people who are the best learners of the society norms and customs have a survival advantage than those people who didn't follow these norms. Simon (1990) suggests that those who are the best learners of societal norms have a competitive advantage. Thus people are genetically programmed to learn social norms and one of these norms is altruism. For example, in the United States, it's customary to give gifts during the winter holiday season. These gifts may vary from baking cookies for your neighbour to receiving a holiday bonus at work. It is so much a part of the culture that most people do it automatically.

Theories of Prosocial Behaviour

The major theory of prosocial behaviour includes Social exchange theory, Social norms theory, Empathy-altruism theory and Evolutionary psychology or socio-biology theory.

Social Exchange Theory

Social exchange theory is the belief that people will help others only when the benefits to themselves outweigh the costs of helping. In fact, social exchange theory argues that much of what we do stems from the desire to maximize our rewards and minimize our costs (Homans, 1961; Lawler, 1999; Thibaut & Kelly, 1959).

According to the social-exchange theory, people help because they want to gain goods from the one being helped. People calculate rewards and costs of helping others, and aim at maximizing the former and minimizing the latter, which is known as a "minimax" strategy.

Rewards are incentives, which can be materialistic goods, social rewards which can improve one's image and reputation (e.g. praise) or self-reward. Rewards are either external (friendship and gratitude) or internal (sense of goodness and self-satisfaction).

Social exchange theory further assumes that individuals are goal-oriented in a freely competitive social system. Because of the competitive nature of social systems, exchange processes lead to differentiation of power and privilege in social groups. Those with more resources hold more power and, ultimately, are in a better position to benefit from the exchange.

Social Norms Theory

The Social Norms Theory was first used by Perkins and Berkowitz in 1986 to address student alcohol use patterns. As a result, the theory, and subsequently the social norms approach, is best known for its effectiveness in reducing alcohol consumption and alcohol-related injury in college students. The approach has also been used to address a wide range of public health topics including tobacco use, driving under the influence prevention, seat belt use, and more recently sexual assault prevention.

Social norms theory provides a model for understanding human behaviour that has important implications for health promotion and prevention. It states that our behaviour is influenced by incorrect perceptions of how other members of our social groups think and act. The theory predicts that overestimations of problem behaviour will increase these problem behaviours while underestimations of healthy behaviours will discourage individuals from engaging in them. Thus, correcting misperceptions is likely to result in decreased problem behaviour or increased prevalence of healthy behaviours.

Social norms interventions focus on peer influences, which have a greater impact on individual behaviour than biological, personality, familial, religious, cultural and other influences (Berkowitz & Perkins, 1986A; Perkins, 2002). These peer influences are based more on what we think our peers believe and do (the "perceived norm") than on their real beliefs and actions (the "actual norm"). This misperception and the effect it has is the basis for the social norms approach.

Empathy-Altruism Theory

According to 'empathy-altruism hypothesis', if you feel empathy towards another person you will help them, regardless of what you can gain from it (1991). Relieving their suffering becomes the most important thing. When you do not feel empathy, the social exchange theory takes control. In other words when we feel empathy for a person, we will attempt to help that person purely for altruistic reasons, regardless of what we have to gain.

The empathy-altruism hypothesis states that feelings of empathy for another person produce an altruistic motivation to increase that person's welfare. In the empathy-altruism hypothesis, the term empathy refers to feelings of compassion, sympathy, tenderness, and the like. Altruism refers to a motivational state in which the goal is to increase another person's welfare as an end in itself. (Altruistic acts are what ordinarily called "good deeds").

The empathy-altruism hypothesis predicts that those feeling high levels of empathy for a person in need will be more likely to help than will those feeling less empathy. This prediction is well supported by research. However, a number of egoistic alternative explanations have been proposed to explain these findings. For example, those feeling high levels of empathy may feel more distress and, consequently, may be more likely to help because they are egoistically motivated to reduce their own distress. Another possibility is that those feeling high levels of empathy are more likely to help because they are more egoistically motivated to avoid feeling bad about themselves or looking bad in the eyes of others should they fail to help. Similarly, those feeling high levels of empathy may be more likely to help because they are more egoistically motivated to feel good about themselves or to look good in the eyes of others should they help.

ANTI-SOCIAL BEHAVIOUR/PERSONALITY

The people who cheat needlessly, lie without reason, are suspicious of others and respond passively to others. They are selfish, irresponsible, impulsive, guiltless and do not learn from punishment. They are not psychotics because they have good grip on reality. They are not fearful, or addicts but their behaviour seems to be odd or abnormal which is a source of distress for themselves and others. This type of disorder is called personality disorder. This is also known as sociopathy and psychopathy.

The above symptoms were first described by J.C. Prichard in 1837. He called it "moral insanity" because the intellect of such person was normal but the moral values were depraved. He felt that such a person lacks self discipline.

The American Psychological Association coined the term antisocial personality in the late 1960. The APA's Diagnostic and Statistical Manual of Mental Disorders, fourth edition (DSM-IV-TR), defines antisocial personality disorder (in Axis II–Cluster B):

A. There is a pervasive pattern of disregard for and violation of the rights of others occurring since age 15 years, as indicated by three or more of the following:
   1. Failure to conform to social norms with respect to lawful behaviours as indicated by repeatedly performing acts that are grounds for arrest;
   2. Deception, as indicated by repeatedly lying, use of aliases, or conning others for personal profit or pleasure;
   3. Impulsivity or failure to plan ahead;
   4. Irritability and aggressiveness, as indicated by repeated physical fights or assaults;
   5. Reckless disregard for safety of self or others;
   6. Consistent irresponsibility, as indicated by repeated failure to sustain consistent work behaviour or honor financial obligations;
   7. Lack of remorse, as indicated by being indifferent to or rationalizing having hurt, mistreated, or stolen from another;

B. The individual is at least age 18 years.

C. There is evidence of conduct disorder with onset before age 15 years.

D. The occurrence of antisocial behaviour is not exclusively during the course of schizophrenia or a manic episode.

ASPD falls under the dramatic/erratic cluster of personality disorders. In the DSM-5, the diagnosis antisocial personality disorder is kept, but it is no longer on another axis as the other mental disorders.

Causes and Characteristics

Factors that contribute to a particular child's antisocial behaviour vary, but as far as family is concerned, the various family problems like marital discord, inconsistent disciplinary practices or actual child abuse, learning or cognitive disabilities, or health problems can force someone to adopt one or the more anti social activities. Attention deficit/hyperactivity disorder is highly correlated with antisocial behaviour. Certain specific stressor such as the death of a parent or a divorce, can also play an important role in developing anti social behaviour. Children and adolescents with antisocial behaviour disorders have an increased risk of accidents, school failure, early alcohol and substance use, suicide, and criminal behaviour.

A salient characteristic of antisocial children and adolescents is that they tend to show aggression and exhibit various behaviours, ranging from disobedience to boisterousness and appear to have no feelings for others or remorse for hurting others. They are incapable to learn from their social and cultural environment as well as in an academic situation. Individuals with antisocial behaviour are less sensitive to stress and show signs of hypo-arousal, or disassociation from emotions, memories, other people, the body and identity. One analysis of antisocial behaviour is that it is a defence mechanism that helps the child to avoid painful feelings, or else to avoid the anxiety caused by lack of control over the environment. Compared to a normal child, the antisocial child does not grow anxious over or dread punishment.

Antisocial behaviour may also be a direct attempt to alter the environment. Social learning theory suggests that negative behaviours are reinforced during childhood by parents, caregivers, or peers. The child will apply the learned behaviour at school and in other social settings and if rejected, becomes angry and attempts to force his will or assert his pride, and is then further rejected by the very peers from whom he might learn more positive behaviours.

Treatment

Psychotherapy is nearly always the treatment of choice for this disorder; medications may be used to help stabilize mood swings or specific and acute Axis I concurrent diagnoses. A variety of methods may be employed to deliver social skills training, but especially with diagnosed antisocial disorders, the most effective methods are systemic therapies which address communication skills among the whole family or within a peer group of other antisocial children or adolescents. Methods used in social skills training include modeling, role playing, corrective feedback, and token reinforcement systems. Special education teachers and counselor's have a better chance at instituting long-term treatment programs. Studies show that children who are given social skills instruction decrease their antisocial behaviour, especially when the instruction is combined with some form of supportive peer group or family therapy.

APPLIED SOCIAL PSYCHOLOGY

Applied social psychology refers to (a) the branch of social psychology that draws on social psychological theories, principles, methods, and psychological theories, principles, methods, and (b) the development of intervention strategies for improving the functioning of individuals, groups, organizations, communities and societies with respect to social and practical problems. In this definition, functioning is broadly viewed as encompassing how well people perform or operate with respect to any one of many criteria, including, for example, emotional and social adjustment, physical health, and performance in school, work, or athletics.

The embracement of the goal of control (manipulation of conditions to cause changes in phenomena) particularly distinguishes applied social psychology as a separate branch of social psychology. That is, at the heart of applied social psychology is a concern with developing social influence strategies (*i.e.*, interventions) to improve people's functioning with respect to social and practical problems. Although the field is particularly concerned with addressing social and practical problems on a general level (*e.g.*, education, environment), individuals also can use social psychology to improve their own lives.

The core assumption of the field of social psychology, and of applied social psychology, is that people's attitudes and behaviour are greatly influenced by situational factors. In fact, intervention strategies may be viewed as involving the use of knowledge about social situational influence to effect improvements in people's functioning. However, applied social psychology also recognizes that to understand and address problems, individual difference variables (*e.g.*, personality) must be considered. Moreover, the social situation can be viewed as reflecting different levels of analysis (*e.g.*, interpersonal, group, community); accordingly, interventions may be directed at different levels.

Applied social psychology requires a broad approach to social and practical problems, including the use of multiple research methods, an interdisciplinary orientation, and recognition of the value of other perspectives (*e.g.*, evolutionary, personality, cultural). In his or her work, the applied social psychologist can assume several roles, some of which include researcher, program designer, evaluation researcher, consultant, action researcher, and advocate.

MULTIPLE CHOICE QUESTIONS

1. .... are mental shortcuts that may be responsible for biases and errors but are efficient and simplify judgement.
A. Alternatives
B. Consensus
C. Heuristics
D. None of the above

2. While making social inferences people behave like "naïve scientists". What does this term "naïve scientist' means?
A. People who are most concerned about the efficiency.
B. People who rationally and logically test their hypothesis about the social world.
C. Both A & B
D. None of the above

3. .... refers to a judgement of something or someone that is based on resemblance to that category.
A. Available heuristic
B. Representative heuristic
C. The actor-observer bias
D. The false consensus effect

4. Internal & external attributions are distinguished in terms of.
A. The co-variation model
B. The inference theory
C. The locus of causality
D. None of the above

5. .... influence the internalisation and interpretation of new information.
A. Schemas
B. Logic
C. Common sense
D. Rules

6. .... perspective in social cognition argues that perceivers don't want to use any more cognitive resources than are necessary.
A. The cognitive miser
B. The naïve scientist
C. The motivated tactician
D. None of the above

7. .... is a cognitive bias whereby a person tends to overestimate the extent to which their beliefs or opinions are typical of those of others..
A. The Congruence bias
B. The false consensus effect
C. The representative heuristic
D. The Attentional bias

8. According to Anderson, which of the following is not a principle model of cognitive algebra?
A. Summation
B. Multiplication
C. Weighted averaging
D. Both (A) & (B)

9. Altruistic individuals tend to have higher level of:
A. Altruism
B. Sympathy
C. Empathy
D. Belief in helping

10. According to which theory the prosocial behaviour is motivated solely by the desire to help someone in need.
A. Empathy-altruism hypothesis
B. Genetic-determinism model
C. Social norms theory
D. None of the above

11. Who is most likely to help people?
A. A person with an altruistic personality
B. A person who is sad
C. A person who is struggling in life
D. A person who is emotionally weak

12. The term "sociopath" or "psychopath" is sometimes used to describe which type of personality disorder?
A. Schizoid personality disorder
B. Antisocial personality disorder
C. Paranoid personality disorder
D. Obsessive compulsive personality disorder

13. Which personality disorder is associated with instability in personal relationships, a lack of well-defined and stable self image, regular and unpredictable changes in moods, and impulsive behaviour?
A. Melancholic personality disorder
B. Associative personality disorder
C. Borderline personality disorder
D. Dissociative personality disorder

14. People who are less likely to help someone because there are a lot of people present would be exhibiting:
A. Group think
B. Group polarization
C. Diffusion of responsibility
D. None of the above

15. .... is a spectrum of disorder proposed to include both avoidant personality disorder and social phobia.
A. Social identity spectrum
B. Social anxiety spectrum
C. Generalised anxiety disorder
D. Antisocial spectrum

16. The main features of avoidant personality disorder include:
A. Feeling of inadequacy
B. Self-imposed social isolation
C. Hypersensitivity to rejection/criticism
D. All of the above

17. People with antisocial personality disorder exhibit which among the following?
A. Poor impulse control
B. Difficulty inhibiting impulsive behaviours
C. Deficits in executive functions
D. All of the above

18. According to which theory we actively help people as a function of how closely related to us they are?
A. Genetic theory of social behaviour
B. Socio biology theory
C. Empathy altruism theory
D. Social norms theory

19. .... personality disorder is characterised by a pervasive and excessive need to be taken care of, submissive and clinging behaviour, and difficulty making everyday decisions without advice from others.
A. Dependent personality disorder
B. Obsessive compulsive disorder
C. Paranoid personality disorder
D. Antisocial personality disorder

20. In personality disorders ...., is a set of dysfunctional beliefs that are hypothesised to maintain problematic behaviour characteristic of a number of personality disorders (*e.g.*, antisocial personality disorder etc).

A. Dysfunctional balance
B. Dysfunctional schemas
C. Dysfunctional memories
D. None of the above

21. Which theory argues that much of what we do stems from the desire to maximize our rewards and minimize our costs?
A. Social exchange theory
B. Social norm theory
C. Socio biology theory
D. Empathy altruism theory

22. The .... theory was first used by Perkins and Berkowitz in 1986 to address student alcohol use pattern.
A. Social norm
B. Social exchange
C. Empathy altruism
D. Socio biology

23. The .... technique is a persuasion strategy that can be used to gain compliance and get someone to agree to a request.
A. The Lowball Technique
B. Reciprocity Norm
C. The Foot in the Door
D. The Feigned scarcity

24. .... is a strong motive in eliciting prosocial behaviour, and has deep evolutionary roots.
A. Empathy
B. Aggression
C. Guilt
D. Shame

25. According to which theory, if you feel empathy towards another person you will help them, regardless of what you can gain from it.
A. Social exchange theory
B. Social norm theory
C. Socio biology theory
D. Empathy altruism hypothesis

26. Components of empathy are:
A. Perceiving and Advancing
B. Advancing and Interpreting
C. Judging and Communicating
D. Perceiving and Communicating

27. When an individual is changing ones behaviour due to the imagined or actual presence of others, it is referred to as:
A. Social impact
B. Conformity
C. Social desirability
D. None of the above

28. A compulsion by decision makers to maintain each other's approval, even at the cost of critical thinking and good judgement, is called:
A. Social conformity
B. Group think
C. Social impact
D. Social desirability

29. A social worker, with a training of Master of Social Work (MSW) who was appointed as an assistant to a psychiatrist, use to administer and interpret Rorschach test. This is an:
A. ethically incorrect practice
B. ethically correct practice
C. ethically correct practice provided the results are kept confidential
D. ethically correct practice provided the results are used only for diagnostic purpose

30. The art of establishing trust, respect and co-operation in a relationship is referred to as:
A. Personal distance
B. Continuation behaviour
C. Use of humour
D. Rapport

31. .... is best known for his research on conformity.
A. Asch B. Schachter
C. Rubin D. Perkins

32. A situation that demands more cognitive resources than we have available is known as:
A. Information overload
B. Cognitive overload
C. Cognitive scarcity
D. Information scarcity

33. Given below are two statements: Assertion (A) and Reason (R). Indicate your answer using codes given below.

Assertion (A): Ingratiation is a technique for gaining compliance from other person in which requester first introduces himself/herself to the target person as an authority and then asks to comply his/her order.

Reason (R): Ingratiation induces liking in target person for requester and attempts to change target person's behaviour in one's favour.

Codes:

A. Both (A) and (R) are true and (R) is the correct explanation of (A).
B. Both (A) and (R) are true, but (R) is not the correct explanation of (A).
C. (A) is true, but (R) is false.
D. (A) is false, but (R) is true.

34. Being persuaded by information that is exclusive is the principle of .... Being persuaded by feeling that you "owe" someone is the principle of ....

A. Reciprocity; scarcity
B. Scarcity, reciprocity
C. Credibility, obligation
D. Exclusivity, credibility

35. Scapegoating is releasing aggression on .... targets.

A. Stronger B. Unsafe
C. Safe D. Stubborn

36. Low levels of which neurotransmitter has been implicated in studies of aggression?

A. Dopamine B. Norepinephrine
C. Serotonin D. GABA

37. Strength, immediacy and the number of people in the group are determinants of conformity in which theory?

A. Social impact theory
B. Conformity theory
C. Social desirability theory
D. Cognitive appraisal theory

38. Which theory holds that a relationship must be profitable to endure?

A. Complementary need theory
B. Social exchange theory
C. Gain-loss theory
D. Social comparison theory

39. Given below are two statements : Assertion (A) and Reason (R). Indicate your answer using codes given below.

Assertion (A): People rebel against the norms of their group.

Reason (R): People desire to be liked and to be right.

Codes:

A. Both (A) and (R) are true and (R) is the correct explanation of (A).
B. Both (A) and (R) are true, but (R) is not the correct explanation of (A).
C. (A) is true, but (R) is false.
D. (A) is false, but (R) is true.

40. The three basic components of prejudice are Effective:

A. Descriptive and Objective
B. Real and Imaginative
C. Focused and Goal-oriented
D. Cognitive and Behavioural

41. The way in which a child's efforts to master a new or challenging task is supported in a flexible and contingent way by teachers, parents or more competent persons is called:

A. Scaffolding
B. Social influence
C. Social mediation
D. Social referencing

42. One reason that people comply with social pressure is to gain approval or avoid rejection; this is called ....; and so understanding rules for accepted and expected behaviour are called ....

A. Social control; norm.
B. Social influence; rule.
C. Normative social influence; norm.
D. Social facilitation; norm.

43. Most of the social psychological research on attitude change has been generated by theories concerning:
A. Consistency in attitudes and behaviour
B. Cognitive dissonance
C. Self-perception
D. Attribution

44. Persuasion is:
A. the process by which a message induces a change in behaviour.
B. the process by which a message induces attitude change.
C. the process by which a message evoke aggressive response
D. the process by behaviour change by an authoritarian leader

45. The social distance scale is mainly a measure of:
A. Attitude
B. Group Cohessiveness
C. Pro-social behaviour
D. Social class differences

46. Situations in which each person can increase his/her individual gains by acting in a certain way, but if all (or most) persons act that same way, the outcomes experienced by all is reduced. This phenomenon is known as:
A. Social loafing
B. Social dilemmas
C. Reciprocity
D. Conflict

47. The social comparison theory would explain the feeling of .... that a person might feel.
A. happiness
B. depression
C. stress
D. relative deprivation

48. Among these which is not a negative consequence of rejection?
A. Decreased level of pro-social behaviour
B. Greater anti-social behaviour
C. Poor cognitive functioning
D. Greater conformity

49. A person showing socially appropriate behaviour, helpfulness, and engaging in good deeds is known to exhibit:
A. Good behaviour
B. Self-regulated behaviour
C. Pro-social behaviour
D. Socially correct behaviour

50. Discrepancies between attitudes lead to:
A. Prejudice
B. Cognitive dissonance
C. The fundamental attribution error
D. Stereotyping

ANSWERS

1	2	3	4	5	6	7	8	9	10
C	B	B	C	A	A	B	B	C	A
11	**12**	**13**	**14**	**15**	**16**	**17**	**18**	**19**	**20**
A	B	C	C	B	D	D	A	A	B
21	**22**	**23**	**24**	**25**	**26**	**27**	**28**	**29**	**30**
A	A	C	A	D	D	B	B	A	D
31	**32**	**33**	**34**	**35**	**36**	**37**	**38**	**39**	**40**
A	B	D	B	C	C	A	B	D	D
41	**42**	**43**	**44**	**45**	**46**	**47**	**48**	**49**	**50**
A	C	C	B	D	B	D	A	C	A

❑❑❑

CHAPTER 10

Developmental Psychology

Developmental psychology is the branch of psychology that studies how people grow and change over the course of a lifetime. Hurlock (1978) defined developmental psychology as the ontogenetic study of the development of organism from conception through childhood, adolescent, adult and senescence till death. Apart from studying chronological and mental ages of human beings, it regulates the structural, functional and behavioural changes that occur in humans before maturity. The goal of study in developmental psychology is to further our knowledge about how development evolves over the entire life span, developing a knowledge of the general principles of development and the differences and similarities in development across individuals.

Development refers to as patterns of change over time which begins at conception and continues throughout the life span. Development occurs in different domains, such as the biological (changes in our physical being), social (changes in our social relationships), emotional (changes in our emotional understanding and experiences), and cognitive (changes in our thought processes).

Heinz Werner (1957) argued that development refers only to changes which increase the organization of functioning within a domain. Werner believed that development consisted of two processes: integration and differentiation. Hurlock (1972), Zanden (1978) and Baller and Charles (1968) defined development as a progressive sequence of orderly, coherent changes. Progressive according to Hurlock signifies that the changes are directional leading forward rather backward. Orderly and coherent suggest that there is a definite relationship between a given stage and the stages which precede or follow it. The progressive series of changes occur as a result of maturation and experience. The developmental changes also occur at each stage of human growth and development. Development leads toward the goal of maturity.

Developmental psychology informs several applied fields, including: educational psychology, child psychopathology, and forensic developmental psychology. Developmental psychology complements several other basic research fields in psychology including social psychology, cognitive psychology, ecological psychology, and comparative psychology.

PRINCIPLES OF LIFE-SPAN DEVELOPMENT

Paul Baltes (1987) has articulated a set of principles which guide the study of human development within a life-span framework. The first of the principles which Baltes (1987) discussed is the belief that development is lifelong. Each period of the life span is affected by what happened before and will affect what is to come. Each period has unique characteristics and value. No period is more or less important than any other.

Second, development may involve processes which are not present at birth but emerge throughout the life span. Development is also multidimensional and multidirectional. Multidimensional occurs along multiple interacting dimensions-biological, psychological, and social-each of which may develop at varying rates. The principle of multidirectional maintains that there is no single, normal path that development must or should take. In other words, healthy developmental outcomes are achieved in a wide variety of ways. Development is often comprised of multiple abilities which take different directions, showing different types of change or constancy.

Another principle of development is the belief that development involves both gains and losses. Baltes argues development across the lifespan is influenced by the "joint expression of features of growth (gain) and decline (loss)." The factors which contribute to gain or loss are not in equal proportions but adjust according to systematic age-related shifts. This relation between developmental gains and losses occurs in a direction to selectively optimize particular capacities which requires the sacrificing of other functions, a process known as selective optimization with compensation.

A fifth principle articulated by Baltes (1987) is that development is plastic. Plasticity refers to the within-person variability which is possible for a particular behaviour or development. . For example, infants who have a hemisphere of the brain removed shortly after birth (as a treatment for epilepsy) can recover the functions associated with that hemisphere as the brain reorganizes itself and the remaining hemisphere takes over those functions. The sixth principle states that development is also situated in contexts and in history. Contextualism as a paradigm is Baltes' idea that three systems of biological and environmental influence work together to influence development: age-graded, history-graded, and nonnormative influences. Baltes wrote that these three influences operate throughout the life course, their effects accumulate with time, and, as a dynamic package, they are responsible for how lives develop. Development is also historically situated; that is, the historical time period in which we grow up affects our development. Finally, Baltes suggests that the study of developmental psychology is multidisciplinary. It is suggested explicitly by life span researchers that the combination of disciplines is necessary to define the origins and directionality of this theory.

MATURATION VERSUS EXPERIENCE IN DEVELOPMENT

In developmental psychology's past, extreme positions have been taken on the nature-nurture debate. Nature refers to the position that our genetic inheritance, through the process of heredity, is the primary influence on development. In contrast, nurture refers to the position that the environment (broadly construed as children's experiences, including parenting, education, learning, cultural influences) is primarily responsible for development.

Those who adopt an extreme heredity position are known as nativists. Characteristics and differences that are not observable at birth, but which emerge later in life, are regarded as the product of maturation. Arnold Gesell (1928) was a strong advocate of genetic factors and believe that the course of our development was largely determined by genetic factors. Our genetic heritage specifies the set of biological processes which determine the patterns of growth that we observe, which Gesell referred to as maturation. Simply put, maturation is the sequence of growth which is specified and controlled by our genes. With regards to genetic and environmental connections that underlie developmental change, the renowned Minnesota twin study on identical twins found that identical twins raised together or apart were far more similar on many psychological tests than non-identical twins and siblings raised in the same family. Likewise Chomsky (1965) also proposed that language is gained through the use of an innate language acquisition device. Another example of nature is Freud's theory of aggression as being an innate drive (called thanatos).

In contrast to nativists, at the other end of the spectrum are the environmentalists — also known as empiricists. Their basic assumption is that at birth the human mind is a tabula rasa (a blank slate) and that this is gradually "filled" as a result of experience (e.g. behaviourism). John B. Watson (1928) argued for the dominance of the environment on children's development. Watson believed that genetic factors placed no limits on how environments could shape the course of children's development. Watson was famous for his belief that if, given the ability to manipulate the environment to his own standards, he could shape the development of any child. While Watson was never able to make good on his boast, he did show how environmental experiences played a role in shaping children's behaviour through the processes of classical conditioning, a type of learning in which a stimulus can come to evoke a response after the repeated pairing of the two stimuli (Watson, 1928). Another example with regards to this is of Bandura's (1977) social learning theory which also states that aggression is a learnt from the environment through observation and imitation. This is seen in his famous bobo doll experiment (Bandura, 1961). Also Skinner (1957) believed that language is learnt from other people via behaviour shaping techniques.

In practice hardly anyone today accepts either of the extreme positions. There are simply too many "facts" on both sides of the argument which are inconsistent with an "all or nothing" view. Today, most developmental psychologists recognize that nature and nurture both play an important role in development. One way we can approach the interaction between nature and nurture is through an examination of the extent to which our biological programming can be altered by environmental influences (Dellarosa Cummins & Cummins,1999; Elman et al., 1996).

STAGES OF DEVELOPMENT

Stage-1: Pre-natal Development

The whole prenatal development involves three main stages: germinal stage, embryonic stage and fetal stage. Germinal stage begins at conception until 2 weeks. Embryonic stage lasts from the beginning of the 3rd week to the end of the 8th week. During this time all major organs are formed and the heart begins to beat. Fetal stage represents 9 weeks until birth of the baby. The major organ systems begin to function and the growth of the organism is quite rapid.

Stage-2: Infancy

From birth until the first year, the child is referred to as an infant. The majority of a newborn infant's time is spent in sleep. At first this sleep is evenly spread throughout the day and night, but after a couple of months, infants generally become diurnal.

Infants can be seen to have six states, grouped into pairs:

- quiet sleep and active sleep (dreaming, when REM sleep occurs)
- quiet waking, and active waking
- fussing and crying

The infant now begin to respond to our five senses *i.e.,* they can see, hear, smell, taste, and touch. Infants respond to stimuli differently in these different states. Also infants of around six months can differentiate between phonemes in their own language, but not between similar phonemes in another language. At this stage infants also start to babble, producing phonemes. With regards to cognitive development, the Piaget's holds the view that, an infant's perception and understanding of the world depended on their motor development. It is through touching and handling objects that infants develop object permanence, the understanding that objects are solid, permanent, and continue to exist when out of sight.

Stage-3: Toddlerhood

Infants shift between ages of one and two to a developmental stage known as toddlerhood. In this stage, an infant's transition into toddlerhood is highlighted through self-awareness, developing maturity in language use, and presence of memory and imagination. During toddlerhood, babies begin learning how to walk, talk, and make decisions for themselves. An important characteristic of this age period is the development of language, where children are learning how to communicate and express their emotions and desires through the use of vocal sounds, babbling, and eventually words.

Stage-4: Early & Middle Childhood

Broadly it covers the period from 2 to 6 years of age. It is also called "pre-school age," "exploratory age" and "toy age." As children mature their locomotion skills become refined and graceful. Body balance while walking and running improves noticeably.

A 3-year-old can run in a straight line and can jump smoothly without falling down. A 4-year-old can skip, jump on one foot and catch a large ball thrown from a distance. By the age six, the child is physically quite capable of coordinated actions which require maintaining body balance. Capacity for sustained attention continues to improve, due to which heir perceptual skills or ability to identify finer aspects of objects also improves.

Mental capacity of children also shows significant improvement during the middle childhood years. Their thinking becomes more logical and systematic particularly in respect of concrete objects, events and experiences. But given abstract situations their thinking fails to follow logical principles. Memory and conceptual knowledge improve facilitating logical thinking beyond the immediate situation. Children can also engage in aesthetic activities such as music, art and dance and develop hobbies of their own.

Stage-5: Adolescence

It is the period from the onset of puberty till attainment of adulthood. Puberty marks the beginning of sexual maturity and reproductive capacity of an individual. Adolescence is characterised by rapid biological and physical change and these changes are associated with many psychological challenge. Intelligence is demonstrated through the logical use of symbols related to abstract concepts and formal reasoning. A return to egocentric thought often occurs early in the period. Only 35% develop the capacity to reason formally during adolescence or adulthood.

It is divided into three parts namely:

1. Early Adolescence: 9 to 13 years (preteen),
2. Mid Adolescence: 13 to 15 years and
3. Late Adolescence: 15 to 18 years

Stage-6: Early Adulthood

The period from the end of adolescence, *i.e.*, from approximately 19 years to about 35 years of age is generally viewed as the early adulthood period. Early adulthood, according to theorists such as Erik Erikson, is a stage where development is mainly focused on maintaining relationships. Examples include creating bond of intimacy, sustaining friendships, and ultimately making a family.

Stage-7: Middle Adulthood

Middle adulthood generally refers to the period between ages 35 to 69. Muscular strength and performance of major organ systems such as digestive and circulatory systems deteriorate. Middle adulthood is characterised by some dramatic changes in the functioning of reproductive system and sexual activity.

Such changes are called climacteric. During the climacteric period women experience menopause and a sharp drop in the hormone estrogen. Men experience an equivalent endocrine system event to menopause. Andropause in males is a hormone fluctuation with physical and psychological effects that can be similar to those seen in menopausal females. As men age, lowered testosterone levels can contribute to mood swings and a decline in sperm count. Sexual responsiveness can also be affected, including delays in erection and longer periods of penile stimulation required to achieve ejaculation. Some cognitive changes are found at this stage. Short-term memory does not decline with age, but recall of information from long-term memory somewhat declines.

Stage-8: Old Age

This stage generally refers to those aged over 70. According to Erickson, those who evaluate their life positively attain a sense of integrity and do not usually have much anxiety over death. Otherwise, old people may experience a sense of despair over not having been able to contribute much to the society and the limited time that is left for them to do something. Erickson characterises this crisis as one of integrity and despair. There are wide individual variations in the way old people prepare to face death and other challenges of old age.

Physically, older people experience a decline in muscular strength, reaction time, stamina, hearing, distance perception, and the sense of smell. Mental disintegration may also occur, leading to dementia or ailments such as Alzheimer's disease. It is generally believed that crystallized intelligence increases up to old age, while fluid intelligence decreases with age. Whether or not normal intelligence increases or decreases with age depend on the measure and longitudinal studies show that speed declines. Some cross-sectional studies suggest that intellect is stable.

THEORIES OF DEVELOPMENT

Psychoanalytic Theory

Psychoanalytic theory originated with the work of Sigmund Freud. The idea of this theory is that, things that happen to people during childhood can contribute to the way they later function as adults. Based on his observations, he developed a theory that described development in terms of a series of psychosexual stages. According to Freud, conflicts that occur during each of these stages can have a lifelong influence on personality and behaviour.

Stages of Psychosexual Development

According to Freud, we all have an innate tendency to seek pleasure since the time of our birth, especially through physical stimulation of parts of the body that are sensitive to touch *i.e.,* the mouth, the anus, and the genitals. These body parts are referred to as erogenous zones, and the pleasure can be seek by just simply touching and rubbing these sensitive zones. Psychoanalytic theory suggested that personality is mostly established by the age of five. Early experiences play a large role in personality development and continue to influence behaviour later in life. If these psychosexual stages are completed successfully, the result is a healthy personality. If certain issues are not resolved at the appropriate stage, fixation can occur. A fixation is a persistent focus on an earlier psychosexual stage.

Stage-1: The Oral Stage (birth to about age 1)

During the oral stage, the infant's primary source of interaction occurs through the mouth, so the rooting and sucking reflex is especially important. According to Freud's theory the infant obtains sexual pleasure first by sucking and later by biting. Feeding and contact with mother, mouthing new objects, and even relief of teething pain by biting, all help to make the mouth the focus of pleasure during the first year. It is believed that if an infant receives too much or too little oral stimulation, they may develop a fixation or a personality trait that is fixated on oral gratification. It is believed that these people may focus on activities that involve the mouth such as over eating, biting the fingernails, smoking, or drinking and may develop dependency in psychological form.

Stage-2: The Anal Stage (1 year to 3 years)

The anal stage is directly related to a child's awareness of bowel control and gaining pleasure through the act of eliminating or retaining feces. Freud's theory puts the anal stage between 18 months and three years. According to Freud, success at this stage is dependent upon the way in which parents approach toilet training. Freud believed that positive experiences during this stage served as the basis for people to become competent, productive and creative adults. However fixation at the first substages results in adult characteristics of messiness and disorder; fixation at the later substage results in excessive compulsiveness, over conformity, and exaggerated self-control.

Stage-3: The Phallic Stage (3 to 6 years)

During the phallic stage, the primary focus of the libido is on the genitals. At this age, children also begin to discover the differences between males and females. Freud believes the phallic stage or the Oedipus or Electra complexes occurs during a child is three to six years of age. The belief is that male children harbor unconscious, sexual attraction to their mothers, while female children develop a sexual attraction to their father. The Oedipus complex describes these feelings of wanting to possess the mother and the desire to replace the father. However, the child also fears that he will be punished by the father for these feelings, a fear Freud termed castration anxiety. The term Electra complex has been used to describe a similar set of feelings experienced by young girls. Freud, however, believed that girls instead experience penis envy.

Stage-4: The Latency Period (6 years to puberty)

During the latent period, the libido interests are suppressed. The development of the ego and superego contribute to this period of calm because as the child learns more about the world, sexuality is largely repressed and the ego expands. According to Freud this period was not considered very important to the development of personality. However this stage is important in the development of social and communication skills and self-confidence.

Stage-5: The Genital Stage (Puberty to Death)

During the final stage of psychosexual development, the individual develops a strong sexual interest in the opposite sex. This stage begins during puberty but last throughout the rest of a person's life. Freud believed that after the unconscious, sexual desires are repressed and remain dormant during the latency stage, they are awakened due to puberty. There are three major sources of sexual arousal during this period: memories and sensations from earlier childhood periods, physical manipulations of genitals and other erogenous zones, and hormonal secretions. The genital stage is the last stage of the psychosexual development theory.

Behaviouristic Theory

During the first half of the twentieth century, a new school of thought known as behaviourism rose to become a dominant force within psychology. Behaviourists explain behaviour in terms of (1) the stimuli that elicit it and (2) the events that caused the person to learn to respond to the stimulus that way. Behaviourists use two processes to explain how people learn: classical conditioning and operant conditioning. Some behaviourists, such as John B. Watson and B.F. Skinner, insisted that learning occurs purely through processes of association and reinforcement. Later, psychologist Albert Bandura rejected this narrow perspective and demonstrated the powerful effects of observational learning.

Behaviourism views the child as basically going along with the flow of her natural development. Development occurs in a continuous way, and children will develop and change their behaviours according to their external environment. This theory holds that kids can unlearn old behaviours and learn new ones if they are rewarded for them.

Behaviourist theory holds that children develop and learn in certain ways based mostly on their environments. Their nature or genes have little to do with how they act in this theory. A child's talents, personality, intelligence and other aspects of his mental being are not that important. With external guidance, Watson believed that he could train a child to become whatever he wanted her to be, despite any supposed genetic predisposition in another direction.

As an advantage behaviourism is based upon observable behaviours, so it is easier to quantify and collect data and information when conducting research. Also effective therapeutic techniques such as intensive behavioural intervention, behaviour analysis, token economies and discrete trial training are all rooted in behaviourism. These approaches are often very useful in changing maladaptive or harmful behaviours in both children and adults.

As far as limitations are concerned the behaviourism does not account for other types of learning especially that occurs without the use of reinforcement and punishment. Secondly, it is considered by many critics a one-dimensional approach to understand human behaviour and that behavioural theories do not account for free will and internal influences such as moods, thoughts and feelings.

Cognitive Theory

Cognitive theories of development look at how thought processes and mental operations influence growth and change. Piaget believed that the childhood plays a vital and active role to growth of intelligence and child learns through doing and actively exploring. In other words, he proposed that children are little scientists" who actively construct their knowledge and understanding of the world. To Piaget, cognitive development was a progressive reorganization of mental processes as a result of biological maturation and environmental experience.

According to him, the children progress through a series of four key stages of cognitive development: the sensorimotor stage, from birth to age 2; the preoperational stage, from age 2 to about age 7; the concrete operational stage, from age 7 to 11; and the formal operational stage, which begins in adolescence and spans into adulthood.

Sensorimotor Stage

This stage has 6 sub-stages including Reflexes (0-1 month), Primary Circular Reactions (1-4 months), Secondary Circular Reactions (4-8 months), Coordination of Reactions (8-12 months), Tertiary Circular Reactions (12-18 months) and Early Representational Thought (18-24 months). In this period (which has 6 stages), intelligence is demonstrated through motor activity without the use of symbols. Knowledge of the world is attained by coordinating experiences (such as vision and hearing) with physical interactions with objects (such as grasping, sucking, and stepping).Infants gain knowledge of the world from these physical actions they perform within it. According to Piaget, the development of object permanence is one of the most important accomplishments at this stage. By the end of the sensorimotor period, the child sees objects as both separate from the self and permanent and also develop some symbolic (language) abilities.

Preoperational Stage

The preoperational stage occurs roughly between the ages two and seven. The main characteristics of this stage are that Children begin to think symbolically and learn to use words and pictures to represent objects. They also tend to be very egocentric, and see things only from their point of view. While they are getting better with language and thinking, they still tend to think about things in very concrete terms. The Pre-operational Stage is split into two substages: the symbolic function substage, and the intuitive thought substage. The symbolic function substage is when children are able to understand, represent, remember, and picture objects in their mind without having the object in front of them. The intuitive thought substage is when children tend to propose the questions of "why?" and "how come?".

Concrete Operational Stage

The concrete operational stage begins around age seven and continues until approximately age eleven. During this stage, children begin to understand the concept of conservation. Thinking becomes more logical and organized, but still very concrete. They begin using inductive logic, or reasoning from specific information to a general principle. Two other important processes in the concrete operational stage are the elimination of egocentrism and logic. At this stage the children became capable of distinguishing between their own thoughts and the thoughts of others. Also they can classify objects by their number, mass, and weight and can fluently perform mathematical problems in both addition and subtraction.

Formal Operational Stage

The formal operational stage begins at approximately age twelve to and lasts into adulthood. Piaget stated that "hypothetico-deductive reasoning" becomes important during the formal operational stage. This type of thinking involves hypothetical "what-if" situations that are not always rooted in reality. It is often required in science and mathematics. At this stage abstract thought emerges. Teens begin to think more about moral, philosophical, ethical, social, and political issues that require theoretical and abstract reasoning. They also begin to use deductive logic, or reasoning from a general principle to specific information. The ability to systematically solve a problem in a logical and methodical way emerges.

VARIOUS ASPECTS OF DEVELOPMENT

Sensory-motor Development

Sensory and motor development is the gradual process by which a child gains use and coordination of the large muscles of the legs, trunk, and arms, and the smaller muscles of the hands. A baby begins to experience new awareness through sight, touch, taste, smell, and hearing.

Motor development refers to the development of a child's bones, muscles and ability to move around and manipulate his or her environment. Motor development can be divided into two sections: gross motor development and fine motor development.

Gross motor skills are those which require whole body movement and which involve the large (core stabilising) muscles of the body to perform everyday functions, such as standing, walking, running, and sitting upright. It also includes eye-hand coordination skills such as ball skills (throwing, catching, kicking). The Fine motor skills are the coordination of small muscle movements which occur *e.g.,* in the fingers, usually in coordination with the eyes e.g drawing, sculpting, clay modeling and knitting.

Motor development also involves the use of muscle tone. Children need a balanced muscle tone in order to develop their muscles and use them with ease when standing, sitting, rolling, walking, running, swimming and all other postures and actions.

Motor development also involves the child's vestibular and proprioceptive systems. Both of these are part of the child's sensory system. The vestibular system is located in the inner ear and contributes to balance in most mammals and to the sense of spatial orientation, is the sensory system that provides the leading contribution about movement and sense of balance. Whereas the proprioceptive system is is located primarily in the cerebellum, and it works closely with the Vestibular System and Tactile System. An individual engages in proprioception during "Heavy Work" activities such as Push-Pull activities - or simply put, during resistance-type, active-engagement-of-muscle activities or exercises.

After extensive observation of infants and toddlers, especially his own three kids, Piaget described the sensorimotor stage as a series of 6 substages. Which are as follows:

1. **Reflexes (Birth-1 month):** During this substage, the child understands the environment purely through inborn reflexes. Three primary reflexes are described by Piaget: sucking of objects in the mouth, following moving or interesting objects with the eyes, and closing of the hand when an object makes contact with the palm (palmar grasp).
2. **Primary circular reactions (1 -4 months):** During this substage, the child becomes more focused on their own bodies and begins to intentionally repeat an action in order to trigger a response in the environment. For example, an infant might repeat the motion of passing their hand before their face.
3. **Secondary circular reactions (4-8 months):** At this stage "Infants become more object-oriented, moving beyond self-preoccupation; repeat actions that bring interesting or pleasurable results". For example, repeatedly picking up and dropping a toy, each time his/her mother gives the toy back to him.
4. **Coordination of secondary circular reactions (8-12 months):** At this stage the child begin to engage in goal directed behaviour and with repetitive observation, acquire knowledge of cause and effect relationship, which means the child came to know that certain actions lead to certain consequences. This stage marks the beginning of goal orientation, the deliberate planning of steps to meet an objective.
5. **Tertiary circular reactions (12-18 months):** This stage is associated primarily with the discovery of new means to meet goals. Piaget describes the child at this juncture as the "young scientist," conducting pseudo-experiments to discover new methods of meeting challenges.
6. **Internalization of Schemas (18-24 months):** Infant develops symbolic thought, and form enduring mental representations. This stage marks the beginning of insight or true creativity.

Cognitive Development

Piaget's theory of cognitive development was first developed by a Swiss developmental psychologist, Jean Piaget (1896-1980). Jean Piaget stressed that children actively construct their understanding of the world. Information does not simply enter their minds from the environment. As child grows, additional information is acquired and they adapt their thinking to include new ideas, as this improves their understanding of the world. In other words cognitive development according to Piaget was a progressive reorganization of mental processes as a result of biological maturation and environmental experience. Through a series of stages, Piaget proposes four stages of cognitive development: the sensorimotor, preoperational, concrete operational and formal operational period.

1. **The Sensorimotor stage (Birth to 2 Years):** In this stage, infants progressively construct knowledge and understanding of the world by coordinating experiences (such as vision and hearing) with physical interactions with objects (such as grasping, sucking, and stepping). During this stage, the development of object permanence is one of the most important accomplishments. Object permanence is the understanding that objects continue to exist even when they cannot be observed (seen, heard, touched, smelled or sensed in any way). During this stage, the children's thoughts are exceptionally egocentric, meaning they cannot perceive the world from another's .The sensorimotor stage is divided into 6 substages: Simple reflexes, Primary circular reactions, Secondary circular reactions, Coordination of secondary circular reactions, Tertiary circular reactions and Internalization of schemes.
2. **Preoperational Thinking (2 to 7 Years):** At this stage the child develops language and the ability to think symbolically. Piaget noted that children in this stage do not yet understand concrete logic, cannot mentally manipulate information, and are unable to take the point of view of other people, which he termed egocentrism. The Pre-operational Stage is split into two substages: the symbolic function substage, and the intuitive thought substage. At the symbolic function substage, the child begins to understand, represent, remember, and picture objects in their mind without having the object in front of them. At the intuitive thought substage, the child wants the knowledge of knowing everything.
3. **Concrete Operations (7 to 11 Years):** At this stage the child begin to think logically but remain very concrete in their logic. Piaget determined that children are able to incorporate inductive reasoning where as on the other hand struggles with deductive reasoning. This stage is centered on rules that now govern the child's logic and thinking. Important processes during the concrete operational stage include: Classification, Conservation, Decentring, Reversibility, Seriation and Transitivity.
4. **Formal Operations (After 11 and 12 Years):** In this stage children develop abstract thought and the person is capable of hypothetical and deductive reasoning. Piaget stated that "hypothetico-deductive reasoning" becomes important during the formal operational stage. This type of thinking involves hypothetical "what-if" situations that are not always rooted in reality. It is often required in science and mathematics. Meta cognition and problem solving in a logical and methodical way emerges. The Children in this stage can now reason from real to other possibilities.

Language Development

There are 6 stages of language development which includes the Babbling, one-word or holophase, Two Words and multi-word sentences, More Complex Grammatical Structures and Adult-Like Language Structures.

Babbling: The first stage of language development is known as the prelinguistic, babbling or cooing stage. During this period, which typically lasts from the age of three to nine months, babies begin to make vowel sounds such as oooooo and aaaaaaa. By five months, infants typically begin to babble and add consonant sounds to their sounds such as ba-ba-ba, ma-ma-ma or da-da-da.

Single words: The second stage is known as the one-word or holophase stage of language development. Around the age of 10 to 13 months, children begin to use one or more words with meaning. Common first words for a child are verbs and nouns, usually people, objects, and what they want in their surroundings. Some common words are papa, mama, etc. Infants begin to comprehend language about twice as fast as they are able to produce it.

Two words: The third stage begins around the age of 18 months, when children begin to use two word sentences. These sentences usually consist of just nouns and verbs, such as "Where daddy?"

Multi-word Sentences: Around the age of two, children begin to produce short, multi-word sentences that have a subject and predicate. Grammatical morphemes in the form of prefixes or suffices are used when changing meanings or tenses. For example, a child might say "Want more toys."

More Complex Grammatical Structures: Children at the two and half and three years of age begins to use more intricate and complex grammatical structures, elements are added (conjunction), embedded and permuted within sentences and prepositions are used. For example- "Take me to the mall."

Adult-Like Language Structures: The five to six year old child reaches this developmental level in which complex structural distinctions and changing the word order in the sentence can also be made accordingly. For example: "He promised to help me."

Socio-emotional development

During infancy the close emotional bond of affection that develops between infants and their parents (caregivers) is called attachment. According to Erik Erikson (1968), the first year of life is the key time for the development of attachment. It represents the stage of developing trust or mistrust. A sense of trust is built on a feeling of physical comfort which build an expectation of the world as a secure and good place. An infant sense of trust is developed by responsive and sensitive parenting. If the parents are sensitive, affectionate, and accepting, it provides the infant a strong base to explore the environment. Such infants are likely to develop a secure attachment. On the other hand, if parents are insensitive and show dissatisfaction and find fault with the child, it can lead to creating feeling of self-doubt in the child.

As far as childhood phase is concerned the important dimension of children's socio-emotional development are the self, gender and moral development. During the early years of childhood, some important developments in the self takes place. The child due to socialisation has developed a sense of who she/he is and whom she/he wants to be identified with. The developing sense of independence makes children do things in their own way. According to Erikson, the way parents respond to their self-initiated activities leads to developing a sense of initiative or sense of guilt. For example, giving freedom and opportunities for play and answering children's questions will create a sense of support for the initiative taken. In contrast, if they are made to feel that their questions are useless, and games played by them are stupid, the children are likely to develop feeling of guilt over self-initiated activities, which may persist through the children's later life also. Self understanding in early childhood is limited to defining oneself through physical characteristics like I am girl and I am a boy. During middle and late childhood, the child is likely to define oneself through internal characteristics such as, 'I am smart' and 'I am beautiful'. In addition to defining oneself through psychological characteristics, children's self-descriptions also include social aspect of self, such as reference to social groups like being a member of school's football club or any other religious group. Children's self understanding also includes social comparison in terms of comparing one's own class performance with another student. Once the children enter school their social world expands beyond their families. They also spend greater amount of time with their age mates or peers. Thus the increased time that children spend with their peers shapes their development.

Moral Development

Piaget described a two-stage process of moral development, while Kohlberg's theory of moral development outlined six stages within three different levels. Kohlberg extended Piaget's theory, proposing that moral development is a continual process that occurs throughout the lifespan. The six stages of moral development are grouped into three levels: pre-conventional morality, conventional morality, and post-conventional morality.

Level 1 (Pre-Conventional)

1. Obedience and punishment orientation
2. Self-interest orientation

Level 2 (Conventional)

3. Interpersonal accord and conformity
4. Authority and social-order maintaining orientation

Level 3 (Post-Conventional)

5. Social contract orientation
6. Universal ethical principles (Principled conscience)

The pre-conventional stage begins with making moral choices to avoid punishment and progresses into the hedonistic stage in which moral judgement is based on self indulgence. The second stage, *i.e.*, conventional stage, begins with interpreting the reactions of others and how they would view the person as a result of decisions made. As this stage progresses, values of honor and duty motivate conduct.

Among the three levels of moral reasoning, Kohlberg called the final level of moral development the Post-Conventional or Principled Level. It's called the Principled Level because people make moral decisions based on a basic set of principles that represent their most important values and beliefs. At this level, people think more abstractly about their values and beliefs.

The Principled Level is subdivided into two stages. Stage five is called the social-contract orientation. At this stage, people understand rules and laws are mere tools intended to create social justice and designed to promote the well-being of all people. The sixth and final stage of moral development is the universal ethical principle orientation. At this stage, universal and abstract values such as dignity, respect, justice, and equality are the guiding force behind the development of a personally meaningful set of ethical principles. Individuals at this level of development believe these ethical principles should guide their actions above all else, including previously established rules, laws, and social contracts.

MULTIPLE CHOICE QUESTIONS

1. Jean Piaget was a:
A. Developmental psychologist
B. Clinical psychologist
C. Genetic Epistemologist
D. Child psychologist

2. During which stage, infants and toddlers acquire knowledge through sensory experiences and manipulating objects.
A. The Sensorimotor Stage
B. The Preoperational Stage
C. The Concrete Operational Stage
D. The Formal Operational Stage

3. Piaget believed that children in the preoperational stage have difficulty taking the perspective of another person. This is known as:
A. Metacognition B. Egocentrism
C. Reversibility D. None of the above

4. According to Jean Piaget, what type of learning do individuals acquire during the formal operational stage?
A. Abstract Thought
B. Auditory Learning
C. Visual Learning
D. None of the above

5. Children begin to develop symbols to represent events or objects in the world during the .... substage of the sensorimotor stage:
A. Tertiary Circular Reactions
B. Preoperational Stage
C. The Formal Operational Stage
D. Early Representational Thought

6. At which stage, kids learn through pretend play but still struggle with logic and taking the point of view of other people.
A. The Sensorimotor Stage
B. The Preoperational Stage
C. The Concrete Operational Stage
D. None of the above

7. Kids at which point of development begins to think more logically, but their thinking can also be very rigid. They tend to struggle with abstract and hypothetical concepts.
A. The Sensorimotor Stage
B. The Preoperational Stage
C. The Concrete Operational Stage
D. The Formal Operational Stage

8. In the nature versus nurture controversy, "nature" refers to
A. The environment
B. Plants and Animals
C. All living things
D. Heredity

9. .... is a branch of philosophy that is concerned with the origin, nature, extent, and limits of human knowledge.
A. Epistemology B. Metaphysics
C. Ethics D. Aesthetics

10. .... is a child's understanding that objects continue to exist even though they cannot be seen or heard.
A. Object permanence
B. Object orientation
C. Object programming
D. None of the above

11. The concrete operational stage begins around age .... and continues until approximately age ....
A. 2; 7 B. 2; 9
C. 7; 9 D. 7; 11

12. In late adulthood, individuals experience a decrease in which of the following?
A. Sexual Desire
B. Creativity
C. Cognitive Abilities
D. Intellect

13. According to Sigmund Freud, what is the correct order of the five psychosexual stages of development?
A. Oral, Anal, Phallic, Genital, Latency
B. Oral, Anal, Phallic, Latency, Genital
C. Anal, Phallic, Latency, Genital, Oral
D. Phallic, Anal, Oral, Latency, Genital

14. A critical period is a stage in development when:
A. Bonding between the child and parent first takes place
B. Specific stimuli have a major effect on development that they do not produce at other times
C. Both A & B
D. None of the above

15. .... is a term referring to another part of the adaptation process initially proposed by Jean Piaget.
A. Assimilation
B. Cognitive development
C. Heredity
D. None of the above

16. The discriminatory ability of infants is better for:
A. Non-social stimuli
B. Social stimuli
C. Auditory stimuli
D. Visual stimuli

17. According to object relation theorists, the primary social relationship upon which all other social relationships were built was:
A. The mother-child dyad
B. The father-infant bond
C. Both (A) & (B)
D. None of the above

18. Those who adopt an extreme heredity position are known as ....
A. Empiricists B. Nativists
C. Functionalist D. Behaviourists

19. According to whom the development is consisted of two processes: integration and differentiation.
A. Werner
B. Hurlock
C. Baller and Charles
D. None of the above

20. The .... and .... emotions are those emotions which include guilt, shame, embarrassment, pride and are related to our sense of self and our consciousness of other's reactions to us.
A. Unconscious and subconscious
B. Initial and latent
C. Primary and secondary
D. Primary and self-conscious

21. .... includes the child's experience, expression, and management of emotions and the ability to establish positive and rewarding relationships with others. It encompasses both intra- and interpersonal processes.
A. Moral development
B. Social-emotional development
C. Sensory-motor development
D. Cognitive development

22. .... refers to the development of a child's bones, muscles and ability to move around and manipulate his or her environment.
A. Motor development
B. Emotional development
C. Functional development
D. Cognitive development

23. Which is a specific emotion related to a successful behaviour?
A. Pride B. Joy
C. Excitement D. Remorse

24. According to which stage, the development involves three main stages: germinal stage, embryonic stage and fetal stage.
A. Prenatal stage
B. Infancy stage
C. Toddlerhood stage
D. Early & Middle childhood

25. Spontaneous movements by the fetus begin around:
A. 2 weeks from conception
B. 3 weeks from conception
C. 5 weeks from conception
D. 6 weeks from conception

26. Mechanistic model of growth focuses on:
1. Role of environmental input and behaviour output.
2. Evolutionary origin
3. Quantitative increase in learned responses

Codes:
A. 1 and 2 B. 1 and 3
C. 2 and 3 D. 1, 2 and 3

27. Match List-I with List-II and indicate your answer using the codes given below:

List-I (Concepts)	**List-II (Explanations)**
(*a*) Person schemas	1. A schema consisting of an organized collection of beliefs and feelings about ourself.
(*b*) Role schemas	2. Mental schemas suggesting that certain traits and behaviours go together and that individuals having them represent certain type.
(*c*) Self schemas	3. The schemas containing information about how persons playing specific roles generally act, and what they are like.
(*d*) Scripts	4. Schemas that indicate what is expected to happen in a given setting.

Codes:

	(*a*)	(*b*)	(*c*)	(*d*)
A.	2	3	1	4
B.	1	3	2	4
C.	4	3	1	2
D.	3	1	4	2

28. Pragmatics is:
A. Learning new words
B. Learning word meanings
C. Understanding how communication works
D. Understanding rules for combining words into proper sentences

29. Development of Super-Ego, according to Freud is a result of:
A. Identification with the opposite sex parent
B. Resolution of Oedipus/Electra complex
C. Age advancement
D. Anatomical superiority

30. Arrange the developmental stages of language given by Vygotsky in correct sequence, given below:
1. Potential concept stage
2. Vague syncretic stage
3. Mature concept stage
4. Complex stage

Codes:
A. 3, 1, 4, 2 B. 2, 4, 1, 3
C. 1, 3, 2, 4 D. 4, 2, 3, 1

31. Which of the following emerges when self-control replaces parental-control?
A. Ego
B. Super ego
C. Identity Achievement
D. Identity Diffusion

32. The two broad types of emotions humans develop are:
A. Primary and secondary
B. Primary and self-conscious
C. Primary and unconscious
D. Primary and real

33. At what level do we understand the complete meaning and sense of a language structure?
A. Phonemes
B. Syntax
C. Prosodic contour
D. Morphemes

34. Primary emotions appear:
A. Within the first 6 months
B. Within the first 8 months
C. Within the first 4 months
D. After 1 year

35. What did Chomsky not argue about language development?
A. There is a universal grammar.
B. It is genetically wired.
C. There is an innate modular language.
D. It is based on reinforced learning.

36. According to whom, moral development evolves from the absolute to the relative.
A. Kohlberg B. Piaget
C. Erik Erikson D. Freud

37. Match the items in List-I with items in List-II and mark your answer with the help of the codes given below:

List-I (Attachment Style)	List-II (Attachment Characteristic)
(*a*) Avoidant attachment	1. Infant, after separation from primary caregiver, shows contradictory behaviour upon his or her return.
(*b*) Secure attachment	2. Infant rarely cries when separated from the primary care/giver and does not make contact upon his or her return.
(*c*) Disorganized-disoriented attachment	3. Infant cries when primary caregiver leaves and actively seek the care-giver upon his or her return.
(*d*) Ambivalent (resistant) attachment	4. Infant becomes anxious before the primary care-giver leaves, is upset during the absence and seeks at the same time avoids contact on his or her return.

Codes:

	(*a*)	(*b*)	(*c*)	(*d*)
A.	1	3	2	4
B.	3	2	4	1
C.	4	1	3	2
D.	2	3	1	4

38. Match List-I with List-II and indicate your answer using the codes given below:

List-I (Accomplishments)	List-II (Cognitive Developmental Stage)
(*a*) Egocentric thought	1. Sensorimotor
(*b*) Object permanence	2. Formal operational
(*c*) Abstract reasoning	3. Pre-operational
(*d*) Conservation reversibility	4. Concrete operational

Codes:

	(*a*)	(*b*)	(*c*)	(*d*)
A.	2	3	4	1
B.	3	1	2	4
C.	4	2	1	3
D.	1	4	3	2

39. Match List-I with List-II.

List-I (Concept)	List-II (Psychologist)
(*a*) Parenting styles	1. Bowlby
(*b*) Attachment	2. Piaget
(*c*) Reciprocal Determinism	3. Bandura
(*d*) Centration	4. Baumrind

Codes:

	(*a*)	(*b*)	(*c*)	(*d*)
A.	2	1	4	3
B.	2	4	1	3
C.	4	1	3	2
D.	4	2	3	1

40. Temporary support that parents provide to a child to do a task until the child can do it alone, is termed as:

A. Ageism
B. Induction
C. Scaffolding
D. Power assertion

41. Which of the following is NOT a stage in Piaget's theory of moral development?

A. Heteronomous Morality
B. Conventional Level
C. Premoral Stage
D. Autonomous Morality

42. Children learn to add new words through a process called:

A. Fast mapping
B. New mapping
C. Extensions
D. Inspiration

43. According to Freud, different types of anxiety are:

1. Neurotic anxiety
2. State anxiety
3. Moral anxiety
4. Reality anxiety

Codes:

A. 1, 2 and 3 only
B. 1, 2 and 4 only
C. 1, 3 and 4 only
D. 2, 3 and 4 only

44. Three mountains task was used by Piaget to study .... in children.

A. Centration
B. Conservation
C. Egocentrism
D. Reversibility

45. Match List-I with List-II and use the following code for your answer:

List-I	List-II
(*a*) Meaning of words	1. Morpheme
(*b*) Rules that govern the order of words	2. Phoneme
(*c*) Smallest unit of sound	3. Semantics
(*d*) Smallest unit of meaning	4. Syntax

Codes:

	(*a*)	(*b*)	(*c*)	(*d*)
A.	4	3	2	1
B.	1	2	3	4
C.	1	3	4	2
D.	4	2	3	1

46. Each individual is different from every other because of which one of the following reason?

A. Chromosomes from the two parents randomly pair up in each child.
B. The female germ cells and the male germ cells contain varying numbers of chromosomes.
C. The male body cells and female body cells have different numbers of chromosomes.
D. The fertilisation of the egg takes place at different times and days in different individuals.

47. In which of Piaget's stages of development would a child be when he has just developed object permanence?

A. Sensorimotor
B. Pre-operational
C. Concrete operational
D. Formal operational

48. Match the List-I with List-II using the codes given below:

List-I (Stages)	List-II (Cognitive development)
(*a*) Operational Concrete	1. Mature adult thought emerges, thinking by deductive logic, abstract thought
(*b*) Pre-operational	2. Develops conservation concepts, classify object in series
(*c*) Sensorimotor	3. Represent the world mentally, thought egocentric, child shows animism
(*d*) Formal operational	4. Lacks of language, does not use symbol, internal behaviour begins

Codes:

	(*a*)	(*b*)	(*c*)	(*d*)
A.	1	2	4	3
B.	2	1	4	3
C.	2	3	4	1
D.	1	3	4	2

49. Read each of the following two statements—Assertion (A) and Reason (R) and indicate your answer using the codes given below:

Assertion (A): Children of permissive-indulgent parents tend to the impulsive, aggressive, inconsiderate and demanding.

Reason (R): Permissive-indulgent parents are high on warmth, discipline and control.

Codes:

A. Both (A) and (R) are true and (R) is correct explanation of (A).
B. Both (A) and (R) are true, but (R) is not the correct explanation of (A).
C. (A) is true, but (R) is false.
D. (A) is false, but (R) is true.

50. According to Piaget, which is the primary motivating force behind development?

A. Accommodation B. Assimilation
C. Equilibration D. Adaptation

ANSWERS

1	2	3	4	5	6	7	8	9	10
C	A	B	A	D	B	C	D	A	A
11	**12**	**13**	**14**	**15**	**16**	**17**	**18**	**19**	**20**
D	B	B	B	A	B	A	B	A	D
21	**22**	**23**	**24**	**25**	**26**	**27**	**28**	**29**	**30**
B	A	A	A	D	B	A	C	B	B
31	**32**	**33**	**34**	**35**	**36**	**37**	**38**	**39**	**40**
B	B	C	A	D	A	D	B	C	C
41	**42**	**43**	**44**	**45**	**46**	**47**	**48**	**49**	**50**
B	A	C	C	A	A	A	C	C	C

❑❑❑

CHAPTER 11

Guidance and Counseling

Motivation is defined by psychologists as an internal process that activates, guides, and maintains behaviour over time. A shift from a behavioural to cognitive perspective in American psychology in the 1960s and 1970s brought a reintegration of motivation with learning (Driscoll, 2000). Thorndike was the first psychologist to document experimentally the link between learning and motivation (Sprinthall, Sprinthall, & Oja 1998).

Motivation has several effects on learning and behaviour.

- **Motivation directs behaviour toward particular goals:** Social cognitive theorists propose that individuals set goals for themselves and direct their behaviour accordingly. Motivation determines the specific goals toward which learners strive (Maehr & Meyer, 1997; Pintrich et al., 1993).
- **Motivation leads to increased effort and energy:** Motivation increases the amount of effort and energy that learners expend in activities directly related to their needs and goals (Csikszentmihalyi & Nakamura, 1989; Maehr, 1984; Pintrich et al., 1993). It determines whether they pursue a task enthusiastically and wholeheartedly, on the one hand, or apathetically and lackadaisically, on the other.
- **Motivation increases initiation of and persistence in activities:** The initiation and persistence in activities that students perform could be increased owing to motivation. It depends on learner's persistence whether they want to begin a task, complete or stop working. Thus motivation can improve student's achievement, since motivation increases students' time on task, an important factor affecting their learning and achievement (Brophy, 1988; Larson, 2000; Wigfield, 1994).
- **Motivation affects cognitive processes:** Motivation affects what learners pay attention to and how effectively they process it (Eccles & Wigfield, 1985; Pintrich & Schunk, 2002; Pugh & Bergin, 2006).
- **Motivation determines which consequences are reinforcing and punishing:** The more learners are motivated to achieve occupational success, the more they will be proud on getting promotion and gets upset by demotion. The more learners want to be accepted and respected by peers, the more they will value membership in the "in" group and be distressed by the ridicule of Colleague will seem.
- **Motivation often enhances performance:** Motivation affects what learners pay attention to and how efficiently they process it (Eccles & Wigfield, 1985; Pintrich& Schunk, 2002; Pugh & Bergin, 2006) leads to improved performance.

Not all forms of motivation have exactly the same effects on human learning and performance. Learners are most likely to show the beneficial effects of motivation when they are intrinsically motivated to engage in classroom activities. Intrinsically motivated learners tackle assigned tasks willingly and are eager to learn classroom material, more likely to process information in effective ways (*e.g.,* by engaging in meaningful learning), and more likely to achieve at high levels. In contrast, extrinsically motivated learners may have to be enticed or prodded, may process information only superficially, and are often interested in performing only easy tasks and meeting minimal classroom requirements (A. E. Gottfried, Fleming, & Gottfried, 2001; Reeve, 2006; Schiefele, 1991; Tobias, 1994). Extrinsic motivation is not necessarily a bad thing, however; often learners are simultaneously motivated by both intrinsic and extrinsic factors (Cameron & Pierce, 1994; Covington, 2000; Lepper et al., 2005).

Bruner opposes the use of the external reinforcement or rewards as a way to motivate students to learn. Rather Bruner favors creating a stimulation environment filled with interesting problems that the students are curious about so that they will be intrinsically motivated to learn. Intrinsic motivation has the advantages of being more robust than rewards, plus it is an inherent part of the learning process not some tack-on goodies that the teacher provides. If a teacher can engage the student's curiosity, then the learning will become intrinsically motivating and will continue. If a teacher manipulates external reinforcement or rewards as a way to engage the learners, this learning will not sustain itself but rather will disappear when the reinforcers are gone.

A key aspect of Bruner's view on instruction is discovery learning. Discovery learning is important according to Bruner because it provides the opportunity for students to construct their own meaning rather than simply memorizing the meeting someone else has assigned to something. Discovery learning has students as active, engaged participants in the process, which also enhances their intrinsic motivation for learning. Discovery learning is also more resistant to forgetting. When students are actively engaged in discovery learning there are also much less likely to be disruptive or "problem students" in the classroom.

However Bandura indicated that motivation had more of an effect on our actions than our learning. Thus, he would not use reinforcers in the same way as behaviourists, such as Skinner. Several factors can influence the motivation of students. One important factor is the student's self-efficacy. Bandura has repeatedly shown that when students have high self-efficacy for a certain learning task. they will put forth more effort to accomplish this task. They will work harder and persist longer with this learning task. As a result they are more likely to be successful than students with lower self-efficacy. Self-efficacy has a motivating effect on students.

Bandura recognizes that our motivation is effected by others through vicarious experiences. Seeing people similar to oneself succeed by sustained effort raises observer's beliefs that they too possess the capabilities master comparable activities to succeed. By the same token, observing other's fail despite high effort lowers observer's judgements of their own efficacy and undermines their efforts. The impact of modeling on perceived self-efficacy is strongly influenced by perceived similarity to the models.

FACTORS IN EDUCATIONAL ACHIEVEMENT

Academic achievement or (academic) performance is the outcome of education — the extent to which a student, teacher or institution has achieved their educational goals. Education plays a vital role in the development of human capital and is linked with an individual's well-being and opportunities for better living (Battle & Lewis, 2002).

The environment and the personal characteristics of learners play an important role in their academic success. The school personnel, members of the families and communities provide help and support to students for the quality of their academic performance. This social assistance has a crucial role for the accomplishment of performance goals of students at school (Goddard, 2003). Besides the social structure, parents' involvement in their child's education increases the rate of academic success of their child (Furstenberg & Hughes, 1995).

The relationship between gender and the academic achievement of students has been discussed for decades (Eitle, 2005). Gender, ethnicity, and father's occupation are significant contributors to student achievement (McCoy, 2005; Peng & Hall, 1995).

Above and beyond the other demographic factors, the effects of Socio-economic-status (SES) are still prevalent at the individual level (Capraro, M., Capraro, R., & Wiggins, 2000). Parental education and family SES level have positive correlations with the student's quality of achievement (Caldas & Bankston, 1997; Jeynes, 2002; Parelius, D., & Parelius, A., 1987; Mitchell & Collom, 2001; Ma & Klinger, 2000). The students with high level of SES perform better than the middle class students and the middle class students perform better than the students with low level of SES (Garzon, 2006; Kahlenberg, 2006; Kirkup, 2008).

The achievement of students is negatively correlated with the low SES level of parents because it hinders the individual in gaining access to sources and resources of learning (Duke, 2000; Eamon, 2005; Lopez, 1995). Low SES level strongly affects the achievement of students, dragging them down to a lower level (Sander, 2001). It is also observed that the economically disadvantaged parents are less able to afford the cost of education of their children at higher levels and consequently they do not work at their fullest potential (Rouse & Barrow, 2006).

Krashen (2005) concluded that students whose parents are educated can better communicate with their children regarding the school work, activities and the information being taught at school. They can better assist their children in their work and participate at school (Fantuzzo & Tighe, 2000; Trusty, 1999).

Theory of Educational Productivity by Walberg (1981) determined three groups of nine factors based on affective, cognitive and behavioural skills for optimization of learning that affect the quality of academic performance: Aptitude (ability, development and motivation); instruction (amount and quality); environment (home, classroom, peers and television) (Roberts, 2007).

The home environment also affects the academic performance of students. Educated parents can provide such an environment that suits best for academic success of their children. The school authorities can provide counselling and guidance to parents for creating positive home environment for improvement in students' quality of work (Marzano, 2003). The academic performance of students heavily depends upon the parental involvement in their academic activities to attain the higher level of quality in academic success (Barnard, 2004; Henderson, 1988; Shumox & Lomax, 2001).

SOCIAL PSYCHOLOGY OF EDUCATION

Social Psychology of Education draws from the disciplines of psychology, sociology, and education in order to help us better understand human behaviour in education. Social Psychology of Education covers wide variety of content concerns, theoretical interests and research methods among which are: Content concerns : classroom instruction, decision-making in education, educational innovation, concerns for gender, race, ethnicity and social class, knowledge, creation, transmission and effects, leadership in schools and school systems, long-term effects of instructional processes, micro politics of schools, student cultures and interactions, teacher recruitment and careers, teachers student relations. Theoretical interests : achievement motivation, attitude theory, attribution theory, conflict management and the learning of pro-social behaviour, cultural and social capital, discourse analysis, group dynamics, role theory, social exchange theory, social transition, social learning theory, status attainment, symbolic interaction, the study of organisations. Research methods: comparative research, experiments, formal observations, historical studies, literature reviews, panel studies, qualitative methods, sample surveys.

Social-Psychological Interventions in Education

In recent years, several rigorous, randomized field experiments have shown that seemingly "small" social-psychological interventions had strikingly large effects on educational achievement even months and years later (Garcia & Cohen, Gehlbach, 2010; Nisbett, 2009; Walton & Dweck, 2009; Walton & Spencer 2009; Wilson, 2006).

Learning and teaching, as currently practiced in most schools, are fundamentally social acts (Goodenow, 1992). Students learn by interacting with their teacher and through working with one another. For the purposes of thinking about social psychology's potential role in schools, Meyer's definition, "Social psychology is the scientific study of how people think about, influence, and relate to one another," (2007) covers three critical aspects of student's and teacher's daily social experiences. It also adequately covers three core domains of the discipline: social cognition, influence and persuasion, and interpersonal relations.

Reducing Biases and Facilitating Social Perspective Taking to Improve Pedagogy

Within social cognition, a long tradition of research has examined how people make sense of and perceive each other. Historically, much of this research has focused on biases and mistakes in person perception (*e.g.,* Ross, 1977). More recently, this research has been complemented by a renewed interest in accuracy in person perception *i.e.,* social perspective taking (SPT) as well as assessing the impact of SPT on other outcomes (*e.g.,* Ames, 2004; Davis, 1996; Ickes, 1997). This strand of social psychological research holds tremendous promise for helping teachers to improve their pedagogy. To the extent that teachers succumb to common biases that decrease SPT accuracy less frequently, they should gain a more accurate perception of their students' understanding of the world. For example, one bias that emerges in classroom settings is the fundamental attribution error (Ross, 1977). According to Ross, this bias consists of people's pervasive and erroneous tendency to make attributions to a person's personality traits rather than to the situation. Those who commit this error less frequently will tend to improve their SPT accuracy. In classrooms, teachers constantly need to assess what causes students to get upset or to not pay attention or to fail to turn in their homework on time. In making these assessments, teachers are likely to be biased towards making dispositional rather than situational attributions. Training teachers to refrain from biased perceptions of their students and to engage in more frequent and accurate SPT should help their pedagogy in multiple ways. Proficiency at the SPT tasks should enhance teacher's capacities to manage classroom behaviour and resolve conflicts in effective ways by virtue of their ability to read the emotional states of their students and to more accurately assess how they perceive different situations.

Using Cognitive Dissonance to Bolster Student Motivation

Social psychologists have maintained a lasting fascination with how people influence and persuade one another in social settings. In particular, the work on cognitive dissonance (Festinger, 1962) has shown that we are adept at self-persuasion and that cognitive dissonance can be a powerful motivating force. Subject to a couple caveats the following rule usually holds true: the more we preach something, the more likely we are to practice it. The untapped potential in this case is that few teachers are familiar with this work might be applied in classrooms *e.g.,* to help bolster student motivation.

Certainly, cognitive dissonance approaches could be used to motivate students to engage in a variety of different behaviours besides trying hard on homework. Students could advocate for the academic goals they would like to achieve in a given school year or how they will strike an optimal balance between school-work and extra-curricular activities. The approaches teachers might employ to invoke the motivating dissonance could be more subtle or stronger than the peer-tutoring intervention. For some students merely submitting a written document of "goals of the year" to the teacher might be enough to arouse dissonance. For others, stronger interventions that encourage students to state their goals to multiple audiences (*e.g.,* teachers, peers, and parents) might be more appropriate.

Enhancing Student Understanding by Learning about Intergroup Bias

A third major domain, in which social psychologists have substantially enhanced our understanding of the social world, is that of interpersonal and intergroup relations. One of the more intriguing phenomena to emerge from this domain is the research on intergroup bias (Devine, 1995). One obvious application of this work to classroom practice is to guide teacher's organization of group work in their own classrooms and to facilitate better intergroup relations between students from different backgrounds or cliques.

Effectiveness of Social Psychological Interventions

One signal of the promise of social psychology as a means to improving education is to examine a couple of the instances where ideas and concepts from this discipline have been applied to education in the past. Scholars studying achievement motivation (*e.g.,* Midgley, 2002), cooperative groupwork (*e.g.,* Johnson & Johnson, 2009; Slavin, 1996), attributions about intelligence (Dweck & Leggett, 1988), and teacher expectancy effects (*e.g.,* Brophy, 1983; Rosenthal, 1991) have applied ideas from social psychology to educational settings. The success of these research programs is, perhaps, unsurprising given that the theories in these domains have obvious applicability to classroom settings.

TEACHER EFFECTIVENESS

Effective teacher is one who quite consistently achieves goals - be they self-selected or imposed - that are related either directly or indirectly to student learning. Effective teachers must possess the knowledge and skills needed to attain the goals, and must be able to use that knowledge and those skills appropriately if these goals are to be achieved. A broader and more comprehensive definition of effective teacher consists of five points, formulated by evaluating discussions of teacher effectiveness in the research literature and reports (*e.g.,* Berry,2004; Brophy & Good, 1896; Campbell et al., 2003,2004).

The five point definition of effective teacher consists of the following:

- Effective teachers have high expectations for all students and help them to learn, as measured by value added or other test-based growth measures, or by alternative measures.
- Effective teacher contribute to positive academic, attitudinal, and social outcomes for students such as regular attendance, on time promotion to the next grade, on-time graduation, self-efficacy and cooperative behaviour.
- Effective teacher use diverse resources to plan and structure engaging learning opportunities; monitor student progress formatively, adapting instruction as needed; and evaluate learning using multiple source of evidence.
- Effective teachers contribute to the development of classrooms and schools that value diversity and civic-mindedness.
- Effective teacher collaborate with other teachers, administrators, parents and educational professionals to ensure students success, particularly the success of students with special needs and those of high risk for failure.

Characteristics of Effective Teacher

Teacher characteristics are relatively stable traits that are related to, and influence, the way of teachers practice in their profession. These characteristics are organized into four 'clusters': professionalism, thinking/reasoning, expectations and leadership.

CLUSTER	CHARACTERISTIC	DESCRIPTION
Professionalism	Commitment	Commitment to doing everything possible for each student and enabling all students to be successful.
	Confidence	Belief in one's ability to be effective and to take on challenges. Being consistent and fair; keeping one's word.
	Respect	Belief that all individuals matter and deserve respect.
Thinking/reasoning	Analytical thinking	Ability to think logically, break things down, and recognize cause and effect.
	Conceptual thinking	Conceptual thinking Ability to identify patterns and connections, even when a great deal of detail is present.
Expectations	Drive for improvement	Relentless energy for setting and meeting challenging targets, for students and the school.
	Information seeking	Information seeking Drive to find out more and get to the heart of things; intellectual curiosity.
	Initiative	Initiative Drive to act now to anticipate and pre-empt events.
Leadership	Flexibility	Ability and willingness to adapt to the needs of a situation and change tactics.
	Accountability	Accountability Drive and ability to set clear expectations and parameters and hold others accountable for performance.
	Passion for learning	Passion for learning Drive and ability to support students in their learning, and to help them become confident and independent learners.

Sources of Evidence of Teaching Effectiveness

There are 12 potential sources of evidence of teaching effectiveness: (1) student ratings, (2) peer rating, (3) self-evaluation, (4) videos, (5) student interviews, (6) alumni ratings, (7) employer ratings, (8) administrator rating, (9) teaching scholarship, (10) teaching awards, (11) learning outcome measures, and (12) teaching portfolio.

NEED OF GUIDANCE IN SCHOOL

The need for guidance had existed at all times. Moreover, the need of guidance is universal. "There is hardly any individual who does not need help". According to Jones (1951): "The focus of guidance is the individual not his problem, its purpose is to provide the growth of the individual in self-direction providing opportunity for self-realisation and self-direction is the key-note of guidance."

Traxler (1957): considers guidance as a help which enables each individual to understand his abilities and interests, to develop them as well as possible and to relate the life-goals, and finally to reach a state of complete and mature self-guidance as a desirable member of the social order.

Guidance is needed from educational point of view because of the following reasons:

(*i*) **Increase in the range of individual differences among school going children:** As each child id unique in themselves. The differences in terms of aptitude, aspirations, interests and achievement of the children calls for the need to understand child aspiration as well as proper guidance in terms of setting realistic achievable goals for the well being of the child . Thus due to this reason the guidance services in the school programmes is essential for modifying the school programme for the best possible unfoldment of the student's potentialities.

(ii) **Guidance as an instrument for the qualitative improvement of education:** As the number of educational institutes are increasing at a much faster pace to cater to the needs of increasing number of children in recent years, the educational standards on the other side are deteriorating at an alarming rate. Consequently, there is a great need of providing guidance services in the school for the qualitative improvement of education.

(iii) **Knowledge explosion or the increase in the types of courses offered in the schools:** Due to the diversity of courses available in the school, at the secondary stage, the educational guidance should help the pupils to understand themselves better, to understand different aspects of the school, to select appropriate courses to get information about different educational opportunities, to develop good study habits. The students should be helped to be acquainted with the vocational implications of various school subjects

(iv) **Expanding Educational Objectives:** Education is not just confined at completing the curriculum of the school. Infact it focuses on the overall development of the child including the emotional, social and civic life of the student. Thus problems of social adjustment and personality orientation require the services of a competent counsellor and availability of appropriate guidance services.

(v) **Solution of Educational Problems:** All students at some point of their educational phase encounter several problems in away or the another such as issues regarding universal and compulsory education, increased enrolment, high per centage of failures and dropout, wastage and stagnation etc. To eradicate these problems, there is an utmost need of proper guidance services in the school. Special guidance services are also required for the gifted, backward, handicapped and delinquent children.

(vi) **Solving Discipline problems:** Problem of discipline is becoming more and more acute in the educational institutions. Even at higher stage of education it has taken a serious turn. Student strikes and agitation has become a common scene of the day. Problems of discipline can be solved with the help of guidance programme.

(vii) **Optimum Achievement of the Students:** As the students of the school didn't invest time and energy properly to utilize the resources and facilities available in their school, the achievement level or performance of the students in the schools deteriorates. Therefore, there is a great need to develop study habits among the students. Proper guidance services can help in this direction.

THE COUNSELING PROCESS

The counselling process is a continuous, cyclical model in which the counsellor and client collaboratively set goals, formulate actions plans, and assess progress toward the goal(s). Throughout the process new information is integrated, the counsellor-client relationship is developed, and progress toward counseling goals is reassessed.

The three fundamental qualities that a counsellor should have, as emphasized by Rogers, are: genuineness of feeling and interest, understanding, and unconditional acceptance of the counselee.

According to Rogers (1957), the conditions necessary for a personality change to take place are:

1. The counsellee and the counsellor are in psychological contact with each other.
2. The counsellee is in a state of incongruence and hence is vulnerable and anxious.
3. The counsellor is congruent and integrated, that is, he is free from anxiety and tension. His relationship with the counselee is genuine and does not cause any disharmony in him.

4. The counsellor has unconditional positive regard for the counsellee.
5. The counsellor experiences an empathic understanding of the counsellee's internal frame of reference and tries to communicate his experience to the counsellee.
6. The counsellor exhibited empathy and warmth of acceptance of the counselee and he appreciates and understands the counsellor's unconditional positive regard towards him to a reasonable extent.

Rogers (1961) describes the counselling process in seven steps or stages which form a continuum. Rogers thought there were seven stages that he could observe, and they enabled him to see whether his clients were making progress in therapy, or whether they seemed to be stuck, for a time unable to move on. Although the process can be erratic, clients do, in general progress step by step, building on their experiences at one stage before moving on to the next. Only when people feel accepted and understood at one stage, do they feel able to take the next step.

Stage-1: People in this stage appear to be rigid in personality and rather remote, cut off from their emotions and from other people. Rogers thought it unlikely that such people would see any value in therapy, and therefore unlikely that they would take part in it. There is unwillingness to communicate about the self; communication if any, is only about externals, such as experiences which have no deep significance for himself. Feelings and meaningful personal experiences are neither recognized nor accepted. They are governed by rigid rules as to how people should behave, and they are strongly judgemental of others, having a rather pessimistic view of human nature.

Stage-2: Here, there is a slight loosening of rigid constructs, though people find it very difficult to accept any responsibility for themselves, or what happens in their lives. When things go wrong, they tend to blame others, and feel like victims of a hostile world, rather than participators in it. Typical of this stage are statements like:

"I'm not responsible when things go wrong, am I?"

"1 don't do anything wrong, other people keep creaing problems for me." * Client may begin therapy at this stage.

Stage-3: The client feels free to express his feelings. The process started in previous stage continues more freely. Another significant improvement is that the client talks about the self as an object. Past feelings and personal feelings which are usually negative are expressed. However, the client does not accept them. For most part, the feelings are revealed as something shameful, bad or abnormal or unacceptable in other ways. Certain experiences are described as in past or as somewhat remote from the self. Personal constructs though rigid, are recognized. Differentiation of feelings and meanings is better and less general. The client is able to see his personal choice as ineffective but not in their proper perspective.

Stage-4: In this stage, clients begin to describe deeper feelings, usually those that happened in the past

"1 felt so desperately unhappy when she didn't seem to care. I've never known such deep feelings it really scared me."

People have difficulty in understanding and accepting these (negative) feelings and would rather they hadn't existed.

"If this is what falling in love means, then l'd rather not have it."

Feelings in the present start to emerge, but they are mistrusted and even rejected. The client started accepting the responsibility for what is happening, even though the fearfulness and hopelessness of it are apparent. Acceptance, understanding and empathy enable the client to move smoothly in the direction of therapy. There is a realization about contradictions and incongruence between experience and self. The client shows feelings of self-responsibility in problems but there is a tendency to vacillate. The client is still wary about close relationships.

Stage-5: Feelings are expressed freely in the present. Feelings are very close to being fully experienced through fear; distrust and lack of clarity are still present. Self-feeling are increasingly owned and accepted. Responsibility for problems is accepted. The client is increasingly able to accept contradictions and incongruencies in experiences. There is an increase in free dialogue within the self and improvement in reducing blockage of internal communication.

Stage-6: Rogers described this stage as being very distinctive and often dramatic. It is characterised by feelings, previously suppressed, becoming fully experienced in the present moment. This awareness is acute, clear and full of meaning. The self which hitherto has been experienced as somewhat fragmented is now experienced as an integrated whole - mind, body, emotion and intellect, and clients experience moments of full congruence. Previously felt ambiguities and uncertainties now start to click into place and become crystal clear. These experiences are irreversible and produce changes in attitude and perception. Feelings start to flow freely and reach their full conclusion. Previous fears about the potential destructiveness of negative feelings evaporate, and feelings are seen as enriching experiences, not ones to be avoided. One of the most striking discoveries made by many people at this stage is the realisation of care, concern and tenderness for oneself.

Stage-7: Rogers thought that changes made by clients in stage six tended to be irreversible, and further change was as likely to occur outside of the therapeutic relationship as within it. By this stage new feelings are experienced with immediacy and richness of details. Changing feelings are accepted and owned. There is a feeling of trust in the total organismic process. All the elements of his experiences are now available to awareness and there is experiencing of real and effective choice in new ways of being. The counselee becomes a "fully-functioning person", by which is meant that each individual has an innate tendency toward actualizing himself that is, realizing his inherent capacities and potentials.

COUNSELLING AREAS

1. Educational Counselling

A term first coined by Truman Kelley in 1914 (Makinde, 1988), educational counselling is a process of rendering services to pupils who need assistance in making decisions about important aspects of their education, such as the choice of courses and studies, decisions regarding interests and ability, and choices of college and high school. Educational counselling increases a pupil's knowledge of educational opportunities.

2. Personal/Social Counselling

Personal counselling deals with emotional distress and behavioural difficulties, which arise when individuals struggle to deal with developmental stages and tasks. Any aspect of development can be turned into an adjustment problem, and it is inevitable that everyone encounters, at some time, exceptional difficulty in meeting an ordinary challenge. For example:

- Anxiety over a career decision
- Lingering anger over an interpersonal conflict
- Insecurities about getting older
- Depressive feelings when bored with work

- Excessive guilt about a serious mistake
- A lack of assertion and confidence
- Grief over the loss of a loved one
- Disillusionment and loneliness after parents' divorce
- Drug and alcohol abuse

3. Vocational Counselling

Vocational counselling is defined as individual contacts with those counselled, in order to facilitate career development. This definition and category encompasses counselling situations such as these:

- Helping students become aware of the many occupations to consider
- Interpreting an occupational interest inventory to a student
- Assisting a teenager to decide what to do after school
- Helping a student apply to a college or university
- Role-playing a job interview in preparation for the real thing

MULTIPLE CHOICE QUESTIONS

1. Which of the following is an example of an intrinsic motivator?
   A. Good working conditions
   B. Promotion
   C. Cash prize
   D. Satisfaction in Job Well Done

2. Which of the following is an example of one of Herzberg's (1966) motivating factors?
   A. Salary
   B. Recognition
   C. Working conditions
   D. Cash prize

3. Career counselling was originally called:
   A. Counselling
   B. Job counselling
   C. Vocational Guidance
   D. None of the above

4. The primary organization representing career counsellors is:
   A. The National Career Development Association
   B. The National Council on Disability Affairs
   C. The National Council on Drug Abuse
   D. None of the above

5. .... are concerned with the educational, academic, career, personal and social needs and encourage the maximum development of every student.
   A. Personal counsellor
   B. Mental health counsellor
   C. Family therapists
   D. School counsellor

6. Among these which is the specific responsibilities and roles of school counsellor?
   A. Individual counselling and advisement
   B. Student appraisal
   C. Career development
   D. All of the above

7. .... is a type of psychotherapy that involves one or more therapists working with several people at the same time.
   A. Group therapy
   B. Individual therapy
   C. Family therapy
   D. Play therapy

8. Family therapy is generally used to·
   A. Attempts to understand the family as a social system.

B. Improve communications between members of the family.
C. Resolve specific conflicts - for example between adolescents and their parents.
D. All of the above.

9. The degree required for independent practice as a social worker is:
A. Ph.D. B. BSW
C. MSW D. All of the above

10. Which of the following is a law of learning?
A. Law of readiness B. Law of effect
C. Law of exercise D. All of the above

11. The rate of progress in learning slows down and reaches a limit beyond which further improvement seems impossible. It is known as:
A. Plateau B. Difficult stage
C. Helplessness D. Both B & C

12. .... is often used when students have a hard time connecting theories to actual practice or when students are unable to understand application of theories.
A. Observation method
B. Task method
C. Demonstration method
D. Lecture method

13. Reinforcement theory of motivation is given by;
A. Skinner B. Pavlov
C. Jung D. Maslow

14. .... is driven by an interest or enjoyment in the task itself, and exists within the individual rather than relying on external pressures or a desire for reward
A. Intrinsic motivation
B. Extrinsic motivation
C. Push motivations
D. Pull motivations

15. According to which theory needs are arranged in order of importance to human life, from the basic to the complex.
A. Flow theory
B. Herzberg two factor theory
C. Maslow need hierarchy theory
D. None of the above

16. According to Piaget, ... is the process of taking new information in one's environment and altering pre-existing schemas in order to fit in the new information.
A. Accommodation
B. Assimilation
C. Conservation
D. Object permanence

17. According to .... theory, there is a tendency for individuals to seek consistency among their cognitions (*i.e.*, beliefs, opinions).
A. evolutionary theory
B. cognitive dissonance
C. transformative learning
D. operant conditioning

18. The book "Childhood and Society" based on the eight stage theory of human development was first published by whom in 1950?
A. Piaget B. Freud
C. Maslow D. Erik Erikson

19. Nativists believe that intelligence is mostly:
A. Inherited B. Learned
C. Empirical D. None of the above

20. One of the main elements of Erickson's psychosocial stage theory is the development of ....
A. psychosexual stages
B. personality
C. trust
D. ego identity

21. Which type of rehearsal involves students imagining certain social interactions (*e.g.*, being teased by another student or group of students)?
A. Structuring B. Overt rehearsal
C. Covert rehearsal D. Mastery learning

22. Which procedure is used by teachers to increases the likelihood that the student will emit a correct response and reduces the possibility of errors being made.
A. Prompting B. Feedback
C. Guidance D. None of the above

23. Any of several branches of psychology that seek to apply psychological principles to practical problems of education or industry or marketing etc. is known as:
A. Practical psychology
B. Human psychology
C. Social psychology
D. Applied psychology

24. Person-centered counselling is a form of
A. Cognitive behavioural psychotherapy
B. Humanistic psychotherapy
C. Psychoanalytic psychotherapy
D. None of the above

25. A person-centered counsellor's role would best be described as a
A. Expert B. Facilitator
C. Counsellor D. Therapist

26. Among the options given below, which is the goal of counselling?
A. Make people intelligent and smart.
B. Give correct medication.
C. Diagnose correctly the issue.
D. Promote personal growth and productivity.

27. Who developed the Rational Emotive Behaviour Therapy (REBT)?
A. Albert Ellis B. Truman Kelley
C. Carl Rogers D. John Dollard

28. Match List-I with List-II and indicate your answer with the help of codes given below:

List-I (Counselling Skills)	List-II (Features)
(*a*) Self-disclosure	1. Telling the client to view the problem from an alternate perspective.
(*b*) Directive	2. Explaining to the client the logical outcomes of sequenstial thinking.
(*c*) Reframing	3. Counsellor discloses about personal experiences from the past.
(*d*) Logical consequences	4. Telling the client how to go about solving the problem/crisis.

Codes:

	(*a*)	(*b*)	(*c*)	(*d*)
A.	4	3	2	1
B.	3	4	1	2
C.	2	1	3	4
D.	1	2	4	3

29. Why is 'learning by doing' important?
A. It develops interest among children
B. It develops intelligence among children
C. Keeps children engaged
D. Promotes meaningful learning

30. What is the ultimate aim of counselling for the individuals to attain?
A. Self-knowledge
B. Self-understanding
C. Self-discovery
D. Self-motivation

31. Empathy, unconditional positive regard and congruence are tenets of which therapy?
A. Cognitive behavioural therapy
B. Client-Centred therapy
C. Humanistic therapy
D. Behavioural therapy

32. Dr. Swati attends to emotionally disturbed students. Which type of service is being provided by Dr. Swati?
A. Charity
B. Help desk service
C. Counselling
D. All of the above

33. Varsha is awaiting her 10th standard result and is confused about choosing the right stream (humanities or science) for her in the 11th standard. How would a school counsellor assist her?
A. Tell her to choose a course that is of her interest.
B. Administer an aptitude test to know about her strengths.
C. Tell her go with her parents wish.
D. Ask her to randomly pick any one, as she is very smart and can handle everything.

34. Match the learning concepts and their explanations given below. Use the following codes:

List-I (Learning Concepts)	List-II (Explanations)
(*a*) Drive	1. The learner must do something.
(*b*) Cue	2. The learner must attend something.
(*c*) Response	3. The learner's behaviour must get him/her something he/she wants.
(*d*) Reinforcement	4. The learner must want something.

Codes:

	(*a*)	(*b*)	(*c*)	(*d*)
A.	1	2	3	4
B.	2	3	4	1
C.	4	2	1	3
D.	3	4	1	2

35. Which of the following is true about the ways of learning for students?
A. Speed of learning is same for all students
B. Each child has a unique learning style
C. Children follow the way other students learn
D. All children immediately follow teacher's instruct

36. Cognitive dissonance occurs when:
A. the attitude to an object and the behaviour towards it are inconsistent.
B. the attitude to an object and the behaviour towards it are consistent.
C. the attitude is negatively inclined.
D. the attitude is positively reinforced.

37. Ravita is very concerned about her grades. She studies 5-6 hours a day to outperform in her class and also in future can choose college of her choice. Which goal orientation best describes Ravita?
A. Subject mastery
B. Performance-approach
C. Self-determination approach
D. Goal approach

38. Among the below given options which should be based upon understanding the needs and problems of the students, competence and interest of the guidance personnel?
A. Guidance principles
B. Guidance techniques
C. Guidance services
D None of the above

39. .... is an endeavour for helping people deal with their psychological problems through a formal, more or less structured interaction between the person(s) seeking help and a trained professional.
A. Psychotherapy B. Medication
C. Consultation D. Meditation

40. What are the attitudes, goals and strategies of Failure Avoiding Students?
A. High fear of failure, very high or very low goals and self-defeating strategies.
B. Expectations of failure, very high or very low goals and self-defeating strategies.
C. High fear of failure, very high or very low goals and learned helplessness.
D. High fear of failure, no goals, learned helplessness

41. .... is the quality of a good teacher.
A. Control over emotions
B. Good command over the subject
C. Physical strength
D. Sense of humour

42. When should a teacher and a student hold a case conference?
A. Before the start of the school
B. After the school gets over
C. Once in a week
D. Whenever need arises

43. Which of the models given below asserts that behaviour is motivated by inner forces over which individuals have little control?
A. Humanistic model
B. Behavioural model
C. Psychodynamic model
D. Cognitive model

44. Read each of the following two statements—Assertion (A) and Reason (R) and indicate your answer using the codes given below:

Assertion (A): Freud's theory holds that many behaviours are caused by unconscious motivation. Personality is determined by biological drives of sex and aggression.

Reason (R): Personality differences results from variations in learning experiences.

Codes:

A. Both (A) and (R) are true and (R) is correct explanation of (A).
B. Both (A) and (R) are true, but (R) is not the correct explanation of (A).
C. (A) is true, but (R) is false.
D. (A) is false, but (R) is true.

45. Among the options given below which one consists of online sessions in which the questions posed to the client and the responses to the client's answers are computer-generated?
A. Automatic response service
B. Electronic therapy
C. Technical based therapy
D. Cybercounselling

46. Which of the following is NOT a factor for poor academic performance among low socio-economic status students?
A. Resistance culture
B. Tracking
C. Learned Helplessness
D. Family size

47. Every psychotherapeutic approach has two components:
A. Theory and case evaluation
B. Theory and practice
C. Practice and intervention
D. Theory, case evaluation and intervention

48. What is the best way for a teacher to resolve the problems in a class?
A. Ask for other teacher's opinion
B. Depends on one's own opinion
C. Think on suggestions offered by the children and implements the good ones
D. Consult principal for a better solution

49. A practitioner counsellor should:
A. develop theories of his kind to treat clients.
B. not be only proficient in existing therapies of counselling and psychotherapy, but also be aware of its relevance and effectiveness with diverse clients.
C. make his/her clients aware of all counselling theories.
D. ignore theories and just focus on practice by developing instant theories by own experiences.

50. Which test should be administered if the teachers/counsellor's purpose is to identify the individuals hidden/inner feelings prejudice, desires and thoughts?
A. Aptitude test B. Interest test
C. Emotional test D. Projective test

ANSWERS

1	2	3	4	5	6	7	8	9	10
D	B	C	A	D	D	A	D	C	D
11	**12**	**13**	**14**	**15**	**16**	**17**	**18**	**19**	**20**
A	C	A	A	C	A	B	D	A	D
21	**22**	**23**	**24**	**25**	**26**	**27**	**28**	**29**	**30**
C	A	D	B	B	D	A	B	A	B
31	**32**	**33**	**34**	**35**	**36**	**37**	**38**	**39**	**40**
B	C	B	C	B	A	B	C	A	A
41	**42**	**43**	**44**	**45**	**46**	**47**	**48**	**49**	**50**
B	D	C	B	D	D	B	C	B	D

❑❑❑

CHAPTER 12

Development of Industrial/ Organizational Psychology

Industrial and organizational psychology (also known as I/O psychology, occupational psychology, work psychology, WO psychology, IWO psychology and business psychology) is the scientific study of human behaviour in the workplace and applies psychological theories and principles to organizations. According to Guion (1965) I/O psychology is "The scientific study of the relationship between man and the world at work: the study of the adjustment people make to the places they go, the people they meet, and the things they do in the process of making a living." Blum & Naylor (1968) define I/O psychology as "the application or extension of Psychological principles to the problems concerning human beings operating within the context of business and industry."

As far as Industrial/Organizational psychology is concerned the industrial approach focuses on determining the competencies needed to perform a job, staffing the organization with employees who have those competences, and increasing those competences through training. Whereas the organizational approach creates an organizational structure and culture that will motivate employees to perform well, give them the necessary information to do their jobs, and provide working conditions that are safe result in an enjoyable and satisfying work environment.

In general industrial psychology focuses on the measurement of job requirements and individual's knowledge, skills, abilities and performance so as to match individuals with the suitable jobs. Organizational psychology is more theoretical and considers psychological processes such as motivation and work attitudes. Organizational psychologists also study phenomenon that occur at a level higher than the individual, such as group and organizational climate as well as organizational change and development.

Origins of Industrial/Organizational Psychology

I/O psychology has its root in the late 19th century movement to study and measure human capabilities & motives. With the outbreak of World War I in 1914, psychologists, played an increasingly large role in the application of science to the workplace. The influence of psychologists was felt first in the military, especially in the selection and training of recruits (Salas, DeRouin, & Gade, 2007). Between the two world wars, the field that would become known as I/O psychology expanded beyond the military into a variety of settings, including private industry, as it became ever more apparent that applying scientific research to the work environment would help employers improve efficiency (Katzell & Austin, 1992).

Neo-Classical School

A change in direction was headed by the Hawthorne experiments, named after western electric company Hawthorne plant in Chicago where the studies were conducted from 1927 to 1932 under the leadership of psychologist and sociologist Elton Mayo. In what became known as the Hawthorne studies, Mayo and his colleagues were initially interested in examining how various work conditions (for example, room lighting, humidity, breaks, work hours, and management style) could influence productivity. The Hawthorne Works had commissioned a study to see if their workers would become more productive in higher or lower levels of light. The workers' productivity seemed to improve when changes were made, and slumped when the study ended. It was suggested that the productivity gain occurred as a result of the motivational effect on the workers of the interest being shown in them. Eventually, they concluded that the workers were responding to the attention they were getting as part of the special research study and this phenomenon came to be known as the Hawthorne effect.

Especially critical of the effects of management's obsession with efficiency on the human side of business, Mayo argued that when a business focuses on micro-level aspects of workers' activities and on initiatives such as creating the most efficient assembly lines, workers become alienated from both their product and their co-workers. Emphasizing the time-and-motion aspects of a job, Mayo said, takes away from both the experience of craftsmanship and the capacity of the worker to identify with the product he or she is creating. Mayo's Hawthorne studies moved researchers away from scientific management and time-and-motion studies toward an emphasis on a human relations approach to management, which emphasizes the psychological characteristics of workers and managers, stressing the significance of factors such as morale, attitudes, values, and humane treatment of workers (Cameron, 2007; Cameron & others, 2006; Hess & Cameron, 2006).

Modern Approaches

Contemporary I/O psychologists no longer feel they have to choose between classical bureaucratic theory or scientific management and neoclassical human relations. The common view today is that taken together, they provide a comprehensive picture of organizational functioning. Environmental forces such as management directives, human capabilities, the state of technology & economic considerations are potent forces on worker performance and cannot be denied. Likewise, human motivation, perceptions and job attitudes are influential and are ignored at management peril.

Where Industrial/Organizational Psychology is Used

The industrial/organizational psychologists might work independently, or for consulting firms as organizational development specialists, career or leadership coaches, as well as trainers and facilitators. Corporations often employ these psychologists as behavioural analysts, employment testing professionals, human resources research assistants, assessment and selection specialists, and compensation analysts. Sometimes, industrial and organizational psychologists enter upper management as directors of divisions within human resources or organizational development departments. Industrial psychologists also work in academia, researching workplace issues.

Large organizations are the primary users of I/O psychological methods, either directly by employing an I/O psychologist services or indirectly by using information from the field (e-g, published articles, books, seminars). Numerous large American Corporations such as IBM, General Motor Corp., Ford Motor Co., Pepsi Co. Inc., to name just a few maintain a staff of I/O psychologists. Many other companies regularly use I/O psychologists as consultants on an as needed basis. I/O psychologists are also employees by government, and all branches of the military employ I/O psychologists to conduct research and applications in leadership, personnel placement testing, human factors and for improving motivation and morale. I/O psychology is widely employed in England, Australia, Germany, Japan and China.

How Industrial/Organizational Psychology is Used

In the process of diagnosing an organization's problems, recommending or implementing changes and evaluating the consequences of those changes, contemporary I/O psychologists employ one or more of four non-mutually exclusive emphasis in addressing;

1. **Personnel Psychology:** Is concerned with individual differences and therefore deals with all aspects of recruiting and selecting personnel. This area of psychology deals with job analysis and defines and measures job performance, performance appraisal, employment testing, employment interviews, employee selection and employee training, and human factors and ergonomics. Since various jobs require different combinations of these human qualities, matching the person to the job involves assessing human characteristics and job characteristics alike in an objective manner in order to achieve a satisfactory person-job fit.
2. **Training:** Is applying the principles of human learning to teaching employee's skills, techniques, strategies and ideas for improving their performance. The development of training programs is another responsibility related to industrial and organizational psychology. Using a job analysis, an industrial and organizational psychologist would assess the skills needed for a particular job and then develop training programs to teach those skills. They would also develop an evaluation method to assess the success of the training programs.
3. **Motivation and Leadership:** This deals with incumbent employees and seeks to create an environment that provides employees with a clear view of what they are supposed to accomplish and promotes the creation of conditions conductive to encouraging people to give their best. Using various theories of motivation, industrial and organizational psychologists develop different ways to increase motivation. Increasing motivation boosts productivity as well as increasing retention rates. Whereas leadership approach teaches leaders the skills and perspectives necessary to meet the local and global challenges of a networked world. Leadership psychology emphasizes the need to understand individual and group behaviours as a complex system in order to achieve positive and long lasting change.
4. **Engineering Psychology:** It addresses the human problems of organizations through the design of machinery and tools that take human limitations specifically into account. In other words it aims to improve the relationships between people and machines by redesigning equipment, interactions, or the environment in which they take place. The work of an engineering psychologist is often described as making the relationship more "user-friendly."

SELECTION PROCESS IN ORGANIZATION

The process of choosing the most suitable candidate for a job from among the available applicants is called selection. It is the process of ascertaining the qualifications, experience, skills, knowledge etc, of applicant with the purpose of determining his suitability for a job. The selection process starts with gathering complete information about the applicant from his application form and ends with inducting the candidate into the organization.

The Selection Process

Selection is the process of picking up individuals (out of the pool of job applicants) with requisite qualifications and competence to fill jobs in the organization. The selection process in an organization depends upon the organization's strategy and objectives, the tasks and responsibilities of the job and the qualifications, experience and characteristics required in an individual to perform these tasks and responsibilities successfully. In other words, the selection procedure is the system of functions and devices adopted in a given company to ascertain whether the candidate's specifications are matched with the job specifications and requirements. The selection procedure cannot be effective until and unless,

1. Requirement of the job to be filled, have been clearly specified
2. Employee specifications (physical, mental, social, and behavioural, etc) have been clearly formulated.
3. Candidates for screening have been attracted.

Most of the organizations, especially the bigger ones, use a combination of selection instruments. For example, many organizations first ask for job application, then conduct written tests and finally interview the candidates for selection. These three instruments are used at three different stages and rejection of unsuitable candidates happens at each of these stages. This is a process of elimination and at the end of the selection process only the most suitable candidates remain, and they are hired.

Process/Steps in Selection

1. **Resume/CV review:** The objective of screening resumes is to eliminate candidates which do not meet the job requirements.
2. **Initial screening interview:** In the initial screening interview a few straight forward questions are asked, to verify information provided on resume or application blank. It can be conducted over phone or in-person.
3. **Application blank:** Application blank is a formal record of an individual application for employment and is considered a good way to quickly collect verifiable and fairly accurate historical data of the candidate. It generally seeks personal information, *e.g.,* name, date of birth, gender, marital status etc.
4. **Conducting tests and evaluating performance:** There are various types of tests conducted depending upon the jobs and the company. These tests can be Aptitude Tests, Personality Tests, and Ability Tests and are conducted to judge how well an individual can perform tasks related to the job. Besides this there are some other tests also like Interest Tests (activity preferences), Graphology Test (Handwriting), Medical Tests, Psychometric Tests etc.
5. **Preliminary interview:** Like screening, the purpose of the preliminary interview is to eliminate unsuitable or unqualified candidates from the selection process.
6. **Core and departmental interview:** A selection or core interview is normally takes place between job applicant and line manager or experts where the applicant's job knowledge, skills, talents are evaluated and ascertained. Interviews can be One-to-One, Panel Interview, or Sequential Interviews. Besides there can be Structured and Unstructured interviews, Behavioural Interviews, Stress Interviews.
7. **Reference & Background Checks:** Reference checks and background checks are conducted to verify the information provided by the candidates. Reference checks can be through formal letters, telephone conversations. However it is merely a formality and selections decisions are seldom affected by it.
8. **Job offer:** The next step in selection process is job offer to those applicants who have crossed all the previous hurdles. It is made by way of letter of appointment.

9. **Medical examination:** Medical examination is part of job specification & organizational recruitment policy. It is done to probe whether candidate is infected with HIV positive/ TB/ Cancer.
10. **Placement:** A proper placement of an employee results in low employee turnover, low absenteeism and low accident rates in the shop floor jobs & increase morale and commitment of the employees.

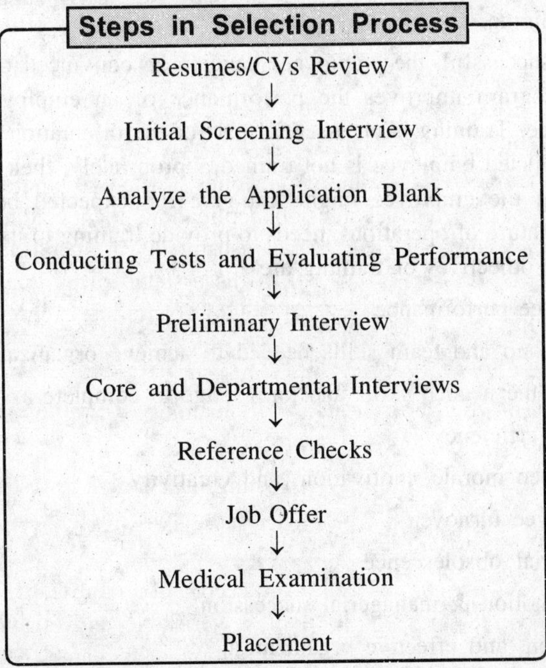

Selection Methods Standards

To ensure a more accurate prediction of the candidate's success in the future job, the selection methods should meet the generic standards of reliability, validity, generalizability, utility and legality.

1. **Reliability:** A selection method is considered to be reliable, if it produces consistent results across different situations and times. If a test produces significantly different results when taken by the same individual at different times, the test is termed to be unrealistic.
2. **Validity:** The validity of a selection method is the degree to which success in the test reflects success in the job.
3. **Generalizability:** It is defined as the degree to which its validity, established in one context, can be established to other primary contexts.
4. **Utility:** It is the degree to which the value provided by the selection method enhances the effectiveness of an organization. The more reliable, valid and generalizable the selection method, the more its utility.
5. **Legality:** Every selection method should comply with the existing laws and legal precedents prevalent in the country.

ORGANIZATIONAL TRAINING

Michael Armstrong defines training as the systematic development of the knowledge, skills and attitudes required by an individual to perform adequately a given task or job. According to Edwin.B. Flippo, training is "the act of increasing knowledge and skill of an employee for doing a particular job". In other words, training as an organizational intervention may be defined as a well thought of set of activities aimed to facilitate learning of knowledge, attitude, and skills among its people in the organization to improve their current job performance and contribute to the achievement of organizational goals. It involves training need analysis (TNA), designing of training program, implementation of the training, and evaluation of the training.

For training to be successful, the employees have to be convinced of its utility & effectiveness. A successful training program improves the performance of an employee which in turn enhances organizational performance. Training is an essential part of the orientation program for new recruits in an organization. If the selected employee is not trained appropriately, then the investment made by the organization in recruiting the employee might not give the expected benefits. Every organization, irrespective of its size or nature of operations, needs to provide training to its employees at various stages of their career. The main objectives of training are:

- Improving employee performance
- Developing the group and team skills needed to achieve organizational goals
- Giving employees the needed skills and knowledge to complete assigned jobs, duties and tasks
- Increasing overall efficiency
- Enhancing employee morale, motivation, and creativity
- Decreasing employee turnover
- Avoiding managerial obsolescence
- Preparing for promotion & managerial succession
- Creating an efficient and effective organization

Training Needs Analysis (TNA)

Before an organization lays out the plan for training, it needs to analyze the organizational objectives, assess the employee needs and then train the employees accordingly. TNA involves the determination of the types and specific training necessary to improve current knowledge, abilities and skills of the workforce. This can be done through personal, task and organizational level of analysis.

These training needs can be assessed by:

- Determining the organizational goals
- Prioritising the tasks in meeting these goals
- Determining the skills required by the employees
- Identifying deficiencies in the skill and knowledge levels of employees

A TNA should always be performed where a major new development in policy, equipment acquisition or procedures is deemed to have potential impact upon the current training regime. The possible sources of training needs includes the data that is gathered from the target participant supervisor's management, and even from customers, using multiple data gathering methods like survey, interview, observation at work, and performance appraisal results. Other possible sources of training needs are the long-range human resource plans of the company, practices of other organizations, requests for training of affiliate/ subsidiary companies, and legislation requirements.

The role of training analysis is to build a formal bridge between the available design data and the training media and training objectives, in order to facilitate the transfer of training elements into the operational environment. Training is a continuous process and the responsibility of a manager is to analyze the performance of employees after the training and to assess the training needs from time to time, keeping into consideration the organizations objectives and the desired standards of performance. Any gap between the desired and actual competency levels of an employee should be bridged through continuous and repeated training.

Area of Training

Training enhances the overall performance of an organization in various ways. Training imparted in one area can benefit the organization in many other areas. For example, training in managing interpersonal relationships in an organization can increase organizational productivity by improving team work. The major areas where employees are normally trained in an organization are discussed below:

1. **Company policies and procedures:** Understanding company policies and procedures is important for any employee of the organization. An employee should acquaint himself with the organizations rules, practices, processes and procedures, apart from the organizational cultures, structure & business. Training in this area the employee work with conviction & confidence.
2. **Skill based training:** Skill based training typically begins with identifying desired skills, assessing the employees for that specific skills, determine the gaps and accordingly structure the training program. Skills can be classified into 'soft skills' and 'hard skills'. The soft skills include the communication skills whereas the training given in Java for example, is a hard skill.
3. **Human relations training:** Human resource training is essential to improve the employee's skills in the areas of self-learning, interpersonal skills, group-dynamics, perception, leadership styles, motivation, disciplinary procedures, grievance redressal & so on.
4. **Problem-solving training:** Every employee encounters problems in the course of his work in an organization. These can range from simple operational problems to major decision-making problems. Training in problem solving skills equips an employee to deal successfully with such problems.
5. **Managerial and supervisory training:** All employees in an organization, at some point of time perform managerial and supervisory functions such as planning, organizing, directing, controlling and decision making. Thus training in these areas is essential for employees as they move ahead in their career paths to assume positions of increased responsibility.

Employee Training Method

A number of factors determine the choice of the type of training methods used by an organization. These are:

- Organizational Culture
- Learning principles
- Content of the program
- Time factor
- Cost effectiveness
- Appropriateness of the facilities
- Employee preferences and capabilities
- Trainer preferences and capabilities

The importance of each of the above factors varies depending on the industry, the business, the job and the criticality of the training.

1. **On the Job Training:** It takes place in a real job environment where the trainee is exposed to an actual work situation. The major advantage of this method is that the trainee can get first hand experience from the job as they learn it through actual equipments and materials. This form of direct learning helps the employee understand and imbibe the training lessons better. Since trainees are involved in actual work process, quick learning and immediate productivity will be obtained from the work performed by the trainees. This will also help in better application of the knowledge and skills gained during training. On the job training methods can also be used if the organization does not have the resources to simulate the work environment. As it is a practical approach, it develops multi-skill in trainees. The employees can get quick feedback about correctness of their performance. The disadvantage of the on-the-job training is that, as the trainee is still going through the learning process, any mistake he commits on the job might result in a loss to the organization.

   Some of the widely used on the job training methods are mentioned below:

   - Job instruction training
   - Apprenticeship and coaching
   - Job rotation
   - Committee assignments

2. **Off- the-job training:** When the training is performed on the job, any mistake by the trainee might result in damage to the organization, especially if it involves a customer or something of value. To avoid such situation, off the job training is used. An advantage of off-the-job training is that the trained employees are placed in the actual work station; hence, high productivity is maintained. Under off-the-job training, a large amount of information can be recovered within a short span of time. During training phase, no production will take place; hence, training requires less time. Also in off-the-job training, a large number of people can be trained at a time. Another advantage is that, the employees in off-the-job training are trained outside the work environment. Therefore, they are not involved in production process as in OJT. As a result, error in production can be minimized. The various techniques of the off-the-job training are:

   - Classroom lectures
   - Simulation exercises
   - Programmed instruction

As a disadvantage the off-the-job training will not be effective as the employees are trained in an artificial classroom. They are unfamiliar with actual work environment. As a result of which, it requires long time for them to learn. Also during training period, no production takes place because employees are kept away from the actual work place. The organization bears only training cost without any physical output. It is also expensive in the sense that the organization has to prepare extra place for training outside the actual work environment. As the employees are trained away from the organizational work environment; it fails to give feedback to employees.

Evaluation of the Training Program

The method to be used for evaluating the training program has to be determined at the planning stage itself. Evaluation helps in auditing and redesigning a training program. The various steps in the evaluation program are:

1. Setting evaluation criteria
2. Assessing knowledge prior to learning
3. Trained or developed workers
4. Assessing the knowledge after training
5. Transfer to the job
6. Follow-up studies

According to Kirkpatrick (1998), there are four levels of evaluating training programs. These are the (1) reaction; (2) learning; (3) behavioural change; and (4) impact to organization.

The reaction level measures the participants' feedback right after the conduct of the training. Feedbacks are taken related to attainment of objectives, processes, methodologies, time, reading materials, resource persons/facilitators, and other logistics of the training. On the other hand, participants' learning level determines what specific skills, knowledge or even what they learned is commonly asked at the end of the training period. Using a questionnaire form is only one of the methods to evaluate training. Other ways to assess training according to Hargraues and Jarius (2000) are: (1) formal or informal interviews; (2) feedback from line managers; (3) feedback from the Training Unit; (4) meet a cross-section of suppliers or customers; (5) discuss with staff who attended; (6) wander into offices and talk to people; (7) number of requests to attend other events; (8) academic or practical standards reached; (9) formal certification; and (10) a cost-benefit analysis.

The behavioural change level assesses the changes on the attitude and/ or habits of the trainees after the training that is usually observable at the workplace. This will involve a follow up of the trainees in coordination with the immediate supervisor. Examples of behavioural indicators are attendance, promptness, courtesy, cooperation, and level of participation.

The impact to organization level measures the effect of the training on the unit where the trainees belong and on the entire organization. This level can focus on productivity sales profits, and customer satisfaction.

PERFORMANCE APPRAISAL

Performance appraisal can be defined as the process of evaluating the performance of an employee and communicating the results of the evaluation to him for the purpose of rewarding or developing the employee. According to Michael Armstrong, "Performance appraisal is a formal assessment and rating of individuals by their managers at usually an annual review meeting". In simple words, performance appraisal is reviewing past performance, rewarding past performance, goal setting for future performance and employee development.

Objectives of Performance Appraisal

1. **Setting targets and goals as performance standards:** These are set at the beginning of the appraisal period. These targets motivate the employee to perform better.
2. **Evaluating employee performance:** It helps understand the strengths and weaknesses of the employee.

3. **Identifying training and development needs:** This includes shortcomings in the individual's performance, which need to be improved upon.
4. **Rewarding performance:** Rewarding a good performance and punishing a bad one encourages employees to perform better.
5. **Improving performance:** Once the strengths and weaknesses are identifies, the employee can be encouraged to overcome his weaknesses and leverage his strengths to optimize his performance.

The ideal way to ensure maximum utility of performance appraisal is to link the performance standards to rewards system and the competency standards to training & development. These gaps in competency levels can be identified and necessary training is imparted to the employee.

Appraisal Practices

The different appraisers are discussed below:

Self-Appraisal: The employee himself is best equipped to evaluate his performance because he understands his strengths and weaknesses the best. He can easily identify the problem areas that need training and development. The employees however have to be trained to be rational and critical in their appraisal. Pre-determined & measurable objectives can help to ensure a more objective appraisal.

Supervisors: It is the responsibility of the supervisor to ensure that his subordinates perform their jobs well. Hence, the authority to evaluate the employee performance has traditionally been with the supervisor.

Peers: Peer evaluation is very sensitive area as it may lead to false and unhealthy appraisal, because of the competition among peers. The organization has to reach an advanced stage of development before it can handle peer appraisal.

Customers/Clients: In service organizations like banks and hotels, customer feedback has become the most important tool in evaluating employee performance.

Subordinates: The Indian culture does not encourage the idea of a subordinate appraisal. However, with more and more MNC's operating in the country today, this concept is likely to gain ground.

Performance Appraisal Methods

These are divided into two categories *i.e.,* traditional methods & modern methods.

Traditional methods includes:

(*a*) **Graphic Rating Method:** This method of appraisal requires the rater to rate the employee on factors like quantity and quality of work, job knowledge, dependability, punctuality, attendance etc. Graphic rating scale includes numerical ranges as well as written descriptions. According to Dessler et al. (2011), Graphic rating scale is a scale that lists a number of traits and a range of performance for each. The employee is then rated by identifying the score that best describes his or her level of performance for each trait.

(*b*) **Work Standards Approach:** This method of appraisal is more suitable in a manufacturing scenario, where the goals are pre-determined work standards. This method compares each employee's performance to a predetermined standard or expected level of output. Several methods are available to determine work standards, including time study and work sampling.

(*c*) **Essay Appraisal:** In essay appraisal method, the appraiser prepares a document describing the performance of the employee. Questions or guidelines are provided to the appraiser, based on which he analyses and describes employee's performance. In this method the rater writes down the employee description in detail within a number of broad categories like, overall impression of performance, promote ability of employee, existing capabilities and qualifications of performing jobs, strengths and weaknesses and training needs of the employee.

(*d*) **Forced Choice Rating Method:** The forced-choice method is developed by J.P. Guilford. It contains a series of groups of statements, and rater rates how effectively a statement describes each individual being evaluated. Common method of forced-choice method contains two statements, both positive and negative. The rater is forced to make a choice. Once the employee attributes are ranked, the human resource department applies the weights and arrives at a score which is the final appraisal score.

(*e*) **Point Allocation Method:** In this method, the appraiser has to allocate points to different members in his team. He has at his disposal, a specific member of points which he has to distribute among his team members, based on their performance, during the appraisal period. The best performer gets the highest score and the last one in the group gets the least score.

(*f*) **Ranking Method:** In this method the rater simply places employees from a group in rank order of overall performance. There are three common used methods of ranking, namely alternation, pared comparison and forced distribution. The first two methods are used when there are only a few employees to be ranked, whereas the forced distribution method is used in large companies like GE, Microsoft & Wipro etc.

(*g*) **Checklist:** In the checklist approach, the rater is given a set of positive or negative descriptive statements that best describe employee performance and characteristics. When weights are assigned to each of the items on the checklist, depending on the importance of each item, it is known as a weighted checklist.

Modern methods includes:

(*a*) **Management by Objective (MBO):** Also called the goal setting approach, MBO is more commonly used for managers & professionals. It is a participating and interactive process whereby supervisors and subordinates jointly determine common objective or goals for the organization and also define each individual's areas of work and responsibilities. These goals have to be in alignment with the organizational goals and have to contribute to their achievement.

Henry Levinson defines, "Management by objectives as a performance appraisal and review which intended to: measure and judge performance, relate individual performance to organizational goals, foster the increasing competence and growth of the subordinates, enhance communication between superior and subordinates, serve as a basis for judgement about promotion and incentives, stimulate the subordinate's motivation, and last but not least it serve as a device for organizational control and integration.

(*b*) **Behaviourally Anchored Rating Scale (BARS):** BARS concentrates on the behavioural traits demonstrated by the employees instead of his actual performance. Some of the other methods like graphic rating scale and checklist also measure the behaviour, based on the assumption that desirable behaviour results in effective performance.

(*c*) **360 Degree Performance Appraisal:** A 360 performance appraisal system aims at a comprehensive and objective appraisal of employee performance. In a 360 degree appraisal system, the employee's performance is evaluated by self, his supervisor, his peers, his internal/external customers, his internal/external suppliers and subordinates.

(*d*) **Team appraisals:** In the team appraisal method, the individual team members evaluate their colleagues in the team and provide feedback. This helps in synergizing individual efforts and taking the group performance to higher levels.

(*e*) **Balance Scorecard:** The implementation of balance scorecard involves formulating a strategy, and deciding what each employee needs to do to achieve the objectives based on the strategy. The Balanced Scorecard implementation process is quite simple insofar as it involves:

1. Agreeing a set of performance measures to be agreed per perspective
2. Agreeing performance targets for each measure
3. Recording actual performance for each performance measure
4. Regularly reporting and acting on any performance deviation

Pitfalls in Performance Appraisal

The performance appraisal system in any organization has to face some of the major challenges because it involves human judgement, which is subject to human error. Some of the common pitfalls of performance appraisal are halo effect, leniency effect, stringency effect, recency effect, primacy effect, central tendency effect, cultural effect, stereotyping, perceptual set, fundamental attribution error.

Uses of Performance Appraisal

1. Problems that stem from a lack of communication can sometimes be resolved with a performance appraisal.
2. Performance appraisal offers an excellent opportunity for a supervisor and subordinate to recognize and agree upon individual training and development needs.
3. Organizational effectiveness can be improved by improving the individual performances of the employees.
4. Appraisals also provide a framework when making decisions about compensation and layoffs, in addition to other methods like market surveys.
5. It can be used as basis for transfers, promotions and other career planning activities of individual employees.
6. Performance appraisals can target a specific area of weakness that needs evaluation and remediation.
7. An effective performance appraisal system also helps in succession planning in the organization.
8. The performance appraisal system also helps in evaluating and auditing the existing plans, process and systems in the organization.
9. Human resource of the firm can be evaluated based on the competency & skills set and potential of the workforce. This provides the base for human resource planning.
10. Performance appraisals often serve as motivational tools for employees. The company may offer a bonus or other perk to employees who are able to improve their performance appraisals from one period to the next.

However for all this to happen, it is essential that the performance appraisal system suits the organizational culture and is in alignment with the other HR systems like training and development, compensation, career and succession planning etc. It is also important that the employees have faith and confidence in the appraisal system and its effectiveness. If the system fails to win the confidence of the employees, it fails to serve its purpose, however good it might be.

MOTIVATION AND WORK

There is an old saying you can take a horse to the water but you cannot force it to drink; it will drink only if it's thirsty-so with people. They will do what they want to do or otherwise motivated to do.

Whether it is to excel on the workshop floor or in the 'ivory tower' they must be motivated or driven to it, either by themselves or through external stimulus.

Motivation can also be defined as a condition that is initiated by a physiological or psychological deficiency or need in an individual, which causes the individual to behave in a certain manner in order to achieve a particular goal or incentive.

According to Stephen P. Robbins motivation is "the willingness to exert high levels of effort towards organizational goals, conditioned by the effort's ability to satisfy some individual need."

Employee Motivation

A worker in any organization needs something to keep them working. Most times the salary of the employee is enough to keep him/her working for an organization. However, sometimes just working for salary is not enough for employees to stay at an organization. An employee must be motivated to work for a company or organization. If no motivation is present in an employee, then that employee's quality of work or all work in general will deteriorate.

Employee motivation shall be defined by Robbins (2004) as: "the willingness to exert high levels of effort toward organizational goals, conditioned by the effort's ability to satisfy some individual need."

There are two kinds of motivation:

1. Intrinsic Motivation: It occurs when people are internally motivated to do something because it either brings them pleasure, they think it is important or they feel that what they are learning is significant.
2. Extrinsic Motivation: It comes into play when someone is compelled to do something, or act a certain way because of factors external to him or her (like money or good grades).

Work-Motivation

Work-motivation is a process to energize employees to the work goals through a specific path.

Theories of Work-Motivation

1. **The Content Theories:** The content theories of motivation attempt to identify and prioritize the needs and drive that motivated people at work. They deal with the goals and incentives that people strive for in their work environment. Although these theories have some limitations and do not always explain motivation and behaviour at work successfully, they have proved useful in providing insights into motivating people.

   (*a*) **Maslow Hierarchy of Needs:** Abraham Maslow's theory is one of the most widely discussed theories of motivation. They can be summarized as follows:

   - Human beings have wants & desires which influence their behaviour. Only unsatisfied needs influence behaviour, satisfied needs do not.
   - Since needs are many, they are arranged in order of importance, from the basic to the complex.
   - The person advances to the next level of needs only after the lower level needs is at least minimally satisfied.
   - The further the progress up the hierarchy the more individuality, humanness and psychological health a person will show.

   The needs, listed from basic (lowest-earliest) to most complexes (highest-latest) are as follows:

   - **Physiological needs:** Basic pay, work-space, heat, water, company cafeteria.
   - **Safety or Security needs:** Job security (benefits like life insurance, safety regulations).

- **Social needs:** Good co-workers, peers, superiors and customers.
- **Esteem needs:** Important projects, recognition, and prestigious office location.
- **Self Actualization needs:** When people realizes or achieve his full potential and is fulfilled, he/she is said to have attained self-actualization.

(*b*) **Herzberg's Two Factor Theory:** Frederick's Herzberg's two-factor theory concludes that certain factors in the workplace result in job satisfaction, but if absent, they don't lead to dissatisfaction but no satisfaction.

The factors that motivate people can change over their lifetime, but "respect for me as a person" is one of the top motivating factors at any stage of life. Herzberg distinguished between:

- **Motivators:** (*e.g.*, challenging work, recognition, responsibility) which gives positive satisfaction, and
- **Hygiene factors:** (*e.g.*, status, job security, salary and fringe benefits) that do not motivate if present, but if absent, result in demotivation.

The name hygiene factor is used because like hygiene, the presence will not motivate if present, but if absent result in deterioration. The theory is sometimes called the "Motivator-Hygiene theory" and/or "The Dual Structure Theory".

(*c*) **Alderfer's ERG Theory:** According to Alderfer, there are three basic groups of core needs:

- **Existence needs:** These are associated with the survival and physiological well-being of an individual.
- **Relatedness needs:** These needs emphasize the significance of social and interpersonal relationships.
- **Growth needs:** These needs are related to a person's inner desire for personal growth & development.

These needs formed the basis on which Alderfer developed his theory which he called the ERG theory.

2. The Process Theories: While content theories of motivation determine "what" motivates people at work, the process theories deal with the "how" of motivation. The process theories of motivation deal with the cognitive antecedents that go into motivation or effort, and more specifically with the way the cognitive antecedents of an individual relate to one another.

(*a*) **Vroom's Expectancy Theory of Motivation:** Victor Vroom was the first behavioural scientist to propose an expectancy theory to explain work motivation. The theory is based on 3 variables-valence, instrumentality and expectancy- and is therefore commonly termed VIE theory.

Vroom's expectancy theory focuses on the relationship between an employee's efforts, performance, rewards and personal goals. Three types of relationships are identified in Vroom's expectancy theory:

- **Effort-Performance Relationship:** It shows an individual's perception of the probability that a specific level of performance would result if he exerts a certain amount of effort.
- **Performance-Reward Relationship:** This shows the extent of an individual's belief that a particular level of performance would result in achieving the desired outcome.
- **Reward-Personal Goals Relation-ship:** It refers to the degree to which an individual's personal goals or needs are satisfied by the rewards given by the organization and his perception of the attractiveness of these rewards.

(*b*) **The Porter Lawler Model:** The Porter- Lawler model was developed by Lyman. W. Porter & Edward. E. Lawler III as an extension of Vroom's expectancy theory. The model holds that performance in an organization is dependent on three factors:

- An employee should have the desire to perform *i.e.,* he must feel motivated to accomplish the task.
- Motivation alone cannot ensure successful performance of a task. The employee should also have the abilities and skills required to successfully perform the task.
- The employee should have a clear perception of his role in the organization & an accurate knowledge of the job requirements. This will enable him to focus his efforts on accomplishing the assigned tasks.

Important variables in the model are efforts, performance, reward and satisfaction of an employee.

3. The Contemporary Theories:

(*a*) **Equity Theory:** Employees compare the outcomes, *i.e.,* what they get from their job in relation to what they give to the job *i.e.,* job input. Input include besides direct contribution, person's experience or previous training, qualifications, personal characteristics etc. The various possible outcomes are pay, fringe benefits, incentives, promotion, prestige etc. Employee generally compares their output-input ratio with that of others. If they perceive the ratio of their outcomes and inputs to be equal to that of their peers & others, a state of equity exists. However, when the employee perceives his outcome-input ratio as being unequal to others, a state of equity tension or inequity exists.

(*b*) **Attribution Theory:** This theory tries to answer the "why" aspect of motivation and behaviour. According to Heider, behaviour is determined by both internal forces or personality attributes such as ability, effort & fatigue and external forces or environmental attributes such as rules, weather etc.

Locus of Control refers to the chief source of factors that creates a result or gives rise to an outcome in the employee's perception. The outcome could depend on either external factors or internal factors. Kelly suggested other dimensions such as consensus, consistency and distinctiveness, having an impact on the type of attributions made by individuals.

Barriers of Work Motivation

1. **Attitude to employees:** Considering employee as cog of the machine rather as a human system having unique needs, abilities, personality traits, values, aptitudes, skills etc.
2. **Work Goal:** Undefined, unachievable and unmeasurable.
3. **Path:** Job responsibilities are undefined, unachievable, unmeasurable and unrelated to work goal.
4. **Leadership:** Leadership failure in manipulation of incentives.
5. **Third party:** Influence of informal communication systems through colleagues, union and family members.

Strategies to Overcome Barriers

1. **Job Analysis:** More emphasis on personal specification and regression analysis to determine weightage on job related individual characteristics.
2. **Human Resource Accounting:** Accounting IQ, EQ, personality traits, aptitude profiles of each employee.

3. **Selection:** Selecting right man for right place at the right time.
4. **Attitude Change:** Employee as human system having specific needs, aptitudes, temperament, attitudes towards job and the organization.
5. **Role Clarity:** Well defined job description & work role.
6. **Training:** Periodical training to the employee about up gradation of skills, work role analysis and to the leaders about leadership development.
7. **Survey:** Periodical survey to study level of employee satisfaction attitude towards organizational health and their relations to individual, productivity and quality of working life for organizational diagnosis.
8. **Work-Culture:** Introduce quality circle, suggestion box system, and intermingle organization to the life style of the employees.

LEADERSHIP

Leadership is probably the most widely researched area of organizational behaviour. This could be because of the crucial role it plays in influencing organizational dynamics. According to Warren .G. Bennis, "Falling organizations are usually over-managed and underled". Even if an organization is bestowed with sufficient resources, in the absence of effective leadership, it will not be able to function smoothly. Inefficient leadership lowers employee morale, promotes dissatisfaction among employees and affects organizational productivity and efficiency.

Definition

A leader may be defined as a person who establishes vision, sets goals, motivates people and obtains their commitment to achieve the goals & realize the vision. The leadership on the other hand involves influencing people to work towards desired goals.

Traits of Effective Leaders

Effective leaders influence people to do things the way they want them done. Relationships play a major role in having the desired level of influence over people. Therefore leaders constantly attempt to build maintain and expand their network of relationships. They take the following measures to enhance the relationships and thus their ability to influences people:

1. They invest time in building and maintaining relationships with people.
2. They try to strengthen their relationships with people by helping them achieve their personal goals.
3. They ignore the negative aspects of a person if these aspects are less than his positive aspects.
4. They do not look for immediate results from relationship. They patiently maintain relationship with people for as long as 10-15 years in order to accomplish long term goals.
5. They recognize that individuals differ in their needs, goals and wishes & therefore modify their behaviour from one relationship to another accordingly.
6. They encourage people to recognize their hidden talents & capabilities.
7. They ignore criticism by opponents on their emphasis on relationships.
8. To maintain a relationship, both parties have to extend cooperation.
9. They strive to maintain enthusiasm & energy in all their relationships. Their high energy levels motivate other people.

Leadership Skills

A behavioural expert, Robert Katz, had identified that the leaders primarily use three skills:

1. **Technical Skills:** Technical skill is proficiency, based on specific knowledge, in a particular area of work. To have technical skills means that a person is competent and knowledgeable with respect to the activities specific to an organization's rules and standard operating procedures and the organization's products and services (Katz, 1974; Yukl, 2006). However, as employees are promoted to managerial positions, these technical skills become less relevant, while other skills become more important.
2. **Human Skills:** An individual's ability to cooperate with other members of the organization and work effectively in teams is referred to as human skills. Human skills also involve developing positive interpersonal relationships, solving people's problems and gaining acceptance of other employees. Effective human skills are an essential requirement at all levels of the organizational hierarchy and especially for people in leadership positions.
3. **Conceptual Skills:** Leaders with high level of conceptual skills are good at thinking through the ideas that form an organization and its vision for the future, expressing these ideas in verbal and written forms, and understanding and expressing the economic principles underlying their organizational effectiveness. It allows leaders to give abstract ideas meaning and to make sense of abstract ideas for their superiors, peers and subordinates. Conceptual skills are of least importance to the employees at the operational level and are of utmost importance to managers at higher levels.

Leadership Theories

There are three important theories that attempt to explain leadership: trait theories, behavioural theories and contingency theories.

Trait Theories: Trait theories of leadership differentiated leaders from nonleaders by focusing on personal qualities and characteristics. As one of the earliest forms of leadership study, trait theories searched for any personality, social, physical or intellectual factors that could describe leaders and differentiate them from nonleaders.

Early researchers studied the personality characteristics that make a person a leader and concluded that leaders are born, not made. For example, the famous personalities in history like Napoleon & Alexander were natural leaders and would have become leaders even if they were made to face situations different from what they actually faced. They also suggested that leaders possess some personality traits that are unique and essential for effective leadership.

One trait theory is the "great person" theory of leadership. This theory were based on the assumption that the capacity for leadership is inherent-that great leaders are born, not made or developed. These theories often portrayed great leaders as heroic, mythical, and uniquely destined to rise to leadership when their skills were needed. The term great man reflects an assumption of these early theories that leadership was a predominantly male quality, especially in the domains of political and military leadership.

Research to identify universal traits applicable to leaders has not yielded significant results. The only trait that was found to be common among all leaders was intelligence. Application of trait theory to organizational leadership yielded even more confusing results. Researchers could not support the theory with the traits observed in successful leaders. Therefore, modern researchers have now begun to emphasize on multiple intelligences of leaders rather than trying to isolate a single most important characteristics leading to their success. For instance, some researchers who studied the emotional intelligence of leaders have suggested that empathy, graciousness, optimism and ability to read non-verbal cues in a social situation are important characteristics of successful leaders. Some general characteristics found in leaders are ambition, high level of emergency, desire to lead, honesty, integrity, self confidence, intelligence and job relevant knowledge. However trait approaches only provide a description of leaders, they have little analytical or predictive value.

Behavioural Theories: There are three important behavioural theories—The Ohio studies, The University of Michigan Studies, The Managerial Grid that have sought to identify the behaviours of leaders.

1. **The Ohio State Studies:** In 1945, researchers from different streams such as psychology, sociology and economics carried out the studies of leadership at Ohio State University. They used a specially developed questionnaire called the Leader Behaviour Description Questionnaire to analyze the differences in the behaviour of leaders across various groups & situations. They wanted to identify the different independent dimensions along which an individual's leadership behaviour could be studied. Initially they defined about 1000 dimensions, which were later consolidated into two dimensions:

   A. **Initiating structure:** This dimension refers to the extent to which a leader is likely to define and structure his or her role and those of employees in the search for goal attainment. It includes behaviour that attempts to organize work, work relationships, and goals.

   B. **Consideration:** This dimension is the extent to which a person is likely to have job relationships that are characterized by mutual trust, respect for employee's ideas, and regard for their feelings. People who are high in consideration show concern for followers comfort, well being, status and satisfaction.

2. **University of Michigan Studies:** Research along lines similar to the Ohio State studies was carried out at the survey research centre at the University of Michigan during the same period. The researcher found that leadership behaviours could be categorized along two dimensions.

   A. **Employee Oriented:** Leaders who were employee oriented were described as emphasizing interpersonal relations. They took personal interest in the needs of their employees and accept individual differences among members.

   B. **Production Oriented:** Leaders who are high on this dimension are more concerned with tasks & goals. They consider employees to be means to achieve goals & pay little or no attention to any problems the employees may face.

3. **The Managerial Grid:** Blake & Mouton developed a to dimensional matrix model of leadership styles based on their own research & the results of the earlier Ohio studies & Michigan studies. The model consists of nine rows & columns. The rows represent the leaders concern for production, while the columns represent the concern for people. With nine possible positions on each side, leaders can be located at any one of a total of 81 positions on the grid. They found 5 intersection points in the model-1, 9; 1, 1; 9, 1; 5,5 and 9, 9.

   1, 9: People who follows the 1, 9 style of leadership have high concern for people but low concern for production.

   1, 1: It is called impoverished style of leadership, exhibit no concern for people or for work.

   9, 1: Those who follow the 9, 1 style of leadership have high concern for production and low concern for people.

   5, 5: Leaders whose behaviour falls into 5, 5 style are considered to be fairly effective.

   9, 9: These people have high concern for both people & production.

Contingency Approaches to Leadership: This approach postulate that leaders have to change their style depending on the situation they face. The theories also suggest that a leader should carefully analyze the nature of the situation before deciding on the appropriate style of leadership to be adopted.

(*a*) **Fiedler's Contingency Theory:** One of the earliest models of contingency leadership was developed by Fred Fieldler and his associates. According to this model, leadership requirements depend on the situation facing the leader; and the choice of the most appropriate style of leadership depends on whether the overall situation is favourable or unfavourable to the leader. The favourability or unfavourability of a particular situation to a leader is analyzed based on the following parameters.

- Leader-Leader Relationship
- Degree of Task Structure
- The Leader's position

Fiedler's model suggests that managers must examine the situation in which they operate in terms of people, task & organization; they must adapt their style of leadership to suit the situation. If this is not possible, they must attempt to change the elements of the job to suit their style.

(*b*) **Leader-Member Exchange (LMX) Theory:** Unlike the other leadership theories mentioned thus far, the LMX theory does not assume that managers treat all workers the same way. The leader-member exchange theory of leadership focuses on the two-way relationship (dyadic relationships) between supervisors and subordinates. The theory assumes that leaders develop an exchange with each of their subordinates, and that the quality of these leader-member exchange (LMX) relationships influences subordinates' responsibility, decision influence, access to resources and performance.

In general a small group of subordinates, who have attitudes and personality characteristics that are similar to the leader, are often selected as in-group members whom the leader trust the most and thus give them more attention, and special privileges in comparison to the out group members, who are left out while making the in-group. According to this theory the in-group people receive high performance ratings and thus obtain rewards and promotions quickly. As a result there is greater satisfaction with the leader and lower turnover among in-group members when compared to out group members.

(*c*) **Hersey and Blanchard's situational theory:** According to the situational leadership or 'Life cycle' model developed by Hersey and Blanchard, there is no single "best" style of leadership. Effective leadership is task-relevant, and the most successful leaders are those that adapt their leadership style to the maturity ("the capacity to set high but attainable goals, willingness and ability to take responsibility for the task, and relevant education and/or experience of an individual or a group for the task") of the individual or group they are attempting to lead or influence. Effective leadership varies, not only with the person or group that is being influenced, but it also depends on the task, job or function that needs to be accomplished.

According to Hersey and Blanchard, there are four main leadership styles:

- **Telling (S1):** Leaders tell their people what to do and how to do it.
- **Selling (S2):** Leaders provide information and direction, but there's more communication with followers. Leaders "sell" their message to get people on board.
- **Participating (S3):** Leaders focus more on the relationship and less on direction. The leader works with the team, and shares decision-making responsibilities.
- **Delegating (S4):** Leaders pass most of the responsibility onto the follower or group. The leaders still monitor progress, but they're less involved in decisions.

The right leadership style will depend on the person or group being led. The Hersey-Blanchard Situational Leadership Theory identified four levels of Maturity M1 through M4:

- M1 — They still lack the specific skills required for the job in hand and are unable and unwilling to do or to take responsibility for this job or task. (According to Ken Blanchard "The honeymoon is over")
- M2 — They are unable to take on responsibility for the task being done; however, they are willing to work at the task. They are novice but enthusiastic.
- M3 — They are experienced and able to do the task but lack the confidence or the willingness to take on responsibility.
- M4 — They are experienced at the task, and comfortable with their own ability to do it well. They are able and willing to not only do the task, but to take responsibility for the task.

Maturity Levels are also task-specific. A person might be generally skilled, confident and motivated in their job, but would still have a maturity level M1 when asked to perform a task requiring skills they don't possess.

(*d*) **Victor-Yetton Decision Model:** According to this model, the leader should assess a situation in terms of its problem attributes. The twelve problem attributes can be broadly categorized into two classes-decision quality and employee acceptance. Once the leader identifies the nature of the problem, he can adopt one of the following 5 styles of leadership.

1. **Autocratic-I (A-I):** Using the information available, the leader takes a decision on his own.
2. **Autocratic-II (A-II):** Leader obtains relevant information from subordinates & find the solution to the problem.
3. **Consultive-I (C-I):** The leader explains the problem to concerned subordinates individually and invites their ideas & suggestions to solve problem. However he takes the final decision.
4. **Consultive-II (C-II):** The leader meets a group of subordinates, discusses the problem with them & listens to their ideas & suggestions. Later he may take a decision that may or may not be in accordance with his subordinated suggestions.
5. **Group II (G-II):** In this case, the leader accepts the solution offered by his subordinates.

(*e*) **Path Goal Theory:** The path goal theory is a contingency theory developed by Robert House. According to this theory, the leader should provide required support & guidance to his followers and help them achieve organizational goals. He should also establish individual (or group) goals for employees that are compatible with the broad organizational goals. Thus, the leader defines the path to achieve goals; he also removes any obstructions that come in the way of employees achieving these goals.

A leader's behaviour is acceptable to subordinates when viewed as a source of satisfaction, and motivational when need satisfaction is contingent on performance, and the leader facilitates, coaches, and rewards effective performance. The original path-goal theory identifies achievement-oriented, directive, participa-tive, and supportive leader behaviours:

1. **Achievement oriented :** The leader sets challenging goals for his followers, expects them to perform at their highest level, and shows confidence in their ability to meet this expectation. It is most effective in professional work environments, such as technical, or scientific; or in achievement environments, such as sales.
2. **Directive:** The leader clearly tells his subordinates what is expected from them, give them work schedules and instructs them on 'how' to do the task.

3. **Participative:** The leader discusses problems and issues with subordinates and asks them to give their valuable suggestions before making a decision.
4. **Supportive:** The leader makes work pleasant for the workers by showing concern for them and by being friendly and approachable. It is most effective in situations in which tasks and relationships are physically or psychologically challenging.

Path-goal theory assumes that leaders are flexible and that they can change their style, as situations require. The theory suggests that the leader's behaviour depends on two contingency variables-environmental factors and the personal characteristics of the subordinates. It also states that the leader's behaviour will be ineffective if it is not consistent with these two factors.

WORK-ENVIRONMENT

Research exists to support both the idea that the environment of the workplace impacts employee health and that the health of employees affects their performance on the job. The classic findings of the Hawthorne studies indicate that physical environment has nothing to do with the level of production. But it cannot be denied that the consideration of physical environment necessary for the very fact that environmental factors affect and influence the workers. Because of the limitations of human sense organs one cannot work in darkness. Low illumination is associated with eye strain, headache, and fatigue, low quality of work, increased number of accidents, low output and ultimately low morale among the employees.

1. Illumination

Several studies conducted on illumination suggest that because of the limited capacity of our sense organs, optimum illumination is essential and desirable for efficient production. In 1937, the Factory Act was approved and only since then have regulations been made for optimum illumination.

Experiments on Illumination

During two and a half years from 1924 to 1927, a series of illumination experiments using different study groups were conducted by the industrial engineers of Western Electric Company Works in Cicero; Illinois. The first, a sequence of illumination tests from 1924 to 1927, set out to determine the effects of lighting on worker efficiency in three separate manufacturing departments. There was no control group and all showed an increase of productivity, whether illumination increased or decreased. In other words the study revealed no significant correlation between productivity and light levels. The results prompted researchers to investigate other factors affecting worker output.

In the next experiments a control group had no change in lighting, while the experimental group got a sequence of increasing light levels. Both groups substantially increased production, and there was no difference between the groups. This naturally piqued the researchers' curiosity.

The researchers decided to see what would happen if they decreased lighting. The control group had stable illumination; the other experienced a sequence of decreasing levels. Surprisingly, both groups steadily increased production until finally the light in experimental group became so low that they protested and production fell off.

It was clear from these studies that there were changes in the productivity of the test participants; however, these changes were not due to the lighting levels. The researchers realized that there was some other reason for the productivity to generally increase.

Problems of Illumination

(*a*) **Distribution of Light:** The illumination research committee in 1933 suggested that it was more desirable to consider the lighting of the total visual field, rather than the field of observation only. Thus a lot of trouble in industry can be eliminated by proper distribution of light.

(*b*) **Intensity of Light:** Moss and his associates, on the basis of the findings of some studies, concluded that increment of illumination should be up to a particular limit, otherwise it would cause various inconveniences with several after-effects.

(*c*) **Duration:** Light should be provided for sufficient duration to facilitate work & efficiency.

(*d*) **Brightness:** Spencer and his associates found that there was a rapid increase in visual acuity with increase in brightness from .01 to 1.00 mm. But excessive light is undesirable as it gives rise to the problem of glare.

(*e*) **Problem of Glare:** Glare is caused due to excessive reflection of light. Because of glare when eyes are over flooded with light, eye strain, fatigue, annoyance and injuries to the delicate cells of the eyes are caused.

(*f*) **Problem of Colour of Light:** It is suggested that in selecting the colour of illumination the following facts should be considered:-

(*i*) The colour of light should be such that the objects can be seen in their true colour.

(*ii*) The amount of reflected light should be such that the objects can be seen in their original colour.

(*iii*) Lastly, the reflection of light should neither too little nor too much to cause discomfort to the workers. It must be optimum.

2. Noise

The most common and acceptable definition of noise is "Any loud, meaningless, disagreeable & discontent sound is referred to noise". It is an accepted fact that every individual in the modern age is daily exposed to some noise in one form or the other. Usually there are two kinds of noise-

1. Periodic or continuous noise
2. Non-periodic or discontinuous noise

Adjustment is easier in the case of continuous noise. But it becomes difficult to adjust in the case of discontinuous noise. The normal range of hearing for a healthy young person is from approximately 20 Hz (Hertz) to 20,000 Hz (20 kHz). Our ears are more sensitive to the middle frequencies, which range from 500 Hz to 4000 Hz - the speech frequencies.

Adverse Effects of Noise

Noise is an unwanted or damaging sound that may damage the hearing and cause other health effects such as stress, hypersensitivity to noise, increased blood pressure and increased heart rate. It can also interfere with communication at work, which could lead to accidents.

Experimental Studies on Noise

Adams (1932) has studied the effect of noise on the output of 11 women weaver in a weaving factory. The weavers were provided with ear defenders on every alternative week. It was found that the use of ear defenders increased production by one per cent on the average during these weeks when they used ear defenders. Moreover, those who used ear defenders wanted to use them in future for the sake of restfulness which they experienced with it. However based on other experiments as well, an overall analysis of the findings justifies the view that though periodic noise is less disturbing than the non-periodic noise, quite situation is the most preferable for mental work in particular, to produce better performance & pleasant feeling.

Control of Noise

According to Oakley (1945), there are two general approaches to noise abatement.

1. Making noise may be stopped
2. Noise may be prevented from reaching the people

Implementing one or more of the following hierarchy of control measures can manage excessive noise levels (in order of effectiveness).

(*a*) Eliminating the noise source.

(*b*) Substituting noisy machinery with quieter machinery ('buying quiet'). (This is a cost effective way to control workplace noise at the source.)

(*c*) Engineering controls by treating the noise at the source or in its transmission path (e.g. using sound dampeners or silencers, noise barriers and isolation).

(*d*) Introducing administrative noise control measures (e.g. training and education, job rotation, job redesign or designing rosters to reduce the number of workers exposed to noise).

(*e*) Providing hearing protectors (e.g. earmuffs, earplugs).

The most effective results may be achieved by implementing a combination of the above control measures

3. Atmospheric Conditions

(*a*) **Temperature:** The minimum temperature in a workroom, as recommended by the Health and Safety Executive, should be 16 degrees Celsius unless much of the work involves severe physical effort in which case the temperature should be at least 13 degrees Celsius. However 16 degrees Celsius is rather cold for sedentary work.

The Chartered Institution of Building Services Engineers recommends 20 degrees Celsius. There are certain exceptions to this, e.g. rooms that have to be open to the outside or rooms where food products have to be kept cold.

The Health and Safety Executive do not recommend a maximum temperature in a workroom, only that it should be 'reasonable'. However the World Health Organisation recommends a maximum of 24 degrees Celsius for working in comfort.

(*b*) **Ventilation:** Ventilation is employed in workplaces to control temperature, replenish oxygen, or remove moisture, odours, heat, dust, airborne bacteria, and carbon dioxide. It is also important to keep interior building air circulating, and to prevent stagnation of the interior air. Adverse health effects due to poor indoor air quality may include: Headaches, fatigue, respiratory irritation, nose bleeds, dry eyes, coughing and allergy symptoms. All these negative effects contribute to poor productivity and absenteeism in the workplace. Ventilation of workplaces is required in terms of the Environmental Regulations for Workplaces, OHS Act (85 of 1993), employers must ensure that:

- The air breathed is safe.
- The time-weighted average of carbon monoxide does not exceed one half per cent by volume air.
- The time-weighted average of carbon dioxide does not exceed three per cent by volume air.
- The occupational exposure limit for substances is not exceeded.
- The concentration of any explosive or flammable gas, vapour or dust does not exceed the lower explosive limit for that substance.

(*c*) **Humidity:** Associated with the problem of temperature is the problem of humidity or the moisture content of the air. Humidity is responsible for interfering with the process of maintaining constant body temperature. With regard to humidity, if it is too high this will cause discomfort (excessive perspiration, exacerbation of the effects of high temperature, feelings of 'closeness', etc) and if it's too low it can cause respiratory problems. Optimum humidity levels are between 40% and 60% - but in any case they should be kept between 30% and 70%. Humidity levels below 40% will begin to cause problems for workers with conditions such as sinusitis.

Conclusion: Keeping in view the above findings on working environment, it can be concluded that adverse atmosphere is not only injurious to health, but it also has got undesirable effects. It gives rise to subjective feelings of headache, drowsiness & a general feeling of discomfort. The objective effects are decreased output, increased sickness & absenteeism and accidents. Besides that the productivity & turnover will also be adversely affected.

ORGANIZATIONAL BEHAVIOUR THEORIES

The various research studies conducted and theories propounded in different parts of the world created a strong base for organizational behaviour. Some of the studies and theories which have served as landmarks in the field of organizational behaviour are Hawthorne studies, Theory X, Y & Z theory. These are discussed in detail below:

1. Hawthorne Studies

In the 1920's, the Hawthorne works of the General Electric Company, Chicago employed around 30,000 workers and manufactured equipment for Bell telephone system. Although it was a progressive organization, its managers were disturbed by the large number of complaints and high level of dissatisfaction among workers. In 1924, the company hired efficient experts to find out the cause of the problem, but the investigations failed. Later, the company requested the National Academy of sciences to help them find a solution. In order to find the relationship between workers efficiency & level of illumination in the workshop, the Academy conducted various experiments which came to be known as the Illumination Experiments.

The Illumination Experiments

In these set of experiments, researchers modified the level of illumination *i.e.*, the intensity of light, to determine its effect on productivity. Two groups of employees, namely, the control group and the experimental group, were selected to study the effect of varied illumination levels on their productivity. Illumination was not changed for the control group throughout the course of these experiments, while it was changed constantly for the experimental group. It was observed that when the illumination was enhanced for the experimental group, its productivity increased as anticipated by the researchers. However, the productivity in the control group also went up despite having no change in illumination level. The researchers then lowered the illumination intensity for the experimental group, but surprisingly, the productivity still shot up. These experiments showed that productivity of workers was influenced by some other variables and not merely by illumination. These experiments revealed that there is some other variables beyond wages, hours of work, working conditions that made a significant impact on productivity.

Relay Assembly Room Experiments

Many management theorists consider this experiment to be the actual beginning of the Hawthorne studies, since the illumination studies failed to come out with any conclusion. In this experiment, a small homogeneous work-group of six girls was constituted and were placed in a test room where they had to assemble telephone relays. These girls were friendly to each other and were asked to work in a very informal atmosphere. An active observer was present to observe them and obtain feedback and listen to their grievances. They wanted to find out how productivity could be improved by introducing certain variables like rest pauses and modifying other variables like cutting down on work hours and decreasing temperature and humidity. Various changes like change in the number of hours in a work week, number of hours in a work day, the number of breaks, lunch timings etc were planned and informed to the girls. Subsequently, these changes were introduced and their effectiveness was measured by noting the increase or decrease in the production of relays.

Findings of the Relay Assembly Room Experiment

The findings of the experiments took the researchers by surprise. Irrespective of the changes made, there was an overall increase in the productivity. Productivity and morale increased considerably during the period of the experiment. Productivity went on increasing and stabilized at a high level even when all the improvements were taken away and the pre-test conditions were reintroduced. The researchers concluded that socio-psychological factors such as feeling of being important, recognition, attention, participation, cohesive work-group, and non-directive supervision held the key for higher productivity. The researchers thus discovered the concept of informal organization. It was also realize that there were factors other than just economic self-interest. An important conclusion drawn from such observation was that every aspect of an industrial work environment had a social value. The self-esteem of the girls was elevated when they were preferred over other factory workers as a part of the study. Moreover, the presence of a friendly observer rather than an authoritarian supervisor at work added to their happiness.

2. Theory X and Theory Y

In his book "The Human Side of Enterprise", Douglas Mc Gregor formulated two sets of assumptions, *i.e.,* Theory X and Theory Y, about how individuals behave at work. Theory X assumes that employees are basically lazy and dislike work. Theory Y on the other hand, assumes that people consider work as natural as play or rest. If employees are happy & satisfied they would be more committed to the achievement of organizational goals. After observing how managers interacted with their subordinates, Mc Gregor concluded that manager's perception about the nature of people depended on the assumption they had about people. The managers molded or improvised their behaviour towards their subordinated according to their assumptions.

Theory X Assumptions

1. The average person dislikes work and tries to avoid it if he can.
2. They have to either coerced by punishment or goaded by means of financial rewards to make them work effectively.

3. The average employee prefers to be given directions about his work & shies away from taking greater responsibilities. They are not too ambitious, seldom take risks and give high importance to their security needs.

The assumption of theory X serve as the basis for most organizational principles and have given rise to "tough/hard" and "soft" management practices. The hard approach relies on coercion, implicit threats, close supervision, and tight controls, essentially an environment of command and control. The soft approach is to be permissive and seek harmony with the hope that in return employees will cooperate when asked to do so. However, neither of these extremes is optimal. The hard approach results in hostility purposely low-output and hard-line union demands. The soft approach results in ever-increasing requests for more rewards in exchange for ever-decreasing work output. The optimal management approach under Theory X probably would be somewhere between these extremes. However, McGregor asserts that neither approach is appropriate because the assumptions of Theory X are not correct.

Theory Y Assumptions

1. People can put in physical and mental efforts in work as naturally as they do while playing.
2. Tight controls and punishments cannot make people deliver the goods. An employee would put in his best effort if he is committed to the goals of the organization.
3. An average person would not only accept responsibility but also seek it if proper conditions exist in the organization.
4. If people find the job satisfying, they would be happier and would stay committed to the goals of the organization.
5. People can solve their work related problems by using creativity & imagination. These qualities can be found in a large number of people and not necessarily in managers only.
6. Generally the intellectual capabilities of an average person are not properly utilized in the modern industrial condition.

Under these assumptions, there is an opportunity to align personal goals with organizational goals by using the employee's own quest for fulfilment as the motivator. McGregor stressed that Theory Y management does not imply a soft approach.

McGregor recognized that some people may not have reached the level of maturity assumed by Theory Y and therefore may need tighter controls that can be relaxed as the employee develops.

Theory Z

In his book, Theory Y: How American Organizations Can Meet the Japanese Challenge, William Ouchi propounded theory Z as an integrative method combining both American & Japanese management practices. He found that the management style adopted by some American companies like IBM, Intel, HP, Eastman Kodak etc was a combination of both American & Japanese management styles. These organizations were referred to as Theory Z organizations. These organizations were American by Origin, but were both American and Japanese in their business operations.

Although theory Z organizations imbibe many features of the Japanese management style, they also have some distinctive American traits. To put simply, the Theory Z approach suggests "that involved workers are the key to increased productivity". The most important well-known characteristics of theory Z organizations are their lifetime employment policy. These organizations offer long term employment for their employees and invest a considerable amount of money and time in training their personnel. Managers and workers are trained not only for a single job, indeed the company offers a non-specialized carrer. The employees can move from one job to another job within the company, which helps them to learn about various aspects of the company rather than only one. Employees are promoted on the basis of their contributions, rather than on their tenure. However, in such organizations, promotions are relatively slow. These organizations use both implicit and explicit controls. Although these organizations have some formal guidelines for control, they also depend on employees judgements for appropriateness or inappropriateness of an action. Decisions are made by consensus that involves employee's participation. The manager is held responsible for the decision taken, which is predominantly an American trait. Thus collective responsibility comes with collective decision making. In theory Z companies, the team, not the individual, is rewarded for success because all achievements are team efforts. Theory Z organization have a holistic concern for their employees; employers express concern for the employee's family life, social life, health and retirement. Therefore, Theory Z organizations try to combine the positive aspects of both American and Japanese styles of management and put emphasizes on building close and trusting relationship among workers, managers and others. The central idea of theory Z is to create an industrial team within a stable work environment, which fulfils employee's needs for affiliation, independence and control as well as organization's need for high quality work.

SOCIALIZATION

When an employee joins an organization, he has to adapt to the new environment-a new work culture, different work activities, a new boss, a different group of co–workers and a different set of procedures and systems. This process of adaptation is commonly termed orientation or induction. When orientation is taken up as a continuous process in the organization, for all employees, it is termed as socialization. The process of socialization is not limited to new employees entering the organization; it is also important for employees moving within the organization as a result of lateral transfers and promotions. However, it is the entry of a new employee into the organization, which demands greater attention, time and resources.

The Process of Socialization

The socialization process is based on certain general assumptions. Some of these underlying assumptions are:

(*a*) **Influence on employee performance:** The process of socialization has an influence on the performance of an employee. It helps an employee to decide what is right and what is wrong and what is acceptable and what is not, in the organizational context. An effective socialization process helps an employee to perform his tasks more effectively and efficiently. An employee performance is an indicator of his fit in the organization.

(*b*) **Influence on organizational stability:** When the socialization process is implemented effectively, it ensures organizational stability. An effective socialization process ensures that a new employee fits well into the organization. This in turn ensures that the employee turnover rate is reduced and the organization becomes more stable. In a stable organization, organizational traditions and customs are transferred smoothly over generations of employees.

(*c*) **Handling new employee anxiety:** Individuals undergoing any organizational transition are in an anxiety producing situation and thus they are more or less motivated to reduce this anxiety by learning the functional and social requirements of their newly assumed role as quickly as possible. The sources of this anxiety are many. To wit, psychological tensions are no doubt by the feelings of loneliness and isolation that are associated initially with a new location in an organization as well as the performance anxieties a person may have when assuming new duties. Thus the new employee must be provided all the relevant information regarding the organization, the business, the rules, the policies etc. This would improve his understanding of his work place and provide him the basic guidelines of working there.

(*d*) **Role of co-workers and work environment in socialization:** Organizational socialization and the learning that is associated with it does not occur in a social vacuum strictly on the basis of the official and available versions of the new role requirements. Colleagues, superiors, subordinates, clients, and other associates support and guide the individual in learning the new role. Effectively, everything and everyone who surrounds a new employee plays an important role in guiding his attitude and behaviour in the organization. Ultimately, they provide the individual with a sense of accomplishment and competence (or failure and incompetence).

Stages of Socialization Process

According to Schien (1979), "Organizational socialization is the process by which an individual acquires the attitudes, behaviour and knowledge she/he needs to participate as an organization member. Socialization is a process that helps employees adapt to the organizational culture. According to them, the process of socialization can be divided into three stages:

1. **Pre-arrival stage:** In this stage, the employee gains an insight into his new job and the new organization. In this stage, the individual does not work on the job but gains an insight into the job. This stage is very important as it gives an individual an idea of what is expected of him. This helps the individual make a career decision depending on own attitude and aptitude.
2. **Encounter stage:** Upon entry into the organization, new members enter the encounter stage. Here the individuals confront the possible dichotomy between their expectations about their jobs, their co-workers, their supervisors, and the organization in general and reality. If the expectations and realities match, then the individual would find it easy to settle down in the job. If in any case do not find the match, it would demotivated him and at times can even force him to leave the job. Hence, while selecting candidates for a particular job, a realistic job description and a true picture of the organization should be given to them.
3. **Metamorphosis stage:** Finally the new member must workout any problems discovered during the encounter stage. This may mean going through changes. Hence the last stage is termed as metamorphosis stage. Metamorphosis is complete as is the socialization process—when new members have become comfortable with the organization and their work teams. The individual tries to reorient himself and work towards fulfilling organizational objectives by following organizational norms. The metamorphosis stage is considered to be successful, if the employee understands and accepts the norms, policies and procedures of the organization and works in accordance with organizational goals.

Socialization Strategies

There are various alternatives that a manager can consider while designing the appropriate socialization program for the organization. Some of these alternative strategies are:

1. **Formal or Informal Socialization Strategies:** The socialization process in which an individual is trained in a formal environment away from the work group is termed as formal socialization. Here, there is a clear demarcation between the new employees and the existing ones. In this process, an individual learns the principles, policies of the organization and norms thoroughly. The disadvantage is that since all the learning takes place off the job, it requires time to actually transfer this learning to on the job performance. In an informal socialization process, the individual works with his co-workers and learns through his own experiences. It can be termed as a trial and error method of learning.
2. **Individual or Collective Socialization Strategies:** In a collective socialization strategy, the socialization programmes are conducted for a group of new employees. Examples are basic training, boot camp, pledging, graduate school; sales training. As a result, most of the employees in the group

have similar learning and understanding. On the other hand the individual socialization programmes are conducted on one-to-one basis. Individual socialization helps groups to present their individual perspectives & differences. This would include apprenticeships, internships, OJT.

3. **Sequential or Non-Sequential Sociali-zation Strategies:** In the sequential method of socialization, an individual accomplish a particular goal through a sequence of activities or an employee will complete a specific task before moving on the next position in the organization. In most banks and government organizations, promotions are sequential in nature. In the non sequential method, the employees are not abide by to follow any discrete or identifiable transition stages or are not forced to complete any sequence of activities before moving to a position.
4. **Fixed or Variable Socialization Strategies:** In some organizations, predetermined time and duration for each activity to be undertaken is laid down by the organization in advance. The time period is standardized and the individual is certain with regard to the time required for the task. This process is called fixed process. In most organizations, the probation period is fixed for a time period of six months. In the variable process of socialization, no such precise time-table is prepared before any task to be assigned. The time period for one employee in completing a particular task may be different from another. Usually apprenticeship programs are variable in nature.
5. **Tournament or Contest Socialization Strategies:** A strategy where new employees are grouped on the basis of their skills, knowledge, educational background and ability for the purpose of socialization is called the tournament strategy. Based on their performance and adherence to the organizational norms, employees are promoted to the next stage or otherwise eliminated from the stage. However in the contest strategy, the channels of movement in the socialization process are kept open and an individual is given the opportunity to perform better in the next stage, even if he does not perform as expected in the ensuing stage.
6. **Serial or Disjunctive Socialization Strategies:** In the serial strategy of socialization, a senior or experienced employee in a similar job trains the new recruits on the various aspects of the job. While on the other hand in the disjunctive process the employee can join the designated position without even attending the socialization programme. It can prove to be costlier for an organization as it involves greater risk, with the individual employee using his own approach.
7. **Investiture or Divestiture Socialization Strategies:** This strategy is usually adopted when there is compatibility between the individual culture and organizational culture. This strategy aims at reinforcing the values and beliefs brought in by the new employees. Divestiture strategies on the other hand try to make new employees unlearn their existing knowledge and skills and dismantle their existing characteristics. This strategy believes that to learn and adapt to new organizational norms, one has to unlearn the previous set of norms.

ORGANIZATIONAL EFFECTIVENESS

Organizational effectiveness is seen as the "ability of the organization, in either relative or absolute terms, to exploit its environment in the acquisition of scarce and valued resources". In simple words Organizational effectiveness is the concept of how effective an organization is in achieving the outcomes the organization intends to produce. Organizational effectiveness is critical to success in any economy. In order to achieve increased and sustainable business results, organizations need to execute strategy and engage employees. Organizational effectiveness is the central theme of organization theory. No management can think of a theory of organization that does not include the concept of effectiveness. Everyone the academicians and corporate people unanimously agree to the significance of effectiveness in organization.

According to Silver and Sherman, organizational effectiveness is the extent to which definite and finite resources can achieve its growth and profit without destroying its internal resources.

Warren. G. Bennils defined organizational effectiveness as the system's capacity to survive, adapt, maintain & growth, regardless of the particular function it performs.

Organizational Effectiveness Model

In the literature, there is not a single model of organizational effectiveness to fit all organizations. According to Balduck and Buelens (2008), the issue of effectiveness in organizations revolves round four main approaches: the system resource approach, the goal approach, the strategic constituency approach and the internal process approach. These are effective and efficient approaches which are contingent upon the type of situation to arise.

1. **The Goal Approach:** The Goal Approach is also called rational-goal or goal-attainment approach. The main focus of this approach is on the output to figure out the essential operating objectives like profit, innovation and finally product quality (Schermerhorn, Hunt, R. N. Osborn, & R. Osborn, 2004). There are some basic assumptions for the goal approach. One of them is that there should be a general agreement on the specific goals and the people involved should feel committed to fulfilling them. The next assumption is that the number of goals is limited and achieving them requires certain indispensable resources (Robbins, 2003).
2. **The System Resource Approach:** This approach explains the effectiveness from the point of view of the ability to obtain necessary resources from the environments outside the organization (Schermerhorn et. al., 2004). The application of system resource can be effective if a vivid relation exists between the resources which an organization receives and the goods or services it produces (Cameron,1981). This approach invites managers to consider the organization not only as a whole but as a part of a larger group as well. The dominating attitude is that any part of the activities of an organization has an effect on all other parts (Mullins, 2008).
3. **The Process Approach:** This approach pays attention to the transformation process and is dedicated to seeing to what extent the resources are officially used to give services or produce goods (Schermerhornet. al., 2004). By effectiveness, it is meant that the organization is internally healthy and efficient and the internal processes and procedures in that place are quite well-oiled. The members are completely part of the system and the system itself works smoothly. The relationship between the members is based on trust, honesty, and good will. Finally, the flow of information is on a horizontal and vertical basis (Cameron, 1981).
4. **The Strategic Constituency Approach:** This approach deals with the effect of the organization on the main stakeholders and their interests (Schermerhorn et. al., 2004). Based on this approach, effectiveness refers to the minimal satisfaction of all of the strategic constituencies of the organization. Strategic constituency involves all the people that are somehow connected to the organization. These people may have different roles such as the users of the services or products of the organization, the resource providers, the facilitators of the organization's output, the main supporters and the dependents of the organization (Cameron, 1981). This approach assumes an exhaustive attitude toward effectiveness and evaluates the factors both in the environment and within the organization. In this outlook, the concept of social responsibility is taken into consideration.

MULTIPLE CHOICE QUESTIONS

1. Who is known as the father of scientific management?
A. Henry Fayol B. Fredrick W. Taylor
C. Herzberg D. None of the above

2. Organizational behaviours are affected by which factors?
A. Human B. Environment
C. Technology D. All of the above

3. Which of these methods can be used for training needs analysis for the organisation?
A. Job interviews
B. Training programmes
C. Learning & development
D. An analysis of longer term objectives and the skills and knowledge required to meet them

4. Which stage of the organizational Behaviour is related to the Hawthorne studies?
A. Industrial revolution
B. Industrial development
C. Human relation movement
D. Organizational behaviour

5. The three phases of systems model of training contains: ...., training, development, and evaluation.
A. Preparation B. Assessment
C. Organizing D. None of the above

6. Which is the best method for conducting a training needs analysis when the data has to be obtained from a large number of employees?
A. observations B. interviews
C. experiments D. questionnaires

7. According to whom humans are essentially motivated by the levels of needs.
A. Maslow B. Herzberg
C. Fayol D. Both B & C

8. Who is known as the "Father of Human Relations"?
A. Fayol B. Taylor
C. Mayo D. None of the above

9. According to which theory 'how' and 'why' people react when they feel they are unfairly treated?
A. Expectancy theory
B. Goal setting theory
C. Motivation hygiene theory
D. Equity theory

10. In leadership trait theory what is a trait?
A. A list of key behaviours a leader show while interacting with followers
B. A list of key characteristics that makes a leader great
C. A list of the things that leaders do which helps him outshines followers
D. None of the above

11. Hersey and Blanchard present a form of situational leadership based on the .... of the people the leader is attempting to influence.
A. motivation B. readiness
C. personality D. intelligence

12. Contingency theories of leadership are based on the belief that:
A. there is no single style of leadership appropriate to all situations.
B. there is a single style of leadership appropriate to all situations.
C. there is a single style of leadership appropriate to all managers.
D. none of the above.

13. In order from lowest to highest, which is the correct order of Maslow's? hierarchy?
A. Self actualization, esteem, safety, social, physiological
B. Physiological, social, safety, esteem, self actualization
C. Social, safety, esteem, physiological, self actualization
D. Physiological, safety, social, esteem, self actualization

14. Which theory suggests that some people have specific characteristics that differentiate leaders from the nonleaders?
A. Contingency theory
B. Path goal theory
C. Trait theory
D. None of the above

15. In .... the social perceiver uses information to arrive at casual explanations for events?
A. Social perception theory
B. Equity theory
C. Attribution theory
D. Path goal theory

16. Which of the following is not a type of performance appraisal?
A. 360 degree appraisals
B. 45 degree appraisal
C. Team appraisal
D. Balance Scorecard

17. The credit of originating the concept of performance management goes to which country?
A. Japan B. France
C. Denmark D. USA

18. What is meant by 360 degree appraisal?
A. A system where a senior manager rates team member performances
B. A system where every employee rates another employees performance
C. A system where the Vice President (V.P) rates managers simultaneously
D. A system where employee performance is evaluated by his peers, subordinates and supervisors.

19. Socialization programmes that aim at reinforcing the values and beliefs brought in by the new employees is called:
A. Investiture strategy
B. Divestiture strategy
C. Tournament-oriented strategy
D. None of the above

20. A strategy where new employees are grouped on the basis of their skills, knowledge, educational background and ability for the purpose of socialization is called:
A. Disjunctive socialization
B. Tournament socialization
C. Investiture socialization
D. Sequential socialization

21. According to which process an appropriate fit between the people and the positions in an organization is found out?
A. Socialization B. Orientation
C. Placement D. None of the above

22. According to Douglas McGregor's view, ... managers assume that people have an inherent dislike of work, while .... managers assume that work is as natural as play.
A. Theory X; Theory Y
B. Theory Y; Theory X
C. Theory Z; Theory X
D. Theory Y; Theory Z

23. According to which theory of Douglas McGregor's the employees exercise self-direction and self-control when they are committed to the objectives of the work?
A. Theory Y B. Theory X
C. Theory Z D. None of the above

24. What does ERG stand for?
A. Employee, related, greatness
B. Existence, relatedness, growth
C. Employee, readiness, goal
D. None of the above

25. During which stage of socialization process the employee gains an insight into his new job and the new organization.
A. Pre-arrival stage
B. Encounter stage
C. Metamorphosis stage
D. None of the above

26. Which one of the following theories predicts that work motivation will be low if an employee perceives that an increased effort will have little, or no effect on his/her performance?
A. Just-world theory
B. Need-drive theory
C. Expectancy theory
D. Normative theory

27. Leaders who adjust their style, from one that is task-oriented and directive to one that is more relations-oriented and less directive, are following the principles of:
A. Democratic Leadership Theory
B. Situational Leadership Theory
C. Consultative Leadership Theory
D. Equity Leadership Theory

28. The term .... was coined by Henry Landsberger who concluded that the act of observing someone changed their behaviour.
A. Socialization
B. Imitation
C. Managerial effect
D. Hawthorne effect

29. .... states that allocating .... rewards for behaviours previously .... rewarded decreases level of motivation.

Codes:
A. Two factor theory; extrinsic; not
B. Theory X; monetary; intrinsically
C. Cognitive evaluation theory; extrinsic; intrinsically
D. Theory Y; financial; selectively

30. According to which motivation theory certain factors in the workplace result in job satisfaction, but if absent, they don't lead to dissatisfaction but no satisfaction.
A. Alderfer's ERG theory
B. Vroom expectancy theory
C. Herzberg's two factor theory
D. The porter Lawler model

31. Hawthorne studies are related to which stage of the organizational behaviour evolution?
A. Scientific management
B. Industrial revolution
C. Digital revolution
D. Human relation movement

32. Read each of the following two statements—Assertion (A) and Reason (R) and indicate your answer using the codes given below:

Assertion (A): Paper-pencil self-report personality inventories are very useful in personnel selection.

Reason (R): In selection situation, paper-pencil, self-report inventories are sensitive to impression management.

Codes:
A. Both (A) and (R) are true and (R) is the correct explanation of (A).
B. Both (A) and (R) are true, but (R) is not the correct explanation of (A).
C. (A) is true, (R) is false.
D. (A) is false, (R) is true.

33. Initiating structure and considerations are the two dimensions of which leadership theory?
A. The Ohio Sate Studies
B. University of Michigan Studies
C. The Managerial Grid
D. Leader-Member Exchange Theory

34. Which of the following is/are the content theories of work motivation?
1. Alderfer's ERG theory.
2. Hertzberg's two-factor theory
3. Maslow's theory of need hierarchy
4. Porter and Lawler's performance satisfaction theory

A. 2 only B. 2 and 3 only
C. 1, 2 and 3 only D. 2, 3 and 4 only

35. Which of these is one of Fayol's fourteen principles of management?
A. Unity of command
B. Employee motivation
C. Cooperation of managers
D. Cooperation of employees

36. Who developed a dimensional matrix model of leadership styles consisting of nine rows & columns?
A. Fiedler's
B. Blake & Mouton
C. Heresy & Blanchard
D. None of the above

37. Annual or semi-annual ratings of each employee's performance, coupled with feedback about the ratings they receive are referred to as:
A. Performance appraisals
B. Rating inventories
C. Behaviourally anchored rating scales
D. Graphic rating scales

38. Who proposed the four principles of scientific management?
A. Herbert Simon B. Daniel Katz
C. Robert Kahn D. Frederick Taylor

39. Given below are two statements, one labelled as Assertion (A), and the other labelled as Reason (R). In the context of the below two statements, which one of the following is correct?

Assertion (A): Entrepreneurs prefer to take moderate risks, as a result of skill and not chance.

Reason (R): Entrepreneurs usually have innovative ideas and they persistently work to implement those ideas.

Codes:
A. Both (A) and (R) are true and (R) is the correct explanation of (A).
B. Both (A) and (R) are true, but (R) is not the correct explanation of (A).
C. (A) is true, but (R) is false.
D. (A) is false, but (R) is true.

40. Which theory assumes that employees have little ambition, dislike work, and avoid responsibility?
A. Theory Y
B. Theory X
C. Self-actualization Need Theory
D. Belongingness Need Theory

41. If a manager gives an employee a positive appraisal on her first evaluation as an employee because he thought that she had been a 'top-notch' performer in her job interview, he may be making an error based on
A. halo effect
B. attributional errors
C. leniency error
D. self-serving bias

42. Which of the following are characteristics of Charismatic leaders?
1. Vision and Articulation
2. Risk taking behaviour
3. Volatile moods
4. Sensitivity to followers' needs

Codes:
A. 2, 3 & 4 B. 1, 2 & 4
C. 1, 3 & 4 D. 1 & 4

43. The perspectives of motivation that identify specific needs:
A. Content Theories
B. Process Theory of Motivation
C. Equity Theory and OB Mode Theory
D. Expectancy Theories

44. Selection is the process of differentiating between .... in order to identify those with a greater likelihood of .... in a job.
A. Applicants; good performance
B. Candidates; good performance
C. Applicants; success
D. Candidates; success

45. Which theory claims that there is no single "best" style of leadership, infact it is task-relevant?
A. Fiedler's Contingency theory
B. Hersey & Blanchard's Situational theory
C. Victor-Yetton Decision theory
D. The Ohio State studies

46. Vestibule Training utilizes equipment which are closely .... to the actual ones, used ....
A. resemble; on the job
B. similar; on the job
C. resemble; off the job
D. similar; off the job

47. The three key elements in the definition of organizational motivation are ...., organizational goals, and needs.
A. personality B. ability
C. effort D. tenure

48. A person while intrinsically motivated does not seek when performing, choose the correct code:
1. Enjoyment
2. Reward
3. Challenge
4. Avoidance of punishment

Codes:
A. 1 and 2 B. 2 and 3
C. 2 and 4 D. 3 and 4

49. A person while intrinsically motivated does not seek when performing? Choose the correct code:

1. Enjoyment
2. Reward
3. Challenge
4. Avoidance of punishment

Codes:

A. 1 and 2 B. 2 and 3
C. 2 and 4 D. 3 and 1

50. Read each of the following two statements—Assertion (A) and Reason (R) and indicate your answer using the codes given below:

Assertion (A): Organizational justice is perception of what is fair in the workplace composed of distributive, procedural and interactional justice.

Reason (R): Employees have greater tolerance of overpayment inequities than underpayment inequities as part of distributive justice.

Codes:

A. Both (A) and (R) are true and (R) is correct explanation of (A).
B. Both (A) and (R) are true, but (R) is not the correct explanation of (A).
C. (A) is true, but (R) is false.
D. (A) is false, but (R) is true.

ANSWERS

1	2	3	4	5	6	7	8	9	10
B	D	D	C	B	D	A	C	D	B
11	**12**	**13**	**14**	**15**	**16**	**17**	**18**	**19**	**20**
B	A	D	C	C	B	D	D	A	B
21	**22**	**23**	**24**	**25**	**26**	**27**	**28**	**29**	**30**
C	A	A	B	A	C	B	D	D	C
31	**32**	**33**	**34**	**35**	**36**	**37**	**38**	**39**	**40**
D	D	A	C	A	B	A	D	B	B
41	**42**	**43**	**44**	**45**	**46**	**47**	**48**	**49**	**50**
A	D	A	C	B	A	C	C	C	A

❑❑❑

CHAPTER 13

Psychopathology

Psychopathology is the scientific study of mental disorders, including efforts to understand their genetic, biological, psychological, and social causes; effective classification schemes (nosology); course across all stages of development; manifestations; and treatment. In general Psychopathology derives from two Greek words: 'psyche' meaning 'soul', and 'pathos' means 'suffering'. Currently, 'psychopathology' is understood to mean the origin of mental disorders, how they develop and their symptoms. Traditionally, those suffering from mental disorders have usually been treated by the psychiatric profession, which adheres to the DSM-IV-TR (APA, 2002) or ICD-10 (WHO, 1992) for classifying mental disorders.

Historically, the concept of psychopathology is rooted in the medical tradition. This is where the terms 'diagnosis', 'symptoms', 'aetiology' and 'prognosis' come from (Murphy, 2010). Psychiatrists categorise severe mental distress into psychopathological disorders whose symptoms they can treat with prescribed drugs, and use the word 'patients'. Counselling psychologists, counsellors and psychotherapists favour the term 'clients' over 'patients' (because of the medical connotations of the word 'patients') and use talking, more than anything else, as a therapeutic 'tool'. They also prefer the concept of 'formulation' instead of 'diagnosis, symptoms, aetiology and prognosis'.

The scientific discipline of psychopathology was founded by Karl Jaspers in 1913, whose object of study was "mental phenomena". Many different professions may be involved in studying mental disorders or distress. Psychiatrists in particular are interested in descriptive psychopathology, which has the aim of describing the symptoms and syndromes of mental illness. Before diagnosing a psychological disorder, clinicians must study the themes, also known as abnormalities, within psychological disorders. The most prominent themes consist of: deviance, distress, dysfunction and danger. These themes are known as the four Ds, which define abnormality. The DSM, or Diagnostic and Statistical Manual of Mental Disorders, is an official guideline for the diagnosis of psychological disorders. Clinicians, researchers and psychologists use this manual as a reference guide to diagnose psychological disorders.

CLASSIFYING PSYCHOPATHOLOGY

Mental illness is classified today according to the Diagnostic and Statistical Manual of Mental Disorders, Fourth Edition (DSM IV), published by the American Psychiatric Association (1994). The DSM uses a multiaxial or multidimensional approach to diagnosing because rarely do other factors in a person's life not impact their mental health. It assesses five dimensions as described below:

Axis I: Clinical Syndromes

- This typically includes the diagnosis (*e.g.*, major depressive episode, schizophrenic episode, panic attack, schizophrenia, social phobia).

Axis II: Developmental Disorders and Personality Disorders

- Developmental disorders include the five Pervasive Developmental Disorders (PDDs), also known as Autism Spectrum Disorders (ASDs), as defined by the Diagnostic and Statistical Manual of Mental Disorders - Fourth Edition (DSM-IV). These include the Autistic disorder, Pervasive developmental disorder, Asperger's Disorder, Rett's Disorder and Childhood Disintegrative Disorder.
- Personality disorders are clinical syndromes which have a more long lasting symptom and encompass the individual's way of interacting with the world. They include Paranoid, Antisocial personality disorder, Avoidant personality disorder, Borderline personality disorders, Narcissistic personality disorder, Obsessive-Compulsive personality disorder and Schizotypal personality disorder.

Axis III: Physical Conditions which play a role in the development, continuance, or exacerbation of Axis I and II Disorders

- Physical conditions such as brain injury or HIV/AIDS that can result in symptoms of mental illness are included here.

Axis IV: Severity of Psychosocial Stressors

- Events in a person's life, such as death of a loved one, starting a new job, college, unemployment, and even marriage can impact the disorders listed in Axis I and II. These events are both listed and rated for this axis.

Axis V: Highest Level of Functioning

- It contains the global assessment of functioning, which is a numerical scale that measures the level of functioning of the client. The scale ranges from 0 (inadequate information) to 100 (high functioning with no symptoms of mental illness present).

COMMON CLINICAL DISORDERS

A Clinical Disorder is a series or group of behaviours that equal or match a list of expected behaviours listed in, "The Diagnostic and Statistical Manual of Mental Disorders (DSM) is the standard classification of mental disorders used by mental health professionals. It is intended to be applicable in a wide array of contexts and used by clinicians and researchers of many different orientations (*e.g.,* biological, psychodynamic, cognitive, behavioural, interpersonal, family/systems). Some of the common mental health disorders include depression, generalised anxiety disorder, panic disorder, obsessive-compulsive disorder, post traumatic stress disorder and social anxiety disorder. Few among them are discussed below:-

1. **Depression:** To be diagnosed as suffering from major depression, a person must have had one or more major depressive episodes—periods that involved more than just "sadness" which includes symptoms like an increase or decrease appetite, altered sleep patterns, loss of interest or pleasure in usual activities, including sex; loss of energy, diminished ability to think and concentrate; feeling of worthlessness or self-reproach; or suicidal thoughts or acts. During depressive episode, the person's mood and thought patterns may be strikingly negative. He/she often appears lost, vulnerable, detached, and unable to find joy in any aspect of daily life. Often the person seems constantly on the verge of tears. The future may seem almost completely hopeless, and this becomes one of the reasons of suicide attacks.

   Life events and changes that may precipitate depressed mood include childbirth, menopause, financial difficulties, job problems, a medical diagnosis (cancer, HIV, etc.), bullying, loss of a loved one, natural disasters, social isolation, relationship troubles, jealousy, separation, and catastrophic injury. Adversity in childhood, such as bereavement, neglect, unequal parental treatment of siblings, physical abuse or sexual abuse, significantly increases the likelihood of experiencing depression over the life course. Certain medications are known to cause depressed mood in a significant number of patients.

Depressed mood can be the result of a number of infectious diseases, neurological conditions and physiological problems. Depression is associated with abusive drug use.

2. **Generalized Anxiety Disorder:** People with generalized anxiety disorder can't seem to get rid of their concerns, even though they usually realize that their anxiety is more intense than the situation warrants. They can't relax, startle easily, and have difficulty concentrating. Such anxiety can make people thoroughly miserable and even upset their health. Symptoms of generalized anxiety disorder may include trembling, fatigue, breathlessness, insomnia, sweating, nervousness, chest pain, dizziness, faintness, headache, and so on. A sense of foreboding, apprehension, and a feeling of impending doom may also be mixed with the physical symptoms.

3. **Panic Disorder:** Panic disorder involves specific, focused, time-bound attacks of intense fear, even terror. The panic attacks, lasting from a few minutes up to an hour or more. People with panic disorder have panic attacks with feelings of terror that strike suddenly and repeatedly with no warning. Symptoms of a panic attack includes difficulty in breathing, pounding heart or chest pain, intense feeling of dread, dizziness or feeling faint, trembling or shaking, sweating, nausea or stomach-ache, tingling or numbness in the fingers and toes, also may include severe physical symptoms such as choking or smothering sensations. Beyond the panic attacks themselves, a key symptom of panic disorder is the persistent fear of having future panic attacks. The fear of these attacks can cause the person to avoid places and situations where an attack has occurred or where they believe an attack may occur.

4. **Obsessive Compulsive Disorder(OCD):** Obsessive-compulsive disorder (OCD) is an anxiety disorder characterized by uncontrollable, unwanted thoughts and repetitive, ritualized behaviours one feel compelled to perform. Obsessions are recurrent and persistent thoughts, impulses, or images that cause distressing emotions such as anxiety or disgust. Compulsions on the other hand are repetitive behaviours or mental acts that the person feels driven to perform in response to an obsession. The behaviours are aimed at preventing or reducing distress or a feared situation. The Common obsessive thoughts in obsessive-compulsive disorder (OCD) includes- Fear of being contaminated by germs or dirt or contaminating others, fear of causing harm to yourself or others, intrusive sexually explicit or violent thoughts and images, fear of losing or not having things you might need, order and symmetry: the idea that everything must line up "just right", superstitions; excessive attention to something considered lucky or unlucky.

   Common compulsive behaviours in obsessive-compulsive disorder (OCD) includes- Excessive double-checking of things, such as locks, appliances, and switches, repeatedly checking in on loved ones to make sure they're safe, counting, tapping, repeating certain words, or doing other senseless things to reduce anxiety, spending a lot of time washing or cleaning, ordering or arranging things "just so", praying excessively or engaging in rituals triggered by religious fear etc.

   People with obsessive-compulsive disorder find their obsessions or compulsions distressing and debilitating but feel unable to stop them.

5. **Post traumatic stress disorder:** Post-Traumatic Stress Disorder (PTSD) is an anxiety disorder that may develop after exposure to a terrifying event or ordeal in which severe physical harm occurred or was threatened. Traumatic events that may trigger PTSD include violent personal assaults, natural or unnatural disasters, accidents, or military combat. PTSD can cause many symptoms. These symptoms can be grouped into three categories: Re-experiencing symptoms, Avoidance symptoms and Hyperarousal symptoms.

Re-experiencing symptoms may cause problems in a person's everyday routine. The symptoms include flashbacks-reliving the trauma over and over, including physical symptoms like a racing heart or sweating, bad dreams and frightening thoughts.

The Avoidance symptoms includes feeling emotionally numb, feeling strong guilt, depression, or worry, losing interest in activities that were enjoyable in the past, having trouble remembering the dangerous event and staying away from places, events, or objects that are reminders of the experience. Things that remind a person of the traumatic event can trigger avoidance symptoms.

Hyper arousal symptoms may includes being easily startled, feeling tense or "on edge" and having difficulty sleeping, and/or having angry outbursts. Hyper arousal symptoms are usually constant, instead of being triggered by things that remind one of the traumatic events. They can make the person feel stressed and angry.

PTSD can develop at any age, including in childhood. Symptoms typically begin within 3 months of a traumatic event, although occasionally they do not begin until years later. Once PTSD occurs, the severity and duration of the illness varies. Some people recover within 6 months, while others suffer much longer.

6. **Social Anxiety Disorder:** Social anxiety disorder (SAD), also known as social phobia, is the most common anxiety disorder. It is characterized by intense fear in one or more social situations, causing considerable distress and impaired ability to function in at least some parts of daily life. The physical symptoms includes red face, or blushing, shortness of breath, trembling or shaking, upset stomach, nausea, tightness in chest, sweating and feeling dizzy or faint. People with social phobia tend to show some emotional symptoms such as feeling very anxious about being with other people and have a hard time talking to them, even though they wish they could, they tend to be very self-conscious in front of other people and feel embarrassed, they feel afraid that other people will judge them and worry for days or weeks before an event where other people will be. They have a hard time making friends and keeping friends.

MENTAL RETARDATION

Intellectual disability (ID) or learning disability or general learning disability is a generalized disorder appearing before adulthood, characterized by significantly impaired cognitive functioning and deficits in two or more adaptive behaviours. Intellectual disability is also known as mental retardation (MR) and mental handicap, although these older terms are being used less frequently. It was historically defined as an intelligence quotient score under 70. It is manifested through defective perceptual and other thought processes and emotional as well as social development. Those who are mentally retarded are also called mental retardates. They show retardation in acquiring intellectual competence, emotional stability, and social maturity. Even when they are physically grown-up they show such emotional and social behaviours which are appropriate to children of much lower age.

According to H.J Grossman (1983)—"Mental retardation refers to significantly sub average general intellectual functioning existing concurrently with deficits in adaptive behaviour and manifested during the developmental period".

Factors Contributing to Mental Retardation

(*a*) **Problems During Prenatal Period:** Use of alcohol or drugs by the pregnant mother can cause mental retardation. Moreover, prenatal causes include congenital infections such as cytomegalovirus, toxoplasmosis, herpes, syphilis, rubella and human immunodeficiency virus; prolonged maternal fever in the first trimester; exposure to anticonvulsants or alcohol; and untreated maternal phenylketonuria (PKU) (Strømme & Hagberg, 2007). Complications of prematurity, especially in extremely low-birth-weight infants, or postnatal exposure to lead can also cause mental retardation (Piecuch et al., 1997). Physical malformations of the brain and HIV infection originating in prenatal life may also result in mental retardation.

(*b*) **Complications During Child Birth:** Although any birth condition of unusual stress may injure the infant's brain, prematurity and low birth weight predict serious problems more often than any other conditions. Injuries at birth, caused by the use of forceps, often lead to mental retardation.

(*c*) **Accidents or Problems During Infancy and Childhood:** Fall from cots or staircases, knockdowns by older children or fall from the mother's or attendant's lap etc. Besides these Postnatal problems include brain infections such as tuberculosis, Japanese encephalitis, and bacterial meningitis. As well as head injury, chronic lead exposure, severe and prolonged malnutrition and gross under stimulation (Leonard & Wen, 2002; Zoghbi, 2003).

(*d*) **Genetic Defects:** These result from abnormality of genes inherited from parents, errors when genes combine, or from other disorders of the genes caused during pregnancy by infections, overexposure to x-rays and other factors. A number of single-gene disorders result in mental retardation. Many of these are associated with atypical or dysmorphic physical characteristics (Sultana et al.,1995). Such conditions include fragile X syndrome, neurofibromatosis, tuberous sclerosis, Noonan's syndrome and Cornelia de Lange's syndrome (Baraitser & Winter, 1996; Jones & Smith, 1997).

(*e*) **Exposure to certain types of disease or toxins:** Diseases like whooping cough, measles, or meningitis can cause mental disability if medical care is delayed or inadequate. Exposure to poisons like lead or mercury may also affect mental ability (Aicardi, 1998; Daily, Ardinger & Holmes, 2000).

(*f*) **Poverty and cultural deprivation:** Children in poor families may become mentally retarded because of malnutrition, disease-producing conditions, inadequate medical care and environmental health hazards. Also, children in disadvantaged areas may be deprived of many common cultural and day- to-day experiences provided to other youngsters. Research suggests that such under-stimulation can result in irreversible damage and can serve as a cause of mental retardation.

Management of Mentally Retarded

(*a*) **Family Responsibility:** Mentally retarded children need family affection, interaction and peer-group identification. Usually the family of a retarded child often feel guilty about the child which results in over protective behaviour, due to which the child cannot make full advantage of his/her limited abilities by learning easy self help skills. Some families even deny retardation which creates more problems for the child who often fails to meet their expectations.

(*b*) **Accepting the Diagnosis:** Parent's reactions to the diagnosis that their child is mentally retarded are often quite different. There are four types of responses to the diagnosis; guilt, anger, disappointment and denial. Parent's reactions are often confusing about their child. On the one hand they are over protective, loving and caring to their child; on the other hand they feel anger, shame and guilt about him/her.

(*c*) **Institutionalization:** Professionals generally advise to keep the mentally retarded child with the family members if possible, and be responsible for his/her care. However, severely and profoundly retarded children may require institutionalization. Institutionalization, or admission in special institutions or hospitals, is determined mainly of two factors, namely (a) degree of behavioural difficulties in the retarded child, and (b) socio-economic factors related to proper adjustment, accommodation, and maintenance of a retardate's.

MENTAL HEALTH

Mental health is a level of psychological well-being, or an absence of a mental disorder; it is the "psychological state of someone who is functioning at a satisfactory level of emotional and behavioural adjustment". In other words mental health is defined as a state of well-being in which every individual realizes his or her own potential, can cope with the normal stresses of life, can work productively and fruitfully, and is able to make a contribution to her or his community.

According to World Health Organization (WHO) mental health includes "subjective well-being, perceived self-efficacy, autonomy, competence, intergenerational dependence, and self-actualization of one's intellectual and emotional potential, among others."

Persons with good mental health have the following characteristics:

- They are not overwhelmed by their own emotions—fears, anger, love, jealousy, guilt or worries.
- They can take pleasure in simple, everyday things.
- A sense of contentment with their lives.
- A zest for living, laughing, and having fun.
- Able to deal with stress and to bounce back from adversity.
- They accept their responsibilities.
- They set realistic goals for themselves.
- They welcome new experiences and new ideas.
- They are able to make their own decisions.
- Flexibility to learn new things, and adaptability to deal with change.
- They have personal relationships that are satisfying and lasting.
- They feel a sense of responsibility to fellow human beings.
- Self-confidence and high self-esteem.
- Good balance between work and play.
- A sense of meaning and purpose in life, including activities and relationships.

Factors Affecting Mental Health

Mental health and mental illness are determined by multiple and interacting social, psychological, and biological factors. Among the globe, poverty and low levels of education correlates with mental disorders, irrespective of their level of the development. An individual's mental health state can also influenced by genetic and biological factors; that is, determinants that persons are born or endowed with, including chromosomal abnormalities (e.g. Down's syndrome) and intellectual disability caused by prenatal exposure to alcohol or oxygen deprivation at birth

Factors such as insecurity and hopelessness, rapid social change, and the risks of violence and physical ill-health may explain the greater vulnerability of poor people in any country to mental illnesses (Patel & Kleinman 2003).

Mental health for each person is affected by individual factors and experiences, social interaction, societal structures and resources, and cultural values. It is influenced by experiences in everyday life, in families and schools, on streets, and at work (Lehtinen, Riikonen & Lahtinen 1997; Lahtinen et al. 1999).

Discrimination, social or gender inequality and conflict are some of the examples of adverse structural determinants of mental well-being. Physical health is inextricably linked to mental health. Poor mental health is associated with other priority public health conditions such as obesity, alcohol misuse and smoking, and with diseases such as cancer, cardiovascular disease and diabetes. Poor physical health also increases the risk of mental illness.

Interventions to Promote Good Mental Health

Some low-cost and cost-effective interventions that can raise the level of individual and community mental health are as follows-

1. Intervention to improve parental health- Home visiting programmes, peer support and telephone peer support for women at high risk of depression reduces rates of postnatal depression. Health visitor training to improve detection also reduces levels of postnatal depression.
2. Pre-school and early education interventions- Systematic reviews of pre-school and early education programmes show their effectiveness in enhancing cognitive and skills, school readiness, improved academic achievement and positive effect on family outcomes including for siblings, as well as prevention of emotional and conduct disorder. Home visiting programmes improve child functioning and reduce behavioural problems.
3. Support to children - Such programs may include skills-building or child and youth development.
4. Violence and abuse prevention programs- At a family level, these include parental mental health promotion, parent training and early intervention for child emotional and behavioural disorders. At a school level, they include school-based mental health promotion, violence prevention; bullying prevention and social and emotional mental health promotion, violence prevention, bullying prevention also prevent sexual abuse. Among the benefits of school-based violence prevention programmes are reductions in aggressive behaviour, conduct problems and attention span problems, as well as improvements in social skills and social relationships, school performance, school attendance, and attitudes towards violence and bullying.
5. Housing policies - designed to improve housing.
6. Empowerment of women - Socio-economic programs to improve access to education and credit, for example. Mental health services have a crucial role to play in alleviating suffering associated with psychiatric illnesses, emotional distress, psychological disorders, and behavioural pathology. Abused women, troubled children, those traumatized by political violence, those who have attempted suicide or are addicted to alcohol or narcotics, and especially those who suffer acute or chronic mental illnesses can be helped substantially by competent mental health care.
7. Social support for the elderly - including day and community centres for the aged and so-called "befriending" initiatives.
8. Mental health interventions in the workplace-Interventions aimed at employees' mental health protection include, at the organizational level- working conditions improvement and work schedule changes. At the individual level, stress management and skills training programs may provide the participants with resources helping them to cope with the detrimental impact of work-related problems.
9. Programs targeted for vulnerable groups - These groups may include migrants, minorities, indigenous people, and people.

Still, being mentally and emotionally healthy doesn't mean that people never go through hard times or suffer through some painful situations. Thus to maintain emotional balance in these situations the need of resiliency comes in. Resiliency, according to the American Psychological Association (APA), is not a trait that people either have or don't have. It involves actions, thoughts, and behaviours that can be learned and developed - in anyone. The APA suggests 10 ways to build resilience. They are briefly included here:

1. Accept that change is a part of living. All of life involves change. Accepting that fact, you will be better served by focusing on things that you can change and putting a plan together to do so.

2. Make connections. Good relationships are important: family, friends, co-workers, and others. Accept help if you need it, and don't be afraid to ask for it.
3. Avoid seeing crises as insurmountable problems. You can't change what's happened, but you can look toward the solution and act accordingly.
4. Take decisive actions. Acting decisively, even during stressful or adverse situations, helps build self-confidence and resilience.
5. Move toward your goals. Create realistic goals and take steps to achieve them. Even small steps are a sign of progress. Keep moving forward.
6. Look for opportunities for self-discovery. You can often learn something good from any situation, even tragedies and hardship.
7. Nurture a positive view of yourself. Develop your confidence and problem- solving ability helps to build resilience.
8. Maintain a hopeful outlook. Try visualizing what you want, instead of worrying about how you'll attain it.
9. Take care of yourself. Pay attention to the physical and mental aspects of personal caretaking. This keeps mind and body primed and ready to deal with situations requiring resilience.
10. Keep things in perspective. Try to look at the broader, long-term view and avoid blowing things out of proportion.
11. Find additional ways of strengthening resilience. These may include journal writing, meditation, or spiritual practices.

PSYCHOTHERAPIES

Psychotherapy, or "talk therapy", is a way to treat people with a mental disorder by helping them understand their illness. It teaches people strategies and gives them tools to deal with stress and unhealthy thoughts and behaviours. Psychotherapy helps patients manage their symptoms better and function at their best in everyday life. In general terms psychotherapy helps people with a mental disorder to understand the behaviours, emotions, and ideas that contribute to his or her illness and learning how to modify them. It helps to understand the behaviours, emotions, and ideas that contribute to his or her illness and learning how to modify them. Psychotherapy also regains a sense of control and pleasure in life and helps to learn coping techniques and problem-solving skills.

There are several main broad systems of psychotherapy. Few among them are briefly mentioned below:-

Psychodynamic therapy: Psychodynamic therapy helps people gain greater self-awareness and understanding about their own actions. It helps patients identify and explore how their unconscious emotions and motivations can influence their behaviour. Sometimes ideas from psychodynamic therapy are interwoven with other types of therapy, like CBT (Cognitive Behavioural Therapy) or IPT (Interpersonal Therapy) , to treat various types of mental disorders.

Behaviour therapy/applied behaviour analysis: Focuses on changing maladaptive patterns of behaviour to improve emotional responses, cognitions, and interactions with others.

Cognitive behavioural: Generally seeks to identify maladaptive cognition, appraisal, beliefs and reactions with the aim of influencing destructive negative emotions and problematic dysfunctional behaviours.

Existential psychotherapy: Is a unique style of therapy that puts emphasis on the human condition as a whole. Existential psychotherapy uses a positive approach that applauds human capacities while simultaneously maintaining a genuine perception of the limitations of the human being, human spirit, and human mind.

Humanistic: Humanistic therapies focus on self-development, growth and responsibilities. They seek to help individuals recognise their strengths, creativity and choice in the 'here and now'.

Interpersonal Therapy: Interpersonal therapy focuses on the behaviours and interactions a patient has with family and friends. The primary goal of this therapy is to improve communication skills and increase self-esteem during a short period of time. It usually lasts three to four months and works well for depression caused by mourning, relationship conflicts, major life events, and social isolation.

Systemic: Seeks to address people not at an individual level, as is often the focus of other forms of therapy, but as people in relationship, dealing with the interactions of groups, their patterns and dynamics (includes family therapy & marriage counseling). Community psychology is a type of systemic psychology.

Transpersonal psychology: Uses positive influences, rather than the diseased human psyche and our defenses, as a model for the realization of human potential. Transpersonal psychology enhances the study of mind-body relations, spirituality, consciousness, and human transformation. Experts disagree as to the specific model and margins of this form of therapy, however the three key areas that are considered through transpersonal psychotherapy are:

1. Combined/holistic and natural psychology
2. Transformative psychology
3. Ego-transcended psychology

MULTIPLE CHOICE QUESTIONS

1. Depressed individuals exhibit which of the following symptoms?
   A. Cognitive symptoms
   B. Physical symptoms
   C. Behavioural symptoms
   D. All of the above
2. In which theory of depression, an individuals exhibit an expectation that positive outcomes will not occur, negative outcomes will occur, and that the individual has no responses available that will change this state of affairs.
   A. Attribution theory
   B. Berne's Humanistic Theory
   C. Beck's Cognitive Theory
   D. Hopelessness Theory
3. Which theory argues that depression is maintained by a 'negative schema' that leads depressed individuals to hold negative views about themselves, their future and the world (the 'negative triad').
   A. Seligman's Learned Helplessness Theory
   B. Freud's Psychodynamic Theory
   C. Beck's Cognitive Theory
   D. Berne's Humanistic Theory
4. In Major Depression, hippocampus abnormalities are regularly linked with which of the following?
   A. High levels of dopamine
   B. High levels of cortisol
   C. High levels of GABA.
   D. High levels of acetylcholine
5. .... disorder is an excessive or aroused state characterized by feelings of apprehension, uncertainty and fear.
   A. Anxiety B. Mental
   C. Depressive D. Phobic

6. Which of the following physical symptoms is not associated with Panic attacks?
A. Choking feeling
B. Heart palpitations
C. Hyperventilating.
D. Feelings of helplessness

7. .... is a set of persistent anxiety-based symptoms that occur after experiencing or witnessing an extremely fear-evoking traumatic event.
A. Post Traumatic Stress Disorder (PTSD):
B. Panic Disorder
C. Obsessive Compulsive Disorder
D. None of the above

8. On which axis of the DSM are medical disorders?
A. I B. II
C. III D. IV

9. Which of the following is not an anxiety disorder?
A. Bipolar disorder
B. Obsessive-compulsive disorder
C. Post-traumatic stress disorder
D. Panic disorder

10. Which of the following would be classified as a negative symptom of schizophrenia?
A. Delusions
B. Visual hallucinations
C. Social withdrawal
D. Aggressive behaviour

11. Which of the following is considered to be a symptom of Post Traumatic Stress Disorder (PTSD)?
A. Re-experiencing the traumatic event
B. Avoiding reminders of the trauma
C. Increased anxiety and emotional arousal
D. All of the above

12. .... includes phobia, panic disorder, obsessive-compulsive disorder, and post-traumatic stress disorder.
A. Anxiety disorder
B. Mental retardation
C. Anti social behaviour
D. None of the above

13. Which among these is not a symptom of generalised anxiety disorder?
A. Constant worries
B. Inability to tolerate uncertainty
C. Social withdrawal
D. Pervasive feeling of apprehension or dread

14. OCD tends to begin:
A. Between 6 and 15 years of age for both genders.
B. Between 6 and 15 years of age for women and between 20 and 29 years of age for men.
C. Between 6 and 15 years of age for men and between 20 and 29 years of age for women.
D. Between 6 and 18 years of age for both genders.

15. Which of the following is an effective treatment for OCD?
A. Exposure and response prevention (ERP)
B. Group therapy
C. Psychodynamic therapy
D. Medication

16. Anhedonia refers to the:
A. Inability to remember things and persons
B. Inability to sleep
C. inability to gain pleasure from normally pleasurable experiences
D. Both (B) & (C)

17. The most common focus of obsessive thoughts is:
A. Repeated doubts
B. Dirt and contamination
C. Sexual impulses
D. All of the above

18. A psychologist associated with the Humanistic approach is :
A. Carl Rogers
B. B.F. Skinner
C. Sigmund Freud
D. None of the above

19. Beck's Cognitive therapy for depression requires the individual to:
A. Alleviate Major negative symptoms
B. Make an objective assessment of their beliefs
C. Set attainable life goals
D. All of the above

20. Systematic desensitisation is an effective therapy for which of the following?
A. Generalised fears or anxieties
B. Specific phobias
C. Depression
D. Schizophrenia

21. Monoamine oxidase inhibitors (MAOIs) are effective for the treatment of:
A. Obsessive compulsive disorder
B. Phobias
C. Schizophrenia
D. Major depression

22. .... is a personality disorder in which individuals show exceptionally perfectionist tendencies including a preoccupation with orderliness and control at the expense of flexibility, efficiency and productivity.
A. Obsessive-Compulsive Personality Disorder
B. Post Traumatic Stress Disorder
C. Generalized Anxiety Disorder
D. Panic Disorder

23. .... therapies focus on self-development, growth and responsibilities.
A. Humanistic
B. Cognitive behavioural
C. Systematic
D. Psychodynamic

24. .... is a psychiatric illness that can occur after experiencing or witnessing a traumatic event, including natural disasters, rape, violent crime, or war.
A. Obsessive-Compulsive Personality Disorder
B. Post-traumatic stress disorder
C. Generalized Anxiety Disorder
D. Panic Disorder

25. Beck's .... represents three types of negative thoughts present in depression. It involves negative thoughts about: the self, the world/environment and the future.
A. Tricychic response
B. Affect-cognition cycle
C. Cognitive triad
D. None of the above

26. According to epidemiology, different types of measures of epidemiology of mental illness are:
1. Prevalence
2. Point prevalence
3. Incidence
4. Percentage

Codes:
A. 1, 2, 4 only B. 1, 3, 4 only
C. 2, 3, 4 only D. 1, 2, 3 only

27. Which among these is a specific learning disability characterised by mathematical ability being substantially below norm for chronological age, intelligence, and educational level?
A. Dyscalculia B. Dyslexia
C. Dysphasia D. Dyspraxia

28. DSM-IV classifies which disorder, also known intermittent explosive disorder under 'habit disorders'?
A. Borderline personality disorder
B. Impulsive personality disorder
C. Dissocial personality disorder
D. Histrionic personality disorder

29. A DSM-IV-TR defined disorder in which an individual has significantly below average intellectual functioning characterised by an IQ of 70 or below is termed as:
A. Reading disorder
B. ADHD
C. Mental retardation
D. Dyslexia

30. Which of the following pairs is not the negative symptom of Schizophrenia?
A. Emotional flattening and Asociality

B. Anhedonia and Amotivation
C. Poverty of speech and Apathy
D. Hallucinations and Bizarre Behaviour

31. Which among these symptoms are related to Narcissistic personality disorder?
A. Increased sense of self-worth
B. Egocentric
C. Sense of superiority
D. All of the above

32. Given below are two statements, Assertion (A) and Reason (R). Indicate your answer using the codes given below:

Assertion (A): The most important neurotransmitter implicated in schizophrenia is Dopamine.

Reason (R): Clinical evidence suggests that drugs which reduce the level of dopamine in the brain also give rise to psychotic states like schizophrenia.

Codes:
A. Both (A) and (R) are true and (R) is the correct explanation of (A).
B. Both (A) and (R) are true, but (R) is not the correct explanation of (A).
C. (A) is true, but (R) is false.
D. (A) is false, but (R) is true.

33. Persistent social inhibition, hypersensitivity to negative evaluation and feelings of inadequacy are the symptoms of which personality disorder?
A. Avoidant personality disorder
B. Dissocial personality disorder
C. Borderline personality disorder
D. Antisocial personality disorder

34. A modern term replacing Mental Retardation to describe the more severe and general learning disabilities is:
A. Behaviour Abnormalities
B. Intellectual Disabilities
C. Distorted Abilities
D. None of the above

35. A child was classified as a case of mental retardation. On DSM IV/ IV (TR), this diagnosis would be recorded on:
A. Axis I
B. Axis II
C. Axis III
D. Axis IV

36. Which of the following do/does not describe an obsession?
1. Continually reliving a traumatic event.
2. An unwanted thought that a person finds intrusive and distressing.
3. A behaviour or mental act that a person feels compelled to perform.
4. Something a person enjoys doing and talking about constantly.

Codes:
A. 1, 2 and 4
B. 2 and 4
C. 2, 3 and 4
D. 1, 3 and 4

37. .... is an excessive or aroused state characterised by feelings of apprehension, uncertainty and fear.
A. Anxiety disorder
B. Panic disorder
C. Bipolar disorder
D. Post-traumatic stress disorder

38. Given below are two statements—Assertion (A) and Reason (R). Indicate your answer using the code given below.

Assertion (A): In case of anxiety disorder, people become inclined to make negative evaluation of themselves, their world, and their future.

Reason (R): People acquire a relatively stable set of cognitive structures or schemas that contain dysfunctional beliefs.

Codes:
A. Both (A) and (R) are true and (R) is the correct explanation of (A).
B. Both (A) and (R) are true, but (R) is not the correct explanation of (A).
C. (A) is true, but (R) is false.
D. (A) is false, but (R) is true.

39. Among the options given below which are the symptoms of Schizotypal personality disorder:
A. Aloof and isolated
B. Suffer from depersonalization
C. Indulgence in magical thinking
D. All of the above

40. .... is characterized by excessive, unreasonable, persistent fear triggered by a specific object or situation?
A. Anxiety disorder
B. Panic disorder
C. Specific Phobias
D. Obsessive Compulsive Disorder (OCD)

41. Read each of the following two statements—Assertion (A) and Reason (R) and indicate your answer using the codes given below:

Assertion (A): Increased metabolic activity in frontal cortex and the caudate nucleus has been implicated in Obsessive Compulsive Disorder.

Reason (R): Current evidence suggests that increased serotonin activity and increased sensitivity of some brain structures to serotonin are involved in Obsessive Compulsive Symptoms.

Codes:
A. Both (A) and (R) are true and (R) is the correct explanation of (A).
B. Both (A) and (R) are true, but (R) is not the correct explanation of (A).
C. (A) is true, but (R) is false.
D. (A) is false, but (R) is true.

42. Using the multiaxial system of DSM-IV-TR paranoid personality disorder and borderline personality disorder would be coded on:
A. Axis I
B. Axis II
C. Axis III
D. Axis IV

43. A phobia of heights is known as:
A. Acrophobia
B. Claustrophobia
C. Hemophobia
D. Glossophobia

44. Match List-I and List-II and indicate your answer using the codes given below:

List-I (Disorder)	**List-II (Explanation)**
(*a*) Depression	1. Classical conditioning
(*b*) Schizophrenia	2. Negative attribution style
(*c*) Phobia	3. Alcoholism
(*d*) Korsakoff's syndrome	4. Dopamine hypothesis

Codes:

	(*a*)	(*b*)	(*c*)	(*d*)
A.	3	2	4	1
B.	2	4	1	3
C.	1	3	2	4
D.	2	1	4	3

45. Match List-I with List-II and indicate your answer with the help of the codes given below :

List-I (Description)	**List-II (Nomenclature)**
(*a*) Number of new cases that occur over a given period of time.	1. Epidemiology
(*b*) Study of the distribution of diseases or health related behaviours in a given population	2. Syndrome
(*c*) Number of active cases in a population in a given period of time.	3. Incidence
(*d*) A group or cluster of symptoms that occur together	4. Prevalence

Codes:

	(*a*)	(*b*)	(*c*)	(*d*)
A.	2	1	3	4
B.	4	2	1	3
C.	3	1	4	2
D.	1	4	3	2

46. The most common cause of mood congruent delusions is:
A. Anxiety and fear
B. Depression
C. Loneliness
D. Paranoia

47. Excessive emotional reliance on other people and poor problem solving skills are symptoms of which personality disorder?
A. Dissocial personality disorder
B. Borderline personality disorder
C. Dependent personality disorder
D. Both A and C

48. Symptoms such as severe impairment in social interaction and in communication can be diagnosed as:
A. Rett's disorder
B. Infantile amnesia
C. Infantile autism
D. Anti-social personality disorder

49. Which personality disorder is characterized by seductive and overdramatic behaviour and is diagnosed more frequently in women than men?
A. Histrionic personality disorder
B. Borderline personality disorder
C. Impulsive personality disorder
D. Dissocial personality disorder

50. The most common cause of mental retardation is:
A. Korsakoffs syndrome
B. Depression
C. Birth asphyxia
D. Kluver-Bucy syndrome

ANSWERS

1	2	3	4	5	6	7	8	9	10
D	D	C	B	A	D	A	C	A	C
11	**12**	**13**	**14**	**15**	**16**	**17**	**18**	**19**	**20**
D	A	C	C	A	C	B	A	B	B
21	**22**	**23**	**24**	**25**	**26**	**27**	**28**	**29**	**30**
D	A	A	B	C	D	A	B	C	D
31	**32**	**33**	**34**	**35**	**36**	**37**	**38**	**39**	**40**
D	C	A	B	B	D	A	D	D	C
41	**42**	**43**	**44**	**45**	**46**	**47**	**48**	**49**	**50**
B	B	A	B	C	B	C	C	A	C

❑❑❑

YOUR SPACE